The Nanjing Massacre and Sino-Japanese Relations

Zhaoqi Cheng

The Nanjing Massacre and Sino-Japanese Relations

Examining the Japanese 'Illusion' School

Zhaoqi Cheng
Shanghai Jiao Tong University
Shanghai, China

Translated by
Fangbin Yang
Wuxi Canal Experimental Middle School
Wuxi, China

This book is funded by "B&R" Book Program.

ISBN 978-981-15-7889-2   ISBN 978-981-15-7887-8 (eBook)
https://doi.org/10.1007/978-981-15-7887-8

Jointly published with Shanghai Jiao Tong University Press
The print edition is not for sale in China Mainland. Customers from China Mainland please order the print book from: Shanghai Jiao Tong University Press.
ISBN of the China Mainland edition: 9787313183620

Translation from the Chinese language edition: 南京大屠杀研究——日本虚构派批判 by Cheng, Zhaoqi, © Shanghai Jiao Tong University Press 2017. All Rights Reserved.
© Shanghai Jiao Tong University Press 2020

This work is subject to copyright. All rights are solely and exclusively licensed by the Publisher, whether the whole or part of the material is concerned, specifically the rights of translation, reprinting, reuse of illustrations, recitation, broadcasting, reproduction on microfilms or in any other physical way, and transmission or information storage and retrieval, electronic adaptation, computer software, or by similar or dissimilar methodology now known or hereafter developed.

The use of general descriptive names, registered names, trademarks, service marks, etc. in this publication does not imply, even in the absence of a specific statement, that such names are exempt from the relevant protective laws and regulations and therefore free for general use.

The publishers, the authors, and the editors are safe to assume that the advice and information in this book are believed to be true and accurate at the date of publication. Neither the publishers nor the authors or the editors give a warranty, express or implied, with respect to the material contained herein or for any errors or omissions that may have been made. The publishers remain neutral with regard to jurisdictional claims in published maps and institutional affiliations.

This Palgrave Macmillan imprint is published by the registered company Springer Nature Singapore Pte Ltd.
The registered company address is: 152 Beach Road, #21-01/04 Gateway East, Singapore 189721, Singapore

Foreword by JianJun Zhang

Zhaoqi Cheng, modest, determined and rich in works, has in-depth research on the Nanjing Massacre and post-war trials. For a newcomer like me who is just engaged in historical works, Zhaoqi is like a tutor and a brother. This year marks the 80th anniversary of the Nanjing Massacre, along with Zhaoqi Cheng's *Nanjing Massacre Research—A Critique of the Japanese Fiction School* which is being published and is worth celebrating.

The Nanjing Massacre took place in the winter of 1937 and was an important event in the history of World War II. Due to its cruelty, the post-war Far East International Military Court conducted a case trial after an extensive investigation. As the oriental main battlefield of World War II, China won the respect of the world with its tenacity and heroism. It established the Military Court of Nanjing for War Crimes Trials according to the international division of labor and also focused on the trial of the Nanjing Massacre. In essence, the Nanjing Trial, in conjunction with the Tokyo Trial, was an international court based on justice. The judgments had irrefutable authority and legitimacy.

The image of the God of justice is a scale in one hand and a sword in another hand. It may be insufficient to weigh the justice through the scale, so upholding justice with a sword is indispensable. In the past few years, the history of the Nanjing Massacre with sufficient evidence and legal basis has been painfully distorted and even tampered with. Faced with this situation, researchers, like Zhaoqi Cheng, took pens as swords and guarded China's historical truth with solid historical evidence and cultural education which is admirable.

This history of blood and fire has been around for 80 years, but no matter how long time goes on, the truth will always remain there, not blurred, or faded. It declares the history and alarms future generations. The poet Oden once said, "After Auschwitz, writing poetry was barbaric". This statement implies a distrust toward human civilization. The existence of the Nanjing

Massacre has no other function than alerting the masses. As is put in the judgment of the Tokyo Trial, "The extent of its brutality is rare in human history. After insulting and raping women, Japanese forced fathers-in-law to rape their daughters-in-law, fathers to rape their daughters, sons to rape their mothers and monks to rape young girls with humiliation". This savagery, destruction of human relations, is far from the essence of what makes us human beings.

In October 2015, UNESCO listed the Nanjing Massacre Archives on the Memory of the World, which represents that the Nanjing Massacre is officially recognized as a common memory for all human beings and is an international event from an archival perspective. Frankly, the painful memories of the Nanjing Massacre belong to all of mankind and is an integral part of the process of human civilization that should be reflected on all the time. It is supposed to have an enduring impact on modern civilization, to urge everyone to rethink what happened at that time, to promote mutual understanding and to form a warm expectation of world peace and to completely reject future massacres.

So far, the history of the Nanjing Massacre needs further attention from the international community. The historical truth of the Nanjing Massacre needs to be further clarified by criticizing and refuting some ridiculous remarks with ulterior motives. In this way, I look forward to more people with lofty ideals and insights to participate in the research and dissemination of the history of the Nanjing Massacre by contributing research, the inheritance of memory and conveying the truth. I would like to take advantage of this opportunity to pay tribute to Zhaoqi Cheng and colleagues who have devoted themselves to the research and dissemination of the history of the Nanjing Massacre.

Jiangdong gate, Nanjing, China
August 2017

JianJun Zhang
Director of Memorial Hall for the Victims of the Nanjing Massacre
Executive Director of the Nanjing Holocaust History and International Peace Research Institute

Foreword by Sun Zhaiwei

Do More Research on Nanjing Massacre in Criticism

2017 marks the 80th anniversary of Anti-Japanese war and the Nanjing massacre. As time passes by, there are fewer and fewer soldiers and survivors of Nanjing Massacre. Only a hundred survivors are registered in the memorial hall of the Victims of the Nanjing Massacre by Japanese invaders. However, the history of Nanjing massacre remains and has great influence. Publishing all kinds of works about the Nanjing massacre is an important means of deepening the memory. At this point, Mr. Zhaoqi's *Nanjing Massacre Research—A Critique of the Japanese Fiction School* (hereinafter referred to "Critique") comes out.

Zhaoqi and I met at the Nanjing Massacre Research Salon held by the research center Nanjing Massacre of Nanjing Normal University in early spring of 2003. Zhaoqi was specially invited to make a speech in the salon, which left me with a deep impression. I was spiritually attracted to Zhaoqi in 2000 when I learned from him about his translation work, "Nanjing Massacre and the Spirit World of Japanese" written by Tsuda Michio. I knew Zhaoqi at an early time. For over ten years, we have been in contact with each other, read many excellent works and I have benefited a lot. Zhaoqi, who is eloquent and of great talent, is known for the essays in *Historical Research* and *Modern Chinese History Studies*. I'm lucky to have had the opportunity to read his new book "*Critique*". After reading, I gained some inspirations from this book and topic.

Since the 1980s, efforts by scholars, documents, pictures and monographs of the Nanjing massacre have sprung up. Among them there are comprehensive researches on the history of Nanjing massacre, such as Gao Xingzu's book, *The Atrocities Committed by Japanese Invaders-Nanjing Massacre*, and the groups' book, *A history of Nanjing Massacre by Japanese Invaders*, (Japan) Tomio Hora's book *The Nanjing Massacre*, (Japan) Kasahara Shijiusi's book

Nanjing Event, and Sun Zhaiwei as the editor-in-chief of *The Nanjing Massacre*, Chen Anji as the editor-in-chief of the *Collection of Papers of the International Symposium on the History of the Nanjing Massacre by Japanese Invaders*, and *Nanjing Massacre-Facts and Records* co-authored by Sun Zhaiwei and Wu Tianwei, and *New Research on Nanjing Massacre* edited by Liu Huishu, and *Collection of Papers on the Exchange of Latest Research Achievements in the History of the Nanjing Massacre by Japanese Invaders edited* by Zhu Chengshan, and *Cry for 300,000 Wrongful Souls—Zhu Chengshan's Collection of History and Literature on the Nanjing Massacre* (Volume I and Volume II) written by Zhu Chengshan, *Clarification of History-Studies and Reflections on the Nanjing Massacre* written by Sun Zhaiwei, *Nanjing Massacre and Japanese War Crimes-Collected Works of Gao Xingzu* written by Gao Xingzu, *The History of Nanjing Massacre* (first, second and third volumes) edited by Zhang Xianwen, *Research on Nanjing Massacre: History and Speech* (the first and second volumes) co-edited by Zhang Lianhong and Sun Zhaiwei, *Research on the History of Nanjing Massacre* (the first and second volumes of the updated versions) written by Zhang Sheng and others, etc. There are many works with authors both at home and abroad, each has his own perspective, each has his own characteristics and each has his own advantages. Most of these works are a comprehensive study of the history of the Nanjing Massacre and have detailed historical materials for research and discussion. Conclusions are based on historical evidence, which makes the whole picture of the Nanjing Massacre clear and detailed for the world.

It should be pointed out in particular that this book *Critique* is distinctive and unique in its research on the history of the Nanjing Massacre. As the name of this book reveals, this book constructs a new world for the study of the Nanjing Massacre and promotes the Nanjing Massacre to new heights by criticizing Japanese fictionalists. Mr. Zhaoqi, who lived and studied in Japan for many years, has a unique advantage. He knows all about the tricks and performances of the Japanese fictionalists who deny the Nanjing Massacre. He has very clear insight and hits his target every time without a miss. Fictionalists' remarks are absurd and uncountable. If you don't feel personally involved and persevere, it will be very difficult to capture their remarks, and it will be even more difficult to probe into the root cause of the problem. In this regard, Mr. Zhaoqi not only took advantage of the situation, but also because of his strict nature, quick thinking and hard work, he was able to calmly collect and sort out the fictional speeches one by one. He was able to refute them one by one by debunking lies and reconstructing the true history of the Nanjing Massacre. Making critique is a battle and an important mode of research. Persuasive criticism can bring forth new ideas and sublimates the theory of academic research. Successful critique requires a strong academic foundation. Mr. Zhaoqi has an excellent academic background and his critical writings are like spears and swords, which are extremely destructive and shocking. This makes his new book a unique academic monograph with a strong fighting color, filling a gap in the research on the history of the Nanjing Massacre.

The publication of Critique is the need of the times and the product of the times. We live in an era of peace and development as the main theme, but not peace and tranquility. The Nanjing Massacre is a disaster and a humiliation that the Chinese people will never forget. The cries and blood of 300,000 dead compatriots have become the alarm bells of history. In the sound of the alarm bell, we seemed to hear the sound of machine guns massacring civilians and the grinning sound of Japanese invaders killing people for fun. This voice, full of terror and blood, is both distant and near. In that barbaric war launched by militarism, human dignity and morality were destroyed. The brutality, barbarity and madness of militarism are the source of all war atrocities. The Nanjing Massacre was a product of the vicious expansion of Japanese militarism.

Since the Meiji Restoration in the 1860s, Japan embarked on a path of militarism. Until the end of World War II, Japan surrendered unconditionally and was forced to terminate. During this period, it experienced Meiji, Taisho and Showa dynasties. Generally speaking, in the Meiji era, militarism began and extorted huge sums of money from China in order to enrich the construction of their navy and army and built a new industrial foundation. In the Taisho era, the degree of militarism developed further, taking advantage of the privileges already seized in China, plundering resources, exploiting labor and grabbing the market. In the Showa era, militarism reached its peak. The invasion of China also changed from a local war to a full-scale war, turning parts of China into Japanese colonies. Japanese militarism is characterized by its endless expansion abroad. Expansion requires conquest, which cannot be achieved without violence. In the history of Japanese militarism, aggression and violence were eliminated simultaneously. Wherever they invaded, they committed violence there. In the process of attacking Nanjing, they also killed people continually from Songhu battlefield to Nanjing. The difference is that the massacre in Nanjing was the most barbaric, craziest and largest.

After World War II, Japanese militarism was destroyed. However, as the Chinese saying goes, "trees want to be quiet but the wind does not allow it". The forces of Japanese militarism and their influence, which brought great disasters to the people of China and the world, are far from being thoroughly criticized and liquidated. The right-wingers and bureaucratic politicians are still there representing the right-wing ideological trend. This was the soil for reviving militarism. Once the conditions were ripe, the poisonous mushroom of militarism broke through the ground. For more than 70 years, the international political situation has not been peaceful. A handful of right-wingers and politicians in Japan have repeatedly set off a counter-current and muddy wave of overturning their verdicts on the issue of invading China, East Asia and the Nanjing Massacre in an attempt to revive militarism, which has been swept into the dustbin of history. They sometimes adopt the method of revising textbooks in order to poison the younger generation and create soil for the revival of militarism. Sometimes, they publish talks which confuse fact and fictional information in influential international magazines to confuse the international audience. Sometimes bureaucratic politicians use their status and position to launch attacks and expand the influence of the fallacy of overturning the verdict. Sometimes they put on cloaks of scholars and write books, seemingly objective, to confuse people who do not know the truth. Sometimes they were led by political leaders, to visit the Yasukuni Shrine which worships Class A war criminals, openly challenge the feelings of the people of China and all Asian countries invaded. This can be said to echo each other, cooperate with each other, and make deliberate efforts to achieve the same results.

History has proved that whenever war maniacs want to launch new wars of aggression and commit new war atrocity, he must first create public opinion and deny his past aggression and atrocities. Reversal of the verdict is intended to revive. The denial of the Nanjing Massacre by a small number of right-wingers in Japan is a denial of the whole history of aggression against China, which is aimed at creating public opinion for reviving militarism. Essentially, such overturning activities are the continuation and extension of Japanese militarism's aggression and violence. Meanwhile, it is also a prelude for the Japanese militarists to launch a new round of aggression and atrocities.

How can we prevent Japan's right-wing forces from overturning the verdict? How can we contain the resurrection of Japanese militarism? It is necessary to hold rallies, issue statements and solemnly denounce in order to crack down on the arrogance of right-wing forces. Fundamentally speaking, being down-to-earth, refuting and breaking lies one by one can make all the fallacies of overturning the verdict and public opinion of reviving militarism uncomprehensible to kind people. Mr. Zhaoqi's *Critique* is exactly the call of the times, which extinguishes the embers of militarism fundamentally. This is the greatest value of *Critique* published today.

The Nanjing Massacre, which took place 80 years ago, is still fresh in the memory of the Nanjing people, the Chinese people and the Chinese people all over the world. The alarm bell of history is ringing in people's ears. The painful history of the Nanjing Massacre calls for people to be alert and never allow the tragedy to repeat. The wheel of history is rolling forward. The Chinese people who overcame the history of the Nanjing Massacre and the Anti-Japanese War will never allow Japanese militarism to come back. The attempt by a very small number of people to revive Japanese militarism will never succeed. Maintaining peace, opposing war and promoting development are the common wishes and responsibilities of people all over the world. The remembrance of the past is the teacher of the future. Peace in Asia and the world can only be guaranteed if we unite as one, learn from history, and constantly guard against the revival of Japanese militarism.

I believe that the publication of *Critique* should be a fruitful response to the historical warning and a fatal blow to the resurgent militarists in Japan. This is a good start. The criticism of various fantastic theories of the fictionalists should be carried out in depth. The struggle has not yet come to an end. There is a long way to go for scholars to continue to deepen, refine and implement this Critique. I would like to share this with Mr. Zhaoqi and other academic colleagues to reach a mutual goal.

Nanjing, China   Sun Zhaiwei
September 2017

About This Book

The fictional claims of the Nanjing Massacre in Japan, which began in the early 1970s, have flourished since then, finally becoming widespread today. Many Japanese scholars, including Tomio Hora who was the first to study the Nanjing Massacre in the world and Mr. Tokushi Kasahara who is still endeavoring to it today, have made unremitting efforts to pursue the truth of the Nanjing Massacre, which is commendable. But so far there has not been a thorough clarification of fictional claims in Japan. This book is the first step in a long-planned and thorough effort to unveil the truth of Japanese fictional claims by focusing on the relevant developments in Japan and reading relevant historical materials.

CIP Data Cataloging in Publication
Nanjing Massacre Research: A Critique of Japanese Fiction School by Cheng Zhaoqi —Shanghai: Shanghai Jiao Tong University Press, 2017
ISBN 978-7-313-18362-0
I. ①Nan... II. ① Cheng... III. ①Nanjing Massacre Research
IV. ①K265. 607

China CIP Data Cataloging in Publication (2017) No. 271020
Nanjing Massacre Research: A Critique of Japanese Fiction School
Author: Cheng Zhaoqi
Publishing House: Shanghai Jiao Tong University Press
Address: No.95, Fanyu Road, Shanghai
Tel: 021-64071208
Postal Code: 20030
Publisher: Tan Yi
Distribution: Xinhua Bookstore
Printing: Jiangsu Suzhong Printing Co., Ltd.
Folio: 710 mm × 1000 mm, 1 / 16

Print: 35
Word Count: 504,000
First Printing: January, 2018
Published: January 1, 2018

ISBN978-7-313-18362-0 / K
Price: 128.00 yuan
Copyright preserved

To readers: If you find any quality problems in this book, please contact the Quality Department of the printing factory at 0523-641646.

Author's Note

First, for historical terms that are ambiguous in meaning, we use what they have been originally used in this book. For example, the "Chinese Army in Central Area" is mostly changed to the "Central China Army". Considering what Japanese call "Central Area in China" and what Chinese call "Central China", whether it is according to traditional geographical area or the administrative divisions after the 1950s, they completely differ. Also, it is true that Chinese army in central area only acted within East China, so this book adopts the original Japanese one.

Second, chapters of this book were written in different periods, spanning more than a decade, so the translations of names are not the same, such as George. A. Fitch, translated earlier to Fitch, has been translated to Fei Wusheng according to the popular translation in recent years. In this book, it is marked with brackets in the index.

Third, the discussion in this book may appear repeatedly in other chapters, and it is retained due to the different emphasis of the issues discussed. However, there are two chapters on the same topic about Kogawa Seijiro, so one of them is omitted in this book.

Fourth, for the pejorative titles, quotation marks are generally used to show it is inappropriate (means "so-called"), without derogatory words added. Such as "Manchukkuo", it is not called "Puppet Manchukuo", "Wang regime" is not called "Wang puppet regime".

Fifth, for nouns that contain negative meaning, such as "fictional", we do not add quotation marks, because fictional is not only commonly used in Japan, but also because it refers to the fact. And adding quotation mark is easy to misunderstand.

Sixth, some of the texts cited in this book are marked with special marks, such as "△, ○, □, ◎" and they remain original in this book, which are usually explained when they first appear.

Contents

Monograph

Who Made Up the "Lies"—An Analysis on Japanese
Annual of the Japan Association for Nanjing Studies   3

A Study of the Bearing and Discipline of the Japanese Army
Invading China—Taking the 10th Army as an Example   39

Re-evaluation of Iwane Matsui's War Guilt—Verifications
of One of the Testimonies on the Nanjing Massacre Given
by the Defendants at the Tokyo War Crimes Trials   81

A Study of the Massacre Order for Japanese Troops   115

Is the Nanjing Massacre a Fabrication Made by Tokyo Trial?   139

Is The Good Man of Nanking: The Diaries of John Rabe an
"Unfounded Fabrication"?—An Examination of The Truth
of Nanjing Incident: An Examination of *John Rabe's Diaries*   193

Re-discussion on "The 100-Man Killing Contest"   225

Re-examination of Ogawa Sekijiro's Testimony—Examination II
of the Testimonies of the Defendants on Nanjing Atrocities
in Tokyo Trial   239

Ogawa Sekijiro and Diary of a Military Legal Affairs Officer	267
The Study on Some Issues Concerning the Nanjing Massacre	273
An Introduction to Japan's Existing Historical Material on the Nanjing Massacre	297

Essays

The "Legitimacy" That Cannot Be Self-justified	375
Impudently Take a Mistranslation as "Rebuttal Evidence"	381
How Can There Be "Not Expansion"	387
The Truth of "Substantial Concessions"	393
The Insincere "Peacefully Opening the City"	397
Three Questions on the Burial	405
Does Iwane Matsui Have Any Grievance to Tell?—An Analysis of OKADA Takashi's Arguments	413
Was What Fitch Said "Wrong"?	421
Questions on the Query Against Rabe	429
How Magee's Explanation Became Contradictory	433
Had the Population of the Safety Zone "Increased"?	437
There "Should Have Been No" Civilians Outside the Safety Zone	445
The Japanese Army's Sex Atrocities Cannot Be Denied Even If Victims Have Never Accused	449
Only Truth Has Power	455

Afterword	459
Appendix	463
References	531
Index	543

Monograph

Who Made Up the "Lies"—An Analysis on Japanese *Annual of the Japan Association for Nanjing Studies*

1 The Emergence of the "Association" and Its Annual in the Context of Right Deviation

After the cold war, especially after the mid-1990 s, Japan's conservatives staged a comeback, not only sharply weakening the left-wing forces (e.g., Japan Socialist Party lost seats in the Diet to such a degree that they had to change the party name) but also severely impacting the educational and academic circles which the right-wing, for a long time, had the most difficulty with. Embracing the full-scale right deviation waves, varieties of groups emerged like the Association for Historical Liberalism Studies, the Society for New Textbook Compilation and so on. They published a large quantity of writing disavowing historical facts[1] and frequently organized a variety of activities demanding for the "settlement" of old scores and "rehabilitation" of the so-called "honor" of modern Japan history. They became a particularly powerful branch of right deviation waves and helped bring about the rightward shift of Japanese society as a whole.

Among the so-called "being wronged" cases, the Nanjing Massacre is considered to be the most notable. For instance, the book *The Alleged "Nanking Massacre"* is subtitled "*Japan's Rebuttal to China's Forged Claims*".[2] Ooi Mitsuru says that the Nanjing Massacre is "made up by words".[3] Yoshimoto

---

[1] For example, National History, National Morality and National Education, etc., whose publication was in charge of the Society for New Textbook Compilation, not only sold for a extremely low price but was gifted in a large quantity. The intention was to "do good to society," which was neither the part of ordinary profit-seekers, nor the publication routine.

[2] Takemoto Tadao, Ohara Yasuo. 日本会議国際広報委員会 (Ed.). *The Alleged "Nanking Massacre": Japan's Rebuttal to China's Forged Claims* (1st Ed.). Tokyo: Meisei-sha, Inc. Tokyo. 2000.

[3] 大井満。『仕組まれた「南京大虐殺」——攻略作戦の全貌とマスコミ報道の怖さ』，東京，展転社1998年6月6日第3次印刷版，第323頁。

says that the Nanjing Massacre just "smears our history with lies".[4] Fuji Nobuo says that the Nanjing Massacre is "a mere fiction by the Tokyo Trial".[5] Matsumura Toshio says that the Nanjing Massacre is "just a lie supported by testimonies without proof".[6] Nobukatsu Fujioka says that the Nanjing Massacre is just "a dark rumor" with "anti-Japan sentiment".[7] And Shudo Higashinakano claims that the "Nanking Massacre" is based on quite indirect historical materials and that there exists no record that can affirm how many people were killed in Nanjing. He even believes that the Nanking Massacre is a globally shared illusion.[8] Kitamura Minoru underlines that the "Nanking Incident" is "closely linked with" "Kuo Min Tang (KMT)'s international propagation and foreign policy".[9] Suzuki Aki doesn't want to be straightforward but says that he, through efforts, has touched the actual kernel of the Nanking Massacre.[10] In other words, the truth is that it was fabricated. Suffering such heated discussion, the Nanjing Massacre has been no more a topic limited to historian circle but a frequent topic of popular publications.

The talk that the Japanese "Nanjing Massacre is fiction" dates back to 1970 s.[11] Since then, supporters (i.e., the school of fiction) and opponents (i.e., the school of slaughter) have been busy with mutual refutation. Before

---

[4] 吉本榮著『南京大虐殺の虚構を砕け』, 東京, 新風書房198年6月1日第1版, 第4頁。

[5] 冨士信夫著『「南京大虐殺」はこうして作られた――東京裁判の欺瞞』, 東京, 展転社198年1月23日第4版, 第323頁。

[6] 松村俊夫著『「南京虐殺」への大疑問』, 東京, 展転社198年12月13日第1版, 第375頁。

[7] Nobukatsu Fujioka, Shudo Higashinakano. 『ザ レイプ オブ 南京の研究――中国における「情報戦」の手口と戦略』(1st Ed.). Tokyo: 祥傳社. 2008: 3.
藤岡信勝, 東中野修道著『ザ レイプ オブ 南京の研究――中国における「情報戦」の手口と戦略』, 東京, 祥傳社199年9月10日第1版, 第3頁。

[8] Shudo Higashinakano. 『「南京虐殺」の徹底検証』, 東京, 展転社200年7月8日第4次印刷版, 第362頁。

[9] 北村稔著『「南京事件」の探究――その実像をもとめて』第一部「国民党国際宣傳処と戦時対外戦略」, 東京, 文藝春秋社201年1月20日第1版, 第25–64頁。

[10] 鈴木明著『新「南京大虐殺」のまぼろし』, 東京, 飛鳥新社199年6月3日第1版, 第508頁。

[11] In 1971, Katsuichi Honda, a reporter of Japan *Asahi Shimbun*, was allowed to visit China. He visited where Japan troops had occupied before, such as Guangzhou, Changsha, Beijing, Shenyang, Fushun, Anshan, Tangshan, Jinan, Nanjing, and Shanghai, during the 40 days from June to July. And his visit was serialized with the title "A Journey to China" in *Asahi Shimbun* from the end of August to December of that year. Katsuichi Honda's severe criticism, along with the particular influence, led Nanjing Massacre to be undeniable fact that Japanese people had to face. As for what the fact caused, reflection or resentment, it cannot be summarized into a word. But its influence make those who opposed the so-called "historical viewpoint of Tokyo Trial" unable to stand by. 鈴木明的「『南京大虐殺』のまぼろし」(此文先刊于《诸君!》1972年4月号, 次年鈴木的论集也以同题为名) became the first to deny Nanjing Massacre. "Maboroshi" was equated with "fansy" or "fiction", so it became the name of those supporters. But recently, faced with the undeniable fact, 鈴木 has said that the current translation is wrong and that the correct one is "puzzle" (『新「南京大虐殺」のまぼろし』, 第31–32頁)。

the mid-1990 s, the school of slaughter had the upper hand—the school of fiction claimed to have won many times, but it was not until modern times that they had an edge over their opponents' voices. This turn of course resulted from the rightward background, but two other factors exist: For one thing, compared to scholars of the school of slaughter who are experienced in Sino-Japanese War studies, such as Tomio Hora[12] and Akira Fujiwara,[13] the earlier fictionalists are mainly those who engage in media or were personally involved in the incident (Suzuki Aki[14] and Aroken-ichi[15] fall with the former group and Tanaka Masaaki,[16] Yamamoto Shichihei[17] and Unemoto Masaki[18] belong to the latter) so that they have neither academic support nor public trust. But in modern times, the school of fiction has not only admitted people of all kinds like Kobayashi Yoshinori,[19] but have active figures, those institution scholars such as Shudo Higashinakano,[20] Nobukatsu Fujioka,[21]

---

[12] Tomio Hora used to be a professor of Waseda University. 著有『決定版,南京大虐殺』,東京,徳間書店1982年12月31日第1版;「南京大卓殺の証明」．東京．朝日新聞社1986年3月5日第1版。 編有洞富雄編『日中戦争史資料』8「南京事件」I, 東京, 河出書房新社1973年1月25日第1版; 9「南京事件」II, 東京, 河出書房新社1973年1月30日第1版。

[13] Fujiwara Akira used to be a professor of Hitotsubashi University. He wrote the *Nanking Massacre* (1st Ed.). Tokyo: Iwanami Shoten, 1985) 東京, 岩波書店, 岩波ブックネットNo. 43, 1985年第1版。

[14] Suzuki Aki first worked at private Tuntai and he later became a freelancer after his work The Myth of the "Nanjing Massacre" suddenly became "an instant hit". See the previous note for his work.

[15] Kenichi Ara used to work as a planner in a publishing house, 著有『き書 南京事件——日本人の見た南京虐殺事件』, 東京, 図書出版社, 1987年8月15日第1版。

[16] Tanaka Masaaki was the secretary of Iwane Matsui at the Greater Asia Association. The year before the incident, he visited Southwest and Nanjing with Matsui. 著有『「南京虐殺」の虚構——松井大将の日記をめぐって』, 東京, 日本教文社1984年6月25日第1版; 田中正明著『南京事件の総括——虐殺否定十五の論拠』, 東京, 謙光社1987年3月7日第1版。

[17] Although Shichihei Yamamoto had nothing to do with the "Nanjing incident", he was also a member of the Japanese army during the war (he was a second lieutenant in the artillery of the 103rd Division of the Japanese Army). 著有『私の中の日本軍』上, 下, 東京, 文藝春秋社1975年1月30日, 12月15日第1版。

[18] When the Japanese conquered Nanjing, Unemoto Masaki was already the captain of an independent light-armored convoy. Although he had taught war history at the Defense University, his status as a general of the Ground Self-Defense Forces was different from that of the scholars in the academy. 著有「証言による南京戦史」1—1, 東京,『偕行』1984年4月号—1985年2月号。

[19] Kobayashi Yoshinori is a cartoonist. In recent years, he directly negates the Nanjing Massacre in the form of cartoons, but also denies the Nanjing Massacre in the form of discussion. 如「「個上公J論京,幻冬舎2000年5月5日第1版。

[20] Shūdō Higashinakano is a professor at the University of Asia. 著有[「南京虐殺」0徹底檢征」,東京,展転社1998年8月15日第1版。

[21] Nobukatsu Fujioka is a professor at the University of Tokyo and has written a variety of books on the negation of Nanjing Massacre. On Nanjing Massacre, he writes 「H .27.才。南京D研究—中国汇书计百「情報戰]0手口上戰略」 with Shūdō Higashinakano.

Watanabe Shoichi,[22] and Kitamura Minoru,[23] a budding one. Some researchers depart from their original stand, propelling the middle-of-the-road and fictionalists to collaborate. For example, Hata Ikuhiko, who has made great efforts in Sino-Japan wars studies, leans toward resistance to China from assistance to China. Since his case is typical, a little bit further introduction is a must. Hata Ikuhiko is a middle-of-the-road representative and has long advocated that during the Nanjing Massacre 40,000 people were killed. Therefore, he is not accepted by Chinese academic circle or overseas Chinese[24] and was attacked by fictionalists.[25] However, his institutional research mainly plays the part in swaying those fictionalists. And he cannot be regarded as deleterious. For example, facing fictionalists' doubt on the figure, he said:

> Some people even falsify the first-hand data and insist that there never exists Nanjing Massacre. Some people merely care about the token figure of 30,000 or 40,000 people that the Chinese government insists on. Should the anti-Japanese group in the United States say that the number recorded in textbooks of people killed in the atomic bomb explosion is 'too large' or 'fabricated' (the real number is still unclear) and begin to protest, what would the victims think of it? The exact figure may be controversial, but the massacre and various illegal acts committed by the Japanese army in Nanjing are undeniable facts. I, as a Japanese, genuinely apologize to the Chinese people.[26]

---

[22] Watanabe Shoichi is a professor at Sophia University and has written a large number of books on denying aggression; although there is no special book on the Nanjing Massacre, he has the greatest influence among the fictionalists because of his high popularity and repeated performances on various occasions.

[23] Kitamura Minoruis is a professor at Ritsumeikan University—Kinugasa Campus. 著有[[南京事件]0)探究一专 0)实像在尼上如了」,東京, 文藝春秋社2001年11月20日第1版。 The basis for attributing Kitamura Minoruis to the fictionalists is his recent conclusion; he will not recognize that he is a fictionalist, because in the postscript, he claims to hold "seeking truth from facts" which China takes as an important code of action after Deng Xiaoping (p. 193). For the time being, no one in Japan has pointed out which faction he belongs to. Recently, some Japanese scholars have criticized the "political" tendency of his work (见山田要一著「歷史改艺人心新意匠一北村稔[[南京事件]0探究」0)灾像I.「人格上教育J34号,東京,社会評論社2002年5月20日, 第139–149页)。

[24] 如1997年在普林斯顿大学召开的南京大屠杀讨论会上,秦郁彦的发言受到了与会华人的嘘声,"一时骚然"(筱原九司著「月川>卜二大学[南京1937年.国際江术沙宁厶J記録」,藤原彰編[南京事件七方及互加一一日, 中, 米研究者汇上石檢征」,東京,青木普店1998年7月25日第1版, 第182页)。 国内学者多以为秦氏 "实质上"否定南京大屠杀.如藉日本学者之口认为是"更巧妙的否定屠杀论"(孙宅巍主编(南京大屠杀)》, 北京,北京山版社1997年5月第1版, 第8页)。 吉田裕曾说:"我和秦郁彦先生在中国的印象都不好"(石川水穂著「徹底橫鉦E「南京論点整理学JJ.「諸君!」.東京, 文藝春秋, 2001年2月号, 第147页)。

[25] 如田中正明批评 秦氏 "没有跨出东京审判史观一步, 仅仅是数字上的不同, 与屠杀派在本质上能说有什么区别么?"(田中正明著[南京事件刀总括一虐 殺否定十五0論狹], 第67页)。

[26] 秦郁彦著『南京事件——虐殺の構造』, 東京, 中央公論新社199年8月20日第20版, 第24页。 (此书初版于1986年2月25日, 基本未改动)。

From such standpoint, his "negation" is made in a more subtle way but can be too overt. But his present standpoint does seem backward, which will be briefly discussed later.

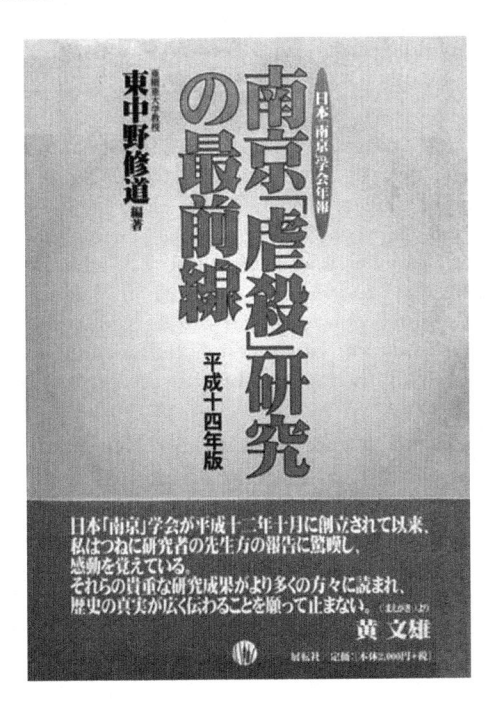

The school of slaughter formed their own academic group the "Association for Nanjing Incident Investigation" as early as 1984 while fictionalists have long been unorganized. It wasn't until 2000 that they began to organize those like-minded individuals, raise a banner and form the "Association for Nanjing Studies". Fictionalists mainly attack the school of slaughter, but without tolerance of dissent, they and middle-of-the-road members attack each other from time to time. However, the Association for Nanjing Studies also admits those middle-of-the-road figures during this time. This may be a major shift in their strategy. (It is said that since the president, vice president and other major figures of the Association are all fictionalists, they actively contributed to the admission.) Recently, the Association for Nanjing Studies has launched the first publication, the Annual of the Association for Nanjing Studies: Studies in Nanjing "Massacre" at the Cutting Edge (hereinafter called "the Annual"). The Annual is composed of four articles respectively written by Hata Ikuhiko, Hara Takeshi, Tomizawa Shigenobu and Higashinakano Shudo, an interview of Susumu Maruyama, a member of the Nanjing Secret Service, a preface and a postscript. Shudo Higashinakano, president of the Association, has put in the postscript as follows: "There can be nothing but discrepancy between the 'Nanjing Massacre' that we talk about today and 'the actual situation at that time', which may be likened to that 'cash on hand doesn't tally with the figure in the accounts.' Hence, the Association for Nanjing Studies is intended to 'check the accounts one by one again'. 'It is not for private interests, nor for certain historical conception.' It is but to 'find out and clarify conflicts and doubts'".[27] Ko Bunyu, who prefaces the Annual, claims:

> According to Chinese "testimony", Japanese armies slaughtered people in all forms. But none have been documented in Japanese history. Why? Because it is simply the depiction of Chinese-style massacre.
> The contradiction between the School of Fiction and the School of Slaughter (in Japan) can be simply presented as that between instigators of anti-Japan sentiment and academics. I agree that the Nanjing Massacre is the outcome of China's "intelligence war." It can be said to be the biggest hit of the Chinese government's anti-Japanese policy after the war. And they oppose the "academic research" of the Japanese because this hit has been challenged.[28]

Apart from "academic research" in the preface written by Huang, and the vicious comment on the massacre claim as "incitement", members from Nanjing Studies Association of Japan neither use coarse language like YOSHINORI Kobayashi, nor behave wantonly as usual, such as "to rip off someone's mask",[29] even nor mark the "Declaration of Victory"[30] on paper tapes, flaps and title pages. Losing temper always means failure while keeping impassivity means success; therefore, whether this kind of low profile is different from the past does it indicate a kind of self-confidence? Questions raised in Annuals mainly include the following aspects: The first is about the death toll, which links with other questions such as the population of Nanjing, interments by Red Cross Society and Zhongshan Hall; the second is about the legality of the judgment of the Tokyo Trial; the third is whether there were any relevant reports at that time. These questions have been put forward for many years; however, this time there are some "innovations" in the way and statements of drawing the conclusion. Although changes in the form generally are not enough to alter the essence of the issue, members in the

---

[27] 東中野修道編著『日本「南京」学会年報——南京「虐殺」研究の最前線』、東京、展転社 202年9月16 日第1版、第252頁。 东中野在后记中说, 此书为学会编辑, 署个人之名纯只是从销路考虑。

[28] 東中野修道編著日本「南京J学会年報一南京[虐殺研究0最前線], 「前言」第3页。 黄文雄为台湾旅日者现为日本拓殖大学客员教授, "南京学会" 副会长, 热中于攻击中国。

[29] For example, in the first half of last year, Higashinakano Shudo said he ripped off the mask of Bates (Higashinakano Shudo, 「南京大学教授ベイツの『化け の皮』」, 『諸君!』, Tokyo, Bungei Shunju, 2002(4), pp. 150–163).

[30] Previous work has such self-praise. For instance, Watanabe Shoichi flattered the evidence of "Nanjing Massacre" written by Tanaka Masaaki "If you continue to talk about the nanjing massacre after reading this book, you will only be branded with the left-wing of anti-japanese agitation" (『「南京虐殺」の虚構———松井大将の日記をめぐって』, he paper tape).

Association only harp on the same string, which is far from their expectation of denying the Nanjing Massacre. But some revised statements do confuse people; therefore, it is necessary for Chinese academia to respond.

2 The "Beguilement" of "Impartial Database"[31]

Tomizawa Shigenobu publishes his article To Clarify the Nanjing Incident in Accordance with Database[32] in Annuals which occupies the largest length and surpasses the sum of the other three articles. Mr. Tomizawa claims that recently he has input all documents related to the early Nanjing Massacre into the computer and established a "system of explanatory concepts" for the Nanjing Incident with events as its longitudes and time as its latitudes. According to him, this system refers to the following:

> The totality of explanatory concepts covers all phenomena that should be expounded, among which there is no gap, showing that extensions of concepts do not overlap. As explanatory concepts, the way of five "W" and one "H" is adopted to classify all events. Five "W" refers to who, what, when, where and why, and "H" is "How"; that is to say, this way is to clarify when, where, why, what and how the victim suffered, as well as who the victim was.[33]

Mr. Tomizawa believes that "there is no subjective effect of the author because all of the data is extracted mechanically". Therefore, a "completely impartial" database (and he regards this database as the national property of Nanjing Incident studies in Japan)[34] can be established as long as original documents inputted are not "influenced by preferences". The author asserts that his "belief" is "to be faithful to the original text", which guarantees all original documents input into the computer are not influenced by his preferences; in that case, the article composed on the basis of the database definitely draws a "completely impartial" conclusion.

There will be a brand new challenge on condition that the "database" is "faithful to the original text". This challenge does not refer to the "way"

---

[31] Beguilement is the word that fiction camp in Japan uses to criticize China; for example, the subhead of the book written by 冨士信夫 to deny Nanjing Massacre is the beguilement of Tokyo trial (冨士信夫著『「南京大虐殺」はこうして作られた────東京裁判の欺瞞』, Tokyo, 展転社, 1st Edition, April 29th, 1995).

[32] Fiction camp in Japan denies Nanjing Massacre; there put quotes around Nanjing Massacre, while they prefer to use "Nanjing Incidents". In recent years, the phrase Nanjing Incidents is also in quotation so as to indicate that all incidents happened in Nanjing are fabricated, such as the Investigation of "Nanjing Incidents" by Kistamura Minoru.

[33] Higashinakano Shudo, ed. 『Annuals of Japanese Association of Nanjing Studies────南京「虐殺」研究の最前線』, pp. 64–65.

[34] Higashinakano Shudo, ed. 『Annuals of Japanese Association of Nanjing Studies────南京「虐殺」研究の最前線』, pp. 71–72.

adopted by "Nanjing Studies Association of Japan", for parallelism of historical records is the basic work of history, and there is no substantive difference between entering it into the computer and writing it on a card. Compared with the card box, "database" is another type of "database", which means there is also no innovation in the "way". The reason why his work may be a challenge is that listing all materials is totally different with previous ways adopted by the school of fiction—not only the school of fiction—after all they only elect sentences and articles in historical materials to support their own views. Nevertheless, it is still a question that whether his "database" including all existing historical records can deuce his conclusion. Because the quantity of historical records is not equal to the truth of the conclusion, historical sources are not fact. Not every historical resource reflects a part of history, and the more parts we have, the more historical facts we know, even though a thorough collection of all historical records plays a vital role in the display of the original. There is no need for history to exist if historical data show fact.

There is always a distance between historical records and historical facts because these records are influenced by objective and subjective factors, such as discernment, preference and horizon of the recorder. The complexity of the Nanjing Massacre is not the same as that of those ordinary historical records; however, records of the Nanjing Massacre concern sensitive national sentiments, which are usually strongly impacted by values and standpoints of recorders. Therefore, contradictions of historical materials have their own difficulties, making it quite tough to deduce historical materials without comparative investigation, textual research, interpretation and other historical research methods. In the above discussion, when talking about the "database" set up by Tomizawa, I always add some words such as "if", "may be" and "although". It is not that I have prejudices against the author, but I have general comprehensions on existing related historical materials, especially for materials related to Japan, and have a general estimation that these historical materials cannot draw the subversive conclusion. That is to say, apart from the meaning that historical records are not facts, his "database" cannot come to the conclusion that the Nanjing Massacre does not exist, even if the database is perfect. In other words, if his "database" is "completely impartial", it should not draw a negative conclusion; otherwise, its "impartiality" will be questioned. After a quick glance at the article To Clarify the Nanjing Incident in Accordance with Database, I find that he made some serious mistakes not only in interpretations but also in his database with arbitrary proof and injustice. The problems that Tomizawa made are comprehensive. As his article has more than 100 pages, to correct all the problems requires the space of a separate article. Therefore, only a few cases are discussed here.

The So-Called "Clearing Fields Combat"

The first question raised by Tomizawa is "Clearing Fields Combat". From Table 1 listed by Rabe (Rabe, John H. D. Rabe), Durdin (Durdin,F. Tillman Durdin), Atchison (George Atchison Jr.), Vautrin (Vautrin, Minnie Vautrin), Abend (Abend, Hallet Abend), Steele (Archibald T. Steele) and the US Life magazine, the US Embassy Espy report and the related materials of the 31st article in the letter from the second governor Zhengyun Jiang to Bates (M. S. Bates), Tomizawa tried to prove that the "scorched earth" plan implemented by the Chinese army, which was to defend against the Japanese army and not to leave a thing for the Japanese army, was destructive. Tomizawa gets into the whole issue from the aspect of the "Clearing Fields Combat", which reveals his intentions. Japanese fictionalists always had such a kind of mind that it is not enough to claim innocence of the Japanese army. What's more, it is to have something on the Chinese side while relieving the guilt of Japanese army. Thus, even if the Japanese army's responsibilities cannot be shirked, putting the blame on the two parties equally will be a balance that alleviates the guilt of the Japanese army. However, it is impossible to get any easy rides when it comes to the topic of "Clearing Fields Combat". Because the Chinese army's self-destruction of homeland is only the result forced by the Japanese army, the bombardment of Japanese aircrafts and cannons and looting and arson everywhere is considered as important aspects of "scorched earth", which is the universal understanding of people with justice. Even if Tomizawa claims "complete justice", he would see this point and create feelings of doubt about his sincerity.

But Tomizawa's problem is not just on the argument. Let us not ask whether there is any reason for the clearance of the fields. Whether the destruction of the Japanese army can be cut off from the "scorched earth", it means that it is reasonable to set the "Clearing Fields Combat" alone. Just looking at the thirty-one materials listed in the "database", Tomizawa has sticky fingers. The short materials drawn by Tomizawa, from the perspective of the context, are garbles without justice because the context of many materials has restrictive records. For example, the 11th citation says that Xiaoling Tomb was burned by the Chinese army, but the main point of the original text was that "that it was completely burned by the Japanese army"[35]; as the 24th citation quoted that the Chinese army committed widespread arson when retreating, the original context said at the same time that "the Americans stressed that the retreating Chinese soldier seldom set fires, destroyed or plundered cities. Therefore, when the Japanese army entered the city, Nanjing was not actually damaged".[36] On the contrary, more materials

---

[35] Nanjing Massacre research center of Nanjing Normal University, *Minnie Vautrin's Diary*, Nanjing: Jiangsu People's Publishing House, 2000(6), p. 216.

[36] 南京事件調査研究会編訳『南京事件資料集』1『アメリカ関係資料編』，東京，青木書店 1992年10月15日第1版，第240页。

include both descriptions and criticisms of Japanese atrocities. Here are just two examples of the beginning and the end. The second citation (the first citation records that the Chinese defenders blew up the railway bridge in order to prevent the Japanese from attacking Jinan, which has nothing to do with the "Clearing Fields Combat" in Nanjing) says that the Chinese army set fires without scruples, Durdin reports. Indeed, Durdin criticizes the Chinese army's clearance of the fields severely. It is believed that there was no effect on blocking the Japanese army and no points in military. However, the original context only said that the clearance of fields outside the city of Nanjing was equal to "the losses caused by the Japanese army". However, the Japanese military aircrafts in the city of Nanjing launched raids around the [safety zone] all day, which made the injured wounded swarm into the [safety zone]. Nanjing was caught in a terrible horror.[37] The 31st citation said that houses around the east and west gates were burned down (a letter from Zhengyun Jiang), but Zhengyun Jiang's original letter not only did not mention that the arson was committed by the Chinese army, but instead mentioned that Japanese soldiers invaded their houses and raped young girls.[38] (This letter was written on December 17th, and the recorded was according to people from "This Morning". At that time, the Chinese soldiers had already suffered from a fingertip search. Those who escaped successfully were in fear of nowhere to hide, so arsonists could only be Japanese soldiers.)

As can be seen from the above, even if the "Clearing Fields Combat" is not discussed alone, the materials in the "database" itself are simply unreliable. Tomizawa starts with this topic with a purpose that is not limited to criticize the destruction of the Chinese army. Moreover, he does not satisfy with this. He also gives "the finishing touch":

> It can be seen that the vast areas in the suburbs of Nanjing have become the targets of the clearance of fields, and nearby residents and houses no longer exist. It is unimaginable to have massacres of Japanese troops and arson in such a region.[39]

The materials intercepted from the materials to criticize the Chinese army cannot cover the Japanese atrocities. Tomizawa had the nerve to make such deductions! The evidence of the Japanese army's destruction and atrocities in this area needs no further search. According to the thirty-one materials cited by Tomizawa, checking the adjacent paragraphs of these materials, and even the words, you can see the contradictions. In addition to the previous citations, the "database" refers to the fourth, fifth, seventh, eighth, ninth, eleventh, twelfth, thirteenth, fifteenth, sixteenth, seventeenth, eighteenth, nineteenth, twenty-first, twenty-second, twenty-third, twenty-fourth, twenty-fifth, twenty-seventh,

---

[37] 南京事件調査研究会編訳『南京事件資料集』1『アメリカ関係資料編』, 第432, 433頁。
[38] 南京事件調査研究会編訳『南京事件資料集』1『アメリカ関係資料編』, 第138頁。
[39] 東中野修道編著『日本「南京」学会年報——南京「虐殺」研究の最前線』, 第74頁。

twenty-eighth or the same paragraph or the same page in the literature, or on the same day or the adjoining days on the diary, you can also see the records of the Japanese atrocities. For example, the next paragraph of the fourth citation from the same article states that "the Japanese army set fire to the siege of the Chinese army"; the same page of the 8th citation refers to the ruin caused by the "battle" between the two militaries; the same page of the 9th citation states that "The most devastating massacre in modern history occurred… all those arrested were shot and is suspected to have been a collective execution". The next paragraph of the 21st citation states that "Japanese military aircraft is omnipresent in the bombing of the city". The same page of the 21st citation states that the Japanese army set fire to drive the Chinese soldiers. On the same page as the 23rd citation, it says that "three Japanese heavy bombers cast bombs on the long queue of the Chinese army entered by the Zhongshan Gate"; the next paragraph of the twenty-seventh citation says that "the Japanese army is openly looting, not only shops, houses, hospitals, but not even refugee areas were spared or survived".[40] The two days before and after the Vautrin's Diary cited in article 6 all mentioned the Japanese bombing of non-military targets. "A mother and her daughter were killed on the spot. When Wilson found the numb father, he still held his child, the upper part of the child's head was blown up". The day diary cited by the 9th article recorded the bombing of the south gate nearby.[41]

From the above, we can see that Tomizawa's "Clearing Fields Combat" is almost a counter-evidence of his conclusions. It's really shocked that Tomizawa practices deception with the public.

Are There Any Records on the Population of Nanjing That Are Roughly Consistent with One Another?

During the studies on the Nanjing Massacre, the most discussed issue is the population. As I once put in the last section of *A Study of the Order for Japanese Troops during Nanjing Slaughter in 1937*, the number of people killed in the massacre is of subordinate importance, considering the figures cannot deny the nature, that the bodies buried have been destroyed in decades of weathering, that large quantities of bodies were pushed into the Yangtze River at that time, and that the documents reserved are incomplete. (This section was deleted before contribution for I suppose it is not prudent to discuss this issue, which is of great importance during the studies on the Nanjing Massacre, incidentally in an article of different theme.[42]) In addition

---

[40] 南京事件調査研究会編訳『南京事件資料集』1『アメリカ関係資料編』, 第392, 387, 553, 461, 536, 402, 468頁。

[41] Vautrin's Diary, pp. 178, 179.

[42] This part was later taken as the postscript of *A Study of the Order for Japanese Troops During Nanjing Slaughter in 1937*, which was included in *Studies on the Nanjing Massacre* by Cheng Zhaoqi, the edition published by Shanghai Lexicographical Publishing House in December 2002: pp. 101–104.

to considering the objective limits, I made this conclusion more based on a point; that is, too much emphasis on this issue is not conducive to further studies. The school of fiction has long fussed about verifying the number, but there is no doubt that the token number cannot deny the nature, be they increased or decreased. However, this is not to say that the number of people killed counts for little.[43] Not only the death toll but the population of Nanjing before and after the Japanese troops captured the city is anything but meaningless to find out the historical truth, though it plays a subsidiary, not a decisive role.

The population issue is important in Tomizawa's article. Not only the second section "The Issue of Population" (the title, the same below) and the third section "The Concentration of Population" are directly related, but the fourth section "No Man outside the Safety Zone" still implies the population issue. Before analyzing Tomizawa's "database", let us first get an idea of his conclusion on the population issue. It is put as follows:

> Two conclusions can be drawn from it. First, one cannot imagine 300,000 citizens were killed when there were 250,000 refugees. Second, more importantly, there is no record on population decline, so there wasn't a small killing, let alone killing 300,000 people.[44]

Tomizawa's conclusion has prevailed among the fictionalists for a long time.[45] But in fact it materially "fools" people for no scholar has put that the mass killing was limited to citizens and the city of Nanjing inside since the issue on the Nanjing Massacre got discussed again in Japan.[46] For example, the late Tomio Hora, a great man specialized in studies on the Nanjing Massacre, once said, "There were no less than 200,000 soldiers and ordinary people killed inside and outside the city of Nanjing".[47] Although there

---

[43] At the end of last year, I had a talk with a Japanese scholar who not only was dismissive of the fictionalists' research on figures but did not agree with the relevant works of the school of slaughter. This is the most extreme view I have ever met. However, he cannot deny that disregard of figures to a full scale will make the issue of the Nanjing Massacre "vague".

[44] Higashinakano Shudo. The Annual of the Association for Nanjing Studies: Studies in Nanjing "Massacre" at the Cutting Edge, p. 79.

[45] For example, Masaaki Tanaka made a typical metaphor: "Wine, if contained in a bottle with a capacity of a half liter, will always have a volume of a half liter, no matter how it is contained and how full it is. So the population was 200,000 and it was impossible that 300,000 people were killed (Masaaki Tanaka, 『南京事件の総括——虐殺否定十五の論拠』, p. 159).

[46] As there was a fierce debate in court during the Tokyo Trial, the debate arising in the 1970 s is a recurrence.

[47] Tomio Hora. 『決定版·南京大虐殺』. Tokyo: Tokuma Shoten Publishing Co., Ltd. 1st Edition published on December 31st, 1982: p. 150.

are different opinions on the time, sphere and target, there were no dissenting voices on that the massacre was perpetrated both inside and outside the city and that people killed not only included "citizens" but also soldiers and peasants. As for the sphere, the majority hold that the massacre was perpetrated "in the jurisdiction of the Nanjing municipal government (the city of Nanjing, the Xiaguan District and suburban areas such as the Pukou District, Xiaolingwei, the Swallow Rock, Shangxin River and the mausoleums) and the six surrounding counties (Jiangning, Jurong, Piaoshui, Jiangpu, Liuhe and Gaochun)".[48] Hence, we have to say that Tomizawa's conclusion is nothing else but a "frame-up", especially untrue.

With a make-believe target, Tomizawa's "database", no matter how effective, is pointless. But how about the population in the safety zone? Can the population of the safety zone represent that of Nanjing? Are the relevant figures in records reserved reliable? All these deserve discussing. Table 2 in Tomizawa's article has listed over 70 pieces of figures about population, which roughly takes the mid-January of 1938 as a watershed: Most of the figures before that time are 200,000 while later figures mostly are 250,000. (The increase has been first discovered by the fictionalists and they think it clear evidence that Japanese troops did not commit the atrocity.[49]) We say the evidence of humanities is different from scientific one which is convincing by an overwhelming majority. But we cannot ignore the main trend shown by more evidence. It thus is necessary to examine Tomizawa's data.

Among the 70 items in Table, 200,000 and 250,000 occupy an overwhelming majority, accounting for 51 in total. The former figure alone totals 27 items. With January 14th that Tomizawa mentioned as a line, we can see that 26 items are before (and on) that day while there is only one after (but excluding) that day, so items before that day are in majority. As for the figure of 250,000, it accounts for 24 but there are only two items before (but excluding) that day while others are all thereafter. So there is also an obvious distinction between figures before and after that day. The distinction is so clear that it can be a strong evidence. However, you can find that Tomizawa has played tricks when selecting the materials, if paying attention to the source. Most of these materials are of the same source, so they cannot be "majority" by nature. For example, the 26 items of 200,000 before January 14th are from the *Documents of the Nanking Safty Zone* by Shuhsi Hsü (accounting for 6 pieces), the Diaries of John Rabe (accounting for 13 pieces), *The Diaries of Minnie Vantrin* (accounting for 1 piece) and letters and reports by Robert O. Wilson (accounting for 2 pieces), James McCallum, Archibald T. Steele, F. Tillman Durdin and George Atchison Jr.

---

[48]「まぼろし派、中間派、大虐殺派三派合同大アンケート」.『諸君!』. Tokyo: Bungei. February 2001: p. 195.

[49] See 『「南京虐殺」の徹底検証』, pp. 232–235. I have refuted it in "Did the Population of the Safety Zone 'Increase'?", the 12th section of *Reading Notes of Nanjing Massacre*, which was published on the 1st issue of Historical Review in 2003 (pp. 113–115).

(respectively accounting for 1 piece). Documents of the Nanking Safety Zone by Shuhsi Hsü, like the book *What War Means: The Japanese Atrocities* in China by H. J. Timperley, has the materials provided by M. S. Bates and others who stayed in Nanjing at that time. Considering that John Rabe, Minnie Vantrin, Robert O. Wilson, James McCallum and M. S. Bates are all members of the International Committee for the Safety Zone or the International Committee of the Red Cross, Documents of the Nanking Safety Zone by Shuhsi Hsü can be anything but inconsistent with others' records, though it is absurd to take the 13 records by John Rabe as 13 pieces of evidence. Hence, among the 26 pieces of items, 23 can be merely regarded as one piece of evidence. It is a similar case with the figure of 250,000. The items before January 14th are from Documents of the Nanking Safety Zone by Shuhsi Hsü (accounting for 12 pieces), The Diaries of John Rabe (accounting for 2 pieces), the Espy Report (accounting for 1 piece) and materials provided by M. S. Bates (accounting for 6 pieces), George A. Fitch and Clarence E. Gauss (respectively accounting for 1 piece), of which only the Espy Report and materials provided by Clarence E. Gauss are not directly from the people in the safety zone. But Allison John Moore has clearly stated in advance that the Espy Report was based on the records by Americans who stayed in Nanjing at that time. Although we cannot specify the author (or the authors), no matter who they are, these materials can still be regarded as the records of the safety zone as M. S. Bates, George A. Fitch, Minnie Vantrin and Robert O. Wilson all related to the safety zone. And Clarence E. Gauss was an American diplomat, so what he was based on probably has something to do with Americans who stayed in Nanjing at that time. But since it is not clearly stated, we prudently regard the material as a separate source. In this case, the items of 250,000 can just serve two pieces of evidence.

Then, we move on to the other items in Tomizawa's "database" excluding 200,000 and 250,000. The figure "million" on September 22nd, 1937, has nothing to do with the theme; no exact figure was mentioned when John Rabe claimed that the Police Chief Mr. Wang told me the true case; as for the two items of December 10th, the item that "non-military departments has been excavated" does not mention any number; it is the same case with the item "Four fifths have been excavated"; the figure "700,000" that F. Tillman Durdin mentioned was his recollection when he was interviewed by the school of slaughter in 1986, which cannot be regarded as the records at that time—except for these five items, the remaining 14 items are as follows: On November 27th, George Atchison Jr. wrote down the figure "400,000"; on December 2nd, Archibald T. Steele wrote down "one third of a million"; on December 9th, Robert O. Wilson mentioned "hundreds of thousands of"; on December 10th, the Washington Post reported "ten thousand"; on December 11th, Hallet Abend marked down "300,000"; on December 14th, Archibald T. Steele marked down "100,000"; on December 15th, the *New York Times* reported "300,000"; on December 18th,

F. Tillman Durdin noted down "over 100,000" and both Archibald T. Steele and the Life recorded "100,000"; on December 22nd, F. Tillman Durdin noted down "100,000"; on January 19th, 1938, The Diaries of John Rabe recorded "hundreds of thousands of" while on February 15 the Hankow herald recorded "150,000" (at least 150,000 in the original).

After examining the items, we can see that Tomizawa's "database" is rather rough "technically" regardless of whether it is "fair". Take the figure "400,000" on November 27th as example. It is put as "300,000 to 400,000" in the original. Another example is Archibald T. Steele's record on December 14th; its original has not marked that date or the writing date and whose publication was as late as February 4th of the next year, having nothing to do with the date, Tomizawa marked. And the Life was marked on December 18th but it was recorded during the days from December 10th to 18th (which was published on January 10th of the next year). As for Steele's records on December 18th, the same figure appears twice. Examples can still go on. Although such non-principle-related problems of Tomizawa's "database" are not the focus of this article, we can still learn that Tomizawa is careless, arbitrary and far from rigorous.

Now let us sort out the foregoing materials. As Steele's record on December 18th is repeated, there remain 13 pieces of useful records: "one third of a million" and "300,000 to 400,000" respectively account for 1 piece, "300,000", "150,000" and "hundreds of thousands of" respectively account for 2 pieces, and "100,000" accounts for 5 pieces. The two pieces about "300,000" respectively from Hallet Abend and the *New York Times*, of which the latter, however, was still from Abend's hand. Hence, they can be just regarded as one. As for the 5 pieces about "100,000", Steele and Durdin respectively contributed two pieces, so they can be only counted as three. With the sources strictly examined, the 70 pieces of materials listed in Tomizawa's "database" are supposed to be as follows:

What should Tomizawa's "database" be

Hundreds of thousands of	1/3 of a million	300,000–400,000	300,000	250,000	200,000	150,000	100,000
2	1	1	1	2	4	2	3

After sorting out Tomizawa's "database", we can know that there did not reach a "consensus" about the population of the safety zone at that time. There was "no overwhelming evidence" that the "records of population decline did not exist at all". If we pay attention to other materials of that time which are omitted from Tomizawa's "database", it can be found that opinions are divided and that most of the figures recorded are different from those mentioned above. For example, The Populace Suffering in Hell, which was published in The Atrocities of Enemies in March 1938, recorded

"400,000"[50]; in the letter of November 13th, 1937, from Nanjing municipal government to the Military Commission of National Government, it was mentioned that "there were about 500,000 people"[51]; the Consulate General of Japan in Shanghai wrote down "about 530,000" in the letter to the Minister of Foreign Affairs[52] and so on. Besides the last two earlier statements being official (the content of the letter from the Consulate General of Japan in Shanghai was from the investigation of Nanjing Police Station), the others, including all the figures listed in Tomozawa's "database", are all conjectured because there was no and there could be no overall statistics based on the investigation at that time. This is the root why opinions vary from person to person. And arbitrarily taking examples from opinions that varied to such a degree, it is impossible to reach a reasonable conclusion.

Was the Population of Nanjing Concentrated in Safety Zone?

The third section "The Concentration of Population" and the fourth section "No Man outside Security Area" of Tomizawa's work concern one thing, i.e., stressing that the population of Nanjing was concentrated in safety zone while no man was outside, which was of great importance for the school of fiction to deny the slaughter. It is self-evident, they suppose, that Japanese troops did not perpetrate the slaughter as long as they can prove that no man was outside the safety zone, because there is no word about slaughter in the safety zone in the International Committee for Safety Zone and its members' individual documents. They no doubt have made a straw man because it has been mentioned above that the Nanjing Massacre was not confined to the city of Nanjing itself. But whether the population of Nanjing was all concentrated in safety zone, or whether there was "no man to be seen" outside the safety zone, is still of great importance to determine whether Japanese troops perpetrated the slaughter in Nanjing.

The materials listed in Table 3 of Tomizawa's work are all from the records of the International Committee members such as John D. Rabe and Lewis S. C. Smythe, the British embassies, the American embassies and Western journals, while those in Table 4 are from Japanese. The difference in the sources just implies the facts at that time. Westerners of the International Committee

---

[50] The Editorial Committee for Historical Records of the Nanjing Massacre & Nanjing Library. (Eds.). *The Historical Records of the Nanjing Massacre Perpetrated by Japanese Invaders*. Nanjing: Jiangsu Ancient Classics Publishing House. The 5th printing edition of the 1st Edition that was published in February 1998, p. 131.

[51] The Second Historical Archives of China & The Nanjing Archives. (Eds.). *Documents of the Nanjing Massacre Perpetrated by Japanese Invaders*. Jiangsu Ancient Classics Publishing House. The 3rd printing Edition published in February 1997, p. 915.

[52] The National Archives Administration of China, the Second Historical Archives of China & Jilin Provincial Academy of Social Sciences. (Eds.). *The Anthology of Documents on Japanese Invasion of China: The Nanjing Massacre*. Beijing: The Book Company. 1st Edition published in July 1995, p. 14.

who stayed in Nanjing at that time were concentrated in safety zone but were too busy with handling Japanese atrocities and daily relief of refugees in large quantities to focus on areas outside safety zone; journalists and embassy personnel were far in Shanghai or Hankou and less likely to know the facts. So the objective condition precluded Westerners from knowing the facts. Although they could testify that refugees were concentrated to the safety zone, they could not judge whether there was any citizen outside. Hence, Table 3 in the Tomizawa's article, even if not a trap made on purpose, does not make any sense.

Then, can the materials in Table 4 prove that there was no man outside the safety zone? The answer, I suppose, is no. The reason does not lie in the feature of historical evidence; that is, it is easier to prove than to deny—one piece of positive evidence means absolute existence while nonexistence proves to be limited no matter how many negative evidences. Besides, Tomizawa's "database" does not include all materials as claimed. It also fails to avoid preferentiality in deciding what to be included. For example, such statements as "there was neither fire nor man as far as to the central roundabout" "in east of Nanjing vast space stayed empty" "no man could be seen but a skinny dog" and "nobody even no dog was seen as far as to Zhongshan North Road, which seemed a 'dead street'" are all excerpted from the Collection on the War History of Nanjing. But the collection not only includes such materials but also opposite examples can be found. For instance, Japanese Major General Sasaki Touichi, head of the 30th Brigade of the 16th Infantry Division, has recorded the mopping-up operations in Nanjing on December 14th in his diary. In terms of those "hidden" remnants, he put it as follows: "Those who resisted or lost their obedience were killed without mercy. Gunshots could be heard here and there".[53] Since the 30th Brigade was one of the major forces who carried out mopping-out operations in Nanjing and the 38th Regiment under the 30th Brigade took charge of the mop-up of a triangle from the east of Zhongshan North Road to Central Road, Sasaki's record is wholly reliable. In this case, there is no need giving other examples, though such records at that time are not rare. But it is of necessity to point out that some materials in Tomizawa's "database" are used out of context. For example, the above-mentioned statement "there was neither fire nor man as far as to the central roundabout" is excerpted from the notes by Yoshio Kanemaru who served the 16th Division, but Kanemaru's original goes like this:

> (December 13th afternoon) I, along with a squad, was going to the central circular intersection by way of Zhongshan Dongche Road (Note: it may refer to the extension of Zhongshan East Road with "che" mistaken for "yan" or

---

[53] Notes by Major General Sasaki Touichi. In Committee for the Compilation of the War History of Nanjing (Ed.). *Collection on the War History of Nanjing* (Not For Sale). Tokyo: Kaikōsha. 1st Edition published on January 3rd, 1989: p. 379.

may refers to roadway). It was scheduled to go north to Yijiang Gate by way of Zhongshan North Road. As we marched, the gunshots became increasingly heavier and fires could be seen everywhere. It was getting darker, so we returned to the camp at the "Nanjing Hotel" (Note: it seems to mean "Central Hotel") near the national government. We then wanted to borrow the blankets that we saw at the enemies' Central Hospital. But strangely, a large number of wounded soldiers of Chinese military as well as the blankets were all gone when we arrived there. After returning to the hotel, we cooked with lunch box in the wholly dark corridor and then slept with candles burning.

Until the central roundabout, there was neither fire nor man. It was comparatively quiet. But no unbroken objects could be found in dwellings, let alone furniture, and some items on shelves had been smashed to pieces. Broken pieces of wood were almost everywhere, leaving no space for a man to stand. And corpses of soldiers and people with plain clothes were here and there. I marked those houses that seemed to be enemies' government offices. However, once passing the central roundabout, I saw fires, weapons and military uniforms scattering on the road, and heaps of dead bodies. Considering that there was fighting near the Yijiang Gate and nearby fires were on, I stepped over the bodies and returned.[54]

The "fighting" Kanemaru mentioned was in fact slaughter of Chinese soldiers who did not resist and tried to escape by crossing the river perpetrated by the 33rd Regiment (under the 30th Brigade), which can be testified by Report on Fightings near Nanjing written by the 33rd Regiment. But Kanemaru's record paints the actual situation of Nanjing on that day. The value and doubts about his record have nothing to do with this article, so it will not be commented on. However, it is obvious that Tomizawa's quotation has totally gone against its original meaning.

A lot of materials cited in Table 4, including Kanemaru's record, are all out of later collection. As mentioned above, since Sasaki was one of the Japanese officers who were in charge of the mopping-out operations in the city and his record was enough to prove the falsity of Tomizawa's argument that "there was no man". But to prove that his argument is indefensible, I prefer to cite a passage just earlier before Kanemaru's latest interview that was published in January. Yasumura Junnitu, who served the 3rd MG Squadron of the 38th Regiment and took charge of the mop-out to the east of Zhongshan North Road, said:

Mopping-out operation was also carried out in the city on the next day after Nanjing had fallen. It was based on the small force as a unit and the 3rd MG Squadron all attended. The next day there were still some enemies who bear arms, mainly rifles. They hid because they, if out, would be arrested and transferred to the Captive Corps. The Captive Corps existed everywhere and captives

---

[54] Notes by Sergeant Yoshio Kanemaru. In Committee for the Compilation of the War History of Nanjing (Eds.). *Collection on the War History of Nanjing*, pp. 361–362.

were concentrated. Captives, if amounting to 10, would be trussed up with a rope and brought there. And they would all be sent to the rear-area troops. But we didn't know the actual situation because we had never dealt with captives.

Mop-up was daily carried out. I did not know whether those captured were soldiers or common people. As long as being seen, people would be captured regardless of sex. Women also resisted and were quite powerful.

Another corps took charge of handling those captives. I never met them. Captives would be taken out of the city and then transferred to the captives corps. But we could not imagine how they would be dealt with, dead or alive. Awaiting them probably was a bad ending. As the corps had none business with me, captives, dead or alive, ….

I merely attacked enemies in fighting and had never heard of captives being killed in large quantities. After the war, I still did not hear of it. I think the Nanjing Massacre is bullshit. And how can 300,000 people be killed? It is not the case!

I did not shoot in that way. I did not spray bullets into people with a machine gun and kill about ten or twenty people. It is not ordinary to bring all Chinese together and fire at once, which I have never done. But it is a fact that some ten or twenty people who gathered together were shot down during the mopping-out operations inside Nanjing. The number of deaths published by Japanese Chiefs of Staff is 84,000, which is likely to be a mistake. This report covers some part of the Regiment's report and I am not as convinced as intended of the death toll. But since it is a statement from the military headquarter, of course, I will not deny it.[55]

As we can see from Yasumura's dictation, it was not the case that "there was no man" outside the safety zone but there were repeated "killing" or "arrest" of people "every day". And if taking into account the population issue of Nanjing mentioned above, we can learn from his recollection that in the safety zone there were civilians besides soldiers—there is no need denying the existence of female soldiers, but most women were civilians.[56] So it is a kind of evasion that Yasumura claimed to "know nothing about it".

---

[55] 安村純一口述「兵士と思ったら、男も女も若いのはみんな引っ張った」. In Tamaki Matsuoka (Ed.).『南京戦————閉ざされた記憶を尋ねて』. Tokyo: 社会評論社. 1st Edition published on August 15th, 2002: pp. 186–187. This book raised great comment from both the left wing and the right wing. For example, 「『南京戦・元兵士102人の証言』のデタラメさ」 written by Kenichi Ara (In 『正論』. Tokyo: 産経新聞社. November 2002: pp. 96–102.) and 「『南京戦』元兵士————疑惑の『証言』」 written by Shudo Higashinakano (In 『諸君!』. Tokyo: Bungei. November 2002: pp. 163–173) try their best to argue what is lost in this book. Japanese left-wing also criticized this book, such as 「『南京戦』何が問題か」 by 小野賢二 (In 『金曜日週刊』. Tokyo: 株式会社金曜日, published on December 20th, 2002: pp. 52–53). Of course, some Japanese scholars hold positive opinion on this book. For instance, 津田道夫 thinks that this book is positively of "great value", though it "does not imply any introspection by nature" (津田道夫著「歴史の真実————松岡環編著『南京戦————閉ざされた記憶を尋ねて』読む」, 東京,『図書新聞』2002年10月12日第2版).

[56] 山田忠义, who also served the 3rd GM Squadron of the 38th Regiment, said, "Corpses could be seen here and there in the city. The bodies of women were in large quantities." 「捕虜に食わす物がないので処分せざるをえず」,『南京戦————閉ざされた記憶を尋ねて』, 第190頁.

Yasumura holds a negative attitude on the Nanjing Massacre and underlines that it is "nonsense". Since he is not willing to imply that Japanese troops perpetrated the massacre, his recollection is more liable in this aspect. (The 1st and 3rd Brigade took part in the mop-out of this area. A Japanese brigade consists of four infantry squadrons, a GM squadron and an artillery squad. A squadron is composed of 3 squads and a squad is divided into 6 detachments. The "small force" Yasumura mentioned can be a squad that is smaller than a squadron or a detachment that is in a much smaller scale. So there were dozens of or even hundreds of "small forces" in the small triangle area to the east of Zhongshan North Road and to the west of Xuanwu Lake. What Yasumura went through, which was also common, was that each small force transferred a large number of captives to the Captive Corps and the small batch of captives, usually ten or twenty, could be transferred or killed on the spot. So in this area alone how many civilians were killed without mercy?)

One cannot help doubting Tomizawa's so-called "impartiality" as he turns a blind eye to Sasaki's and others' records. His work consists of 11 sections, each with one or more tables. After skimmed through, it is discovered that generally, there are foregoing problems in each section and each table. But the length of this article does not allow them being respectively analyzed in detail.

3 "Valuable Findings" Which Cannot Bear Examinations

The expression "valuable findings" is from the preface written by Huang Wenxiong. From the article of Tomizawa, the most important content in Annals, the self-praise is not consistent with the truth. And how about the rest contents of Annals? Are there any "valuable findings"? We will give a further discussion.

As the president of Japanese Association of Nanjing Studies, Higashinakano Shudo writes the most articles and is the most active character in the school of fiction in Japan. This time he provides an article named Why did the Japanese know about Nanjing Massacre before the Tokyo Trial? Just before the publication of Annals, I have composed an article about this title.[57] The coincidence indicates that this issue has been of great significance which cannot be ignored so far. The parlance of "do not know Nanjing Massacre" is an old topic that proposed by Tanaka Masaaki and others in the 1980 s and also a vital contention from various camps in Japan.[58] However, there are some

---

[57] *Is the Nanjing Massacre a Fabrication Made by Tokyo Trial?*, Beijing, Modern Chinese History Studies, 2002(6), pp. 1–57.

[58] Tanaka Masaaki said, "The so-called Japanese army did something inhuman and terrible in Nanjing and massacred hundreds of thousands of Chinese, including women and children. Besides, the sadistic acts of arson, atrocities, rape and plunder continued for seven weeks. This "chilling fact" was first known to Japanese nationals through the Tokyo trial (the heavy dot number is what the original text has the initiator).『「南京虐殺」の虚構──松井大将の日記をめぐって』, 第287頁.

changes in its connotation between today and 1980 s. "Nanjing Massacre" is a kind of generalization, including homicide, pillage, rape and arson, and other atrocities. In face of these undeniable facts, someone in the school of fiction has to adjust their strategies. They deny the crucial and symbolic "slaughter", and simultaneously admit some lesser crimes.[59] The strategy that "sacrificing minor to save major ones" makes materials which can prove atrocities of the Japanese troops at that time flexible. For instance, Ishii Itaro, the East Asia Director of Ministry of Foreign Affairs of Japan at that time, once said in his book The Life of being a Diplomat:

> The telegram brought by the Consul Fukui who followed our army back to Nanjing, and the written report sent by the consul in Shanghai, shocked us. These reports recorded that Japanese armies occupied Nanjing and committed pillage, rape and arson to Chinese.[60]

This record has always been treated as the evidence that Japanese senior leaders know the incident at the beginning. However, in the Tokyo Trial, Ishii answered the question about the specific content of "atrocities" in his testimony (No. 3287), proposed by lawyer Kiyoshi Itō differently. He said,

> Atrocities included such things as rape, arson and plunder by Japanese troops who occupied Nanjing.[61]

In general, the court defense reflects that there is no big difference between atrocities of the Japanese army and records. But the school of fiction regards the small inconsistencies that "slaughter" isn't mentioned in the defense note as a significant difference and makes a fuss about it. They also think they are holding the upper hand. For example, the article The Review of "Nanjing Massacre" takes this to prove that there is no "slaughter".[62]

So does Higashinakano. His article focuses on the topic that before the Tokyo Trial, strictly speaking, at that time, Japanese do not know "slaughter"

---

[59] For example, Ooi Mitsuru, a member of fiction school, said in *The Fabricated Nanjing Massacre*, of course, I am not saying that the Japanese army has done nothing illegal. It is impossible for an army with 70,000 soldiers that nothing happens. Staff officer Onishi punished and arrested the gendarmes, which undoubtedly happened everywhere (『仕組まれた「南京大虐殺」——攻略作戦の全貌とマスコミ報道の怖さ』, 第297頁) 而在《諸君!》. In the questionnaire of February the year before last, he filled in "12" in the answer to the first choice of the number of people killed, and "12" means "infinitely close to zero" (「まぼろし派、中間派、大虐殺派三派合同大アンケート」,『諸君!』, 東京, 文藝春秋社, 2001年2月号, 第179頁).

[60] 石射猪太郎著『外交官の一生——対中国外交の回想』, 東京, 太平出版社1974年4月15日第4次印刷版, 第267頁.

[61] 洞富雄編『日中戦争史資料』8「南京事件」I, 第221頁.

[62] 日本会議国際広報委員会編『再審「南京大虐殺」——世界に訴える日本の冤罪』, 東京, 明成社2000年11月25日第2次印刷版, 第64頁. *The Alleged "Nanking Massacre"* is different from Ooi Mitsuru, which not only denies slaughter, but also does not admit the Japanese atrocities.

from five perspectives: news blackout at wartime, records from Japanese, reports from America, the earliest "propaganda materials" in English, and reports received by the Japanese embassy.

Is There No News Blackout in Japan at Wartime?

The discussion of news blackout by Higashinakano is based on the viewpoint from the Japanese school of slaughter. The school of slaughter thinks that the news of the slaughter at that time failed to circulate because of news blackout in Japan. Aiming at the famous case of the book *Soldiers Alive* by Ishikawatatuzou,[63] Higashinakano said that Ishikawatatuzou "never believes" there had been slaughter and his work was composed in accordance with the book The Testimonies of 48 Japanese People About "Nanjing Incident" written by AroKen-ichi.[64] However, if Ishikawa did not believe the slaughter, why he run the risk to write it? If it is merely a work of fiction, why did his descriptions, for instance, the description of Xiaguan slaughter, correspond with many other records? Why did he tell Yomiuri Shimbun at the Tokyo Trail that he had witnessed the slaughter? (May 9th, 1946) If what he said was totally wrong, why did not he correct it? Why did he only tell Ara Kenichi who denied Nanjing Massacre? Why Ara kept it secret when Yomiuri Shimbun was alive. These questions need to be answered if Higashinakano persists on his view that Ishikawatatuzou "never believes" there was slaughter. Even what Ishikawatatuzou means is a truth, it cannot be related to the denial of news blackout at wartime in Japan because there are reasons like "anti-troop" and "disturbing the social order" and cases such as the violations of news blackout rules except that "taking the fiction as a fact" is a label on the work living soldiers, the blackout of publication and prosecution against

---

[63] Japanese writer Ishikawa Tatsujo came to China after the war broke out. He spent ten days (from February 1st, 1938, to the 10th) writing this book. The book was originally intended to be published in March 1938 on *Central Public Comment*, which was banned in the name of so-called "anti-military content that is not conducive to the stability of the current situation" because it contains many contents such as plunder, rape, arson, and murder by Japanese troops. Not only was the book banned from publication, authors, editors, and publishers were all charged with the violation of press law on the grounds of "regarding fiction as a fact and disturb peace and order". Ishikawa was sentenced to four months' imprisonment (suspended for three years). The verdict said: "The killing and plundering of non-combatants by imperial soldiers and the lax military regulations are described as disturbing the peace and order".

[64] 阿羅健一編『「南京事件」日本人48人の証言』，東京，小学館2002年1月1日第1版，第312頁。此书为15年前出版的『聞き書南京事件』（東京，図書出版社1987年8月15日第1版）的"文庫本" (Bunkoben is the size of a postcard and its target is to be easy to carry. It can be read during commuting and any break). The arrangement has been adjusted, with some deletions. Sakurai's recommendation and the publisher's "written in the Bunkoben" have been added. Ara rewrote the postscript. Sakurai called this book the first-level data of the "Nanjing Incident". The biggest difference between Ara's new postscript and the old postscript is that the new postscript emphasizes that the Japanese army only "punished" soldiers in Nanjing and did not commit crimes against civilians.

relevant people.⁶⁵ Therefore, it brings no benefits for Higashinakano to cite this example in the beginning of his article.

After 918 Incident, the Japanese military government enforced news blackout, and when July 7th Incident of 1937 occurred, news blackout was very severe. On July 13th, Police Security Station of the Cabinet Office ordered that all photos and records relevant to the Japanese invaders were not allowed to publish except for army headquarters. On July 31st, "Article 27 of Newsprint Law" stipulated that the secretaries of the army and the navy and foreign ministers have the right to prohibit and restrict the publication of military and diplomatic matters. On that day, the army headquarter published the corresponding "No. 24 decree" and "standards for the prohibition of news release". Among these "prohibited items", atrocities of Japanese army were important. Three days before the adoption of article 27 of the newsprint law, the news agency of army headquarters has already implemented "key points for determining the permission of news release", in which what is not permitted to publish is clearly stipulated as follows: "No. 6 Bloodcurdling things of photos and records about arrests and interrogations of Chinese soldiers or Chinese persons; No. 7 Pictures showing people were abused, but records of sadistic behaviors of Chinese soldiers could be published".⁶⁶ At the night of December 1st, the eve of the invasion of Nanjing, the Japanese garrison ruled that "publicity strategies and espionage are in charge of major generals of front army command, but other strategies should be instructed when the reports are published in the form of "released by the news agency".⁶⁷ Later, in the specific outline of publicity, there is another stipulation that "disciplined acts, Bushido attitudes of the imperial army and its benevolent acted in the occupied territories shall be publicized".⁶⁸

Obviously, it is the most elementary fact but Higashinakano totally ignored it. Apart from the example of Ishikawatatuzou, he also takes the example of at least 200 journalists from Tokyo Asahi Shimbun, Tokyo Nichinichi Shimbun, Yomiuri Shimbun, alliance news agency, Fukushima Minpo and Fukushima Nichinichi Shimbun and so on who entered Nanjing with the Japanese army at the time of the occupation of Nanjing as proof that there is no news blackout. Since there was neither news blackout nor any reports about Nanjing Massacre, it could prove that no slaughter happened in Nanjing. This logic is so surprising. How could allowing journalists to enter Nanjing be equivalent to no news blackout? Blackout means restricting

---

⁶⁵For example, the Tokyo Imperial University Professor Tadao Yanaihara's *Country's Dream* has ideas against the war reviewed by the Police Security Bureau of the Ministry of Internal Affairs. Later, his book *Nations and Peace* was also reviewed to have anti-war ideas. So, he was punished and forced to resign in December 1937.

⁶⁶转引自山中恒著『戦時国家情報機構史』, 東京, 小学館2001年1月1日第1版, 第225页.

⁶⁷大陸指第九號, 臼井勝美, 稲葉正夫編集, 解説《現代史資料》9《日中戦争》2, 東京, みすず書房1964年9月30日第1版, 第217页.

⁶⁸转引自『戦時国家情報機構史』, 第283页.

news release with power rather than canceling or forbidding news—here the distortion is not considered (for instance, the so-called "publicity" and "benevolence"). If news is completely prohibited, why do they need to regulate "prohibited items of no permissions"? Therefore, it is precise because these explicit and harsh regulations that contents which are not permitted still cannot be reported even there are 200 journalists. It is a quite shallow fact, how could Higashinakano reverse cause and effect?

Although he disregarded the facts and says nothing about previous institutional regulations at wartime, he gave no explanations about regulations. Hence, he cited what Hashimoto Tomisaburo, the deputy director of Shanghai branch of Tokyo Asahi Shimbun (the Chief Cabinet Secretary in the Sato Cabinet), said when being interviewed, "I do not feel any illiberality and I have said and recorded what I think of and see".[69] Then, Higashinakano writes that to say the least,

> supposing there is news blackout, … if (slaughter) exists, journalists will talk about it and never keep it to themselves. After the war, testimonies about Nanjing massacre must be broadcast by related personnel. However, there is only the following testimony after half a century of the fall of Nanjing….[70]

"The following testimony" refers to that "Nanjing Massacre is unheard of" said by Kanazawa, the press photographer of Tokyo Nichinichi Shimbun. According to Higashinakano, what the witness saw is the same as what Kanazawa saw; therefore, he only cited the example of Kanazawa to show there was no slaughter. Last year, I once took an example to prove that Higashinakano stood facts on their heads.[71] Though the words were harsh, I could not claim that he made mistakes deliberately. Later, I didn't found that he was wrong in basic ethics in addition to his negligence until I researched his representative *A Thorough Examination of "Nanjing Massacre"*.[72] In fact, here the so-called "only" cited by Higashinakano is a new one, and there are many other evidences to prove that journalists who entered Nanjing definitely hear of Nanjing Massacre. Imai Masayoshi, the journalist of Tokyo Asahi Shimbun at that time, once witnessed many "executions" at the side of Guanjiang River[73]; Masayoshi Arai, Maeda Yuji and Fukasawa, journalists

---

[69] 阿羅健一編『「南京事件」日本人48人の証言』, 第39頁.

[70] 東中野修道編著『日本「南京」学会年報——南京「虐殺」研究の最前線』, 第175頁.

[71] The diaries of Central China Army's military doctor and Colonel Hatatakashi Hiromichi recorded a large number of corpses in Shimonoseki and Yijiangmen. However, Higashinakano said there was no corpse (*Details in the Fabricated Nanjing Massacre*? Beijing, Modern Chinese History Studies, 2002(6), p. 48).

[72] *Japanese Right-Wing's Comments on the Nanjing Massacre(6th)*, Nanjing Massacre Research, pp. 354–401.

[73] 今井正剛「南京城内の大量殺人」, 猪瀬直樹監修, 高梨正樹編『目撃者が語る日中戦争』, 東京, 新人物往来社1989年11月10日第1版, 第4859頁. 今井文初刊于『特集·文藝春秋』1956年12月号.

of alliance news agency, "directly saw" a lot of burned bodies "at the place from Xiaguan to the direction of Caoxie Xia", "at the original military-political compound, in the name of training new recruits, young officers ordered them to bayonet Chinese captures" and "at military academy, captures were shot to death".[74] Anyone who witnessed atrocities of the Japanese troops would never keep it to himself as long as he has a conscience. "After the war, testimonies about Nanjing massacre must be broadcast by related personnel". Apart from the memory, records sprung up continuously after the war, and I have already discussed them before.

Besides, various photo albums which were not permitted at wartime are published by Mainichi Shimbun, Asahi Shimbun and so on. Lots of common photos in these albums were labeled "no permission", indicating the strictness of news blackout at that time. No news blackout said by Higashinakano at wartime cannot withstand the test of facts.

Why Is "Slaughter" Not Mentioned?

After denying news blackout at wartime in Japan, Higashinakano continues to explain why Japanese "did not know Nanjing Massacre" at wartime. The conclusion is that no slaughter happened in Nanjing since neither was news blackout nor Japanese knew Nanjing Massacre at that time.

At the beginning of this chapter, we point out that the school of fiction now insists that what Japanese did not know is only "slaughter". The second part of Higashinakano's article tries to prove "no one talks about slaughter" in accordance with Japanese documents at that time. In response to recollection of the slaughter, he quotes Ishikawa's diary, "The detailed report from Shanghai recorded atrocities committed by our troops in Nanjing. They committed plunder and rape".[75] It indicates that there is no such word as "slaughter" in the original diary.[76] Therefore, there is no slaughter actually. It is necessary to trace back to the original and to explore historical resources as early as possible to know things. Except documents are contradictory with each other, it is very common for different people to record the same thing with different emphasis and details. It is natural for an official in a hurry to jot down an outline of his daily doings and to recount these calmly after retirement. If what Ishii recorded is different before and after, the latter must be wrong. By loosely comparison, not only the word "slaughter" but also "arson" is found only in the recollection rather than diaries. So whether does it indicate that arson is made up? If "arson" is made up, in his recollection, Ishii said he received "the telegram sent by the Consul Fukui" and "the written report sent by the consul in Shanghai", while his diary only recorded

[74]松本重治著『上海時代』,東京,中央公論社1977年5月31日第1版,第675–676頁。
[75]石射猪太郎著「石射猪太郎日記続」,『中央公論』,東京,中央公論社,1991年6月号,第271頁。
[76]東中野修道編著『日本「南京」学会年報——南京「虐殺」研究の最前線』,第179頁。

"letters from Shanghai", whether is his recollection true or not? If his recollection is not true, who wrote "letters from Shanghai"? Who could be? Isn't any specific person excluded in accordance with the standard of "no record"?

We do not need to guess whether Higashinakano believes the criterion of "no record" which is beyond reason, and he factually does not obey it. After the example of Ishikawatatuzou, he denies what Takigawa, a scholar of legal history, said in his book Judge Tokyo Trial that he heard of "the hearsay of slaughter" in Beijing at that time. It is an easy way to deny it that he only depends on the interview with Takigawa by Hatakenaka Hideo (Ara Kenichi). Hatakenaka claimed that Takigawa said to him "Do I write it? I do not remember that I heard of "Nanjing Massacre" in Beijing. If I write so, I must make a mistake".[77] This statement is dubious. *Judge Tokyo Trial* was published in 1953, while Hatakenaka's interview happened over 30 years later. Isn't it strange that an old man forgets what he said when young but remembers the things he said are by mistake? What's more, take the consistent performance of Hatakenaka into consideration, we are suspicious about whether Takigawa said this. However, Higashinakano never doubts it, and regardless of his newly established criterion that worships the superiority, he denies early serious and well-founded records only because of the interview in Takigawa's late years, which naturally makes people feel that Higashinakano is totally unscrupulous.

His viewpoint also cannot be valid because of the motivation. Fabricating facts purposely must be motivated just like faults of carelessness also have reasons. So why did Ishikawa and Takigawa fabricate facts? Higashinakano cannot point out reasons and we also cannot find them.

The title of this part is "why is "slaughter" not mentioned. According to what I discussed above, it is impossible not to mention "slaughter". However, in my opinion, it is still necessary to discuss why Japanese still insist that "slaughter is not mentioned" in some records. Although the necessity of discussion arises from the school of fiction, it aims at centrists who admit slaughter partly and think themselves objective (they are also called central school of slaughter or small school of slaughter in Japan). There is no need to calmly discuss it at this level because the school of fiction always holds the concept of the first. Centrists in Japan basically do not admit evidences that presented by the prosecution in the Tokyo Trial and Nanjing Trial, especially investigations and testimonies presented by China, which is the same as the school of fiction.[78] What they totally believe and partly believe is mainly records from "the third party" such as Bates, Rabe, Smythe and others who

---

[77]聞き書き昭和12年12月南京 (続)」, 東京, 『じゅん刊世界と日本』1985年3月15日号 (第447号), 第15–16页。

[78]At that time, due to the haste of the incident, some of the testimony did have doubts. For example, Jasu, who provided testimony for the Tokyo trial, said that "it was physically impossible to accurately count such a huge number of 57,418 people who had seen the enemy's slaughter" and "cut off their food and starved to death by freezing".

were in Nanjing at that time. We have already discussed that most Westerners in Nanjing at that time were members of the International Committee for Safety Zone or of Red Across. They tried their best to rescue and protect refugees in safety zone. It is impossible for them to help people outside Nanjing and outside safety zone where it was very dangerous, which is the main reason why Western documents reflect the limited scale of "slaughter". And it is not surprising for the school of fiction to deny records about slaughter done by Japanese, but why do centrists even the school of slaughter also turn blind eyes to these records? I think it is because they treat the slaughter happened outside Nanjing as a combat. I once combed the existing Japanese military records and found there was a great disparity in casualties between two sides in "combats" occurred in surrounding areas of Nanjing, "many enemies were killed" and there were no captures, and these were hand-to-hand combats which could not use heavy weapons. Therefore, I claimed that these dead were captures who abandoned resistance, and the so-called "combat" was used to gloss over slaughter to gain merits.[79] Once knowing about it, we can easily find that Japanese documents at wartime are the records of slaughter but not "fail to mention slaughter".

Do Durdin's Records Come from the "Information Sources" of Bates?

The scale of the slaughter recorded by Westerners is much smaller than that affirmed by postwar trial. However, records from Westerners also have special values about the determination of Japanese atrocities because at that time records were few and some parts of these records were spread to the world at the first moment. For this reason, the school of fiction has always tried hard to overturn these early records. In recent years, the school of fiction even has a parlance that the "Nanjing Massacre" is an "achievement" of "information warfare" of Chinese government. Higashinakano Shudo also probes into "information sources" from three parts that are American newspapers, English publicity materials and reports to Japanese embassy given by safety zone committee in the article. Higashinakano said that reports written by American journalists such as Steele and Durdin were based on Bates's information source rather than what they saw; in addition, five documents compiled by Timperley, Xu Shuxi and others also are from Bates, Feige and others, and reports to Japanese embassy are the collection of individual opinions including Bates, Feige and other Westerners who were in Nanjing. These influential reports composed by Steele, Timperley and others were related to Bates who was so-called "the counselor of Republic of China"[80] instead of "a neutral history professor and devout missionary". Bates served for the

---

[79] See details in *A Study of the Massacre Order for Japanese Troops*, Beijing, History Studies, 2002(6), pp. 68–79.

[80] 東中野修道編著『日本「南京」学会年報——南京「虐殺」研究の最前線』,第191頁。

international publicity division of publicity department of the Kuomintang and "fabricated" atrocities of Japanese troops. So the information source was not impartial.

We will discuss the issue of "counselor" in the next part, and now let's continue to check the so-called "information sources" of Bates and others.

Based on the "similarities" between reports from the two journalists and Bates and "disparities" between what Durdin said in his later years and what he wrote in his early years, Higashinakano drew the conclusion that reports of Steele and the others were written by Bates. Examples he listed as follows (the omitted part follows the original quote). Steele gave a description as the following:

> The story of t0he occupation of Nanjing was chaotic and panic which could not be expressed by trapped Chinese troops, and the story was about the horrible occupation by conquering armies. Thousands of people were sacrificed, among who were innocents. ......They were killed like mutton. ......The above record was account of observations of myself and other foreigners in besieged Nanjing.

Durdin said,

> Slaughters are frequent...Mass plunder, atrocities against women and killings of noncombatants happened......Nanjing was surrounded by terror. ......People running in fear and nervous were all shot instantly no matter who they were. Foreigners witnessed many killings.

Bates said,

> Japanese troops fell into disrepute in Nanjing and lost chances to be respected by Chinese and praised by foreigners. After two days of frequent killings and large-scale semi-organized pillage and assaults on women, prospects were completely destroyed. According to reports from foreigners patrolling Nanjing, many corpses of noncombatants lay across streets. In accordance with statistics yesterday, in center districts of Nanjing, each district had one corpse....... People running in fear and nervous as well as those arrested by patrols in the streets and lanes were shot instantly at dusk no matter who they were.

Do these three paragraphs have similarities? Of course. However, just like the news that no one will deny that Higashinakano is a stalwart of the school of fiction does not copy from others because it is the truth that he is a stalwart. If someone thinks that Higashinakano is a member of the school of slaughter or of centrist, his thought actually is caused by trusting the wrong "information source". Therefore, it is not strange at all that various records of the same thing have similarities. But independent records must have differences for each recorder due to the different positions and fields of vision. If different records have similarities in detail, we also cannot exclude the possibility of being from the same information source.

And we do not need to compare one by one to make sure that the above three records are quite similar. Although "similar" is an adjective without strict boundaries, we still can reach the conclusion that if these records are "quite similar", they only have few similarities. Even in light of standards of restatement, these three paragraphs are "slightly similar" at most. However, the "slightly similar" is elaborately organized by Higashinakano. He added quotation marks and apostrophes in these paragraphs, which seems to be very strict but in fact there are many "omissions". For instance, the third paragraph consists of three parts while only one part is added apostrophes. Another example is that some sentences and words are weakened or intensified and so on. But I do not think these are "rough" because he wants to provoke "fighting" and naturally has his "careful" considerations. Nevertheless, "materials" he adopted are not successful. If we compare original texts of the above three paragraphs, it is easy to find that they have "discrepancies". For example, Bates mentioned in the paragraph that four hundred policemen were arrested by Japanese army. "It is very obvious that their lives come to the end".[81] If the report of Steele originated from that of Bates, Steele definitely adopted these materials because they are supporting evidences to expose atrocities of Japanese army, but he did not mention it; Durdin mentioned that someone was arrested but not specifically mentioned that they were arrested by policemen. Both Steele and Durdin mentioned that the Japanese army executed Chinese people at the riverside on 15th, and Steele recorded that "there were three hundred Chinese people while Durdin mentioned that "there were two hundred men".[82] But Bates did not mention it at all. We can list more than ten examples about their "discrepancies". They are conclusive evidences to attest that their reports are not written by Bates. Moreover, differences between reports of both Steele and Durdin prove that they are not arranged to acquire materials from "information sources" and they are not accomplices in collusion. Their reports are based on their own observations. (They witnessed it when leaving Nanjing on the USS Crock.) This strongly negates the so-called "information sources"; therefore, it is in vain for Higashinakano to make trouble out of nothing.

The Problem About the So-Called Chinese "Counselor"

As precisely mentioned, the biggest obstacle for the school of fiction to topple the parlance that Japanese troops committed atrocities in Nanjing are records from Westerners at that time. Therefore, members in the school of fiction have always been trying to negate all records. The viewpoint that Bates is the "counselor" is firstly presented in the article The Mask of Professor Bates at Nanjing University written by Higashinakano last year. Suzuki Aki

---

[81]洞富雄編『日中戦争史資料』9「南京事件」II, 第24頁。
[82]南京事件調査研究会編訳『南京事件資料集』1『アメリカ関係資料編』, 第466, 418頁。

is the first one who "finds" the problem about "counselor". In his book The New Mysteries of the "Nanjing Massacre", there was a statement: According to the report of The Guardian about the death of Timperley (November 29th, 1954), Timperley was not only the "counselor of publicity department of the Kuomintang", but also the "counselor of intelligence department of China". Suzuki Aki did not frankly point it out but his implication was clear enough. Kitamura Minoru followed his discussion to write the book The Investigation of Nanjing Incident. He said in the book that intelligence department of China actually was publicity department of the Kuomintang. As the counselor, Timperley published the book What is the War (the book is also called as Japanese Atrocities Witnessed by Outsiders and Records of Japanese Atrocities) at the command of the international publicity division of publicity department of the Kuomintang; at that time, the persons who were in charge of the plan were Dong Xianguang, the deputy minister of publicity department, and Zeng Xubai, the chief of international publicity division who was the specific person to manipulate the plan. Therefore, Kitamura came to the conclusion that "Timperley was not "the third party of justice but he just worked for the diplomacy of the Kuomintang".[83] "The counselor of the republic of China government" presented by Higashinakano comes down in a continuous line from the view of Kitamura. Scholars from home and abroad including the Japanese school of slaughter do not respond to the issue of "counselor". Members in school of fiction gloat to catch the tripping, therefore always mention it.

There is no doubt that the identity of "counselor" definitely has an impact on "neutrality", but this does not mean that being a "counselor" will ignore facts. So we do not need to "be ashamed to associate" and to think that they get goods on us. Here is what Zeng Xubai said in his book Autobiography of Zeng Xubai:

> We agreed that the international publicity in this period should be carried out by foreign friends who knew truths and policies of the wars of resistance against Japan instead of Chinese people. Timperley was the ideal candidate. Therefore, the first step we took was to pay Timperley and Smythe who was invited by Timperley to write two books about authentic records of witnessing atrocities of Japanese troops in Nanjing and to publish the two books. Timperley followed our instructions. His book Records of Japanese Atrocities and the book Photos of Disaster of War in Nanjing of Smythe were very popular and became bestsellers, achieving the purpose of publicity. At the same time, we invited Timperley to be the host of the international publicity division who did not show up and distributed news in America in the name of Transpacific News Service...[84]

---

[83] 『南京事件の探究——その実像をもとめて』, 第44页。

[84] *Zeng Xubai's Anthology*, Taipei, Liming Cultural Inc. In March, 1980, the 1st version, p. 201.

This paragraph is treated as "a confess" by Kitamura and others. It is easy to consider it unscrupulous to "pay money" in peacetime. But making allowance for the extremely difficult situation encountered by China at that time, measures the Kuomintang adopted could be understood. At that time, Japanese invasion was only symbolically opposed by British, America and other Western countries through verbal condemnation; meanwhile, it was the period that the advantage of modernization of Japanese troops was brought into full play. In the war of resistance against Japan, China neither had external strong supports (the Soviet air force volunteer corps and others were limited in scale) nor had internal effective measures; therefore, land was occupied everyday and both soldiers and civilians were dead or injured each day. Facing such urgent crisis of national subjugation and genocide, it was hard for people to consider that whether measures were proper or not. However, it does not mean that at that time "publicity" of China had no principles at all. Zeng Xubai gave a clear exposition in his another book *The Recollection of Publicity of the War of Resistance Against Japan* (hereinafter referred to as The Recollection):

> Our policies have been implemented (refer to international publicity) and the purposes are clear. But in what way could we advance our policies to achieve our purposes? Although we carried out international publicity later than Japan, their failures in publicity provided us with valuable references and we learned correct skills of publicity. We all knew that <u>publicity is neither a sophistry nor a whitewash and not a guile to cheat people. Effective publicity is the publicity without a guile; it is the imperceptible work of the backstage manipulation</u>; it is the undertaking of <u>treating people sincerity and earning trust with honesty</u>……
>
> As mentioned before, at the beginning of the war of resistance against Japan, British, America and other countries did not estimate China's strength accurately and also did not have a proper comprehension about atrocities and conspiracies committed by Japan. We could state it publicly, but could not be believed easily. It was only with the help of spokesmen that we could be trusted. Nevertheless, where did we find our ideal spokesman? <u>The spokesman who was hired by money was not real. The true spokesman was the sincere enthusiast who neither could be forced to work for money nor could be forced to do what his conscience did not allow him to do</u>. We wanted to make outsiders imperceptibly become our spokesmen with the sincere and honest attitude. We did it indeed. On the one hand, we achieved it because of our efforts, on the other hand, because of many valuable publicity chances provided by our enemies. For example, the slaughter in Nanjing and various cruel atrocities even made foreigners very angry. ……We did not need to exaggerate facts, but to expose facts to arise the attention of British and American people…….
>
> We came to an agreement with Timperley from British and Fansibo from America to publish their books Japanese Atrocities Witnessed by Outsiders and Japanese Spies. These books shocked the world and made conspiracies and atrocities committed by Japanese warlords known to the world.[85]

[85] *Selected Works of Zeng Xubai's Anthology*, Taipei, Liming Cultural Inc. In March 1980, the 1st version, pp. 295–297.

Zeng Xubai emphasized "treating people sincerity and earning trust with honesty". There is no space for the sophistry, whitewash or a guile to cheat people with the principles of "sincerity" and "honesty".

In this recollection, it is particularly worthwhile to pay attention to the view about "employment by money". I think this view can be an important footnote of "paying money" in Autobiography. Because the book Autobiography and the book Recollection were accomplished many years after the Nanjing Massacre, there were some discrepancies between the two books. For example, the two books published by the international publicity division mentioned Timperley but used different names. As for the other books, the book Autobiography was called as Photos of Disaster of War in Nanjing written by Smythe, while this book was called as Japanese Spies written by Fansibo. Even if so, the two books had no contradictions in the main aspects. In my view, "paying money" in the book Autobiography meant the cost of compilation and publishing instead of "bribe". This can be seen not only from the decisive attitude expressed in the book Recollection that "the one who was hired by money was not true spokesman", but also from the expression in the book Autobiography that "moving people with sincerity and honesty" and "exposing facts of the war of resistance against Japan without any exaggerations and concealment".[86] If "paying money" referred to "bribe", it neither accorded with the statement of the book Recollection nor the book Autobiography itself.

Now, we do not need to insist that those Western people who recorded atrocities of Japanese were "neutral third parties" and we should realize that it is not important whether they were "neutral third parties". The so-called "neutrality" and "third parties" are expressions out of the angle of "interests".[87] Different parties have totally different interests. However, human behaviors are not only governed by interests, but also by morality. From the perspective of morality, there is neither "neutrality" nor "third party". Timperley, Bates and other enthusiasts "moved by sincerity and honesty" indeed were not and did not have to be "neutral third parties". It is impossible for Japanese right-wing not to know about it since they have huge

---

[86] *Zeng Xubai's Anthology*, p. 199.

[87] Fictional school denied western people's records of Japanese atrocities on the grounds of "interests". For example, Masaki said that Rabe's Siemens company has great commercial interests in China, so "Rabe cannot be said to be neutral and fair as a third party" (畝本止凸著『真相・南京事件――ラーベ日記を検証して』序章, 東京, 文京出版1999年2月1日第2版, 第5頁). Matsumura Toshio said, as Rabe, it is unbelievable to say that he has no hatred for the Japanese army because the Japanese army occupied Nanjing and he lost the business that he has cultivated all the year round. There is no doubt that he feels desolate" (『「南京虐殺」への大疑問』, 第213頁).

interest in talking about Sugihara Chiune.[88] It only can prove that members in the school of fiction have no morality that they think the identity of "third party" and "counselor" is related to the authenticity of records or they limitlessly exaggerate the impact on the authenticity.

4 Epilogue

Annuals also include two articles from Hata Ikuhiko and Hara Takeshi, which are published in the first and second pages. Both of them are not members of the school of fiction. And their articles also are not composed "elaborately" like "database" established by Tomizawa Shigenobu (the article from Hata Ikuhiko is one of his speeches at Nanjing Studies Association of Japan). The arrangement of the two articles is out of the consideration for the "united front" of Higashinakano Shudo and others. Therefore, the two articles themselves cannot be discussed. However, in my opinion, it is still worth talking about Hata Ikuhiko—to be exact, talking about the position of Hata Ikuhiko. Hence, I want to offer my superficial view before wrapping up this article.

The number of people is an important issue in researches of the Nanjing Massacre; meanwhile, it still only is "one" issue. Overemphasizing the number of people not only avails the comprehensive understanding of historical truth, but also attenuates the seriousness of this issue (the question whether it is right or wrong becomes arithmetic), even it makes the nature of the Nanjing Massacre ascribe to the number of people. After the middle 1990 s, someone in the school of slaughter thought that Hata Ikuhiko overemphasized the issue of the number of people and gave sharp criticisms about it.[89] Related works of Hata Ikuhiko reflect that he is knee on numbers. Besides, he claimed several times that "Only God knows the true figure".[90] The two performances seem to be opposite but actually are complementary to each other. Then, on the other hand, he has not revised the book Nanjing Incident so far (until 20th press printed books of 1999) which indicates that he does not abandon the standpoint of "Nanjing Incident". Moreover, under

---

[88] During World War II, the Japanese Consul in Lithuania, out of the moral sense of protecting Jews from persecution by fascist Germany, resisted the Japanese Foreign Ministry's order to issue a large number of visas to Jews. Israel awarded the State Medal of Honor after its foundation in recognition of its "humanitarian exploits".

[89] Kasahara Tokushi said, "However, Hata Ikuhiko has recently made a comparison of the profound significance of the Nanjing incident and made little evaluations of the number of victims. In particular, today he is more dedicated to determining the number of victims in difficulty, giving people the impression that various theories coexist and the reality of the Nanjing incident is unclear. It makes people feel that he has retreated to the position of a historical revisionist who holds the same position as the Jewish Holocaust". 笠原十九司著「プリンストン大学『南京1937年・国際シンポジウム』記録」, 藤原彰編『南京事件どうみるか──日, 中, 米研究者による検証』, 第179–180頁.

[90] 如「南京事件の真実」,『産経新聞』, 東京, 産経新聞社, 1994年7月1日.

all circumstances, he never denies all atrocities of Japanese troops including slaughters.[91] Therefore, his performance reflects the complexity of Nanjing Massacre to some extent though I suppose that his excessive "prudence" of document identification restricts his judgment.[92] Such statement is not the evaluation on Hata Ikuhiko. The individual evaluations abet disputes caused by personal feelings but are adverse to clarifying historical facts. Also, the purpose of such statement is not to win over centrists from the perspective of "strategy" because rights and wrongs of academia are not determined by quantities. Besides, this statement is not only to show our tolerance. How to treat the research of Hata Ikuhiko, or how to treat different opinions, has a direct bearing on whether the research can be further developed.

Different from common academic projects, the project of the Nanjing Massacre concerns sensitive "national emotions". Hence, "value neutrality" does not work.[93] For two sides of debate, they have to set "the most important viewpoint", which is the step that they must take on major issues of principles. Kitamura Minoru, who styled himself as "seeking truth from facts", sneered at it as "a theological debate".[94] Aside from whether the metaphor is appropriate and whether Kitamura Minoru keeps out of the affair, we can find that the so-called master narrative seriously neglects details of history from the perspective of the concept of the first held not only by the school of fiction. While knowing the school of fiction, I think that we should have to admit that many difficulties remain to be solved in this important historical project. And

---

[91] For example, when discussing war crimes in the twentieth century last year, Hata Ikuhiko said that "the Nanjing massacre is still a symbolic existence as Japan acted as an offender (here "symbolic" also contains representative meaning-initiator)." (秦郁彦, 佐藤昌盛, 常石敬一「戦争犯罪ワースト20を選んだ——いまなお続く『戦争と虐殺の世紀』を徹底検証」,『文藝春秋』, 東京, 文藝春秋社, 2002年8月号, 第160頁). In the discussion with the fictionalists, although the solemn attitude towards Tanaka Masaaki had softened, there was no change in the point of disagreement with the fictionalists. 詳見秦郁彦, 東中野修道, 松本健一「問題は捕虜処断をどう見るか」,『諸君!』, 東京, 文藝春秋社, 2001年第2期, 第128–144頁.

[92] The Nanjing Massacre Research Center of Nanjing Normal University in 2003 plans to hold a monthly seminar with relevant scholars in Nanjing. The first meeting was held on March 29th and I reported on the relevant research in Japan. Before the end of the meeting, Mr. Sun Zhiwei, who made the greatest estimate of the number of people killed, once again said that as long as the premise of Japanese atrocities was recognized, any scholars could have "academic" discussion (Sun tried to say in "*Nanjing Massacre*" edited by him: "As long as we 'respect historical facts', 'specific figures' and 'of course, we can discuss them'" [*Nanjing Massacre*, pp. 9–10]). This statement has attracted the attention of overseas scholars, who think that for the "possibility" of discussions in mainland China, this "may be regarded as a small step forward." [ジョシュア・A・フォーゲル編『歴史学のなかの南京大虐殺』, 東京, 柏書房2000年5月25日第1版, 第219頁].

[93] Even in foreign academic circles, it is difficult for such subjects to be completely neutral and "impartial". On December 10th, 2002, Frederic Wakeman of the University of California at Berkeley (former president of the American Historiography Association) came to my report on the research situation in the American historiography field and expressed his great disapproval of the "pure academic" tendency of the "younger" generation of scholars, such as Chongqing, Yan'an, and Nanjing as three parallel regimes during the Anti-Japanese War.

[94]『「南京事件」の探究——その実像をもとめて』, 第21頁.

some conclusions are still not decisive and even historical documents themselves need to be explored, clarified and known. If we do not strictly abide by the basic principles of history, the research comes to nothing even though we have the heart of "academic examination" (no matter whether there is a guise or not) and change research methods (e.g., "database"). Annuals are the newest counterexample.

(Originally published in *Modern Chinese History Studies*, 2003(6))

Excursus:

A professor at Ritsumeikan University recently has published an article in the most important journal of Japanese right-wingers. He said that my book The Study on the Nanjing Massacre is "overall" among "Chinese research works". Then, yet in the next breath, he criticized that through reading this book, he found that it was still impossible to have one's own views which are different from the will of the state in China when discussing the history of Nanjing.[95] But quite strangely, the example he listed was "the exaggeration of death toll". My works cover a wide range of topics, but just do not involve specific figures (I never discuss specific figures in my books). Therefore, it is the strong evidence to prove that school of fiction holds the concept of the first.

---

[95] アスキュデイ—●ヴィッド著「南京大虐殺の亡霊」,『諸君!』, 東京, 文藝春秋社, 2005年12月号, 第164页。

A Study of the Bearing and Discipline of the Japanese Army Invading China—Taking the 10th Army as an Example

Among the armies that invaded China in modern times, the Japanese army undoubtedly left the worst impression on the Chinese. There are many reasons for it. Firstly, the Japanese army invaded China for the longest time, with the widest area and the greatest harm—at the critical period in the development of the Chinese nation, it blocked the path of Chinese modernization twice. Secondly, the Japanese army invaded China the most recently and the people's memory is most clear. Thirdly, the Chinese political mainstream with resistance to "Japan" as an important resource played a tortuous role.[1] However, if the reasons are listed, I'm afraid that the most important reason is the atrocities committed by Japanese army which is deeply rooted in the minds of the Chinese people. Perhaps it is for this reason that the Chinese academic circle talks a lot about Japanese atrocities, but little argues about the bearing and discipline of the Japanese army—since they are "beast soldiers" or "devils",[2] is there any bearing and discipline? Not only does the Chinese academic circle not see it, but also in my limited reading, the bearing and discipline of the Japanese army have never been discussed in Japan. On the other hand, it does not prevent the Japanese from praising the bearing and

---

[1] For example, some photos in the publicity materials published under the auspices of the International Publicity Department of the Kuomintang Central Propaganda Department have been technically processed. Although it is true in general, it cannot but be said that they have exceeded their original appearance.

[2] They were the most common titles at that time: "beast soldiers" in Guo Qi's *Record of Blood and Tears in the Captured Capital*, "devils" in(unknown)'s *Common People in the Dark Hell*, *Historical Materials of the Nanjing Massacre Made by Japanese Invaders*, compiled by Editorial Committee of the Historical Materials of the Nanjing Massacre Made by Japanese Invaders and Nanjing Library, Jiangsu Ancient Books Publishing House, the 1st edition and 5th printed edition in February 1998, pp. 159, 131, 133.

© The Author(s) 2020
Z. Cheng, *The Nanjing Massacre and Sino-Japanese Relations*,
https://doi.org/10.1007/978-981-15-7887-8_2

discipline of the Japanese army. For example, Komuro Naoki in the book Questions of Nanjing Massacre from International Law said,

> In the impression of the Japanese, the Japanese "soldiers" are strong and positive.
>
> In the Japanese military education, it especially emphasizes honor. ... "soldiers are the model of the nation" is one of the themes of education.
>
> "Soldiers don't do evil" and "soldiers don't lie", which the citizens believe firmly.
>
> Because of the high pride, <u>the criminal rate of Japanese Army is the lowest in the world</u>.[3] (The key numbers are added by the writer and hereinafter added by the writer, and will not indicate one by one.)

Such statements are very popular today. For example, during the second Songhu Battle, Genda Minoru with the 2nd Air Fleet of the Imperial Japanese Navy was transferred to Shanghai. In his later years, he denied that Japanese army committed atrocities in an interview because it is in violation of "the spirit of Bushido".[4] Unemoto Masaki's *The Truth About the Nanjing Incident* said that most Japanese soldiers are kind and bear the injustice.[5] Takemoto Tadao and Ohara Yasuo's *The alleged Nanking massacre* said that the Japanese army who occupied Nanjing has strict discipline and few criminals, and they were punished severely by the council of military tribunal.[6] Tanaka Masaaki's *What Really Happened* in Nanking uses "bravery and tenacity" to disprove the solemn discipline of the Japanese army because "only with the strict bearing and discipline can the Japanese army become a fine and strong army. Regardless of the time and location, the rule that a strong army is equal to a strictly disciplined army is unchanged".[7] "Refined and strong" and "solemn military discipline" are by no means equivalent. There are numerous examples from ancient and today. For example, Unemoto Masaki likes listing the strong army of "cruel" and "inhuman" Genghis khan and Hitler.[8] This point is irrelevant to this article and there is no need to discuss it.

---

[3]国際法から 見た「南京大虐殺」の疑問、小室直樹、渡部昇一著『封印の昭和史―――「戦後五〇年」自虐 の終焉』、東京、徳間書店1995年10月15日第4次印刷版、第107頁。

[4]阿羅健一編『「南京事件」日本人48人の証言』、東京、小学館2002年1月1日第1版、第269頁。

[5]畝本正己著『真相・南京事件―――ラーベ日記を 検証して』、東京、文京出版1999年2月1日第2版、第230頁。In the preface of the same book, Hanae Shou says the Japanese Army is "clear" (p. 11).

[6]日本会議国際広報委員会編『再審「南京大虐殺」―――世界に訴える 日本の冤罪』、東京、明成社2000年11月25日第2次印刷版、第64頁。

[7]田中正明著『南京事件の総括―――虐殺否定十五の論拠』、東京、謙光社1987年3月7日第1版、第135頁。

[8]Unemoto Masaki stressed that the Japanese attack on Nanjing "was not Genghis Khan's conqueror against Europe, nor was it Hitler's genocide. It's a decent 'real war' - punishing and abstinent war." 畝本正己著『真相・南京事件―――ラーベ日記を 検証して』総括、第229頁。

Actually, the defense talked about the bearing and discipline of Japanese army as early as the Tokyo Trial. For example, the witness Wakisaka Jiro (the general of 36th Alliance of the 9th Division) said,

> My army had just entered Nanjing when an accountant lieutenant found a shoe abandoned by the woman on his way out on business. He wanted to show his friends its beautiful style and brought it back to the army. After the matter was discovered by the gendarmes, they sent the materials as the suspicion of robbery to the council of the military tribunal. This lieutenant therefore cried in front of me and claimed that he was innocent. I accepted the fact and conveyed it to the superior. I remembered it turned out to be a minor crime and was rejected. At that time, the Japanese gendarmes in Nanjing were disciplined strictly and would never forgive any minor crimes.[9]

According to Wakisaka Jiro, the Japanese army not only committed no minor crimes, but also was worthy of being an "army of righteousness". What Wakisaka said is an extreme example in the testimony at that time, but it is also a vivid example of our understanding of the defense.

This argument cannot be accepted by the Chinese in that it deviates from the empirical facts. That Wakisaka and other people said this indicates they have no introspection. From this point, these arguments are not worth mentioning. However, in the recent years, I also wonder why all sorts of anecdotes that can be seen at a glance still have room for discussion, whether atrocities have something with Japanese army and Japanese army doesn't behave well (every Japanese called the atrocities of the US-Soviet army and the Chinese army), whether it is because of the "war" rather than the atrocities by Japanese soldiers that the great disaster occurred, or whether most Japanese soldiers follow laws and few have been punished severely, and thus offsets the crime, whether the firsthand record leaves room for different opinions. To persuade the Japanese right-wing and Japanese people, if not from Japanese army's own records, I'm afraid that it is useless to turn their arguments against them.[10]

---

[9] 洞富雄編『日中戦争史資料』8「南京事件」I，東京，河出書房新社1973年11月25日第1版，第239頁。

[10] A considerable number of people in Japan do not recognize the evidence left by China and the West, thinking that it is the propaganda of "enemy countries" or countries that help the enemy in wartime. For example, Suzuki Aki, Kitamura Minoru, and Shūdō Higashinakano have "found out" that H. J. Timperley and M. S. Bates are Chinese consultants and the evidence from China and the west is "made" by the Kuomintang itself or by Westerners who followed Kuomintang's advice. (见鈴木明著『新「南京大虐殺」のまぼろし』第十三章 "田伯烈の『外国人の見た日本軍の暴行』"，東京，飛鳥新社1999年6月3日第1版，第281295頁; 北村稔著『「南京事件」の探究———その実像をもとめて』第一部 "国民党国際宣傳処と 戦時対外戦略"，東京，文藝春秋社2001年11月20日第1版，第25 64頁; 東中野修道著，南京大学教授ベイツの「化けの皮」，『諸君!』，東京，文藝春秋，2002年第4期，第150 163頁)。

1 Relevant Documents and Military Law System of the 10th Japanese Army

Japanese army burned and destroyed a large number of written documents when Japanese army was defeated and during the Tokyo Trial. Because of this point, Wakisaka Jiro and others gave such arrogant testimony. (Also, there are people cheating themselves, such as Iwane Matsui, the first responsible person for the Nanjing Massacre. The diaries are still here but he lies that the dairies have been burned.) However, on the other hand, from another perspective, aside from Wakisaka's declamatory statements (such as "a shoe"), we can also see that Japanese council of military tribunal seems to be more than a decoration. The lost things always leave room for imagination. Thus, if the diaries of the council of military tribunal of Japanese Expeditionary Forces existed, the questions of the fictionalists would fall themselves. This is an outstanding experience when I collected relevant Japanese documents to respond to the school of fiction. Thus, when I visited Japan at the end of last year and saw the published diaries of Okawa Sekiziro, Minister of Justice of 10th Army (the main force attacking Nanjing), I was surprised and regretted not to search carefully. Okawa's diary has been treasured so far but is unknown to us. Even his daughter, who lived with him in his later years, was "surprised" and "didn't remember it".[11] I realized from diaries that the dairies of the 10th Army with a large number of cases are the important materials as the military documents at that time.

It was an "accident" that the diaries of judicial department of the 10th Army were kept. The editor of the Japanese modern history materials said,

> Even though the 10th Army existed half a year (actually from October 13th, 1937 to March 9th, 1938[the order of Japanese Army removed on February 18th], less than 5 months—original note), its diaries recorded the crimes of Japanese Army during Japan-China wars and pacific wars – it is certain that other armies and divisions also set up military tribunal[12] and only kept this record—now it was left to us totally and really <u>rare dairies of judicial department</u>.[13]

The diaries of the judicial department of the 10th Army were kept by Okawa Sekiziro. "Only kept this record" is a generalized statement because

---

[11] 長森光代著「わが父, 陸軍法務官 小川関治郎」, 載小川関治郎著『ある 軍法務官の日記』, 東京, みすず書房2000年8月10日第1版, 第210頁。

[12] The "military tribunal" is generally translated as "military court". However, Japan also had a "military law conference" to hear the army and people of the occupied territories, and the courts set up by the occupying forces during the US occupation of Japan used the Chinese character "military court". This "military court" is about the same as the "military law conference". In order to avoid confusion, this article directly uses the "military tribunal".

[13] 高橋正衛編集, 解説『続・現代史資料』6「軍事警察」, 東京, みすず書房1982年2月26日第1版, 前言第32頁。

the one-month diary of the council of military tribunal of the newly built Central China Army in January 1938[14] also depends on Okawa Sekiziro to keep. (The cases recorded in the dairies of the council of military tribunal of Central China Army are mainly about the 10th Army and few cases are about Shanghai Expeditionary Force.) Although the two kinds of diaries don't involve Nanjing, it can be considered as the "only" valuable evidence in terms of the bearing and discipline of Japanese army.

The dairy of the 10th Army is from October 12th, 1937 (the following 1937 is not noted one by one) to February 23rd, 1938. The dairy of the Central China Army starts from January 4th, 1938, to 31st of the same month. Okawa Sekiziro's diary is from October 12th to February 22nd, 1938, almost the same period as what the dairy of the 10th Army recorded. The latter is mostly coincident with the former in contents, but the latter is a private one and considers little benefits. It is not strictly controlled and has more truth to supplement the diary.[15]

This article is centered with the 10th Army. Before entering the topic, it is necessary to give a brief introduction about the 10th Army.

After the second Songhu Battle broke out, Japanese army immediately decided to dispatch army to support. Because there is controversy about whether to enlarge the war in the Japanese army, the newly built Shanghai Expeditionary Force (August 14th) consists of the 3rd and 11th Divisions and is limited to conquer the enemies near Shanghai and occupy the northern areas in Shanghai.[16] On August 23rd, the two divisions landed in

---

[14] 中支那方面军 is often translated as "Central China Army". Considering that the so-called "中支" in Japan and China's "Central Area" are different or completely different in the traditional natural areas and the administrative divisions referred to after the 1950s, and the active scope of the 中支那方面军 has never exceeded that of East China, which is commonly referred to today, so this article still uses the old name in Japan. For example, the first note on the first page of the Chinese translation of the *Thorough Examination of "the Nanjing Massacre"* states: 支那 is Japan's disparaging term for China before the war. *Thorough Examination of the Big Nanjing Massacre* still uses this term, which shows the author's anti-China position. In order to objectively reflect the political reactivity of the book, the translator has not made any changes." (*The Thorough Examination of the "Big Nanjing Massacre"* [the original work does not have the word "big", "Nanjing Massacre" is in quotation marks, because the Japanese fictionalists do not recognize the "massacre", so the massacre must be in quotation marks], Beijing, Xinhua Publishing House, July 2000, Inner Press, p. 1.) Today, Japan still insists on using the term "支那" to call China, it must be the right wing, but when it uses the historical name, such as the "中支那方面军" neither the left wing nor the right wing will change it.

[15] 详请见拙文《小川关治郎和〈一个军法务官的日记〉》, 上海, 《史林》2004年第1期。

[16] 「臨参命第七十三号」, 白井勝美等解説『現代史資料』9『日中戦争』2, 東京, みすず書房1964年9月30日第1版, 第206頁。 Senior General Iwane Matsui, commander of the Expeditionary Force, disagreed with this restriction, and before the troops set out, he said: "We should abandon the policy of local solution and not expansion", and "we should resolutely use the necessary forces and make a quick decision in the traditional spirit". "Rather than use the main force in the northern branch, it is more necessary to attack Nanjing". We should capture Nanjing in a short period of time". (「飯沼守日記」, 南京戦史編集委員会編『南京戦史資料集』, 非売品, 東京, 偕行社1989年11月3日第1版, 第67 68頁).

Wusong areas one after another. The stubborn resistance of the Chinese army was beyond the expectation of the Japanese army, so the Japanese army and Navy demanded an urgent surge. After much effort (the minister of General Staff ISHIHARA Kanji opposed the surge and believed that it was the top priority of the Japanese army to guard against the Soviet Union and Manchukuo.[17] However, this standpoint was not sanctioned by the Japanese army), in early September, the surge was approved by the emperor. The Japanese army then dispatched the 9th, 13th and 101th Divisions, Shieto detachment (Taiwan reserve, the general is Shieto Chiaki), the 5th Artillery Division and the 3rd Flight Regiment (at the end of October, the 16th Division was transferred to the command of the Shanghai Expeditionary Force) to Shanghai Expeditionary Force. However, the national government tried its best to resist. The frontline soldiers fought bravely and were ready to sacrifice themselves. Although Japanese army had surge, their attempt to win was hampered. In October, the situation remained a stalemate. (ISHIHARA Kanji resigned.) The 6th, 18th and 114th Divisions and the 10th Army (the 7th army) of the 105th Division were built in such situation. (The mobilization order was issued on October 12th.)

Giving description of this process firstly is because the revenge aroused by the difficult battle and heavy casualties is one of the reasons for the atrocities committed by the Japanese army, which has become common.[18] In fact, it is not only revenge, but also the impermanence of life and death caused by the fierce war itself will shake the normal values and constraints, resulting in

---

[17] 参见防衛庁防衛研修所戦史室編『支那事変陸軍作戦』1，東京，朝雲新聞社1975年7月25日第1版，第295页。

[18] This view has existed for a long time in Japan, and many parties have also confessed to it. For example, a corporal of the second company of the first battalion of the 65th Regiment said: "It is really tragic. They all died fighting for their country. We hope to regard the attack on Nanjing as an extension of this fierce battle (the Battle of Shanghai). In the end, there was no atmosphere in which the prisoners who came to surrender were easily released. It is the revenge of a comrade-in-arms who has been hurt like that! In such a mood, I want the Chinese soldiers fighting at that time to understand. If we kill 100,000 or 200,000, it will also be the result of continuing to fight. From the mood at that time, it was not a 'slaughter' at all" (本多勝一著『南京への道』，東京，朝日新聞社1987年1月20日第1版，第209页). In recent years, Chinese scholars have also begun to admit the reason for China's resistance, such as: "In the Nanjing Defense War, the heroic resistance of the Chinese soldiers also increased the vengeful mentality of the Japanese invaders, making them even more cruel and crazy in the subsequent atrocities. It is in this sense that the Nanjing Defense War and the heroic resistance of the Chinese army have become one of the basic reasons for the Nanjing Massacre" (Nanjing Massacre, compiled by Sun Zhiwei, Beijing, Beijing Publishing House, the 1st edition published in May 1997, p. 13). However, the term "resistance" here is different from that of Japan, which refers to the Battle of Songhu rather than the "Nanjing Defense War". In terms of reality at that time, the resistance to the Japanese attack on Nanjing was far less fierce than that in Shanghai. For example, Shanghai fought for nearly three months, while Nanjing fought less than a week, and the Japanese casualties were only one-tenth of those in Shanghai. If Nanjing's "heroic resistance" is regarded as "one of the basic reasons", it will inevitably leave questions as to why the Japanese army's "atrocities" are not more "cruel and crazy" in Shanghai.

perverse and even frenzied actions. However, I'd like to draw special attention to the following: Although the 10th Army was built during the fierce wars between China and Japan, Chinese army in Shanghai started to retreat when they landed in Jin Shanwei on November 5th. In the several months in China, the 10th Army didn't encounter fierce resistance, nor did it suffer as many as casualties as the Shanghai Expeditionary Force except for occupying Nanjing with absolute priority. There have been almost no wars since then, such as occupying Hangzhou without costing a shot or a bullet. Therefore, the experience of the 10th Army was different from that of Shanghai Expeditionary Force. Its atrocities had nothing with the so-called fierce wars and revenge. It is because of this that we can more rely on what the 10th Army did to know the bearing and discipline of Japanese army.

The Ministry of Justice of the 10th Army was set up when the 10th Army was built on October 13th. At the beginning of its establishment, there were 5 persons including minister of justice and later one was added.[19] On October 30th, the military tribunal was set up (in accordance with "Dingji Day Order No. 12" and the military discipline conference was set up on December 5th). The members of the ministry of justice included prosecutors, examining justices and judges.[20] In addition to the full-time legal officers, the judges were served by soldiers with swords. Theoretically speaking, there is no difference between a legal officer and a judge with a sword in terms of their functions. Also, there is no difference between specialized judges who tried their best to make the trial fair with their special knowledge and the so-called judges with swords in terms of the limitation of their functions. They have the same function in the determination of facts and the interpretation of the decrees.[21] However, as the editor of the Materials of Japanese Modern History Military Policeman said, a legal officer is under the commissioned officer, a judge with a sword, and also acts as an officer without authority.[22] Actually, it is not only "also" but the Japanese council of military tribunal stipulates that the chief of the military tribunal shall be the commander of the army, the head of the division and other heads (the

---

[19] When the ministry of justice was established on October 13th, the Ministry of Justice included Minister 小川关治郎 (second grade, army judicial officer), members 田岛隆弌 (fifth grade, senior officer), 增田德一 (seventh senior officer, etc.), 部附加藤七兵卫 (second grade army officer) and 龟井文夫 (third grade officer), with a total of five people. On October 20th, the 部附笹木特务 was added (named as the third officer) and two soldiers on duty. After 小川 was transferred to Central Area Army on December 28th, the Minister of Justice of the Ninth Division of the left army, 根本庄太郎, took over as the minister.

[20] 小川 is the prosecutor of the military tribunal, 田岛 is the magistrate and pre-adjudicator of the military tribunal, 增田 is the pre-adjudicator and prosecutor of the military tribunal, and 加藤, 笹木 and 龟井 are attached to the military tribunal. 小川 and 增田 served as pre-adjudicator and magistrate, respectively.

[21] 日高巳雄述著「陸軍軍法会議法講義」, 油印本, 无版权页, 第41页, 转引自高橋正衛編集, 解説『続·現代史資料』6「軍事警察」, 前言第26页。

[22] 高橋正衛編集, 解説『続·現代史資料』6「軍事警察」, 前言第27页。

chief of high military tribunal shall be the minister of army), in order to show "the consistency between the judicial power and the command power of the army". This institutional provision has restricted professional legal officers from performing in accordance with law.

Besides the institutional provisions, the ministry of justice is not taken seriously in the headquarters. For example, the adjutant officer intentionally separated the ministry of justice from commander such as the discrimination against the ministry of justice in terms of treatment, which is recorded in Okawa's diary. This situation is connected with the low positions of officers. What Okawa's dairy on December 12th said really reflected this situation. It said that "the soldiers were more and more violent and fierce"; "we were actually considered as a burden".[23] However, the discrimination against the ministry of justice is not only due to the military attaché's contempt for civilian officials in the war environment, but also because of the conflicts between the function of the ministry of justice and the corrupt bearing and discipline of the Japanese army.

Okawa's diary on December 8th recorded, "Minister Tsukamoto is negative in everything and does not do anything". Tsukamoto Hirotsugu is the minister of the justice of Shanghai Expeditionary Force. The reason for "omission" and "negativity" is that Okawa's diary said that he heard of "internal disharmony".[24] However, as far as the situation of the Japanese army concerned, it is hard to imagine that "nothing can be done" because of interpersonal relationships. I believe that the omission should be related to the difficulty of ministry of justice in carrying out their work. During the Tokyo Trial, many Japanese soldiers including Tsukamoto Hirotsugu mentioned the protests of the various armies against ministry of justice because of the too severe penalties imposed by the ministry of justice. He said, "All the armies criticized the severe punishment of the ministry of justice of Shanghai Expeditionary Force and the attitudes of correcting the minor crimes". The Chief of Staff of Shanghai Expeditionary Force IINUMA Mamoru also said, "because the military discipline is extremely solemn (according to the diary, it should be too strict), the 16th division protested with the ministry of justice".[25] The so-called "severity" is totally false from a large number of cases of minor or no penalties for felonies in the diary, which will be described in detail below. However, even though the ministry of justice is lenient, its nature determines that it cannot be accepted by the Japanese soldiers.

The blame said by Minister Tsukamoto could be proved through the experience of Okawa. In January 1938, Okawa went to the Japanese Area Army (it didn't set up a ministry of justice and Okawa was attached to the headquarters). He felt that the obvious difference between the Japanese Area

---

[23] 小川関治郎著『ある 軍法務官の日記』, 第109頁。
[24] 小川関治郎著『ある 軍法務官の日記』, 第97頁。
[25] 洞富雄編『日中戦争史資料』8「南京事件」I, 第191, 252頁。

Army and Japanese army is that there was no direct army under the central government, so he didn't have to think deeply with trepidation as facing the "equivalent opinions" at all levels in the army.[26] The so-called "equivalent opinions" should be regarded as the "critique" of various armies said by Tsukamoto Hirotsugu. At that time, the professional judge was in a weak position and Okawa's daughter had a symbolic experience when she was young. Mitsuyo (Okawa) Nagamori said that when she was in primary school, the color of her father's official collar and the hat was special (white; red symbolized the army; black symbolized the navy; green symbolized the cavalry; blue symbolized the air force) and their number was rare, so people were always curious. Her classmates even asked: "Is your father a Chinese soldier?" For this reason, the teenager Nagamori was very upset. She thought: "I would be so proud if my father was an ordinary soldier, but I feel sorry for myself".

The council of military tribunal of the 10th Army was abolished on February 14th, 1938, with the dissolution of the 10th Army. The original council of military tribunal was transformed into the council of military tribunal of the newly established Central China Expeditionary Force.

The laws on which the council of military tribunal of the 10th Army was based were mainly the Army Criminal Law and the Army Penalty Orders. At the same time, Because of the new areas and problems, the judicial department had made corresponding provisions on the subject of the jurisdiction of the council of the military tribunal, slaves, international laws, the setting up of the prison field, the custody of the detainees, confidentiality measures and other principles and specific rules. From the system, the judicial department of the 10th Army was fairly detailed, such as the handling of the custody goods, and detailed provisions on cashier, verification, recording, management, credentials, responsible person, writing format, signature and stamps.

The chief of the 10th Army prison field was Honma Hikotaro, the lieutenant of the Japanese gendarmerie. The director was Kobayashi Katsuji, a gendarmerie, and governed 8 people.

There was no firsthand information on the specific number of the gendarmeries but the number of the gendarmerie should be limited. At that time, when the Tokyo Trial, Japanese embassy staff officer in China Hidaka Shinrokuro said, "the attitude of the Japanese gendarmeries is generally fair". The comments of the foreigners and Chinese are good. At the beginning, the population is few and I hear that there are only 17 people (in Nanjing–quotation)[27] under the captain on December 17th. The original adjutant captain of the 10th Army Kamisago Shoshichi once said, "the number of gendarmes attached to the Shanghai Expeditionary Force and the 10th Army

---

[26] 小川関治郎著『ある軍法務官の日記』, 第149頁。
[27] 洞富雄編『日中戦争史資料』8「南京事件」I, 第182頁。

with 200,000 soldiers is less than 100".[28] If the proportion of gendarmes in each army is roughly equal, the number of gendarmes in the 10th Army will not exceed 40.[29] The significance of this point is because the gendarmes who maintain the discipline of the Japanese army is too limited, even of the gendarmes spare no effort,[30] what they can do is in a limited range, the crimes discovered by the Japanese gendarmes and trialed by the council of military tribunal are only the tip of the iceberg.

The limited population of gendarmes mainly limits its function. Besides, the authority of the gendarmes must be a problem. According to the system of the army officers (Meiji 41th year, Emperor's Order No. 340), the gendarme's affiliation can be interpreted as belonging directly to the minister of the army. For example, Yinoue Kentaro was entrusted to the emperor. However, in actual implementation, the challenge to the authority of the gendarmes can sometimes become a crisis. On November 18th, when the ministry of justice recorded the terrible bearing and disciplines in the army command, it was said that there were sacrifices to correct the disciplines.[31] The word "sacrifice" is not meant to be alarmist, because the arrogant soldiers and fierce generals of the Japanese army think that they can enjoy the privilege of running amok and don't regard the gendarmes as important.

---

[28] 上砂胜七著《宪兵三十一年》，東京，ライフ社1955年4月10日第1版，第177页。

[29] What Shōshichi Kamisago is should be the initial situation, because it has increased slightly in the local area later. For example, on January 24th, 1938, the Central Area Army decided that the 11st Division should send one officer (lieutenant or second lieutenant), 12 non-commissioned officers and 155 soldiers to enrich the Shanghai Gendarmerie. However, the increase in Shanghai is because the atrocities of the Japanese army have been widely criticized by international public opinion. The Japanese army thinks that "the international relations in Shanghai and its vicinity are complex"; in particular, they should prevent the atrocities of the Japanese army from being used by foreigners for propaganda (「中支那方面軍軍法会議陣中日誌」，高橋正衛編集，解説『続·現代史資料』6「軍事警察」，第141页). Therefore, since this increase is intended to cover people's ears and eyes, it can only be used as a special case.

[30] 井上源吉, who was a gendarmerie during the war, later wrote the book *The Gendarmeriein the Field*, one paragraph of which was recorded as a "positive image" of the Japanese gendarmerie. One battalion of the Japanese 110th Division, which returned to Shanghai after the battle in Xuzhou, occupied a mansion of one Chinese businessman as the headquarters of the battalion. At that time, Private First Class of the gendarmerie, 井上, went to ask for evacuation. "The adjutant of the battalion saw that I was a low-level first class, showed arrogance and did not take my request seriously at all". The captain came out and said, "Hey, private first class of the gendarmerie, what nonsense? This area is occupied by us. Where we want is none of your business, go back and tell it to your division leader". In desperation, I could only use the last resort, pulled out the precious knife of the family heirloom, and said: "Stand still! Army private first class 井上 has now, on the order of his Majesty the Emperor, ordered the 大島 army to hand over the house immediately!" He retorted, "I'm a major in the army. Can you order me as a private first class?" But maybe he felt that the situation was unfavorable, suddenly changed his attitude and said, "I will go to the gendarmerie tomorrow and say hello to the team leader" (井上源吉著『戦地憲兵』，東京，図書出版社1980年11月5日第1版，第102 103页).

[31] 「第十軍(柳川兵団)法務部陣中日誌」，高橋正衛編集，解説『続·現代史資料』6「軍事警察」，第37页。

According to the above-mentioned testimony of the Tokyo Trial, the minister of justice himself admitted the "blame" of all the armies, which showed that it was common that the superiors shielded the subordinates. The attitude of the commanders and the army, even if not to exempt the crimes, would objectively have the effect of connivance. Thus, criminals didn't give in easily when confronted with gendarmes and armed resistance also occurred from time to time. For example, the secret service soldier of the second field hospital of the 101th Division[32] Haku□□□(considering the reputation of the party concerned, only one word was left in his name at the time of publication, the same below) stabbed gendarmes with the bayonet.[33]

Even the low-status secret service soldiers were treated like this, and the arrogant frontline armies would not take the gendarmes seriously. At that time, Japan's diplomatic department also lamented the runaway Japanese atrocities. Ishii Itaro, the head of the Bureau of Asiatic Affairs of the Japanese Foreign Ministry, said in his memories,

> Nanjing fell on the 12th of December. The telegrams of the Consul Fukui who followed our army back to Nanjing and the written report from Shanghai Consul were deeply regrettable. There was information that Japanese army in Nanjing plundered, raped, set fire to and massacred the Chinese. Even if there were few gendarmes, they couldn't be banned. It was reported that the Consul Fukui was in danger because they tried to stop it.[34]

Not only the gendarmes but also the members of the Japanese Consulate "attempted to stop", which was also dangerous. In such a vicious environment, even if some people in the top ranks of the Japanese army wanted to maintain the bearing and discipline, it ended in failure.

Therefore, although the Japanese army has urged the military discipline from time to time, for example, on November 9th, after hearing Okawa's opinions on the atrocities committed by the Japanese army that bearing and discipline should be strictly observed and military actions should avoid causing international issues,[35] the commander required that "no useless killing" and "plunder" should be prohibited at the gathering of the army commanders that night.[36] On the 11th, "once again, all armies were demanded observing the bearing and discipline". On the 18th, the armies were warned

---

[32] The soldiers who take care of the horses are called secret service soldiers of traffic, also called secret service soldiers or soldiers of traffic. Because the soldier of traffic is not a frontline unit, it has a low status among the Japanese army.

[33] 「第十軍法務部陣中日誌」, 高橋正衛編集, 解説『続・現代史資料』6「軍事警察」, 第80頁.

[34] 石射猪太郎著『外交官の一生―――対中国外交の回想』, 東京, 太平出版社1974年4月15日第4次印刷版, 第267頁.

[35] 「第十軍法務部陣中日誌」, 高橋正衛編集, 解説『続・現代史資料』6「軍事警察」, 第29頁.

[36] 小川関治郎著『ある軍法務官の日記』, 第19頁.

to observe the bearing and discipline,[37] but the aggressive army still didn't restrain. It demonstrated that the praise for the Japanese army and the assertion of the lowest crime rate in Japanese army were far from the truth.

2 The Sexual Atrocities Everywhere

From the diaries, we can see that the Japanese army's basic integrity disintegrated. The Japanese army was unscrupulous and rebellious. The things that could not have happened at home frequently occurred. For example, in the evening of November 25th, the 3rd Squadron of the 124th Regiment of the 18th Division Taka□□ killed someone in Huzhou, because a soldier in the dormitory coerced Chinese women to commit adultery in public.[38] The lack of Japanese integrity directly resulted in a large number of rape. This is the most serious physical and psychological injury to Chinese women, which is still firmly denied by many Japanese today because the victims themselves rarely accuse them. (Not only were the records at that time falsely described as "hearsay", but what's more, they believed that "the actual state of rape" was either "voluntary prostitution", or "the act of the Chinese posing as Japanese soldiers" or "the anti-Japanese disruption of the work of the Chinese soldiers".[39]) I once said in the book *The Japanese Sexual Atrocities although the Parties Didn't Accuse the Japanese*,[40] except the weak position of facing the occupying forces, it was also related to Chinese view on virtues and chastity. The Chinese people always put emphasis on the righteousness from ancient times. When moral integrity, they had no alternative but to sacrifice

---

[37]「第十軍法務部陣中日誌」,高橋正衛編集,解説『続・現代史資料』6「軍事警察」,第30, 36頁。

[38] Because the "adultery happened before the Tablet of the dead team leader while ignoring military discipline",高□□ "strongly advise", then they drew swords to kill each other, resulting the woman being killed.「第十軍法務部陣中日誌」,高橋正衛編集,解説『続・現代史資料』6「軍事警察」,第47頁。

[39] 詳見日本会議国際広報委員会編『再審「南京大虐殺」―――世界に訴える 日本の冤罪』第二章之「強姦事件の真相」小节,第85 87頁;藤岡信勝,東中野修道著『ザ・レイプ・オブ・南京の 研究―――中国における「情報戦」の手口と 戦略』第三章之「真実は安全地帯の住民が知っいた」小节,東京,祥傳社1999年9月10日第1版,第168, 170頁;東中野修道著『「南京虐殺」の徹底検証』第十二章「南京安全地帯の記録」, 東京, 展転社2000年7月8日第4次印刷版,第257, 282頁. The above comment was made in response to the 361 cases of rape and attempted rape recorded by the International Commission on security zones. However, after the fall of Nanjing, the officers and soldiers of our army who laid down their arms faced robbery, endured humiliation, kept a low profile to protect themselves and reduce unnecessary sacrifices, and there was absolutely no resistance. The Japanese searched for disabled soldiers, abolished the security zone, and imposed a "self-government committee" and a "reformed government". The so-called "latent" soldiers (including citizens) accepted it silently. The so-called "pretending to be a Japanese soldier" and the so-called "disrupting work" are difficult to understand, and there is no basis for the facts at all.

[40] For details, see Section 14 of the *Notes of the Nanjing Massacre*, Shanghai, Historical Review, No. 1, 2003, pp. 117, 119.

their life for righteousness. A woman's duty of righteousness was her supreme chastity (when Guo Qi discussed the atrocities of rape of the Japanese army in A Record of the Blood and Tear of the fall of Nanjing, he said that woman's chastity was above everything[41]). Therefore, if a Chinese woman was raped, especially by a brutish soldier, her whole life was completely destroyed. Even if she did not commit suicide, she could only swallow the insult and humiliation silently rather than standing out to initiate a prosecution. As a result, a report to the Japanese occupying forces was a doomed request, so few people intended to find justice with their real names.[42]

Negative explanation of "no report" is due to the difficulties in evidence. So when I saw Okawa's diary, I couldn't help thinking that although the firsthand evidence of the rape in Nanjing left by the Japanese army was destroyed with the burning of the diaries of the ministry of justice of the Shanghai Expeditionary Force—maybe they were "lost"—a large number of rape cases in Shanghai, Hangzhou, Huzhou, kept in the diaries were the most valuable evidence.[43] After a rough reading of these cases, it was found that there were not only the pleadings and judgments drawn up by the ministry of justice, but the complaints of the aggrieved party and the statements of the two parties were recorded in detail. The latter was so surprising. Therefore, although these charges basically did not play a role in punishing the culprits (section IV will state otherwise), the previously inferred reason of "no charge" cannot be established, nor can "no charge" itself. The so-called rape is only "hearsay" and can never stop.

[41] *Historical Materials of the Nanjing Massacre Made by Japanese Invaders*, compiled by the Editorial Committee of Historical Materials of the Nanjing Massacre Made by Japanese Invaders and Nanjing Library, p. 8. Guo Qi, who served as the commander of the garrison when the Japanese invaded Nanjing, was trapped in Nanjing for three months. This article was published in Xijingping Daily after his fleeing.

[42] According to the investigation conducted by Nationalist Government after the war, most of those identified by their families, neighbors and other witnesses were dead or missing, and a very small number of victims who reported themselves had all their families or male families killed or missing, and all their situation was very difficult. For example, Xu Hong, who lived in Dabaihua Lane in Nanjing, tried to jump in a well to kill herself after being raped but failed, and later, all her families were killed except for her 70-year-old mother and her daughter who also jumped in a well. They then lived in "a very shameful and difficult life" and so they dared to come out to clear the "national shame and family feud". *Archives of the Nanjing Massacre Made by Japanese Invaders*, compiled by the Second Historical Archives of China and Nanjing Municipal Archives, Jiangsu Ancient Books Publishing House, the 3rd edition published in December 1997 (p. 354). From the moral point, there is no doubt about the significance of the victim complaint after the 1980s, but it has to be discounted from the legal and academic point of view.

[43] Although the 6th and 18th divisions and the 国崎 detachment of the 10th Army were the main forces attacking Nanjing, the Military Legal Department only participated in the Nanjing Entry Ceremony and was not stationed in Nanjing. The security and management of Nanjing were successively carried out by the 16th Division and 天谷 Detachment of the Shanghai Expeditionary Army, and the activities of the gendarmes of the 10th Army were also outside Nanjing, so there was no or almost no content of Nanjing in logs and diaries. Therefore, although journals and diaries can infer Japanese atrocities in Nanjing, they cannot be said to be direct evidence in a narrow sense.

From the dairies, Japanese rape has brought great disasters to Chinese women. Wherever and whenever the Japanese army went, all the women would inevitably become victims.

The Japanese Army Raped Regardless of the Place

As mentioned above, "somebody" killed by Ta ka□□ was engaged in the lascivious activities in the dormitory publicly. Another example was the raping case of the 7th Squadron of the 45th Regiment of the 6th Division Private First Class.

> When the accused went to Feng Ting town to collect grains and fodders in the daytime of November 27th, the 12th year of Showa, he saw a Chinese girl (15-year-old) trying to run away, then he caught her and raped her.[44]

The accused undertook the official business and raped in the daytime, which was arrogant. From the following examples, we can see the rapes everywhere.

The Japanese Army Raped Regardless of Time

For example, the case of Private First-Class Ka□□□□ of the 3rd Squadron of the 16th Regiment of the sapper company was on the morning of December 12th; the Private First-Class Mae□□□□ of the 1st Squadron of the 14th Regiment of Heavy Artillery Field Forces committed crimes twice on December 27th, one was at 12 p.m., another was at 5 p.m.; the Private First-Class Ko□□□□ of stretcher-team of the 100th Division committed crimes at 1 p.m. on December 21st; the Private First-Class Ko□□□□ of the field artillery of the tenth army raped two women once a time, at 3:30 p.m. on the January 1st of Showa period.[45]

Evening is a "good time" for raping, such as the rape of the Private First-Class Ike□□□ of the second team of Machine Guns of 23rd Regiment of the infantry of the 6th Division:

> The defendant, in Songjiang camp and on the night of November 2nd of Showa period, saw Shina going in and out of suspiciousness in the neighboring houses near the North Gate. The defendant then entered into a certain room, occasionally saw the Shina woman (30 years old) in the bedroom and raped the woman out of malevolence.[46]

---

[44] 「第十軍法務部陣中日誌」, 高橋正衛編集, 解説『続・現代史資料』6「軍事警察」, 第47頁。

[45] 「第十軍法務部陣中日誌」, 高橋正衛編集, 解説『続・現代史資料』6「軍事警察」, 第61, 72, 63, 89頁。

[46] 「第十軍法務部陣中日誌」, 高橋正衛編集, 解説『続・現代史資料』6「軍事警察」, 第50頁。

Ike□□□ was not on duty, and the so-called "midnight", "search", "occasionally" and "see" were "suspicious". Even if Ike□□□ indeed raped "occasionally", the situation of hunting out at night can be found everywhere. The case of Private First-Class Furu□□□ and Kawa□□□ of the 13th Squadron of the 6th Regiment is an example:

> (December 27th) In the same night, the Japanese army set up camps at the farmer's house in the Building Shijia in Jinshan county and invaded into the neighboring house at midnight. They raped the sleeping Shina woman (32 years old) with violence. The defendant Kawa□ who set up camps together with above mentioned people, heard the rape from Furu□ and rushed to the same house immediately. He frightened the woman with bayonets and raped her.[47]

In this case, Furu committed crimes repeatedly. Not only did he rob the boat and shoot Chinese in Caojia Bang during the day, but also raped a young woman while collecting vegetables in the past two days.

The Japanese Raped Regardless of Age

As mentioned above, Soto□□ raped 15-year-old girls. In the Bates documents, "girls as young as eleven and women as old as 53 years old were raped".[48] There were quite such a few records in the Western records. For example, James McCallum in the letter said that "the eleven and twelve-year-old girls, 50-year-old women also failed to escape (sexual violence)".[49] Raping children at the age of eleven and twelve years old sounds horrible, but the diary showed us that this was not the lowest limit of age. In the case of the Private First-Class Taka of the 1st Squadron of the 114th Regiment of the sapper of the 114th Division, the victim was younger.

> The defendant, in Huzhou camps and at 2:30 p.m. in the afternoon on December of 31st in Showa period, saw a Shina girl aged 8 years old walking past the Moss Bridge in Huzhou, then seduced the girl into the empty house with a sweet talk and raped the young girl (this case was convicted as "rape" cited). He was arrested by the gendarmes.[50]

Even not let slip a child who can be deceived with "sweet words" and has no discretion at all, it can be seen that no "age-appropriate" problems

---

[47]「第十軍法務部陣中日誌」、高橋正衛編集、解説『続・現代史資料』6「軍事警察」、第77頁。

[48] *Archives of the Nanjing Massacre Made by Japanese Invaders*, p. 694.

[49] 转引自「一九三七――一九三八年冬季の日本軍の南京虐殺に関する 報告」、南京事件調査研究会編 訳『南京事件資料集』1アメリカ 関係資料編、東京、青木書店1992年10月15日第1版、第258頁。

[50]「第十軍法務部陣中日誌」、高橋正衛編集、解説『続・現代史資料』6「軍事警察」、第75頁。

existing in the eye of Japanese army. The daily records of the Central China Army recorded that one major forcibly entered the shelter and raped the "fifty or sixty-year-old woman" when camping in Songjiang on November 29th.[51] (This case had not detailed complaint, according to the daily record of the Tenth Army, this person should be Shi□□ of the transport corps of the 6th brigade of field heavy artillery. However, the daily records of the Tenth Army did not record this rape.) Hou□□□ of the first field hospital of the 18th Division was also an example:

> The defendant and his troops were together in the camp of Hangzhou, Zhejiang Province, on January 28th during Showa period, completely drunken and entered a house on the Labor Road in the center of the city. He intimidated the Shina woman (56 years old) with the carried pistol and raped her.[52]

Eight-year-old girls and fifty-six-year-old women, who could be grandparents and grandchildren, can't escape from the sexual violence of the Japanese army. Who can escape from the violence?

The Gang Rapes Committed by the Japanese Troops

Except for wandering individuals, it is typical that the Japanese troops committed rape in groups. Take as example the case of Agent Judayi□□□ and Private First-Class Ishi□□□, who served as a part of the Service Corps in the Bridging Material Squadron of the 12th Division.

> Two defendants and their units were camping in Huzhou. At first, on the afternoon of December 21st, the 12th year of the Shōwa period, Ishi □ along with an agent, was hunting Chinese women nearby the camp. He learnt from Judayi □, who was coming out from a Chinese house and became his co-defendant later, that the hostess was at home. Then Ishi □ went in and, with his sword, forced the Chinese man therein out. He rapped the Chinese woman (forty years old) who got scared. And then, knowing that Ishi □ had raped the Chinese woman with no sweat, Judayi □ also went in and raped the woman who was still under fear.[53]

The Japanese troops explicitly collaborated to hunt women and they acted in the same way in rapes, without any shame. For example, Private First-Class

---

[51] 「中支那方面軍軍法会議陣中日誌」、高橋正衛編集、解説『続・現代史資料』6「軍事警察」、第205頁。

[52] 「第十軍法務部陣中日誌」、高橋正衛edited and noted:『続・現代史資料』6「軍事警察」、第97頁。

[53] 「第十軍法務部陣中日誌」. 高橋正衛 edited and noted:『続·現代史資料』6「軍事警察」, p. 63.

Sake□□□ and Private Second Class Honjitsu□□□, who served the Small Transport Corp[54] in the 2nd Regiment of Individual Engineers, committed violent gang rape[55] in a Chinese house close to the Japanese concession outside Hangzhou on February 7, 1938.

Gang rapes could be seen here and there at that time. For instance, Private First-Class Chi□□□□, along with his fellow Private First-Class To□□□ and Private Second Class Togo □□□, who all served the 10th Squadron of the 6th Engineer Regiment of the 6th Division, violently took away Mr. Cai's wife from his house which located on the Station Front Road in the Nanshi District, and gang raped her in an empty house nearby.[56] And it was the same case with Agent Kichi □□□, Ino□□□ and Tou□□□, who served the Signal Corps of the 18th Division. On February 3rd, 1938, they were "the duty stableman of their unit and saw Ms. Zhao, a 30-year-old Chinese woman who lived in No. 3, Hengzi Lane, Hangzhou City, not far from their camp, entering her house". They then followed her in and raped her.[57]

From the foregoing cases, we can know that Japanese troops committed rape for entertainment not only when they were off duty but also on duty. One example is the "unreported-absence" of Agent Wata□□□ and Tsuka□□, members of the Service Corps, serving in the second field hospital of the 18th Division. On January 25th, 1938, when "on guard at the front door thereof", they "molested a woman" and "left for a house nearby"[58] "without permission". As the case mainly dealt with their unauthorized absence, it is unknown whether they committed "rape". But leaving at the risk of punishment, they were unlikely to give up even if they failed "at the house nearby".

The Extremely Violent Rapes Committed by the Japanese Troops

The cases above have proved that the rapes committed by Japanese troops are accompanied with threat of violence, but we have to deal with it separately due to its significance. Japanese troops wounded or killed those who disobeyed them without scruple, which hardly can be seen in the modern history.

---

[54] Japanese Transport Corps, either large or small, are responsible for brigade-level or over-brigade-level cargo transportation. The Small Transport Corp transports ammunition and other cargo that directly relates to combat (while Large Transport Corp is responsible for cargo not directly related to combat, such as army provisions).

[55]「第十軍法務部陣中日誌」. 高橋正衛edited and noted:『続·現代史資料』6「軍事警察」, p. 106.

[56]「中支那方面軍軍法会議陣中日誌」. 高橋正衛edited and noted:『続·現代史資料』6「軍事警察」, p. 164.

[57]「第十軍法務部陣中日誌」. 高橋正衛edited and noted:『続·現代史資料』6「軍事警察」, pp. 98–99.

[58]「第十軍法務部陣中日誌」. 高橋正衛edited and noted:『続·現代史資料』6「軍事警察」, p. 95.

The typical case, which involved Service Corps Agent To□□□ who served in the 3rd Brigade of the 13th Infantry Regiment of the 6th Division, Private First-Class Tana□□□ who served in the 12th Squadron of the 3rd Brigade, Sergeant Nayi□□□ and Turu□□□ who served in the 9th Squadron of the 3rd Brigade, is hereby cited as an example:

> Firstly, at 10 a.m. on November 24, Nayi□□□ stayed around the empty house mentioned above, and other defendants To□□□, Tana□□□, Turu□□□ and Togo□□□ (Note: He was a Private First Class of the 12th Squadron and met other defendants at Jinshan on his way to Fengjing. According to Okawa's Diaries, he later committed suicide.) left for the nearby village to hunt Chinese to carry their luggage. On the half way, Turu□□□ returned to where Nayi□□□ stayed while others jointly hunted Chinese women to rape them.
>
> 1. At about 11 a.m. that day, To□□□ saw Pan △△ (18 years old) in a hush to avoid other defendants near her house on Dingjia Road. He then caught up and, with the riffle carried, forced her to stop. Pan feared and gave up her effort to escape and was brought to the house. At about 4 p.m. that day, he broke into Li △△'s house (18 years old) in that village and forced her in the same manner.
> 2. At the noon that day, Tana□□□ met Zhang △△ (20 years old) while hunting Chinese women in that village. He chased her and, with the riffle carried, forced her to stop. Zhang feared and gave up her effort to escape and was brought to the empty house.
> 3. At about 4 p.m. that day, Togo□□□ saw Zuo△△ (23 years old) and Zuo◎◎ (22 years old) working on a boat moored in the river near the foregoing village. He approached, aimed his gun at them and then forced them to the empty house when they were in fear. Togo□□□ also entered the nearby house of Lu △△ and asked her to follow him. Lu did not. He kicked her and forced her to the house when she was in fear.
>
> For plunder, the foregoing six Chinese women were taken in a boat moored in the river to the empty house mentioned above, which was about 1 Li (Note: Li is mistaken for Jeli, which amounts to 4 km.) far from the village.
>
> Secondly, Nayi□□□ and Turu□□□ returned to the foregoing camp at about 8 p.m. that day and saw those Chinese women locked in the room. Knowing that those women were forced here by To□□□ and other defendants to sate their lust, Togo□□□ proposed that they each chose a woman for rape. Then Nayi□□□ chose Pan △△ and Turu□□□ chose Zuo◎◎.
>
> Thirdly, at about 9 a.m. that day, To□□□, Tana□□□, Nayi□□□, Turu□□□ and Togo□□□ agreed and each entered their own room at the empty house to rape the Chinese women who were too scared to resist. To□□□ raped Li △△, Tana□□□ raped Zhang △△, Nayi□□□ raped Pan△△, Turu□□□ raped Zuo◎◎ and Togo□□□ raped Zuo△△.
>
> Fourthly, defendant To□□□
>
> 1. saw Tan Youlin (53 years old) near Pan's house at about 11 a.m. that day. He beckoned her over but Tan did not, and he wanted to kill her. To□□□ aimed

his rifle at Tang and shot in her left chest, around the heart. Tang died outright due to the perforating wound.
2. saw He-Chen Shi (26 years old) at her house's vestibule in the foregoing village at about 2 p.m. that day. He said to her, "Come here! Come here!" But He-Che Shi was so scared that she fled back home, which triggered To□□□'s killing intent. He fired his rifle behind her back but did not kill her as He-Chen Shi's right leg was wounded but not perforated.
3. saw a Chinese man, who previously led the way for them and other Japanese soldiers, appear nearby when he was monitoring those Chinese women confined in the above-mentioned boat. He believed that man was to rescue those women and wanted to kill him. He fired two shots but missed him. So the man was not killed.

......

On November 24th, a report was sent from Shajiabang, Jinshan County, Jiangsu Province that there were Japanese soldiers killing Chinese women. And then at about 11.40 p.m. that day, defendants being sought, who were on those women's bed according to the arrest document, along with Togo□□□ were arrested at the empty room of Lu Longqing's house, which located on Dingjia Road, Jinshan County.[59]

(According to in Okawa's diaries on December 26th, there were actually three Chinese people killed and three wounded in this case.) Tang and He did not resist but To□□□ shoot them at his will, which reveals that he disregarded not only Chinese people but Japanese military discipline.

The records and the Diaries deal with many crimes committed by the Japanese troops, with rape ranking top. Japanese troops committed rape "at all times" without scruple and often resorted to violence and blood, exactly the same as what was engraved on our nation's mind.

3   Reckless Murder, Arson and Looting

According to Okawa's diaries, he used to see the brutally murdered dead bodies of the Chinese soldiers and civilians along the road. On November 14th, for example, he made such description of the way to Zhangyan town, "there was corpse after corpse in the river, pond and field"; "countless corpses". According to his diaries, upon arriving at Jinshan village in the afternoon, he even saw some naked corpses. On November 17th, on the suburb of the Jinshan village, "I still saw some Chinese corpses today". On November 28th, on the way to Huzhou, he saw "heap of dead bodies", some of whom wore civilian clothes. He wrote, on December 10th, "the number

---

[59]「中支那方面軍軍法会議陣中日誌」. In 高橋正衛 edited and noted:『続・現代史資料』6「軍事警察」, pp. 175–177.

of corpse along the road was countless".[60] Some Japanese debated that the death comes with the war. On landing Huzhou, however, the 10th Division didn't confront large-scale resistance. Thus, undoubtedly, most corpses are not the result of the war. We can see from the diary that the Japanese soldiers killed people randomly to his satisfaction, reflecting the indifference to the Chinese people's life. For example, Tsuji□□, the lance corporal of the 1st Squadron of reserve artillery, killed men as he likes:

> On November 29th in 1937(the 12th year of Showa), the defendant stationed in Jiaxing city. At 5 p.m., he was dead drunk after drinking the Chankoro wine. Driven by the strong hatred of enemy, he killed three Chankoro on street.[61]

When he was as drunk as skunks, he murdered three men with his bayonet. It is hardly possible unless the victims surrendered or possible accomplices collaborated him. He got so drunk that he couldn't recognize anybody. The defendant's so-called hatred is nothing but an excuse to avoid taking responsibility. But the written records of hearings just noted it down. The case was not prosecuted. Even if such act cannot be deemed as being partial to the Japanese side or conniving in an injustice, it is a dereliction of duties by pushing the boat with the current. The list of such murder of the Chinese in the records can go on and on. For example, Asa □□□, lance corporal in the 124th Regiment of 4th Squadron under the 18th Infantry Division, committed murder:

> On November 29th in the 12th year of Showa, the defendant stationed in Huzhou city. In the nearby field, he and his associate picked some vegetables that weighed about 18.75 kilograms. The defendant went to the nearby farmers' house and asked three Chankoro women to wash the vegetables. One of the women (her name is Liu Asheng according to the Front Army Journal, the information added by the author) spoke something fast as if she was unwilling to do so. The defendant thought she was insulting the Japanese soldier and shoot her with his rifle.[62]

Though the defendant had no clue of what she said, he still shot her because of his ambiguous feelings. Obviously, the defendant "felt" the life of the Chinese insignificant. On December 14th, Chi □□□, lance corporal in 10th Regiment of 6th Squadron under the 6th Engineer Division, and his associate took turns to rape a woman whose family name was Cai. After that, they came back to rape her once again in the same month.

---

[60] Okawa. The Diary of Military Law Code Officer. P27, 30, 44, 102.

[61] *The Military Law Department Journal in the 10th Division*. Takahashi Masae. The Record of Contemporary History.[6] Military Police. P46.

[62] *The Military Law Department Journal in the 10th Division*. Takahashi Masae. The Record of Contemporary History.[6] Military Police. P60–P61.

At 3 p.m. on December 17th, imbued with a lust for the woman, he left his dormitory to rape her. On the way, he met Fuji □□□ (He also participated in the rape last time, the information added by the author) and invited him to the house of women together. They called her outside in front of the house. Standing at the door, her husband Cai shouted at them while walking towards them (The defendant) deduced that her husband was preventing him to rape her wife. Having the intention to kill Cai, the defendant fired 3 shots from his pistol, with 2 bullets in his brain and left chest. He died on the spot for the penetrating wound.[63]

It is extremely insolent that he exposed his attempt to rape and called the woman out publicly. When he saw the victim's husband, the defendant not only had no sham but also shoot him immediately. The defendant's deep contempt for Chinese is beyond description. The following holocaust is a typical example:

First, Oka □□□, the second lieutenant of logistics branch, worked in the clothing and food factory of Jinshan field operations branch. He was disturbed by the nearby Chankoro as they often spoke and behave unappropriately and stole things. He explained his worried to the sergeant in the same factory. Second, as a result, on December 15th in the 12th year of Showa, Yoshi □□□ led 26 soldiers to arrest the above-mentioned 26 Chankoro. On the way they took them back to the military police office, the japanese soldier decided to kill them as someone tried to escape. (The list of murder and accomplice is attached in the end of the book, the information added by the author.)[64]

26 men were all murdered. However, Jinshan town was a solid base of the Japanese troops. Therefore, there is no way that the civilians would dare to challenge the authority of them. (At that time, my mother lived in Zhapu, a town next to Jinshan. She said the civilians tried to avoid the Japanese soldiers, not to mention dare to upset them.) Even if Oka really felt disturbed by the Chankoro, they should not be murdered for his doubt of "stole things". As such "crime" shouldn't be penalized, of course, the so-called attempt to escape can't be a charge. What's more, as 26 civilians were escorted by the same number of soldiers (in Nanjing Massacre, the number of escorted Chinese soldiers is 10 times as the number of Japanese escorts), any reasonable man has no attempt to escape. Even if they have such intention, they have no courage to do. Even if one of them escaped, the rest wouldn't risk their life to escape if the Japanese soldier fires rifles into the air or shoot the fugitive. Unless something strange happened, I doubt the truth behind is intentional slaughter.

[63] *The Military Law Council Journal of the Chankoro Front Army*. Takahashi Masae. The Record of Contemporary History.[6] Military Police. P164.

[64] *The Military Law Department Journal in the 10th Division*. Takahashi Masae. The Record of Contemporary History.[6] Military Police. P67–P68.

Such massacre was rampant in those days. As mentioned in the diary written by Okawa, the corpses of Chinese were common in any place the 10th Division passed. At least part of the corpses was the result of slaughter. As I write here, I remembered two relevant materials. In the diary of soldiers belong to Shang expeditionary forces, there are many records of slaughtering prisoners. The earliest record about the holocaust of captives since the landing of Japanese troops was written in the September 6th and 7th diaries of Iinuma Mori. As the two records were never cited, I hereby noted them for the reference of interested researchers.[65] According to the record, on the one hand, the holocaust of prisoners already began since the battle of Songhu and happened in regions beyond Nanjing. On the other hand, the claim of "slaughtering prisoners was the last resort" is untenable.[66] But what makes the murder case of Yoshi special is that it has the firsthand clear records.

"Murder and arson" is often put together because arson is another major atrocity of the Japanese troops.

The denial of the arson by the Japanese troops appeared as early as the Tokyo Trial. For example, as for the testimony of witness (Xu Chuanyin) about Japanese troops setting Nanjing embassy on fire, Itou Shimizu, the defense attorney of Matsui Ishim, framed the Chinese troop by claiming that they used to set fire when they occupy or left a city.[67] Today, some politicians still say the same words by highlighting Japanese soldiers didn't set fire on the one side and pass the buck to the Chinese soldiers on the other side. For example, to show that Japanese soldiers didn't set fire, Nakano cited "fire prevention" written in the Guidelines for Mopping-up Operation of the 7th Regiment. Meanwhile, to prove the prisoners set fire, he also cited the deduction of the Chinese soldiers set fire from the Diary of Miyamoto as a Soldier.[68] For example, Matsumura cited the records of "looting and arson" written by Cabot Coville, an ambassador in the American Embassy in Japan. Then, Matsumura said,

> The trace of looting and damage Coville saw was often viewed as the "act of Japanese troop". But after comprehensive observation, he deduced that "arson happened after the looting", which means arson is cover the trace of looting. If

---

[65] *Diary of Iinuma Mori*. The Collection and Editing Committee of Nanjing Battle History. The Records Collection of Nanjing Battle History. P99, 100.

[66] In Japan, many people think the Japanese troops have to massacre Chinese because they were threatened by the great number of prisoners. For example, on the one hand, Tonakano didn't amidst the massacre. On the other hand, he remarked the massacre is a "pity", because "it's an urgency as they were surrounded with the enemy civilians and soldiers." (The Way to Deal with the Prisoners Problems. Gentlemen. Tokyo. The Spring and Autumn of Literature and Art Press. 2001(2): 140.)

[67] Hora Tomio. *The Information about the History of Sino-Japanese War* (8). Nanjing Issue (I). 38.

[68] *The Thorough Investigation of Nanjing Massacre*. P180, 135.

the looting was done by Chankoro, then arson was also the act of Chankoro. ... It will bring the Japanese troop no good if arson occurred in Nanjing after the Japanese side occupied the city.[69]

Higashinakano and Miyamoto only mentioned Nanjing because the debate was focused on Nanjing. It doesn't mean the situation in other regions is different from Nanjing. There are many doubts of every sentence in their citing, but the facts speak for themselves.

Lack of evidence and witnesses, most fires happened in the war became unsolved mysteries. There is no way to know who the perpetrator is. Besides, the Chinese troop once adopted the strategy of "emptying the house and clearing up the field". And some Chinese leaders said such words like leave "nothing" to the enemy (Wang Jingwei's word in the Last Moment) while the Japanese troops did put forward the instruction of "fire prevention". Given all of this, it provided some evidence for the smear of "wounded soldier" and "prisoner" set fire. The claim of the Japanese can be traced back to the war. For example, here is the November 15th diary written by Okawa:

> When I patroled in the city (Jinshan, the information added by the author), I saw most part of the city was in ruins for men's act. Once in a while, I saw some houses turned into ashes. The messy situation after looting is beyond description. For example, when I walked into a big bookstore and dispensary, I found the stores were designed as great as the Japan's Sanseido but the medicine and books were in shambles. The rest of the remaining shop looks the same. The mess is definitely not caused by the Japanese soldiers. Then I guess it is the atrocity of the Chankoro soldiers. I heard the Chankoro has declared that they would not leave anything to the Japanese soldiers and damaged and burned down everything when they escape.[70]

The reason why Okawa made such deduction is that he believed the rumor or he overrated the discipline of Ja the truth. Even if some Chinese witnesses proved it wrong, it is still hard to change the view. But the later diary of Okawa exposed the real perpetrator:

> It is said that the Japanese soldiers are violent. But I still have some doubts about it. Today, Nakasa, the army surgeon, said, "Arriving on Jinshan at November 10th, the shops in the city, including the bookstore as great as the Japan's Sanseido, has no trace of damage. Later, when I saw the same store, it was in a mess. Obviously it is not damaged by the Chankoro soldiers but the Japanese soldiers." It is shocking to know that truth.[71]

---

[69] Matsumura Toshio. 『「南京虐殺」への大疑問』. Tokyo. Tenden Sha Press. 1998.12.13 (1). P49–150.

[70] 小川関治郎著『ある軍法務官の日記』, 第36页。

[71] 小川関治郎著『ある軍法務官の日記』, 第45页。

The judgment of Nakasa and Okawa can't be false. As the Japanese soldiers had occupied Jinshan since November 10th and the city became a mess overnight, it is Japanese troops brought destruction to the area. Okawa's change of view is a typical example. In those days, the Japanese observers, soldiers, journalists, diplomats, etc., always hold the opinion that the atrocities are not the acts of Japanese troops when they had no clue of the truth. The unique value of the diary written by Okawa is that it is the authentic records of what he had seen and heard on the Japanese troop stand. His standing in the Japanese troop position is of great importance, because he wouldn't let the Japanese soldier under suspicion. Therefore, the records of Japanese troop's atrocities should be valid evidence.

At that time, the arson of the Japanese soldiers became a regularity. The motives behind are not always about interests, for example, the arson case of Furu□□□, Matsu □□□, Kita □□□, the spy soldiers of a regiment under the 12th Division.

> On November 12th in the 12th of Showa, the defendant's troop landed on somewhere near the House of Li in Songjiang town of Zhejiang province. On 13th, the next day, they took breakfasts and left the camp to search for wine, tobacco and other items. Furu□□□ and Ishi □□□ and several other soldiers, the spy soldiers of a regiment, left the camp without permission. From time to time, they saw some houses were set into fire on their way. The defendants regarded it as an act done by the Japanese troop. With strong hatred of the enemy and the Chankoro, they decided to set fire on the civilians' houses. At 11:40 on the same day, arrived on the Dongmen village, Jinshanwei town, Tong county, the defendant Furu□□□ went to the kitchen in an empty house of Lu Xiaoyun, a trader that sold rice and cotton. He used his lighter (exhibit 1) to set the old newspapers on fire as a way to burn all the wallpaper and bamboo cage in the home, burning a house that covers about 63 square meters. The defendant Matsu□□□ also set the wallpaper and ragged clothes in wildfire in another nearby house, owned by Lu Liren, a trader that sold rice and cotton. The defendant Kita□□□, lighted the ragged clothes on the bed in the same room, burning a house that covers 99 square meters. The two fires also burned down the two brick houses with each covers about 99 square meters, the houses owned by Lu Liwen and Lu Liru respectively.[72]

The motive that Furu □□□ and others set fire is that they became fretful as they failed to get tobacco and wine, while their "hatred of enemy" is only an excuse. But burning down the empty house of Lu Xiaoyun and others does them no good. While they looted to get profits and they raped to satisfy their lust, arson is another thing. All of this proved that the so-called "fire

---

[72]「中支那方面軍軍法会議陣中日誌」, 高橋正衛編集, 解説『続・現代史資料』6「軍事警察」, 第180頁。

prevention",[73] the military discipline in a broad sense, was an empty talk for Furu□□ and his compliance. At that time, Furu□□ didn't participate in the war, but he already had "hatred of enemy" as he claimed, proving that his "revenge for his comrade" is an excuse. (The written judgment of this case put the poor education as a reason, which will be explained in detail in the following text.) Such arson for no reason is very common during the period—for example, the arson case of Take□□□ and Ko□□□, spy soldiers of the first field hospital of the division.

Except murdering and arson, looting is a major crime committed by the Japanese army. There are many related records in the diary of Okawa, for example, the November 14th diary:

> We saw village after village on the way, with larger houses still smoking in the fire. About 1 p.m., we finally saw the first town nearby, which is said the Zhangyan town of Jinshan county. We ate lunch in Tongsuo, a lively place that is filled with stores owned by capitalists. On a two-floor restaurant that hangs a plaque written "the No. 1 Teahouse in South Lake", the japanese soldiers on the second floor called us when they saw our boat. Though Tongsuo was less damaged, the goods in the merchandise has been took away by the Japanese soldiers openly, which is a kind of looting.[74]

As a minister of military law, Okawa didn't stick to the principle when he saw the openly looting. He didn't blame or arrest them, but only wrote "which is a kind of looting" in his diary. The Japanese troop has no effective mechanism to punish those perpetrators. According to his diary, the Japanese soldiers' booty has nothing valued. We have to doubt that the records avoid the important and dwell on the trivial. Take a look at the case of Mae□□□, lance corporal of 1st Regiment, 103rd Squadron under the 101th Infantry Division. (The division originally belonged to the army stationed in Shanghai at first, and then, it was directly under the Japanese army in the battlefield of China. At that time, as the army didn't have its own council of military court, the council of military court of the 10th Division represents the front army to deal with their cases.)

> From September 25th to December 28th, in the Japanese occupied areas such as Jiangwan town, Jiading and hangzhou, under the broad daylight, the soldiers have broken in the houses of Chankoro in busy streets for 6 or 7 times. As the Chankoro family left because of the war, they openly stole the five 5-yuan paper money of Transportation Bank, two 1-jiao paper money of China Bank,

---

[73] At the beginning of its departure, the Tenth Army stressed that "special attention should be paid to fire prevention" and issued a ban on "strictly prohibiting fire burning" on November 7th, 8th and 14th after landing (高橋正衛編集, 解説『続・現代史資料』6「軍事警察」, 第14, 24, 25, 33頁). Although this is targeted at resident areas, it is also applicable to the occupied areas.

[74] 小川関治郎著『ある軍法務官の日記』, 第28頁。

seven 1-jiao paper money of China bank, 30 Chankoro silver coin and copper coin, 4 silver rings and other items (exhibit 1–17).[75]

The looting was mainly the act of soldiers and corporals(private), but sometimes the lieutenants and officers would join. For example, the case of Sibu□□□, the solider of field heavy artillery in the 6th brigade:

> From November 22nd to December 1st, he stolen over 10 scrolls, a blanket and over 10 valued items. (The Army Journal also listed the booty: hundreds of ancient coins, the white cotton as long as 9 meters and as wide as 0.2 m and 2 ink stones. The information added by the author.)[76]

The Japanese army legalized looting in the name of "collection", as a task of the soldier by openly organized looting. I once said, the houses of civilians, grocery stores, official residence, the embassies and all the public and private companies are our target of "collection". As for what should be "collected", anything valued or useful is in our range.[77] Therefore, even though the Japanese military discipline has a regulation on forbidden looting, Okawa, the minister of military law, didn't follow the rules. Based on his diary, he only blamed the perpetrators once in a while, with very light punishment. Few of them suffered heavy punishment for several crimes with looting as a relatively minor charge. For example, two cases of heavy punishment were accused of "violence or threat against superiors". Even if some common looting cases would be accepted by the ministry of law, the perpetrators would not be punished or be imposed on light punishment. There are many examples to prove that. In the case of Yama□□□, lance corporal of field heavy artillery 14th Regiment, 2nd Squadron, he looted fortunes in Jiaxing on November 15th and in Huzhou on December 2nd. Buku□□□ and the other four soldiers, lance corporal of 2nd Regiment, 14th Squadron, were involved in the looting in Pingwang on December 10th. Ko□□□ and Kou□□□, lance corporal of field heavy artillery 13th Squadron, had looted in Jiaxing for several times from November 20th to 24th.[78] In this case, only Ko□□□ was charged for looting camera and other 95 valued items, with the rest given warning of reading "300 regulations".[79] In the next section, the degree of punishment of Japanese conducted by council of military court will be discussed. Here, we

---

[75] 「中支那方面軍軍法会議陣中日誌」, 高橋正衛編集, 解説『続・現代史資料』6「軍事警察」, 第158頁。

[76] 「第十軍法務部陣中日誌」, 高橋正衛編集, 解説『続・現代史資料』6「軍事警察」, 第71頁。

[77] For more information, see Is the Nanjing Massacre a Fabrication of the Tokyo Trial?, *The Study of Modern History*, Beijing, No. 6, 2002, p. 42.

[78] 「第十軍法務部陣中日誌」, 高橋正衛編集, 解説『続・現代史資料』6「軍事警察」, 第46, 63, 79頁。

[79] If no public prosecution or preliminary hearing is initiated by the officer, the prosecutor (military Advocate) shall be notified immediately for his release.

will continue to see the cases of looting. It is important to note that the victims of the looting cases are different from other cases. For example, the victim was only the Chankoro in a rape case, while the looting case is different. As crime became a regularity among the army, the Japanese soldiers themselves sometimes would become "victims". We will look at crimes on this aspect in particular.

The regularity of crimes occurred in various occasions in troops, personnel and regions at all levels. Meanwhile, the criminal would continue to loot, rather than one-time activity. The criminal would loot fortunes by hook or by crook and even stole things from their comrades, ending up shooting themselves in the foot. Such things happened regularly. For example, Togo□□□, lance corporal of 10th Regiment, 124th Squadron under the 18th Infantry Division, "looted (the original text used this word. The information added by the author) Chankoro paper money and coins that worth 10,000 yuan" in the military warehouse".[80] (Togo□□□ "and his unit robbed a Chankoro by taking his paper money and a leather suitcase filled with silver coins that valued 10,000 yuan".) Such inside job was not only existed in the 10th Division, but also other troops. As written in the journal of front army, Buku□□□,lance corporal in the clothing and food factory of Shanghai expeditionary forces, was prosecuted for theft. This case is also an inside job.

> The defendant Buku□□□ was called up right at the beginning of war in China battlefield and assigned in the 1st infantry squadron. On September 10th in the 12th year of Showa, his troop landed on the Wusong town, Jiangsu province, China. As a soldier in the troop (refers to the clothing and food factory. The information added by the author), he always had ulterior motives when served as the warehouse keeper. From November 20th to December 16th in the same year, he stole 100 packs of Chankoro cigarettes that belong to the troop from the affiliated factory, a substitute bread producing factory located in the Broadway Street 35th in Shanghai. He also stole many goods that belongs to the troop from the warehouse of the factory in Shanghai's Gongxiang wharf. Here is a list of the stolen things: 1450 kilograms of rice, 10 L of soy sauce, 300 L of Japanese wine, two boxes of wine (one box includes 12 bottle of three boxes of malt liquor), a box of golden bat tobaccos (including 50,000 cigarettes), 96 boxes of Areca brand tobaccos (including 48,000 cigarettes), 3 boxes of Ruby Queen tobaccos (each box has 500 cigarettes).[81]

They would steal whatever can turn into fortunes, no matter it belongs to the Chankoro or their army. For example,

> On December 26th in the 12th year of Showa, when they were sent to Shanghai for tasks, the defendants decided to steal something in Nanjing. They

---

[80] 「第十軍法務部陣中日誌」、高橋正衛編集、解説『続·現代史資料』6「軍事警察」、第80頁。
[81] 「中支那方面軍軍法会議陣中日誌」、高橋正衛編集、解説『続·現代史資料』6「軍事警察」、第184页。

drove the car to receive tobacco, wine and dessert that should be sent to the office of division from the army service station. Without permission, they sold them to 2 Chankoro in Shanghai for over 1,000 yuan and divided the money. They returned to Shanghai to have access to travel in the inland provinces. Besides, on January in the 13th year of Showa, Ni□□□,stole two cars owned by division headquarters. Then they allow the cars used by a Japanese in Shanghai for free as a thanks gift to provide him convenience on his trip.[82]

Togo□□□ was sentenced for a year; Buku□□□ was sentenced for year and a half; Ni□□□ and other 5 persons were not sentenced (recorded in the unsentenced part of the journal) but heavily punished. The value of things that Togo□□□ stole is more than the others. More importantly, the reason why he was sentenced was that he did harm to his own side, which was strictly forbidden in the Japanese troop. I will explain this point in the later section with more materials.

Larceny is one of the crimes committed inside the Japanese troop. I will give 3 more examples. Sibu□□□, lance corporal of 2nd Regiment, 3rd Independent Infantry Squadron, involved in the case of death by injury.

Camped in Hangzhou, Zhejiang province, on January 8th in the 13rd year of Showa, the defendant was under the order of squadron to take two coolies outside. They found a broke rickshaw on the way. When they were trying to find something to mend the rickshaw, an officer from other squadrons sat on it. He forced and beaten the two cookies to drag it. Seeing this, the defendant suggested the officer not doing so. As a result, they began quarreling and fighting. Driven by a sudden fury, the defendant stabbed officer's chest by his bayonet and caused his death immediately.[83]

If he did suggest the officer not doing so, Sibu□□□ has good cause. According to the interrogation record by army justice police Yamamoto Toushirou in the front army journal, however, there is no description of "suggestion" and "quarrel". It noted that the defendant "attacked him from the behind". Therefore, there is still a possibility that the beating cookies was only an excuse to hide the real reason behind the quarrel. The Japanese soldiers argued on petty benefits, or even fought over trivial things with no interests involved. Such thing happened a lot at that time. For example, in the case of Sibete□□□, lance corporal of 7th Regiment, 47th Squadron under the 6th Infantry Division, he committed mayhem.

The defendant's troop camped in Wuhu, Anhui province. On December 27th in the 12th year Showa, they went to a village in the Wuhu suburban area to

---

[82]「第十軍法務部陣中日誌」, 高橋正衛編集, 解説『続・現代史資料』6「軍事警察」, 第105頁.

[83]「第十軍法務部陣中日誌」, 高橋正衛編集, 解説『続・現代史資料』6「軍事警察」, 第84, 85頁.

collect things. When they rest after lunch near the villager's house, two soldiers shouted "two Chankoro girls". Hearing that, they ran to find the girls. The other soldier ran before him jumped down from the earth wall while the branches of the willow tree near the wall hit the face of the defendant. When they quarreled over it, the defendant became impatient and stabbed his back with the Chankoro's scissors.[84]

(In the case, the description of the eager of the Japanese soldiers for girls is vivid.[85]) There is another example of the mayhem case of an airman second class of 115th Regiment under the 18th Infantry Division.

The defendant and his squadron stationed in Huzhou, Zhejiang province. On February 7th in the 13rd year of Showa, the defendant was drunk and went to the special comfort station ran by the Chankoro. When he picked the whore on the upstairs, he shouted "I will stab you if you come nearer" at the two soldiers. He stabbed one of them in his bayonet, with the one stab cut into his right abdomen.[86]

If the claim of "revenge" for Chinese is untenable, then fight among the Japanese soldiers proved that the Japanese military discipline is not effective.

4 The Dereliction of Military Code Council Reveals No Effective Institutional Restrictions upon the Crime Committed by the Japanese Army

I have to admit that the Japanese military law and its system had certain regulations on the military discipline. Yet compared to the law enforced in Japan, the fact is that the constraints were rather limited. The reason behind is complicated. Some reckoned that the Japanese "aggressiveness" and "education" contributed to it. For example, the above-mentioned judgment of the arson case of the Furu and other 3 soldiers considered "poor education" and "violate the military discipline" as the cause. On the contrary, the Chinese

---

[84] 「第十軍法務部陣中日誌」, 高橋正衛編集, 解説『続・現代史資料』6「軍事警察」, 第91頁。

[85] 前田光繁, a Japanese soldier who was in the Eighth Route Army, said when talking about the Eighth Route Army in his later years, "What is particularly touching is that we do not talk about issues of woman. Almost no one talks about issues of woman among Chinese cadres or soldiers. …… It turns out that when we were on the Japanese side, we used to play comfort women. But later, among us (referring to the former Japanese soldiers in the Eighth Route Army), we gradually stopped saying those obscene words." He believes that this "noble discipline", which contrasts most with the Japanese army, cannot be achieved without "political consciousness" (香川孝治, 前田光繁著《八路軍中的日本兵》, 北京, 长征出版社, 1985年5月第1版, 第134頁).

[86] 「第十軍法務部陣中日誌」, 高橋正衛編集, 解説『続・現代史資料』6「軍事警察」, 第103, 104頁。

think that the crimes of Japanese soldiers are deeply embedded in the "poisoned militarism-oriented education". Some deem that the limited number of Japanese soldier and some other problems existed in the institution led to it. Meanwhile, others hold the opinion that the "war" itself triggered the disaster. But the discussion is just a tip of the iceberg, because no one knows the immense bulk hidden beneath the water for the lack of the evidence. As it doesn't facilitate the understanding of truth, I will not elaborate on this. In general, the crux of the matter is the nature of the war launched by Japan which is to invade China. In other words, the nature decides that the fighting capacity won't be limited or reduced by the military law. From the perspective of the Japanese high command, nothing is more important than fighting capacity, even military code. The above-mentioned November 18th records in the journal of military meetings have noted that safeguarding military discipline requires "sacrifices", reflecting the "determination". However, the discussion about the issue went even further on the meeting. According to the diaries written by Okawa, he wrote down the important fact "ignored" in the journal. It turns out that the provision not only noted "sacrifice" but also had a premise:

> The rear units shall obey the military discipline while the frontline troop is another matter.[87]

It is a noteworthy finding and a crucial point that can't be neglected. However, the Japanese left-wing and right-wing politicians began to make corresponding response and the central leaders warned soldiers about the military discipline after the Japanese high commands were laid pressure because of the Nanjing atrocities. It is aimed to show that the Japanese troop's "focus" on military discipline or the seriousness of discipline problems. Of course, we can't simply regard the "another matter" written by Okawa as an encouragement of committing crimes or the frontline enjoy privileges. But prior to the end of December, the 10th Division Shanghai expeditionary forces should have clearly expressed that the regulation of "maintaining military discipline" can postpone its enforcement. That means the shocking atrocities occurred in Nanjing arc caused by ruthless Japanese soldiers and indulgent troop units as well. The records of Okawa provide the direct evidence.

Therefore, the Japanese military law department had strict regulations on the surface while its enforcement depended on the interests of the troop. As a result, the measurement of penalty was so random that the provisions existed in name only, lacking seriousness of law. For example, Yoshi□□□ and others were not charged for killing 26 civilians; Tsuji□□ who murdered 3 civilians was also not charged. Even if some malefactors were sentenced, most received probation. For example, Furu□□□ and 2 soldiers who set houses into fire

---

[87] 小川関治郎著『ある軍法務官の日記』, 第46页。

were given 1-year sentence respectively and the two years of probation. At the same time, however, those who "insult superior" were imposed on heavy penalty and the Chinese who "committed crimes" got tougher punishment. For example, Li△△, Zhou△△ and Lu△△ and other cases of Chinese were sentenced to death.[88]

This section elaborates military law council's punishment of Japanese soldiers who committed crimes recorded in the journal and diaries, so as to prove that institutional problems also caused the disrupted discipline of Japanese troop.

First, the prosecutors' statement of criminal facts reflects evident indulgence of perpetrators. For example, the indictments of many cases used such expression "by accident" or something like that. It was used in the indictment of the above-mentioned rape case of Ike□□□, lance corporal of 11th Squadron, 56th Regiment under the 18th Infantry Division (detailed description in section 2.2). "By accident" also appeared in the indictment of the rape case by Mae□□, lance corporal of the 11th Squadron, 56th Regiment of the 18th Infantry Division. The indictment of Mika□□□□, lance corporal of the 3rd Squadron of the 16th Engineer Regiment, also adopted such expression.[89]

Rape is different from accidental discharge because the perpetrators consciously force somebody to do something. There is no "by accident" in such thing. But the indictment still used the expression. No matter it is the statement of the criminal, it reflects the persecutor took an indulgent attitude.

All the cases of the crimes against Chinese, including rape, have various excuses. For example, the case of Ta□□□, lance corporal of the 124th Machine Gun Squadron under the 18th Infantry Division.

> The defendant and his unit camped in Hangzhou, Zhejiang province. On February 18th, the 13th year of Showa, in a village near the Japanese concession in Hangzhou, the defendant shot the dog barking towards him and thus shot the foot of a nearby Chankoro. Then he went to into two Chankoro shops and looted money, shooting two Chankoro. On the way back to his camp in Hangzhou, he threatened the Chankoro he came across, looted their money and shot them, causing every Chankoro injured.[90]

He intended to murder, hurt and loot Chinese, but the indictment noted the "barking" of the dog on purpose in particular. If Ta□□□ is bad at using

---

[88] It is said the journal only has brief statement of the Zhou's case, without any details of hearing, judgment and implementation. The journal has no statement of Lu's case as well. I deduced that records have been tampered to cover its crimes against Chinese. (The detailed description is in my article *Ogawa Sekijiro and 'The Diary of Military Law Officer'*.) The records of Li's case haven't been deleted because Li escaped from the prison after he was given death sentence.

[89] 「第十軍法務部陣中日誌」, 高橋正衛編集, 解説『続·現代史資料』6「軍事警察」. P49, 61.

[90] 「第十軍法務部陣中日誌」, 高橋正衛編集, 解説『続·現代史資料』6「軍事警察」. P105–106.

guns and the "person's feet" is accidentally near the barking dog, the case still should focus on shooting the "person's feet". But according to the indictment, the motive is all about the "barking dog" and all subsequent events accidentally happened. Even if such indictment is not on purpose, it still admits the lame arguments of the defendant (it even can't be called as an excuse). Many cases had such "excuses". For example, the above-mentioned murder case of Tsuji□□ whose excuse was "dead drunk", the most common used excuse at that time. I will list more cases used "dead drunk" as an excuse. On January 6th, 1938, Yama□□□□, lance corporal of the 10th Squadron, 149th Regiment under the 110th Infantry Division, committed rape in Huzhou because of "drunkenness". At 3 p.m. on January 6th, 1938, Ko□□□, lance corporal of the field artillery factory in 10th Division, threatened two women by bayonets and raped them in Nanshi "after drinking wine".[91] Ji□□□□, lance corporal of the 10th Squadron, 6th Regiment under the 6th Engineer Division, committed murder and rape for the same excuse.

> First, on December 14th in the 12th year of Showa, camped in Shanghai, the defendant got very drunk during dinner. Then he came to the house of a Chankoro who worked as a dogsbody in the southern Shanghai guard. He used his rifle to threaten and raped the dogsbody's wife aged 28 years old. Second, on December 17th, the defendant who was drunk during lunch led the other two soldiers to the house of the dogsbody. He let the two soldiers stay outside of the house, shot the man with his rifle and raped his wife.[92]

Using "drunk" as an excuse is full of flaws in these cases. Some of them were lies, which were revealed at that time. The case of Ji □□□□ is an example. According to the survey of army military police toward Fuji, Ji □□□□'s accomplice in the rape case happened on December 14th (the front army journal reveals that 3 soldiers raped the woman by turns on December 14th), Ji □□□□'s two rapes happened "on the way go out for business" and "on the return trip from outside" had nothing to do with "drinking wine" or "dead drunk". There is no doubt about the evidence because it was exposed from the Japanese troop's records.

As many indictments adopted such excuses and the judgment of the criminal is light, it reflects the Japanese military law council didn't conduct any thorough investigation toward the exculpatory explanations at least. I used "at least" because the situation depends on case by case. For example, based on the front army journal, some cases exculpated perpetrators by using excuses like "getting drunk". For example, a second lieutenant of infantry (the front army journal didn't note the specific troop of the defendant), he beat 3 waitresses in a restaurant in the Zhapu Road in Shanghai on January

---

[91] 「第十軍法務部陣中日誌」, 高橋正衛編集, 解説『続・現代史資料』 6「軍事警察」, P83, P89.

[92] 「第十軍法務部陣中日誌」, 高橋正衛編集, 解説『続・現代史資料』 6「軍事警察」, P68.

2nd, 1938. The judgment didn't impose any penalty on him because he was "drunk".

> ......The corpus delict has enough evidence. The defendant, a military officer, was in a position that is higher than civilians and is not allowed to do such thing. But his behavior is driven by the excitement after getting drunk. When he sobered up, the defendant regretted for what he had done and promised to stop drinking to save his reputation. Given his deep regret about it and the victim wished to get leniency, the council decided not to prosecute him.[93]

"The excitement after getting drunk" became an excuse for "leniency".

As the victim in this case is Japanese, it is no surprise that they would like to ask for leniency. There is no doubt to take the requirements of the victims as an excuse for "leniency". The demands of the victim will be considered when grant the perpetrator leniency. But the key is how military law council will deal with the case if the victim didn't "wish" for "leniency" but "wish" for severe punishment. We assume that council would meet the demands of victims. The paradox of the assumption is that the history records proved things on the contrary. For example, Yama□□□, lance corporal of the 1st Regiment, 12th Infantry Squadron, committed rape. The victim Ying△△ required "severe punishment", yet got no response from the front army military law council.

> According to law, the defendant objected the 177th provision in the penal code. As the indictment wrote, however, the defendant's crime is only an accident that can be forgiven. Therefore, based on the condition, according to the 66th and 71st provision and section 3 in 68th provision, I granted him commutations of sentences.[94]

The victim's "wish" for "heavy punishment" ends up with "forgiveness" and "commutations of sentences". Is anything wrong? We can draw the conclusion later. Check out the results of other "wishes" before we make judgment. As for the above-mentioned rape case of Mae □□□, lance corporal of 1st Regiment, 14th Field Heavy Artillery Squadron, the requirements of victim Zhang △△ also ended up with such judgment from military law council.[95] Zhang described how Mae raped her and how military police arrested them. The military police recorded "Zhang wished to severely punish Mae. Her confession matched with the fact". But the judgment was:

---

[93] 「中支那方面軍軍法会議陣中日誌」, 高橋正衛編集, 解説『続·現代史資料』6「軍事警察」. P136, 137

[94] 「中支那方面軍軍法会議陣中日誌」, 高橋正衛編集, 解説『続·現代史資料』6「軍事警察」. P151.

[95] 「中支那方面軍軍法会議陣中日誌」, 高橋正衛編集, 解説『続· 現代史資料』6「軍事警察」, 第162, 168页。

According to the law, defendant's accomplished crime shall be governed by the forepart of 177th provision of penal law. The defendant's attempted crime shall be applicable to the forepart of 177th and 179th provision of penal law. The defendant's continuing offence shall be applicable to 55th provision of this law. He should be given corresponding sentence for accomplished rape according to the applicable law. The judgement, however, declared that the drunken defendant saw the victim by accident and forced her to have sex with him. He would never do such thing when he was sober. Now, the defendant realized his alcohol problems, decadence and debauchery. He swears that he will stop drinking to change himself. Therefore, the defendant's crime can be forgiven. According to 66th, 71st, 68th provision of the penal law, his sentence shall be reduced based on his condition.[96]

Mae was arrested when he raped the woman and the victim "wish" was "approved" by the Japanese military police. If the military law council is intended to maintain the military discipline, it would severely punish the perpetrator for his excuse of "by accident". But the council exculpated Mae by using the statement like "accident" and "drinking wine". Besides, using such frivolous expressions like "teasing woman" showed no consideration for victim's sufferings. Unless military law council was a puppet agency, it has no sincerity at all.

Except using the excuse of "the crimes can be forgiven", the council even blamed victims in some cases. For example, Kawa □□□, lance corporal of 2nd Medic Regiment under the 101th Division. When the victim Wang △△ was investigated for obtaining evidence, she said:

That day, three Japanese soldiers came to my house and asked me to prepare dinner. When I was washing vegetables in sink in the backyard for the dinner, at about 5:30, a Japanese soldier tailed after me and gestured to have sex with me. He clutched my hand and dragged me while I tried to resist him. I was afraid something bad would happen to me if I resist his requirement, so I let him rape me as he please. After he dragged me into the toilet, he undressed my trouser and raped me.

For this, the judgment wrote:

According to the law, the defendant's behavior governed by the forepart of 177 provision of penal law. He should be sentenced to two years' imprisonment, but his crime as here recorded is totally happened by accident. And the victim Wang didn't strongly resist the atrocity of defendant. Her calm reaction is also a reason that leads to the crime. Overall, the defendant's crime can be forgiven.[97]

---

[96] 「中支那方面軍軍法会議陣中日誌」，高橋正衛編集，解説『続・現代史資料』6「軍事警察」．P166.

[97] 「中支那方面軍軍法会議陣中日誌」，高橋正衛編集，解説『続・現代史資料』6「軍事警察」．P163.

Her calm reaction even became a reason that leads to rape. From the perspective of the judgment, it seems that the defendant has the suspicion of enticing him unless she is stabbed by the defendant! Seeing such a cunning scheme of calling white black, I doubted the guideline of the military law council is "leniency". The so-called "wishes" are nothing but an excuse to clear Japanese soldiers' names. As "leniency" is put at the priority, anything can become their excuse. As the above-mentioned judgment, it used the excuse "the defendant was excited after drinking wine…he was deeply regretful" to exculpate the defendant. Here is another example. In the judgment of lance corporal Taka□□□, cavalryman, the council decided not to prosecute.[98]

Except the defendant's "wish", the victims' relatively calm response, instead of dying to resist, to be precise, is also an excuse of "the crimes can be forgiven". Meanwhile, there are excuses like "drinking wine", "by accident" and "deeply regretful". But the next example will let you have a deep understanding of their almighty power. The above-mentioned arson case of Furu□□□, Matsu□□□ and Kita□□□, special agents in the 12th Division. They set civilian Li's house on fire on their day of arriving. The council made such judgment:

> According to the law, the defendant's behavior governed by the of 60 and the first section of 109 provision of penal law. But the defendants' motives can be ascribed to under-trained soldiers who received poor education. Therefore, they had the hatred of the enemy's country and superficial understanding of innocent civilians. Overall, their crimes can be forgiven. According to the 66th and the 3rd section of 68th provision of the penal law, the defendants' sentences will be reduced, with each of them be sentenced to 1 year. However, the defendants have deeply regretted for their superficial understanding and decided to work harder in the front line to save their reputation. Therefore, compared to prison them, it is better to give them the opportunity to satisfy their desires. According to the 25th provision of penal law and the second section of 402nd provision of the military law council, the council granted two-year probation to the defendants since the judgement came into effect. Lighter (exhibit 1), the tool of the defendant Furu□□□ used to set fire, was confiscated according to the 2nd article of the first section and second section of 19th provision of penal code.[99]

"Poor education" even became an excuse for "commutation of sentence". In this way, anything can be used for excuses. The confiscation of lighter in this case is a signal that symbolizes the military law council's indifference of crimes against the Chinese.

---

[98] 「中支那方面軍軍法会議陣中日誌」, 高橋正衛編集, 解説『続・現代史資料』 6「軍事警察」. P137.

[99] 「中支那方面軍軍法会議陣中日誌」, 高橋正衛編集, 解説『続・現代史資料』 6「軍事警察」. P181.

Such situation is rather common among the cases accepted and heard by the Japanese military law council. Unlike the "rare" miscarriage of justice, it is a problem that deeply rooted in the fundamental institution. We will verify this point from the measurement of penalty in the following case. The above-mentioned murder case of Asa□□□, lance corporal of 124th Regiment, 4th Squadron of the 18th Infantry Division. He killed a Chinese Liu Asheng. Written in his judgment:

> According to the law, the defendant's behavior shall be sentenced to fixed-term imprisonment, governed by the 199th provision of the penal law. Given his crimes can be forgiven, the council granted him commutation according to the 66th, 71st and article 3 of the 68th provision.[100]

At the end, Asa was sentenced to one year and a half in prison. Unlike many murder cases that were not prosecuted, it happened in broad daylight with enough evidences that the crime can't be exempted. But it is still a light punishment for murder cases. The "light" is not measured by common standard (the criminal who committed murder faces at least a long-term sentence according to the regulations of Japanese army), but compares to other cases accepted and heard by the military law council of front army. I will elaborate on it by several examples. For example, Turu□□□, a Japanese soldier in the 2nd unit, 55th Regiment of the 18th Infantry Division, committed mayhem. Being drunk, he stabbed and shot another Japanese soldier. Even if the victim didn't die of shooting, the perpetrator still be sentenced to "heavier punishment according to the law", instead of being forgiven.[101] Compared to the last case that involved shooting and stabbing, Matsu□□□, a platoon leader in the 4th Division, was punished for his inappropriate words.

> The defendant, a platoon leader in the unit stationed in Shanghai, witnessed a second lieutenant in the same unit beat the soldiers who led by the defendant for several times. He was unpleasant after seeing the scene. He deduced that the reason why this happened is the superior didn't regulate and monitor his men. Therefore, at 8 p.m. on November 30th in the 12th year of Showa, the defendant asked the superior to rebuke the second lieutenant. Taking out the pistol, the defendant threatened him to accept his requirement, otherwise something bad will happen to him. The defendant's gesture of taking out his pistol is to show his violence and unpredictable behavior under such circumstance.[102]

For this case, no crime had been committed and the requirement was fair enough. Besides, the defendant's will threaten him if he didn't accept the

---

[100]「中支那方面軍軍法会議陣中日誌」，高橋正衛編集，解説『続・現代史資料』 6「軍事警察」．P168–169.

[101]「中支那方面軍軍法会議陣中日誌」，高橋正衛編集，解説『続・現代史資料』 6「軍事警察」．P169–170.

[102]「第十軍法務部陣中日誌」，高橋正衛編集，解説『続・現代史資料』 6「軍事警察」．P52.

condition. But just as the above-mentioned case of Zuru, the defendant was sentenced for 2 years. Compared to the punishment to Asa who committed murder, Matsu and Zuru who only caused slight injury and potential damage received heavier punishment. Though it seems contradictory, the difference is that the latter made a mistake of principle that disordered the Japanese troop.

Looking through the journal of military law office, I found the standard applied to all the judgment, instead of several cases. Ara□□, lance corporal of the medical unit in the 2nd Squadron under the 11th Division, was sentenced for same reason. Written in the judgment, Ara has made 3 mistakes. First, "he disobeyed the platoon leader's (Fukuoka Yoshio) order of do some preparations for camp". Second, "he took the bayonet to stab the platoon leader" ("he was prevented by the soldiers beside and not achieve his goal"). Third, he "said inappropriate words" to "insult" the superior.[103] There is some doubt in the judgment. It is hard to explain why Ara who is a reasonable man would often "insult" his superior and tried to kill him on a whim for something that doesn't matter his interests. If Ara was a villain, it is not difficult for him "seeking a chance" to kill him. If the judgment was true, then Ara was obviously a stupid and impulsive man. In the above-mentioned case of Ko, special agent in a squadron of the 12th Division, set fire on the civilian Li's house in Songjiang district on the second day of their arriving. As Furu's crimes were "forgiven" for his "poor education", Ara who didn't cause substantial injury deserved to be "forgiven". In this case, it should conduct a psychiatric examination of Ara at least.[104] Let's see the judgment.

> According to the law, the defendant's first act was governed by the section 2 of 57th provision of the army penal code. The second act was governed by 72nd provision and the section 2 of 62nd provision of the code. The third act was governed by section 1 of the provision 73rd of the code and 56th provision of the penal law. He shall be sentenced to fixed term imprisonment for his second and third acts. He once had committed crimes that governed by the section 1 of the 56th provision and 57th provision of the code. Given his criminal records, the punishment for his second and third act will be heavier for recidivism.

---

[103] 「中支那方面軍軍法会議陣中日誌」, 高橋正衛編集, 解説『続·現代史資料』 6 「軍事警察」. P189.

[104] 植, a lance corporal worked as a triarii, committed murder. The case has enough evidence but 早尾虎雄, the lieutenant in military medical team (the professor in金沢医科大学) still conducted a "psychiatric" examination of him. The "psychiatric" examination includes nearly 30 tests in 7 categories, such as "sense of direction", "understanding ability", "memory ability" (especially to remember new things), "common sense", "judgment ability", "delusion and illusion", "concept", "threatening", "emotion" and "will". The conclusion of the test was very complicated. It concluded that he drank too much wine that caused him became unaware of what he was doing. Driven by his primary consciousness, he mistakenly confessed the fact and done inappropriate behavior. After such thorough examination, I'm afraid the result would show nobody is "normal". It is not a psychiatric examination, but an act of trying to find excuses for the criminal.

The three crimes and his previous crimes shall be concluded in. According to the 47th, 10th, 14th provision of the penal law, the punishment for his second act shall be heavier based on the law. The defendant shall be sentenced for 2 years.[105]

The first act, "disobey order", that had no substantial injury seems cannot take it as a crime. Based on the judgment, however, it was counted as a "criminal record" to impose severe punishment. In the above-mentioned cases, the council had attempted to cover the Japanese soldiers' crimes against the Chinese. On the contrary, Ara was punished for every single mistake. Ori□□□, lance corporal of the infantry artillery in the 115th Squadron of the 140th Infantry Division, was sentenced for 5 years. It's the second heaviest punishment after the case of Taka, lance corporal of the 12th Squadron, 56th Regiment of the 18th Infantry Division. Taka committed the crime of "discarding and damaging weapons and escaping in the battle". His punishment is another example.

On December 15th in the 12th year of Showa, under the instruction of the platoon leader, the defendant was on the way to carry four trucks of ammunition to Mouling, Nanjing. He came across another baggage unit that get in his way and he came forward to negotiate with the unit. Finally, the defendant's trucks can pass first. In the negotiation, the leader wanted to pass first and leave the defendant's trunks behind. The defendants lost his temper and said, "Leader is nothing in this occasion". "Don't think me as a coward. The gun is not a mere form." He said while he fired over their heads to throw a scare into the leader.[106]

In this case, the "victim" "leader" (Takahashi Eizo) was unscathed but the defendant was sentenced for 5 years. The defendants in only two cases were sentenced for 5 years by the 10th Division military law council. The other is the murder case of Hashi, special agent of the 2nd Squadron, 12th Baggage Regiment of the 18th Division. He committed murder.

The defendant and his unit were stationed in Jinshan, Jinshan town of Jiangsu province. He was distant with another lance corporal in the same regiment. At 11 a.m. on December 29th in the 12th year of Showa, the defendant was beaten by a soldier for he did something inappropriate. The two began fighting each other and was prevented by others. At 3 p.m., the soldier came to the defendant's unit and forced him to walk with him. Driven by hatred, the defendant decided to kill him. Seeing the defendant carried a rifle, the soldier tried to escape and was shoot in the chest. He died on spot.[107]

---

[105]「中支那方面軍軍法会議陣中日誌」, 高橋正衛編集, 解説『続·現代史資料』6「軍事警察」. P190.

[106]「第十軍法務部陣中日誌」, 高橋正衛編集, 解説『続·現代史資料』6「軍事警察」. P62.

[107]「第十軍法務部陣中日誌」, 高橋正衛編集, 解説『続·現代史資料』6「軍事警察」. P62.

This case reflects a common problem existed in the Japanese troop. That is the superior bullies the subordinate. As Hashi was so brutally bullied that he killed the superior, he is "forgiven" yet received severe judgment. Based on these cases, I found the Japanese military council has completely different standards on the punishment. The life of the Chinese is nothing compared to the life of Japanese soldier. In the judgment, the life of Chinese isn't equal to a slight injury, threatening with a gun and even an intimidating word.

The difference in judgment also vividly reflects in the conviction. Japanese soldiers injured the Chinese, which is not a crime. For example, the case of Fuku, lance corporal of the 9th Squadron, 41st Regiment under the 5th Infantry Division.

> First, on the way the defendant and his unit to Wangjiang town, they passed through Songjiang and Jiashan. On November 17th in the 12th year of Showa, in somewhere that was 500 miles away from the Wangjiang town, the defendant left his unit and came to a Chankoro village. On 19th of the same month, he decided not to go back the troop and hided in some nearby Chankoro villages. Second, on 17th of the same month, in the village of Wangjiang town, under attack of hundreds of Chankoro, he shot three of them and jumped into a nearby stream. He threw everything that distributed by the troop, including pistol, bayonet, medicine boxes, cap, pants, jacket and socks. Third, from December 20th in the 12th year to January 12th in the 13th year, he escaped from the unit and stole things from the civilian's houses for several times, including rice, chicken, duck and eggs. Fourth, he wore military uniform without approval when he left the army. (101)

It is evident that the major crime of this case is murder, but the conviction was "escape from the troop, steal and damage military items and used badges without approval". As the judgment didn't mention murder at all, we can see the Japanese troop's indifference of Chinese life. It is an absolute fact that no question can be raised. But I found something was covered after my deduction. Among these convictions, the fact "escape from the troop" can't be denied. As for "wearing military uniform without approval", it should be referred to the clothes he wore when was arrested (because everything else attributed by the troop was "thrown into the stream"). Thus, this statement is also true. Then, only two convictions, "throw and damage military goods" and "steal things", lack evidence, particularly the first one. As no one knew the process of the two crimes (the above-mentioned second and third points), it should be Fuku's confession. Clearly aware that "throw and damage military goods" is a felony, he confessed the second and third acts to show that was the last resort in order to reduce his crimes. For the second act, the situation he described was a close call to touch the nerves of the judges. It is understandable to shot 3 persons if he was surrounded with hundreds of people. Therefore, the military law council would regard it as "forgiven". Based on Fuku's description, he showed himself as a lone ranger with high-profile behavior. But something was illogical in his story. First, it is a miracle to pit one against ten. Then, Fuku became a mythological figure if he can remain unscathed when hundreds of people attack him. Second, the enemy would not stop especially when he shot 3 of them and threw his own weapons. Third, he should have no way to escape under such circumstances. But he jumped into a "stream" (ク リ — ク) and escaped. It is possible to escape if he swims with the current in a big river. But how can he do that in a stream? Given the three reasons, his statement is dubious. As for the third act, he confessed "stealing things" because he had to explain how can he survive for months when he left the troop with no penny in his name. Although he "stole" things, he admitted he had to steal food for survival. It is misdemeanor that can be "forgiven". Today, the truth of the case is hard to know. But, obviously, he racked his brains to make up a lie that is full of loopholes. Wandered along the villages, Fuku committed offenses against law and discipline and hided himself from place to place to avoid being arrested by the Japanese troop or "attacked" by the Chinese. If he did murder 3 persons, he might have been blocked when he tried to steal things. It's a reasonable deduction. But the council just believed his statement and wrote in judgment. If the deduction is true, Fuku's perjury offered us an important piece of information. It is, in Fuku's eyes, as long as he has some reasons, killing "Chankoro" was as insignificant as stealing things. On the contrary, "throwing and damaging martial weapons" is a more severe crime. As Fuku's murder didn't count as crime, we can see that military law council had no care for murdering "Chankoro" just as Fuku's expectation.

5 Brief Conclusion

To sum up, we can generalize the military discipline and the function of military law council in the 10th Japanese Division, an epitome of the Japanese troop against China.

First, during the several months that the 10th Division stayed in China, Japanese troop steadily controlled the southern China because both Kuomintang (Nationalist Party) and Communist Party didn't organize large-scale resistance. If the Japanese soldiers' atrocities are related to the so-called "revenge", the number of outrages should be the lowest during the war. Based on the description of the military offices journal of the 10th Division and Chankoro front army and the diaries of Ogawa, we can see the savage act done by the soldiers in the 10th Division is quite severe.

Second, the Japanese troop's atrocities include reckless murder, arson, looting and rape. Among these crimes, rape is frequently and ubiquitously existed.

Third, the military law office that is responsible for regulating military discipline is small and has limited function; especially, it has few police ready for use. Therefore, only few atrocities were seen by the police and accepted and heard by the military law office. The atrocities reflected by the journal and diaries are only a tip of the iceberg of the crimes committed by the Japanese soldiers.

Fourth, the Japanese troop set military law office to maintain military discipline. On the one side, it limited the Japanese soldiers' inappropriate behavior. On the other hand, the office has some side effects as the soldiers resist it and the leaders of various levels protected their men on purpose. This further limits the military law offices to play its role.

Fifth, it is the military law office's responsibility to maintain military order and discipline. But, as a part of the Japanese troop, the agency can't "harm" its troop on essence. Thus, most criminals were acquitted or treated with exceptional leniency. Even if it has some "pressure" from the outside, the key is the concession of the military law office. Despite the office only dealt with limited cases (even a small piece of it) among the enormous outrageous acts, the office didn't conduct thorough investigation. Objectively speaking, the indulgent attitude of the office exasperated the Japanese soldiers' frequencies of crimes on a broader scale.

Sixth, compared to the indulgence of Japanese soldiers' crimes, Japanese military law office imposed extremely cruel penalty on the "violation of law" by the Chinese. Based on the limited description of the remaining journals and diaries, any Chinese who had the suspicion of trying to escape ends up with being executed. This is a persuasive evidence. As for the day-to-day regulation, any Chinese that showed a hint of rebellion was heavily punished by the violent Japanese police. Therefore, for Chinese, the Japanese law office is a machine to brutally suppress the Chinese.

Seventh, thus, we can draw a general conclusion. Even if it is based on the firsthand information left by the Japanese troop, the claimed "strict military discipline of the Japanese troop" and "the lowest crime rate" have proved groundless.

(Originally published in *Modern Chinese History Studies*, 2004(2))

Re-evaluation of Iwane Matsui's War Guilt—Verifications of One of the Testimonies on the Nanjing Massacre Given by the Defendants at the Tokyo War Crimes Trials

Preface

Regarding Japan's war crimes, only the Nanjing Massacre has been in dispute in Japan for a long time. Walking into the bookstores in Japan, we can see that there is no works related to Chinese historical events more than the Nanjing Massacre, which shows that this debate is no longer limited to a narrow professional scope, but has become a topic of high social attention. Why is there so much debate merely in the Nanjing Massacre in Japan? First, we think that the Nanjing Massacre is the largest atrocity committed by the Japanese army. Second, the Nanjing Massacre is considered as the "symbol" of the "historical disputes" between the two countries. Third, the Nanjing Massacre's verdict was given by the post-war trials. (At that time, the experiments and usage of biochemical weapons weren't accused.[1]) Fourth, in Japan, some people claim that the Nanjing Massacre is "made up" in line with the "crime against humanity". These reasons are all related to the "standpoint" which has nothing to do with academics. Indeed, without the factors of the standpoint, the Nanjing Massacre couldn't have caused such a heated debate. At the same time, it is difficult to form a lasting debate just for the difference in standpoint. I think the reason why the Nanjing Massacre has become a continuous "hot-spot" is indeed related to the inadequate records of the incident and the "missing" of the firsthand data. Inadequate records mean that there is no comprehensive investigation and record, and it is also impossible to make a comprehensive investigation and record Japanese atrocities about the massacre; the "missing" of the firsthand data refers to the non-transmission of Japanese documents such as the journal of the Legal Ministry of the

---

Aiming at memorizing the 60th anniversary of the ending of Tokyo (October 1948).

[1] The prosecution mentioned the use of poison gas, which wasn't included in the formal cause of action.

Shanghai Expeditionary Force. The reason why we say "missing" rather than destroyed is that the documents may still exist, just as the fact that the journal of the 10th Army Legal Ministry existed for a long time while not be found. Since some people insist that the dispute in Nanjing Massacre has been resolved properly in the Nanjing Trial, it is necessary to specify those things: First, there are much information about the Nanjing Massacre—including words, objects, images, and oral transmissions nowadays. For instance, "The Nanjing Massacre Historical Data Collection" published in batches has reached 72 volumes. "Inadequacy" I mentioned is just limited to the "first time" records and the "first hand" materials in the historical sense. Second, "Inadequacy" is by no means an indication that the evidence of the Japanese atrocities in Nanjing is not sufficient, but that for the Tokyo Trial, especially the conclusion of the Nanjing Trial has to be further enriched. It is an important reason why the Nanjing Massacre has the value of research as a historical event. On the contrary, it is safe to say that if the issue of the Nanjing Massacre has been resolved in the Nanjing Trial, not only the efforts in unearthing new historical materials today would become meaningless, but the study of the Nanjing Massacre also would become unnecessary. In this sense, it is totally different between the challenge of the Japanese right-wing and the research Nanjing Massacre today. Of course, reviewing the entire controversy, especially after the 1990s, the Japanese right-wing as an interactive party did take the initiative offensive, and many issues were indeed triggered by them.

The idea of verifying the testimonies on the Nanjing Massacre given by the defendants at the Tokyo Trials is related to the Japanese right-wing. For a long time, the Japanese right-wing has always claimed that the Tokyo Trial is the winners' trial. It is unfair, especially it is considered that the court only received one-side statements of the Nanjing Massacre case. For example, Fuji Nobuo wrote in "Nanjing Massacre is a Fabrication-The Deception of the Tokyo Trial" that the evidence of the Tokyo Trial for the prosecution and the defense is extremely unfair:

> The opinion of the court (referring to the court's description of the evidence), is that neither the evidence from the defense nor the final debate of the defense has any effect on the court, so it is equivalent to say, "The court's decision was based on the evidence submitted by the prosecution and the final statements of the prosecution."
>
> I don't mean that all the evidence submitted by the prosecution is wrong, and the evidence presented by the defense party is correct. I just mean that any Japanese with common sense, reading the evidence of both the prosecution and the defense, will deeply feel that there are lots of distortion, exaggeration, and fiction in the evidence submitted by the prosecution, and it is more reasonable for the evidence presented by the defense.[2]

---

[2]冨士信夫著『「南京大虐殺」はこうして作られた――東京裁判の欺瞞』，東京，展転社 1995年4月29 第1版, 第291、348頁.

Since the Tokyo court did not stand in the position of a "neutral" arbitrator, the Nanjing Massacre was naturally thought "untrue". Some Japanese think the suspicion about the Nanjing Massacre caused the denying of the truth is reasonable; I think this is one of the main reasons for the long-term failure of the clarification of the strong questioning of the Tokyo Trial.

When the Tokyo Trial heard the Nanjing atrocities, the caliber witnesses and defendants who participated in the attack on Nanjing were not exactly the same, and some did not leave any room for negation. One of the most typical examples is that the officer Wakisaka Jiro of the 36th regiment said one of his subordinates is jailed for a shoe.[3] While some people admitted that there exist some "individual" military disciplines problems[4]; but even if they do not completely deny that the Japanese army has military discipline problems, they all agree that the Nanjing atrocities proposed by the prosecutors have not been heard or seen. Although we think that whether we hear about isn't equal to whether it is true, if it is certified that a certain number of parties' similarities are contrary to reality, it is necessary to prove it. Therefore, the necessity to respond positively to this issue is not just for those who deny the truth of Nanjing Massacre repeatedly today. Perhaps it is because there is already a conclusion of the Tokyo Trial, or some people think these "testimonies" will be overturned as long as the facts can be clarified. The specific re-evaluation of these "testimonies" has not been seen so far. I have analyzed the question of the important testimony of the defendant who was not questioned by the Tokyo Trial, but did not write a specialized article. In fact, as long as comparing the first-time records of the personal diary opened in public with the testimonies of the defendants and witnesses in Tokyo, it is not difficult to find that the inconsistency between the two is not an accidental "error" but a basic difference. This verification is intended to be carried out one by one through examining the testimonies of related persons of the Japanese Expeditionary Forces, Shanghai Expeditionary Force and the Tenth Army to figure out what the "reasonableness" of the defense evidence is all about.

This article re-evaluates the testimonies of the first person that bears the responsibility of the Nanjing Massacre, the commander of the Shanghai Expeditionary Force (dismissed on December 2nd, 1937) and the commander of the Japanese Expeditionary Forces (taking office on November 7th), Iwane Matsui.

---

[3]洞富雄編『日中戦争史資料』8「南京事件」I, 東京, 河出書房1973年11月25日第1版, 第239頁.

[4]如小川关治郎"宣誓口供书"(辩方文书第2708号)称: "在到达南京为止处罚了约二十件军纪犯和风纪犯。"洞富雄編『日中戦争史資料』8「南京事件」I, 第256頁.

1 PUT FORWARD THE ISSUES

Three of the Class A war criminals in Tokyo Trial were charged with the Nanjing Massacre.[5] They are Koki Hirota, who was the Minister of Foreign Affairs at the time of the incident (the same below), Akira Muto, Vice Chief of Staff of the Central Branch and Iwane Matsui, the commander of the Japanese Expeditionary Forces, all of whom were hanged. Among them, Koki Hirota's main crimes are the "co-conspiracy" of the war of aggression (the 1st cause of action), the "committing the aggression against China" (the 27th cause of action) and "negative prevention" (the 55th cause of action) of the Nanjing Massacre is only one of the crimes; in addition to "co-conspiracy" and "committing the aggression against China", Akira Muto also "committed the aggression against the United States, Britain, and the Netherlands" (the 29th, 31st, 32nd cause of action) and the "command permission" (the 54th cause of action) and "ignorance of prevention" for the violation of the law. Compared with those crimes, the Nanjing Massacre was dismissed at the time of the verdict. In the prosecution, Iwane Matsui's charges included 38 items such as "co-conspiracy", "committing the aggression against China" and "command permission" to the Nanjing Massacre.[6] Finally, the court only judged the "ignorance of prevention" of the Nanjing Massacre is guilty. He is not only the only Class A war criminal who was sentenced to death for a single crime, but also the only Class A war criminal who was convicted of a single crime except for Shiratori Toshio, the civil official of the lowest rank.

The judgment leads to two issues. The first one is the issue of negative responsibility and maximum punishment. Even if the Nanjing Massacre is considered as the biggest atrocity in the Tokyo Trial, after all, the "inaction of prevention" and the "command permission" are different. This is one of the reasons why some people (except those who deny the fact of the Nanjing Massacre) are still aggrieved. Another one is the responsibility of Class A war criminals. Although there is little controversy about this, it is of great significance that it cannot be ignored, because it involves the charge of "class A war criminal".

After the war, the trial of Japanese war crimes, in the 51 courts outside the new China and the Soviet Union, except for the quasi-A-level trial in Tokyo "Marunouchi" (the defendants only include Toyota Deputy Wu, the Admiral of the Navy and Lieutenant General Tamura), Only the Tokyo Trial is a Class A trial, and trials scattered throughout Asia are Class B and C trials. The

---

[5] In Tokyo Trial, the crimes of Japanese armies related to Nanjing are translated into Nanjing Massacre in China. In the translation of *Verdict of the International Military Tribunal for the Far East* (Published by Masses Publishing House in February 1986), ZhangJiaolin translated just like this. In fact, the original title of judgment and verdict is "Nanjing atrocities". This article uses "Nanjing Massacre".

[6] The Tokyo Trial just adjudicated 10 crimes of the 55 crimes in the end; Iwane Matsui's crimes covered 9 of those crimes.

biggest difference between the Tokyo Trial and other trials is that the main criminals of Class A war criminals are "crime against peace" and "crime against humanity", which were the verdict of the London Conference, while Class B and C war criminals are traditional ordinary war crimes. From this point of view, if the "crime against peace" and "crime against humanity" are not guilty, there are some suspicions about whether they can be considered as the Class A war criminals.

The Tokyo Trial denied the prosecution of Iwane Matsui's "crime against peace", which is quite clear as mentioned above. The problem is the "crime against humanity". For a long time, we have always believed that the Tokyo Trial judged the Nanjing Massacre as "crime against humanity", which is a negative responsibility, and there is no question of whether the crime is a conformity. However, in the actual trial of the Tokyo Trial, the "crime against humanity" and ordinary war crimes are not clearly distinguished. Therefore, technically, the "crime against humanity" of the charter of the International Military Tribunal for the Far East (Tokyo Charter) is equivalent a nominal charge in the trial. Regarding this, it is necessary to state that the genocide is common in human history.

But in modern times, in "civilized society" especially in Western civilized society, the extinction of specific races like Nazi Germany is unprecedented; when it comes to the comprehensive plans, "scientific" artifice, the extremely large scale, nothing has made a more evil influence in the world than the Nazi genocide. Therefore, for the genocide of the Nazis was classified as traditional war crimes, their crimes and the intensity far from enough. This is the special need for the "crime against humanity" when the London Conference established the Charter of the International Military Tribunal (Nuremberg Charter). Therefore, in the Article 6 of the Nuremberg Charter, the "crime against humanity" lists "inhumane" acts such as mass killing, annihilation, slavery, forced migration and other sever persecution crimes based on politics, race and religion. The term "and other inhumane acts" added after those crimes listed above cover a broader scope, but we generally emphasize those following characteristics: First, for civilians, it is subject to all countries in any time, and this is the biggest difference from ordinary war crimes; second, it is especially for the specific races, which is closely related to the Nazi genocide, especially to the slaughter of the Jews. From this, "crime against humanity" is indeed tailored for Nazi Germany.

The Tokyo Charter is adapted from the Nuremberg Charter. Compared with the Nuremberg Charter, there are two deletions of "crime against humanity" in Article 5 of the Tokyo Charter. One is "all civilians" and the other is "religion".[7] The latter was deleted, according to the report of the

---

[7] The 3rd item of the Article 5 of the Tokyo Charter is "Crime against humanity": 『人道ニ対スル罪 即チ、戦前又ハ戦時中為サレタル殺人、殲滅、奴隷的虐使、追放、其ノ他ノ非人道的行為、若ハ犯行地ノ国内法違反タルト否トヲ問ハズ、本裁判所ノ管轄ニ属スル犯罪ノ遂行トシテ又ハ之ニ関連シテ為サレタル政治的又ハ人種的理由ニ基ク迫害行為』.

United Nations War Crimes Commission: "For Japanese Class A war criminals do not have such crimes, so there is no practical significance for the existence of this crime provision".[8] This inference is reasonable. While for the deletion of the former one,[9] as stated in the above report, it seems to take into account of the differences between Japan and Germany:

> The charter of the International Military Tribunal for the Far East does not explicitly regulate that "crime against humanity" is a crime against peaceful residents, however, this is emphasized in the Nuremberg charter. The main purpose is to cover the crime–human rights violations against German citizens by the Nazi authorities.[10]

It is generally believed that the deletion of "civilians" has widened the coverage of "crime against humanity". For example, Antonio Cassese, an Italian jurist who had documented the Tokyo Trial of the Dutch judge, B.V.A. Roling's thinking about the Tokyo Trial, said:

> The term "all civilians" was deleted at the beginning of the Tokyo Charter, which resulted in the expansion of crime against humanity (one of the purposes of the expansion was to make it possible to punish those massive killing of combatants in illegal warfare – from the author).[11]

---

[8] R.Zivkovie drafted the *Report of the United Nations War Crimes Commission*, Zhang Xianwen edited the *Nanjing Massacre Historical Materials Collection 7*, Yang XiaoMing edited *Tokyo Trial* (p. 25.), published by Jiangsu People's Publishing House and Phoenix Publishing House in July 2005, the 1st edition (p. 25.) word "may" in this citation may cause doubts, while when I wrote this article, I asked Mr. Xia Ming to reconfirm again and the original text is right.

[9] The Chinese judge of the Tokyo Trial, Mei Ruao, has wrote the phrase—"any peaceful population" in the relevant writings (refer to Mei's book—International Military Tribunal of the Far East, Law Press China, People's Court Press, 1st edition, July 2005, p. 14). There is no such term in the official document of Japan, so it has been ignored before. When I was writing "From 'the Tokyo Trial' to the Tokyo Trial" (in *Historical Review*, No. 5, 2007), I noticed that Yang Xiaoming's newly translated Tokyo Charter refers to this term (civilian population, refers to Charter of the International Military Tribunal of the Far East, Nanjing Massacre Historical Materials, No. 7, Tokyo Trial, p. 6). Mr. Xia Ming said that he was based on the "original English document" in the National Archives of the United States. At that time, he didn't know why it is different and wrote it need to be reconfirmed. Later, he read such a record, "A few days before the indictment, the court regulations (the charter—my word) deleted the 'restrictive words for the civilians', recorded by Radha Binod Pal, the India judge, the only person who advocate that all members are not guilty. But the court did not explain the reasons for the deletion. Refer to the Tokyo Judicial Research Association, 『共同研究パル判決書』 (the second volume), 東京, 講談 February 22nd, 1996, the 12th edition in p. 524. So they are 2 "original documents" in different periods.

[10] *Nanjing Massacre Historical Materials Collection*, 7, Yang Xia Ming, edited *Tokyo Trial*, p. 25. In addition, 「人道ニ対スル罪」 is translated into "crime against humanity", and the Chinese literature is quoted in accordance with the original work.

[11] 小菅信子訳、粟屋憲太郎解説『レーリンク判事の東京裁判』 (Italian jurist Antonio Cassese), Tokyo, New Wave Society, 1st edition, August 31st, 1996, p. 8.

The "expansion" may be those "massive killing of combatants" should be included, which Cassis once said. Of course, there will be different considerations of Japan and Germany, but in terms of the stressed "crime against humanity" from the Tokyo Trial prosecution and the court, Japan is not exempt from the crime of "humanity crimes" for the difference between Japan and Germany, which is different from the prevailing view in Japan. In addition to the few people who insisted on rebelling against war crimes in Japan, there have been people who believe that the Tokyo court "intentionally confuses" the "inexistent" "crime against humanity". Before the trial of the squadron of the B-class war criminals, the Allied Legal Minister interpreted the A, B and C levels as "levels". For example, "the B-class refers to the heads of the army generals like the Yamashita and Honma, and their criminal responsibility is killing, ill-treating and slavery. C-level refers to the actual execution of the above crimes. The A-level is a political leader like the Prime Minister of the Tojo". Although it is not accurate enough to distinguish level-A, level-B and C in this way, there is nothing wrong with it in general. However, there are still Japanese who believe that this distinction is deliberately distorted. For example, Yoshio combined this conversation with the Yokohama Trial Procedure of the Ordinary War Criminals published before the conversation, saying that the abc means nothing about the distinction:

> There is no C item in Japan (crime against humanity=genocide – from the author), which is the reality of the US military investigation. Therefore, the GHQ (the General Headquarters of the Allied Forces in Japan) is proposed to be a level, adding the impression of c-level=class-C=soldier crime, or even deliberately associates with genocide and causes confusion.[12]

As mentioned above, in the Tokyo Trial, Japan is not exempt from the crime of "crime against humanity" for the difference between Japan and Germany. Therefore, the "intentional" is just a misinterpretation of the tea garden himself. On the other hand, however, the "crime against humanity" is not clearly distinguished from the ordinary war crimes in the actual trial of the Tokyo Trial. Lerin said:

> "Crime against humanity" were also applied in the Tokyo Trial, but they were all made under the packaging of "(ordinary —from the author) war crimes." The killing of prisoners and civilians with no reason is a war crime and can be applied to death penalty. Therefore, the concept of "crime against humanity" did not work in the Tokyo trial.[13]

---

[12] 茶園義男著「戦犯裁判の法的正当性を問う」, Pacific Judging Research Association edited *Tokyo Referee*, Tokyo, newcomers Society, 1st edition, July 15th, 2003, p. 62.

[13] 『レーリンク判事の東京裁判』, p. 92. A lot of Japanese scholars also think "crime against humanity" is not used in the actual trial and judgment of the Tokyo Trial. 細谷千博、安藤仁介、大沼保昭編『東京裁判を問う———国際シンポジウム』, Tokyo, 講談社, 1st edition, July 10th, 1984, pp. 61–62, pp. 173–176; 幼直吉著, 東京裁判をめぐる諸論点——「人道に対する罪」と時効, Tokyo, Iwasaki Bookstore *Ideas* May 1984 (Total No. 719).

The "common war crimes" mentioned here is translated from Japanese. Although the Tokyo Charter clearly lists "crime against humanity", in the third category (fifth-five to fifty-five items) of the fifty-five appeals, the meaning of the "ordinary war crimes and crime against humanity" merely means "ordinary war crimes".[14] In addition, the second category of "crimes of murder" (the thirty-seventh to fifty-two items) outside this crime and the first category of "crime against peace" (the first to thirty-six items) is only ordinary war crimes.[15]

There is an evident difference between the Class A war criminals in Tokyo Trial and the Class A war criminals in the Nuremberg Trials in their crimes. In Nuremberg Trial, 12 members of the Class A war criminals who were hanged were convicted of "crime against humanity", while only 7 people were charged with "crime against peace". Among them, there are "co-conspiracy crime" which is the general principles of the "crime against peace" and only 5 people are charged with this crime. In addition to Iwane Matsui and civil officer Shigemitsu Mamoru, the 25 Class A war criminals in Tokyo were all found guilty of "co-conspiracy crime", and Shigemitsu Mamoru was also found guilty in the crime of "crime against peace" and "commit invasion against China, the United States, Britain, the Netherlands and France". Only Iwane Matsui was acquitted of "crime against peace". In the third category of the crimes, the Tokyo Trial sentenced only seven people with the crime of omission, and only five were sentenced with the crime of active "command permission". Obviously, the Tokyo Trial and the Nuremberg Trial each have their own emphasis.

This difference between the Tokyo Trial and the Nuremberg Trial has led some Japanese to equate the Tokyo Trial and the "crime against peace" trial. For example, the earlier specific book—Review of Tokyo Trial written by Sugawara Masahiro about the Tokyo Trial wrote: "The crime against peace" is a crime that the defendants' co-conspiracy in planning, preparing, starting and committing the invasion to disorder the world. This is the reason why we call them Class A war criminals. Such equivalent comments are still common today, just like the only specialist of Chinese modern history, Kitamura (Professor of Ritsumeikan University) wrote in his first book about "Nanjing Massacre":

> In the trial of war criminals in the United Nations, the crimes are classified into Class A, Class B, and Class C. The A-level is "crime against peace", that is the planning, the beginning, and the committing of the invasion war. Class

---

[14] The Tokyo Trial indictment clearly states that the 53rd and 54th are "violation of the law of war and customary law" and "violation of the law of war". General prosecutor Jinan also stated in the opening speech of the Tokyo Trial: "The third group of indictments are ordinary war crimes". (Yang Xia Ming translated *Tokyo Trial Indictment, General Prosecutor Keenan's Hearing Speech, Nanjing Massacre Historical Materials*, 29, *International Prosecutor Documents US Newspapers and Periodicals' Report*, Jiangsu People's Press, 1st edition, October 2007, pp. 18, 19, 73.) The 8th chapter of the Tokyo Trial Judgment, which includes crimes such as the Nanjing Massacre, is entitled "General War Crimes".

[15] The second type of murder is not tried for it is "included in the crime against peace".

B is "ordinary war crimes", that is an act of violating the wartime international law. Class C is "crime against humanity", which refers to the killing and abuse before and during the war. The trial of the Nuremberg Trial and the Tokyo Trial trials are the Class A war criminals, and the trial of military courts in cities of various countries are Class B and Class C war criminals.[16]

Although the classification of ABC of the Minister of Justice is not rigorous, it is generally reasonable. It is obviously unrealistic for Kitamura to equate the ABC-level trial with the abc in the Nuremberg and Tokyo Charters. However, for there are some differences in the war crimes between Japan and Germany, highlighting "crime against peace" without paying attention to "crime against humanity" is indeed a feature, which distinguishes the Tokyo Trial from the Nuremberg Trial.

This feature of the Tokyo Trial causes a problem[17] that whether Iwane Matsui, who is the only one acquitted of "crime against peace" in those 25 Class A criminals mentioned above, is the "Class A" war criminal or not. This leads to the central question of this article: What kind of war responsibility should Iwane Matsui undertake? The main purpose of this paper is to re-evaluate the defense testimony of Iwane Matsui in the Tokyo Trial. I hope there is a new understanding of the real responsibility of Iwane Matsui through this re-evaluation.

2 The Evaluation of Iwane Matsui's "Affidavit"

Iwane Matsui's "Affidavit" (Defense Document No. 2738, Court Evidence No. 3498) include 11 articles, and some important articles will be evaluated as follows.

Attacking Nanjing Is Not an "Accident" to Iwane Matsui

The first article of the "Affidavit"—"The purpose of the motive for sending troops to Jiangnan in the 12th year of the Showa", which mainly concerns about "the threat of Japanese military and civilians staying in Shanghai after the July 7th", the formation of the Shanghai Expeditionary Force. "The purpose of the military is to support my naval forces and protect the lives and property of residents living near the area". Article 2 "The reason for me to change from the reserve personnel to the commanders of the Shanghai

---

[16] 北村稔著『「南京事件」の探究―――その実像をもとめて』, 東京, 文藝春秋社, 1st edition, November 20th, 2001, p. 89.

[17] Some scholars in Japan said: "Matsui Iwane should be acquitted of the 'co-conspiracy for the preparation of the invasion war' and 'the guilty of the crime of peace'", which should be guilty for the 'Violation of the obligation to comply with the laws of war', while he was sentenced with hanging. In other words, he is not guilty of being a Class A war criminal and is guilty of being a BC-level war criminal". Shimizu Masahiro wrote, International Military Tribunal, Article 6c, 「人道に対する罪」に関する覚書, 東京, 『東京女学館短期大学紀要』No. 14, 1991, p. 88.

Expeditionary Force and my mood at the time", he also said that "the main purpose of the government's policy supporting was to quickly resolve the incident there and then, so as to avoid the expanding of military struggle. In the fourth article, in "The composition of Japanese Expeditionary Forces and the decision to attack Nanjing", it said that "the army that is based in Nanjing has gradually developed to the north branch to echo my large-scale battle. The gathered troops from various places in Jiangsu and Zhejiang is also preparing to launch the war. It is impossible to maintain our security and our interests without occupying the base areas near Nanjing. For this reason, in order to restore the overall peace of the south of China, I decided to capture Nanjing".[18]

How did the Battle of August 13th break out? Was attacking Nanjing a plan or "accidental"? It was originally a different issue that has nothing to do with the atrocities in Nanjing. There are two meanings of the word "unrelated". First, I don't think the historical reasons that Japanese emphasize can be the "reasons" of atrocities. Nor do we think that some Japanese scholars believe that the purpose of attacking Nanjing by the Japanese army includes atrocities (so-called "punishment") is in line with reality; second, Japan attacked Shanghai, whether it is as a nominal Saying "To protect the residents" or not, Iwane Matsui did not have to take responsibility for obeying orders. There are two points to consider in this matter: First, the statement made by Iwane Matsui in the Tokyo Trial covered up his performance; second, this covering affects the identification of Iwane Matsui's responsibility.

Since the publication of the timely memory[19] Zhang Zhizhong's, the early Chinese commander of the Shanghai-Shanghai Campaign, domestic scholars no longer avoid "preemptive strikes".[20] By examining the Japanese literature, we can learn that the initial military command of the Japanese high-level officials has indeed limited the purpose to "extracting the enemy near Shanghai and occupying the northern part of Shanghai".[21] Even with the increasing military strength of the two sides, the war is comprehensive escalated. The staff

---

[18] 洞富雄編『日中戦争史資料』VIII「南京事件」I pp. 273–275.

[19] For details, refer to *The Memoirs of Zhang Zhizhong*, section 5, "Re-anti-Japanese-- the August 13th campaign of Shanghai", the 1st–5th subsections, China Literature and History Publishing House, 1st edition, February 1985, pp. 111–122

[20] Although we all say "preemptive strikes", the difference is that some clearly believe that "the August 13th Campaign was launched by China" (for instance, Ma Zhendu's work, *The Causes of the August 13th Campaign of Shanghai, Research on Modern History*, No. 6, 1986, p. 223); others believe that it is both China's"preemptive strikes" and Japan's "deliberately strategic plan" (Yu Zidao, Zhang Yun, *Anti-Japanese Campaign in Shanghai in the August 13th*, Shanghai People's Publishing House, 1st edition, November 2000, pp. 10, 75). It seems worthy to explore the effect of the actual historical process about Japan's "strategic plan". For details, refer to *Re-discussing the Causes of the August 13th Campaign of Shanghai*.

[21] 「臨参命第七十三号」, 臼井勝美等解説『現代史資料』IX「日中戦争」II, 東京, みすず書房, 1st edition, September 30th, 1964, p. 206.

headquarters has set two restrictions on war area lines successively.[22] On the other hand, the reason why the scale of the war was escalating after the outbreak, both sides have responsibility, however, the continuous breakthrough of their plan from the Japanese army, especially the attack on Nanjing, is completely a result of the "enterprising" of the Japanese army. There is no doubt that Iwane Matsui is largely responsible. From the diary of Matsui himself and his family, his statement in the Tokyo Trial masked his performance.

Iwane Matsui once lied that his diary had been burned when he was interrogated in the Tokyo Trial.[23] When the Nanjing Massacre caused fierce controversy in Japan in the 1980s, the representative of the group that deny the truth of Nanjing Massacre, Tanaka Masaaki, based on the clues provided by Iwane Matsui's daughter Matsui Shoji, found a batch of documents in the Relic Storage Room of Archive of the Self-Defense Force's 34th Joint (United) team after the war, and the most important one was the wartime diary of Iwane Matsui. The diary was from November 1st, 1937 (the Suzhou River battle) to the second year of February 28th (the so-called "Triumphal"), missing the part before October. When the remnant was published by the Furong Publishing House in the title of The War Journal of the Iwane Matsui General, Japanese scholars pointed out that the organizer Masaaki Tanaka tampers with the original text for more than 900 places.[24] After this part of the diary, the Japanese old military group Minhang Publishing Housing re-edited the punctuation and slightly abridged, finally it was classified into The Nanjing War History Data Collection. In 1992, the researcher of the War Department of the Japan Defense Research Institute went to the archive and found the August 15th to October 30th part of Iwane Matsui's diary. This part and the supplemented part that has been published later were collected in The Nanjing War History Data Collection II. (Perhaps in order to avoid misreading, the reprinting part canceled the original punctuation.) Let's take a look at how Iwane Matsui himself wrote in his diary.

On the day after the "August 13th" broke out, Japan decided to form the "Shanghai Expeditionary Force", and Iwane Matsui was appointed as the commander. In the afternoon, the army provincial vice-officer sent him an express telegram to come to Tokyo, and he rushed to the residence of

---

[22] It has been regulated that staying in the Suzhou JiaXing line and Wuxi Huzhou line successively.

[23] The International Prosecutor's Office documents clearly record: "In the interrogation, the defendant Matsui said: ... All my records have been burned, including my diary." Yang Xia Ming translated *Summary of Prosecution Analysis of Evidence by the International Prosecutor's Office Documents (VIII), The Nanjing Massacre Historical Materials*, Vol. 29, p. 165. (Matsui's "Affidavit" said that "all documents were burnt down" and did not explicitly mention the diary, details in Tomio Hora's work—*Historical Materials of Japanese-Chinese War* 8 「Nanjing Incident」 I, p. 276.)

[24] I have introduced in this work—*Is the Nanjing Massacre a Fabrication of the Tokyo Trial?*, which is collected in *Research of Modern History*, No. 6, 2002, p. 18.

the Army Minister Hajime Sugiyama from Mount Fuji where he lived. He recorded the feelings of this meeting in the beginning part of his diary:

> The Army's intentions are still not determined to regard Chinese troops as the main propose. Instead, it is only sent the army as the reinforcement to Shanghai to response the request of the Navy… This time the Chinese troops sent army and our government withdrew the policy of partial settlement and no expansion, which is a strong demand for the Nanjing government to reflect on the whole fight to restore a comprehensive Japanese-Chinese relationship. The naval authorities have a determined attitude toward this, while the Army, especially the headquarters of the General Staff, has not yet decided such a plan. The main objectives of the Army are still limited to the North Branch. The attitude of the government is still unclear. The foreign authorities are also afraid of diplomatic negotiations on the front line. The intention to try to avoid force oppression is still exist. I deeply worried the future development of the situation for the attitude of my government and the military.[25]

Okada and other defense witnesses have said that Matsui is holding a "pity" for the Sino-Japanese War (which will be described later in Okada's testimony). Is Iwane Matsui "anxious"? Matsui's diary has a clear answer from the first day. In his diary of August 15th, he said: "The pain is that we should have hold the hammer to awaken the Chinese authorities".[26] The next day, Matsui met Sugiyama and said:

> The current situation has entered a stage of dissolving the so-called non-expanding policy to comprehensively solve the problem. Considering the comprehensive policy of the war with the Chinese army and the national army, it is best to aim at the Chinese army, especially the Nanjing government and use the force and economic oppression to realize our strategic plan. If the army reviews the past, or excessively cares about Russia and other foreign relations, it is possible to get our national policy into trouble in the future. … For the above reasons, our military should aim at attacking Nanjing and dispatch the required troops (five divisions) to confront Chinese army, so that we can destroy the Nanjing government. In addition to the strength of force, the oppression of the Nanjing government will be more effective in economic and fiscal oppression.

Iwane Matsui said that for his suggestion, Sugiyama "seems to have no objection himself", but "doesn't show his agreement" because of considering the opinions of the staff headquarters. Matsui expressed "special regret" for the "deficient decision of the army department". On the afternoon of the same day, Matsui met with the Navy Minister Mitsumasa Yonai. "The

---

[25] 「松井石根大将戦陣日記」, 南京戦史編集委員会編『南京戦史資料集』II, 非売品, 東京, 偕行, 1st edition, December 8th, 1993, p. 34.
[26] 「松井石根大将戦陣日記」, 南京戦史編集委員会編『南京戦史資料集』II, p. 4.

opinions of the minister related to the current situation are almost the same as what I mentioned above". So Matsui is "very grateful".[27] In the days before the departure, Matsui visited the heads of military and political affairs and continued to promote his own idea of "extinguishing the Nanjing government in a second". Because the Japanese high-ranking troops sent to Shanghai at that time were still fighting a local war, Matsui received some echoes in the military and political officials who did not have to be responsible. The attitude of the important officials still disappointed him. For example, on the 17th, he visited the Prime Minister Konoe Fumimaro, and Konoe Fumimaro's "unclear attitude" made Matsui feel "regretful".[28] On the 18th, Matsui met with Tada Jun, the new Minister of General Affairs, and the Minister of General Affairs, Nakajima, the Minister of Operations (the 1st operation), Ishihara, the Minister of Information (the 2nd), Yasushi Masaru, and others. In particular, the attitude of Ishihara was "negative", which made Matsui "extremely disappointed".[29] The specific content of the meeting was not recorded in Matsui's diary. The diary of the chief of staff of Shanghai Expeditionary Force, Iinuma Mamoru, has a detailed record. The main purport of his dairy is that Matsui thinks that "we should give up the plan of partial settlement and no expansion", and "the necessary force should be used categorically, the traditional combat style should be followed in order to expect a short campaign". "It is more necessary to use the main force in Nanjing than to use it in the North Branch". "We should capture Nanjing in a short time".[30]

Before the Japanese high-level decided to attack Nanjing, Iwane Matsui has never changed to constantly propose the plan that attacking and occupying Nanjing. For example, on September 17th, when the Battle of Shanghai in Baoshan area was still difficult to tell who will win, he set the third stage of the war as "attacking Nanjing", which can be seen in his "My Personal Opinion" attached to the assistant chief of the general staff's "Representation of the Army's Opinions".[31] At that time, it was completely unexpected that the Chinese army would collapse and drawback in the end of October, so the third stage is expected to be from March of the following year. This also shows that Matsui's determination to attack Nanjing is unshakable. In the end of October, the war in Shanghai was nearing the end. Matsui said in the diary of the 20th: "I asked Suzuki in the military headquarters to convey my opinion to assistant chief of the general staff". "With the end of the battle in the west of Shanghai, the formation of the army contains at least two armies, and the

---

[27] 「松井石根大将戦陣日記」, 南京戦史編集委員会編『南京戦史資料集』II, pp. 6–7.
[28] 「松井石根大将戦陣日記」, 南京戦史編集委員会編『南京戦史資料集』II, p. 8.
[29] 「松井石根大将戦陣日記」, 南京戦史編集委員会編『南京戦史資料集』II, p. 11.
[30] 「飯沼守日記」, 南京戦史編集委員会編『南京戦史資料集』, 非売品, 東京, 偕行社. The first edition, November 3rd, 1989, pp. 67–68.
[31] 「松井石根大将戦陣日記」, 南京戦史編集委員会編『南京戦史資料集』II, p. 49.

military's operational target should be Nanjing".[32] The diary of the three days later: "This day, Lieutenant Nakayama came from the army returned to Tokyo, and I filed a letter to the Minister of Sugiyama. The keynotes are: … Three, anyway, the goal of in the South areas should be Nanjing… Four, at present, Japan's policy should be centered on destroying the Nanjing government.[33] On November 15th, the department head of the military headquarters of the Ministry, Mr. Sasuke and the department head of the Military Affairs Division of the Army, Kaneshiro Shibayama, went on a business trip to Shanghai Expeditionary Force, and Matsui strongly shows his opinion "the necessity of capturing Nanjing".[34] On November 22nd, the Japanese army's "Remarks on the future battles" showed again: "We should take advantage of the current enemy's strength to occupy Nanjing" (Matsui's opinion in the day's diary is clearly "my opinion").[35] On November 25th, Tada Jun, the assistant chief of the general staff, indicated that the action of the army can be extended to Wuxi and Huzhou area, but it should not go west further. Matsui is angry about this and rebuked him in his diary "pedantic, unbelievable".[36]

Whether Iwane Matsui Continued to Emphasize the Military Discipline

In the second article of "Affidavit", when talking about his 12-year tenure in China, he said he was dedicated to "Japanese-Chinese peace", and mainly stated "… In order to avoid long-term bitter civil relations between the two countries for sending troops, and pursue the peaceful and friendly relationship between the two countries, I especially asked the subordinates to thoroughly implement this spirit, and made the following instructions on the occasion of sending troops: 1. The battles near Shanghai are specially designed to target the enemy forces that challenge our troops, and we will treat the officials and the government friendly. Second, pay attention to avoid affecting the residents and the army in various countries, and to keep close contact with officials and the military in order to avoid misunderstanding". It said in the Article 3 about "The fighting situation near Shanghai", the war in Shanghai "I have repeatedly ordered to protect the residents, respect the rights and interests of foreign countries. One example is that under my command, no resident has been harmed in the South City battle". In Article 5 about the "Disposal at the time of Nanjing's occupation and the so-called Nanjing plundering atrocities", it said "in the middle of the battle, based on the consistent policy of the Japanese government, I tried to limit the

---

[32] 「松井石根大将戦陣日記」, 南京戦史編集委員会編『南京戦史資料集』II, pp. 91–92.

[33] 「松井石根大将戦陣日記」, 南京戦史編集委員会編『南京戦史資料集』II pp. 95–96.

[34] 「松井石根大将戦陣日記」, 南京戦史編集委員会編『南京戦史資料集』II, p. 119.

[35] 「松井石根大将戦陣日記」, 南京戦史編集委員会編『南京戦史資料集』II, p. 125.
「中方参電第一六七号·中支那方面今後ノ作戦ニ関スル意見具申」p. 130.6.

[36] 「松井石根大将戦陣日記」, 南京戦史編集委員会編『南京戦史資料集』II, p. 127.

war to the general fighting range, and in conformity with the faith in my heart, that Japan and China will be prosperous together. So I try my best to avoid this fight becoming the overall national struggle, thus I am required to be careful in the war". "To realize the purpose mentioned above, I specially strengthened to emphasize the military discipline".[37]

Iwane Matsui's statement emphasizing the military discipline has been consistently "proven" by the defense. For example, IINUMA Mamoru said that "General Matsui has repeatedly instructed the entire army to stop the illegal act"[38]; Ogawa, the 10th Army Minister of Justice said: Commander Matsui demanded strict observance of military discipline and spirit, and also required strict application of the law in order to protect the interests of the people and foreigners.[39] Because of the special circumstances of IINUMA Mamoru and Ogawa, IINUMA Mamoru said that some of the "words" were conveyed by himself (such as December 4th), Ogawa's position is the military discipline and spirit, without the strong internal evidence, it is difficult to make a substantial refutation. Therefore, the Tokyo Trial prosecution and the court did not refute for it is difficult to do so without internal evidence.

Turning the diaries of these parties today, people were surprised to find that the records of these incidents appeared to be prepared as the counter-evidence of the testimony they made in the Tokyo Trial. Checking the diary of Iwane Matsui, there was no record of so-called "ordering to supervise the discipline and the spirit of the military" during the entire battle, no matter in the Battle of Shanghai or Nanjing. Not only we can't see this in Matsui's diary, we can't see any records of Matsui's request for attention to the military discipline between August 15th and December 17th in IINUMA Mamoru's Diary either. In general, there are no records doesn't simply mean that it is the truth or it is not the truth. If the diary is just a rough sketch, and something doesn't important for him, we couldn't rule out the possibility that they didn't remember. Iwane Matsui and IINUMA Mamoru's diary are different from others', for their diaries are both very detailed, and the key is that like Matsui and IINUMA Mamoru, the other witnesses of the defendant all say that these "discipline requirements" are emphasized by Matsui. The relevant records cannot be completely "missed". Therefore, the diary does not contain those part only proof that their proof in the Tokyo Trial is not true. The IINUMA Mamoru's diary and Matsui's diary began to record the military discipline on December 18th, the time after the highest military and political authorities of Japan feeling pressure under the Western medium's protest. The inconsistency between the two can also prove that, before

---

[37] 『日中戦争史資料』 VIII 「南京事件」 Iwritten by Tomio Hora, pp. 274–275.

[38] IINUMA Mamoru's "Affidavit" (Defense Document No. 2626, Court Evidence No. 3399), 洞富雄編『日中戦争史資料』VIII 「南京事件」I, p. 252.

[39] IINUMA Mamoru's "Affidavit" (Defense Document No. 2708, Court Evidence No. 3400) 2, 洞富雄編『日中戦争史資料』VIII 「南京事件」I, p. 256.

December 17th, Iwane Matsui has not issued the so-called "instructions" of the "supervise the discipline and the spirit of the military".

If Iwane Matsui and IINUMA Mamoru are intentionally confused, the testimony of Ogawa's is entirely fabricated by himself. Because Ogawa had only met Matsui from a distance in the ceremony of getting into Nanjing and "comforting the spirit" in Nanjing. Before the transfer to the Central Military Academy in early January 1938, he had never had any contact with Matsui. Ogawa mentioned Matsui twice in the "Affidavit", the first time he said that the principles and laws should be "strictly adhered to" and "strictly applicable", another time he said about "special emphasis", and his tone is prudent. It should not be a formality. According to Ogawa's daily, the habit of detailed records of personnel encountered, this two indications cannot be omitted. Therefore, when reading the full story of Ogawa's diary without seeing Matsui's similar speech, we can naturally conclude that the so-called "testimony" is not the truth. But the reason why I dare to assert that Ogawa's testimony is fabricated is not only because the diary is not recorded, but the diary directly exposes that Ogawa has overshot himself. The fifth part of the "Affidavit": "During the time meeting with Matsui on January 4th, 1938, the general emphasized that the punishment for crimes should be strict".[40] The concrete time, place and witness are very specific and detailed. Therefore, it is conceivable that the accused party couldn't find any disproof to refute it. But for its concrete and precise, we can follow the clue and compare it with their diary. On January 4th, Ogawa's diary recorded his second visit to the 10th Army Commander, Heisuke Yanagawa, they talked about the case of Major and attending the farewell party of weapons, military doctors, veterinarians and legal departments. He did not leave the 10th Army Command Station which set in Hangzhou. On the 7th, Ogawa left for Hangzhou to Shanghai to register to Japanese Expeditionary Forces.[41] It was not until the 15th that he saw Matsui. The diary on the 15th detailed the situation with Matsui, and Matsui talked about the strategy to treat China. Such as how to overthrow Chiang Kai-shek's political power, how to establish a pro-Japanese political power, how to achieve "a hundred-year plan for a large number of Japanese immigrants", etc. The word speaks of the military discipline can't be found anywhere.[42] So no matter whether Ogawa as the officer has professional personal integrity or not,[43] there is no doubt that the testimony he provided to the Tokyo Trial was a perjury.

[40]『日中戦争史資料』VIII「南京事件」ITomio Hora, p. 257.

[41] There is no Ministry of Justice in the Japanese Expeditionary Forces, Ogawa is responsible for the daily affairs of the military law conference.

[42] 小川関治郎著『ある軍法務官の日記』, 東京, みすず書房 the 1st edition, August 10th, pp. 153–155.

[43] In Ogawa's diary, there are many records of "abhorring" against Japanese criminals, which has introduced in my article—Ogawa and 'A Military Law Officer's Dairy', *Historical Review*, No. 1, 2004.

Whether Iwane Matsui Have the Intention of "Full Cooperation and Negotiation with the Chinese Government"

In Article 6 of the "Affidavit" about the "Action after the occupation of Nanjing", it said that he "considered the necessity for a comprehensive cooperation with the Chiang Kai-shek government to promote the Chinese in Shanghai worked hard with them together, Matsui also sent people to Fujian and Guangdong to contact Chen Yi and Soong.[44]

It is impossible to say that whether Iwane Matsui's self-report is possible or not. The previous citation of Matsui's capture of Nanjing and the overthrow of the Chinese government (the so-called "Chiang Kai-shek government" by Iwane Matsui) already showed Matsui's plan. Although Matsui said in "Affidavit" that "cooperation and negotiation" is after the occupation of Nanjing, it contradicts with what were recorded in the diary on January 15th by the Ogawa cited hereinbefore. Therefore, I might as well check the diary of Matsui after the Japanese occupied Nanjing, and estimate if Matsui did have different considerations at the time. December 30th and 31st diary:

> On this day, I met with Li Zeyi, Chen Chung-fu, and Kayano, instructed the future strategies and listened to their opinions. It is said that the Shanghai Peace Movement has gradually matured and its momentum has been high recently.
>
> Li recently went to Hong Kong and liaised with Soong to explore the future trends of the National Government. I told them we can use Soong, while he can't participate in the new political power.
>
> According to what Chen has said, KUI CHING's wife left Hankou to Shanghai to know our intentions. Generally speaking, she said there is no special requirement except for the prevention of the Communist Party and the promotion of Asianism. In addition, KUI CHING and some members of the National Government hope to negotiate peacefully with Japan under the precondition that Chiang Kai-shek fell out of power. I told him the prerequisite for organizing a new regime is that Chiang Kai-shek falls out of power and dissolved the current National Government.

The diary on this day also writes:

> As a representative of Tang Shaoyi, Wen Tsung yao said that Jiang must fall out of power anyway (referring to go to foreign countries), and Guangdong, Guangxi should be independent and must cut off the relations with the United Kingdom. I agree to what Wen Tsung yao said. Wen Laichun went to Guangdong in accordance with the meaning of Tang, and we also sent Wachi

---

[44] 『日中戦争史資料』VIII「南京事件」Iwritten by Tomio Hora, p. 27. When the prosecutor in the court asked Iwane Matsui about leading the army to China, "Do you have any advice to your government not to negotiate with Chiang Kai-shek?" Matsui clearly said: "No." 『日中戦争史資料』VIII「南京事件」Iwritten by Tomio Hora, pp. 280–281.

to assist their work. Our army intends to attack Guangdong, so it is necessary to do the work of Guangdong and Guangxi. This matter is worth considering.[45]

On January 2nd, the report of the Chief of Staff of the Japanese Expeditionary Forces, Tsukada, who returned from Tokyo and the view of Iwane Matsui:

The chief of staff Tsukada returned from Tokyo. According to his report:
First, regarding to the operations of the military (referring to Japanese Expeditionary Forces - the leader), the headquarters of the staff is extremely negative and does not want to expand the scope of future operations.
Second, the government has not yet made any decision on the future plan. It is surprising that there is no plan for whether to let the National Government compromise or to establish a new political power.
Third, there is no enthusiasm for the military's strategy. Naturally, they didn't agree with my proposal that sending personnel. In particular, I did not get any response for writing letter directly to the Minister, even worse, they let Major General Putian negotiate with the undersecretary. Its indecisiveness makes me surprising.
In short, the government regard the National Government at this time as a prerequisite for future operations and strategies.[46]

On January 4th, Iwane Matsui discussed with the Japanese ambassador in China, Kawagoe Shigeru and the Minister of Foreign Affairs, Kawai, "The rehabilitation of the situation". The first one is that "the government must deny the National Government in some form". The next day, Matsui called the Navy and the Army officials, Tasuichiro Funatsu and conveyed the discussion plans on the previous day. Tasuichiro Funatsu (publicly known as the director-general of "China Textile Association" and later the "Annual Government" consultant) came to China to make a private negotiation with Chinese after the war broke out.[47] The diary about January 6th wrote:

Wen Tsungyao visited and discussed the independence movement of Guangdong and Guangxi with me. On the 8th, Wen left Shanghai for Hong Kong and made agreement with the local comrades. I made an agreement with him, we will send Wachi to assist him, and if possible we will also send Nakai Nakajima to Hong Kong to assist their work.[48]

January 7th dairy:

The result of the recent liaison with the embassy and the navy (I have known), is that our government has decided to deny the National Government. We all

[45] 「松井石根大将戦陣日記」, 南京戦史編集委員会編『南京戦史資料集』 II, pp. 149–150.
[46] 「松井石根大将戦陣日記」, 南京戦史編集委員会編『南京戦史資料集』 II, pp. 150–151.
[47] 「松井石根大将戦陣日記」, 南京戦史編集委員会編『南京戦史資料集』 II, p. 152.
[48] 「松井石根大将戦陣日記」, 南京戦史編集委員会編『南京戦史資料集』 II, p. 153.

agree that issuing statements in and out of the country in some form is crucial to future campaigns and strategies. I presented this opinion to the Minister and the Chief, and let the Navy and the Embassy each write their opinion to the Minister and the Chief. I also asked the Director of Personnel to submit a private letter to these person, the Prime Minister of the Konoye, the Foreign Minister of Hirota, and the Minister of the Army, Sugiyama. The letter mentioned the future operations and tasks accompanying the above-mentioned major policies, the establishment of a special agency under the jurisdiction of the executive authorities in Shanghai, and gathering all important personnel to research and propose a solution of the military and economic affairs in the future.

The diary of the day also recorded on the page:

Liaison with the 10th Division to occupy the Longhai Railway near Xuzhou, cut off salt transportation, and expand the scope of power in Zhejiang.[49]

January 10th diary:

According to the mainland news report, in yesterday's Tokyo cabinet meeting, the cabinet and supreme headquarters negotiated and talked with the participants, it seems that a more specific decision on the future policy has been decided. Although the content is still unclear, my government policy is gradually becoming clearer. Which will not only make the military's strategies more clear and operations more quickly, but also cause the attention of the Chinese. I am more positive and motivated to act after I see the policy and strategies clearly.[50]

January 15th diary:

Minister Ito came to inform the government's attitude. As the German mediation activities have not been extinguished today, the government still hesitated to move forward (Ito said) we should prompt the government to make a decision, which is amazing. In the call for Major General Harada to raise the opinions of the military on the current situation, he also ordered Major General Harada to return to Tokyo and supervise and urge the work of the authorities...[51]

January 16th diary:

Today, the government of Japan issued a statement that "not regard the National Government as a (negotiating) opponent" (it means they don't recognize the existence of the National Government—from the author), although its true meaning is not yet known, but there is no doubt that it is closer to

[49] 「松井石根大将戦陣日記」, 南京戦史編集委員会編『南京戦史資料集』II, pp. 153–154.
[50] 「松井石根大将戦陣日記」, 南京戦史編集委員会編『南京戦史資料集』II, p. 155.
[51] 「松井石根大将戦陣日記」, 南京戦史編集委員会編『南京戦史資料集』II, p. 157.

my claim. While the government's determination still makes me disturbed. Therefore, I feel that all aspects of this should be directed to the government. While consolidating future understanding, of course we must go further in both making the relevant decisions and conducting operations in the future. Having discussed with the general of Ito, Tsukata, and Harada, we made the above decisions and ordered to quickly formulate local policies.[52]

On January 15th, the cabinet liaison meeting of the Japanese supreme headquarters decided not to recognize the Chinese government, so the content cited above ended from Matsui being informed that the Japanese government no longer recognizes the Chinese government. Because although Iwane Matsui's activities to actively overthrow the Chinese government have far exceeded the boundaries of "following the orders", we just regard this responsibility as the highest level of Japan's.

The reason why this section details the diary of Iwane Matsui during this period is mainly that it is crucial to determine what kind of responsibility Iwane Matsui should take.

Whether Iwane Matsui Is Especially Concerned About the Protection of Western Interests

The second article of the "Affidavit" mentions "noticing that don't affect residents and military forces of various countries", and the third article says "I have repeatedly ordered officers and soldiers under my control" and "respect foreign rights and interests". Article 6 states: "Keep in touch with the British and American naval commanders and the civilian and military officers of the various countries to deal with the incidents in the fighting".[53]

Does Iwane Matsui especially respect the "foreign rights"? Let's check the diary.

On August 26th, 1937, British Ambassador to China Xu Gesen (S. M. Knatchbulll-Hugessen) drove from Nanjing to Shanghai and was shot by a Japanese military plane near Wuxi. He was seriously injured, which caused strong dissatisfaction by Britain and other Western countries. Japan immediately apologized. Matsui recorded this in his diary on 30th, and after a few days, he still remembered to record his emotions in his diary shows he really cares about what happened about this accident. He said that he thought it was "my navy plane". Yesterday, there was a "chino plane" and it was painted with "Hinomaru". Therefore, this matter "cannot be asserted that our army did it":

> Even it is our army who shoot the man, it is evitable for internal and external personnel who passed through the battlefield without notice are killed by

---

[52]「松井石根大将戦陣日記」, 南京戦史編集委員会編『南京戦史資料集』II, p. 157.

[53] 洞富雄編『日中戦争史資料』VIII「南京事件」I, pp. 274–275.

the fighting. Therefore, there is no need for our government to rush to express regret, which makes people feel that the attitude of my government, Shanghai's foreign affairs, and the navy is too flustered.[54]

In the diary on the same day, Matsui also recorded dissatisfaction with the ongoing trade activities of British merchant ships after the war began. Matsui felt uncomfortable for the navy hadn't made a total blockade along the sea areas of China. Matsui held a hostile attitude not only to Britain, but also to the normal cruise of all Western ships on the Huangpu River and Wusongkou. On September 1st, when the Third Division attacked Wusong Town, a French warship passed by. Matsui called it a "prank" in the diary of that day, demanding that the Third Fleet and the Japanese embassy make a "serious protest" against France, and stated "If such a thing happens again in the future, our army cannot guarantee the safety of French ships".[55] After September 20th, he thought the British merchant ship in the lower Huangpu River should leave, recording as following:

> If these ships do not comply with this warning and remain at the current location, our army will not take responsibility for the result of fighting in the future.[56]

In the diary of the next day:

> Today, a number of shells were fired against British ships that were temporarily moored downstream of the Huangpu River, which aims at threatening British ships and all these shells land in the water near the ships, two of which hurriedly set anchor and tracked back, which means we have achieved our goal while one still stubbornly stopped in place ...[57]

This is the true attitude of Iwane Matsui. If Matsui is not completely without the consciousness of "foreign rights", this consciousness compared to the weight needed by the Japanese army is at least insignificant. In his diary on October 1st, Matsui wrote about his request for the Japanese embassy to influence Western journalists. It can be seen that Matsui is not completely indifferent to foreign public opinion, but Matsui's concern is not to require his army to behave properly, but only to ask others to follow his will and against foreign media's negative reports on the Japanese army. Matsui used the Chinese character "manipulation" to influence Western journalists. He said that his idea that it was necessary to "manipulate" because the National League passed an "illegal" resolution condemning Japan for bombing

---

[54] 「松井石根大将戦陣日記」, 南京戦史編集委員会編『南京戦史資料集』II, pp. 22–23.
[55] 「松井石根大将戦陣日記」, 南京戦史編集委員会編『南京戦史資料集』II, p. 25.
[56] 「松井石根大将戦陣日記」, 南京戦史編集委員会編『南京戦史資料集』II, p. 54.
[57] 「松井石根大将戦陣日記」, 南京戦史編集委員会編『南京戦史資料集』II, p. 56.

Chinese cities on September 28th. The Resource Book has a note under the word "illegal", saying that it refers to a "condemnation" resolution. Then he remembered the following paragraph:

> It is reported that in the Shanghai embassy, it is really surprising that foreign journalists have not used any means of purchase. The Army and Naval military officer who never make effort and if they do not take urgent measures, it will bring very unfavorable results to future wars' propaganda. I really worry about his situation.[58]

Iwane Matsui has a special preference for Chinese culture. Even during the fierce battle, he continues to write poems (most of which are seven words quatrains). Therefore, his true thoughts can be clearly expressed to Chinese people at their first those Chinese characters such as "manipulation" and "illegal".

After the Chinese army's defense line in the large battlefield and other places were breached, Japanese artillery fire ignited the urban area, which directly conflicted with the interests of Western countries. On October 29th, artillery from the Third Division of the Japanese army bombarded many parts of the city. The bombardment in the Jessfield Park caused many British soldiers' death or injury. Therefore, the British protested to the Japanese. Although Matsui wrote down "regret" in his diary, he thought that the reason was that "the British army did not retreat near Zhongshan Bridge according to our request". On the same day, the Japanese army shelled Avenue Road in the French Concession, and Matsui thought that it was "a prank and a strategy of the Chinese army".[59] On October 31st, Matsui recorded in his diary that the artillery fire affected the British military area were due to the British army "connecting with the support area of the Chinese Army". There was a sentence that reflected Matsui's unhappy heart knot: "The British and French army always hold an attitude of sympathy and support for the Chinese army". Therefore, he believed that the Japanese army should take a "strong standpoint".[60]

With the defeat of the Chinese army, the attitudes of Western embassies and consulates in Shanghai and the army became less tough than before, therefore, Matsui's treatment to them seemed more "relaxed" than before. In the diary of November 2nd, he recorded "Britain, the United States, France, Italy, and other countries" gave "general understanding" of "our policy", so Matsui did not add a "proviso" when asking divisions to "protect property of foreigners in southwest Shanghai".[61] But this doesn't mean that Matsui's

---

[58] 「松井石根大将戦陣日記」, 南京戦史編集委員会編『南京戦史資料集』II, p. 69.
[59] 「松井石根大将戦陣日記」, 南京戦史編集委員会編『南京戦史資料集』II, p. 103.
[60] 「松井石根大将戦陣日記」, 南京戦史編集委員会編『南京戦史資料集』II, p. 105.
[61] 「松井石根大将戦陣日記」, 南京戦史編集委員会編『南京戦史資料集』II, p. 107.

position has fundamentally changed. The basic points in Matsui's position that the West should obey the Japanese army have not changed. One of the paragraphs records of November 10th in the diary can reflect the meaning of Matsui:

> I met the British fleet chief for the first time.
> Today I met with the British fleet chief and army commander at the school in Jiangwan. The British chief changed his previous tough attitude and very attentive. He repeatedly stated that the British army had no intention to hinder the Japanese army's operations. I can't help smiling his behavior in my mind. After a formal greeting to him with general international etiquette, I foretell that our army will use the Suzhou River, Huangpu River, and railways for resupply, and will take necessary self-defense measures against the obstructionists, no matter who he is. The British chief said that he would take measures in consultation with the Consul General. I thought it was necessary for them to act completely in accordance with the wishes of the Japanese army. …
> After the above-mentioned meeting, I also met with military officer of the embassies of British, America, French and Italian in China, and talked about what the preface said to the British chief, hoping that the official constitutions of the countries and the military would properly handle them. Military officers from all countries have a humble attitude and show reverence for the Japanese army and me. In fact, they are afraid of the power of the Japanese army.[62]

It can be seen from this record that the prerequisite of Iwane Matsui's display of "international etiquette" is first and foremost that western countries "have no intention of obstructing the Japanese army". On November 17th, Matsui returned to the British Navy's flagship to visit the British fleet chief. The British navy chief was "extremely attentive" and Matsui's "moderate" attitude was not just the same as the day before, but he also added something like "avoiding infringing the rights of other nations" and "Oriental peace". But on the same day, when he called the Minister of "their own person"—Ito Shushi, Matsui's "bottom thoughts in his heart" was another tone:

> On the same day, Minister Ito was called to the headquarters to discuss my opinion on the future measures of the Shanghai Concession. He fully agreed with me, and agreed to work hard to urge the work of the foreign authorities in the future. In addition, for the navy, observing from the general international situation, there is no need to worry about Britain and the United States. Our words and actions should take advantage of the current combat situation in our favor. In the future, the common concession and of course the French concession should do their best to ban the Chinese government and the Chinese people's activities which against Japan. To make the Chinese government abandon the so-called will of relying on Europe and the United States that in Shanghai

---

[62]「松井石根大将戦陣日記」, 南京戦史編集委員会編『南京戦史資料集』II, p. 114.

and continuing the war of resistance against Japan. They must have a clear and conscious attitude.[63]

On November 21st, Iwane Matsui ordered Japanese military officer Harada, who stayed in China, to convey to the French Concession authorities a request to ban anti-Japanese activities and threatened that "if you can't meet our requirement, our army will take decisive measures according to the needs of the battle".[64] On November 24th, the French army commander in China visited Matsui for the first time, and his attitude was similar to that of the British military officer—"extremely attentive", but because the French embassy and the concession authorities contradicted the requirements of the Japanese army, Matsui spoke bluntly and harshly, "If the authorities of France can't recognize our sincerity (referring to the French obedience to the Japanese army— from the author), and blindly advocate the privileges of the French Concession, we will take decisive measures against the French army near the South City".[65] On November 26th, the French Navy Chief and Chinese Consul General in Shanghai visited Matsui. Matsui wrote in his diary on that day:

> In addition to their courtesy visits, their main purpose is to hope that our military will take a stable attitude towards the French Concession in the future. I said that the French army must cooperate with the Japanese army to maintain the safety and order in the French concession, especially in the South City. Therefore, in order to communicate with our army's supply in South City, our army needs to use part of the river bank in the French Concession for transportation. They have no objection to cooperating with our army, but they consider it difficult to recognize the treaty and French rights through the French concession by armed soldiers. I said that we would then have to consider taking measures against the French army in South City. While intimidating, I hope that they will block the National Bank of China in the concession…[66]

On December 3rd, the Japanese army's No. 101 Division was marching in the Shanghai Public Concession and when they arrived in Nanjing Road, a grenade was thrown by passersby, causing three Japanese soldiers and one embassy patroller injured (the young bombers was shot and killed on the spot). The concession authorities were forced to agree that "if the Japanese army thought that it was necessary to defend themselves, they could take an independent 'cleanup' operation in the concession". Matsui said after recording the incident, "this is the contribution of the explosion accident".[67]

[63] 「松井石根大将戦陣日記」, 南京戦史編集委員会編『南京戦史資料集』 II, pp. 120–121.
[64] 「松井石根大将戦陣日記」, 南京戦史編集委員会編『南京戦史資料集』 II, pp. 124–125.
[65] 「松井石根大将戦陣日記」, 南京戦史編集委員会編『南京戦史資料集』 II, pp. 126–127.
[66] 「松井石根大将戦陣日記」, 南京戦史編集委員会編『南京戦史資料集』 II, p. 128.
[67] 「松井石根大将戦陣日記」, 南京戦史編集委員会編『南京戦史資料集』 II, p. 136.

It can be seen from the above quote that Iwane Matsui is not completely without the consciousness of "foreign rights and interests", he is just friendly to those who take actions in accordance with his will, and he is definitely not a model who protects foreign rights and interests like his self-present in the Tokyo Trial.

Whether Iwane Matsui apologizes for "Ladybird Incident"

Finally, let's take a look at the actual performance of Matsui during the Ladybird incident. Article 11 in the "Affidavit", about "Ladybird, Panay and other foreign-related matters", he said "Hashimoto Daisuke found several ships carrying Chinese soldiers sailing in the Yangtze River in the dense fog on the morning of the 12th, and carried out shelling and occasionally hit the Ladybird. I immediately ordered the Commander of the 10th Army to apologize to the British Navy Chief. After I returned to Shanghai from Nanjing, I also immediately visited Little, the British Navy's Governor to show my apology.[68]

On the morning before the fall of Nanjing on December 12th, four British warships and merchant ships, such as the Ladybird, were shelled and wounded by the 13th Regiment of the Japanese 10th Field Artillery near Wuhu; in the afternoon of the same day, the USS Panay and Three Mobil oil companies were sunk at the upstream of Nanjing by the Japanese Navy's 12th Air Force.[69] The incident caused strong protests in Britain and the United States. At that time, Japan was not ready for a full-scale military showdown with Britain and the United States, so the Japanese government expressed apology on the 13th, and the Japanese Minister of Foreign Affairs, Koki Hirota sent a letter to the British and American ambassadors to Japan, in addition to expressing apologies, he also promised to make a loss compensation. The actual pressure on this accident for Japan exceeded the Nanjing atrocities at the time. Not only did the Japanese government respond quickly, but all circles have expressed their apologies to the United States and Britain, especially the United States. For example, Yamamoto, the undersecretary of the Navy apologized to the US ambassador, and the famous publisher Iwami Shigeo donated a thousand yen in response to the Tokyo Nichinichi Shinbun initiative to raise funds for shipbuilding compensation.[70] At that time, the army was under pressure, and the army and navy sent commissioners to investigate on the spot. There were also some measures. For example, Hashimoto

---

[68] 洞富雄編『日中戦争史資料』VIII「南京事件」I, p. 277.

[69] 会編纂『南京戦史』, 非売品, 東京, 偕行社, 1st edition, November 3rd, 1989, p. 288. 『中國方面海軍作戦』consider it's the Japanese Navy's 12th Air Force that bombed the USS Panay, 防衛庁防衛研修所戦史室編『戦史叢書·中國方面海軍作戦〈1〉昭和13年3月まで』, 東京,朝雲新聞社, 1st edition, March 28th, 1974, p. 512.

[70] 转引自南京战史编集委员会编纂『南京戦史』第五章第十四節"揚子江事件 (Ladybird, Panay incident)", pp. 288–290.

Kingoro, who became "a prestigious" Class-A war criminal, was forced to be removed from the captain position in the 13th Regiment of field heavy artillery by this incident.

It was the naval aviation that sank the USS Panay, which was not under the jurisdiction of Iwane Matsui. Therefore, we only check Matsui's attitude toward the Ladybird Incident. The first time that Matsui recorded the incident in his diary was the next day of the incident. At that time, he had anticipated that this incident would "somehow cause problems in the future", but at the same time said: "It is also helpless for the third-country nationals and ships remaining in this dangerous area to suffer innocent disasters. Moreover, we have already reminded the danger of the battlefield in this area".[71] This day's diary ended with this sentence. Apparently, Matsui did not think it's the Japanese army's fault. The second time that Matsui mentioned the Ladybird Incident was on 16th, three days later after the incident. At this time, he had learned the Japanese government had apologized, so he wrote those down at the beginning of the diary:

> Wuhu British Ship Incident
> Regarding the damage of British warships and merchant ships on the 12th, my government immediately apologized to the British protests without knowing the truth, it a kind of trepidation. But that has happened, what I can do is to investigate the truth, and I have telegraphed to Tokyo the unnecessary result of the punishment about the responsible person.[72]

After that, there is no further record about this accident in Matsui's diary. According to Matsui's habit of setting down his daily actions, if it's really as what he said in the Tokyo Trial, "I immediately ordered the Commander of the Tenth Army to apologize to the British Navy Chief. After I returned to Shanghai from Nanjing, I also immediately visited Little, the British Navy's Governor to show my apology". It is impossible that there is nothing record in his diary about this accident. There are indeed some mutual "visits" between Matsui and the British Navy Chief, Little. While these "visits" happened before the incident, so there is no apology. The meeting between Matsui and Little was only cited in the diary on November 10th, the "British Navy Chief" "visited" Matsui and Matsui's return visit on the 17th of the same month. It can be seen that Matsui's testimony on the Ladybird Incident in Tokyo was a high degree of perjury: not only because there is no "immediate visit", but also because the "apology" was the exact opposite of his actual performance.

Some aspects reviewed in this section, such as the performance of Iwane Matsui in the "Ladybird Incident", will not have any impact on sentencing even if they are stated truthfully. The reason why I did not hesitate to identify them in detail is mainly to explain that Matsui's falsehood testimony provided

---

[71]「松井石根大将戦陣日記」, 南京戦史編集委員会編『南京戦史資料集』II, p. 140.
[72]「松井石根大将戦陣日記」, 南京戦史編集委員会編『南京戦史資料集』II, p. 141.

in Tokyo Trial was not an occasional misconduct, but an explicit fabrication for the purpose of the trial. Neither the Tokyo Trial Procuratorate nor the court made substantive doubt about Matsui's testimony. Therefore, pointing out that the testimony is not true, which makes it reasonable and possible for us to re-examine Matsui's war responsibility today.

3   Re-evaluation of Iwane Matsui's War Guilt

At the beginning of this article, we mentioned that there were as many as 38 charges for Matsui's trial in Tokyo, while the court finally convicted only "inaction", which showed that even at that time, among all his crimes, they are not sufficiently targeted. For example, for "preparation of war plans" to the countries, including China, the United States, Britain, Australia, New Zealand, Canada, India, the Philippines, the Netherlands, France, Thailand and the Soviet Union that involved in the indictment, he is guilty. At the same time, through the review in the previous section, we can say that the court completely acquitted the other crimes out of the 55 items, which is not appropriate today.

The description about the opposition of Iwane Matsui's crime, about "anti-peace crimes" in the Tokyo Trial verdict, is just like this.

> Matsui was a senior general of the Japanese Army and was promoted to general in 1933. He has extensive experience in the Army, including work in the Kwantung Army and the Staff Headquarters (However), although he has close ties with those who planed and implemented "co-conspiracy crime", and he should know the purpose and policy of co-conspirators. As far as the evidence presented to the court, he is considered to be the co-conspirators are still unreasonable (the original text was "Legitimate" –from the author).
>
> His deeds in the military positions in China between 1937 and 1938 could not be regarded as aggression wars. In order to make the 27th cause of action become reasonably guilty, as an obligation of the prosecutor, it is necessary to provide reasonable evidence that can derive Matsui knows the criminal nature of the war, but the prosecutor did not put forward.[73]

In this statement in the verdict, the 27th item explicitly referred to in the latter paragraph is "the crime of aggression against China". If the previous paragraph refers only to the first "co-conspiracy crime", the public prosecutor's allegations reserved in the judgment—29th, 31st, 32nd, 35th, 36th of the war about the aggression against the United States, Britain and the Netherlands, as well as the incidents of Zhang Gufeng and Nomenkan—are all ignored. If the statement in the previous paragraph contains these allegations, the time is unreasonable. Because although Matsui's position in the army was "powerful", he had left the central department with

---

[73] 「松井石根大将戦陣日記」, 南京戦史編集委員会編 『南京戦史資料集』I, p. 398.

decision-making authority before he retired from service in 1935 (serving as the Minister of Part Two of the Staff Headquarters in the mid-1920s), the resumption in Shanghai Battle only lasted a few months, and the time of the wars against the nations was far behind. Therefore, the "deserved understanding" in the preceding paragraph is an unrealistic inference, and there is no probative value of the "evidence" proposed, naturally without any "irrational" points. The prosecution's allegations are widespread, but have nothing to do with the purpose of this article, so there is no need to discuss details about whether the verdict is appropriate or not.

I think the improper judgment of the Tokyo Trial on Iwane Matsui is mainly the pardon of the 27th cause of action.

Originally, "anti-peace crimes" included all aspects of planning, preparation, initiation and implementation of the war of aggression. It was not a narrow and easy-to-evade charge. Looking back at the Tokyo Trial of Iwane Matsui, we can see that the public prosecutor was not easily given up researching the Nanjing Massacre. The reason why Iwane Matsui was exempted from the crime of "anti-peace" was that his actual performance during the time of sending troops in Shanghai and the Central China Army, especially the effect of his performance in promoting the war, after being whitewashed, was completely covered up. This cover of truth is even deeper than the ordinary cover, because it also creates the illusion which is totally opposite to the truth, that Iwane Matsui is really distressed at the war. This illusion not only affected the verdict of the Tokyo Trial, but also had a lasting "infectivity" that continues today.

This illusion can be established, which is closely related to Matsui's "love" China's statement that is also uncontested. Therefore, it is necessary to explain briefly when re-evaluate Iwane Matsui's war responsibility. Iwane Matsui said in the "affidavit":

> I was in office about twelve years in China. Not only did I focus on working together for the relationship between China and Japan, but since I was young, I have been helping and supporting a good relation of China and Japan for the rest of my life and devoting my life to the revival of Asia.[74]

This statement by Iwane Matsui was echoed in the defense testimony. For example, Shinrokuro Hidaka, who was an officer of the Japanese embassy in the Shanghai Campaign, said in "Affidavit" (Defense Document No. 1165, Forensic Evidence No. 2537):

> General Matsui has been a Japanese-Chinese mutualist for a long time. He understands Chinese culture and has a deep attachment to China and the Chinese people.[75]

[74] 洞富雄編『日中戦争史資料』VIII「南京事件」I, p. 274.
[75] 洞富雄編『日中戦争史資料』VIII「南京事件」I, p. 181.

Among all the testimonies of the defense, the relevant testimony that Okada was "commissioned"[76] by Shanghai Expeditionary Force (defense Book No. 2670 and Forensic Evidence No. 3409) is the most detailed. Okada said that Iwane Matsui had a real love for China. When he was appointed, Matsui said to him:

> He inherited the ideas of Kazuo Kawakami, the predecessor of the Japanese Army, and Sun Yat-sen, the founding father of the Republic of China. For decades, he has taken the responsibility of supporting Japan as a good friend of China and liberating and rejuvenating Asia. This time, in the unfortunate incident between China and Japan, he was unexpectedly appointed as a dispatcher commander of the army, which makes people feel a lot.
>
> In particular, I was transferred from the reserve personnel to the commanders of the Shanghai Expeditionary Force, and it can be inferred that, it is more important for me, the one who totally understand China and love China, to handle the incident with the least sacrifice under the principle of absolutely no expansionism, rather than to become a great military commander who can achieve great achievements... It is my dream to open up the road of Sino-Japanese integration with minimal warfare.[77]

If it were not for the testimony of Iwane Matsui from 1937 to 1938, there is some doubt that China is "most understandable" and "Dearest" for Matsui. While saying "nostalgia" Chinese culture is generally reasonable. When Matsui was a teenager, it was a time when the western tide struck into Japan and Japanese society was undergoing drastic changes. However, in the world of culture, belief and value, the tradition deeply influenced by Chinese culture was not fundamentally shaken, which is totally different from the modern China. Matsui seemed to have admired China when he was young. Otherwise, after he graduated with the 18th "chief" of the Army University, he could have chosen to go to Europe and the United States instead of volunteering to go to China (Qing Dynasty). We mentioned in the previous article that Matsui continued to write poems even during the fierce battles, while we can hardly find his records of reading Chinese classics in his diary today. If he hadn't studied hard in his youth, it is impossible for him to use Chinese skillfully in writing poems. Although his poems are not difficult to understand, his love for Chinese poetry is also evident from his behavior of "writing Chinese poetry" [78] while waiting for his verdict. In fact, it is not only Matsui, if you look at the writings of modern Japanese "military attaché" remained today, it is easy to find that there are many people who like

---

[76] It is usually translated into "consultant". While "commissioned" doesn't reach the level of the Chinese word "consultant". From the specific situation of Okada, he is actually just a general attendant of Iwane Matsui.

[77] 洞富雄編『日中戦争史資料』VIII「南京事件」I, pp. 261–262.

[78] 朝日新聞東京記者団著『東京裁判』下, 東京, 朝日新聞社 the 1st edition in July 1995, p. 96.

Chinese poetry and calligraphy. Such as Fukushima Yasumasa, whose poem skills are no less than contemporary Chinese.[79] The banner inscribed at the Omori Detention Center by Tojo Hideki, who is still alive today. The content is "every day should be different" from Terminus Technology Inc.[80] As for civil administration's nostalgia for Chinese classics, the proportion of Chinese literatures which those Class A war criminals have read in Sugamo prison is far more than the West literatures. It is a kind of microcosm. Of course, these "Chinese classic literatures" have long been dissolved in the blood of Japanese culture, and it is not easy to tell whether they can be used as a proof of loving "Chinese" cultures. But for those people, concluding Iwane Matsui, their passionate about Chinese culture can't offset their war responsibilities, for they are totally different things.

If Iwane Matsui's "nostalgia" in Chinese culture is not completely groundless, Takashi Hamada's testimony said that Matsui was "heartbroken" about the Sino-Japanese War. Okada claimed that the next day of the "Congratulations on Victory" (the evening of December 17th, 1937), he went to visit Matsu, and Matsui was completely unhappy. Matsui "has always been wishing for peace between China and Japan for more than 30 years", while it is now a "miserable result" when we cross swords with each other, which makes him "extremely regret". Okada said, "Listening to every painful sentence, I feel sympathy for the general's feelings". On December 19th, Okada accompanied Matsui to the Qingliang Mountain and the Observatory. He said that Matsui "passionately" expressed regret for the miserable setback of Chiang Kai-shek's unification efforts, and thought that Chairman Chiang would be patient for another two or three years without causing any wars. If things happened like this, Japan would also have realized the disadvantages of using force to solve China's problems, and today's unfortunate result of brothers' ramparts wouldn't have occurred. It's really regretful". Okada also cited a poem given to him by Matsui's on New Year's Day in 1938: "I have been praying the peaceful development of Asia during the several decades in China. Looking back, I feel shamed for my worthless. I will never obtain the peace mind if I couldn't realize my dream. It is claimed that the poem "shows the general's mood" is "to pray for peace and development of Asia". In his testimony, Okada also said that Matsui "amiably comforted" the refugees during his "inspection of the refugee area", and sternly ordered that "they will never harm the innocent", and promised that "the age of living and working peacefully and happily will definitely come".[81]

---

[79] 太田阿山編『福島将軍大陸征旅詩集』, 東京, Kuwabunsha October 20th, 1939, 1st edition. Fukushima Yasumasa, he was the military attaché when he was young. In 1892, he returned at the end of his term as the military attaché in German Legation, it took him one and a half year. His legend of crossing the Euro-Asian alone was astonishing at that time. He was promoted as the Colonel General between 1912 and 1926.

[80] It is collected by Yoshio, more details, please refer to『東京裁判』, p. 106.

[81] 洞富雄編『日中戦争史資料』VIII「南京事件」I, pp. 263–264.

The prosecutors did not question the testimony of Okada, and the reason is as it mentioned above, the problem of the evidence. This testimony is not true from the detailed claim of Iwane Matsui, he constantly advocated to attack Nanjing between the time of the formation of Shanghai Expeditionary Force and November 25th. Here is another strong and sufficient proof from Matsui's self-report to prove the falsity of Okada's testimony. Matsui received the decision of the staff headquarters to attack Nanjing on November 28th. In the diary of that day, he set down such a sentence: "My enthusiastic representations have worked, and I am extremely pleased".[82] Matsui couldn't wait to attack Nanjing, and his "enthusiastic" desire was revealed in this sentence, which is completely contrary to the helplessness and regret described by Okada. Maybe some people think that Matsui's state of mind and his understanding have changed after the capture of Nanjing. However, there are persuasive evidence which can prove Matsui cannot have the feeling of "regret" after entering the city. This evidence is also a confession by himself. On December 18th, the day that Okada claimed Matsui felt "infinite regret", he wrote this kind of sentence in his "Nanjing Strategies' Feelings": "It's a great honor for our army to win the wars".[83] On December 21st, Matsui returned to Shanghai. In his diary of that day, he wrote a sentence: "It took just two weeks to complete the successful entering to Nanjing, and the mood of return to Shanghai is particularly comfortable".[84] This is totally different from Okada's testimony.

This shows the reason why Iwane Matsui, as a commander in chief of the Japanese army in the "implementation" of the war in the early days, could be exempted from the "implementation of the crime of aggression against China" is that he and the defense deliberately fabricated a negative illusion of justification, which is more effective than the reason of "acting according to orders"; we have revealed this illusion through the records left by Iwane Matsui himself, which made the verdict (he was not guilty for the 27th cause of action) sentenced by Tokyo Trial be on shaky ground. Why can't Iwane Matsui be exempted for taking a positive attitude in the war? There are two reasons: First of all, we believe that "the crime of aggression against China" is a substantial crime. If an "executive" officer can be exempted from

---

[82] 「松井石根大将戦陣日記」, 南京戦史編集委員会編『南京戦史資料集』, p. 10. In November 22nd, after he received the order from emperor of Japan: "Be brave and decisive in the battle, and we are honored for your loyalty". Matsui answered: "We will overcome obstacles to show our army's strength" (same as it mentioned above in 『南京戦史資料集』, pp. 196–197), Matsui's active action is consistent.

[83] 「松井石根大将戦陣日記」, 南京戦史編集委員会編『南京戦史資料集』, p. 21. The purpose that Okada cited Matsui's poem is try to show Matsui's pursuit of peace. While "showing Japanese army's strength" is what Matsui really considered. There is a sentence on the day he went on an expedition to Shanghai: "it is the right time to show off our strength" (「松井石根大?戦陣日記」, 南京戦史編集委員会編『南京戦史資料集II, p. 12), the meaning and words are almost same with what cited above.

[84] 「松井石根大将戦陣日記」, 南京戦史編集委員会編『南京戦史資料集』, p. 23.

responsibility, there is merely one situation, he is only "acting according to orders" in a negative attitude. Suppose his performance does not exceed the "military duties" stated in the Tokyo Trial Judgment, while Iwane Matsui was highly engaged after he was appointed and performed positively. Therefore, it is safe to say that Iwane Matsui can't be exempted from liability. In other words, the crime of aggression become meaningless if Iwane Matsui can be exempted from his committing one of the most important contents of the "anti-peace crime"—"implementation", not limited to against China. Secondly, what is more important is that the war between China and Japan became irreversible, of course, there are many complicated reasons, including Iwane Matsui's essential role. Although we cannot assume whether the history will be different if Iwane Matsui strictly followed the orders of Japanese Central Committee. However, Matsui repeatedly "advocate" his "impelling claim" (it is used frequently in Matsui's diary). His purpose is to expand the war and push the war forward. He took action without permission, leading the Japanese army to continue to break through the restrictions on fighting in Shanghai and areas around Shanghai. He disobeyed orders, violated the Wufu Line and the Xicheng Line and attacked Nanjing. All of those lead to the irreversible relationship between China and Japan. Furthermore, unlike ordinary technical soldiers, Iwane Matsui has his own "mature" proposition and overall consideration of politics. The decision, not regarding the national government as its opponent, is precisely accomplished by him after he realized the occupation of the capital Nanjing and strongly opposed Chinese government.

The reason why Iwane Matsui cannot be exempted here is related to the active engagement that we have already discussed in detail above. The impact on Matsui's performance is simply explained here. Firstly, after the Lugou Bridge Incident, the war in North China has been expanding. Because the Japanese political and military officials at the time did not make up their minds to fight a full-scale war with China immediately, so we call "the July 7th Incident" as the beginning of the outbreak of the comprehensive anti-Japanese war, while different with us, Japan called it the "North Chinese Incident". Japan announced on September 2nd in the name of "Conference" that it would change the "Northern Chinese Incident" to the iconic "Chinese incident". The background is the continuous escalation of the Shanghai campaign. Secondly, after the war broke out, although China and Japan fought fiercely on the battlefield, diplomatic negotiations have not been interrupted. On July 17th, Chiang Kai-shek published The Last Moment and he set down his "determination" of resistance the next day in his diary, saying that this last resort to Japan was also the "only" resort.[85] On the third day of the publication of The Last Moment, Xu Shiying, the Chinese Ambassador to Japan still visited Koki Hirota, Japanese Foreign Minister. In the following days, the

---

[85] サンケイ新聞社著『蔣介石秘録』(II), 東京, サンケイ published the special version revised on October 31st, 1985, p. 205.

Japanese ambassador to China, Kawagoe Shigeru and other people also had frequent contact with Chinese officials. Until the eve, Japan announced that it "does not take the National Government as its opponent", the German ambassador to China and Japan also intervened between China and Japan. Even excluding whether there exists the effect of Matsui's opposition in negotiation, the path of mediation became narrower and finally got to the point of failure. Matsui's "completely victory" is the most important reason of attacking Nanjing.[86]

Now we can come to the following conclusion: Even with the strictest standards, Iwane Matsui's performances consist to one of the main crimes of "anti-peace crime", "the crime of aggression against China". Without sufficient evidence, the Tokyo Trial made the improper exempted responsibility judgment. That Iwane Matsui was listed as the Class A war criminal is indeed appropriate, and there is no "injustice" at all.[87]

4 Further Discussion

In the Tokyo Trial, the Indian judge, Radha Binod Pal, is the only one to plead that all the defendants are innocent. He said in his "judgement", which refuted the verdict of the Tokyo Trial over a thousand pages:

> Although this tribunal (referred to the charter of the International Military Tribunal for the Far East—from the author) is in a legal form, it is essentially for political purposes only.[88]

Nowadays, Radha Binod Pal's extreme proposition still has a wide influence in Japan. There are ideological reasons such as national emotions and other legal reasons, like the so-called "anti-peace crime" and "anti-human

---

[86] Seen from the whole process of mediation, the price of the Japanese negotiations has been rising with the favorable conditions on the battlefield. At the beginning, the declaration of "not regarding the National Government as the opponent" means there is no room for the National Government negotiating to reclaim Nanjing.「『國民政府ヲ相手ニセズ』政府聲明」, 外務省編『日本外交年表竝主要文書』（下）「年表」, 東京, 原書, 1st edition, November 25th, 1965, p. 386.

[87] In the Tokyo Trial, Dutch Judge Lehring thought: "even if the 'anti-humanity crime' and 'anti-peace' is guilty, it shouldn't be sentenced to death if the person who doesn't commit a common war crime".『レーリンク判事の東京裁判』, p. 92. Some Japanese scholars have similar ideas. For example, Onuma Yasuaki, who held some doubt for "Criminal Statutory", thought the crime of anti-peace violated Criminal Statutory, while it shouldn't be used to verdict that it violated the existing international. There is no doubt that it is right for people who advocate the "Criminal Statutory" just hope to protect their rights.
Onuma Yasuaki's work『東京裁判から戦後責任の思想へ』, 東京, 有信堂高文社, 1st edition, May 30, 1985, p. 33. We don't discuss the measurement of penalty in this paper.

[88]『共同研究 パル判決書』(II), p. 739.

crime" are ex post facto laws. But under the limited conditions at that time, the prosecution and the court have not closely refuted the evidence presented by the defendant and the defense at the fact level is the basic meaningful reason. Therefore, to eliminate the stubborn view that the "Tokyo Trial is the trial of the Victors", reconstructing the evidence that can withstand the test is a more powerful and effective work than "arguing".

Although the Tokyo Trial took place in 60 years ago, for the historical issues, neither China nor Japan has completely known the true history. As the largest victim of East Asia in World War II, this work still has its own special meaning.

Originally published in the Modern Chinese History Studies, 2008(6)

A Study of the Massacre Order for Japanese Troops

I

Japanese troops, after occupying Nanjing on December 13th, 1937, violated the international rules and customs of warfare[1] and committed a series of crimes. On the top was the slaughter of prisoners. Over the past years, fictionalists[2] have specially wrote about this. They claimed Japanese troops did not slaughter war prisoners, except that a few plainclothes soldiers who undermined public security were legally executed, and that large numbers of war prisoners were freed, enslaved or imprisoned. The Battle of Nanjing, the so-called Japanese "official" record of the Nanjing Incident,[3] puts as follows:

[1] There is a popular argument in Japan that the Tokyo Trial is subject to ex post facto law and thus is illegal since the law is not retroactive. For instance, Susumu Nishibe once said, "It is kind of legal fraud that the International Military Tribunal for the Far East (IMTFE), or the Tokyo trial, delivered its judgement based on 'crimes against peace' and 'crimes against humanity'. Since these crimes are ex post facto provided for, the Tokyo Trail openly violated the principle of nulla poena sine lege, at least in terms of legal procedure." (Susumu Nishibe. Atarashii Rekishi Kyokasho Tsukurukai (Ed.). The Moral of Nationals. Tokyo: Fusosha. 1st Edition published on October 30, 2001: pp. 131–132.) Higashinakano Shudo also said that the Tokyo Trial was based on ex post facto law, trampling on the principle of 'Non-Retroactivity of Law'." (Higashinakano Shudo. A Thorough Examination of the "Nanjing Massacre". Tokyo: Tendensha. 4th Printing in July, 2000: p. 375.)

[2] In Japan those who have different opinions on the Nanjing Massacre are divided as the "Great Slaughter School" (who affirm the Nanjing Massacre), the Fabrication School (who deny the Nanjing Massacre) and the Moderate School (who affirm part of the Nanjing Massacre). As the Fabrication School and the Moderate School have similar opinion on the slaughter of captives, fictionalists mentioned herein include those who stand in middle of the road.

[3] Many Japanese fictionalists also refer to the "Nanjing Massacre" as "Nanjing Incident". For instance, Kasahara Tokushi said, "The Incident of the Nanjing Massacre is called Nanjing Incident for short." (Kasahara Tokushi.「数字いじりの不毛な論争は虐殺の実態解明を遠ざける」. In Association for Nanjing Incident Investigation (Ed.).『南京大虐殺否定論13のウソ』. Tokyo: Kashiwa Shobo. 4th Printing on March 30, 2001: p. 92.) But the reason why they refer to it as an incident is that they did not admit the "Nanjing Massacre", so the words "Nanjing Massacre" are in quotes so as to indicate it is an "alleged" slaughter.

© The Author(s) 2020
Z. Cheng, *The Nanjing Massacre and Sino-Japanese Relations*,
https://doi.org/10.1007/978-981-15-7887-8_4

... The foregoing words have specified as much as possible how our troops respectively dealt with soldiers who surrendered, defeated and injured or wore plain clothes regardless of war situation or missions. But there still remain a lot to be clarified.

Five situations may follow: One is that they were officially imprisoned as captives; they were disarmed and then freed; they fled after taken prisoners; things remained unknown after they were imprisoned. And the last is that they received awarding sentence...

It can be inferred that the awarding sentence is Japanese troops' combat act based on task command or due to the outbreak of resistance riots or concerns thereof. But further explanation about this are rarely seen in combat reports.[4]

The Army Operations during the China Incident, an authoritative work of Japanese military history, puts as follows:

It is impossible to cite the exact figures of all items. But most of the corpses in the vicinity of Nanjing were the result of combats, which cannot be described as a planned and organized "slaughter".[5]

Unemoto Masaki puts in *The Truth: The Naking Incident*,

In the Dairy and articles, Scharffenberg and John D. Rabe compared Japanese troops' acts to Genghis Khan's war of conquering the Europe or to the holocaust started by Hitler, Stalin or Pol Pot without any specific examples. They even offer anything but a specific example about separate, or accidental events.[6]

And *The Alleged "Nanking Massacre": Japan's Rebuttal to China's Forged Claims*,[7] a newly published representative work of Japanese fictionalists, claims that even plainclothes soldiers arrested in the mopping-up operations who were most likely to be executed were still not.

---

[4] Battle of Nanking Editorial Committee (Ed.). The Battle of Nanjing (Not For Sale). Tokyo: Kaikosha. 1st Edition published on November 3rd, 1989: p. 336.

[5] The Office of War History of the National Institution for Defense Studies under Ministry of Defense. Japanese Army Operations in the China Incident: Volume 1. Tokyo: Asakumo shimbunsha. 1st Edition published on July 25, 1975: p. 437.

[6] Unemoto Masaki. The Truth about the Nanjing Incident: Scrutiny of John Rabe's Diary. Tokyo: Bunkyo-shuppan. 2nd Edition published on February 1, 1999: p. 224. For further argument for why Unemoto's "scrutiny" are completely invalid, please refer to my article A Scrutiny of the Scrutiny of John Rabe's Diary (Beijing: Modern Chinese History Studies. 2002(2): pp. 150–183).

[7] This book is a "representative work" for the following reasons: First, it completely negates the "Nanjing Massacre", which can be seen from the subtitle "Japan's Rebuttal to China's Forged Claims"; second, instead of making a scrutiny as those of the same pinion, this book is an amalgam of comments, more like an editorial; third, this book, bilingual in Japanese and English, is not directed against Japanese slaughter school as what other writings has done, but against the world, as is expressly stated in the first sentence on the end paper "A First Round

Most Chinese soldiers arrest by Japanese troops in the mopping-up operations were put into the Nanjing Jail. The number of prisoners amounted to about 10,000, of which a half were sent to Shanghai as labor force at the end of December and others were incorporated into the Nanjing Government Army which was founded by Wang Zhaoming in 1940. They could be anything but executed.[8]

All the fictionalists do not agree with the assertion of "no execution". Some admit the existence of "execution" but denies it to be "an organized action", let alone a top-down order. Nakamura Akira put in *China: Who should Reflect on History*,

> It is true fact that some Chinese people were illegally killed but this was a kind of accidental, sporadic event and could not be a planned large-scale action of troops.[9]

As there are large numbers of written or video records about the slaughter of prisoners (of which the relevant records by Japanese organizations and individuals at that time matter most[10]) as well as incontestable evidence such as remains, the so-called "no execution" at the factual level matters little. Hence, this essay focuses on whether Japanese troops' slaughtering prisoners was a top-down order.

II

During the Japanese Invasion of China, Japanese troops at all levels kept a lot of records but later to avoid sanctions, burnt quite a lot. Besides, private records, more as they were, mostly have not been published in deference to

---

of Counterattacks on Anti-Japan Activities in the U.S."; fourth, although from the end paper we can see the rebuttals were aimed at activities "in the U.S.", but in the preface it is said that this book is intended as an "inform letter" to those directed against... and intended to raise concern over China's claims of the "Nanjing Massacre" since ... the origin of the message in international anti-Japan network, which press Japan to take responsibilities for war crimes, lies in China; fifth, it is frequently mentioned that China has "anti-Japan" sentiment but what we can see in the book is rampant anti-China sentiment; sixth, although on the cover is the signature of Takemoto Tadao and Ohara Yasuo, on the copyright page "Japan Committee for Communique of International Conference" and "Representative Takemoto Tadao" were used to replace individual signature—Japan Committee for Communique of International Conference is a major right-wing group, this book thus can be regarded as an "official" document of the right-wing forces.

[8] Takemoto Tadao, Ohara Yasuo. Japan Committee for Communique of International Conference (Ed.). The Alleged "Nanking Massacre": Japan's Rebuttal to China's Forged Claims. Tokyo: Meisei-sha. 2nd Printing on December 25, 2000: p. 73.

[9] San Nakamura. 「過去の歴史を反省すべきは中国の方だ」. Seiron, Tokyo: Sankei Shinbun. February 2010 Issue: p. 67.

[10] Cheng Zhaoqi. Was the Nanjing Massacre Fabricated by the Tokyo Tribunal?. Beijing: Modern Chinese History Studies. 2002(6): pp. 1–57.

the will of the author or his family as the Second Sino-Japanese War is universally known as a war of aggression and has been thoroughly discredited—even in Japan, those who are "advocates of the Great East Asia War",[11] like Fusao Hayashi, are also in a minority. As a result, only a few remain today and available to us is a smaller fraction.[12]

However, this small number of records have included a significant number of Japanese troops' atrocities. They, written by those perpetrators, particularly can be valid evidence. Hence, to deny the atrocities Japanese troops perpetrated in Nanjing, fictionalists have to refute these records first. To refute these records, the way to deal with evidence from Chinese, i.e., showing a total disregard or claiming it "made up", does not work. Instead, a "reasonable" explanation is a must. Radically, it is a paradox as far-fetched notions cannot turn the "existence" into "nonexistence". But fictionalists' persistence in "explaining" it does make things unclear. And therefore, discussions nowadays on the atrocities of Japanese troops can anything but avoid the clarification of those "explanations".

Among the records of Japanese troops' slaughtering captives, three pieces that indicate the massacre order "contradict" each other. One is Lieutenant General Kesago Nakajima's diary on December 13th, who then served as Head of the 16th Division, one of the major forces attacking Nanjing. Another is the battle report of the 1st Battalion of the 66th Infantry Regiment of the 114th Division. The third is some notes in Major General Yamada Senji's diary on December 15th, who then served the 103rd Infantry Brigade of the 13th Division. We then move on to discuss these three pieces of records.

Among Japanese armies' clear records of killing captives that have remained, the one by Kesago Nakajima on December 13th marks the highest level. It puts as follows:

> <u>Firstly, in principle, we would not take prisoners</u> (Note: bullets here are marked by me and the same case will no longer be pointed out), so captives were dealt with in the first place. But as a group of 1000, 5000 or 10000 people, they were unlikely to be disarmed immediately. They, already-given-up, just streamed following us. It seemed to be in a safe condition, but once a riot broke, things would just run away. So some forces were dispatched through trucks to oversee and guide them.

---

[11] Fusao Hayashi. The Great East Asia War was A Just War. Tokyo: Bancho Shobo. 1st Edition on August 5, 1964. Nowadays, the right-wing forces dominate and the assumption of the "Great East Asia War" has become widely popular, but in the 1960s, it was a innovation.

[12] After finishing writing this article, I read a recently published spoken reminiscences of Japanese veterans, but here is no such thing in Japan as it claims that 102 veterans were interviewed. (Tamaki Matsuoka. The Battle of Nanjing—Searching for Forbidden Memories. Tokyo: Shakai-Hyoron-sha. 1st Printing on August 15, 2008.)

In the evening of December 13th, a large quantity of trucks were needed but the plan was delayed because just finished a battle, the Staff was too busy to carry out it – a plan not the same as designed at the start.[13]

In recent years, this piece of record has been adopted by some textbooks, like *The History of the World* (Version B) published by Hitotsubashi University and *The History of Japan* (Version B) published by Practical Education Press. Fictionalists and the so-called middle-of-the-road then have regarded it as a major weak point and tried to find excuses to deny this record. Yoshiaki Itakura wrote *The Truth of the Nanking Incident* and put as follows:

> The big problem is that there are various explanations about the "policy of not taking prisoners in principle". And I have to say that the same idea lies in the order of the 30th Infantry Brigade –"All levels are allowed to take prisoners under instructions of the divisions", mentioned in the battle report of the 38th Infantry Regiment on December 14th. It means that "<u>captives were disarmed and then released</u>", which is the most powerful evidence. However, disputes arise as it has not been <u>clearly stated in positive words</u>.[14]

Higashinakano Shudo and Yoshiaki Itakura are like-minded but the former has expressed himself more clearly. In the Naking Massacre: Fact Versus Fiction—A Historian's Quest for the Truth, he claims that there are many "questionable points" about taking Kesago Nakajima's order as "an order to kill captives", which can be summarized into seven points:

> First, if the order for not taking prisoners meant "immediately executing soldiers who surrendered", words must be passed not only to the 16th Division but also the other ones. However, official records except the 16th Division's have mentioned anything but the "execution order".
>
> Second, it is also argued that Mr. Nakajjima, the division commander, gave the "execution order" only to the 16th Division. If so, there must be words about the questionable "execution order" in the official records of the 16th Division. But in fact, there was none.
>
> Third, it has been mentioned that the 16th Division "has dealt with this from the very beginning". If it meant that they indiscriminately killed people they have encountered, no matter 10 or 20, gunshots no doubt could be heard from the start. If so, why did "groups of 1000, 5000 or even 10000 who wanted to flee but failed" surrender?
>
> Fourth, at the sight of mountainous corpses, why didn't soldiers go into panic but instead streamed to surrender?

---

[13] Kesago Nakajima's Diary. In Battle of Nanking Editorial Committee (Ed.). Documents on the Battle of Nanjing (Not For Sale). Tokyo: Kaikosha. 1st Edition published on November 3, 1989: p. 336.

[14] Yoshiaki Itakura. 『本当はこうだった南京事件』. Tokyo: Nihon Tosho Kankoka. 2nd Printing on January 20, 2000: p. 370.

Fifth, Division Commander Mr. Nakajjima "called for trucks to oversee and guide those who surrendered". If he favored the policy of "immediately killing them on the spot", why did he not do but bothered to ask for some forces?

Sixth, could Mr. Nakajjima disobey orders? If the answer is yes, why he still insisted on "disarming them"? Had he carried out the plan designed at the start, forces and trucks would not be hurried there.

Besides, there is another point; that is, if <u>the policy of immediately killing captives was designed at the start</u>, Mr. Nakajjima would obey and tried his best to carry out the "order for killing soldiers who surrendered", but as it was impossible to kill such a big group of 1000, 5000 or 10000, he must say a few words about it.[15]

Ruling out a diverse variety of explanations, Higashinakano Shudo claimed to have understood the "true meaning": As put in Miyamoto's Diary, had soldiers not disarmed, it would be impossible to fully implement the "policy of not taking prisoners". That is to say, "disarming" Chinese soldiers is a means to an end—"not taking prisoners". <u>In other words, "the so-called 'policy of not taking prisoners' means that 'soldiers who surrendered would be disarmed and told to leave instead of being taken as prisoners'"</u>. Also, Miyamoto stressed that if the "policy of not taking prisoners" means shooting the captives, it would be clearly stated as "a policy of shooting all the captives".[16]

The Alleged "Naking Massacre" shares the mere thoughts mentioned above and says,

> In context, "the proper disposal of captives" cannot be simply interpreted as "execution" but appropriately as "release in a proper manner".[17]

What does "disposal" mean? Does it mean "release" This is not up to the "context", and in the context, their thoughts, which we will examine and explain one by one, make no sense.

The "execution order" is never touched on in official records other than that of the 16th Division—the first point cannot vouch for the nonexistence of the order. Reasons are as follows: First of all, to avoid accountability, Japan burnt a large quantity of records before the Tokyo Trial, and then records that still remain today are incomplete, which cannot prove that other divisions did not keep a record. Second, even if other divisions did not receive the command, it does not mean that the 16th Division did not take the order, because all commands are not taken by troops at all levels, which is often the case in peacetime and more often in difficult situation of wartime, and different troops can carry out either the same task or different ones. And last, changes may occur at any time in a war, and the troops enjoy autonomy

---

[15] Higashinakano Shudo. A Thorough Examination of the "Nanjing Massacre". pp. 116–117.
[16] Higashinakano Shudo. A Thorough Examination of the "Nanjing Massacre". p. 119.
[17] The Alleged "Nanking Massacre": Japan's Rebuttal to China's Forged Claims. p. 76.

in dealing with them. This does not corroborate the old saying "A general at the front may even refuse an emperor's order" but means the "execution order" might be a decision exclusively made by the 16th Division.

The second point says that the "execution order" should have been touched on in the official records of the 16th Division. But the word "should" does not make sense, because The Status Report of the 16th Division and A Summary of the Battle by the 16th Division—these two "official records" are too brief to a proof. The Report does not touch on the "enemy forces", whether captured or killed, in the Part of Status, Military Discipline, Education, Weapons, Management, Sanitation and Horse Health, while the Summary just briefly refers to their destroying enemies who gained advantage, for instance, at the fork road of Yaohua Gate on December 13th but not mention whether those enemies were captured or slaughtered. These brief documents taken for reference, neither major elements of Kesago Nakajima's diary nor the commands of Japanese Central China Area Army (CCAA) or Shanghai Expeditionary Army (SEF), can be found in the "official records of the 16th Division". Didn't these exist? Obviously, the answer is no.

The third point says that "captives has been dealt with from the beginning" ... and that 10 or 20 people were absolutely executed at the start. But the problem is that at the start had came groups of 1000, 5000 or even 10,000 so that Kesago Nakajima was taken unawares.

The fourth argument that soldiers who surrendered, at the sight of mountainous corpses, did not go into panic but instead obediently followed can be challenged because where they went was not the killing field and they were lured to other place and then be slaughtered, of which the details can be seen in Kesago Nakajima's diary mentioned later.

The fifth point and sixth point argue that Mr. Nakajjima "called for more trucks to oversee and guide those who surrendered" and insisted on "disarming" instead of "immediately killing them on the spot". These can be challenged due to the same reason for the third point: Japanese troops were facing large corps rather than stragglers, and it was impossible to "immediately kill them on the spot". Mr. Nakajjima did not "insisted" and had no choice but to "disarm them" so as to avoid loss and to "deal with" those soldiers.

As for the argument that captives "were in such a large quantity that could not be killed", I agree. But since this point is true, why did the third, fourth, fifth and sixth points develop? Don't they constitute a paradox? Higashinakano Shudo's so-called questions make no sense.

After those cited above, there are still two paragraphs in Kesago Nakajima's diary, which can be an answer to forgoing question.

> First, it was learned later that Sasaki's force alone had dealt with 150,000 people and a squadron leader who garrisoned at the Taiping Gate handled 1300 people. And near the Xianhe Gate gathered about seven or eight thousand people. Besides, people came one after another to surrender.

And this paragraph is followed by the assumption of those who were not be "dealt with".

> First, to hold seven or eight thousand people, a big ditch was needed but could not be easily found. In that case, they were divided into groups of one or two hundred and then <u>lured to a right place for disposal</u>.[18]

These two pieces of records, respectively, referring to the result and the plan of "disposal", is the clear evidence of slaughtering captives and such intention.

And the argument that if meaning "shooting the captives", "the policy of not taking prisoners" would be clearly stated as "a policy of shooting all the captives", is ridiculous, otherwise it can also be said that if referring to "release the captives", "the policy of not taking prisoners" would be clearly stated as "a policy of releasing all the captives".

These two paragraphs and the foregoing quotations combined, Kesago Nakajima's diary on this day can be said to a complete, top-down record, from the assumption to result, of Japanese troops' slaughtering captives, which allows no leeway to those "questions". One who is objective will know there exists no weak points in such record. But Higashinakano Shudo has a different understanding and with a slim chance, still tries to make a difference. He quoted the first paragraph mentioned above and said:

> The "disposal" can be explained in three ways:
> One is that it refers to the disposal of all the soldiers who surrendered. If there were 15 thousand people killed in the area to the north-east of Purple Mountain and the Nanjing City, 1300 people killed at the Taiping Gate and around seven or eight thousand people killed near the Xianhe Gate (Note: To be specific, near the Xianhemen County), there must be a record of the burial site (and even so is the witness testimony). But there are no corpses. Without corpses, it cannot be taken into account the possibility that all the soldiers who surrendered were killed.
> Another is that it refers to the disposal of soldiers who surrendered but later resisted. Article 8 of Laws and customs of war on land (Hague, IV) provides that harsh tactics can be imposed on captives in case of any disobedience, which was legal under the international rules and customs of warfare. But could there be such a large quantity of soldiers killed?
> Last, it can, as the foregoing materials put, refer to "disarming and releasing soldiers who surrendered instead of being taken as prisoners." [19]

The questionable points in Higashinakano Shudo's "explanation" are in fact beyond dispute: Kesago Nakajima searched for "ditches", lured soldiers

---

[18] Kesago Nakajima's Diary. In Battle of Nanjing Editorial Committee (Ed.). Documents on the Battle of Nanjing. p. 326.

[19] 東中野修道著『「南京虐殺」の徹底検証』,第122页.

who surrendered to appropriate places and disposed them—this paragraph has stated clearly. Isn't it the most powerful evidence? Higashinakano "disregards the whole picture" and picks out some passages that can be used to his advantage, which just indicates that he has no intention of seeking out the truth.

The foregoing account written by Kesago Nakajima is believable not only because it is reasonable within the "context" but because a lot of records by Japanese troops at all levels and personally by soldiers can be positive evidence of it. When again examining relevant war records by Japanese troops on other days, I noticed some that have been ignored. A piece of record, not direct as it is, can be a powerful indirect evidence of slaughtering captive. That is a brigade-level command issued by the 30th Infantry Brigade of the 16th Division at 4:50 before the dawn on December 14th. Article 6 of the command provides that all divisions, if without new instructions, are not allowed to take prisoners.[20] The so-called "not allowed to take prisoners" can be explained in many ways. But Major Yoshio Kodama, who served as Lieutenant of the 38th Regiment under the 30th Brigade, once wrote about this incident:

> It was when we were involved in a terrible fight against enemies one or two kilometers away from Nanjing that the division lieutenant phoned and gave the order that Chinese soldiers who surrendered were not allowed to be taken prisoners but disposed. It was surprising to receive such an order. Although Lieutenant General Kesago Nakajima, the director of the Division, was a greathearted general with charm, we could be anything but pleased to accept this order. Surprised and confused as the whole army was, we still had to pass the order to the battalions. And then no battalion reported on this matter.[21]

Yoshio Kodama's account was written before Kesago Nakajima's diary and thus cannot be directed against any issue. His account of "not allowed" is just the most direct and clearest evidence that the order for "not allowed to take prisoners" was issued by the 30th Division. And taken into account the situation in that time and the documents that have remained, the order can only be understood as killing all the captives. Kesago Nakajima's diary, the order of the 30th Division and Yoshio Kodama's account are of a piece and completely involve all the levels up to down, i.e., the division, the brigade and the battalions. Hence, the record in Kesago Nakajima's diary is reliable without any doubt.

---

[20] Order of the 13th Infantry Brigade. In Battle of Nanking Editorial Committee (Ed.). Documents on the Battle of Nanjing. p. 545.

[21] Battle of Nanking Editorial Committee (Ed.). The Battle of Nanjing. pp. 341–344 (Table occupies two pages).

III

The battle report of the 1st Battalion of the 66th Regiment of the 114th Division is also positive proof that the slaughter of captives was based on a top-down order.

The record was as follows:

> Eighth, the following orders were received from the Head of superior battalion at 2 p.m.
> The Document was as follows:
> First, kill all the captives in accordance with the order from the Brigade;
> You can divide captives into groups of 10 and then shoot them group by group. How do you like it?
> Second, collect the weapons and send troops for surveillance before receiving new instructions;
> Third, all the regiments send the major forces to carry out the mopping-up operations in the city in accordance with the order from the division;
> And your battalion still carry out the previous commission.
> Ninth, in accordance with orders mentioned above, the first and the fourth Squadron were ordered to collect all the weapons and send soldiers for surveillance.
> At 3.30 p.m., heads of the squadrons were gathered to discuss how to execute those captives. And it was decided that captives were distributed equally to the squadrons (the 1st, 3rd and 4th Squadron) and taken out of the cells in batches of 50 one by one to certain place and then killed them. The 1st Squadron took captives to the valley on the south of the camp, the 3rd Squadron took them to the hollow on the south-west of the camp and the 4th Squadron took them to the valley on the south-east of the camp.
> But please mind that send soldiers to guard the cells and put them on alert and make sure captives do not know why they were taken out. Squadrons had prepared them by 5 p.m. and then started to kill them. The slaughter ended at 7.30 p.m.
> Then report was submitted to the Regiment.
> The 1st Squadron did not follow the schedule proposed and intended to incarnate the captives in a place and burned them but failed.
> Some captives learned what would happen and became no longer afraid: Their heads were erect and their backs were straight before the sabers and bayonets, totally in a calm manner. Also, there were some lamenting and begging for mercy. Especially when squadron heads came to make an inspection, laments could be heard here and there.[22]

If Kesago Nakajima's diary which involves part of senior military orders cannot be relied on, this pieced of record by the 1st Battalion of the 66th Regiment involves not only the order but how it was carried out and thus

---

[22] The 1st Battalion of the 66th Infantry Regiment. The Battle Report. In Battle of Nanking Editorial Committee (Ed.). Documents on the Battle of Nanjing. pp. 673–674.

is specific evidence to killing captives perpetrated by Japanese troops at primary level. And since the 114th Division is attached to the 10th Army and the 16th Division attached to the Shanghai Expeditionary Army, we can infer that slaughtering the captives was not "accidentally" perpetrated by certain troop but all the troops.

This piece of record, like Kesago Nakajima's diary, was questioned by Japanese fictionalists. "The 66th Infantry Regiment The Yuhuatai Incident", a section in the 3rd chapter of *The Truth of the Nanking Incident* by Yoshiaki Itakura[23] specially discussed on this matter. It puts as follows:

> If examined totally and carefully, this battle report would be found to be of quite dubious value and to be likely to have been revised later.
> To examine the battle report of the 1st Battalion of the 66th Division, the following types of first-grade materials can be taken for reference:
> Orders from the D Army (the 10th Army);
> The battle reports by the 114th Division and other documents thereof, and those by Mr. Isoda, Chief of Staff;
> The reports on battles near Nanjing (including the orders from the 128th Brigade) and the wartime logs by the 150th Infantry Regiment and the 2nd Battalion of the 66th Infantry Regiment.
> ......
>
> Generally speaking, there are three questionable points about the battle report by the 66th Infantry Regiment. <u>One is there are confusing words about the order issued from the Command to the battalions. Another is that the account of the battle situation greatly differs from that of the real conditions. And the third is that the date mentioned in the report and the timing of the operations cannot be determined.</u>[24]

When examining Kesago Nakajima's diary, we cannot just conclude the existence of the slaughter based on documents written in the same perspective, without other evidence—since records are partly lost, orders vary from person to person and some operations are limited to certain troop. But we are still willing to take the foregoing documents, the so-called "first-grade materials", for reference to check whether the battle report of the 1st Battalion is consistent with the "context" and whether it "distorts the facts".

---

[23] Yoshiaki Itakura admitted that Japanese troops killed one thousand people and thus falls into the category of the "Small Slaughter School" under the Moderate School. (Some of the moderate school believe the number of people slaughtered were around ten thousand, such as Hata Ikuhiko argues for the figure of 4 thousand, and they are called the "Medium Slaughter School".) But the viewpoints of the small slaughter school are basically similar to those of the fabrication school, especially opinions on the scrutiny of certain facts, so Yoshiaki Itakura herein is referred to as a member of the fabrication school.

[24] Yoshiaki Itakura. 『本当はこうだった南京事件』. pp. 125–126.

Lieutenant General Yanagawa Heisuke, the commander of the 10th Army once made a famous speech, saying that our enemy includes every mountain and river, every bush and tree.[25] Adhering to this general policy, the 10th Army continuously ordered the subordinate troops to "wipe out" the enemies in the entire process of attacking Nanjing. For instance, Article 3 of "Class-A Combat Order No. 66 of the 10th Army" on December 12th provides that the main force of Kunisaki Brigade shall occupy the neighboring area of Pukou and <u>wipe out remaining enemies</u> while Article 2 of the "Extra to Class-A Combat Order of the 10th Army" on December 13th provides that the 10th Army shall <u>wipe out the enemies in the Walled City of Nanjing</u>.[26]

When attacking Nanjing, the 114th Division also continuously issued the same order. Article 2 of the "Class-A Combat Order No. 62 of the 114th Division" issued at 9.30 a.m. on December 13th provides that the Division shall continue to attack Nanjing and <u>wiped out the enemies in the city</u> and Article 3 thereof provides that the flanks shall enter the city and <u>by all means, wipe out enemies</u>, in addition to shelling.[27]

The 66th Regiment was not subordinate to the 128th Infantry Brigade but the 127th Brigade. But since orders of the latter has been lost and the 128th Brigade acted, as Yoshiaki Itakura mentioned, "near the Nanjing City", their orders can be taken "for reference". Article 1 of "Order No. 66 of the 128th Infantry Brigade" provides that the Division shall continue to attack Nanjing and wipe out enemies in the city and Article 3 thereof provides that the two regiments at the front shall launch an all-out attack to enter the city and shall <u>wipe out the enemies at all costs and if necessary, burn the city</u> to allow no leeway for any cheating by remaining enemies.[28]

And as Yoshiaki Itakura put, the 66th Regiment "did not engage in combat" and merely kept a record of the orders, so we don't have to cite the records again.

From the foregoing analysis, we can see that

For one thing, the 10th Army issued the order for "wiping out the enemies in the city" at 8.30 a.m. on December 13th; the 114th Division issued the order for "by all means wiping out enemies" one hour later, i.e. at 9.30 a.m.; under the command, the 128th Infantry Brigade issued the order for "wiping out enemies at all costs" at 12 o'clock; and the 1st Battalion of the 66th Regiment received the order for "killing all the captives in accordance

---

[25] Naoki Inose (Supervisor). Masaki Takanashi (Ed.). 『目撃者が語る日中戦争』. Tokyo: Shin Jinbutsu Ōraisha. 1st Edition published on December 10, 1989, p. 69.

[26] No. 66 Class-A Combat Order of the 10th Army. In Battle of Nanking Editorial Committee (Ed.). Documents on the Battle of Nanjing. p. 554.

[27] No. 62 Class-A Combat Order of the 114th Division. In Battle of Nanking Editorial Committee (Ed.). Documents on the Battle of Nanjing. p. 556.

[28] No. 66 Combat Order of the 128th Infantry Brigade. In Battle of Nanking Editorial Committee (Ed.). Documents on the Battle of Nanjing. p. 557.

with the Brigade order" from the Regiment at 2 p.m.—from the perspective of timing, the foregoing orders do not contradict the battle report by the 1st Battalion of the 66th Regiment and are logically consistent with each other.

For another, from the perspective of content, although there are a few differences between the expressions of the orders by the 10th Army, the 114th Division and the 128th Brigade, they are totally consistence with each other in the principle of "wiping out enemies". And "at all costs" mentioned in the division and brigade order is particularly noteworthy. Armed with this dispensation, Japanese troops disregarded those "cautions" mentioned in the "Advice concerning the Capture of and Entry into the Walled City of Nanjing, such as the so-called "no damage to the reputation of Imperial Japanese Army", on which fictionalists have based their argument. Hence, the actions the 1st Battalion of the 66th Regiment took did not violate the provision but instead was logical consequence of the "wiping-out" order.

According to many Japanese records at that time, Chinese troops who surrendered followed one after another and did arouse Japanese authority's concern, as Kesago Nakajima had, over "out-breaking of riots". Therefore, even if disregarding the possibility of "revenge" or "venting their rage", it was quite natural for Japanese troops to kill all the captives from their standpoint, about which there exists no questionable point. So the account in the battle report by the 1st Battalion of the 66th Regiment can be one piece of important evidence to Japanese troops' slaughtering captives.

IV

In addition to foregoing two pieces of materials, records by Major General Yamada Senji, commander of the 103rd Infantry Brigade, are also very controversial. One of the troops under the 103rd Infantry Brigade (attached to the 13th Division) encountered large quantities of captives at the neighboring area after capturing the Mufu Mountain and commanding officer of the Brigade Yamada Senji called for the Shanghai Expeditionary Army and the superior division to imprison those captives. His diary on December 15th put as follows:

> A cavalry second lieutenant was sent to Nanjing to report on issues concerning disposal of captives.
> <u>The reply was killing all of them</u>.
> It is confusing that troops at all levels have no reserve of food.[29]

---

[29] Battle of Nanking Editorial Committee (Ed.). Documents on the Battle of Nanjing (Not For Sale). Tokyo: Kaikosha. 1st Edition published on December 8, 1993: p. 331. Before the publication of this diary, fictionalists, if citing it, would fiddle with key paragraphs. For example, Suzuki Aki replaces "killing all" with "the whole story" in The Illusion of the "Nanking Massacre", the first edition 1973, and the change remained in later editions. (Suzuki Aki. The Illusion of the "Nanjing Massacre". Tokyo: Bungei Shunjû. 15th Printing on May 30, 1989: p. 193.) As Suzuki Aki also replaced "disposal" with "the whole story", it was difficult to point

Next day, Yamada Senji sent his adjutant Lieutenant Colonel Shunji Aida for Shanghai Expeditionary Army to imprison those captives and again received the "killing" order[30]. Suzuki Aki once interviewed Yamada Senji and wrote the following words:

> Mr. Yamada said, almost to himself, at this point, "it will be confusing if these words are published." It was the royal family (Prince Yasuhiko Asaka) that supported Mr. Yamada's advocacy of "protecting captives under a regular procedure" but forced him to "dispose" those captives. This point might still be the focus. But based on the sequence of those words, we can know it was Colonel Mr. Cho (Note: Isamu Cho was a Lieutenant Colonel then).[31]

Whether Suzuki Aki was more eligible to make a conclusion than individuals involved and whether he blamed on Isamu Cho to cover up the royal family's wrong decision[32]—these points set aside, however, Brigade commander Yamada Senji's diary and the account for his memory is still a clear proof that the 103rd Brigade received the massacre order.

Japanese fictionalists later mostly have argued about this. For example, Ooi Mitsuru spends one chapter to specially argue on this matter in The Fictitious "Nanking Massacre".[33] The chapter is named as "The Yamada Brigade and Captive Riots", from which we can see that Ooi Mitsuru blames the slaughter on those "captives"; that is, he thinks it was "captives who raised a riot" that caused Japanese troops to take "defensive" actions. Ooi Mitsuru quotes Second Lieutenant Sadaharu Hirabayashi as saying that "why we bothered a lot if we really did intend to kill them". He also said,

---

out the different meanings of "the whole story". And this puzzling expression remained until the publication of Document on the Battle of Nanjing: Volume II which was edited by the Battle of Nanjing Editorial Committee.

[30] Noboru Kojima. The Sino-Japanese War: Volume III 1937–1945. Tokyo: Bungei Shunjû. 1st Edition on July 1, 1984: p. 203. This record was paraphrased by Noboru Kojima, not the original diary, and it also differs from that in Documents on the Battle of Nanjing: Volume II, edited by the Battle of Nanjing Editorial Committee. Hence, Kenji Ono, the editor of the Imperial Japanese Soldiers Witnessing the Nanjing Massacre, thinks Yamada's Diary included in Documents on the Battle of Nanjing: Volume II is likely to have been partly deleted. (「虐殺か解放か―――山田支隊捕虜約二万の行方」. In Association for Nanjing Incident Investigation (Ed.). 『南京大虐殺否定論13のウソ』. Tokyo: Kashiwa Shobo. 4th Printing on March 30, 2001: pp. 146–147.)

[31] Suzuki Aki. The Illusion of the "Nanjing Massacre". p. 193.

[32] Iwane Matsui claimed to take all the responsibilities in the Tokyo Trial because he did not get Prince Yasuhiko Asaka involved in. Up to now, Japanese still have a tendency to cover up the wrong decisions of the royal family.

[33] 「山田旅団と捕虜の暴動」. In Ooi Mitsuru, Chapter 5 of 『仕組まれた「南京大虐殺」―――攻略作戦の全貌とマスコミ報道の怖さ』. Tokyo: Tendensha. 3rd Printing on June 6, 1998: pp. 139–173.

First, nine of our soldiers were killed, which, in a powerful manner, has spoken for itself that there were battles.

Second, on the following day, Maeda Yuji, Masayoshi Arai and Fukasawa Kanosamu in the Domei Tsushin mentioned above, went to the spot for materials and reported on it in detail:

"The captives raised a riot and led to a battle."

The Current of Fighting by Yuji Maeda has dwelt on things of this area, and what Suzuki Aki mentioned was accidental, not least because Yuji Maeda's fellows have added a postscript that it was far from the truth like the Gagging order. However, much of the account was based on supposition, for example,

"The slaughter was planned."

"The Gagging Order was issued to cover the truth".[34]

Whether the fact that "nine of our soldiers were killed in battle" can the most powerful evidence—this is not up to Ooi Mitsuru. At the Mufu Mountain, facing Japanese troops were soldiers who surrendered ten times as many as themself. Ooi Mitsuru himself also mentioned in his book Eiichi Kakuta's squadron took in prison "soldiers who surrendered 30 times as many" and that the total number of captives were up to "40 times as many as guarding soldiers",[35] which has been greatly under-reported to hide the true number of those killed.[36] If at that time did a "riot" take place, how unimaginable it was that thousands of people (the smallest number claimed) were killed while the other side only "nine" were killed (The Battle of Nanjing claims a smaller number, saying that there were totally seven people killed, with a guarding soldier killed on December 16th and an officer and five soldiers killed on the next day[37]). We don't have to deny the possibility that individual soldiers stood against the slaughter, but it was more likely that those nine people were accidentally killed by their fellows. The 2nd Battalion of the 65th Regiment took charge of the neighboring area of the Navy Wharf and started the slaughter at dusk on December 16th while the main force of the 65th Regiment took charge of the waterfront 4 kilometers on the east of Shangyuan Gate and the slaughter lasted from the dusk to midnight on December 17th—"Firefight" could not be avoided even in the day, let alone at such night.

As for why the assertion that the so-called "Gagging Order" is "far from the truth" is "not true", I have dwelt on it in Section 3 of Was the Nanjing Massacre Fabricated by the Tokyo Tribunal and will not go further here. And you, if interested, can take for reference the long article.

---

[34] Ooi Mitsuru. 『仕組まれた「南京大虐殺」―――攻略作戦の全貌とマスコミ報道の怖さ』. pp. 161–162.

[35] Ooi Mitsuru. 『仕組まれた「南京大虐殺」―――攻略作戦の全貌とマスコミ報道の怖さ』. pp. 144+153.

[36] The number is one-third of that recorded by Major General Iinuma Mamoru, Chief of Staff for Shanghai Expeditionary Army.

[37] Battle of Nanking Editorial Committee (Ed.). *The Battle of Nanjing*. p. 325.

Higashinakano Shudo also went into this piece of record. And he made the following comment on Yamada Senji's diary on December 15th.

> It is difficult to understand why Mr. Yamada wrote "it is confusing that troops at all levels have no reserve of food" since the order for "killing all the captives" has nothing to do with the food reserve.
>
> And isn't the shortage of food a great fodder for naturally weakening the enemies? Naturally weakened, enemies will not resist as before, which will avail them to implement the so-called "All-killing" Order. The shortage of food thus could not be a barrier to "killing all the captives".
>
> But if lacking reserves of ammunition, Japanese troops will cannot "kill all" of the enemies. So we will not get confused if Mr. Yamada wrote "It is ordered captives shall be all killed but it is confusing that there is no reserve of ammunition for troops at all levels".[38]

Higashinakano Shudo's explanation about why Yamada Senji's diary is hard to understand really sounds far-fetched because Yamada Senji's account can be anything but "hard to understand": First, if Yamada Senji, as what he told Suzuki Aki in his late years, did not support killing captives but had to obey the order for "all-killing" order, the so-called "no reserve of food" could be "a great fodder" for saving his conscience because "no reserve of food" promised the captives not only death but pain for a longer time. Second, even if Yamada Senji supported the order issued by the Army and the Division, considering Japanese troops were nominally subject to Laws and customs of war on land (Hague, IV) by which killing captives is expressly forbidden, "no reserve of food" still could be "a great fodder" as it could be a good excuse to avoid liability in future. Third, in his diary Yamada Senji did not make an adequate account but briefly took notes. It is uncertain whether there is a causal link between "killing all the captives" and "no reserve of food" and the two sentences might be irrelevant.

Hence, we can see that Yamada Senji's record makes sense and can be anything but incomprehensible. For one thing, it is an undeniable fact that the 65th Regiment slaughtered large quantities of captives, regardless of any reason; for another, Higashinakano Shudo made a "groundless" and "counter-factual" argument as it was impossible that there was "no reserve of ammunition" in the slaughter. Hence, it was Higashinakano Shudo who denies one sentence based on the following one that makes it "hard to understand" and "far from the truth".

Higashinakano Shudo's "explanation" goes further but is basically absurd. So here is cited one point and to be brief, others will not be detailed.

V

Among Japanese records that have remained and published, those that belong to what Japanese fictionalists called "Class-A materials" only have

---

[38] Higashinakano Shudo. *A Thorough Examination of the "Nanjing Massacre"*. p. 131.

included foregoing three pieces that expressly mentioned the order for killing the captives. But many records can be seen in other materials and a account of Sumi Yoshiharu's memory in his late years is quite well-known. He said Tenente Colonnello Isamu Cho who then served as Chief of Staff in the 2nd Department of Shanghai Expeditionary Army's Staff was at the spot and ordered the 6th Division to kill the captives. Since Sumi Yoshiharu is the regular adjutant of General Iwane Matsui, commander of Japanese Central China Area Army, considering his status, what he said is noteworthy. But Sumi Yoshiharu also said Iwane Matsui originally ordered to "release" those captives but Isamu Cho "disobeyed the order".[39] So if what he said is true, Isamu Cho's order for killing the captives is "individual decision" and cannot be taken as official Japanese order. However, there is no doubt that this can be taken as a proof that Japanese troops from the top down slaughtered captives.

The above-mentioned three pieces of records that Japanese troops' slaughtering captives were "systematic murder" are of special value to discover the true history. They are reliable not only because they are reasonable within the "context" but more because they are consistent with the fact. Examining the "context" is an important means to authenticate materials since a piece of material, if against the truth, cannot be "exactly within" the context and even carefully designed, it is unlikely to be flawless and will give itself away. However, written records are subject to certain elements, both subjective and objective, such as the writer's capacity, preference, feeling and acknowledge of the study object. The relationship between the fact and the account thereof is not like that between an original and its copies—a true record cannot always be logical in the "context", so "opinions may vary" from the perspective of "context". This is why things are complicated, why "humanities" are more complicated than "science".

Therefore, when a true material is attacked for no reason, the best response is providing supporting facts.

Japanese fictionalists have always said that Japanese records at the wartime, especially those by Japanese troops, have a tendency to exaggerate their achievements. This statement cannot make sense from the perspective of both "reasoning" and "fact"—those records, even if exaggerating something, do indicate their neglect of moral obligation. And based on Instructions by General Iwane Matsui, commander of Japanese Central China Area Army and Japanese documents concerning enhancing military discipline, which still remain today and have always been mentioned by those fictionalists, records written by Japanese military and other agencies have a tendency more of "under-reporting" than of "exaggerating" Japanese troops' atrocities. Besides, as has mentioned above, after defeated Japan burnt relevant powerful

---

[39] 「角証言」の信憑性について. In Battle of Nanking Editorial Committee (Ed.). *Documents on the Battle of Nanjing*. pp. 758–759.

evidence that they slaughtered captives to avoid after-war trial and in addition to "systematic" killing, a lot are "individually perpetrated" that have not been recorded, leading those relevant materials that still remain today to be a reflection of just part of, or even a tiny part of the truth. Yet all for that, existing records written by Japanese military at the wartime are enough to deny the so-called "no possibility of being executed" that fictionalists have been claiming, such as in *The Alleged "Nanking Massacre"*.

As stated above, Shanghai Expeditionary Army and the 10th Army both ordered "thorough mopping-up operations" and "wiping out" "enemies". Receiving such order, Japanese troops at many levels started to slaughter captives, some even in a large scale, about which many records can be seen in the battle reports by troops at different levels and in relevant wartime logs.

The 7th Regiment, attached to the 9th Division of Shanghai Expeditionary Army, recorded "no captive" but 505 "corpses of enemies" in the List of Captives (December 7–13).[40] Considering soldiers who surrendered followed one after another, the reason why there were no captives alive must be the 7th Regiment shall "take no prisoners". Section 2 of The List of Mopping-up Operations in the Nanjing city (December 13–24) read "6670 'defeated soldiers' stabbed to death,[41] and no prisoner". The No. 111 Combat Order of the 7th Infantry Regiment expressly provided that "remaining defeated troops shall be thoroughly captured and wiped up"[42]—"Wiping-up" could mean "capture" but considering the foregoing order and the follow-up, the "wiping-up" measure taken by the 7th Regiment when attacking and after entering Nanjing, no doubt, meant physical annihilation. And the number of soldiers killed showed a surprisingly sharp increase when Chinese troops surrendered after the fall of Nanjing on December 13th. This increase cannot be justified unless on the slaughter of captives.

The 16th Division of Shanghai Expeditionary was the main force attacking Nanjing and his subordinate troop, the 33rd Regiment put as follows in Report on the Battle near Nanjing:

> At 2.30 p.m. on December 13, the advance guard arrived at the Xiaguan and searched for enemies. And it was found that many defeated soldiers were on rafts fashioned from bamboo and others down the Yangtze River. The Regiment then organized the advance guard to shoot them with high-velocity gun and annihilate almost 2000 soldiers in two hours.[43]

---

[40] The 7th Infantry Regiment. Appendix to the Battle Report. In Battle of Nanking Editorial Committee (Ed.). Documents on the Battle of Nanjing. p. 629.

[41] The 7th Infantry Regiment. The List of Mopping-up Operations in the Nanjing City. In Battle of Nanking Editorial Committee (Ed.). *Documents on the Battle of Nanjing*. p. 630.

[42] No. 111 Class-A Combat Order of the 7th Infantry Regiment. In Battle of Nanking Editorial Committee (Ed.). *Documents on the Battle of Nanjing*. p. 622.

[43] The 33rd Infantry Regiment. The Report on the Battle near Nanjing. In Battle of Nanking Editorial Committee (Ed.). Documents on the Battle of Nanjing. p. 601. There are

In Annex 3 "Reference" to the above-mentioned battle report, it was recorded that from December 10th to 13th, defeated soldiers that were executed and corpses of enemies were up to 6830.[44] The 38th Infantry Regiment, also attached to the 16th Division, took charge of "thoroughly mopping up" the city and clearly stated in Annex 5 to Report on the battle in Nanjing (December 14th) that "enemies were all wiped out", although it did not list the exact number of "copse remained" or "soldiers killed".[45]

The 114th Division attached to the 10th Army recorded a total of 6000 "corpses of enemies remained" in 3rd Annex to the battle report on December 15th and a total of 229 Japanese soldiers killed or injured in 1st Annex, with numbers of Table 1, 2 and 3 added up.

And it was the same case with the 1st Battalion of the 66th Infantry Regiment attached to the 114th Division. 9 of their soldiers were killed but they killed "700 enemies who fiercely resisted the day before they entered Nanjing (December 12th)[46]; From December 10th to 13th, 17 of their

---

many records concerning the seaborne "mopping-up operations against enemies" in Japanese official and private documents. For example, the 1st Seaborne Mopping-up Platoon wrote in A Summary of Seaborne Operations near Nanjing, "We go down from Wulong Mountain to Xiaguan of Nanjing. And at 13: 23, the advance guard left the port to bombard the enemy position on the north-shore of the Yangtze River. We broke the blockade and launched a fierce assault on the major enemy force on the shore and those who tried to flee on ships and rafts, killing almost 10,000 enemies." (The Education Department under the Ministry of the Navy. 『事変関係掃海研究会記録』. cited in Kasahara Tokushi, The Nanking Incident. Tokyo: Iwanami Shoten. 1st Edition on December 20, 1997: p. 159.) This has been proved by Major General Iinuma Mamoru's diary, which mentions Major General Eijiro Kondo, commander of the 11th Navy Army claimed "about 10,000 enemies were killed". (Battle of Nanking Editorial Committee (Ed.). Documents on the Battle of Nanjing. p. 217.) And Tatsuzo Ishikawa, a famous Japanese writer, once followed Japanese troops entering Nanjing and a month later wrote the Soldiers Alive, which was forbidden to be published in wartime. "Japanese troops did not attack the Yijiang Gate, so defeated troops in the city fled to Xiaguan Wharf via this only gate. But then facing them was the vast river without any ferryboat and no alternative land route, and they had to swim across the vast river to the Pukou Wharf with floating objects such as table, log or door plank, of which the number was up to 50,000 -- it seemed there was a dark cloud floating on the river. But when they approached the opposite shore, awaiting them was Japanese MG Column. Japanese soldiers opened fire and the rain of bullets broke the silence of the water. They also could not swim back as it is the case with the Xiaguan Wharf. Then Japanese destroyer delivered coup de grace to those defeated soldiers adrift in the river." (Tatsuzo Ishikawa. 著『生きている兵隊』, 昭和戦争文学全集3『果てしなき中国戦線』. Tokyo: Shûeisha. 1st Edition on June 30, 1965: p. 78.) Although it is a novel, Soldiers Alive is based on personal experience and thus has special information value.

[44] The 33rd Infantry Regiment. The Report on the Battle near Nanjing. In Battle of Nanking Editorial Committee (Ed.). *Documents on the Battle of Nanjing*. p. 605.

[45] No. 82 Battle Report of the 38th Infantry Regiment: The Report On the Battle in the Walled City Of Nanjing. The Condition Report of the 16th Division. In Battle of Nanking Editorial Committee (Ed.). Documents on the Battle of Nanjing. p. 591.

[46] The 1st Battalion of the 66th Infantry Regiment. The Battle Report. In Battle of Nanking Editorial Committee (Ed.). Documents on the Battle of Nanjing. pp. 668–689.

soldiers were killed but they killed over 80 times as many "enemies", almost up to 1400.

The 11th Squadron of the 45th Regiment, attached to the 6th Division of the 10th Army,encountered enemies at the Jiangdong Gate and had 3300 "enemies killed" but their own soldiers killed and injured were just totally 80. The battle at the Jiangdong Gate was not the only case. According to the battle report by the 6th Division, during the battle from the Xiahe Town to Xiaguan, the 2nd and 3rd Battalion of the 45th Regiment, one troop of the 2nd Mountain Gun Regiment directly under the 10th Army, and one troop of the 6th Infantry Regiment of the 6th Division defeated Chinese troops with one-ten of their forces and killed 11,000 "enemies" but only 58 of their soldiers were killed, almost one hundred and ninety to one.[47]

In terms of the foregoing materials, noteworthy are two points: One is that there were no captives but "corpses of enemies"; another is that there was a big gap between the number of "corpses of enemies" and that of Japanese soldiers killed. This could not happen in a fight unless there existed a contrast between their weapons or on one side were captives disarmed. With the materials that remain, it will not be difficult to figure out the case. For instance, we can know the Battle of the Jiangdong Gate was a "close combat" and a "hand-to-hand combat", both sides with the same weapons.[48] SEF's Deputy Chief of Staff Colonel Uemura Toshimichi got surprised at the scale of underground bunkers after shown around the defensive facilities on southern highland of Yijiang Gate and the battery at Fugui Mountain on December 26th. But on January 6th of the next year (1937), he visited the 16th Division for the "proof firing of weapons captured" and recorded it in his diary on that day.

> This afternoon I accompanied the Prince to the 16th Division and watched the "proof firing of weapons captured" (Note: The Prince refers to Lieutenant General Yasuhiko Asaka, commander of Shanghai Expeditionary Army and "D" means division). Sadly, equipment such as automatic rifle, rifle, pistol, LG, MG (Note: LG refers to light machine gun while MG refers to heavy machine gun), artillery, worked as well as ours.[49]

Major Yoshikiyo Ninomiya, a member of the 3rd Department attached to the General Staff, visited China and wrote an investigation report. He said, "Compared to Chinese troops, [Japanese troops] were at a disadvantage in the

---

[47] The 6th Division. No. 13 and No. 14 Battle Report. In Battle of Nanking Editorial Committee (Ed.). *Documents on the Battle of Nanjing*. p. 692.

[48] In this battle, Japanese troops and Chinese soldiers were both armed with Sanpachi-shiki hohei-ju. (Battle of Nanking Editorial Committee (Ed.). *Documents on the Battle of Nanjing*. p. 692.)

[49] Uemura Toshimichi's Dairy. In Battle of Nanking Editorial Committee (Ed.). *Documents on the Battle of Nanjing*. pp. 279+286.

quality or in the quantity of weapons used in close combat".[50] When Shanghai Expeditionary Army fought at Baoshan in October, it occurred many times that 240 mm mortar shell and 300 mm carronade shell failed to explode after fired; after crossing the Suzhou River in November, it occurred many times that 240 mm mortar shells exploded in the barrel—Japanese troops were apparently not competitive in heavy weapons. And when it comes to small arms, things got worse. Colonel Sahishige Nagatsu, who served as Head of China-concerned Department under the General Staff before attacking Shanghai and then as commander of the 22th Regiment after the outbreak of war, once got fussed at the Colonel Onishi, the staff officer of Shanghai Expeditionary Army due to the poor quality of grenade which would not explode after thrown out. Coincidentally, Captain Haruo Kano, commander of 101st Regiment under the 101st Division who was killed in the battle near the Baoshan Section of Wenzao River on October 11, mentioned the problem that grenade "could not be fully fired" in his letter to the division Chief of Staff. Such was the case not only with regular weapons but with "high-tech" ones. Flaks shipped from German to Nanjing before the battle and set up on eastern highland of the Jiming Temple had an electric aiming system and were the most advanced ones at that time. They were a great threat to Japanese naval aircrafts. Lieutenant Hanae shou, who was the 3rd Squadron leader under the 1st Battalion of the 20th Infantry Regiment, once said German's military aid to Chinese troops, in his suppose, dealt a "German blow" to Japan.[51] These materials are not intended to prove Chinese military equipment of advantage over Japanese—in general, it was Japanese troops that got an advantage, especially in terms of heavy weapons such as aircraft, heavy artillery and tank and they can take advantage of this mainly in uphill battles and remote sabotage—but to prove in close combat, hand-to-hand combat and night battle, a Japanese soldier could not magically defeat ten or hundred enemies.

Therefore, I can see no other explanation for the gap between the death toll of two sides in the battle near Nanjing except that Japanese troops slaughtered captives disarmed. And the so-called "battle", the so-called "close combat" and "hand-to-hand combat" were the excuse troops at different levels gave to claim more credit.

In a word, we can reach a positive conclusion that Japanese troops' slaughtering captives during the process of capturing Nanjing were based on a top-down order instead of being an accidental, sporadic event limited to individual soldiers and that Japanese fictionalists' absurd argument on this issue cannot make any sense. Through this article, we can sure that Japanese military at the division level did issue a massacre order, although the massacre order by the army who captured Nanjing and the Area Army cannot be affirmed.

Originally published on Historical Research, 2002(6)

---

[50] Battle of Nanking Editorial Committee (Ed.). *The Battle of Nanjing*. p. 6.

[51] Hanae shou. Preface *Three to The Truth about the Nanjing Incident: Scrutiny of John Rabe's Diary*. p. 7.

PS:

Note 1: (There was another section dealing with the importance of studying the Massacre order and arguing that the number of people slaughtered is of minor importance. But considering this issue has been the focus of current studies in the Nanjing Massacre, it is not proper to deal with it incidentally in an article with another theme. Hence, this section was deleted before contributed and has been included as a postscript to Study on the Nanjing Massacre,[52] which you can refer to in Appendix.)

Was the slaughter of Chinese soldiers and people perpetrated by Japanese troops in Nanjing independent action by troops at grassroots level or subject to a top-down order?—this is one of the key issues in the study of the Nanjing Massacre. And others also matter, like the scale of the slaughter. But three points must be noted: First, figure cannot cover the nature, so even if the exact number of people killed is larger or smaller than that widely known, the existence of the slaughter is undeniable; second, corpses buried then, like by The Word Red Swastika Society, have been weathering for a variety of reasons over the past 60 years and at the riverside area of Xiaguan large quantities were pushed into the Yangtze River, so in Nanjing still buried underground were much fewer than before.[53] In other words, even the remaining bodies all discovered (which is theoretically possible), they just account for part of those killed in the slaughter and thus it is hard to learn about the overall scale of the slaughter; third, little firsthand information can be seen in the documents. Memoirs written in one's late years, testimony and investigation reports, of value as they are, are evidence of limited probative value from a law or academic perspective. Therefore, this issue or issues of this kind are of minor importance to the study of the Nanjing Massacre in history and it is impossible to get a whole picture of them.

The massacre order is not the case. Although most of Japanese military documents have been lost, the remaining ones give us a clue to find out

---

[52] Cheng Zhaoqi. Study on the Nanjing Massacre. Shanghai Lexicographic Publishing House. The Edition published in December 2002. pp. 101–104. A certain scholar with Ritsumeikan University recently published an article in the most important right-wing journal, regarding my book as a writing of comparatively "complete examination" among "Chinese works of studies therein". However, he also said, "From this book, we can see it is impossible to deal with the Nanjing Incident in a manner against the national will or the national custom." (アスキユデイ――.ヴイッド.「南京大虐殺の亡霊」. Shokun. December 2005 Issue: p. 164.) Ridiculously, he says so because, for example, he thinks "the number of corpses has been exaggerated". My book, however, does not refer to exact figure although covering a wide range. And to argue that Japanese fictionalists are biased, this can be a small but powerful new example.

[53] Masaaki Yoshida, 4th Detachment leader of the 1st Platoon under the 3rd Squadron of the 30th Infantry Regiment, mentioned many killings in his diary. On December 14, it was recorded that about 7000 captives were taken to the riverside and killed, i.e. the so-called "feeding to fish foregoing 7000 captives". (Masaaki Yoshida's Diary. In Battle of Nanking Editorial Committee (Ed.). Documents on the Battle of Nanjing. p. 519.) The words "feeding to fish" proves that Japanese troops killed the captives and pushed the corpses into the river.

the truth. We need to clarify whether the slaughter perpetrated by Japanese troops was a up-down decision—it is not about whether this issue can be solved or about how many false statements Japanese fictionalists have made—because this issue is of importance that cannot be ignored. If the slaughter was independent action by troops at grassroots level, Japanese military also shall shoulder the responsibility and be punished—the overall responsibility Japanese military and Japan shall shoulder, however, would be of a different nature and be much more serious if the slaughter was based on a top-down decision. And the study of the massacre order for Japanese troops thus specially matters since after the war Japanese military did not take the full responsibility for their atrocities in Nanjing.

Although in the Tokyo Trial Iwane Matsui was sentenced to be hanged, the severest punishment, which, however, was not for his "command, authorization and permission in an illegal manner" as the prosecutor requested, but for his negative "inaction".[54] What's more, in the Tokyo Trial the Japanese troops' atrocities were not questioned from the institutional perspective, bringing about the following consequences: First, it gave some leeway for Iwane Matsui to appeal his conviction as there was no direct proof that Iwane Matsui "illegally ordered, authorized or permitted" the atrocities perpetrated by Japanese troops but records about his intention to "enhance military discipline".[55] The special institutional nature of Japanese troops ignored, Japanese military at large was charged for mere negligence in the Tokyo Trial—a much lesser charge. Consequently, many Japanese including

---

[54] Judges put as follows in the Judgment of the Tokyo Trial, "from December 13, 1937 to early February 1938, 'six or seven weeks, thousands of women were raped, more than 100,000 people were killed, and countless properties were stolen or burned down. The most terrible day was December 17. Iwane Matsui arrived in Nanjing on this day and stayed for five to seven days. His observation and reports from his staff should have informed him of what had happened. He himself admits that he heard about the illegal acts of his soldiers from the Kempeitai and the embassy and appeal to the Japan Diplomatic Representative in Nanjing (Note: the International Committee) to report this situation to Tokyo government. This court holds that there is strong evidence that Iwane Matsui knew what had happened but he took no action against this horrible incident or did something without effect. He did issued the order for enhancing the military discipline before capturing Nanjing and did the same thing in latter days. But as we have known and as he knew, these orders did not work. It was suggested (Note: by the defense) that he had been sick at that time. However, he was not so sick as to be incapable of commanding the army, and his inaction also was not because of his stay in Nanjing for several days during the period of the atrocities. He was the commander of the troops that shall the responsibilities; he knew the facts; he had the obligation and had the power to regulate his troops and protect those unlucky Nanjing citizens. He fell to perform his duty and one cannot help thinking that he shall take responsibilities for those crimes. This court therefore finds the defendant Iwane Matsui guilty on the 55th cause of action, not guilty on the 27th, 29th and 31st, 32nd, 35th, 36th, and 5th cause of cation.

[55] Such as Iwane Matsui's Diary on December 26–28 (jointly covered in one) and on December 29 of 1937 and on January 6, on February 16 and on February 19 of 1938. For further please refer to General Iwane Matsui's Wartime Logs. (In Battle of Nanking Editorial Committee (Ed.). Documents on the Battle of Nanjing. pp. 24+28+43++44.)

those who do not study this issue have cried foul on behalf of Iwane Matsui. Second, many people who should have taken the responsibility escaped punishment. Third, fictionalists highlighted the relatively weak discipline of US army and Soviet army in wartime to make Japanese troops' atrocities not the only case and to justify the so-called argument that "The Tokyo Trial was a party for winning states".

Based on the foregoing arguments for the Japanese massacre order, this important point needs to be noted.

Note 2: Although it was mentioned above that "it was impossible to prove the massacre order issued by the army who captured Nanjing and by the Area Army", that is not to say that there is no clue to be followed. After the publication of this article, I found two pieces of records that can be indirect evidence to suggest that Major General Iinuma Mamoru, Chief of Staff for Shanghai Expeditionary Army, had known and acquiesced in the slaughter of captives as early as when attacking Baoshan, of which further details please refer to my article The Record of Historical Documents Concerning the Defensive Battle of Baoshan.[56] Iinuma Mamoru had no time lost in learning that Yamada Column slaughtered the captives and on December 21st he wrote, "it was said that Yamada Column under the Rippei Army captured over ten thousand people and killed them one by one with bayonet. And on the following day many people were taken to the same place and a riot occurred. Yamada Column then had no choice but to sprayed them with machine gun. Several of Yamada Column soldiers were killed in the fusillade of bullets and many people fled".[57] "Kill… one by one with bayonet" is almost the same as what was mentioned in the battle report by the 1st Battalion of the 66th Regiment (which proves the large-scale slaughter of captives was not limited to certain troop at that time).

[56] On the History and Classics. Shanghai: Shanghai Classics Publishing House. 1st Publication in August 2004. pp. 448–459.

[57] Iinuma Mamoru's Diary. In Battle of Nanking Editorial Committee (Ed.). *Documents on the Battle of Nanjing*. p. 222.

Is the Nanjing Massacre a Fabrication Made by Tokyo Trial?

I

Twenty years ago, Japanese Textbook Incident[1] caused a strong backlash from Japanese right-wing groups. In the uproar of denying Japan's invasion, the Nanjing Massacre is a major attack point of Japanese right-wing groups, of which *What Really Happened in Nanking: The Refutation of a Common Myth* (hereinafter referred to as *Myth*) written by Tanaka Masaaki is the most important representative in this attack round. In order to deny the Nanjing Massacre from its source, the *Myth* "fabricated" a so-called "fact", that is, before the Tokyo Trial, the world did not know about the "Nanjing Massacre" and the "Nanjing Massacre" was completely fabricated by the Tokyo Trial. There is a section in chapter seven of the *Myth*, of which the title is The First Time I Know about the "Nanjing Massacre". The section is not very long that could be copied down as follows:

> In December of the 12th year of the Shōwa era (1937), the internal and external defenses in Nanjing, the capital of China, was easily broke through by rapid attack of the Imperial Army. On the 13th of the same month, Nanjing fell. Japan was jubilant nationwide as parades held flags and lanterns to bless the victory and celebrate the illustrious military achievements.
>
> However, eight years later, Japan lost in the Greater East Asia War and subdued before the Allied Powers. As a result, eleven victorious allies formed the International Military Tribunal for the Far East to try Japan. It is unprecedented

---

[1] On June 26th, 1982, Japan's *Asahi Shimbun* and other major media reported the results of the Ministry of Education, Science, Sports and Culture's examination of textbooks that finished just the day before. Since the results tended to downplay Japanese invasion, they had been strongly criticized by China, South Korea and other countries. On the other hand, the Japanese right-wing groups insisted that the report of crucial significance in this incident which changed the "invasion" to "in and out" was a "false report".

© The Author(s) 2020
Z. Cheng, *The Nanjing Massacre and Sino-Japanese Relations*,
https://doi.org/10.1007/978-981-15-7887-8_5

for the victorious countries to try the defeated countries through an international trial. Germany and Japan, the defeated countries in World War II, received such international trials.

Japan was unilaterally tried for war crimes committed worldwide (whether existed or not) during about 17 years from January 1st of the 3rd year of the Shōwa era (1928) to September 2nd of the 20th year of the Shōwa era (1945) when Japan signed the Surrender Agreement.

In the trial, Japanese army was alleged to have committed inhumane and evil deeds in Nanjing such as massacring hundreds of thousands of Chinese, including women and children, and the sadistic acts of arson, atrocity, rape, plunder, etc. continued in seven weeks. Such <u>"chilling facts" were known to Japanese nationals for the first time</u> (the emphasis marks are retained according to original texts and hereinafter the same shall apply—noted by the quoter). All the Japanese nationals who heard the news was shocked, deeply felt guilty and ashamed from the bottom of their hearts.

Until then, none of the Japanese nationals had ever mentioned such massacre in Nanjing, so it was like a bolt from the blue. Even General Iwane Matsui, commander of the Expeditionary Army sent to China, who was executed for this incident, heard such news just after the defeat in August 20th of the 20th year of the Shōwa era. He said,

Shortly after the end of the war, it was surprising to hear from the American radio that Nanjing had gone through an organized mass massacre and atrocities against ordinary people, prisoners, women, etc. After inquiring my former subordinates, I found that such rumors were completely false. Neither I received such reports and intelligence when I was in power nor received them after my return and until the end of the war. When I was in Shanghai, I often met with correspondents of newspapers of various countries, and I never heard of the incident, so they are completely false statements.

The news of the so-called "Nanjing Massacre" was also a bolt from the blue to General Iwane Matsui. Like General Iwane Matsui, Lieutenant General Hisao Tani, Head of the 6th Division, who was tried by Chiang Kai-shek's Provisional Government of the Republic of China after the war for his role in the "Nanjing Massacre" and shot dead outside Nanjing, also said in his confession, "I first knew about the Nanjing atrocity when I read newspapers last year (the 20th year of the Shōwa era) after the war and I was deeply terrified. As a defendant in the battle, this is also the first time I have heard of it". That is to say, this is an incident even the army commander and division head are completely unaware of.

Not only the army commander and division head, but also the more than 100 media workers who entered the city at the same time when occupation happened did not know the incident. Hara Shiro, commissioner of the aforementioned Yomiuri Shimbun, also made it very clear about this matter. Moreover, another war correspondent of Tokyo Nichi Nichi Shimbun, Ujima Hiroshi, who entered the city with the troops that first entered Nanjing, also published an article entitled The Truth of the Battle of Nanjing in the magazine Osamuoya (published in May of the 43rd year of the Shōwa era), which said:

Shortly after returning to Shanghai from Nanjing, rumors of torture murders in Nanjing spread to my ears. So I tried to call various newspapers, and they all said that they had neither seen nor heard of such a thing. It was Chinese people's consistent exaggerated propaganda, or the bodies are who killed by enemy troops in a regular battle in Hsiakwan district. Those bodies were abandoned in streams and lakes and were described as torture murders.

Not only the commanders, division heads and soldiers, but also the war correspondents did not know about the incident, not to mention Japanese nationals.

In a letter to the author, Soki Yoshinobu (Kumamoto) said: "I think everyone knows that the "Nanjing Massacre" was firstly broadcast on December 9th of the 20th year of the Shōwa era 20 by NHK[2]. Everyone who heard it at that time thought it was not the facts and therefore they lodged a large number of protests against NHK. The broadcast script was said to have been provided by the occupying forces. It can only be recognized as a fabrication."[3]

Why did the Tokyo Trial "frame" Japan? The Myth holds that there are three main purposes: The first one is "condemning the history". It regarded the consistently imperial historical concepts—patriotism, nationalism and familism centered on the Emperor of Japan as inferior, barbaric and incorrect concepts in order to deny all past history, tradition and culture of Japan. The second one is "fostering the consciousness of sin". Not only all external wars since the Meiji Restoration were regarded as "wars of aggression", but also the performance of Japanese army abroad was portrayed as plundering, setting fires, raping, killing people and being utterly devoid of conscience. It can thus implant indelible "sense of criminal record" and "sense of self-abuse" into the hearts of Japanese people.

The third one is "retaliating". In words of Pal from India, the only one who had reservations about Japan's crimes among the eleven judges: "It merely took advantage of legal procedures to satisfy the desire for revenge. It had nothing to do with international justice". It made people feel that "it went back to the barbaric era centuries ago".[4]

---

[2] NHK is a Japan's national broadcasting organization whose policy is adhering to the objective and justice, and not be affected by politics and commerce. It therefore was often attacked by Japanese right-wing groups after the war. For example, the right-wing main publication *Seiron* called NHK's behavior a "traitorous act" because NHK early reported sexual slavery in Japanese army. (Kase Hideaki,「NHKよ、それを売国行為と呼ぶのです」,『正論』, Tokyo, Sankei Shinbunsha, April 2001, pp. 56–67.) Meanwhile, NHK's "neutral" position has also been criticized by the left-wing groups. For example, as to the aforementioned report, the left-wing groups pointed out that NHK bowed to the right-wing pressure and deleted some original content which led to damaging its original "meaning". (Nishino Rumiko,「NHK——消された映像」,『マスコミ"民』, Tokyo,マスコミ"民月刊, May 2001, pp. 2–9.)

[3] Tanaka Masaaki,『「南京虐殺」の虚構——松井大将の日記をめぐって』, Tokyo, Nihon Kyōbunsha, 1st edition, June 25th, 1984, pp. 287–289.

[4] Tanaka Masaaki,『「南京虐殺」の虚構——松井大将の日記をめぐって』, pp. 282–284.

According to the *Myth*, it seems that without the Tokyo Trial the Japanese would not have known about the Nanjing Massacre. In light of this, they also would not have known about the Japanese atrocities such as plunder, rape and arson. Therefore, the Japanese army's atrocities in Nanjing are inevitably suspected of being imposed by the "winners". Such argument does not need to be debated for a simple reason that "hearing nothing" does not mean "nothing". The existence of the "Nanjing Massacre" is unquestioned. No one can deny it by the reason "not knowing". The reasons why this issue is still brought up for review today are as follows: First, the "not knowing" itself is a lie; second, Japan's "slaughter school" once tried to clarify the issue, but it was too rough; third, such rough clarification consistently appeals more followers who share the same views with the Myth. "Muddleheadled men and women"—some Japanese nationals—are also willing to "spread rumors"; and fourth, this issue is the most painful part in Japanese modern national history which is a matter of "sense of honor".

To begin with, please review the use of words from the *Myth* by the works written by Japanese right-wing groups in recent years. In *Breaking the Myth of Nanjing Massacre* written by Yoshimoto Sakae:

> The incident "Nanjing Massacre" was first introduced in Japan on December 8th of the 12th year of the Shōwa era (1945). On that day, a special note provided by the U.S. military command was published in Asahi Shimbun under the title "History of the Pacific War - Collapse of False Japanese Militarism" under the name "Provided by the Allies' Command". It was written like this when Nanjing fell: "The Japanese army committed heinous acts of cruelty. As the largest cruelty in modern history, according to the accounts of witnesses, it can be confirmed that 20,000 men, women and children were killed at that time." To the Japanese at that time, the note was like a bolt from the blue.[5]

Nanjing Massacre Was Fabricated in this Way—The Deception of Tokyo Trial written by Fuji Nobuo has a section entitled "*No Massacre Was Reported at All in December of the 12th Year of the Shōwa Era*". It said:

> When Nanjing was captured, not only about 120 journalists and photographers entered the city, but also famous critics, poets and writers such as Sōichi Ōya, Kimura Ki, Sugiyama Heisuke, Noyori Hideichi, Saijo Yaso, Kusano Shinpei, Hayashi Fumiko and Ishikawa Tatsujo. In addition, from spring to summer of the 13th year of the Shōwa era, a great number of other celebrities also visited Nanjing.
>
> War correspondents and war photographers often moved together with the front-line soldiers with their missions to report on the activities of the front-line troops and the war situation. If, after the Japanese army occupying Nanjing, a

---

[5]Yoshimoto Eiichi,『南京大虐殺の虚構を砕け』, Tokyo, Shinpû Shuppansha, 1st edition, June 1st, 1998, pp. 7–8.

massacre did happen like what was prosecuted by the procurator, then the incident would definitely be known by war correspondents, war photographer and the aforementioned critics, poets and writers who entered Nanjing.[6]

In *The Truth of Nanjing Incident* written by Yoshiaki Itakura:

The "Nanjing Massacre" became a problem for the first time because of the International Military Tribunal for the Far East. In fact, there was no such expression "Nanjing Massacre" at that time.[7]

In *The New "Nanjing Massacre" Mystery* written by Suzuki Aki:

"International Military Tribunal for the Far East" is commonly known as "Tokyo Trial". It was this "Tokyo Trial" that made the existence of the "Nanjing Massacre" known to the world.[8]

In *Questions about the Nanjing Massacre* written by Matsumura Toshio:

It has clearly shown the development of this issue as a rumor by the above-detailed review of the contemporaneous materials of the 12th and 13th year of the Shōwa era, the materials of the International Military Tribunal for the Far East and the Nanjing Military Court, as well as the newly prepared materials and the testimony of witnesses from the Chinese side after the problem was brought up again.[9]

In *The Alleged "Nanking Massacre"* written by Takemoto Tadao and Oohara Yasuo:

At that time, there were no senior Japanese officials who knew about the Nanjing Massacre.[10]

---

[6] Fuji Nobuo, 『「南京大虐殺」はこうして作られた——东京裁判の欺瞞』, Tokyo, Tendensha, 4st printed version, November 23rd, 1998, p. 339.

[7] Yoshiaki Itakura, 『本当はこうだった南京事件』, Tokyo, Nihon Tosho Kankôkai, 2nd printed version, January 20th, 2000, p. 44. The "expression" appearing late cannot deny the fact, just as Kasahara Tokushi, a representative of new generation of Japan's "slaughter school", said: "the 'Bombing of Tokyo' is also a post-war term. But no one could say that it was fabricated for the reason that the expression 'Bombing of Tokyo' appeared after the war. The incident happened firstly and then came the expression which might be changed someday". (「まぼろし派、中間派、大虐殺派三派合同アンケート」, *Shokun*, Tokyo, Bungei Shunjû, February 2001, p. 199.)

[8] Suzuki Aki, 『新「南京大虐殺」のまぼろし』, Tokyo, Asuka Shobô, June 3rd, 1999, 1st edition, pp. 408–409.

[9] Matsumura Toshio, 『「南京虐殺」への大疑問』, Tokyo, Tendensha, December 13th, 1998, 1st edition, p. 396.

[10] 日本会議国際広報委員会編『再審「南京大虐殺」——世界に訴える日本の冤罪』, Tokyo, Meiseisha, November 25th, 2000, 2nd printed version, p. 65.

In *History the Textbooks Do Not Teach* written by Association for Advancement of Unbiased View of History:

> Before the war, the Nanjing massacre was regarded as a complete false statement even in international documents. No official document proving the massacre can be found. However, the Tokyo Trial after Japanese defeat suddenly brought up the Nanjing Massacre. Keenan, the Chief Prosecutor, vaguely stated that tens of thousands of people were killed, while Provisional Government of the Republic of China expanded the number to seven times as 300,000 people.[11]

In *Statements about the Nanjing Incident* written by Ara Kenichi:

> Most alleged evidence and testimony of the Nanjing incident are believed to contain false contents. Starting from the materials submitted to the Tokyo Trial, the number of reports in the most famous newspapers and other media is also very large. Thus, it is even more difficult to see the truth of the Nanjing incident. People also become more confused when it comes to the question that what kind of evidence and testimony can convince them.[12]

The Study of Nanking Atrocity written by Nobukatsu Fujioka and Higashinakano Shūdō not only says that the Japanese did not know about the Nanjing Massacre, but even has a section titled "The League of Nations, Mao Zedong and Chiang Kai-shek Did Not Know about the Nanjing Massacre".[13]

The above quotations are just a few works written by the right-wing groups which the Japanese book market currently is full of.[14]

---

[11] 藤岡信勝、自由主義史観研究会編『教科書が教えない歴史』2, Tokyo, Sankei Shinbunsha, December 30th, 1996, 1st edition, p. 72.

[12] Ara Kenichi, 《聞き書 南京事件》, Tokyo, Tosho Shuppansha, August 15th, 1987, 1st edition, p. 298.

[13] Nobukatsu Fujioka and Higashinakano Shūdō, 『ザ・レイプ・オブ・南京の研究──中国における「情報戦」の手口と戦略』, Tokyo, Shodensha, September 10th, 1999, 1st edition, p. 196.

[14] Apart from the denial of the Nanjing massacre, the denial of Tokyo Trial's affirmation of Japan's invasion is also extensive. Some people believe that "the illegality of the so-called Tokyo Trial…is unanimously recognized by jurists all over the world". (Ooi Mitsuru, 『仕組まれた「南京大虐殺」──攻略作戦の全貌とマスコミ報道の怖さ』, Tokyo, Tendensha, June 6th, 1998, 3rd printed version, p. 299); "From a legal perspective, anyone would say that the Tokyo Trial is unreasonable!" (Komuro Naoki and Watanabe Shoichi, 『封印の昭和史──「戦後五〇年」自虐の終焉』, Tokyo, Tokuma Shoten, October 15th, 1995, 4th printed version, p. 165); "The biggest reason for Japanese servility after the war was the judgement 'Japan is the aggressor' decided by the International Military Tribunal for the Far East". (Harako Shojo, 『世界史から見た日本天皇』, Tokyo, Tendensha, May 27th, 1998, 1st edition, p. 114); "The so-called Tokyo Trial…is a lynching imposed by the will of the winners". (Komuro Naoki, 『大東亜戦争ここに甦る──戦争と軍隊、そして国運の大研究』, Tokyo, クレスト社, October 10th, 1995, 2nd printed version, p. 5); "The International Military Tribunal for the Far East is illegal. The trial is a vile drama centered on 'warning' or 'revenge'". (Nishibe Susumu, 新しい歴史教科書をつくる会編『国民の道徳』, Tokyo, Fusôsha, October 30th, 2000, 1st edition, p. 135); "Supranational judges reveal criminal countries in the name of human beings. But essentially it is some countries

Here, main problems to be solved in this article are as follows: First, whether Iwane Matsui and the Japanese military and political authorities knew about the Japanese atrocities or not; second, why ordinary Japanese people did not know the (hypothetical) Japanese atrocities; third, whether the Japanese "correspondents", "photographers", "critics", "poets" and "writers" who entered Nanjing and the Japanese soldiers themselves as perpetrators knew about the Japanese atrocities or not. The answer of the third problem will be divided into two sections.

II

Before proving Iwane Matsui knew about it, let us see whether the Japanese military and political authorities knew about it and to what extent did they know?

The Japanese army entered Nanjing on December 13th. At first, some citizens and foreign nationals in Nanjing held high hopes for the Japanese army, thinking that the bombing since mid-August, especially the plunder and arson by the defeated troops on the eve of the fall of Nanjing, could be ended and the order in Nanjing could be restored. However, the atrocities committed by the Japanese army after entering the city broke people's illusions. F. Tillman Durdin, the New York Times reporter, was ordered to leave Nanjing by Japanese army on December 15th. He issued his first report on the 17th on an American warship moored in Shanghai. This was also the first report by a Western reporter on Japanese atrocities, which said:

> Because of the disintegration of the Chinese authorities and Chinese army, many Chinese in Nanjing think that order and organization can be established with the Japanese army entering the city and they are ready to accept it immediately. They think that if the Japanese army controls the city, the horrible bombing can be stopped, and the disaster brought by the Chinese army can be ended. Therefore, peace of mind is spreading among the Chinese residents.
> Of course, it is also believed that at least until the end of the war, the Japanese army's rule will be severe. However, the wait-and-see situation has changed after mere three-day occupation by Japanese army. Things happen in

---

that control supranational organs decide the results of the defeat by force in order to occupy a more favorable position on the earth, which is totally unreasonable and intolerant". (Nishio Kanji, 新しい歴史教科書をつくる会編『国民の歴史』, Tokyo, Fusôsha, October 30th, 1999, 1st edition, p. 467); "Everyone knows that the testimony given at this time is false, but the counter-argument is not allowed". (Higashinakano Shūdō, 『「南京虐殺」の徹底検証』, Tokyo, Tendensha, July 8th, 2000, 4th printed version, p. 375); And "The Tokyo Trial is wrong from the perspective of law, procedure and especially factual cognition. The ending is just a 'winners' judgment'". (Nobukatsu Fujioka, 『汚辱の近現代史——いま克服のとき』, Tokyo, Tokuma Shoten, October 31st, 1996, 1st edition, p. 102, quoted from Victors' Justice: The Tokyo War Crimes Trial.)

Nanjing such as large-scale plunder, violence against women, massacre of ordinary citizens, expulsion from residents' homes, collective execution of prisoners and forcible capture of adult men. Nanjing has already become a scary city.[15]

The Japanese army's performance spread like wildfire and soon spread to the outside world. Judging from the available data, Japan's top officials also learned the truth almost at the same time.

Japan's local military and political authorities learned about the Japanese army mainly through two channels. The first channel is extensive coverage by foreign media. In third section of this article, relevant coverage will be listed in detail. The second channel is the information obtained by the Japanese embassy and consulates, mainly the embassy and other institutions in Nanjing. The sources of information can be roughly divided into two types: the grievances reports, protests and other documents received by the embassy and consulates as well as various types of information collected by embassy and consulates, Japanese News Agency and other institutions.

It can be seen from The Good Man of Nanking: The Diaries of John Rabe and other records that on the second day of the Japanese army entering Nanjing, John H. D. Rabe had drafted a text in the name of the chairman of the International Committee for the Nanking Safety Zones and was ready to submit it to the Japanese army. Rabe met with Japanese army and Japanese embassy officials on the 15th and delivered letters to them, respectively, hoping that the Japanese army would maintain order in Nanjing and treat the Chinese soldiers who laid down their arms "with leniency". On the 16th, the International Committee in a letter to the Japanese embassy said that after the Japanese army robbed the cars of the members of the International Committee with appendix 15 "Carefully Verified Incidents" (No. 1–15).[16] In a long letter to the Japanese embassy on the 17th, the International Committee talked about the robbery of the Red Swastika Society's cars for collecting corpses, the capture of the Red Swastika staff and "volunteer police", "horrible activities such as robberies, rapes and massacres made by your soldiers and so forth".[17] On the 18th, the International Committee in a letter to the Japanese embassy talked about large-scale rapes, and the captured 50 uniformed police from the Ministry of Justice and 45 "volunteer police"

---

[15] 『日中戦争史資料』9「南京事件」II, compiled by Hora Tomio, Tokyo, Kawade Shobô Shinsha, November 30, 1973, 1st edition, p. 280. Quotation in Nanjing Incident written by Hata Ikuhiko and the quotation here have some differences. For example, after the first paragraph, there is an additional sentence "Even citizens greet the first Japanese army with cheers". Besides, in the second paragraph, it is the "mere two-day" instead of "mere three-day". (See Hata Ikuhiko's 『南京事件──虐殺の構造』, Tokyo, Chûô Kôronsha, August 20th, 1999, No. 20, p. 3.)

[16] John Rabe, The Good Man of Nanking: The Diaries of John Rabe, translated by the translation group of this book, Jiangsu People Publishing, Jiangsu Education Publishing House, August 1997, 1st edition, pp. 185–189.

[17] The Chinese version of The Good Man of Nanking: The Diaries of John Rabe, pp. 191–196.

with appendix "Incident Memorandum of the Ministry of Justice" signed by Lewis S. C. Smythe, the secretary of the International Committee.[18] On the same day, robberies, rapes and murders were also mentioned in a letter written by M. S. Bates, chairman of the Relief Committee of Ginling College. From the 16th, the International Committee for the Nanking Safety Zone almost daily reported the Japanese atrocities to the Japanese embassy.[19] At that time, the embassy officials dealing with Rabe and other people were mainly alternate officials such as Fukuda Tokuyasu,[20] Consul General of Shanghai Okazaki Katsuo,[21] Second Secretary Fukui Kiyoshi[22] and others.

Fukuda Tokuyasu once said in an interview:

> I became the bearer of dissatisfaction from them (referring to the International Committee for the Nanking Safety Zones - noted by the quoter). Their causal protests are mixed truths and falsehoods. It is my role to convey protests to the military like "Please deal with the happened incident no matter in what way."[23]

Such a large number of protests were conveyed to the local garrison as well as to the highest military and political authorities in Japan. On December 22nd, Major General Anami Korechika, the Director of Personnel, after attending the meeting of directors of the Ministry of the Army, wrote down the following words in his notes on the same day: "the Nakashima Division has acts of treating women (this is the original expression and it should mean rapes or violence against women - noted by the quoter), killing, and violating military discipline. It

---

[18] The Chinese version of *The Good Man of Nanking: The Diaries of John Rabe*, pp. 201–207.

[19] As Bates said, "We visit the Japanese embassy every day to present our protests, our demands, and the exact records of violence and crime". (*Selected Archives of Japanese Aggression against China: Nanjing Massacre* jointly edited by Central Archives, the Second Historical Archives of China and Jilin Provincial Academy of Social Sciences, Zhonghua Book Company, 1st edition, July 1995, p. 1023.)

[20] The Chinese version of *The Good Man of Nanking: The Diaries of John Rabe* mistakenly translated it into "Fukuda Tokuko", such as line 2 on page 180, line 12 on page 183 and line 13 on page 185. After Fukuda Tokuyasu became the secretary of the Prime Minister Yoshida Shigeru, he had served as the chief of the Defense Department, the chief of the Administrative Department, the Postmaster General and other positions as well as a member of parliament.

[21] The Chinese version of *The Good Man of Nanking: The Diaries of John Rabe* mistakenly translated it into "Okazaki Katsutake", such as the line 7 by counting backwards on page 190 and the line 6 by counting backwards on page 191. Okazaki Katsuo served as the Minister for Foreign Affairs in the 1950s.

[22] The Chinese version of *The Good Man of Nanking: The Diaries of John Rabe* mistakenly translated it into "Fukui K", such as line 13 and line 16 on page 191, line 10 on page 201, etc. At present, in many historical data collections, the name is mistakenly translated as "Fuguyi" (the pronunciation of the surname "Fukui"), such as Selected Archives of Japanese Aggression against China: Nanjing Massacre, line 4 on page 1034; Archives of Nanjing Massacre Made by Japanese Invaders jointly compiled by the Second Historical Archives of China and Nanjing Municipal Archives, line 18 on page 657, edition produced in December 1997. Fukui Kiyoshi was serving as Consul General of Japan in Nanjing.

[23] Tanaka Masaaki, 『「南京虐殺」の虚構——松井大!の日記をめぐって』, p. 36.

has reached an unspeakable condition in terms of the decadence of the national morality and the tragic situation of the war".[24] Due to the atrocities committed by Japanese army in Nanjing, the South China battle targeting Guangdong, which was scheduled to start on December 25th, had to be cancelled.[25]

According to the memoir from Ichigayadai-machi to Ichigayadai-machi written by Colonel Kawabe Torashiro, the Chief of the War Instruction Section of the first division (Operations Department) of the Staff Headquarters, Kawabe then drafted a "serious warning" to Matsui Iwane in the name of the Chief of Staff Prince Kan'in Kotohito.[26] The so-called "serious warning" here is the Ultimatum on Military Discipline issued on January 4th, 1938. The ultimatum raised the Japanese atrocities to the level of "harming the holy business of the entire army".[27] The War history of Nanking records this event with title "Special and Significant expectation from the Chief of Staff",[28] which reveals the significance of the event. Meanwhile, as early as on December 28th, 1937, there was an ultimatum "Reinforce and Maintain the Military Discipline" required and signed by the Chief of Staff and the Secretary of State for War. At the same day, the Deputy of the Ministry of the Army also called the Chief of Staff and Director of Secret Service of the Japanese Central China Area Army on Japanese atrocities. Due to the pressure of the international public opinion, the Japanese army was forced to take measures to constrain the acts of the army.[29] At the end

---

[24] Quoted from Hata Ikuhiko, 『南京事件——虐殺の構造』, p. 172.

[25] In general, much emphasis has been placed on harming the interests of the west, like said, "The reason is that the U.S. ship Panay was sunk and a British ship was shelled during Japanese attack on Nanjing. Diplomatic negotiations on this incident are under way. Now the relationships with Britain and the United States are very dangerous. Therefore, the implementation of this operation will be considered seriously". (Imoto Kumao, 『作戦日誌で綴る支那事変』, Tokyo, Fuyo Shobo Publishing, June 30th, 1978, 1st edition, p. 184.) However, judging from the original documents, this matter should also be connected with the Japanese atrocities, as in the Iinuma Mamoru's diary on December 30th: "Staff Officer Nakayama of the Area Army has come to convey the regret to see Japanese army' illegal acts against foreign embassies and other violations of military discipline to the Chief of staff, which is frightening. He showed a telegram jointly issued by Secretary of State for War and Chief of Staff with the main idea that the Area Army is requested to be careful when the movements of various countries are extremely delicate. There is a tone that the Guangdong battle has been consequently suspended". (「飯沼守日記」, 南京戦史編集委員会編『南京戦史資料集』, 非売品, Tokyo, Kaikōsha, November 3rd, 1989, 1st edition, pp. 229–230.) At that time, Japanese atrocities were an important aspect to cause severe international public opinion.

[26] Kawabe Torashiro, 『"ケ谷台から"ケ谷台へ』, Tokyo, Jiji Tsûshinsha, 1962, 1st edition, p. 153.

[27] 「軍紀風紀に関する件通牒」, 南京戦史編集委員会編『南京戦史資料集』, p. 565.

[28] 南京戦史編集委員会編纂『南京戦史』, 非売品, Tokyo, Kaikōsha, November 3rd, 1989, 1st edition, p. 398.

[29] Nukata Tan who then was Anami Korechika's retinue said, "On New Year's Day of the 13th year of the Shōwa era (1937), I was following the Director of Personnel Anami who was reporting to Commander of the Army Matsui. He said, 'the battle guidance of the 16th division led by Nakashima Kesago violated humanity' and therefore condemned it and lamented the decadence

of December, the Japanese army sent Anami Korechika to China to investigate and deal with the discipline of the Japanese army as one of his missions. At the end of January of the following year, Major General Honma Masaharu[30], the Minister of the second division (Intelligence Agency) of the Staff Headquarters, was sent to China and one of the missions of him was also the discipline of the Japanese army.

At that time, the first Secretary of the Japanese embassy in China, Aiyi Tanjiri, said:

> The atrocities such as plunder and abuse made by the Japanese Army when they entered the Nanjing city, which was too cruel to hear, was personally told by Okazaki Katsuo (who later became the Minister of Foreign Affairs). Okazaki Katsuo at that time followed General Iwane Matsui in Nanjing and took preventative measures with foreign missionaries and professors.[31]

Ishii Itaro, then the Chief of the East Asia Bureau of the Ministry of Foreign Affairs, testified at the Tokyo Trial and said:

> On December 13th, our army entered Nanjing city, and then our Acting Consul General of Nanjing (Fukui Kiyoshi) returned to Nanjing from Shanghai. The Acting Consul General's initial local report to the Ministry was about our army's atrocities. The telecom report was immediately sent by the East Asia Bureau to Chief of the Military Affairs Bureau of the Ministry of the Army without stopping. At that time, the Foreign Minister was astonished and worried about the report. He said to me that measures must be taken to deal with it as soon as possible. Therefore, I replied to the Minister that since the telecom report had been sent to the Ministry of the Army, it should be me to warn the army authorities in the liaison meeting of Ministries of Army, Navy and Foreign Affairs. After that, the liaison meeting was held in my office (it was a practice that a meeting would be held in the office of the Chief of the East Asia Bureau at any time when necessary. The Chiefs of the Military Affairs Bureau of the Ministry of the Army and Navy and the Chief of the East Asia Bureau should have attended the meeting. But in reality, it was the first Section Chiefs of the Military Affairs Bureau of the Ministry of the Army and Navy that attended

---

of Bushido". (『陸軍省人事局長の回想』, Tokyo, Fuyo Shobo Publishing, May 1st, 1977, 1st edition, pp. 321–322.)

[30] Honma Masaharu later defeated MacArthur in the Philippines and his was then quickly executed after Japanese defeat. Tanaka Masaaki was very dissatisfied with the execution and said, "MacArthur was extremely keen on revenge for Lieutenant General Honma Masaharu who caused MacArthur's failure and loss of face in the Philippines. The Lieutenant General Honma was executed only two months after the trial began. Moreover, both the judges and the prosecutors of this trial were his subordinates, so the trail was tantamount to lynching". (Tanaka Masaaki, 『南京事件の総括——虐殺否定十五の論拠』, Tokyo, 謙光社, March 7th, 1987, 1st edition, p. 24.)

[31] Tajiri Akiyoshi, 『田尻愛義回想録』, Tokyo, Hara Shobô, October 11th, 1977, 1st edition, p. 62.

the meeting which was hosted by the Chief of the East Asia Bureau.) At the meeting, I raised the issue on the atrocities mentioned above with the first Section Chief of the Military Affairs Bureau of the Ministry of the Army, saying that since it was called holy war and Imperial Army, rapid and severe measures should be firmly taken to eliminate such grave situation. The Section Chief totally agreed with me and accepted my proposal. Shortly thereafter, the written report from the Acting Consul General of Nanjing arrived at my ministry. The detailed report on the atrocities of our army was made by the International Committee for the Nanking Safety Zones organized by people from third countries that resided in Nanjing. It was typed in English and received by our Consulate General of Nanjing and was then sent to my Ministry. After reading through the report carefully, I reported the gist to the Minister. According to minister's intention, I was required to mention this report at the next liaison meeting to the first Section Chief of the Military Affairs Bureau of the Ministry of the Army and to put forward the hope of taking severe measures. The army said that it had already instructed the local army in the first place to pay strict attention to military discipline. Later, the atrocities committed by the local army have greatly eased. I remember that around the end of January of the following year, the Army Center specially dispatched personnel to the local army. I know the dispatched personnel were Major General Honma. After that, the atrocities in Nanjing ended.[32]

One of the records of the Tokyo Trial said that Lieutenant Colonel Hirota Minoru specially served as the staff of Shanghai Expeditionary Army in China was also due to the military discipline. According to the memory of Utsunomiya Naokata (Minister of Foreign Affairs on the Army, who was succeeded by Hirota Minoru), Hirota Minoru once told him that "The Japanese consuls in Nanjing and I knew merely from the clearest information that many women and young women have been brutalized and killed in Ginling College. Such a regrettable fact is really shameful".[33] Lieutenant General Okamura Yasuji, who came to China as commander of the 11th army in June 1938, said that "In Tokyo, I once heard rumors of massive atrocities during the Battle of Nanjing". After arriving in Shanghai in July, he confirmed the following facts:

> During the Battle of Nanjing, there were massive atrocities such as plunder and rape of tens of thousands of citizens.
> The first-line troops had the fault of killing the prisoners due to shortage of supplies.[34]

---

[32] 『日中戦争史資料』8「南京事件」I, compiled by Hora Tomio, Tokyo, Kawade Shobô Shinsha, November 25th, 1973 1st edition, p. 220.

[33] Utsunomiya Naokata, 『黄河、揚子江、珠江――中国勤務の思い出』, 1980, 非売品, quoted from 南京戦史編集委員会編纂『南京戦史』, pp. 402–403.

[34] Inaba Masao, 『岡村寧次大將資料(上)』, Hara Shobô, 1970, quoted from 南京事件調査研究会編『南京大虐殺否定論13のウソ』, Tokyo, Kashiwa Shobô, March 30th, 2001, 4th printed version, p. 32.

Ishii Itaro later said in his memoirs:

Nanjing fell on the December 13th. The telecom report made by Consul Fukui who followed our army back to Nanjing and the written report immediately sent by Shanghai Consul are deeply regrettable. Because the Japanese army entering Nanjing had information about plunder, rape, arson and massacre of the Chinese. There are too few military police to maintain military discipline. It was reported that even Consul Fukui was in danger because of the attempt to stop it. In the diary on January 6th, 1938:
A letter from Shanghai reported in detail the atrocities committed by our army in Nanjing, including plunder and rape, which were horrible. Alas, is this still the Imperial Army?[35]

Shigemitsu Mamoru, the later ambassador to Nanjing, also said that "When I got to know the truth of the Nanjing incident, I had to feel indignant at the degeneration of our army and the Japanese nationals".[36]

Since the atrocities committed by the Japanese army had heard by senior military and political officials in Tokyo, those who was at the scene of the incident Nanjing had no reason for "not knowing". Even if the victim's pain was completely ignored, passive "knowing" was inevitable. And this kind of "knowing" would always remain in the records intentionally or unintentionally. Major General Iinuma Mamoru, then Chief of Staff of Shanghai the Expeditionary Army, wrote in his diary on December 19th that:

According to a report by the military police, the buildings in Dr. Sun Yat-sen's Mausoleum were set on fire on the 18th and are still burning. In addition, army officers led troops to invade refugee areas and commit rapes.[37]

In the diary on December 21st:

It is said that more than ten thousand prisoners captured by the Yamada detachment of the Ogisu army (i.e., the 103rd brigade of the 13th division—noted by the quoter) were successively executed with bayonets, and one day, many people were brought to the same place, resulting in riots. The soldiers were forced to shoot them with machine guns. Many officers and soldiers of our army were also shot dead and many prisoners escaped.[38]

---

[35] Ishii Itaro, 『外交官の一生――対中国外交の回想』, Tokyo, Taihei Shuppansha, April 15th, 1974, 4th printed version, p. 267.

[36] 伊藤隆、渡辺行太郎編『続・重光葵手記』, Chûô Kôronsha, 1988, quoted from 『南京大虐殺否定論13のウソ』, p. 31. The performance of the Japanese army in Nanjing, even completely from the standpoint of Japan, was regrettable to some extent. As Horiba Kazuo said in a summary of "national governance" in the late 1940s, "The invasion of Nanjing brought up ten years of hatred and hurt the prestige of the Japanese army". (堀場一雄著『支那事変戦争指導史』, Tokyo, Jiji Tsûshinsha, September 10th, 1962, 1st edition, p. 111.)

[37] 「飯沼守日記」,南京戦史編集委員会編『南京戦史資料集』, p. 220.

[38] 「飯沼守日記」,南京戦史編集委員会編『南京戦史資料集』, p. 222.

In the diary on December 24th:

> Vicious plunder was mainly committed by soldiers. From the perspective of the military discipline and the spirit of the Imperial Army, the Army must be resolutely revitalized.[39]

Iinuma Mamoru also frequently mentioned military discipline in his later diaries. For example, on December 30th, adjutants stationed in Nanjing and nearby areas were required to pay "serious attention" to military discipline (Nanjing garrison commander Major General Sasaki Toichi, head of the 30th infantry brigade, also put forward "attention and expectation" on the same occasion), and Zhongzhi army staff officer Major Nakayama Neito, Staff of the Japanese Central China Area Army, conveyed the Area Army's "deep regret" for "noncompliance" and actions of "having no military discipline".[40] On January 6th, "great attention" was paid to "military discipline".[41] On January 14th, "extreme indignation" resulted from the arrest of illegal officers by military police.[42] On January 2th, "real regret" was shown for the robbery and rape.[43] On January 26th, "squadron leader Tenya" of the 8th Squadron of the 45th Regiment led soldiers to commit rapes.[44] On January 29th, the Minister of Justice's report on rape, injury and especially seizure was record. On February 12th, "true lament" was shown for the report on Japanese soldiers' misbehavior made by the military police,[45] etc.

Colonel Uemura Toshimichi, Deputy Chief of Staff of Shanghai Expeditionary Army, also recorded something in his diary. As early as December 12th, the day before the Japanese army entered Nanjing, the diary of Uemura Toshimichi already recorded that:

---

[39] 「飯沼守日記」,南京戦史編集委員会編『南京戦史資料集』, p. 224.

[40] 「飯沼守日記」,南京戦史編集委員会編『南京戦史資料集』, pp. 229–230. The "affidavit" submitted to the court by the Nakayama Neito during the Tokyo Trial said, "General Matsui was very worried when he heard that the Japanese army in Nanjing committed illegal acts. He sent me to convey the following instructions 'Rumors of illegal acts of the Japanese army spread in Nanjing. Attention should be paid in order to keep image of the Japanese army. This is especially important because the commander Asakanomiya is here with us and the military discipline should be obeyed more strictly and those who misbehave should be severely punished'". (『日中戦争史資料』8「南京事件」, compiled by Hora Tomio, p. 204.) Nakayama Neito spared no effort to excuse Ishiguro Matsui in the Tokyo Trial, but this statement is supposed to be true.

[41] 「飯沼守日記」,南京戦史編集委員会編『南京戦史資料集』, p. 234.

[42] 「飯沼守日記」,南京戦史編集委員会編『南京戦史資料集』, p. 237.

[43] 「飯沼守日記」,南京戦史編集委員会編『南京戦史資料集』, p. 237.

[44] According to the table compiled on December 10th by the 33rd regiment, the leader of the 8th squadron is Senior Captain Tasawa. According to the Detailed Report of Battles near Nanjing and the List of the Death and Injury from December 10th to 14th produced by the same regiment, Tasawa was not included and there was no battle after December 14th. Besides, in diaries of Uemura Toshimichi and others, Amano was the only one called as Lieutenant. Thus, there are doubts about the title "squadron leader".

[45] 「飯沼守日記」,南京戦史編集委員会編『南京戦史資料集』, p. 248.

The lack of military discipline in the Imperial Army was early heard and that is quite a pity.[46]

In the diary on December 16th:

As for the military discipline in the city, it is regrettable that those who heard it all made bad comments.[47]

In the diary on December 27th:

The valuable cultural relics with academic value in Nanjing city were gradually destroyed by the soldiers who were seeking goods and materials for the second section.[48]

The so-called "demands of second section" shows that plunder is more than "individual" act for the Japanese army.[49]

In the diary on January 8th:

According to the report of the military police, there were quite a number of violators of military discipline. Second lieutenants and warrant officers were called in. They were extremely regretful for the shameless behavior.[50]

The diary on January 26th recorded that "extreme regret" was caused by "the misconduct of Lieutenant Tenya".[51]

The record of "handling" prisoners in the diary on December 13th of Lieutenant General Nakashima Kesago, head of the 16th Division of the Shanghai Expeditionary Army, has been taken as clear evidence of the Order of Killing Prisoners of War. Japan's military attaché in Shanghai, Okada Yuuji, who was also affiliated to the secret service department of the Shanghai Expeditionary Army after the establishment of the Shanghai Expeditionary Army, later said:

Since we belong to the special service department of the Expeditionary Army, we tried to make some contribution to the political work of the war, but the speed of the war exceeded our expectation, making a blank timing, thus becoming eternal regret.

---

[46]「上村利道日記」,南京戦史編集委員会編『南京戦史資料集』, p. 270.
[47]「上村利道日記」,南京戦史編集委員会編『南京戦史資料集』, p. 272.
[48]「上村利道日記」,南京戦史編集委員会編『南京戦史資料集』, p. 280.
[49] As to plundering daily necessities, it was a "work" of the Japanese army. For example, in the "Results Table" of the 7th infantry regiment recorded from December 13th to 24th, there are tens of thousands of "seized things" in 77 kinds ranging from various types of vehicles (32 vehicles) to compressed biscuits (1600 boxes). (步兵第七聯隊〈南京城内掃蕩成果表〉,南京戦史編集委員会編『南京戦史資料集』, p. 630.)
[50]「上村利道日記」,南京戦史編集委員会編『南京戦史資料集』, p. 287.
[51]「上村利道日記」,南京戦史編集委員会編『南京戦史資料集』, p. 292.

The capture of Nanjing, the capital, not only missed the chance for peace, but unfortunately, the news of the massacre of some ordinary residents was especially propagandized by the China's society, which made the international situation worse for Japan and also led to the result that China's anti-Japanese front became even more strong.[52]

A large number of relevant records in the diaries and notes of the soldiers of the Shanghai Expeditionary Army and the 10th Army will be quoted in the fourth and fifth sections of this article and will not be transcribed here.

Matsui Iwane was dismissed in early February.[53] From a military point of view, the Japanese army led by Matsui Iwane captured Nanjing one month earlier than expected, which was a great "success".[54] But it seems unreasonable for him to be dismissed. Matsui himself was also extremely dissatisfied with the result. On February 10th, 1938, Iwane Matsui was ordered to resign. He left this dissatisfaction in his diary on that day that "The Army Center made a false decision".[55] In fact, the Army had more intense opinions on Matsui Iwane. Major General Tanaka Ryukich, a former director of the Bureau of Military Affairs of the Ministry of the Army, said in response to a question from the International Prosecution Section after the war that "In the spring of 14th year of the Shōwa era (1938), we had advocated that General Matsui and the head of the Nakashima Division should be sent to the military law conference, but this was not realized due to the firm opposition of the Deputy Chief of Staff of Nakashima (Tetsujo)".[56]

According to the above quotation of the memory of Kawabe Torashiro and the words of Tanaka Ryukich, it is enough to see that the atrocities committed by the Japanese army in Nanjing shocked the top Japanese military officials. Akira Fujiwara thus judged that "Matsui's title 'commander of the Area Army' was dismissed in February 1938 due to his responsibility for this incident".[57] Akira Fujiwara's judgment should be right. The reason is that

---

[52] Okada Yuuji, 《日中戦争裏方記》, Tokyo, 東洋経済新聞社, November 25th, 1975, 3rd printed version, p. 110.

[53] The Tokyo Trial decided that "Due to such unfavorable reports and the pressure of public opinion around the world, the Japanese government recalled Matsui and about 80 of his subordinates". (The Judgment of the International Military Tribunal for the Far East translated by Zhang Xiaolin, the judgment of the far east, Qunzhong Publishing House, February 1986, 1st edition, p. 487.)

[54] On November 22nd, Matsui recorded in his diary what he said on the 15th to the General staff and the army provincial officials (Kagesa Sadaaki and Shibayama Kenshiro)—"the goal can be reached within two month". (「松井石根大将戦陣日記」,南京戦史編集委員会編『南京戦史資料集』, p. 8.)

[55] 「松井石根大将戦陣日記」,南京戦史編集委員会編『南京戦史資料集』, p. 41.

[56] Quoted from Hata Ikuhiko's 『南京事件——虐殺の構造』, p. 31. 見粟屋憲太郎ほか『東京裁判・田中隆吉尋問調書』, Tokyo, Ōtsuki Shoten, November 18th, 1994, 1st edition, p. 151.

[57] 『南京大虐殺否定論13のウソ』, p. 17.

Kawabe and Tanaka were not at high official titles who were not directly related to the incident (Tanaka was then in North Korea) and it was a long-term memory, so it is a narrow reason for Matsui's dismissal based on the above-cited materials. However, we do can find more direct materials than these two remarks. This material is the diary of General Hata Shunroku who was Matsui's successor. In Hata Shunroku's diary:

> After the battle, the military discipline of the Expeditionary Army in China is gradually decadent, and there are many abominable acts such as plunder and rape. At this time, the troops of reserve service and further reserve service[58] are called back to Japan and are replaced by active soldiers. General Matsui in Shanghai is also replaced by active general.[59] (Matsui Iwane had become reserve service after retiring from the commander of the Taiwan army, and was reused after the Shanghai battle - noted by the quoter)

What Hata Shunroku has written can prove that Matsui Iwane's dismissal did resulted from "taking responsibility".

But does Matsui's dissatisfaction indicate his not knowing?

Matsui Iwane claimed during the pre-trial phase of the Tokyo Trial that his diary had been burned down. In reality, his diary still exists in the world. Why did he lie about the diary when it still exists? Did he want to conceal something by the lie? These are all questions that people cannot help asking.

The diary written by Matsui Iwane during the war was edited by Tanaka Masaaki, which was published by Fuyo Shobo Publishing in 1985. In the same year, Asahi Shimbun published critical articles consecutively on November 24th and 25th under the titles "Tampering with historical materials of the 'Nanjing Massacre' - 900 Texts Different from the Original Texts" and "Keep 'Nanjing Massacre' Bottled up - Tanaka's tampering with the diary of General Matsui". In response, Tanaka Masaaki argued that "the General's unique cursive script cannot be interpreted in many ways". He stressed that "The purpose of compiling the General's diary is to widely convey the General's behavior, emotion and true intention during the war to 'society' through such first-level information as the army commander's diary. As for the mistakes, they are not to distort the true intention of the General. It could be said that the purpose has been completely achieved. The slaughter school led by Asahi Shimbun, Hora Tomio and others, listed fake photos

---

[58] At that time, Japan's Military Service Law stipulated that people aged 20 or above would be called up for active service, discharged from active service after two years, and would be in reserve service for the next five years and four months, and in further reserve service for the next ten years.

[59] 〈陸軍大将畑俊六日誌〉,南京戦史編集委員会編『南京戦史資料集』, p. 52. The original text was dated "January 29th, 1938", but there were events on February 5th and 6th in the text, and the next day of this article was the 7th, so the record should cover content from February 29th to February 6th.

and inflated notes and publicized the 'massacre' of 200,000 or 300,000 people that did not exist. Such things are real <u>falsification of history</u>".[60] Hora Tomio and other Japanese scholars had refuted this excuse.[61] Even from the incomplete diary of Matsui Iwane,[62] we can still see many records of Japanese atrocities.

As in the diary on December 20th:

At that time, officers and soldiers had a few robberies (mainly furniture, etc.) and committed some rapes, which were more or less the truth.[63]

In the diary on December 26th to 28th:

Robberies and rapes near Nanjing and Hangzhou were also heard. Special staff demanded a severe ban and punished person in charge in order to sweep away the foul atmosphere. Serious demands were made on the armies.[64]

In the diary on December 29th:

There were incidents in Nanjing in which our soldiers looted cars and other things from embassies of various countries. The Army's ignorance and rudeness are surprising. It is regrettable that the reputation of the Imperial Army has been consequently damaged. Staff Officer Nakayama (Nakayama Neito, the Staff Officer of the Japanese Central China Area Army and Major of Air Arm) was sent to Nanjing quickly to deal with the aftermath immediately. He ordered the punishment of those involved and, of course, the person in charge also was punished. In particular, Shanghai Expeditionary Army is under the command of his royal highness, which is related to royal morality and dignity. Therefore, strict disciplinary measures would be taken.[65]

In the diary on January 6th in the following year:

Chiefs of staff of the two armies were called into pay attention to the situation and be given instructions on future matters. The military discipline of the two armies is gradually under control and efforts are being made to eliminate the situation so that it will no longer be the biggest worry in the future.[66]

---

[60]Tanaka Masaaki,『南京事件の総括──虐殺否定十五の論拠』, pp. 340 and 341.
[61]Such as Hora Tomio's「松井大将陣中日誌改竄あとさき」and『南京事件を考える』, compiled by Hora Tomio, Akira Fujiwara and Honda Katsuichi, Tokyo, Ōtsuki Shoten, August 20th, 1987, 1st printed version, pp. 55–68.
[62]此处所本南京戦史編集委員会編『南京戦史資料集』中所收「松井石根大将戦陣日記」, and the proofreading is fine, but there are too many deletions.
[63]「松井石根大将戦陣日記」,南京戦史編集委員会編『南京戦史資料集』, p. 22.
[64]「松井石根大将戦陣日記」,南京戦史編集委員会編『南京戦史資料集』, p. 24.
[65]「松井石根大将戦陣日記」,南京戦史編集委員会編『南京戦史資料集』, p. 24.
[66]「松井石根大将戦陣日記」,南京戦史編集委員会編『南京戦史資料集』, p. 28.

On February 6th, Matsui Iwane went to Nanjing for the last time. His diary on that day recorded this:

> Many people have no fundamental understanding of this incident. On the one hand, the problem of military discipline has not yet been fully resolved. On the other hand, cadres are all merciful and indulgent. I deeply feel that it is rather harmful and useless for the army to conduct local propaganda and caresses, and cannot help sighing with great regret… Military discipline problems are indeed caused by the staff under the head of the 16th division.[67]

Matsui Iwane received the order of dismissal on February 10th. In his farewell speech to the headquarters of the Area Army on February 16th, he still stressed that "It is still urgent to reinforce military discipline".[68] On February 19th, General Hata Shunroku, the new commander of the Japanese Expeditionary Army in China, arrived. During the handover, Matsui Iwane also stressed that "In order to maintain military discipline, the Army should stay in the camps in groups to reduce direct contact with the ordinary people".[69] It can be seen that Matsui Iwane had already lost the hope that the Japanese army could "come to reason".

Judging from the diary of General Matsui quoted above, although he did not mention the massacre at that time,[70] he was very clear about the atrocities such as robbery and rape committed by the Japanese army. Not only was he very clear about the atrocities committed by the Japanese army, but these atrocities had made him feel the irreparable damage to the "reputation of the Imperial Army".[71] As the commander-in-chief of the Shanghai Expeditionary

---

[67] 「松井石根大将戦陣日記」,南京戦史編集委員会編『南京戦史資料集』, p. 39.

[68] 「松井石根大将戦陣日記」,南京戦史編集委員会編『南京戦史資料集』, p. 43.

[69] 「松井石根大将戦陣日記」,南京戦史編集委員会編『南京戦史資料集』, p. 44.

[70] However, the main reason for the massacre was his sweeping order, which had been made known to every soldier at that time, and officers and soldiers of the Japanese army "courageously rushed forward". On Matsui Iwane's responsibilities of killing prisoners, there will be another article that describes it in detail. Here is only one example and that is the words in the diary of Mizutani Sho who was the Private First Class in the 1st Infantry squadron of the 7th regiment. He wrote in his dairy *War Dust* "…36 people were shot dead. Everyone cried desperately and begged for mercy, but there was no way. Since it was hard to distinguish the targeted people, we had no choice but to kill some poor victims. These victims are necessary. 'Thoroughly sweeping the anti-Japanese people and defeated soldiers' is an order issued by the army commander General Matsui. The order is severe". (Mizutani Sho, 「戦塵」,南京戦史編集委員会編『南京戦史資料集』, p. 502.)

[71] According to the diary kept by Iinuma Mamoru on February 7th, Matsui said at the spiritual consolation ceremony held on the same day: "recalling the boasting when we first entered Nanjing and the feeling in the spiritual consolation ceremony held on the next day (the December 18th), today we just feel grief. Several forbidden things happened in the past 50 days, which have halved the achievements made by the officers and soldiers died in the battles. Don't we feel ashamed of meeting them someday?" (「飯沼守日記」,南京戦史編集委員会編『南京戦史資料集』, p. 246.) The word "several" recorded by Iinuma Mamoru should be a fuzzy word even if it was the original word used by Matsui, because it is impossible that "several" things could halve "the achievements".

Army and the "elite" 10th Army, Matsui Iwane had unobstructed information. Therefore, his declaration that he did not know about the serious atrocities committed by the Japanese army at the pre-trial stage of the Tokyo Trial, just as he claimed that his diary had been burned down, could only be regarded as false statement—if he "forgot" them, he would not leave no room for words.

Although Matsui Iwane did not admit the massacre and mass atrocities committed by the Japanese army in Nanjing, there are still traces to follow from what he said after the death sentence to Hanayama Shinshou, a Buddhist professor at the University of Tokyo and a "trymoaris" at the Sugamo Detention House where Class-A war criminals are held. On December 9th, 1948, he left words like this:

> The Nanjing incident was shameful… When I was engaged in the Japan-Russia war, I joined the Army as a senior captain. Today's division head is worse than that of that time. During the Japan-Russia war, even the handling of Russian prisoners was good, not to mention Chinese prisoners. I didn't do well this time.
>
> After the spiritual consolation ceremony, I called everyone together. As the commander of the Army, I wept and expressed anger. Asakanomiya was also on scene. So was Lieutenant General Yanagawa, the commander of the Army. The glory of the imperial power was overshadowed by the atrocities of the soldiers. Later, everyone laughed. What's more, a division chief even said, "Why so strange about this?"
>
> Therefore, even if I was the only one who got such an ending, I would be very glad to see that the military people at that time, even one more, reflect deeply.[72]

The "atrocities of the soldiers" here which can "overshadow" the "glory of the imperial power" at one stroke is obviously not the so-called "several illegal incidents" committed by "one officer and three soldiers" mentioned by Matsui Iwane in the pre-trial phase. Such regretful remark made by Matsui Iwane "on his deathbed" has already made a clear meaning, although he had not directly stated the scale of the atrocities.

According to the above statement, we can be sure that Matsui Iwane was deeply aware of the severity of the Japanese atrocities when he was in office, and his consequent dismissal further gave him no reason to forget it. His pretense of not knowing the atrocities during the Tokyo Trial is meant to not only safeguard the "Imperial Army" but also to safeguard himself—Matsui Iwane was the only Class A war criminal among 28 who was sentenced to hanging for "failure to prevent breach of contract" (Cause of Action 55).

---

[72] Hanayama Shinshou,《平和の発見》, quoted from Hata Ikuhiko,『南京事件――虐殺の構造』, pp. 45–46.

The above-mentioned facts have shown that the Japanese military and political authorities and Matsui Iwane were aware of the atrocities committed by the Japanese army. Hence, the gist of this section is clear. However, whether Japanese atrocities are known to Japanese Emperor Hirohito is still a question worthy of attention. Hirohito did not direct the war, but he was the "spiritual leader" of the whole war, not only the spiritual leader, he was also highly committed to the war[73]:

> The situation was urgent on the 11th. At half past seven in the morning, Anami, the Director of Personnel of the Ministry of the Army, first came to the royal residence to attend. Later in the morning, Prince Kan'in, the Chief of Staff, paid a formal visit. In the afternoon, Prince Fushiminomiya, the Minister of Military Orders, paid a formal visit and Prince Kan'in, the Chief of Staff, paid another visit. Later in the afternoon, Prime Minister Konoe and Secretary of State for War Sugiyama came and paid formal visits. His Majesty got up at 7 o'clock earlier than usual and stayed indoors until late at night. As daily exercise, walks along the coast were all cancelled. He dressed in military uniform and worked hard in the office all day long. All those close to him were deeply fearfully and grateful.[74]

Although this was just "one common day" after July 7th, it was also a microcosm that Hirohito was diligent in discharging his official duties.

Hirohito gave Matsui Iwane "imperial rescript" after the establishment of the Shanghai Expeditionary Army, saying that "I hereby appoint you to command the Shanghai Expeditionary Army" and "we should quickly conquer the enemy troops and show the Imperial Army's prowess at home and abroad so as to meet my trust".[75] Hirohito then issued "royal instruction" the day after the Japanese army captured Nanjing, expressing "deep satisfaction" with the Japanese army's "bravery" and its rapid capture of Nanjing.[76] Before the invasion of Nanjing, "royal wine" was long before prepared for the "celebration". However, after the war, he avoided all issues including the responsibility for the war. When returning from a visit to the United States in the autumn of 1975, he said in response to a reporter's question that "I cannot answer this question because I don't know much about "linguistics"

---

[73] Only Hirohito is mentioned here. In fact, the whole royal family is highly devoted. For example, when the Japanese army reached the gates of Nanjing, Asakanomiya gave the silk vest and refreshments given by the empress dowager to the high-ranking officers as encouragement. Iinuma Mamoru said in his diary on December 9th, "I feel extremely grateful". (「飯沼守日記」, 南京戦史編集委員会編『南京戦史資料集』, p. 209.)

[74] 全國各縣代表新聞五十社協力執筆『支那事變皇國之精華』「畏し事變時の竹の園生」, 上海毎日新聞社, January 25th, 1939, 1st edition, p. 1.

[75] 防衛庁防衛研修所戦史室編『大本営陸軍部』1, Tokyo, Asagumo Shimbunsha, September 25th, 1967, 1st edition, p. 471.

[76] 南京戦史編集委員会編『南京戦史資料集』, p. 18.

and literature".[77] (Hirohito's prevarication was severely criticized by Japan's left-wing groups.) After Hirohito's death, his dictation was published in 1946 in Emperor's Monologue, which said he had a "peace" talk before attacking Nanjing.[78] However, from the later published The Will of the Chief of the Samurai, Hirohito "may" also be an insider of Nanjing's atrocities. In *The Will of the Chief of the Samurai*,

> The debate over the existence of the Nanjing Massacre was mostly known to the relevant personnel at that time. I am not sure whether His Majesty knew about it or not, but occasionally he said that "it is different from the Army in the Japan-Russia war".[79]

As for whether Hirohito knew about it or not, the existing materials "may" not be conclusive, but as Japanese scholars said that:

The Emperor was "deeply satisfied" with the severity of the Nanjing Massacre. Although the emperor was not engaged in the massacre or directly ordered the killing of the prisoners, he was the only head of the Great Japanese Empire and it was he who was the "Grand Marshal" of Imperial Army and Navy. After the Manchurian Incident, the name of the Japanese army changed from "National Army" to "Imperial Army". The war of aggression against China was carried out as a "Holy War" in the name of the emperor. This concept "Holy War"

---

[77] On October 31st, 1975, He answered a question from the Japanese Press Club. (quoted from Tsuda Michio's 『南京大虐殺と日本人の精神構造』, Tokyo, Shakai Hyôronsha, June 15th, 1995, 1st edition, pp. 259–260.)

[78] Memoirs of Hirohito translated by Chen Pengren, Taipei, Taiwan Shin Sheng Daily News Publishing Department, 1st edition, September 1991, p. 36. The commentary following this section further reads: "The Sino-Japanese peace work mediated by German Ambassador to China Trautmann made great progress in December 1937. On the 7th, Chiang Kai-shek told Trautmann that he was willing to hold Sino-Japanese talks on the basis of Japan's peace conditions. Hirohito, who was informed of the news by Foreign Minister Hirota Koki, said happily 'That's great.' However, at that time, the general staff had issued an order to attack Nanjing according to the strong reporting of opinions of the army commander Hata. What a turning point in history" (ibid., p. 37). There seems to be no evidence for the so-called That's great. However, judging from mistaking Matsui Iwane as Hata Shunroku and the translation lacking precision, this statement is not convincing. Hirohito was exempted from liability suggested by the United States. China, the Soviet Union and other countries all held different opinions. The Japanese right-wing groups also expressed dissatisfaction from an opposite standpoint that Hirohito was never guilty and therefore was not responsible. Hirohito's Innocence theory was widely accepted with the intensification of right-wing groups in Japanese society after the end of the Cold War. For example, Tahara Soichiro, the critic who has the most influence on Japan's mainstream society in recent years, also maintains in his recent works that Hirohito was always opposed to war. (see Tahara Soichiro's 『日本の戦争——なぜ、戦いに踏み切ったか?』第7章「八紘一宇」之「天皇の『戦争反対』はなぜ通らなかったのか」小节, Tokyo, Shôgakukan, January 1st, 2001, 4th printed version, pp. 441–452.)

[79] 『侍従長の遺言』,Asahi Shuppansha, 1997, quoted from 『南京大虐殺否定論13のウソ』, p. 37.

complemented the contempt for China, relieved guilt and rationalized all sadistic acts. Therefore, it is beyond doubt that the emperor must at least bear the highest moral responsibility for the Nanjing Massacre.[80]

III

Whether the Japanese local public "did not knew" the Japanese atrocities in Nanjing during the war? Before solving this problem, we may as well make a reverse assumption, assuming that the Japanese public was completely "ignorant" of the Japanese atrocities, and then let us see what causes this "ignorance"?

There are many possibilities for individual "not knowing", but the overall "not knowing" is nothing more than two possibilities: First, nothing had happened; and second, they merely did not know the matter. The primary reason for not knowing is that the channel of "knowing" had been blocked. Therefore, if we want to draw an equal sign between "not knowing" and nonexistence, unobstructed information is a necessary condition. At the beginning of this article, a passage in the Myth is quoted, which includes the following sentence "Hara Shiro, commissioner of the aforementioned Yomiuri Shimbun, also made it very clear". The so-called "made it very clear" refers to such a passage:

> I got information that a massacre seemed to happen in Nanjing after three months of the fall of Nanjing, when the army did not issue a gag order. I wonder why currently there is such news… It is strange. I contacted several authorities to confirm it but got no satisfied result. Most people think that this was another propaganda made by the Chinese army.[81]

If this statement is true and "no gag order had been issued", then there is a reason to doubt "information on the massacre". Since Japanese rightwing groups are passionate about social identity, believing that "identity" is

---

[80] Tsuda Michio, 『南京大虐殺と日本人の精神構造』, p. 259. Japanese Admiral of the Fleet 56 Yamamoto Isoroku expressed his ambition with a poem in his death note that "Lofty is the grace of the emperor and long is the kingdom of the emperor. When it comes to the prosperity of the kingdom for hundred years, individual's death or honor is tiny," which indicated that he will "repay the kingdom and the emperor with his life". (Yamamoto Yoshimasa, 「わが父山本五十六最後の晩餐と遺書」, 『正論』, Tokyo, Sankei Shinbunsha, September 2001, p. 61.) At that time, the actions of countless Japanese soldiers were inspired by "the emperor's mercy".

[81] Tanaka Masaaki, 『「南京虐殺」の虚構——松井大将の日記をめぐって』, p. 243. The so-called "Propaganda" by China theory is very popular among the right-wing groups in Japan. For example, seeing the Sino-Japanese War from the Reporting Front said that "Since the war began, the words that the Nanjing Massacre was made by the Japanese army and 20,000 people were raped in Nanjing have been prevalent. It can be said that this is the victory of Chiang Kai-shek's propaganda". (Nishioka Kaori, 『報道戦線から見た日中戦争——陸軍報道部長馬淵逸雄の足跡』, Tokyo, Fuyo Shobo Publishing, June 25th, 1999, 1st edition, p. 127.)

the guarantee of responsibility and credibility[82] and Hara Shiro was the former consultant of the Japan's leading newspaper Yomiuri Shimbun, his words should be the most credible, but in reality it is nothing but a lie!"

After the Manchuria Incident, the Japanese military and political authorities began to control the news. By the July 7th Incident, the blockade of the news had reached a rather severe level. On July 13th, the Home Ministry Police Affairs Bureau ordered that all records and photos of the Japanese invaders, except those of the Ministry of the Army, cannot be published. On July 31st, "Article 27 of the Newspaper Law" was passed, stipulating that the Ministers of the Army, Navy and Foreign Affairs have the right to prohibit and restrict the publication on military and diplomatic matters. On the same day, the Ministry of the Army announced the corresponding "Ministerial Decree No. 24" and "Standards for News Disclosure of Prohibited Items". Among these "Prohibited Items", Japanese atrocity was an important part. As early as three days before the "Article 27 of the Newspaper Law" was passed, the media division of the Ministry of the Army had implemented the "Essentials for Permission or Not of News Disclosure Items", which clearly stipulated the contents of "No Permission" for news disclosure:

6. Horrible notes or photos that give people a feeling of maltreatment about the arrest and interrogation of Chinese people or soldiers;
   7. Ruthless pictures, expect those about sadistic behavior of Chinese soldiers.[83]

These facts should not have been unknown to Hara Shiro and the *Myth*.

On December 1st, the eve of the attack on Nanjing, the Imperial General Headquarters stipulated that "publicity strategies and general intelligence shall be the responsibility of major generals of the headquarters of the Area Army. But reports will be 'issued by the Report Department' and strategies will be given further instructions".[84] Later in the "Outline of Specific Publicity" for "external publicity":

---

[82] For example, Sono Ayako, a female writer and current chairman of the Nippon Foundation, said recently when talking about bin Laden that his mother came from a family in Yemen and "could never enter the upper class in Saudi Arabia". She then said that "He turned 'personal resent' into 'public resent'. From this point of view, it is left-wing thinking. The left wing has always turned all its hatred into the 'public resent', that is, the so-called 'evil of society'". (Talks of Sono Ayako and Tokuoka Takao「我ら、キリスト教徒から見たイスラム」, *Shokun*, Tokyo, Bungei Shunjû, December 2001, p. 28.)

[83] Quoted from Yamanaka Hisashi's『新聞は戦争を美化せよ！――戦時国家情報機構史』, Tokyo, Shôgakukan, January 1st, 2001, 1st edition, p. 225. This book written by Yamanaka Hisashi contains a detailed account of the Japanese government and military's control of speech during the war.

[84]「大陸指第九號」,『現代史資料』9「日中戦争」2, compiled and interpreted by Usui Katsumi and Inaba Masao, Tokyo, みすず書房, September 30th, 1964, 1st edition, p. 217.

The disciplined actions of Imperial Army, Bushido's spirit and merciful behavior in occupied areas should be publicized.[85]

We can see from these materials that: First, the Japanese government strictly controlled the news during the war; second, the publication of notes and photos reflecting Japanese atrocities was strictly prohibited the so-called "No Permission"; third, not only reflecting the atrocities of the Japanese army was strictly prohibited, but it was required to publicize the "mercy" of the Japanese army; and fourth, the "sadistic behavior of Chinese soldiers" was highlighted. In other words, there was not only the strict control, but also distorted propaganda. Japanese scholar Kikuchi Masanori said 30 years ago that:

It was almost impossible to learn about the Nanjing Massacre from the Japanese newspapers at that time. The newspapers were flooded with such news as the outstanding victory, the humanitarianism of the Japanese army and the unreserved solidarity of Japanese nationals in the rear…

After reading the newspapers before and after the Nanjing incident, the first thing I felt was that by that time there was the harsh fact that the major newspapers had completely become lackeys of the imperial fascists…

It is extremely hard to see clearly the cruelty and aggression of the "Imperial Army" from such newspapers.[86]

Under such distorted publicity, what the Japanese public could get was only an illusion, which was far away from the truth than from the ignorance. Such illusion was actually clearly seen by foreigners in Nanjing at that time. After the establishment of the Nanjing Self-governing Committee, in order to create a festive atmosphere, the Japanese army held a celebration and asked the Safety Zones to send thousands of personnel to attend it. Minnie Vautrin's Diary depicted the participants' feeling that "One of our representatives felt sick about this and did not even eat dinner". However, the following sentence is that "There is no doubt that you will see movies about people's enthusiastical support for the new regime".[87] Such taunt is obvious because it can be easily understood by outsiders. The reason why Japan's right-wing groups still use these "enthusiastic support" materials as evidence is that their position is completely consistent with the Japanese national policy in wartime. Not only were there so many false appearances in Japan, but there the situation of Nanjing was hidden by false appearances. George Fitch, a former deputy director of the Nanking Safety Zones, later said in his memoirs,

[85] Quoted from Yamanaka Hisashi 『新聞は戦争を美化せよ!——戦時国家情報機構史』, p. 283.

[86] Kikuchi Masanori, 「南京事件と日本の新聞報道」, 『日中戦争資料』8付録, pp. 2–4.

[87] The Diary of Vautrin, written by Minnie Vautrin and translated by the Nanjing Massacre Research Center of Nanjing Normal University, Jiang People's Publishing House, 1st edition, October 2000, p. 220.

These pictures were posted everywhere by the Japanese in Nanjing, saying that they were considering the welfare of the people. One poster showed a smiling woman and her child kneeling in front of a Japanese soldier and receiving a piece of bread from him. The caption was that "The Japanese army pacify the refugees, and the harmonious atmosphere in Nanjing is becoming more and more gratifying." At the same time, they also spread outright lies that "The people were oppressed by the anti-Japanese army, suffering severely, without food and medicine, but when the Imperial Army entered the city, it put away the bayonet and stretched out a merciful hand…to give mercy and concern to the good and sincere citizens … tens of thousands of refugees gave up their former foolish attitudes against Japan, clapping and cheering for the assurance of their lives." There were several paragraphs of such disgusting words. Finally, there was a picture that showed "Japanese soldiers and Chinese children play together in the park: Nanjing is the best place in the world and we can see that people live and work in peace and contentment." These texts were translated by many of my colleagues, so I guarantee that they were accurate and not fabricated. [88]

Georg Rosen, the administrative secretary of the German embassy in China, said in a letter to the Ministry of Foreign Affairs that "The Japanese brought a beautiful color poster: A kind Japanese carries a lunch box and a Chinese child sits on his shoulder. Meanwhile, the child's parents who are poor and honest peasants look at the kind-hearted uncle with gratitude and happiness. Unfortunately, color posters like this were not in conformity with reality and can only be regarded as advertisements to attract tourists!"[89]

Such "propaganda", especially the "No Permission" policy, was thoroughly implemented at that time. For example, one and a half months after the Japanese captured Nanjing, the Japan's Dōmei News Agency sent back an introduction of a report about the Japanese atrocities on British conservative newspaper The Daily Telegraph, and the Intelligence Department of the Cabinet ordered "not to publish".[90] The Asahi Shimbun reporter, Mori Kyojo, who was sent to New York at the time, said in My Stories in Asahi Shimbun,

I thought seriously about the "duty of notification" of news when I went overseas as a special correspondent. The Nanjing Massacre made by the Japanese Army (December 1937) was widely reported in American newspapers. As a special correspondent of New York, I certainly had to send this telegram back in detail. However, no newspapers sent from Tokyo reported that. In addition, the instructions from the editorial department in Tokyo were all "successful bombing in Chinese mainland made by the naval air force departing from Taiwan

---

[88] 《日本帝国主义侵华档案资料选编•南京大屠杀》, p. 1045.
[89] 《日本帝国主义侵华档案资料选编•南京大屠杀》, p. 161.
[90] 《绝密、内阁情报部一•三一、情报第三号》, quoted from Yamanaka Hisashi's 『新聞は戦争を美化せよ!——戦時国家情報機構史』, p. 285.

base, response in America of this landmark feat and immediate call" and so on. I couldn't help but feel the rift between the correspondent and its press.[91]

According to Published Police Newspaper No.111 and No.112 sponsored by Japanese Home Ministry Police Affairs Bureau in wartime, it can be seen that from December 1937 to February of the following year, a large number of imported newspapers were prohibited from circulating in Japan on the ground that these newspapers reported the atrocities committed by Japanese army in Nanjing, including:

During December 1937

The Shanghai Evening Post & Mercury (Shanghai), on 23rd— "Atrocities in Nanking City Shock the Headquarters, and the Army is out of Control"

Ibid, on 24th— "Exposure by The Times"

Ibid, on 25th— "Witnesses Claim that Japanese Atrocities in Nanking do Happen"

The North-China Daily News (Shanghai), on 25th— "Rape and Plunder Committed Immediately after Occupation of the Capital"

The China Press (Shanghai), on 25th— "Hard Evidence of Brutal Acts by Japanese Army"

The North China Herald (Shanghai), on 29th— "Rape and Plunder after Occupying the Capital"

The China Critic (Shanghai), on 30th— "The Rape of Nanking"

South China Morning Post (Hong Kong), on 25th— "Terror Activities after the Fall of Nanking"

The People's Tribune (Hong Kong), on 26th— "The Japanese Culture Mission in Nanking"

The Tien Kwong Morning News (Hong Kong), on 25th— "Enemy is Massacring People in our Capital and How the Chinese People Clear the Blood Debts"

The Kung Sheung Evening News (Hong Kong), on 25th— "Enemy Troops Commit Wanton Killings after Occupying Nanking and 50 thousand Able-bodied Men were Killed"

Universal Circulating Herald (Hong Kong), on 27th— "Foreigners from Nanking give Angry Accounts of the Rape of Nanking by Japanese Army"

Yuet Wa Po (Guangzhou), on 25th— "U.S. Journalist Reports on Horror Scenes of Rape, Plunder and Ravaging in Nanking by Enemy Troops"

The Kung Sheung Daily News (Hong Kong), on 25th— "Enemy Troops Commit Wanton Killings in Nanking"

Ibid, on 26th— "Enemy Troops Commit Wanton Killings in Nanking"

Kwok Wa Po (Guangzhou), on 26th— "Rape, Plunder, and Massacre Committed by the Enemies in Nanking"

Peking & Tientsin Times (Tianjin), on 31st— "Rape and Plunder after the Fall of the Capital"

Sin Chew Daily (original text, Singapore), on 26— "Japanese Army Show Animal Brutality and Commit Mass Killings in Nanking"

[91] Mori Kyojo, 『私の朝日新聞史』, Tokyo, 田畑書店, September 30th, 1981, 1st edition, p. 24.

Xin Bao (Jakarta), on 27th— "Atrocities of Japanese Army in Nanking"
The New York Times (New York), on 18th— "the Captured were all Killed"
Ibid, on 19th— "Japan is Trying to Control the Atrocities in Nanking"
New York Herald Tribune (New York), on 25th— "A Letter Unveiling the Horrors in Nanking after its Fall"
The Times (London), on 18th— "Terrorist Activities in Nanking"

During January 1938
The Times Weekly Edition (London), on 23rd— "Horror in Nanking"
Life (Chicago), on 10th— "Reports and Photos of the Fall of Nanking"
Zhongshan Daily (Guangzhou), on 23rd— "Enemy Troops Show Animal Brutality and Commit Mass Killings in Nanking"
The Natal Mercury (Durban), on 29th— "Cruelty and Lust Hanging over Nanking"
News (Seattle), on 10th— "Japan under the Threat of Trends"
During February 1938
The Manchester Guardian (Manchester), on 7th— "Terrorism in Nanking"
The Manchester Guardian Weekly (Manchester), on 11th— "Atrocities in Nanking"
The Chinese Mail (Hong Kong), on 21st— "Conversation with a Survivor who Escaped from Nanking to Hankou"[92]

According to Hora Tomio's statistics, the above citations are far from the whole of the banned newspapers.

Just looking at the above citations, one may mistakenly think that although the Japanese government and military strictly prohibited the spread of Japanese atrocities in Japan, they didn't prohibit the news spread outside Nanjing, the place of the incident. This is certainly not the truth. Few days ago, I reread Iinuma Mamoru's Diary and found a piece of material that I didn't notice before. It is now quoted below:

> The Deputy called and said that "according to the report of the U.S. consul in Nanjing, from January 15th to 18th, Japanese soldiers took eight women from institutions of the U.S (it seems to refer to those American properties - noted by the quoter) and stole pianos by breaking the wall of Jinling University. Diplomats in Nanjing were powerless and the military were not regulated, so the U.S ambassador in Tokyo protested it. It is really regrettable that there are still such soldiers nowadays. However, soldiers who broke into houses with an American flag and robbed things were detained today by military police that walked with the secretary of the U.S. embassy. Protests of the U.S. seemed to be real. <u>But our side sent a suspicious telegram to the central government in order to protest against the consul who breached the original agreement. He denied everything on sending the telegram.</u>[93]

---

[92] Quoted from Hora Tomio's 『南京大虐殺の証明』, Tokyo, Asahi Shinbunsha, March 5th, 1986, 1st edition, pp. 225–227.

[93] 「飯沼守日記」,南京戦史編集委員会編『南京戦史資料集』, p. 240.

The "agreement" between the Japanese army and the United States (and perhaps other countries) was not recorded in Iinuma Mamoru's Diary. But according to the above quotation, there should be an "agreement" that the atrocities committed by the Japanese army should be reported by the United States only to the Japanese army stationed in Nanjing who took the responsibility to solve the issue, instead of being reported directly to the Japan's central government. We can see from this record that news was definitely prohibited from spreading to the outside. There was also a record in Uemura Toshimichi's Diary which can be compared with this to show that this was a "standpoint" of the Japanese army and was not occasional. In Uemura Toshimichi's Diary on January 21th:

> In terms of military discipline such as plunder and abuse of women, the U.S. ambassador to Tokyo said that "diplomats are powerless and the will of military governance is lacking." The Deputy Staff Officer called for an investigation into it. <u>Negotiations will be led by local staff officers and consul will offer an apology</u>…[94]

Instead of verifying the situations, the Japanese army stationed in Nanjing blocked sources of the news. It can be seen that the senior officers of Japanese army stationed in Nanjing were aware of the atrocities. (In this regard, the Tokyo Trial was not excessive in judging Matsui Iwane as "failure to prevent".)

At that time, not only the Japanese army but also other Japanese organs spared no effort to prevent the spread of Japanese atrocities. In *The Good Man of Nanking: The Diaries of John Rabe*, there was a record on February 9th as following, which shows the "effort" of the Japanese embassy:

> In order to settle my application for returning to Shanghai, Mr. Fukui invited me to go to the Japanese embassy early this morning. Perhaps he would like to remind me again that I should not forget to say only <u>good things</u> about the Japanese when I arrive at Shanghai! If he thought I will say no, he would be totally wrong. Of course, he would not be wrong in this respect, nor would I. He has already known me very well. He knew that I will promise him to say what he wants to hear in the same Asian hypocritical way.[95]

What Fukui said to Rabe was indeed as Rabe's "perhaps" speculation:

> Yesterday I went to the Japanese embassy to see Mr. Fukui but did not meet him. At 6 o'clock that night, he came to see me and discussed my trip to Shanghai. As expected, he could not help but threaten me that "If you <u>speak ill of</u> us to the corrspondants in Shanghai, you are against the Japanese army."

---

[94] 「上村利道日記」,南京戦史編集委員会編『南京戦史資料集』, p. 292.
[95] The Chinese version of *The Good Man of Nanking: The Diaries of John Rabe*, p. 599.

He told me that Kroeger's report was very bad and took a long telegram from London as an example to show Kroeger's bad thought. He believed that the telegram was sent to him from Hong Kong. I comforted Fukui immediately and said, "In my opinion, Kroeger was not in Hong Kong at all at that time." This was obviously meaningless because the telegram was probably sent from Shanghai. I knew from the following letter of January 28 from Kroeger that he made a detailed report in Shanghai and agreed to publish it. When I asked Fukui what I was allowed to say in Shanghai, he replied that "It's up to you, Sir." In response, I said: "In my opinion, you expect me to tell the press that the situation in Nanjing is getting better day by day and please stop publish any more reports on the criminal acts of Japanese soldiers. Reporting such news is equal to adding fuel to the flames and generating more dissonal atmosphere between the Japanese and the Europeans." "Good!" he said joyfully, "that is really great!" "Well, my dear Mr. Fukui, now please give me a chance to talk with General Asabu and Major Honato about this thing. I heard that Mr. Honato can speak German fluently. I think there will always be an understanding and friendly cooperation between you and me, I mean, between the Committee and the Japanese military. We arduously got several foreign doctors and nurses for the Drum Tower Hospital. Why do you refuse to issue passports to them to Nanjing? Why are we not allowed to ship food from Shanghai to Nanjing? Why are we forbidden to enter the Red Cross Hospital inside the Ministry of Foreign Affairs? The hospital is still provided with food by our committee!" His reply was a shrug of the shoulders or the repeated sentence that "If you speak ill of the Japanese, you will infuriate the Japanese military and you will not be allowed to return to Nanjing."

It can be seen from what has been mentioned above that the Japanese embassy would never permit others saying, "bad things" against the Japanese.

H. J. Timperley, a reporter of The Manchester Guardian, is the author of What War Means: the Japanese Terror in China, the first book to expose Japanese atrocities. He was detained by Japan when he sent back his electric manuscripts to the newspaper.[96] He later said that,

In December last year, after the Japanese army captured Nanjing, they shot, raped and plundered innocent Chinese civilians everywhere, stopping at no evil. I thought that as a journalist, it was my duty to report it. And I drafted what I

---

[96] Yoshiaki Itakura once questioned it and said that "In Shanghai, the international city at that time, the Japanese army did not have the authority to prevent foreign news agencies from sending messages". (Yoshiaki Itakura,「南京大虐殺」の真相(続)——ティバーリの陰謀,『じゅん刊●世界と日本』, 内外ニュース社, June 15th, 1984.) Hora Tomio refuted him according to the diary of Matsui Iwane. (In the diary of November 28th: On this day, our officials are in charge of the Telegraph Bureau, Press Inspection Office, and Customs of the Chinese Government in the Common Concession".『松井石根大将戦陣日誌』, Tokyo, Fuyo Shobo Publishing, 1985, p. 115, this section was omitted in 南京戦史編集委員会編『南京戦史資料集』. Hora Tomio refuted it in his 『南京大虐殺の証明』, pp. 41–42.) Yoshiaki Itakura never confessed, but this article has not been included in his collection. (Yoshiaki Itakura,『本当はこうだった南京事件』, Tokyo, Nihon Tosho Kankôkai, December 8th, 1999, 1st edition.)

saw and heard about the atrocities committed by the Japanese army then sent the electric manuscripts to The Manchester Guardians. However, after asking local authorities for instructions, the telegraph inspector of the Japanese side in Shanghai thought the content was "too exaggerated" and detained it. After repeated negotiations, still no satisfied result had been achieved.[97]

In addition to the strict ban on the press issued by senior officials, there were also strict warnings against ordinary insiders in order to prevent Japanese atrocities from spreading to Japan. Sone Ichio, who took part in the attack on Nanjing, said in Nanjing Massacre and Battle:

In order not to let the people know the evil side of the Army in the battlefield, apart from strengthening control of the news, soldiers in the battlefield were strictly forbidden to leak anything. After the Nanjing battle, some veterans were gagged when they returned to Japan. I also returned to Japan in autumn of the 15th year of the Shōwa era. When leaving troops, we were warned that "when you return to Japan, you will be out of troops and become local people. However, the reputation of being a soldier is something to be proud of and you must not spread negative things that defile the Imperial Army".
It was a complicated statement. The main point was that "Even if you return to Japan and leave the troops, you are absolutely not allowed to say anything bad you did on the battlefield."[98]

---

[97] *What War Means: the Japanese Terror in China* written by Timperley and The Historical Materials of the Nanjing Massacre of the Japanese Army in China compiled by the Editorial Committee of the Historical Materials of the Nanjing Massacre of the Japanese Army in China and Nanjing Library, Jiangsu Ancient Books Publishing House, 1st edition, February 1998, pp. 157–158. Timperley said that "the reason why he wrote this book is that he wanted to make the information blocked by Japan "public in the world" (ibid., p. 158) but Kitamura Minoru recently wrote that the reporting channels at that time were not only telegrams, but also air mail and radio. For example, F. Tillman Durdin, a reporter of the New York Times, once sent a long record by air mail. Besides, the gist of Tian's report was published in the North China Daily News on January 21st, 1938. Therefore, Timperley's acts are just the "conspiracy" of the Ministry of Propaganda of the Government of the Republic of China. (See Kitamura Minoru's 『「南京事件」の探究——その実像をもとめて』第一部「国民党国際宣傳処と戦時対外戦略」, Tokyo, Bungei Shunjû, November 20th, 2001 1st edition, pp. 25–64.) Kitamura thinks that he seeks truth from facts, but someone in Japan has written a work to point out that Kitamura's work is political. (See Yamada Youichi,歴史改ざんの新意匠——北村稔『「南京事件」の探究』の実像,『人権と教育』No. 341, Tokyo, Shakai Hyôronsha, May 20th, 2002, pp. 139–149.)

[98] Sone Ichio, 『南京虐殺と戦争』, Tokyo, Tairyûsha, April 24th, 1988, 2nd printed version, p. 106. At that time, the Japanese authorities paid considerable attention to the words and deeds of "soldiers who returned back". For example, in 1941, the Chief of Military Affairs specially said at the Chief of Staff's meeting that returning soldiers "exaggerated the bad military discipline, although not maliciously, and it gradually cultivated anti-military and anti-war ideas". Therefore, special attention should be paid to them. (「参謀長会同席に於ける兵務局長口演」,『資料日本現代史』1「軍隊内の反戦運動」, compiled and interpreted by Akira Fujiwara, Tokyo, Ōtsuki Shoten, July 25, 1980, p. 343.) In reality, many Japanese veterans do strictly keep quiet so far in order to never "lose face" of "the Imperial Army". Yamada Masayuki, a professor of the Akita

These bans should be said to have achieved good results. However, when Japan was defeated and its control over the media was removed, the atrocities committed by the Japanese army in Nanjing were soon made public. The spread actually occurred before, what is commonly said, the International Military Tribunal for the Far East brought up the Incident in August 1946. Moreover, nor was it "forced" to be published by the occupying forces as stated in Myth. As early as in March 1946, in People's Review, Kaneko Renji had introduced H. J. Timperley's What War Means: the Japanese Terror in China under the title "Emperor's Army". Kaneko Renji added that:

> Such atrocities are not innated to the Japanese nation. This is a terrible result of years of militarism education. <u>The citizens' sense of justice has been intentionally paralyzed for a long time</u>. Japan's so-called military education is to create such inhuman robbers and such tame tools. In order to achieve this goal, schools, newspaper industry, magazine industry, movie industry and all other institutions have been mobilized… Today, the Japanese society for the first time wants to achieve justice. The first task we got is to thoroughly hold the leaders and their followers' responsibility of committing those chilling crimes. They will be handed to the people to be tried and punished severely. Only in this way can we remove all the elements of crime in our Japanese nation and apologize for such crimes, or we will always be sinners to all people of the world.[99]

The above quotation can prove that: First, if the claim that the Japanese nationals "first knew" the atrocities committed by the Japanese army in Nanjing from the Tokyo Trial, which right-wing groups such as the Myth sticks to, is true, it is completely caused by the blockade news made by the Japanese military and political authorities during the war; and second, at the same time, it can be proved that although the Japanese occupying forces were trying to prevent the spread of Japanese atrocities, their effectiveness was limited because, outside Japan, Japanese army had been known to the whole world for burning, killing, robbing, plundering and raping people in Nanjing.

University, in recent years, has interviewed a veteran (then was a lieutenant) many times who had reached extreme old age. The veteran was one of the soldiers who invaded Yunnan. The veteran denied the "comfort women" and said that he had never heard of such a thing. However, when talking about other topics, the old lieutenant casually said something that "Troops send us condoms. But when they can't even supplement weapons, ammunition and food, the condoms can't be distributed. The soldiers can only clean and dry the used condoms for reuse". Yamada said teasingly after the words, "It is confusing that the troops 'distributed condoms' to officers and soldiers who knew nothing of 'comfort women in the army'". (Yamada Masayuki,『アイデンティティと戦争——戦中期中国雲南省滇西地区の心理歴史研究』,鹿沼[栃木],グリーンピース出版会, May 20th, 2002 1st edition, pp. 103–104.)

[99]『人民評論』,伊藤書店出版,『日中戦争南京大殘虐事件資料集』第2巻英文資料編, compiled by Hora Tomio, Tokyo, Aoki Shoten, October 15th, 1986, 1st edition, pp. 3–4. (『日中戦争史資料』9「南京事件」, compiled by Hora Tomio, p. 7.)

IV

The situation that the world outside Japan knew everything while Japan inside knew nothing can only prove that the control of the Japanese military and political authorities during the war was effective, but it can never prove the inexistence of Japanese atrocities which has been demonstrated above. Japan's senior military officers and political officials were fully aware of the atrocity, which has been also proved above. Therefore, "not knowing" in the Myth and other works has been overturned. However, according to the consistent practice of the Myth and other parties, they will not accept it because they think they still have trump cards in their hands such as "neither seen nor heard" said by "Ujima Hiroshi". Therefore, it is still necessary for us to review it "repetitiously". Let us just regard the above records as "misinformation" and explore whether the "correspondents", "photographers", "critics", "poets", "writers" and Japanese soldiers who entered Nanjing "knew" it—temporarily "presumption of innocence" for the perpetrators. Such action is certainly a concession, but more than a concession, because only by thoroughly clarifying this point, can totally change the views on the Myth and related works.

In the last section, we talked about the severity of Japan's press censorship after the outbreak of Sino-Japanese War, which was the most important obstacle to the publication of Japanese atrocities in Japan. As Kazuo Minamata, reporter of Yomiuri Shimbun, said in Nanjing at the time of the incident that "Not only it cannot be published, but we will certainly be punished for writing it. So we can just focus on "courageous and skillful Imperial Army in battle".[100] Tadashi Imai, reporter of Asahi Shimbun, who was also in Nanjing at that time, witnessed a large number of "executions" near the River of Hsiakwan area and wrote down "unspeakable pain mood" (Hata Ikuhiko said):[101]

"I really want to record it."
"What's the time? Alas, I can't record it at present. But we really saw it."
"It was really worth watching again, with the eye."
"I stood as I said. Somehow, the machine guns stopped."[102]

At that time, many Japanese correspondents in Nanjing were the witnesses. Matsumoto Shigeharu, Shanghai Bureau Chief of the Dōmei News Agency, said in his memoir Shanghai Times that:

---

[100] Kazuo Minamata, 『侵掠』, quoted from Hata Ikuhiko, 『南京事件——虐殺の構造』, p. 17.
[101] Hata Ikuhiko, 『南京事件——虐殺の構造』, p. 18.
[102] Imai Masatake, 「南京城内の大量殺人」, 『目撃者が語る日中戦争』, revised by Inose Naoki and compiled by Takanashi Masaki, Tokyo, Shin Jinbutsu Ōraisha, November 10th, 1989, 1st edition, p. 58. 今井文初刊于『特集・文藝春秋』, December 1956.

Recently, for reference, I heard directly from what my former colleagues, Arai Masayoshi, Yuuji Maeda and Fukasawa Kanosamu, who have interviewed people for several days after the fall of Nanjing as war correspondents, said about the situation at that time. Especially, Fukasawa has kept a diary since he joined the Army. I also read his diary, which is of great value. They saw directly on December 16th and 17th that first there were burnt bodies along the bank from the Hsiakwan area to Straw Shoe Gorge. Some said there were about 2,000 people while others said about 3,000 people. They were probably shot dead by machine guns and burned with petrol. In addition, thousands of people might be driven into the Yangtze River from the bank. Besides, in the former courtyard of the military and political department, young officers asked recruits to stab Chinese prisoners with bayonets and then threw them into the air-raid shelter there. The activity was called "recruits training" by the young officers. Maeda started to feel sick and vomit after seeing 12 or 13 people being killed, and then he left. In the courtyard of the military academy, the prisoners there were shot with pistols. After seeing several prisoners being shot dead, he couldn't see any more.[103]

Although some Japanese "were unwilling to see any more", influenced by extreme nationalism, the Japanese at that time hardly had the "consciousness" to resist it. Hata Ikuhiko[104], one of the representatives of Japan's research of the "Nanjing Incident", once lamented that "There was no correspondent challenging this taboo, which really makes people feel regrettable". However, Hata believed that "If we explore deeply, we will not be unable to find any clues about the Nanjing Incident". He demonstrated his opinion by quoting the words "it's really frightening" said by Asahi Shimbun's reporter Masao Nakamura when he met with New York Times' reporter Durdin the day after Japanese army captured Nanjing, and "meaningful" words of other reporters such as "capturing 15,000 prisoners on the riverbank", "searching for the latent 25,000 defeated soldiers" and "traces of plunder".[105]

---

[103] Matsumoto Shigeharu, 『上海時代』, Tokyo, Chûô Kôronsha, May 31st, 1977, 1st edition, pp. 675–676.

[104] Although Hata Ikuhiko does not belong to the "slaughter school", his academic research still contributes to shaking up the "fabrication school". Japan's "slaughter school" also agrees with him in some ways. For example, Honda Katsuichi thinks that although he "basically has big doubts about the definition and number of massacre", he still "deserves [positive] estimation". (『裁かれた南京大虐殺』, compiled by Honda Katsuichi, Tokyo, Banseisha, June 1st, 1989, 3rd printed version, p. 5.) Tanaka Masaaki who reserves comments on the name of the "fabrication school" and completely denies the Nanjing Massacre criticizes that "both Katogawa Kotarou and Hata Ikuhiko have still not got rid of the Tokyo Trail. The mere difference in the number is in line with the slaughter school". (Tanaka Masaaki, 『南京事件の総括——虐殺否定十五の論拠』, p. 67.) Katogawa refers to Katogawa Kotarou, who ranks first in the compilation of *The Battle of Nanjing*. Although denying the Nanjing Massacre is the basic idea of *The Battle of Nanjing*, there is a slight difference in Katogawa's own position. He once said that "Nanjing was captured on December 13th and we left the stigma of 'Nanjing Massacre'". (Katogawa Kotarou, 『中国と日本陸軍』下, Tokyo, 主文社, 1978 [no precise date], 1st edition, p. 201.)

[105] Hata Ikuhiko, 『南京事件——虐殺の構造』, pp. 18 and 17.

However, the invisibility of reports criticizing the Japanese army does not mean that reports exposing Japanese atrocities are not visible. Hata and some Japanese scholars believed that there were only "traces" of the atrocities because their recognition of materials was too "reserved" to allow clear evidence to enter their sights—because there was no lack of records of atrocities in the flattery of "courageous and skillful Imperial Army in battle". One of the most famous records was the killing contest between two second lieutenants, Mukai Toshiaki and Noda Tsuyoshi of the "Katagiri Troop",[106] which was unanimously (Japan's right-wing groups hold quite different views on other issues) "vindicated" by Japan's right-wing groups. The report was published in the Tokyo Nichi Nichi Shimbun (the predecessor of Mainichi Shimbun) in four times at that time. On December 13th, there was also a large photo of the two holding Japanese machetes. Both of them were sentenced to death by the Nanjing Military Court after the war. The truth of the matter[107] is not discussed in this article for the moment, but the news was published by a Japan's first-class newspaper, and no one came out to "refute the rumors" during the wartime, so the Japanese people indeed had no reason of "not knowing" the Japanese atrocities. If they were really "not knowing", then it must be, as Kaneko Renji said, that people turned a blind eye due to their complete "paralysis".

Since late Meiji Period in Japan, extreme nationalism had become the mainstream of social thoughts. The Japanese public's "sense of justice" had not only been "paralyzed", but had nationalism itself become the main motivation for outward expansion.[108] Throughout the wartime, especially

---

[106] Before Japan's defeat, the army was made up according to geographical position with the aim of enhancing its combat effectiveness through sharing weal and woe. "Katagiri Troop" is referred to the 9th regiment of the 19th brigade of the 16th infantry division—"Kyoto Regiment", led by Colonel Katagiri Goro.

[107] Suzuki Aki in 1972 published an article titled "The Mystery of the 'Nanjing Massacre'" in *Shokun* which is a vital publication of Japan's right-wing groups with the aim to ask for justice for Mukai Toshiaki and Noda Tsuyoshi. A book of the same name was published in the next year, which became the beginning of the wave of denial of the "Nanjing Massacre" since the 1970s. (Suzuki Aki, 『「南京大虐殺」のまぼろし』, Tokyo, Bungei Shunjû, March 10th, 1973 1st edition.) In recent years, Japan's "slaughter school" has acquiesced that the "competition" is a fabrication by the media in a militaristic environment, but there should be no doubt about the mass killings made by the two men. For example, Akira Fujiwara, the first living person of the "slaughter school", thought that the incident "was made as a brave biography in the battle, which yet can be considered as killing the captives who did not resist" (「まぼろし派、中間派、大虐殺派三派合同大アンケート」, p. 193). The author thinks that even if the evidence provided by Japan's the "fabrication school" is true, it is not enough to shake the record of the "100-man killing contest" in wartime. For more details, please refer to the article "Re-discussion on "The 100-man Killing Contest"", Nanjing, *Jiangsu Social Sciences*, No. 6, 2002.

[108] Japanese scholar Tsuda Michio disagrees with the popular saying that "the Japanese people were also victims". He thinks that the war Japan launched against China is a "General War", that is, the so-called "Holy War" that "a war in which every citizen is engaged as the executive body of the war. Even if citizens are different from the war leadership, the Japanese public should be held accountable for the war." (Tsuda Michio, Chinese Preface of 《南京大虐

at the beginning of the war, Japan's war policy was highly supported by the Japanese people. After the Lugouqiao Incident had just erupted, on July 12th the Japanese Trade Union Confederation issued a statement to call for assistance for the war. On July 14th, the women in Ginza, Tokyo, launched the so-called "Thousand Stitch Belt"[109] campaign to "send warmth" to the frontline soldiers. Later, various types of blessing such as "blessing bags", "blessing articles" and various forms of "supporting the front" activities were quite commonly seen. On July 30th, the Ministry of the Army announced that it had received amounted to more than 2.69 million yen (a considerable amount according to the current currency value) of "pension" and materials worth about 60,000 yen since the outbreak of the war. Therefore, it is extremely rare to see such inner pain as that of Tadashi Imai. So, does "not only it cannot be published, but we will certainly be punished for writing it" force everyone to keep silent?

In fact, there is a particularly famous "exception". Ishikawa Tatsujo, a famous Japanese writer, lived with the Army in China after the outbreak of the war. Shortly after the Japanese army captured Nanjing, he alone wrote (February 1st to 10th, 1938) the famous novel Living Soldiers. Plunder, rape, arson, murder and other acts committed by the Japanese can easily be found in this book. For example, as for properties in China, the book reads:

> The soldiers are in a good mood. This land is full of unlimited wealth which can be obtained at we wish. The ownership and private things of the residents in this area are like wild fruits open to the demands of the soldiers…

As for abusing women, the book reads:

> Requisition is an excuse for them to go out. There are also obscure expressions like the following example. The special expression of "the requisition of flesh" refers to looking for women.

殺と日本人の精神構造》,《百年》, Tokyo, 百年雜誌社,May 1999, No. 3, p. 74.) The author even thinks that "The Japanese public are the beneficiaries of Japan's war of aggression. Even if they are also the victims of militarism, their suffering cannot be compared with the suffering of the people of the invaded country." (Views on Japan of China's Mainland, *History Monthly*, Taipei, Lianjing Publishing Company, June 2001, p. 46.)

[109] "From the Japanese-Sino War to the Pacific War, the 'Thousand Stitch Belt' is popular among women in the rear. Women stitch on a white or yellow cloth with red threads one by one to embroider a thousand circles, and five or ten white copper coins will be tied to this cloth. It is usually made into a belt. Wearing five coins means 'exceeding four coins (the homophonic of death line in Japanese)' and wearing ten coins means 'exceeding nine coins (the homophonic of bitter struggle in Japanese)'. In addition, according to the saying "the tiger that travels thousands of miles know the way back", the women born in the year of Tiger will sew stitches of which the number is same as their ages. The so-called "thousand" also means the majority. People want to use these numbers to avoid danger through their combined efforts." (『日中戦争への道』, compiled by Harada Katsumasa et al., Tokyo, Kôdansha, October 20th, 1989, 1st edition, p. 270.)

As for the killing, the book reads:

> Yijiang Gate was not attacked by Japanese army in the end. The residual defeated soldiers in the city took it as the only way to retreat and fled to the Hsiakwan Dock. The front was water and there was no boat to cross and no land to escape. They held tables, logs, door panels and all floating objects and swam across the vast Yangtze River towards Pukou area on the other side. The number of them was totally 50,000, crossing the already dark river. While the other side was already visible, what was waiting for them was the Japanese army that had arrived first! The machine guns started. The surface of the water looked as if it had been roughened by rain. If they went back, the Japanese machine gun array was waiting for them in the Hsiakwan - and the last blow to these drifting defeated soldiers was the destroyer's attack.[110]

Ishikawa Tatsujo's book was originally intended to be published in The Central Review in March 1938 (the 13th year of the Shōwa era), which was banned because it contained so-called "anti-military content that is not beneficial to the stability of the current situation". Not only was the publication prohibited, the author, editor and publisher were all prosecuted for "violating the Newspaper Law" on the grounds of "taking the fabrication as fact and disturbing the peace and order". Ishikawa was sentenced to four-month imprisonment (suspended for three years). The verdict said that "The work describes the killing and plundering of non-combatants by imperial soldiers and the lax military regulations, which has disturbed the peace and order".[111] This book of Ishikawa Tatsujo was preserved to publicate until the war ended. Although this book is only a "novel", the author's special experience and the special reason for writing it make it possible to be regarded as a faithful history when it comes to the Japanese army's "killing, plundering and lax military regulations".[112]

So, was the humanity of the Japanese in wartime completely swallowed by the darkness of the times? Was there really no "exception"? The speech by Yanaihara Tadao published in Japanese Christian publication Good Faith in the wartime finally shows us the tenacious struggle of humanity, which also shows us that even though the Japanese military and political authorities had

---

[110] Ishikawa Tatsujo, 『生きている兵隊』,昭和戦争文学全集3『果てしなき中国戦線』, Tokyo, Shûeisha, June 30th, 1965, 1st edition, pp. 23, 27 and 78. The narration on the river here is consistent with the diary records of many Japanese soldiers.

[111] Quoted from Tanaka Masaaki's 『南京事件の総括』第六章「虐殺否定十五の論拠」之十四, Tokyo, 謙光社July 10th, 1987, 2nd edition, p. 226.

[112] The Living Soldier has long been criticized by Japanese left-wing intellectuals, who think that it has "no criticism" of the war of aggression and is not fundamentally different from "aggressive literature" and "imperialist war literature" that "blindly cater to" the war of aggression. (Odagiri Hideo,「『生きている兵隊』批判——戦争と知識人の一つの場合」, Tokyo, 『新日本文学』March 1946[創刊号], pp. 23–31.) However, from the perspective of "faithfulness", Ishikawa's "naturalistic" attitude does make his works closer to reality.

strict control, they could not help covering up the sky. Yanaihara Tadao was a famous economist.[113] He said in a speech in November 1939,

> On November 3th last year, a Christian meeting was held in Aoyama, Tokyo. In the morning, there was a Christian speech. In the afternoon, I heard a speech by the director of Religious Affairs of the Ministry of Education, Science, Sports and Culture. A General of the Army also gave a speech. Before the General of the Army delivered his speech, the host said that we were so honored to have the Army General here and asked everyone to stand up and welcome the General walking to the rostrum. So everybody stood up.
>
> Do the director and General come here as a political liberator for Christians in modern society? No, never. The Army General was the supreme commander of the <u>Nanjing Incident</u>. When Nanjing fell, he made a big mistake to the Christian Girls' School established by the American Order. After the incident was reported, the feelings against Japan by foreign countries, especially the United States, were irritated again. If the organizers of the Christian meeting were not informed of this, it could be said to be a blasphemy. If they knew it, it could be said to be impudent. <u>The person in charge of this incident must plead guilty in front of the Christian Church</u>. Shouldn't the Christian meeting demand the apology in the name of Japanese Christians?

The "General" denounced in the speech was Matsui Iwane, who was regarded as a hero by the Army and nationals at that time!

Now let look back at what the Japanese army did in Nanjing through the records of the Japanese officers and soldiers.

Major Kisaki Hisashi, the rear staff of the 16th division, wrote in his diary on January 15th:

> Translator Kichi brings two girls in order to protect their lives from the military police. I had no negative attitudes towards the military police, but this time I am extremely disgusted. Who is responsible for the loss of the national army's reputation and the loss of military discipline in Nanjing? Even such poor girls would be deprived of their lives, and I couldn't help feeling strong indignation.[114]

---

[113] Yanaihara Tadao, a former professor at the University of Tokyo, resigned from his teaching position in December 1937 because the Home Ministry Police Affairs Bureau identified that his article National Ideal (Chūōkōron, September 1937) had an "anti-war" ideology, and subsequently identified that his article Nation and Peace (Iwanami Shoten, June 1936) had an "anti-war" ideology which were both banned and he was also punished for these articles by the Ministry of Education, Science, Sports and Culture. (「筆禍の矢内原教授辭表を提出」, 讀賣新聞社編集局編『支那事變實記』第5輯, p. 12. The book did not specify the place and time of publication, but judging from the preface by Mabuchi Itsuo, head of the Reporting Department of the Ministry of the Army, who said that "it has been four years since the outbreak of the China Incident", the publication time should be 1941.)

[114] 「木佐木久日記」, 南京戦史編集委員会編『南京戦史資料集』, p. 431.

The quotation here is slightly questionable, so it is hard to judge whether the military police themselves had bad behavior. However, at least it shows that the military police had failed to fulfill their responsibility for the "loss of military discipline". Japanese military police are very strict with military discipline (especially at home). If the military police were powerless-the military police are not considered the accomplices for the moment, it is clear that the "loss of military discipline loss" has reached a high level. Major Yamazaki Masao, staff officer of the 10th army, also said in his diary "The Record of the Words of Colonel Fujimoto" on the 18th that "I deeply believe that it is necessary for soldiers to achieve spiritual education". It also mentioned the "integrity and reputation" lost by the Japanese army.[115]

Lieutenant Maeda Kitsuhiko, squad head of the 7th Squadron of the 45th Regiment, wrote in his diary on December 19th,

> On the way back to the south by car, black smoke suddenly came out of a three-story western-style building in Qinhuai area of which the precise location was unknown. Then flames began to come out from below. When I came here this morning, there was no sign of fire at all. It must have been set off by the plunder group here.

Their actions were without any sense of caring about the reputation of the Imperial Army.[116]

Lieutenant Orita Mamoru, head of the 2nd artillery squad of 23rd Regiment wrote in his diary on December 17th,

> In the dusk, celebration of entering the city was held and heads of the squadrons and squads was ordered to assemble at the brigade headquarters at 6 o'clock in the evening. The head of brigade at table reminded everyone to pay attention to:
> Yesterday, two soldiers of II MG (MG refers to the machine gun squadron and II MG refers to the machine gun squadron of the 2nd brigade—noted by the quoter) raped two Chinese women, which was discovered by Lieutenant Yugi and caused a problem at the R headquarters (R refers to regiment—noted by the quoter). The two are currently being interrogated. Therefore, special attention should be paid to such acts.[117]

Private First Class Mizutani Sho of the 1st Squadron of 7th Regiment recorded in his diary on December 19th that "the squad leader Komura" admonished everyone "to be especially <u>cautious</u> about such shameful things as arson and rape".[118] "The squad leader Komura" said "cautious" rather

---

[115]「山崎正男日記」,南京戦史編集委員会編『南京戦史資料集』, p. 411.
[116]「前田吉彦少尉日記」,南京戦史編集委員会編『南京戦史資料集』, p. 468.
[117]「折田護日記」,南京戦史編集委員会編『南京戦史資料集』, pp. 448–449.
[118] Mizutani Sho,「戦塵」,南京戦史編集委員会編『南京戦史資料集』, p. 503.

than "forbidden", which was not accidental because in situation at that time, bans had no real power.

From the official letter sent to the Japanese embassy by the International Committee for the Nanking Safety Zones, as well as the records of many Westerners such as Rabe, Bates, Fitch and Vautrin, we can see that the number of rape cases in Nanjing was huge at that time. However, since "rape" is an especially "shameful act" and people concerned are eager to clear away traces, it is difficult for us to see relevant records in the diaries of Japanese soldiers today.[119] However, individual or organized robbery—the so-called "requisition"—was different, which was not only the Japanese soldiers' "daily lesson" but also was overt. Some soldiers even called it "Chiang Kai-shek's allowance". Therefore, we can see a large number of relevant records from the diaries of the Japanese grassroots officers and soldiers. The robbery of private properties was sometimes covered up. The "requisition" was almost daily content in some diaries. All public and private properties such as "houses of ordinary people", "grocery stores", "mansions" and even foreign embassies and consulates were inevitably the targets of "requisition". As for the things to be requisitioned, they included all valuable and useful things, ranging from cooking equipment to a pig, a chicken, a bag of rice, a cabbage, a watch and a pen… Here are two examples selected from the plainest diaries of Private First Class Makihara Shouta and Private First Class Kitayama Atae who were both in the 3rd Machine Gun Squadron of the 20th Regiment. In Makihara Shouta's Diary on December 19th,

> At half past eight, according to the order of Second Lieutenant Okamoto (the head of the 3rd squad), Private First Class Ootsuki and I went to collect non-staple food for the squadron after the meal. First, we went out of the city through the south gate, but found that outside the city there was the 13th division (at that time it was Yamada branch of the 13th division - noted by the

---

[119] The scenes of abusing women recorded in The Hidden Regiment History (Shimozato Masaki, 『隠された聯隊史——「20i」下級士兵の見た南京事件の実相』「婦女凌辱現場の記録」, Tokyo, Aoki Shoten, December 16th, 1987, 2nd printed version, pp. 55–57), are based on Azuma Shiro's "Diary Kept in Wartime". Azuma Shiro also has many records in his diaristic work "We the Nanjing Detachment". (Azuma Shiro, 『わが南京プラトーン』, October 10th, November 25th, December 21st, Tokyo, Aoki Shoten, October 25th, 1996, new edition [The first edition was in 1987], pp. 41–43, 61–64 and 112–113. This book is part of *Azuma Shiro's Diary* that was published later, but there are many differences in the dates.) The dairy on the 21st recorded the author his own confession of abusing women. After the publication of this book in 1987, it was besieged by the Japanese right-wing groups. The famous "Azuma Shiro Trial" in recent years is caused by this book. Japan's left-wing scholars and slaughter school also hold an "indifferent" attitude to it. After the publication of *The Diary of Azuma Shiro* (Jiangsu Education Publishing House, 1st edition, March 1999), the author received one from Azuma Shiro as a gift. After comparing the contents of the work with various historical materials, the author holds that although there are indeed some "suspicious" points, the contents are generally convincing. The Japanese version of the book finally came out last year by Kumamoto Syuppan Bunka Kaikan. Azuma Shiro's experience provides a meaningful example for why published diaries of Japanese soldiers seldom record rapes.

quoter) and other teams, so we got nothing there. After taking one-hour rest, we burned the house... At two o'clock, we started from the same place into the city. There were still many abandoned bodies. Within the city, we required the Chinese to carry cabbages, carrots and briquettes back by using three wheelbarrows. On the way back, we passed a grocery store and collected many notebooks, pencils and ink.[120]

Outside the south gate, the other troops had already arrived in advance, but they could always get something from the ordinary people in Nanjing. Such robberies and arsons are almost recorded in each diary of the Japanese officers and soldiers who attacked Nanjing.

Kitayama Atae wrote in his diary on December 16th:

On my way back, I passed a shop which name was "Beiyang Beverage Store". I went in it and saw a pile of sodas. Then I pulled out a bottle and drank. It was so delicious. I immediately went to the nearby and got a rickshaw. I asked a "ni gong" (a scornful address used by Japanese to address the Chinese at that time - noted by the quoter) to drag the rickshaw full of sodas back. Other soldiers also brought back a large number of beds, furniture, liquors, granulated sugar, sugar, phonographs and other items. The stove burned brightly, we drank beers and sodas until twelve o'clock.[121]

The records by people concerned have special significance for us to know the truth. It is not only because these records are based on personal experience, but also because even according to the values publicly advocated by the "Imperial Army, "violating military discipline" is a disgrace. Therefore, as for the Japanese army officers and soldiers' records of Japanese atrocities, it is likely that the situation was severer and the records were closer to the truth. In other words, although the records of the Japanese officers and soldiers are far from presenting all of the Japanese atrocities, it has provided basic solid fact, which is a "baseline". Japan's right-wing groups have always thought that the response of the top Japanese army to military discipline was "misguided" by the "propaganda" of the west,[122] which was of low credibility in front of the records of the Japanese army's lower-level soldiers and officers.

---

[120] 「牧原信夫日記」,南京戦史編集委員会編『南京戦史資料集』, p. 513.

[121] Sone Ichio,『続私記南京虐殺──戦史にのらない戦争の話』, Tokyo, Sairyûsha, December 10th, 1984, 1st edition, p. 60.

[122] In the third section, Japan's propaganda that was "inconsistent with reality" has been cited, but some people in Japan always like to say that it is the China's propaganda, such as the former citation of Kitamura Minoru's recent book of which the first chapter "Kuomintang's International Propaganda". (See Kitamura Minoru's『「南京事件」の探究──その実像をもとめて』第一部「国民党国際宣傳処と戦時対外戦略」, pp. 25–64.) In fact, this kind of false accusation has a long history. Japan had the following representative statement in wartime that "It is a very obvious fact that after this incident, (the Chinese government) accelerates the international propaganda and extremely vilifies Japan for getting sympathy and support from third countries". (『「中支に於ける教育、思想、宗教、宣傳、外國勢力」に關する調査報書』第四

In fact, at that time the Japanese military discipline was deeply corrupt. Not to mention fighting for the Chinese public and private properties, even fights and competitions among "friendly troops" were very fierce. Nakashima Kesago recorded in his diary on December 19th that the 9th Regiment of the 16th Division was expelled from the principal's office of the Military Academy by the 5th brigade of the field heavy artillery. He wrote the following indifferent words after his "sincere regret":

> This is the manifestation of denying ownership in the battlefield. We also make the Chinese feel scared. Meanwhile, the denial of ownership among the Japanese can be seen as a manifestation of developed utilitarianism, egoism and individualism.[123]

Even people within the Japanese army did such things to each other, how could they show mercy to the Chinese?

Now we are going to solve the primary problem, that is, did the Japanese officers and soldiers know about the massacre? (Japanese officers and soldiers were originally the perpetrators, so the correct statement should be "whether there was a massacre", and the so-called "know" here is a statement limited by the problem and context).

V

In the past 30 years, especially in the past 10 years, with the discovery of some important historical materials, it has become more difficult to deny the Japanese atrocities in Nanjing. Meanwhile, the Japanese right-wing groups are forced to make strategic adjustments when continuing to deny the Japanese atrocities. Faced with the undeniable facts, they have no choice but to condemn some "inessential" crimes—the blood and tears of the ancestors are the greatest thing in the world and should be misunderstood—but they still deny the "Massacre", which is essential and symbolic, without any concession. Here is an example of such strategy. Ooi Michiru, who believed in the "fabrication school", said in The Fabricated Nanking Massacre that "Of course, I'm not saying that the Japanese army had not committed any illegal acts. There was no possibility that an army of 70,000 people committed no illegal acts during the war, which is common sense. Staff officer Oonishi slapped the rapist heavily who then was sent to the military police, which undoubtedly happened everywhere".[124] In the February of last year, he filled

---

篇「宣傳」,參謀本部April 1940 [no precise date], pp. 168–169. The original book did not indicate the place of publication, but there was only a printed sticker on the title page, stating that the "Shanghai Institute of Natural Sciences" was entrusted to conduct investigation.)

[123] 「中島今朝吾日記」,南京戦史編集委員会編『南京戦史資料集』, p. 333.

[124] Ooi Mitsuru,『仕組まれた「南京大虐殺」——攻略作戦の全貌とマスコミ報道の怖さ』, p. 297.

in "12" in the answer to the number of people killed in the war in a questionnaire in the Shokun,[125] where"12" referred to "infinitely close to zero".

However, the Japanese army's massacre is not easily denied. Let's see the following records of Japanese army officers and soldiers.

Major Sumi Yoshiharu, Matsui Iwane's full-time adjutant, wrote an article Battle in the First Six Months of the Chinese Incident" in his late years and sent it to Kaikōsha in August 1983. As the article talked about mass killings by Japanese army, it was not published before Sumi Yoshiharu died. Not only was it not published, but, according to Yoshiaki Itakura, that "This testimony and letter was kept secret from the editorial board of The Battle of Nanjing for a long time, and I was able to see it in January of the 61th year of the Shōwa era (1986), more than two years later".[126] It was not until the third year after the death of Sumi Yoshiharu (January 12th, 1985) that this article was published (Kaikōsha, January 1988). However, some content had already been quoted in article General Description: The Battle of Nanjing Based on Testimony published earlier (Kaikōsha, March 1985). Since Sumi Yoshiharu was Matsui's full-time adjutant and had a special status, his review was extraordinary important and once the review was disclosed, it immediately caused controversy between the left and right-wing groups. The most controversial point was the "about 130,000 bodies near Hsiakwan". According to Sumi Yoshiharu, the one responsible for the deaths was the 6th Division, and the massacre order was issued by Lieutenant Colonel Cho Isamu, Chief of Staff of the 2nd section of the Shanghai Expeditionary Army. Sumi Yoshiharu said that he was on the scene when Cho Isamu issued order. As for this, the "fabrication school" and the "moderatists" are quite skeptical. The Battle of Nanjing holds that Sumi Yoshiharu's memories are "contradictory and lack of credibility". "Notes on the War History Research" attached to Data Collection of The Battle of Nanjing also holds that "Sumi Yoshiharu's misunderstanding, prejudice and wrong memory are too numerous to mention". However, what Sumi Yoshiharu said is not single evidence.

Major Yamazaki Masao, staff officer of the 10th army, once recorded in his diary on December 17th,

> After the celebration, Major Donowaki led us to visit the downtown… then we arrived at Zhongshan Dock by the Yangtze River. The Yangtze River was relatively narrow here. There were seven or eight navy destroyers anchored here. Numerous dead bodies were abandoned on the riverbank and immersed in the water. The so-called "heaps of dead bodies" had different types. Here, the Yangtze River was really crowded with dead bodies. If the bodies can be placed on flat ground, it will really be the so-called "mountain of dead bodies". Since I have seen dead bodies many times, I am not surprised at all and have dinner as usual.[127]

[125]「まぼろし派、中間派、大虐殺派三派合同大アンケート」, p. 179.
[126] Yoshiaki Itakura,『本当はこうだった南京事件』, p. 287.
[127]「山崎正男日記」,南京戦史編集委員会編『南京戦史資料集』, p. 408.

The "Zhongshan Dock" area is exactly the same place as Sumi Yoshiharu said.

Navy Medical Officer Colonel Yasuyama Koudou, Chief Medical Officer of the Headquarters of the "China Fleet", took a seaplane to Nanjing on December 16th. At two o'clock in the afternoon, he visited the battlefield along with Chief of Fleet Forces and Chief Accountant. He wrote in his diary on that day.

> From the Hsiakwan Dock, we were driving on the vast and straight road. The road was strewn with rifle bullets like brass-covered sand. The dead Chinese soldiers, flesh and blood, were lying in the grass beside the road.
>
> Soon, from the Hsiakwan area to Yijiang Gate leading to Nanjing, under the towering stone gate was an arched road, about one third of which was buried with soil. When entering the gate, there was a ramp in the Hsiakwan area. We drove slowly forward, feeling that we drove slowly forward on a rubber bag filled with air. The car was actually driving on bodies of countless buried enemies. Somehow, we drove on a plot with thin soil layer, and meat pieces were suddenly secreted out of the soil when we drove. The miserable situation was too hard to be described.[128]

The area from Hsiakwan Dock to Yijiang Gate mentioned here is also the same place as Sumi Yoshiharu said. From the same records of the three unrelated persons, there should be no doubt about the irrefutable facts of the matter.[129] In addition, no matter whether there are civilians or not, since the riverside was not a battlefield, "dead bodies" were at least the result of killing prisoners.

There is a special "comment" on one of Sumi Yoshiharu's statements in "Notes on the War History Research" attached to Documents on the Battle of Nanjing. Sumi Yoshiharu stated that "In the end, I only want to record one thing among many mistakes. It is perhaps true that I, who respect General Matsui heartily, took a car with General Matsui to Hsiakwan area. But such record that "We walked quietly for two kilometers on the river bank road where dead bodies lying. All sorts of feelings welled up in the mind. The Commander of the Army sobbed, tears streaming down' is really surprised. A General who loved China would never drive on the abandoned dead bodies of the battlefield. Moreover, a car with low body could never drive two kilometers long above the bodies. In my opinion, in this regard,

---

[128] Yasuyama Koudou,「上海戦従軍日誌」,南京戦史編集委員会編『南京戦史資料集』, pp. 527–528.

[129] Matsui Iwane's diary of December 20th also said: "I set out at 10 o'clock in the morning to inspect Hsiakwan, near Yijiang Gate. This area is still in a mass. Bodies and other objects are still abandoned and must be cleaned up in the future." (「松井石根大将戦陣日記」,南京戦史編集委員会編『南京戦史資料集』, pp. 21–22.) Matsui's record is also a strong proof. Considering the possible homology of the relationship between Kado and Matsui, in order to avoid-from the most cautious standpoint-circular demonstration, Matsui's diary is only appended for future reference, not as evidence.

it was completely fabricated and anyone can affirm it".[130] However, such an "assertion" seems to be arbitrary. In fact, the so-called "driving on the abandoned dead bodies" can serve as a good evidence of the reliability of Sumi Yoshiharu's testimony. Because it can not only be supported by what Yasuyama Koudou and others said,[131] "driving" "on numerous bodies", but it was so uncommon that it took risks to make such fabrication.

It doesn't matter whether the order was given by Cho Isamu[132] because: First, Cho Isamu's order was only a personal act, not a military order; second, massacres were widespread at that time and were not limited to certain time or place, meaning that even if there were no order by Cho Isamu, massacres would never have been avoided. In the absence of a formal Order of Killing Prisoners of War at army level today,[133] we would rather say that massacres were spontaneous acts in the whole Japanese army. Such "inevitable" spontaneous acts resulted from long-term influence of the militarism.

Excessive massacres at that time could be reflected in the records of the Japanese officers and soldiers. Let us take a look at the following records in the diary of Yasuyama Koudou on the 16th.

> Through the doorway the army entered in Nanjing. There are <u>numerous enemies' bodies</u> that were charred. Iron pockets and bayonets were also blackened. Metal wires of barbed wires overlapped residual burnt-down doorposts. The piled was also burnt to black. The scene was too mess and smelt acrid to describe.
>
> On the hillock at the right head of the doorway, there were engraved words "China and Japan cannot coexist", showing Chiang Kai-shek's propaganda against Japan. When we were close to the downtown, plain blue-cloth cotton-padded jackets abandoned by enemies made the road look like ragged

---

[130] 「『角証言』の信憑性について」,南京戦史編集委員会編『南京戦史資料集』, p. 764.

[131] Durdin, the *New York Times*' special correspondent in Nanjing, said in the report on December 18th that "The capture of Hsiakwan Gate by the Japanese was accompanied by the mass killing of the defenders, who were piled up among the sandbags, forming a mound six feet high. Late on 15th the Japanese had not removed the dead, and two days of heavy military traffic had been passing through, <u>grinding over the remains of men, dogs, and horses</u>."(『日中戦争史資料』9「南京事件」, compiled by Hora Tomio, p. 283.) Suzuki Aki's *The Mystery of the "Nanjing Massacre"* is the first book focused on questioning the Nanjing Massacre. However, in his interview, there is an important oral testimony to prove the massacre, that is, Fujii Shinichi (recording technician of the film *Nanjing*) who was then embedded with the army said, "There were a large number of corpses near <u>Yijiang Gate, with wooden plates on the corpses, and cars ran on them</u>". (Suzuki Aki, 『「南京大虐殺」のまぼろし』, Tokyo, Bungei Shunjû, May 30th, 1989, 15th printed version, p. 228.) Suzuki Aki was interviewed as early as the early 1970s when this matter has not yet become a "dispute", so it is impossible to be recognized as intentional words. Therefore, such oral statement can be used as strong evidence.

[132] As to whether the order is given by Cho Isamu, it was first said by Tanaka Longji, who has been mentioned before, and Tokugawa Yoshichika also said that he had heard of it indirectly from Fujita Isamu. (Tokugawa Yoshichika, 『最後の殿様』, Tokyo, Kôdansha, 1973, 1st edition, pp. 172–173.) It is now difficult to find more direct evidence.

[133] More details on Order of Killing Prisoners of War, please refer to article "Research on Japanese Order of Killing People", Beijing, Historical Research, No. 6, 2002.

clothes while the bodies of enemy officers, dressed in khaki military uniforms with vigorous leather leggings, could be seen everywhere, lying on their backs with stiff and rigid hands and feet.[134]

The above quotation is only a part seen by Yasuyama Koudou's on his first day in Nanjing. During his three days in Nanjing, he encountered a large number of bodies everywhere. For example, on the morning of the second day (17th), he saw "numerous bodies" in other two places in Hsiakwan area. And he personally saw a Chinese soldier "bleeding" and "begging for mercy" being shot dead by a "reserve soldier" who just stood behind him. In the morning, he saw "numerous bodies" along Zhongshan North Road. In the afternoon, he, with Ōkawachi Denshichi, Commander of the Shanghai Special Marine Corps "inspected" the plain in lower reaches of Hsiakwan area, seeing "countless blackened enemy bodies" and "60 or 70 enemy bodies that 'tasted Japanese machetes'" in the dyke.[135] On the 18th, in Lion Forest Garden, he first saw "bodies abandoned everywhere by enemies". Then outside the barracks that were stationed in the foothills, he saw "scattered bodies". When arriving at Zhongshan Park, he also saw "scattered enemy bodies".[136] After this article finishing, I occasionally read the so-called "Latest Report on 'Nanjing Incident'". In the Report, Higashinakano Shūdō, regardless of "numerous bodies" recorded by Yasuyama Koudou, unexpectedly said,

> Kado's testimony did not prove that the bodies were drifting in the river. He said that on December 18th, 100,000 bodies of citizens were found around Hsiakwan area.
>
> However, in detailed diaries from 17th to 19th of Navy Medical Officer Yasuyama Koudou who then stayed in Hsiakwan area, these bodies were not even mentioned. Even if there were drifting bodies, they must come from the upper reaches. It is too indiscreet to link it with the assumption that Japanese army threw bodies into the river.[137]

The records are crystal clear. How dare Higashinakano Shūdō fool the readers by saying no "bodies thrown into the river"!

We might as well look at the relevant materials. Second Lieutenant Maeda Kitsuhiko, team leader of the 7th Squadron of the 45th Regiment, wrote in his diary on December 15th:

> On the 2000-meter stone road from the East River Gate to the West River Gate, many paving stones were covered with miserable blood.

---

[134] Yasuyama Koudou,「上海戦従軍日誌」,南京戦史編集委員会編『南京戦史資料集』, p. 528.

[135] Yasuyama Koudou,「上海戦従軍日誌」,南京戦史編集委員会編『南京戦史資料集』, pp. 528–30.

[136] Yasuyama Koudou,「上海戦従軍日誌」,南京戦史編集委員会編『南京戦史資料集』, p. 531.

[137]「南京事件最新報告」『問題は「捕虜処断」をどう見るか』, Tokyo, Shokun, Bungei Shunjû, February 2001, p. 129.

I thought about it as I walked, feeling incredible. Later I heard that the situation was as follows: on the afternoon of the 14th, 100 prisoners of the 3rd brigade were sent to West River Gate. It happened that the second supplementary soldiers from Japan (reserve soldiers, led by Warrant Officer Soejima and Warrant Officer Tame, enlisted from the 11th year of the Taishō era to the 4th year of the Shōwa era, namely, these soldiers aged roughly from 28 to 38) arrived, and therefore were appointed to escort the prisoners. Here came the problem that since these reserve soldiers just came from the Japan and lack experience in fierce battlefield, it was improper to appoint these soldiers who lacked morale[138] to undertake such a task.

The cause was only a small matter. Since the road was narrow, the Japanese soldiers with bayoneted guns on two sides seemed to have been squeezed or slipped into the pond. [Japanese soldiers] were outraged and decided to beat or scold these prisoners. Prisoners were afraid and suddenly dodged aside. The guard soldiers there also jumped up. Weapons are long called dangerous tools. The guard soldiers swore "you bastard", shaking their bayoneted guns, beating and stabbing prisoners. Panic prisoners began to escape. "Things cannot go on like this", they said, firing and shouting "Prisoners are not allowed to escape" and "Shoot those who escape". This must have been the case at that time. It is said that such a small misunderstanding led to a great tragedy.

It was too late for Major Ohara, the head of the 3rd brigade, to be angered. He could not make any excuse for committing atrocities against prisoners who eventually had surrendered and laid down their arms.

I have to say that this has tarnished the image of the Imperial Army. In order to conceal this tragic incident, these reserve soldiers stayed up all night and bodies were not buried until this morning. This is a real example of immoral behavior that cannot be imagined by human in common sense under "extraordinary" or extreme conditions.[139]

Such "manslaughter" occurred frequently at that time. This article does not discuss whether it was "manslaughter" or not for the present, but the fact of killing prisoners is beyond doubt.

Private First Class Makihara Shouta of the 3rd Machine Gun Squadron of the 20th Regiment wrote in his diary on December 14th:

At half past eight in the morning, the 1st unit assisted the 12th squadron to collect horses. I heard that the residual enemies staggered out because of lacking food, so they immediately set off by bus. When they arrived, about 300 enemies disarmed by the rifle squadron were waiting who then were all shot dead quickly and our soldiers came back……. On the side of the railway bifurcation, there were more than one hundred Chinese soldiers attacked and all killed by

---

[138] At that time, Colonel Tanaka Shinichi, Military Section Chief of the Bureau of Military Affairs of the Ministry of the Army, was deeply worried about these over-age conscripts and said that "the root of the decadence of military discipline lies in the conscription and those over-age conscripts." (『田中新一／支那事変記録其の四』, Quoted from Kasahara Tokushi's 『南京事件』, Tokyo, Iwanami Shoten, November 20th, 1997, 1st edition, p. 62.)

[139] 「前田吉彦少尉日記」, 南京戦史編集委員会編『南京戦史資料集』, p. 464.

our cavalry in the night... At six o' clock in the afternoon... six defeated soldiers were caught and shot dead... Today there is strange scenery of a garage somewhere, 150 or 160 enemies being poured with gasoline and burned to death. But today we have no reaction no matter how many bodies we see.[140]

In just one day, Makihara Shouta and his unit saw and participated in so many massacres. This was not a special "luck" for Makihara Shouta and his companions but showed a miniature of the whole Japanese army in Nanjing at that time. Yasuyama Koudou wrote in his diary on December 19th that "It was said that the number of Chinese soldiers who defend Nanjing resolutely in the end was about 100,000, of whom about 80,000 were exterminated..."[141] Most of the "80,000" should be those who were "disarmed" as mentioned above. Here may as well give two more examples.

Private First Class Matachi Ike of the 2nd Squadron of the 7th Regiment wrote in his diary on December 16th:

We went out again in the afternoon and caught 335 young men... These 335 defeated soldiers were brought to the Yangtze River and shot dead by other soldiers.[142]

Shoji (Yoshida) Masaaki, head of the 4th unit of the 1st squad of the 3rd Squadron of the 20th Regiment, mentioned killings many times in his diary. Among them, in diary on the 24th, 7000 "prisoners" were taken to an area near the Yangtze River and shot dead as the record "7,000 prisoners mentioned before also became bait".[143] There are two points in Shoji Masaaki's record worth noting. First, in the above quotation, Yasuyama Koudou, Yamazaki Masao and others stated that a large number of bodies were found on the 16th and 17th along the river and prisoners were still being killed on the 24th, indicating that the river had become a abattoir at that time. Second,

---

[140] 「牧原信夫日記」,南京戦史編集委員会編『南京戦史資料集』, pp. 511–512.

[141] Yasuyama Koudou,「上海戦従軍日誌」,南京戦史編集委員会編『南京戦史資料集』, p. 532. The number "80,000" seemed to be a "statement" at that time. For example, Nanjing's War Traces and Places of Interest compiled by the "Reporting Department of the China Dispatch" said wiping out "80,000" enemy troops. (quoted from 『南京』第七篇第二章「南京攻略史」, compiled by Ichiki Yoshimichi, 南京日本商工会議所, September 1st, 1941, 1st edition, p. 626.) For example, Nanjing, the collection of "verses" published in 1940, contains "Song" written by Senior Captain Horikawa Shizuo, the team leader of the Military Police, which also has the words "80,000 abandoned bodies". (quoted from 『南京事件を考える』, p. 206.) "The Diary of Iinuma Mamoru" said on December 17th that "According to today's judgment, there are about 20 divisions and 100,000 people in the vicinity of Nanjing, with about 50,000 of them destroyed by our dispatching divisions, about 30,000 of them destroyed by the navy and the 10th Army, and about 20,000 scattering. The number of destroyed troops is expected to increase in the future". (「飯沼守日記」,南京戦史編集委員会編『南京戦史資料集』, p. 217.)

[142] 「井家又一日記」,南京戦史編集委員会編『南京戦史資料集』, p. 476.

[143] 「林正明日記」,南京戦史編集委員会編『南京戦史資料集』, p. 519.

Japan's right-wing groups regard the denial of pushing bodies into the river as part of the denial of massacres near the river (if no body was pushed into the river, there are as many bodies as there are bones of the dead). The so-called "bait" here proves once again that the bodies were pushed into the river after the massacres made by the Japanese.

The quoted details of the massacre said by Maeda Kitsuhiko are just "hearsays". Matachi Ike provides us with a personal experience in his diary on December 22th:

> At 5 o'clock in the afternoon, the sky was getting dark and we gathered at the headquarters of the brigade to kill the residual defeated soldiers. We saw that 161 Chinese stayed in the courtyard of the headquarters, waiting for the gods and looking at us without knowing that death was coming. We led them, shouting at them in Foreigner Street in Nanjing, and later approached the essential place near Gulin Temple where machine guns were hidden. As the sun sank, only moving figures could be seen. The houses also became black dots. Prisoners were led to a pond (maybe lake? the meaning here is not clear - noted by the quoter) and were locked in a house here. Five people were brought out of the house and stabbed dead. The five people walked, screaming, muttering and crying. It could be easily seen that they had already known their results judging from their depressed faces. <u>Defeated soldiers are doomed to be killed by Japanese soldiers</u>! Their wrists and necks were tied by iron wires, being beaten by sticks while walking. There were also brave soldiers singing and walking. Some soldiers pretended to be dead after being stabbed. Some jumped into the water and gasped for breath. Some hid in the roof in order to escape. Because they firmly refused to come down, we poured petrol and set fire on them. After the burning, two or three people jumped down and were stabbed to death.
>
> In the darkness, we tried hard to stab the escaped guys and shoot them. At that time, this place became hell. When everything was over, we poured petrol on the dead bodies lying on the ground and set a fire. Those who were still alive and moved in the fire were killed. Then the flames grew bigger. All the tiles on the roof fell down and the flames scattered. Looking back on the way back, the fire was still burning.[144]

If the "righteous indignation" in above quotations of Kisaki Hisashi and others still does not lose the sense of humanity, Matachi Ike's position is totally inhuman. It is Matachi Ike's behavior and mentality which the majority of the Japanese officers and soldiers had that the Nanjing went through such tragic disaster.

Most of the above quotations are from Documents on the Battle of Nanjing. The Collection was sponsored and published by the old military group "Kaikōsha", which held a denial attitude toward the atrocities committed by the Japanese army in Nanjing. Members of the editorial board, such as Unemoto Masaki and other old soldiers, held denial attitudes toward

---

[144] 「井家又一日記」,南京戦史編集委員会編『南京戦史資料集』, p. 479.

Japanese atrocities. The only one who was not a veteran, Yoshiaki Itakura, was also a "moderatist" in recent years (the so-called "moderate" was actually a euphemism for "denial", and he died in February 1999). Therefore, the selection of historical materials in this collection cannot be without bias. But if they wanted to prove that the Japanese atrocities in Nanjing were just "sporadic" individual acts, they would have recorded something of Japanese atrocities since this was a historical data collection—no matter what the position is, as long as what is recorded is true, the Japanese atrocities cannot be "clean" without leaving any traces.

Atrocities in Nanjing are a great sin of the Japanese army and a sinful debt of the Japanese nation, so it has long been a taboo topic in Japan. In 1971, after series of A Journey to China written by Honda Katsuichi were published in Asahi Shimbun, this incident began to raise public concern[145] and caused prolonged debates between Japan's left and right-wing groups. However, compared with "incidents" such as "the May 15th Incident" and "the February 26th Incident" (the atrocities committed by Japanese army in Nanjing are also neutrally referred to as "incident"), its impact is quite limited and the published works are not rich enough. For example, apart from Data Collection of The Battle of Nanjing (Collection II was published in 1993), there are only two serious historical data collection, Data Collection of Nanjing Atrocities in the Sino-Japanese War (Data Collection I: International Military Tribunal for the Far East, 1985 and Data Collection II: English Materials, 1986, see the previous note; The Nanjing Incident Volume II compiled by Hora Tomio [1973] in Data of Sino-Japanese War published by Kawade Shobo Shinsha has same content as this book) and Documents on the Nanjing Incident compiled and translated by Nankin jiken chōsa kenkyūkai (divided into two volumes: Data Collection of the United States and Data Collection of China, 1992). However, from relevant records scattered in various publications in recent years, we can still see many valuable materials. Here are two more examples.

Ohara Koutarou, from the 19th Class of the 4th unit of the 2nd squad of the 4th Squadron of the 16th Regiment of the transportation corp, was a primary school teacher in Chiba County when he was enlisted. He kept a diary from September 1st, 1937, the day he joined the army, to August 7th, 1939, the day he left the army. In his diary on December 15th, 1937:

> That area seems to be Nanjing. Over the mountain, there was a village built on a slightly flat place. I saw astonishing sights there. In a square surrounded by bamboo fences, as many as 2,000 prisoners were carefully guarded by our army, which is shocking. I later knew that they were the prisoners captured during the

---

[145] Honda Katsuichi late said that "I have written all kinds of communications so far, but I have never had such a strong and profound reaction as that caused by the serial of A Journey to China". (『裁かれた南京大虐殺』, compiled by Honda Katsuichi, Tokyo, Banseisha, June 1st, 1989, 3rd printed version, p. 85.)

attack on Nanjing. It is said that there are about 7,000 prisoners. They came with white flags and were disarmed. Of course, among them were some people captured in the battle, and other situations. Some of them wore casual clothes outside the military uniforms that were firstly checked here and then the army decided to shoot, conscript or release them. It is said that <u>the bodies of prisoners shot dead in the back mountain are piled up</u>. Most areas in Nanjing seem to have been cleaned up.[146]

In the diary on December 17th:

The 27th class went to collect hay. They found four hidden defeated and disabled soldiers in the haystack of the farmhouse and brought them back. △△△ (original text used such signs - noted by the quoter) pulled out the machete, snapped the head off, and the head hang down. Then the △ △ △ △ of △ △ △ drew the machete and cut it again, but the head still did not fall down. Then △ △ △ △ started to cut it and said an obscene word. He wielded the machete quickly and the head rolled to the front with spattering blood. His wrist strength is amazing! In the afternoon, the 16th class also captured some defeated and disabled soldiers…

The prisoners were brought here, which were the prisoners in the village yesterday. About a squad with bayonets was inserted in the procession. The procession was too long to count. I ran over and asked someone the amount of the prisoners and was told that there were 4,000 prisoners. All of them were captured by the 33rd, 38th and 20th regiments in the battles of this area. The guards are also from these regiments. Why bring these prisons? Were they brought to Nanjing? Some people said they were all shot dead. Others said they were taken to Nanjing to serve. Anyway, no one certainly knew the answer. There were 20,000 prisons, but now we just have these.[147]

On his way to Nanjing on the 18th, Ohara Koutarou also encountered a large number of corpses. In his diary on that day, he wrote that "<u>The bodies are piled up like mountains</u>. Imagine [our army] climbing over the bodies and chasing the enemy all the way to Nanjing".[148] The body "mountain" was, of course, composed of the prisoners seen by the narrator because people died in battle cannot be "piled up".

Private First Class Kitayama Atae in the 3rd Machine Gun Squadron of the 20th Regiment mentioned above was arrested in the early 1930s for joining a left-wing organization and was recruited on August 31th, 1937. His diary was checked by his squadron. In his diary on December 13th, Kitayama Atae recorded a Chinese student soldier who "begged" the Japanese to shoot

---

[146] 愛知大学国学叢書1,『日中戦争従軍日記——輜重兵の戦場体験』, compiled by Eguchi Keiichi and Shibahara Takuji, Tokyo, Hôritsu Bunkasha, April 25th, 1989, 1st edition, p. 134.

[147] 江口圭一、芝原拓自編『日中戦争従軍日記——輜重兵の戦場体験』, pp. 136 and 137.

[148] 江口圭一、芝原拓自編『日中戦争従軍日記——輜重兵の戦場体験』, p. 137.

himself in the throat because he could not bear the atrocities of the Japanese. Kitayama Atae said that:

> Killing people like this that did not resist, pointing at their throats and begging to "shoot here", was a disgrace to the Japanese soldiers.[149]

In the diary on December 14th, Kitayama Atae also mentioned the killing of prisoners:

> After twelve o'clock in the evening, the sweep was over and people came back. It seems that 800 soldiers were disarmed and all killed. Enemy soldiers may not think of being killed. It seems that they were mainly students. I heard that there are many college students.[150]

In addition to the records at that time, in recent years, occasionally people concerned broke their silence and testified. For example, a mountain artillery soldier from the 3rd brigade of the 19th Regiment of the 13th Division (saying that "the name cannot be made public due to fear of intimidation") testified that:

> [On the way to Nanjing] the army was stationed in a village. All the men of the village were taken out of houses and shot with pistols or rifles. The women and children were all locked up in the room and raped at night. I didn't do such things myself, but I think many others had committed rape. Moreover, on the next morning, all the raped women and children were killed and even the houses were burned down. This is a killing march without reserving residences for returning. I couldn't believe why we were so stupid. The answer I got was that the anti-Japanese ideology in this area was quite fierce, so we were ordered to kill them all. In short, this is a sinful war of arson, robbery, rape and murder.
>
> I think this is a war that we really should apologize for. When we arrived near the shogunate hill of Nanjing city, the number of prisoners was incalculable. The 65th Morozuno regiment ("Morozuno" refers to head of the regiment Colonel Morozuno Sakuhajime; at that time, the main force of the 13th division was in the north of the Yangtze River, and only the 65th regiment was sent to attack Nanjing with one part of the 19th regiment - noted by the quoter) captured about 20,000 people. These "prisoners" were covered from 12-year-old children to wrinkled old men, including all men.
>
> … [5,000 bound prisoners were held under the shogunate hill artillery] This time, it was a two-column row, headed for somewhere of the Yangtze River. Japanese soldiers were armed with ammunition and pulled ropes about two or three meters away from the two sides of the row. Suddenly, one prisoner fell down and other prisoners fell down one after another. Before them get up, they were all stabbed dead with bayonets.

---

[149] 『南京事件　京都師団関係資料集』, compiled by Iguchi Kazuki et al., p. 71.
[150] 『南京事件　京都師団関係資料集』, compiled by Iguchi Kazuki et al., p. 71.

The following prisoners had to make a detour of about one kilometer to reach the Yangzi River. I didn't know whether there was a soldier's shed or a building on the south of the Yangtze River. When we arrived at the place, it was already evening. There were infantries with guns pointed at them form windows of second and first floors. Five thousand prisoners were sitting here in the square. A several meter-high stone wall was in the north. I could felt its height even though it was quite late. Therefore, no prisoners could escape from that side. The prisoners all sat there. Some Japanese soldiers wanted to pull prisoners out for beheading in order to try military swords while others wanted to stab them with bayonets, and all did as they wanted.

In fact, since the war began, I have not cut someone's head. I had borrowed staff sergeant's machete and used it to cut the sleeping prisoners, but only half of head was cut down. Actually, beheading is not easy. It is strenuous to cut the head down. Then, there was a screaming and [prisoners] all stood up. It should have shot prisoners under the command of the machine gun team leader before we could shoot them. However, at that time, five thousand prisoners stood up and we cannot control the situation. Therefore, without the command of "shooting", the machine guns were started. I also wanted to try one shot, but I did not shoot again because I felt that it was dangerous. When the machine guns were fired together, all 5,000 captured soldiers fell to the ground.

Then, we used bayonets to stab them because there might be someone alive. I was not holding a Japanese gun, but a Chinese gun, and the Chinese gun could not be equipped with Japanese bayonet. So I had to borrow comrade's Japanese gun. I walked on the bodies with a Chinese gun in my back, stabbing more than 30 people. On the next morning, my arms were too painful to lift.[151]

The specific statement made by the former Japanese soldier whose name cannot be made public due to "intimidation" is another solid evidence that the Japanese army violated both international law and war ethics. The former Japanese soldier heard that the "Morozuno regiment" had killed 20,000 prisoners. This is just the number of people killed by one regiment!

The texts cited above, although far from what has been found at present, are sufficient to illustrate the issue. I had lived in Japan many years ago and felt deeply about the absurdity of Japan's right-wing view of history and the misunderstanding of the history by the Japanese public.

However, I still don't want to doubt the motives of others. I would rather regard the fallacies of the Japanese public and even the Japanese right-wing groups as "misunderstanding" caused by ignorance. Therefore, while proving that the relevant viewpoints put forward in the works of right-wing groups such as the Myth can't stand the test of facts and thus are not true, this article also wants to help the Japanese public objectively understand this historical "minor issue"—in the eyes of Chinese people, it will always be a "state affair".

(Originally published in Modern Chinese History Studies, No. 6, 2002)

---

[151] 南京大虐殺の真相を明らかにする全国聯絡会編『南京大虐殺——日本人への告発』, Tokyo, Tôhô Shuppan, September 21st, 1992, 1st edition, pp. 34–37.

Is The Good Man of Nanking: The Diaries of John Rabe an "Unfounded Fabrication"?—An Examination of The Truth of Nanjing Incident: An Examination of *John Rabe's Diaries*

Among many Japanese works denying the "Nanjing Massacre", The Truth of Nanjing Incident: An Examination of John Rabe's Diaries[1] (hereinafter referred to as Examination) is a more important and more recent book. The author's purpose of writing this book is to prove that The Good Man of Nanking: The Diaries of John Rabe (hereinafter referred to as Rabe's Diaries) is a book of "exaggeration, hearsay, conjecture"[2] and "obvious fabrication, inconsistency, artificiality and unreason"[3] that are caused by "author's belief, standpoint, view of history and view of war" and to prove that the Rabe's Diaries is not "superior information" that "has great influence on the debate direction of the Nanjing Massacre"[4] in order to deny the truth of the Nanjing Massacre.

---

[1] *The Truth of Nanjing Incident: An Examination of John Rabe's Diaries*, Tokyo, Bunkyô Shobô, 1st edition, November 10th, 1998 and 2nd edition, February 1st, 1999. The citations in this article are all from the 2nd edition.

[2] Unemoto Masaki, *The Truth of Nanjing Incident: An Examination of John Rabe's Diaries*, page 1.

[3] Unemoto Masaki, the Recapitulation in *The Truth of Nanjing Incident: An Examination of John Rabe's Diaries*, page 220.

[4] See "A Commentary on Nanjing's Tragedies and Rabe's Diaries" of the Japanese edition of the *Rabe's Diaries*, written by Yokoyama Hiroaki, a professor at Meiji Gakuin University. 見ジョン•ラーベ著,エルヴィン•ヴィッケルト編,平野卿子訳『南京の真実』, Tokyo, Kôdansha, 3rd edition, November 21st, 1997, page 329. Japan's right-wing scholars mostly hold negative attitudes to the *Rabe's Diaries*. For example, in 『ザ•レイブ•オブ•南京の研究』 written by Nobukatsu Fujioka and Higashinakano Shūdō, the *Rabe's Diaries* is regarded as "three class information" (東京,詳傳社1999年9月10日第1版,第283页). Not long ago, Japan's famous right-wing publication *Shokun* published the results of a questionnaire on the "Nanjing incident." As for the *Rabe's Diaries*, Tanaka Masaaki, the author of 『「南京虐殺」の虚構』(東京,日本教文

The author, Unemoto Masaki, is a retired professor at National Defense Academy of Japan. He was the leader of the independent light armored fleet when the Japanese captured Nanjing. This experience was not only specially marked on the cover of the book, but also frequently noted in the writing, presumably to emphasize his special right to speak as a "witness". However, Unemoto Masaki held that Rabe, who was also a witness, cannot be an objective and impartial witness due to his "belief, standpoint, view of history and view of war". In Unemoto Masaki's view, what Rabe's wrote probably was "exaggeration" and "conjecture". For the time being, we do not discuss the author's prejudice caused by strong emotions and physical limitations. After a rough reading of Examination, I deeply feel that the author is too harsh on others and has no self-reflection, so that his accusation against Rabe can be used as his own mirror.

I

The Rabe's Diaries is famous for recording atrocities committed by Japanese troops. Therefore, the first purpose of the Examination is to deny the reliability of these records. In general, due to the limitation of the narrator's vision, it is inevitable that some records are distorted. However, if the proportion of distorted content is too large, there must be special reasons. And such special reasons are most easily related to the subjective intention of the narrator. The Examination's denial of the Rabe's Diaries starts with the motivation of the Rabe's Diaries.

The Examination specifically states in the preface and introduction chapter that the Siemens Company that Rabe worked for had great commercial interests in China, so Rabe could not hold a "neutral" and "impartial" standpoint.[5] Not only Rabe could not hold a "neutral" and "impartial" standpoint, but the "editor"[6] Victor who visited China in his early years and later served as of the ambassador to China could not hold a "neutral" and "impartial" standpoint due to his "pro-China gestures", so the author specially reminded

---

社1984年6月25日第1版)『南京事件の総括』(東京,謙光社1987年3月7日第1版), said: "The book is full of arbitrary words of arson and rape and it is unreliable and anti-Japanese"(『諸君!』月刊,東京,文藝春秋社,2001年2月号,第177页). Fuji Nobuo, the author of『「南京大虐殺」はこうして作られた———東京裁判の欺瞞』(展転社1995年4月29日第1版), said: "It is a diary that is hardly worth comment" (『諸君!』,2001年2月号,第172页). Watanabe Shoichi who wrote a large number of works denying the war of aggression said: "The only right thing that written by him (referred to John Rabe - noted by the quoter) is people's gratitude to the Japanese army when it entered the city"(『諸君!』,2001 年2月号,第167页).

[5] Other right-wing scholars in Japan also hold the same view, such as Matsumura Toshio, who said: "Rabe lost his business that had been cultivated for many years because the Japanese army occupied Nanjing. People will not believe it if someone says he did not hate the Japanese army. At least he would feel hopeless, which is no doubt." 松村俊夫著『「南京虐殺」への大疑問』, 東京,展転社1st edition, December 13th, 1998, page 213.

[6] The Japanese edition of the *Rabe's Diaries* is marked that the book is edited by Victor while the Chinese edition is not marked.

readers that the victor' "impact on the impartiality and neutrality of the diaries must be paid attention".[7] Coincidentally, in the third part of the introduction chapter, Hanae Shou (who was the team leader of the 3rd Squadron of the 20th Regiment when the Japanese army captured Nanjing) also emphasized in his "The Truth of Nanjing: Reading Rabe's Diaries" that the "proximity" between Germany and China was "beyond imagination", Germany's military aid to China made him feel that Japan was "struck by Germany" and especially Rabe's "affection for Chinese people" made his diaries "totally in favor of China",[8] etc. Hanae Shou was Azuma Shiro's superior when he conquered Nanjing, and he was also the important mastermind of the famous Azuma Shiro case in recent years. He said that Azuma Shiro's My Nanjing Infantry[9] was an "unfounded" fabrication and the Rabe's Diaries was "just the same".[10]

There is no denying that Rabe sided with China instead of Japan. However, this emotional tendency is neither inherent nor generating in his days living in China. Rabe's emotional tendency is precisely triggered by the behavior of the Japanese army. Before the arrival of the Japanese army, Rabe was rather contemptuous of the Chinese people. For example, once in Yantai, he was not satisfied with a rickshaw puller who took him to a hotel, and he used "the worst swear words" to reprimand the rickshaw puller:

> I had to use one of China's worst swear words I know "wangbadan" to reprimand him. Although the word is not civilized, it is very useful. Then, the rickshaw puller had to take his tired legs and pull me to the Seaside Hotel near the end of Seaside Avenue.[11]

What we see here is an unsympathetic Rabe. There is no denying that some contempt for the Chinese is caused by some Chinese's behavior. In the diary of Rabe on September 22nd, there is a passage,

> There are about 28 Chinese people squatting in my dugout, of whom I know less than 14. Among the people I know, there is a shoemaker. I never agree with him on the price of shoes in peacetime, because he always takes into account the deduction he gives back to his servant, but I would like to turn a blind eye to it.[12]

---

[7] Unemoto Masaki, the Introduction Chapter in *The Truth of Nanjing Incident: An Examination of John Rabe's Diaries*, page 5.

[8] Unemoto Masaki, the Introduction Chapter in *The Truth of Nanjing Incident: An Examination of John Rabe's Diaries*, page 7 and 9.

[9] Azuma Shiro, 『わが南京プラトーン』, Tokyo, Aoki Shoten, 1st edition, 1987.

[10] Unemoto Masaki, the Introduction Chapter in *The Truth of Nanjing Incident: An Examination of John Rabe's Diaries*, page 11. In the page 10 of the same book, the author rebuked that *Rabe's Diaries* was to "say one thing and do another."

[11] John Rabe, *The Good Man of Nanking: The Diaries of John Rabe*, translated by the translation group of this book, Jiangsu People Publishing, Jiangsu Education Publishing House, August 1997, 1st edition, page 6.

[12] The Chinese version of *The Good Man of Nanking: The Diaries of John Rabe*, page 14.

Rabe later discovered that the shoemaker and his servant were relatives! This shoemaker is undoubtedly a cynical person in Rabe's eyes. Specific experience like this is a source of Rabe's contempt. However, it was indeed common for westerners of that era to treat China and Chinese with "superiority" gestures or even contempt.

Rabe's "total" "affection" for China" was entirely caused by Japanese atrocities. After Rabe returned to Nanjing from the north on September 7th, 1937, he faced Japanese bombings every day. He said in his diary on September 24th,

> All the newspapers published protests from all European countries and the Regiment States against air strikes against civilians in Nanjing in violation of the international law. However, the Japanese calmly replied that they had just bombed buildings or military targets as usual and had absolutely no intention of harming civilians in Nanjing or nationals of friendly European countries. In fact, this is not the case at all! So for, the vast majority of bombs did not hit military targets, but fell on the ordinary civilians, and a survey showed that the poorest civilians suffered the most.[13]

In the eyes of the Chinese, Japan's behavior absolutely represents a living rogue. In the eyes of Rabe, the Japanese all tell lies boldly. How can the Japanese be credible? As Rabe said in his diary on September 27th when he talked about the protest against Japan: "No one will believe that the Japanese will respond to this protest"![14] As long as someone still has his conscience, he, in addition to Rabe, will have Rabe-style emotional turning—a convincing proof is that the westerners who then stuck to Nanjing unanimously condemned the Japanese. Therefore, Mr. Unemoto and Mr. Hanae blindly blame others and only see "totally in favor of China" but not see the reason, which cannot help but make people feel that their consciousness still remained 60 years ago.

Why was Rabe "totally in favor of" China as mentioned above (Rabe's Diaries actually did not lack criticism of the Chinese government and the Chinese army at that time). However, although the author's likes and dislikes had some influence on his "neutrality" and "impartiality", the key to judging the "neutrality" and "impartiality" of author's statement is the statement itself. If affection and hate is tantamount to misrepresentation, outsiders like Rabe[15] may not avoid misrepresentation. Furth more, is it a little bit

---

[13] The Chinese version of *The Good Man of Nanking: The Diaries of John Rabe*, page 17.

[14] The Chinese version of *The Good Man of Nanking: The Diaries of John Rabe*, page 23.

[15] Rabe stated in a special report to Hitler after returning home that "I can't help but feel sympathy for China in its misery, but first I am for Germany." ジョン•ラーベ著『南京の真実』, page 290. This report is not included in the Chinese version of the *Rabe's Diaries*. The so-called "full report" attached to page 704 of the Chinese version is actually only a letter written before the report, not the "full report". Rabe's attitude has always been lenient. For example, in his

strange that Mr. Unemoto, who is so eager to "justify" the Japanese army and is also the culprit, can maintain "neutrality" and "impartiality"[16]? Does Mr. Unemoto himself think it makes sense?

Of course, the negative evaluation of Rabe's Diaries by the Examination is only one aspect. In view of the final purpose of the Examination, negation is only at the first level. The final purpose of Examination is to prove the "innocence" of the Japanese army, so its focus on the Rabe's Diaries is not only to "destruct" it but also to "construct" something else by finding useful evidence in the Rabe's Diaries. Therefore, while the Examination is harsh and critical, it also has to say that the Rabe's Diaries is "a mixture of truth and falsehood".[17]

Under such utilitarian motive, the judgment of the "truth" and "falsehood" made by the Examination is to conceal the violent behavior of the Japanese army. Any record that is unfavorable to the Japanese army is denounced as "falsehood" by the Examination; otherwise, it may be called "truth".[18] It is unreasonable to explain that the contradictions in

commentary to the documentary on Japanese atrocities by the American Anglican priest John Magee, he said that "the scenes were filmed not to stir up the feelings of revenge against Japan, but only to hope that all people, including the Japanese, will remember the terrible consequences of the war and make people understand that all legal means should be used to end the dispute provoked by the Japanese army. Maker of the documentary often goes to Japan and is familiar with Japan's scenic spots and historical sites, knowing that many Japanese people have noble spirits. If the Japanese people knew how this war took place and how it was carried out, their hearts would be filled with disgust!" The Chinese version of *The Good Man of Nanking: The Diaries of John Rabe*, page 614.

[16] Unemoto once said that "outside the city, it is true to get involved in the battle. But there was no deliberate killing of citizens. There was of course no citizen in the city being killed. Only when food was requisitioned outside the city, there may be atrocities, rapes, killing, etc. But no one in my army ever did that. Smith's so-called investigation that 15,000 citizens were killed is simply unauthentic. Even if there were killed citizens, it would only be 5000 citizens, one-third of 15,000 citizens. Each division killed about 1,000 citizens. No, it should be less. In short, since it was a battlefield, citizens cannot be seen there." (Cited from Ooi Mitsuru's 『仕組まれた「南京大虐殺」——攻略作戦の全貌とマスコミの怖さ』,東京,展転社3th printed version, June 6th, 1998, page 232.) This can be said to be Unemoto's general attitude towards the Nanjing Massacre.

[17] Unemoto Masaki, *The Truth of Nanjing Incident: An Examination of John Rabe's Diaries*, page 1; Recapitulation, page 220. Due to the same motive, most other right-wing scholars in Japan also said the same thing, for example, Higashinakano Shūdō held that "in conclusion, Rabe's *The Truth in Nanjing* has the following four features: first, its description is based on facts; second, its description is of exaggeration; third, its description omits key facts; and fourth, its description takes the rumors made by Chinese as facts." 『「南京虐殺」の徹底検証』付章「改めて『ラーベ日記』を読む」,東京,展転社4th printed version, July 8th, 2000, page 385.

[18] Although the *Examination* thinks the statement is of ambiguity, saying that "The so-called civilians should only simply refer to the 'peaceful citizens' and, besides the army (directly taking part in the battle-the original note), Nanjing also had anti-enemy organizations such as civilian volunteer corps and requisitioned army men, the capital's anti-enemy support society, the women's consolation society, the students' anti-enemy support society, etc. Nanjing had already been a "soldiers' city" (Page 202 of the Part 4), it still says with certainty that "The fundament of the so-called 300,000 killed people of the Nanjing Massacre has collapsed" (page 224 of the Recapitulation).

the description made by the same author are simply cause by the so-called "commercial interest" and the emotional bias caused by this interest. If Rabe wanted to "charge" the Japanese army with crimes, why would he record "true" feelings that are "in favor of" the image of the Japanese army? Why would he leave room for Mr. Unemoto to judge after several decades? Therefore, whether from the perspective of necessity or possibility, it is unreasonable to say that Rabe made misrepresentation. The consistent emphasis in the Examination can only show that the book itself is partial.

In the following, we may as well take a look at the so-called "falsehood" and "truth" in the Rabe's Diaries as judged by the Examination with some specific "examinations".

II

Did the Japanese army enter the safety zone on December 13th? Were there any plunders and other atrocities?

The Rabe's Diaries has such a record:

> Ten to twenty Japanese people form a small team. These teams walk through the city and ransack shops. If I hadn't seen it with my own eyes, I wouldn't have believed it. They smashed the doors and windows of shops and took whatever they wanted, probably because they lacked food. I witnessed the plunder of the German Kiessling cake shop. The Hempel Hotel was also smashed, as was almost every shop on Zhongshan Road and Taiping Road. Some Japanese soldiers dragged away the looted goods in boxes while others commandeered rickshaws to transport the looted goods to safe places. We came along with Mr. Foster to see his Anglican church on Taiping road. There are several houses near the church, one of which was hit by two bombs.[19]

This record was originally dated December 14th, but the Examination changed it to December 13th. However, "the Japanese army did not enter the safety zone on the 13th" is the so-called "fact" in the Examination.[20] Therefore, the Examination believes that the above-mentioned record is "unfounded fabrication". Whether the Examination made a misrepresentation or not, it does use incorrect date and is so confident to think that others made misrepresentation, from which we can see that the Examination is good at arbitrarily identifying "facts".

Since the date of the record in the Rabe's Diaries is not the 13th, it is no longer necessary for the Examination to make a further argument, whether

---

[19] The Chinese version of *The Good Man of Nanking: The Diaries of John Rabe*, page 176. There are quite a few omissions when the *Examination* cited it.

[20] Unemoto Masaki, the Part 2 in *The Truth of Nanjing Incident: An Examination of John Rabe's Diaries*, page 70.

it is intentional or negligent. However, although the authenticity of this section in the Rabe's Diaries is be beyond question, did the Japanese army enter the safety zone on the 13th? Were there plunders and other atrocities? These questions are still worth discussing.

The basis of the statement in the Examination is some so-called "testimonies". In order to remove Mr. Unemoto's worry of being treated unfairly, we might as well give the copy of these "testimonies" below.

Hanae Shou (see previous for details) said,

> We were not allowed to enter the refugee camps, so we had no contact with refugees.

Iba Masuo (leader of the 10th squad of the 20th Regiment—refers to the position during the occupation of Nanjing, similarly hereinafter) said:

> After entering the city, we strictly obeyed the order that we were not allowed to enter the foreign concessions and refugee camps.

Kuribara Naoyuki (acting leader of the rapid-fire squadron of the 20th Regiment) said:

> In the mop-up area, there were neither residents nor abandoned bodies, not to mention the firefight and the mop-up operation ended peacefully and smoothly.

Muguruma Masajiro (adjutant of the 1st Battalion of the 9th Regiment) said:

> All was silent. No gunfire was heard. No fire was seen… The city was extremely peaceful and stable, and there was no change.

Kisaki Hisashi (the rear staff officer) said:

> Two or three days after the occupation… According to the strict order of the General Matsui and the Army commander Asakanomiya, military discipline was strictly enforced, and even staff officers toured the city to guard against illegal incidents.

Yoshimatsu Hideyuki (adjutant of the 6th brigade) said:

> After the brigade entered the city, we adjusted and prepared to move to Suzhou. During this period, plunders, atrocities or the killing of residents were never heard.

About the mop-up in the city, Yoshimatsu said:

> When we entered the city, the enemy's retreat was unexpectedly fast and we did not meet the expected resistance, nor residents. Therefore, we left very quickly.

During the stay of our troops in the city, the residents were silent and therefore we were able to leave without making any incident.

Hijiya Masaharu (leader of the 4th Squadron of the 19th Regiment) said:

The more deeply we entered the central street, the more deeply I feel it was really a "dead street". Not to mention enemy's bombs, we did not even see a person.

Agawa Sadayoshi (lieutenant of the 1st brigade of the 19th Regiment) said:

After we entered the city through Guanghua Gate, we swept in the southwest and there was no enemy soldier and no firefight.

Orikono Suetaro (leader of 3rd Squadron of the 23rd Regiment, acting leader of the 1st Battalion) said:

At night there was not even a dog's bark in the distance. It was really quiet within Nanjing city.

Orita Mamoru (leader of the artillery squad of the 2nd Battalion of the 23th Regiment):

The battalion began sweeping the city around eleven o'clock and move to attack Qingliang Mountain. I thought there would be street battles like situations happened in Shanghai, but the situation was "extremely peaceful and stable". Only from the east gate came the gunfire... It was strictly prohibited to requisition things in the city...[21]

With just these "testimonies", it seems that there are no signs of Japanese troops entering the safety zone and atrocities committed by Japanese troops on the 13th. However, the relation between these "testimonies" and facts is not self-evident as the Examination wishes. Here are the reasons. First, most of these "testimonies" are long memories with inevitable memory errors. Second, these "testimonies" are partial that are not enough to be used to make an overall judgment, nor be used to make a negative judgment—like the old saying "It is easier to say that there is something than to say that there is nothing". Third, what is more important is that the providers of these "testimonies" all participated in the attack on Nanjing. If we judge from the emotional bias of the Examination, these "testimonies" can only be regarded as the defendant's self-justification, and only have the least significance in terms of the validity of "evidence".

[21] Unemoto Masaki, the Part 2 in *The Truth of Nanjing Incident: An Examination of John Rabe's Diaries*, page 73, page 73, page 74, page 75, page 77, page 78, page 79, page 80, page 87 and pp. 87–88.

Then, did the Japanese army enter the safety zone on the 13th? Did the Japanese army commit atrocities after entering the safety zone?

Jiang Gonggu, who was a military doctor of the Nanjing garrison at that time, witnessed the atrocities committed by the Japanese troops after they entered the city. After he escaped from Nanjing, he wrote Three-month Experience in Nanjing to record his experience, of which there is a record on 13th that:

> At three o'clock in the afternoon, Qi Mingjing went to me for shelter hastily and fearfully with his package. He said that "The hospital was defended by all officers and soldiers in the hospital last night until dawn. Only then did they find out that the enemies had indeed entered the city and they had to retreat into the refugee camps. There are still more than 300 wounded in the hospital, and the American Anglican priest Magee agreed to take care of the hospital. However, although we retreated into the refugee camps in Yaohuali, Jianyin lane (originally a director's residence), and thought we could live in peace, enemy soldiers still unexpectedly came and robbed wantonly. We cannot stay there any longer. Xu Xianqing, Huang Ziliang and other colleagues once moved to Yaohuali with me. I'm afraid they have to find another place."[22]

This work was written shortly after the author escaped from Nanjing. Since it was written just after the author's crucial moment of life and death, the author's memory should be clear and should be in the most reliable state. If the work's authenticity is still questioned, how can "authenticity" exist in the world?

What War Means: the Japanese Terror in China, written by British Manchester Guardian reporter Harold John Timperley, was compiled in March 1938, which is an almost simultaneous record, saying on the 13th:

> This brief but illuminating description of events immediately after the Japanese entry of Nanking is taken from a letter, date December 15, written to friends in Shanghai by one of the most respected members of Nanking's foreign community who is noted for his fair-mindedness:..."But in two days the whole outlook has been ruined by frequent murder, wholesale and semi-regular looting, and uncontrolled disturbance of private homes including offences against the security of woman. Foreigners who have travelled over the city report many civilian bodies lying in the streets. In the central portion of Nanking they were counted yesterday as about one to the city block. A considerable percentage of the dead civilians were the victims of shooting or bayoneting <u>in the afternoon and evening of the 13th</u> (the emphasis marks are retained according to original texts and hereinafter the same shall apply - noted by the quoter), which was the time of the Japanese entry into the city".[23]

---

[22] *Historical Materials of the Nanjing Massacre Made by Japanese Invaders*, compiled by editorial committee of this book and Nanjing Library, Jiangsu Ancient Books Publishing House, 1st edition, February 1998, page 72. The author compared the records made by Chinese people records and thought that Jiang Gonggu's record was most authentic and credible.

[23] *Historical Materials of the Nanjing Massacre Made by Japanese Invaders*, pp. 166–167.

Jiang Gonggu is a Chinese victim and Mr. Unemoto can still be picky about his motives. But Timperley is an "outsider" and his account should be credible. Maybe in Mr. Unemoto's eyes, Timperley's account is only "hearsay" that is not seen personally, which is not very reliable. Maybe Mr. Unemoto is just like Suzuki Aki and others, believing that Timperley was a Chinese employee[24] whose record is as untrustworthy as Chinese records. We might as well make a concession and not draw a conclusion on this for the time being.

When the Japanese army invaded Nanjing, the disaster suffered by Nanjing can be described as "overwhelming disaster". The disaster was a great misfortune. However, it is a "fortune" for today's evidence collection, because the Japanese army's actions were everywhere and therefore can be found everywhere. In recent years, there have been records of that time that are discovered. Among them, Minnie Vautrin's diaries are of special value, and there is a paragraph like this on the 13th:

> At four o'clock in the afternoon, we were told that there were several Japanese soldiers on the western hill. I went to the South Mountain Apartment where I found several Japanese soldiers standing on top of the "western hill". Shortly after, another worker called me and said that a Japanese man came into our poultry farm to ask for chickens and geese. I immediately got there and gestured to tell him that the chickens here were not for sale, and he soon left. Luckily, he is a polite person.
> …
> At seven thirty-nine in the afternoon, the head of the canteen reported that Japanese soldiers were occupying the house with rice across from our school gate. F. Chen and I tried to get in touch with the leaders of these Japanese soldiers, but failed. The guards at the gate are very fierce. I really don't want to see them. Later, I met with the Chairman of the International Committee for the Nanking Safety Zones for this matter. They said that the problem would be solved tomorrow and all agreed that they must be cautious in dealing with this problem.[25]

The above quotation can be said to be strongest evidence for it has three elements "outsider", "seeing personally" and "record of that time". Vautrin

---

[24] The 『新「南京大虐杀」のまぼろし』 of Suzuki Aki said that "Timperley was not only a well-known adviser to the Kuomintang Central Propaganda Department, but also an adviser to the 'Chinese Ministry of Intelligence" according to Timperley's obituary in the Manchester Guardian on November 29th, 1954. Therefore, Timperley is not a neutral person." Tokyo, Asukashinsha, 1st edition, June 3rd, 1999, page 294. Recently, Kitamura Minoru thought that "Chinese Ministry of Information" should be translated as "Central Propaganda Department". But he further said that "Timperley is not a third party with a sense of justice, but only an existence serving the Kuomintang's diplomatic strategy." 『南京事件の探究――その実像をもとめて』, Tokyo, Bungei Shunjû, 1st edition, November 20th, 2001, page 44.

[25] *Minnie Vautrin's Diary*, written by Minnie Vautrin and translated by the Nanjing Massacre Research Center of Nanjing Normal University, Jiangsu People's Publishing House, first edition, October 2000, pp. 190–191.

is said to be an "outsider" not only because she does not belong to China or Japan side, but also because she has no prejudice against Japanese troops. In her diary on the 13th, she recorded that "After experiencing heavy shelling and bombing, the city is unusually silent. Three dangers have passed - soldiers' robbing, planes' bombing and artillery' shelling, but we still face a fourth danger - our fate is in the hands of the victorious army. People are very anxious tonight because they don't know what will happen in the future. Mills said that so far it has been pleasant to deal with the Japanese, but after all, there has been very little contact".[26] Vautrin had personally seen the Japanese soldiers "seizing" the "houses with rice" on that day and had faced the "fierce" Japanese soldiers, but she still had expectations from the Japanese troops and spoke straight the "politeness" of the Japanese soldier. It can be seen that Vautrin had no "emotional bias"[27] at that time. Vautrin's "neutral" and "impartial" attitude is

Now, we can make a certain judgment that on December 13th the Japanese army did enter the safety zone, and the Japanese army who entered the safety zone did plunder.

III

We can see that the *Examination* ignores facts and is deeply biased from the above example. Most of the accusations against Rabe in the Examination are of this kind. A few more examples will be given below.

Did the Japanese army that captured Nanjing have mark?

The third part of the introduction chapter of the *Examination* is written by Hanae Shou, saying,

> There is no specific record on the Japanese soldiers' troops in Rabe's Diaries at all. The untrustworthiness of the diaries is precisely from this point. At least one or two of the Japanese soldiers can be recognized. It can be said that at

---

[26] The Chinese version of the *Minnie Vautrin's Diary*, page 190.

[27] She even said in her diary of the previous day that "Why not hand over the city intact instead of 'suffering from destruction'?" (The Chinese version of the *Minnie Vautrin's Diary*, page 188.) In fact, the westerners at that time were dissatisfied with the Japanese bombing, but they did not expect the Japanese army to perform so badly. Rosen, secretary of the German embassy, wrote the following representative passage in "The Nanjing Situation and Japanese Atrocities" on January 15th, 1938 that "The gloomy scene depicted in this report shocked foreigners in Nanjing because none of them would have believed that the Japanese would have committed such heinous crimes. People had prepared to guard against the atrocities of the Chinese soldiers who fled on a large scale, especially the Sichuan army. <u>People never thought to guard against the atrocities of the Japanese before</u>. On the contrary, people expected that with the arrival of the Japanese, peace and prosperity will be restored. Therefore, how can people accuse those gentlemen who testify against Japanese cruel crimes with their honest conscience of jealousy and prejudice?" (The Chinese version of *The Good Man of Nanking: The Diaries of John Rabe*, page 432.)

that time the Japanese soldiers had to avoid detection by spies (referring to the absence of a mark—noted by the quoter), but at that time the Japanese soldiers had marks on the sleeves of their uniforms to show the troops they belonged to. Our regiment is △white cloth. As soon as people saw it, people can immediately know that he was a member of the Oono Army (the 20th Regiment).[28]

The *Examination* quotes the speech of Reuters' reporter Smith that is attached to the Rabe's Diaries,[29]

> At noon on the 14th, six to ten people formed a group. They took down the regiment insignia to make no one recognize them and they carried out organized and thorough plunders. All things in Chinese families and most things in European families were plundered.[30]
> The *Examination* refutes that,
> All troops joining in the war were removed of their regiment insignia, which did not represent exemptions from plunders but to avoid detection by spies. They sew "troop insignia" on the arm part or chest part of their clothes instead.[31]

The *Examination* has such an arbitrary attitude that it cannot be considerate. Among the photos at the beginning of the Examination, only in one photo health soldiers wore Red Cross armband and in other photos there are no marks on the chests or arms of the Japanese officers and soldiers! Moreover, the testimony of Kiyomizu Sadanobu (leader of the 3rd Squadron of the 35th Regiment) quoted in the Examination also said that "Allies constantly entered the city and <u>there were troops that cannot be identified</u>".[32] "Cannot be identified" is certainly because there was no recognizable mark.

The tone of Hanae Shou and others seems so unquestionable, which is the very reflection of their arbitrary attitude.

Can "nervousness" be used as a reason to excuse plunder?

As for the plunders of the Japanese army at the beginning of entering the city which is mentioned in Rabe's Diaries, the Examination said that "Did the troops that entered the city forget to fight but plunder shops on Taiping

---

[28] Unemoto Masaki, the introduction chapter in *The Truth of Nanjing Incident: An Examination of John Rabe's Diaries*, page 10.

[29] Smith's speech is not included in Chinese version.

[30] Unemoto Masaki, the introduction chapter in *The Truth of Nanjing Incident: An Examination of John Rabe's Diaries*, Part 2, page 95. Quoted from ジョン・ラーベ著『南京の真実』, page 117.

[31] Unemoto Masaki, *The Truth of Nanjing Incident: An Examination of John Rabe's Diaries*, Part 2, page 97.

[32] Unemoto Masaki, *The Truth of Nanjing Incident: An Examination of John Rabe's Diaries*, Part 2, page 80.

Road and Zhongshan Road? They should only have the nervousness of fighting the residual enemy soldiers after entering the city!"[33]

The Japanese army plundered the city on the very day it entered the city. There is already hard evidence such as the *Minnie Vautrin's Diary* and the truth cannot be changed. After the fall of Nanjing, not all the Chinese soldiers in the safety zone gave up the intention to resist, but according to the result, there was no resistance. Moreover, in order to prove that the Japanese army did not commit atrocities, the Examination quotes the words of the former soldier "the city was extremely peaceful and stable" (said by Muguruma Masajiro), "the mop-up was completed without firing a single shot", "the city was extremely quiet and stable with few guards working at night", "extremely relaxed" (said by Hanae Shou), "shops quickly reopened and barbershops and fast food restaurants were full of people"[34] (the diary on December 15th of Matachi Ike, Private First Class in the 2nd Squadron of the 7th Regiment) and other testimonies. These testimonies are used to prove that there was no "tension" at that time. However, even if there is no evidence such as the Minnie Vautrin's Diary and the record of the Japanese army's performance is completely authentic, there is no inevitable connection between "nervousness" and plunder—for example, it is common that "profit makes wisdom blind". So "nervousness" cannot be a reason to deny plunder in any sense.

When someone tells truth from falsehood, inference is also one of the available methods given that some information is difficult to find, but he should be as meticulous as he can. The Examination makes arbitrary judgments base on soldiers' "nervousness", which is either intentional or presumptuous! Such arbitrary judgments can be found everywhere in the *Examination* and some of them will be discussed later.

Was there any battle on the 13th?

The testimonies of many former soldiers quoted in the *Examination* say that on the 13th "there were neither dead bodies nor the sound of gunfire",

---

[33] Unemoto Masaki, *The Truth of Nanjing Incident: An Examination of John Rabe's Diaries*, Part 2, page 69. Such tone is very popular in the works of the Japanese right-wing groups. For example, 『再审「南京大虐杀」——世界に诉える日本の冤罪』(日本会议国际广报委员会编集,东京,明成社, 1st edition, November 25th, 2000), published in Japanese and English at the end of last year, said that "there were no such things as plunders and rapes because of the lack of intention and time" (page 72) and "the motivation to take great risks to commit illegal acts is extremely lacking" (page 85). Yoshiaki Itakura also said in his book 『本当はこうだった南京事件』 (this book is one of the most important works in recent years written by Japanese "objectivists" who deny the Nanjing Massacre) that "in addition to mopping up the residual enemy soldiers, the Japanese army 'had to deal with the surrendered Chinese soldiers and seemed to have no contact with the majority of the citizens, and therefore there was little chance of committing crimes'." Tokyo, Nihon Tosho Kankôkai, 2nd printed version, January 20th, 2000, page 107.

[34] Unemoto Masaki, *The Truth of Nanjing Incident: An Examination of John Rabe's Diaries*, Part 2, page 73 and page 100.

"all was silent" just like "dead streets" and "no one heard of" the massacre, such as the above words of Kuribara Naoyuki, Muguruma Masajiro, Kisaki Hisashi, Yoshimatsu Hideyuki, Orikono Suetaro and Orita Mamoru. However, Kiyomizu Sadanobu's testimony quoted in the Examination said that the Japanese troops met "hundreds of enemy soldiers", "began a mop-up battle in the dark" and "the enemy soldiers threw a large number of grenades" while the battlefield was slightly southeast of the city center. Nomura Toshiaki (lieutenant of the 2nd Battalion) who was also in the same 35th Regiment with Kiyomizu, wrote a letter to Kiyomizu, saying that "on the evening of the 13th, there was fierce gunfire".[35] This is an obvious contradiction significant not self-rounding. This matter is not worthy of mention, but it involves another matter of great importance:

Did the Japanese army slaughter prisoners at the beginning of entering the city?

The Rabe's Diaries has the following record on the 14th:

> We ran across a group of about 200 Chinese workers. They were picked up off the Safety Zone by Japanese soldiers. They were tied up and driven out of the city. All protests were in vain. We quartered about 1,000 Chinese soldiers at the Ministry of Justice and between 400 and 500 of them were driven from it with their hands tied. We assume that they were shot because we heard several salvos of machine gun fire. We were stunned by these conducts.[36]

The *Examination* says the date of the above record is 13th and used the above so-called "testimonies" to "prove" that "all was silent" on the 13th. Therefore, it holds that Rabe's record is not the truth but "unnatural" and "contradict" "hearsay".[37] Since on the 13th there was a fierce grenade war according to the above citation, "all was silent" and similar accounts are just misrepresentations. But did the Japanese army kill prisoners at the beginning of entering the city?

In recent years, Japan has not only the "fabrication school"[38] who openly denies the Japanese army's atrocities in Nanjing, but also has so-called

---

[35] Unemoto Masaki, *The Truth of Nanjing Incident: An Examination of John Rabe's Diaries*, Part 2, page 81 and page 82.

[36] The Chinese version of *The Good Man of Nanking: The Diaries of John Rabe*, page 176.

[37] Unemoto Masaki, *The Truth of Nanjing Incident: An Examination of John Rabe's Diaries*, page 70.

[38] 最早称南京大屠杀为"まぼろし"(『「南京大虐殺」のまぼろし』,東京,文藝春秋社1973年3月10日第1版)的铃木明,面对铁的事实,不能不说将"まぼろし"译成"虚幻" "是明显的误译。"并曲辩说:"现在日本人使用的'まぼろし',除了'虚''实''秀'等各种各样的汉字(指对应的汉字——引者)外,还有想捕捉也无法捕捉的恍惚的意味,这一极其日本化的、'情绪的'题名,以正确的中国语译出,我想大概是不可能的。"从铃木对『文藝春秋』1951年7月号坂口安吾『飞鸟の幻』的"幻"之解释——"难解之历史之谜",铃木现在对"まぼろし"的解释似已转为(铃木自不会承认自己有转变)"谜"。见『新「南京大虐殺」のまぼろし』,第31、32页。

"moderate school" and "objective school" who maintain that they "respect the historical truth". "Respecting the historical truth" is actually a euphemism for denying the Nanjing Massacre. Therefore, the so-called "objective school" and "fabrication school" have something in common. Since the "objective school" maintains that it "respects the historical truth", it cannot ignore everything like the "fabrication school" and has to provide "evidence" to deny the Nanjing Massacre. However, if it provides evidence, there must be some loopholes. About killing prisoners at the beginning of entering the city, Isa Kazuo (leader of the 7th Regiment) kept a diary like this:

> After a three-day mop-up, on the 16th about 6,500 people were severely punished (the original Japanese can be explained as "dealt with" or "executed").[39]

According to the "Detailed Report of the Battle" of the 7th Regiment, from the 13th to the 24th, a total of 5,000 rifle bullets and 2,000 heavy machine bullets were consumed and 6,670 residual enemy soldiers were killed.[40] *The Fabricated Nanjing Massacre* is also an important work denying the Nanjing Massacre in recent years. Although it ignores facts to some extent, it has to admit,

> It is impossible to accurately distinguish those who were shot in running fight, those who were shot after surrender and those who were shot after surrender but showed resistance expression.[41]

Therefore, it is also unreasonable for the *Examination* to question the *Rabe's Diaries* in this regard.

Is Sekiguchi Minami visit a fabrication?

In the *Rabe's Diaries* on December 15th:

> Sekiguchi, Second Lieutenant of the Japanese navy, came to visit us and he conveyed greetings from the captain and fleet officers of the gunboat "Seta". We gave him a copy of the letter to the supreme commander of the Japanese army.[42]

The *Examination* called the record "completely strange" and marked "it is not true that the date of the visit is the 15th" with emphasis marks.[43] The

---

[39]「伊佐一男日記」,南京戦史编集委员会编『南京戦史資料集』,非売品,Tokyo,偕行社 November 3rd, 1989, page 440。

[40] The 7th regiment's "The Mop-up Result Table in Nanjing City", 南京戦史编集委员会编『南京戦史資料集』, page 630.

[41] Ooi Mitsuruis,『仕组まれた「南京大虐殺」——攻略作戦の全貌とマスコミの怖さ』, page 200.

[42] The Chinese version of *The Good Man of Nanking: The Diaries of John Rabe*, page 179.

[43] Unemoto Masaki, *The Truth of Nanjing Incident: An Examination of John Rabe's Diaries*, Part 2, page 90.

Examination has two grounds: first, Sekiguchi Minami was a navy senior captain instead of a second lieutenant; and second, Sekiguchi Minami himself said that he only met an American named Fitch (フイッチ) and did not say that he met Rabe.

The grounds given in the *Examination* are not enough to prove that what Rabe said "is not true". Here are the reasons: First, Rabe did make the mistake with the titles senior captain and second lieutenant—perhaps Rabe did not know the rank of Japanese navy,[44] perhaps he did not care about the rank at all, or perhaps it was just a slip of the pen in the record, which is not surprising—but the Japanese navy officer named "Sekiguchi" did make a visit. Second, Sekiguchi himself did not say that he met Rabe, but his memory maybe wrong after decades; and even if Sekiguchi kept a diary, he may not record everything he did. In other words, only by proving that the Sekiguchi made an "all-round" record of his daily activities, can "what he not said" is equivalent to "what he never met". Third, the Examination said that "according to The Private Record of Major General Sasaki Toichi, on December 13th the leader of the 33rd Regiment ordered the regiment's communications monitor Hirai Akio to visit the gunboat 'Seta' that was moored in Hsiakwan area. As a 'reply', on the afternoon of the 14th, Senior Captain Sekiguchi, the liaison officer, visited Major General Sasaki Toichi".[45] However, in "The Private Record of Major General Sasaki Toichi" collected in Documents on the Battle of Nanjing, there is only "Sekiguchi came" but no "reply".[46] Why did it happen? Sasaki Toichi was the leader of the 30th brigade who was superior to the leader of the 33rd Regiment. As an insider, his record should be authentic. However, according to Sekiguchi's record, he went into the city to "investigate the situation in Nanjing city so as to report to the upper command"[47] and never mentioned the "reply". As for Sekiguchi's retrospective, he may forget something or perhaps his purpose was to "investigate" while the "reply" was incidental that can be omitted in the record. However, no matter what is the reason, this matter proves that Sekiguchi's record is not all-round. Fourth, whether a matter is recorded or not, in detail or not, it depends on the relation between the author and the matter. For Rabe, his letter to the Japanese army commander is of significance and should be definitely included in the diary. However, meeting Sekiguchi is occasional for

---

[44] Sekiguchi himself said that when he passed the sentry post, an army sentry said his marine corps clothing was "similar to the clothing of enemy officers, and there was a risk of being mistaken for a Chinese officer" (南京戦史編集委員会編纂『南京戦史』,非売品, Tokyo, 偕行社 November 3rd, 1989, page 265).

[45] Unemoto Masaki, *The Truth of Nanjing Incident: An Examination of John Rabe's Diaries*, Part 2, page 90.

[46] 「佐佐木到一少将军私記」,南京戦史編集委员会編『南京戦史资料集』, pp. 369–380.

[47] Unemoto Masaki, *The Truth of Nanjing Incident: An Examination of John Rabe's Diaries*, Part 2, page 90.

Rabe, so not recording the meeting is common. The reason why Sekiguchi mentioned Fitch was that Fitch drove him a long way for his safety, which certainly impressed Sekiguchi deeply. Fifth, Fitch's record[48] is consistent with what Sekiguchi said. The record in the Minnie Vautrin's Diary should be the same matter that "Mr. Rabe and Mr. Lewis Smythe have made contact with the Japanese army commander, and the man has just arrived who is not too bad".[49] Besides, the letter sent to the Japanese embassy in Rabe's name by the International Committee for the Nanking Safety Zones on the 17th also recorded it in detail. All of these records can improve that this matter is authentic.

Can the lack of "ceremony of the Japanese army entering the city" in the Rabe Diaries be used as a criterion for authenticity?

The *Examination* says that the Japanese army held a ceremony of entering the city on the afternoon of the 17th, but the *Rabe's Diaries* "did not mention the ceremony at all", which shows that the Rabe's Diaries is unreliable.[50] The reason given by the *Examination* is that the Japanese army's entry into the city is "the entry ceremony of the century" which is of great importance and should be recorded. The Examination quotes detailed records in the diaries of Matsui Iwane (General, Commander of the Central China Area Army, and the chief executive when the Japanese army attacked Nanjing), Iinuma Mamoru (Chief of Staff of Shanghai Expeditionary Army), Yamazaki Masao (Staff Officer of the 10th Army), Orita Mamoru (Second Lieutenant), Matachi Ike and other people as its grounds. This method is so astonishing. Why people who were not Japanese should think that the ceremony was a great event just like what the Japanese thought and, moreover, should record it? Let us still take the Minnie Vautrin's Diary as an example, on this day Vautrin kept a very detailed diary. At the beginning the diary, there were rapes of women aging from 12 to 60 by the Japanese soldiers, but there was no record of Japanese army entering the city. The implication is obvious. The Japanese' entry ceremony will never bring the outsiders—not to mention the victims—positive feelings. (The establishment of the Nanjing "Self-governing Committee" was also a great event for the Japanese. In order to create a festive atmosphere, the Japanese requested the safety zone to send thousands of personnel to attend the ceremony and therefore this event was recorded in the Minnie Vautrin's Diary. Vautrin mentioned the feeling of the participants that "one of our

---

[48] フィッチ is George Fitch, author of *My Eighty Years in China* in which Fitch mentioned the meeting with the Sekiguchi. See *Archives of the Nanjing Massacre Made by Japanese Invaders* compiled by the Second Historical Archives of China and Nanjing Municipal Archives, Jiangsu Ancient Books Publishing House, 1st edition, December 1997, pp. 652–653.

[49] The Chinese version of the *Minnie Vautrin's Diary*, page 194.

[50] Unemoto Masaki, *The Truth of Nanjing Incident: An Examination of John Rabe's Diaries*, Part 2, page 107.

representatives felt sick about this and did not even eat dinner", and after this, "there is no doubt that you will see movies about people's enthusiastical support for the new regime".[51] The latter sentence is still a good footnote quoted by some Japanese today from documentaries and written records.)

Did the Japanese army kidnap "prostitutes" in the refugee camps?

In the *Rabe's Diaries* on December 25th:

> The Japanese ordered that every refugee must be registered and the registration must be completed within the next ten days. There are a total of 200,000 refugees, so the registration is not an easy task. The first trouble thing has occurred: A large number of strong civilians have been selected, and their fate is either to be forced to toil or to be executed. And a large number of young girls have also been selected in order to build a large-scale brothel for soldiers.[52]

On the basis of the Iinuma Mamoru's Diary on December 19th that

> The task of quickly opening brothels was entrusted to the Lieutenant Colonel Cho.

and on December 25th that

> Lieutenant Colonel Cho returned from Shanghai and had a meeting with Huang Jinrong, leader of the Green Gang... The girls will be jointly recruited from the Japan and the China. The brothel is expected to open by the end of the year.[53]

The *Examination* holds that "it can be seen from this that the brothel was set up by professionals and consisted of Japanese and Chinese girls",[54] so as to deny Rabe's record.

However, what is recorded in Iinuma Mamoru's Diary cannot be the basis for denying the Rabe's Diaries. Here are the reasons: First, from the perspective of the validity of the evidence, Iinuma Mamoru's Diary is the same material as the Rabe's Diaries and therefore it cannot be used to deny the Rabe's Diaries. Second, there is no exclusive record in Iinuma Mamoru's Diary. It says that senior Japanese officers "entrust professionals to recruit Japanese and Chinese", which cannot prevent the professionals from "selecting" girls in the safety zone to build the "brothel for soldiers". Third, the Rabe's Diaries is not a single case. Many records at that time have similar records, such as in the Minnie Vautrin's Diary on December 24th:

---

[51] The Chinese version of the *Minnie Vautrin's Diary*, page 220.
[52] The Chinese version of *The Good Man of Nanking: The Diaries of John Rabe*, page 279.
[53] *Iinuma Mamoru's Diary*, 南京戦史編集委員会編『南京戦史資料集』, page 220 and page 226.
[54] Unemoto Masaki, *The Truth of Nanjing Incident: An Examination of John Rabe's Diaries*, Part 2, page 134.

Tomorrow is Christmas. At ten o'clock, I was called to the office to meet with a senior military adviser from a Japanese division. Fortunately, he brought an interpreter, an elderly Chinese interpreter from the Japanese embassy, who asked us to allow them to select 100 prostitutes from the 10,000 refugees. They believe that if a legitimate place is arranged for the Japanese soldiers, they will not harass women from good families. After they promised not to take the women from good families, we allowed them to select women. During the selection, the adviser sat in my office. After a long time, they finally found 21 women.[55]

The reason "a legitimate place is arranged" mentioned here is in line with the thinking of senior Japanese officers such as Iinuma Mamoru. Therefore, it is very natural, if not the first choice, to seek solutions locally.[56]

Did Rabe say that the 28th is the "final day of registration"?

The "Examination 1" of the record in the Rabe's Diaries on December 28th made by the Examination says: "The investigation and registration of the separation of soldiers and civilians continued until January 5th of the following year. The December 28th was not the final day".[57] But the original words in the Rabe's Diaries are "<u>Rumors</u> that today is the final registration day seem to be spreading", and there was no certainty that it was the final day. Mr. Unemoto's indiscretion and purposelessness cannot help but make people wonder whether he was too careless, too casual or just intentional.

Is a record that does not describe the establishment of the Nanjing Self-governing Committee also false evidence?

When I first read the "Recapitulation" II "Omissions of Important Matters" of the Examination, I was quite astonished that "the establishment of the Self-governing Committee on January 1st" was also included in it. The reason is that the Rabe's diary on December 31st says "tomorrow, January 1s, 1938, the Self-governing government will be ceremoniously established (formed)". After the attachment of the invitation letter and an agenda, Rabe also wrote about the personnel arrangement that "Mr. Sun, Mr. Wang and Mr. Tao are members of the Red Swastika Society affiliated to us. We

---

[55] The Chinese version of the *Minnie Vautrin's Diary*, page 209.

[56] Such things can easily be found in Chinese records at that time. For example, Guo Qi's *Record of Blood and Tears in the Captured Capital* recorded that "There was a Mr. Tang who had a special pass to show that he was asked to run a house of prostitution." *Historical Materials of the Nanjing Massacre Made by Japanese Invaders*, compiled by the editorial board of this book and the Nanjing Library, Jiangsu Ancient Books Publishing House, 5th printed version, February 1998, page 11.

[57] Unemoto Masaki, *The Truth of Nanjing Incident: An Examination of John Rabe's Diaries*, Part 2, page 137.

were a little surprised by these appointments but we ignored them".[58] With this record, how can anyone say there were omissions? After carefully reading the Examination, I found that the author had another reason that was even more surprising. In the Part 3 of the Examination, the author says that: Rabe should have seen the establishment ceremony of the Self-governing Committee, but he did <u>not say a word</u> about <u>the situation of the establishment ceremony</u>.[59] His reason is so absurd. The establishment ceremony was disgusted by the upright people at that time, like the quotation from the Minnie Vautrin's Diary. Why people who disliked the "disgusting" matter had to record it? The Examination denies the truth of the Rabe's Diaries on the grounds that it did not record the "situation" of the ceremony, which can only show that the Examination lacks strong arguments!

Why did Rabe keep raising the issue of burying dead bodies?

By quoting the records in the Rabe's Diaries on December 28th and January 7th that the Japanese army did not approve the burial permits, the Examination said that it is untrue that the burial statistics put forward by the Red Swastika Society in the Tokyo Trial began on December 22nd.[60]

The Red Swastika Society's statistics on the burial of dead bodies began on December 22nd. In the following year (1938) on April 4th, the Society wrote a letter to the Nanjing Self-governing Committee for financial support in which there was a paragraph like this:

> Since last July, we have dealt with the military disaster and have provided relief, such as setting up factories to supply porridge, setting up clinics to treat patients, and distributing rice, clothes, and money, which are very costly. Among them, <u>the burial of the dead</u> is of great importance. Since <u>last autumn</u>, a total of 30,000 bodies have been buried, and the burial is still in progress.[61]

The Japanese army bombed Nanjing from August 15th. People are dying one after another and the Red Swastika collected the dead bodies and buried them at all times. Even if the Japanese army entered the city, the Society did not stop the burial. In a letter to the Japanese embassy signed by Rabe on the 17th sent by the International Committee, there was a sentence that

---

[58] The Chinese version of *The Good Man of Nanking: The Diaries of John Rabe*, page 313 and page 315.

[59] Unemoto Masaki, *The Truth of Nanjing Incident: An Examination of John Rabe's Diaries*, Part 3, page 144.

[60] Unemoto Masaki, *The Truth of Nanjing Incident: An Examination of John Rabe's Diaries*, Part 2, page 139 and page 146.

[61] *Archives of the Nanjing Massacre Made by Japanese Invaders* compiled by the Second Historical Archives of China and Nanjing Municipal Archives, Jiangsu Ancient Books Publishing House, 3rd edition, December 1997, page 460.

"Since Tuesday morning, our Red Swastika Society has begun to send cars to collect the dead bodies in the safety zone".[62] Since some employees of the Red Swastika Society were captured by the Japanese army when they collected bodies on the 16th, the "Tuesday" should be the 14th. Therefore, it can be seen that the collection and burial conducted by the Red Swastika Society began on the second day after the Japanese army entered the city. Moreover, the arrival of the Japanese army did greatly interfere with the work of the Red Swastika Society. Some Japanese hold a lame argument that the Japanese army, as a ruler, had no need to obstruct the collection and burial. However, is there a normal path to predict what the Japanese army would do? In addition, the fact is the fact, which cannot be changed by some <u>arguments</u>. In a letter to the Japanese embassy from the International Committee on the 17th:

> When the Red Swastika Society, under our command, picked up bodies in the refugee camps, the trucks were either robbed or not robbed successfully. Moreover, 14 workers from the Red Swastika Society were tied up yesterday.[63]

In the Rabe's Diaries on December 26th:

> The Chinese soldier who is tied to a bamboo bed and shot dead ten days ago is not far from my house. His body has not been collected. No one dares to approach the body, not even the Red Swastika Society, because it is the dead body of a Chinese soldier.[64]

It doesn't matter whether the Japanese soldiers tied up the workers because they "collected the bodies". Meanwhile, it doesn't matter whether the Japanese soldiers really wanted Chinese soldiers to be exposed on the streets. What is important is that the Japanese army did rob trucks and tie workers up. What is more important is that the performance of the Japanese army after entering the city completely broke people's fantasies. If not, why did Rabe keep "asking" and protesting?

Was there no fire after the Japanese army entered Nanjing?

The Rabe's Diaries on December 20th, 21st and 27th, 1937, January 1st, 2nd, 9th and 18th, 1938 and so on record many fires set by the Japanese

---

[62] The Chinese version of *The Good Man of Nanking: The Diaries of John Rabe*, page 193.

[63] *Archives of the Nanjing Massacre Made by Japanese Invaders*, page 598. There are some differences between the same letter in the *Archives* and in the *Rabe's Diaries*. For example, the above-quoted sentence "...Tuesday..." is not included, which may be a translation mistake. The tied workers incident on the 16th was also compiled in the document "Japanese Soldiers' Atrocities in Nanjing Safety Zone" (No. 23) sent by the International Committee for the Nanking Safety Zones to the Japanese embassy on the 19th. See the Chinese version of *The Good Man of Nanking: The Diaries of John Rabe*, page 218.

[64] The Chinese version of *The Good Man of Nanking: The Diaries of John Rabe*, pp. 281–282.

army. In the third part of the introduction chapter of the Examination, Hanae Shou said that:

> I was the leader of the 3rd squadron. In addition to the guards on duty, I also rode a horse to doing the rounds of the guard area, but I did not see any violation. We were not allowed to enter the safety zone when did the rounds, but if there was any violation or fire, we are requested to report it to the superior for disposal, but none of this happened. When it was said that the day of triumph was approaching, there should be no soldiers who dare to break the law. The streets of Nanjing gradually returned to normal around the January. Illegal acts by the Japanese soldiers for consecutive days in the Rabe's Diaries were completely fabricated.[65]

There have been many violations mentioned above, but is there any fire?

Hanae stayed in Nanjing from December 13th to the middle of January of the following year, the same as what Rabe recorded. However, the records of the westerners in Nanjing at that time can fully corroborate Rabe's records. For example, the Rabe's Diaries on December 20th said that "As I write this, a good number of houses not far away are on fire again, including the YMCA building".[66] Fitch recorded that "Later, when we arrived at the YMCA Hall, it was smoking and burning".[67] For another example, the Rabe's Diaries on New Year's Day said that "The courtyard and house are brightly lit. Two buildings are on fire in the North Gate Bridge area, which are two rows of houses away from us".[68] The Minnie Vautrin's Diary said that "The fire near North Gate Bridge is raging and the robbery is continuing".[69] In addition, the Rabe's Diaries on January 4th said that "When I write this, another cloud of smoke is rising in the south".[70] The Minnie Vautrin's Diary said that "Tonight, from the South Mountain Apartment, I see two big fires, one near the South Gate".[71] The area "near the south gate" was located in the "south" of Rabe's residence. (The fire that happened on this day was also proved by the memory of photographer Koyanagi Tsuguichi in his later years who belonged to the Japanese Secret Service stationed in Shanghai. He said that "the fire on the night of his arrival in [Nanjing] on the 4th seemed to be set by plainclothes teams".[72])

---

[65] Unemoto Masaki, the introduction chapter in *The Truth of Nanjing Incident: An Examination of John Rabe's Diaries*, page 9.

[66] The Chinese version of *The Good Man of Nanking: The Diaries of John Rabe*, page 228.

[67] *Archives of the Nanjing Massacre Made by Japanese Invaders*, page 658.

[68] The Chinese version of *The Good Man of Nanking: The Diaries of John Rabe*, page 317.

[69] The Chinese version of the *Minnie Vautrin's Diary*, page 220.

[70] The Chinese version of *The Good Man of Nanking: The Diaries of John Rabe*, page 339.

[71] The Chinese version of the *Minnie Vautrin's Diary*, page 224.

[72] Ara Kenichi, 『「南京事件」日本人48人の証言』, Tokyo, Shôgakukan, 1st edition, January 1st, 2002, page 291.

Even in the materials quoted by the Examination, there are clear records of fires. For example, the diary of Orikono Suetaro (the leader of the 3rd Squadron of the 23rd Regiment and the acting leader of 1st Battalion) on 17th said that "There was a fire nearby". The diary of Matachi Ike on 18th said that "The fire in the distance reflected the red sky". Nomura Toshiaki said in the letter that on the evening of the 13th "two fires were set in one night, which caused difficulties for the moving". The first testimony quoted from the "testimonies of combatants" in the section six of the final chapter Recapitulation of the Examination is that "There were many fires, but all were set by Chinese soldiers and local ruffians. We were strictly prohibited from setting fires. We were not only strictly prohibited, but also we went out to put out the fires".[73]

There are many similar records in Japan's historical materials. For example, Makihara Shouta (Private First Class of the 3rd Machine Gun Squadron of the 20th Regiment) said in his diary on December 15th that "Everyone went to bed after dinner. In the capital of the enemy country, they peacefully dreamed about our hometown. Here and there, fires break out in three or four places". Makihara's diaries also have many other relevant records. For example, on December 17th, "There are also two or three fires tonight. (Since the fire is set by the plainclothes team, we are forbidden to go out.)" On December 21st, "Fires happen every night. Why? As expected, some Chinese sprinkled gasoline and set fires near the Japanese's residence. We caught one today and killed him". On December 22nd, "today there was a fire behind the artillery (dormitory)".[74]

The aforementioned Yamazaki Masao, Staff Officer of the 10th army, recorded in his diary on December 15th,

> When the Japanese soldiers entered Nanjing, all were warned not to plunder or set fires by the Area Army. Fires were relatively few. However, at one time slow-moving fires could not be extinguished due to the lack of special fire extinguishing system and proper fire extinguishing methods. Fortunately, there was no wind and the fires did not get serious. In night, the columns of fire everywhere were very spectacular.[75]

Major General Sasaki Toichi, leader of the 30th brigade of the 16th Division, wrote the diary on December 14th,

> The remains of the houses were burnt out, and the fires were still raging everywhere. None of the residents were seen. There were only skinny dogs, walking expressionlessly or stretching legs and lying down.

---

[73] Unemoto Masaki, *The Truth of Nanjing Incident: An Examination of John Rabe's Diaries*, Part 2, page 110, page 115 and page 82; and Recapitulation, page 227.

[74] 「牧原信夫日記」,南京戦史編集委員会編『南京戦史資料集』, page 512, page 512, page 513 and page 514.

[75] *Yamazaki Masao' Diary*,南京戦史編集委員会編『南京戦史資料集』, page 403.

Major Nakayama Neito, Staff Officer of the "Central China Area Army", appeared in court as a witness for the defense during the Tokyo Trial. He had the following dialogue with the prosecutor:

> *Prosecutor*: Have you ever seen a fire in Nanjing?
> *Witness Nakayama*: Yes.
> *Prosecutor*: Did you see fires burning in different places in Nanjing? Where were the fires?
> *Witness Nakayama*: In one place, that was the west side of the airport that was in the south of Nanjing.
> *Prosecutor*: Was it outside or inside the city?
> *Witness Nakayama*: It was in the city.[76]

Major General Iinuma Mamoru, Chief of Staff of the Shanghai Expeditionary Army, the highest-ranking witness of the Nanjing case in the Tokyo Trial, said in part 7 of his "affidavit" (Defense Document No. 2626, Court Evidence No. 3399):

> I patrolled the city three times on December 16th, 20th, and the end of 1937… I admitted that there were fires, but I did not see any organized arsons and did not receive any report.[77]

Nakayama Neito went to Nanjing after the Japanese troops captured Nanjing and at the end of December. Nakayama Neito, Iinuma Mamoru and Hanae Shou were all staying in Nanjing at that time. Both Iinuma Mamoru and Nakayama Neito testified that the Japanese army was innocence at the Tokyo Trial. They either denied or diminished the Japanese army's atrocities. However, it was unexpected that Hanae Shou surpassed them and he distorted the facts more boldly than his officers.

Matsumura Toshio quoted the "plunders and fires" reported by Cabot Coville who was a military officer of the US embassy in Japan in his Big Questions about the Nanjing Massacre and said that "The traces of plunders and destructions seen by Cabot Coville here were mainly regarded as the 'acts of the Japanese army'. However, he deduced from his calm observation that 'the fires were set after plunders', that is, the fires were set to cover up the traces of plunders. (We believe) If the plunders were done by Chinese, the fires should also be done by Chinese" because "any fire occurred after the Japanese army occupied Nanjing could not bring any benefit to the Japanese army".[78] Fuji Nobuo quoted what Colonel Nakazawa Mitsuo (Chief of Staff of the 16th Division) said in How the Nanking Massacre Was

---

[76] 『日中戦争史資料』8「南京事件」I, compiled by Hora Tomio, Tokyo, Kawade Shobô Shinsha, 1st edition, November 25th, 1973, page 212.

[77] 『日中戦争史資料』8「南京事件」, compiled by Hora Tomio, page 252.

[78] Matsumura Toshio, 『「南京虐殺」への大疑問』, pp. 149–150.

Manufactured—Deception of the Tokyo Trial and said "fires were not only 'common means' of the Chinese army", "but also there was an incident that a Chinese woman with a residence certificate was arrested at the scene of a fire".[79] As long as it was not Japanese soldiers who set fires, there could be fires. As long as it can be proved that it was the Chinese who set fires, there must be fires.

This is a good example to show that the determination of the facts in the Examination—as well as other works denying the Nanjing Massacre—is entirely arbitrary: If the Japanese army "had nothing to do" with fires, it can be quoted that "there was a fire nearby" and if they tried to deny Rabe's accusation against Japanese army, they would say that fires "had never happened"!

Were there dead bodies when the Japanese entered Nanjing?

The determination of this point in the Examination is exactly the same as the determination of fires. In the Rabe's Diaries on December 13th, "we turn onto Shanghai Road and the street was full of dead civilians".[80] When the Examination quoted this sentence, it omitted "and drive on toward the advancing Japanese soldiers" and then said firmly,

> Before the Japanese army entered the city, there were <u>dead bodies of the citizens</u> which may be caused by defeated Chinese soldiers. Perhaps they were killed by Chinese soldiers of the 212th brigade of the 36th division to prevent the defeated soldiers.

However, among the quotations used to prove that the Japanese army did not commit atrocity when they entered Nanjing in the Examination, there were words "no corpses" (Iba Masuo), "<u>there were neither residents nor abandoned corpses</u> in the mop-up area" (Kuribara Naoyuki) and "no corpses were seen when I patrolled the city"[81] (Hijiya Masaharu).

There are both records of corpses and no corpses. People with normal thinking can't help but ask: Were there corpses or not?!

Was it impossible for Rabe to meet Japanese soldiers who know German?

In the Rabe's Diaries on December 13th, "we drive on toward the advancing Japanese soldiers and a German-speaking doctor of the Japanese detachment

---

[79] Fuji Nobuo, 『「南京大虐殺」はこうして作られた──东京裁判の欺瞞』, Tokyo, 展転社, 4th edition, November 23rd, 1998, page 179.

[80] The Chinese version of *The Good Man of Nanking: The Diaries of John Rabe*, page 171.

[81] Unemoto Masaki, *The Truth of Nanjing Incident: An Examination of John Rabe's Diaries*, Part 2, page 66, page 74 and page 80.

tells us that the Japanese general is not arrived until two days later".[82] The Examination asserted that "there was no German-speaking military doctor".[83] The Japanese right-wing groups had frequently questioned the "German-speaking", thinking that they had found Rabe's "fabrication". For example, Thorough Examination of the Nanjing Massacre by Higashinakano Shūdō quoted this paragraph in the section "Contradictions in the Over-polished Rabe's Diaries" and marked the "German-speaking" with emphasis marks to indicate that it was a fabrication.[84] But "German-speaking" soldiers can be commonly seen in the Japanese army at that time. Since the Meiji Restoration, Japan had formed a system of compulsory education and all Japanese officers and soldiers came from schools. German was the most important language taught in schools besides English at that time and military doctors especially had a higher level of education. Therefore, "German-speaking" soldiers can be commonly seen. Moreover, when Japanese army entered Nanjing, they took "foreign rights and interests" into account and specially selected officers and soldiers who knew foreign languages to take part in the "mop-up". The order of the 7th Regiment included the requirement of "selecting people with competent language skills".[85] Relying only on imagination can't deny the Rabe's Diaries.

Did Rabe say the specific time?

As for the Rabe's record quoted above, the Examination has another reason for its negation:

> According to Rabe's "A Report to Hitler" (page 312), "on December 13th, at about 5: 00 a.m., I was awakened by the air strikes by the Japanese army and then went to the south of the city with several Americans. We tried to contact the Japanese military command to investigate the damage."… (the emphasis marks and the ellipsis are retained according to original texts)
>
> The diary and the report were different in Rabe's acts. On the morning of the 13th, the Japanese military command did not enter or leave the city. It was unable to investigate the war situation (seemingly referring to the "damage" - noted by the quoter) in the city.
>
> … The time was completely unmatched. (the emphasis marks are retained according to original texts)[86]

---

[82] The Chinese version of *The Good Man of Nanking: The Diaries of John Rabe*, page 171.

[83] Unemoto Masaki, *The Truth of Nanjing Incident: An Examination of John Rabe's Diaries*, Part 2, page 67.

[84] Higashinakano Shūdō, 『「南京虐殺」の徹底検証』付章, pp. 386–387.

[85] The 7th regiment「捕虜、外国権益に対する注意」, 南京戦史編集委員会編纂『南京戦史』, page 193. Major Yamazaki Masao, staff officer of the 10th army, encountered an acquaintance, Senior Captain Fujimori Yukio, on December 11th. Fujimori "was enlisted when he studied in the language school (Tokyo University of Foreign Studies) in August this year" (「山崎正男日記」, 南京戦史編集委員会編『南京戦史資料集』, page 397). There are indeed many talented people who master foreign languages in the Japanese army.

[86] Unemoto Masaki, *The Truth of Nanjing Incident: An Examination of John Rabe's Diaries*, Part 2, pp. 66–67.

When I first read the above quotation, I thought it was a small error in Rabe's memory. Because his report to Hitler was written nearly half a year later after the incident and had nothing to do with the key point—there was no value of fabrication in any sense—so "the time was completely unmatched" can only be a human error. Therefore, when I sent this article to Modern Chinese History Studies, I did not write it. Recently, I have read The Truth of Nanjing again and found that the Examination tampered with the Rabe's original text, which made the quotation significantly different from the original text. The original text of Rabe's report is:

> On December 13th, at about 5 a.m., I was awakened by the fierce air strikes by the Japanese army and felt particularly surprised for the first time. However, I became calm when I thought that the defeated Chinese soldiers might not have been swept away. In fact, the daily air strikes have made people quite accustomed to it, so I didn't care too much. I went to the south of the city with several Americans. We tried to contact the Japanese military command to investigate the damage.[87]

The difference between the original text and the quotation in the Examination is crystal clear. The Examination didn't use quotation marks or even full stops for omitted content, which showed that the Examination have ulterior motives.

After the above quotation, Rabe's report also said that "there were opportunities almost every day" to meet with people of the Japanese embassy, but there was no specific date mentioned in the report—certainly no specific time. Therefore, as long as someone has reading ability, he should not have any doubt that the original text by no means meant that Rabe "went to the south of the city with several Americans" after "about 5 a.m." Therefore, the so-called "time" issue is entirely concocted by the Examination.

IV

The Examination was aimed at "vindicating"[88] the Japanese army. It has high self-expectation but it cannot cope with real problems and is full of loopholes. It says that Rabe had "emotional bias". However, it is itself that is trapped in "emotional bias". With such "emotional bias", anyone, no matter what "experienced person" he is or whether he is familiar with this "discipline" or not,[89] he can only judge the world and other people from the "political perspective", not to mention that he can be "impartial" and "neutral". Here are a few more examples:

---

[87] ジョン・ラーベ著『南京の真実』, pp. 311–312.

[88] Unemoto Masaki, the Recapitulation in *The Truth of Nanjing Incident: An Examination of John Rabe's Diaries*, page 230.

[89] Unemoto Masaki once wrote many works, such as 有「証言による南京戦史」(一—十七,『偕行』April 1984 to November 1985).

Who is the first responsible person?

Scharffenber[90] said that the ruins of Nanjing and the impoverished life of refugees were entirely caused by the Japanese army.

As for the Nanjing battle, as mentioned before, Tang Shengzhi who refused to accept General Matsui's "advice of peacefully opening the city" and Rabe's "proposal for a three-day truce" strengthened the defenses, cleared the fields and upheld the scorched-earth policy. Then he irresponsibly ignored 200,000 citizens and fled.

As the journalist F. Tillman Durdin and Rabe said, the first responsibility should lie with China.

The fundamental reason of the so-called "Nanjing Massacre, 300,000" publicized by the Chinese is, first of all, the "rigid operational guidance of the Chinese" pointed out by German Rabe and American journalist Durdin. This point must be recognized.

As for the so-called "rape", we went out on public duty or led by superiors and we were not allowed to move freely. The buildings in the safe zone in which the women lived were strictly forbidden to enter. The fear of going out alone in the dark night made people absolutely not dare to do that.

Our young sergeants only played mahjong under the candles.

As for the so-called "plunder", the houses had been plundered before we entered them. All we took from the empty houses in wartime were some seasonings, pots and cans.

…There was absolutely no military discipline disorder. The officers and soldiers strictly followed the orders and fought hard. (These are the testimonies of combatants quoted in the Examination.)

"Fires ordered by the Japanese army, arbitrary plunder and rape" written by Rape is by no means the fact. From the superior command to the inferior leaders in the first line, everyone was doing their best to prevent illegal activities.

The miserable wounded people and corpses that Rabe saw in the Drum Tower Hospital were entirely regarded as the result of the illegal and cruel acts of the Japanese army. <u>However, not all of them were illegally killed by abuse</u>. Was it common in wartime?

The atomic bombs in Hiroshima and Nagasaki and the Tokyo Raid were the same. Legitimate and unavoidable killing and unlawful killing must be distinguished.

After reading through the Rabe's Diaries, we could see that it lacks a fair understanding of the war and the Japanese army, and it has the bias of treating the Japanese army as an illegal group and a villain.

Even shooting and killing the defeated soldiers was also combat behavior. If ordinary citizens were hijacked, it was unavoidable to say that they were killed by abuse. Combat behavior and so-called illegal killing should be strictly distinguished.[91]

---

[90] He was a member of the German Embassy in China.

[91] Unemoto Masaki, *The Truth of Nanjing Incident: An Examination of John Rabe's Diaries*, Part 4, pp. 164–165; Part 1, page 28; Recapitulation, page 227; and Part 2, page 126, page 131 and page 103.

Our officers and soldiers were by no means like "the violent soldier ベルゼルカ[92] who tried to seize everything" and "kept reaching Nanjing to get girls." On the contrary, they held the faint hope that they might be able to go home after conquering Nanjing and they warned each other that if they did something bad, they would not be able to go home, so they fought bravely.

Isn't the killing and destruction brought about by the war an inevitable fate and "karma" of mankind? However, Rabe's praying to God was only hatred and revenge against the Japanese army. Combatants, onlookers and third parties have different standpoints and they have different hopes and understanding of harsh reality, but truly "purity" and "justice" cannot be felt (in the Rabe's Diaries—noted by the quoter).

The "handling captives" in the Nanjing battle was distorted and publicized as the division leader Nakashima's "policy of not accepting captives". However, General Matsui adopted the policy of "disarming surrendered soldiers and liberating them", including "liberating, releasing", "taking in surrendered captives" and "killing defeated soldiers and plainclothes soldiers" instead of killing them all. (The emphasis marks are retained according to original texts.)

The Japanese army's attacks from Shanghai to Nanjing, as this article said, were unlike Genghis Khan's conquest of Europe or Hitler's genocide. It is an upright "just war"—a war of moderation and punishment.

(The thing that Chinese soldiers strengthened the defenses and cleared the fields had hardly hindered the Japanese army from the military perspective. On the contrary, it brought incalculable disaster to the peasants, reflecting the organized destruction since the era of Genghis Khan. (The original text here is very unsmooth.)

Japanese heavy artillery raised balloons on the Zijin Mountain to watch the air for shooting in order to avoid damage to refugee camps.

In refugee camps, the Chinese men and women of all ages were unexpectedly calm and looked at the benevolent country called "Japan" in hesitation, expressing their deep gratitude. (This paragraph is the diary of Yamazaki Masao, Staff Officer of 10th army. The Examination specially added a note after the quotation that "Yamazaki Masao has well shown the Chinese people's view".)

We came by car. The Chinese thought we were major characters, so they flocked to watch us and the reporters could only run away (the diary of Matachi Ike on December 16th).

We took back scallions, radishes and green vegetables and asked the refugees to wash them. We also asked them to clean up and do other things. Because we gave the refugees leftovers, they were very happy to work for us (the diary of Matachi Ike).

The superiors issued strict instructions on military discipline and we carefully protected the cultural heritage (said by Muguruma Masajiro, and the emphasis marks are retained according to original texts).

Strict control over Nanjing city's gates was to prevent the entry of unscrupulous people and was not to control the news as Rabe said. Embassy staffs from various countries and news organizations had entered Nanjing and news spread all over the world through Shanghai.

[92] A powerful god in Nordic mythology.

The kendo teacher related to the navy came with a letter of introduction and demanded to slay the captives, which was contrary to common sense. His application to the head of division was certainly rejected.

<u>There were no women in the city</u> (from the posthumous manuscript of Miyamoto Shiro, adjutant of the 16th Division, and the emphasis marks are retained according to original texts).

Ginling College took in women and had walls. Other people were forbidden to enter it. According to the records of the International Committee on December 17th, there were 4,000 to 5,000 people in the college, of whom more than 100 were raped. What kind of rape can be carried out in front of the public? <u>There was no disproof</u>, but all of the records were "hearsay" that <u>were suspicious</u>.[93] (The emphasis marks are retained according to original texts.)

The record "Zhang told me" is just like that the author was at the scene. The story seemed to be true at the beginning, but as for "that part[94] was inserted with a bamboo pole" and so on, Japanese (people) would not do that. Only Chinese people have such custom in the past. If Rabe knew this point, would he still think it was done by the Japanese soldiers? In addition, 70-year-old women and others were also raped, which was really unnatural.

It was too courageous to commit atrocities in hospitals. But when? What kind of atrocities? There was no specific description. The Rabe's Diaries was just like this. The facts and hearsay were mixed, which can make people fall into danger.

The 16mm film produced by Magee, including photos of "a stunned old woman whose family members were killed", "corpses floating in a pool", "a scene in which children's corpses were transported in a cage", "a woman receiving treatment in a hospital" and so on, was published in Life in 1938.

I have also seen the copy of the film, but can we say that this is a film that can be used as evidence for "Nanjing Massacre"? I don't think so.

Why wasn't this film mentioned in the "Tokyo Trial"?

There were a large number of violent incidents in the Rabe's Diaries. All of these <u>records</u> were made up of reports given by the Chinese. (The emphasis marks are retained according to original texts.)

"Seventeen people in a family of eighteen were killed". When? Where? How were they killed? <u>Rumors</u> after <u>rumors</u>, how can there be such cruel killings just after the New Year's Day?

As for the so-called "knowing the message", there should be no stationed Japanese soldiers nearby. As for the so-called looting coffin lids and throwing corpses on the streets, soldiers in Kyoto division (16th Division) and Kanazawa division (9th Division) were mostly Buddhists who were all benevolent and generous. Could they conduct such barbaric acts? Although it was wartime, it was still hard to imagine that with common sense. (The emphasis marks are retained according to original texts)

---

[93] Unemoto Masaki, *The Truth of Nanjing Incident: An Examination of John Rabe's Diaries*, Part 4, page 167; Part 2, page 132; Part 4, page 186; Recapitulation, page 229; Part 1, page 35 and page 42; Part 2, page 109, page 101, page 125 and page 76; Part 4, pp. 177–178; and Part 2, page 77 and page 107.

[94] In the Chinese version of *The Good Man of Nanking: The Diaries of John Rabe* (page 563), it is directly translated into "vagina".

According to the petition from refugee camps in Guangzhou Road, young women who will be abused were taken away by trucks every night. Was there such a troop? If there was no record of <u>the name and place of the troop that took away women</u>, then it cannot be used as evidence. (The emphasis marks are retained according to original texts.)

Japanese soldiers were forbidden to go out at night. Those Japanese soldiers who invaded the home of German Rabe must be very stupid. Rabe should not just drive them out, but also catch them. Otherwise, how can this be eradicated?

Rabe, as Chairman of the International Committee, must take an absolutely neutral position, but he harbored cadres of the national government. One of the cadres, Luo Fuxiang (air force officer, whose real name was Wang Hanwan), left Nanjing by the British Bee gunboat and headed for Shanghai on February 23rd.

This was a clear proof that <u>Rabe himself</u> cannot be "neutral" and "impartial".[95] (The emphasis marks are retained according to original texts.)

Some of the above quotations were quotations in the Examination, but since the Examination quoted them, these quotations can be regarded as parts of the Examination. What does the Examination think of these words? Are they reasonable words or nonsense? The answer is self-evident.

V

The above passages in the "examination" (sections two and three) and excerpts from the translation (section four) are not deliberately selected but unconsciously marked by me when I read the Examination. These marks have "shortcomings". For example, it cannot show the extent of absurdity. But we can get the big picture from small details. Therefore, through the above several examples, we can draw a relatively comprehensive conclusion that the denial of authenticity of the Rabe's Diaries by the Examination, the so-called "exaggeration, hearsay, conjecture" and the so-called "obvious fabrication, inconsistency, artificiality and unreason" are totally untenable.

In a postscript to the translation of The Nanjing Massacre and Japanese Spiritual Structure, I once said that the repeated defeats of the Azuma Shiro case "had a significant value for 'understanding history' of Japanese court and commonalty".[96] Similarly, the false accusation of "Examination" is not only untenable as to the Rabe's Diaries, but also it is a "sample". Through this sample, people can see that a considerable number of former Japanese

---

[95] Unemoto Masaki, *The Truth of Nanjing Incident: An Examination of John Rabe's Diaries*, Part 4, page 181; Part 2, page 112; Part 4, page 184 and page 185; Part 3, pp. 150–151; Part 2, page 123 and page 124; and Part 4, page 187.

[96] Tsuda Michio, *The Nanjing Massacre and Japanese Spiritual Structure*, The Commercial Press (HK), 1st edition, June 2000, page 210.

soldiers—certainly more than the former soldiers—still have no introspection and still hold the same values and ideologies as before. People can also see how the "Nanjing Massacre" denied by the Japanese right-wing groups through "exaggeration", "conjecture" and "fabrication".

(Originally published in Modern Chinese History Studies, No. 2, 2002)

Re-discussion on "The 100-Man Killing Contest"

1　I

The Nanjing Massacre has received widespread attention in Japan since the 1970s. The direct cause is the A Journey to China serialized in Asahi Shimbun from late August to December 1971.[1] Asahi Shimbun is Japan's most influential newspaper. As a journalist of Asahi Shimbun, Honda Katsuichi was permitted to come to China in 1971. He successively visited Guangzhou, Changsha, Beijing, Shenyang, Fushun, Anshan, Tang Mountain, Jinan, Nanjing and Shanghai for 40 consecutive days from June to July. A Journey to China is the record of his trip. Wherever Honda went, he looked for the former sites of Japanese atrocities and the surviving victims. These records became the main content of A Journey to China. Therefore, A Journey to China is not an ordinary "travel notes", but a denunciation of Japanese atrocities in those days. The book was also serialized in Asahi Journal and some photos in the book were published in Asahi Graph. In the second year, a separate edition of A Journey to China was published by Asahi Shimbun. Apart from the original chapters "Pingdingshan" and "Manninkō" (Hushigou), "Nanjing" and "The Policy of Burn All, Kill All, Loot All", the separate edition added chapters such as "The Image of Militarism of Japan Made by Chinese", "In the Former Workshop of 'Sumitomo'", "House of Correction", "Human Bacterial Experiment and Vivisection", "Fushun", "Epidemic Prevention and Brutal Killing", "Anshan and the Former 'Kubota' Workshop", "Around Lugou Bridge", "Forced Escort to Japan", "Shanghai", "Port", "The Reality of the 'Punitive Expedition' and

---

[1] Honda Katsuichi late said that "I have written all kinds of communications so far, but I have never had such a strong and profound reaction as that caused by the serial of *A Journey to China*". 『裁かれた南京大屠殺』 edited by Honda Katsuichi, Tokyo, Bunseisha, 3rd printed version, June 1st, 1989, p. 85.

'Bombing'". The "Nanjing Massacre" then became a reality that the Japanese public had to face due to the severe criticism of Honda Katsuichi and the special influence of Asahi Shimbun. Whether this "reality" aroused introspection or antipathy cannot be easily judged by a few words. However, its influence has disturbed those who oppose the so-called "Tokyo Trial Historical View".[2] Consequently, surging waves of negating the Nanjing Massacre, each stronger than the last, have come into being.

Suzuki Aki was the first one to "refute" Honda Katsuichi. Suzuki Aki was born in 1929 and once worked in a private radio station before becoming a freelance writer. In 1972, he published The Myth of the "Nanjing Massacre" (hereinafter referred to as Myth) in Japanese famous right-wing journal Shokun in April. Suzuki Aki's collection of essays published the following year was also named after "Myth".[3] Since then, the word "myth"[4] has been regarded as the same meaning of the Chinese "fiction" and has become the generic name of the "fabrication school" that completely denies the "Nanjing Massacre". The first challenge posed by the Myth to A Journey to China was the "100-man killing contest". The "100-man killing contest" refers to the killing contest between Second Lieutenant Noda Tsuyoshi, adjutant of the 3rd Battalion of the 9th Regiment of the 16th Division of the Shanghai Expeditionary Army, and Second Lieutenant Mukai Toshiaki, team leader of infantry artillery of the same battalion, on the way to Nanjing. The contest was famous at that time, and the two were sentenced to death by Nanjing War Crimes Tribunal after the war. Myth believes that the "100-man killing contest" is a fabrication by the media, and it is not the truth. As a result, Japan's left-wing groups and right-wing groups have launched fierce debates. Akira Fujiwara, the living leader of Japan's "slaughter school", said recently in response to a relevant questionnaire that this contest "was concocted for the purpose of writing heroic episode of the battle, but it can be said that some captives who did not resist were killed".[5] If we take the answer as a result of

---

[2] Japan's right-wing groups always think that the Tokyo Trial was a "winners' trial" and in order to prove the Japanese's "guilt", the "winners" would do everything, even fabricating rumors. Therefore, the Japanese army's behavior in World War II was greatly vilified. Among all the false accusations against the Japanese army, the "Nanjing Massacre" is the biggest one. The reason is that before the Tokyo Trial, the world did not know about the "Nanjing Massacre" and "not knowing" was due to "not existing", so the "Nanjing Massacre" was completely fabricated by the Tokyo Trial. For details, see my article "Is the Nanjing Massacre a Fabrication Made by Tokyo Trial?" in *Modern Chinese History Studies*, Beijing, No. 6, 2002, p. 157.

[3] Suzuki Aki, 『「南京大虐殺」のまぼろし』, Bungei Shunjû, 1st edition, March 10th, 1973. The quotation in this article is from the 15th printed version, May 30th, 1989.

[4] Regarding Suzuki's denial of the old translation of "まぼろし" and approval of the new translation "myth", please see the footnote in the section three of my article "Is *The Good Man of Nanking: The Diaries of John Rabe* an 'Unfounded Fabrication'—An Examination of *The Truth of Nanjing Incident: An Examination of John Rabe's Diaries*", *Modern Chinese History Studies*, Beijing, No. 2, 2002, p. 166.

[5] 「まぼろし派、中間派、大虐殺派三派合同大アンケート」, *Shokun*, Tokyo, Bungei Shunjû, February 2001, p. 193.

the debate, as far as the "justice" of this matter is concerned, it can still be said that each side has its own argument (the so-called "killing" of captives), and as far as the matter itself is concerned, it has to be said that the "fabrication school" has won the game (the so-called "concocted").

This matter is brought up again today because this year marks the 65th anniversary of the Nanjing Massacre (this article was published in 2002) which is also a "symbolic event".[6] What is more important is that the relevant discussions have not really ended.

2   II

Regarding the "100-man killing contest", A Journey to China said like this:

"These famous words were also reported in Japan at that time," said Mr. Jiang, who introduced the following killings committed by Japanese soldiers.

> As for the second lieutenant "M" and second lieutenant "N", one day their superior instigated them to carry out a killing contest. On the way from Gourong to Tang Mountain on the outskirts of Nanjing, about 10 km, the one who firstly killed 100 Chinese people will be rewarded ...
>
> Then the two-man contest began. The result was that "M" killed only 89 people and "N" killed only 78 people. When they arrived at Tang Mountain, their superior gave them another order that on the way from Tang Mountain to Zijin Mountain, about 15 km, they were requested to kill another 100 people respectively. The new result was that "M" killed 105 people and "N" killed 106 people. This time they both reached their goals, but the superior said that "Since no one knows who firstly killed 100 people, the contest is invalid. On the way from Zijin Mountain to Nanjing City, about eight kilometers, I wonder who can firstly reach the goal of killing 150 people."
>
> Mr. Jiang held that this area was close to the city wall and had a large population. Although the result was not known, both of them were highly likely to reach their goals.[7]

The "Mr. Jiang" in this article refers to Jiang Genfu, who was a crew in inland waters of Nanjing Port Authority during the interview. "At that time" there were also reports in Japan, referring to the reports in the Tokyo Nichi Nichi Shimbun (the predecessor of the Mainichi Shimbun), an important Japanese media at the time of the incident, on the "100-man killing contest" between Mukai Toshiaki and Noda Tsuyoshi on November 30th, December 4th, December 6th and December 13th, 1937, respectively (In the report on December 13th, there was a large photo of the two holding Japanese swords).

---

[6]The expression used in the recent questionnaire in the Japanese journal Shokun. 「まぼろし派、中間派、大虐殺派三派合同大アンケート」, Shokun, p. 166.

[7]Honda Katsuichi, 『中国の旅』「南京」注4, Tokyo, Asahi Shimbun, 19th printed version, January 20th, 1993, p. 234.

Myth compares the record in A Journey to China with the record in The Nanjing Incident written by Hora Tomio, and holds that:

> The subtle difference between the two records is obvious to anyone. First of all, Oomori's (Oomori refers to Oomori Minoru. Hora Tomio quoted Oomori's quotation of the words of "the Chinese People's Association for Friendship with Foreign Countries" in the book. – noted by the citer) quotation was "before entering Nanjing", which indicated the achievements in the battle. However, Honda's words were ambiguous which can be applied to both the wartime and peacetime. The so-called "this area <u>had a large population</u>" (the emphasis marks are retained according to original texts and hereinafter the same shall apply – noted by the citer) is probably concluded according to the usual situation. It is clear that the determination of "cruelty" is mainly different in peacetime and wartime. Although the line "One murder makes a villain, millions a hero" in Chaplin's movie are exaggerated, the killing in the battlefield, at least in the eyes of the Japanese living in the 12th year of the Shōwa era, is the cruelty that "can be accepted". But even in Japan's wartime, there were no people who accepted "killing games" other than the killing in the battlefield.[8]

The frequent mention of the killing contest between Mukai Toshiaki and Noda Tsuyoshi is due to the hard evidence reported by Japan itself "at that time". Therefore, the key lies not in what people said decades later, but in what they thought of the reports at that time. In this regard, the Myth says like this:

> In view of the present station, the words at that time are unbelievable, absurd and ridiculous. These words had been spread to China and some changes had taken place in the course of the spread. First, the killing in the battlefield was changed into the killing game in peacetime. Second, the "superior's order" which was not found in the original text was added. Third, the "100-man killing contest" had three repeated stages, and so on. In my opinion, this report in the Tokyo Nichi Nichi Shimbun was not without traces of exaggerating the facts regarding militarism. It is true that we can think of such brave men on the battlefield, but how can they who just held Japanese swords confront enemies with guns behind reinforced concrete bunkers? Those authors who regarded it as something to boast about and tried their best to polish it cannot be regarded as normal people.[9]

The words of Suzuki Aki are certainly not convincing for the victims. Even if some people have "peace of mind" and regard it as an objective event completely unaffected by emotion, Suzuki Aki's words cannot deny the truth recorded at that time and the cruelty of Japanese atrocities. Here are the reasons: First, war will bring a large number of deaths and there is difference between the "peacetime" and "wartime". However, it does not mean that "cruelty" can be allowed in wartime. Laws against maltreatment of prisoners

---

[8] Suzuki Aki, 『「南京大虐殺」のまぼろし』, pp. 10–11.
[9] Suzuki Aki, 『「南京大虐殺」のまぼろし』, pp. 14–15.

of war on land were promulgated as early as 1899, and the strict prohibition of "cruel" behavior to civilians was the world consensus since the era of great powers. The so-called "the determination of 'cruelty' is mainly different in peacetime and wartime" can only show that Suzuki Aki's maintenance of the Japanese army's "cruel" behavior has reached the level of no principle at all. Second, the Tokyo Nichi Nichi Shimbun did not—nor did the book of Honda Katsuichi and the book of Hora Tomio—say that Mukai Toshiaki and Noda Tsuyoshi were holding swords to fight against the guns in bunkers. The dead under the swords of Mukai Toshiaki and Noda Tsuyoshi could be soldiers without weapons, captives who had laid down arms,[10] and civilians completely unrelated to the war. These situations can be found in a large number of written records in China and Japan, and can also be verified by a large number of photos taken by the Japanese army.[11]

Third, if the reports of the killing contest between Mukai Toshiaki and Noda Tsuyoshi "exaggerated the facts regarding militarism", concrete evidence of "exaggeration" should be provided firstly, and if there is no evidence, people will definitely ask that: Why "exaggerate" the event of Mukai Toshiaki and Noda Tsuyoshi instead of others? Why "exaggerate" the killing contest instead of others—such as the war situation? Fourth, if all the reports regarding militarism at that time were "exaggerated", it is suspicious that the "inflated" reputation of Mukai Toshiaki and Noda Tsuyoshi was not investigated by others due to the fierce competition for merits in Japanese army at that time. Besides, Mukai Toshiaki and Noda Tsuyoshi who gained the benefits should bear moral responsibility since they did not give any explanation of the event. Moreover, even if it was "propaganda", it was also wrong to promote militarism.

3   III

After this, many people started to defend Mukai Toshiaki and Noda Tsuyoshi. For example, Ooi Mitsuru's The Fabricated Nanjing Massacre said that not only did the killing contest not exist, but also "Mukai had a noble heart".[12] The Alleged "Nanking Massacre" written by Takemoto Tadao and others said,

---

[10] Regarding the order of killing massive prisoners from top to down when the Japanese army captured Nanjing, please see my article "A Study of the Massacre Order for Japanese Troops", *Historical Research*, Beijing, No. 6, 2002, pp. 68–79.

[11] Japan's "fictionalists" challenged the authenticity of these photos. The most extreme argument is that "there was not a single photo that can prove the Nanjing massacre". Nobukatsu Fujioka and Higashinakano Shūdō, 『ザ・レイプ・オブ・南京の研究』第二章「『写真検証編』写真捏造、暴かれた手口」, Tokyo, 祥伝社, 1st edition, September 10th, 1999, p. 108. The authenticity of these photos will be discussed in a special article.

[12] Ooi Mitsuru, 『仕組まれた「南京大虐殺」——攻略作戦の全貌とマスコミの怖さ』第八章「記事に殺された原軍人」之一、二, Tokyo, 展転社, 3rd printed version, June 6th, 1998, pp. 247–269.

There were no Chinese who witnessed the "the 100-man killing contest" and the court sentenced Mukai Toshiaki and Noda Tsuyoshi to death on the single evidence of news records. Was this absurd trial in accordance with evidentiary adjudication?

There is no need to argue about the "witness" because Mukai Toshiaki and Noda Tsuyoshi were killing innocent people and were in a "race" when they wanted to meet and kill more living people. Those "lucky witnesses" must have "been killed with swords" in the contest. How can they be the living "witnesses"? The Alleged "Nanking Massacre" further said:

> It is easy to understand for those who understand the military system. Second Lieutenant Mukai Toshiaki was the commander of infantry artillery, and Second Lieutenant Noda Tsuyoshi was the adjutant of the battalion. Both of them should not take part in the first-line hand-to-hand combats. Samurai movies often have scenes of beheading one after another. However, it is not easy to cut someone because blood contains fat which causes difficulties in cutting people. According to the quality of Japanese swords, the sword edge will be damaged and the blade will bend, which is clear from the opinions of specialists at that time. Japanese swords are different from the Chinese Green Dragon blades, which rely on their own weight to increase the cutting force.
>
> The "100-man killing contest" that caused two Japanese officers' death was treated as a representative case of the Japanese army's crazy killing in the Nanjing battle. However, the sentence is infinitely close to the wrongful conviction.[13]

Yoshiaki Itakura's The Truth of Nanjing Incident said,

> The "100-man killing contest" was well known to the ordinary people after the war due to the journalist Honda's A Journey to China. In this regard, Suzuki Aki has used nearly perfect demonstration in The Myth of the "Nanjing Massacre" to prove that the contest is a fabrication. Yamamoto Shichihei also has detailed demonstration. Besides, from the testimony of Mainichi Shimbun's photographer Sato Shinju who took the photos of Second Lieutenant Mukai Toshiaki and Second Lieutenant Noda Tsuyoshi, as well as the army's organization, the physical features of Japanese swords and the war situation at that time, the "the myth of the 100-man killing contest" theory can be recognized as the final conclusion.[14]

Among all the arguments on "100-man killing contest", Yamamoto Shichihei's arguments were the most "detailed" ones. He not only

---

[13]Takemoto Tadao and Oohara Yasuo, 日本会議国際広報委員会編『再審「南京大虐殺」――世界に訴える日本の冤罪』, Tokyo, 明成社, 2nd printed version, November 25th, 2000, pp. 90–91.

[14]Yoshiaki Itakura,『本当はこうだった南京事件』, Tokyo, 日本図書刊行会, 2nd printed version, January 20th, 2000, p. 121.

comprehensively revised and supplemented Suzuki's so-called "work", but also wrote a long article against Honda Katsuichi's criticism. Suzuki once quoted the appeal of Mukai Toshiaki to "prove" the fabrication of the killing contest on the grounds that Mukai met the journalist Asami Kazuo only in Wuxi, he did not meet Noda Tsuyoshi again after December 6th and he did not take part in the frontline battle. Such verbal statement without any proof naturally cannot be evidence, just as the Nanjing War Crimes Tribunal did not recognize it at that time. Moreover, two important testimonies appeared during the serialization of Honda's A Journey to China. First, the journalist Suzuki Jiro who made third report of the "100-man killing contest" said "I witnessed the 'tragedy of Nanjing'" regarding the interviews with Mukai Toshiaki and Noda Tsuyoshi in the magazine Maru.[15] Second, Shishime Akira (who worked in the Promotion Department of the Central Labor Protection Organization) told the magazine China his memory of Noda Tsuyoshi' return to his primary school in hometown. Noda directly said to him,

> It was all about me in the newspaper, such as the warrior from home village and the warrior of the 100-man killing contest... In reality, there were only four or five people who were killed in the assault.
>
> Facing the enemies' trenches that had been occupied by us, I shouted "You come, you come" (the original was the Chinese "nilai" - noted by the citer). The Chinese soldiers were fools and gradually came out. I asked them to stand in line and then chopped one person and another ...
>
> The "100-man killing contest" was actually like this ...[16]

This is a remark that exposes the cruelty of Noda Tsuyoshi, which is in line with the wartime reports. However, in regard of this, Yamamoto Shichihei had a lame argument that:

> This was the content of Shishime Akira Shishime's contribution to the monthly magazine China. He said that he heard it in the spring of 14th year of the Shōwa era, about one year and four months after the reports of the "100-man killing contest". This is very accurate testimony no matter how people think of it. How can Honda Katsuichi take it as "evidence"? Later, he mentioned about forced human experiment. As for this point, I will not discuss it here because Bungei Shunjū had already explained it. Now I would like to review Second Lieutenant Noda's testimony.
>
> First of all, there is no doubt that this testimony confirms that the "records" such as the "100-man killing contest" reported by journalist Asami do not exist in reality, which have been proved by me. Of course, since it was a wartime remark, no one would feel incredible and the great praise of it was normal when

---

[15] The monthly 『丸』, November 1971, quoted from Honda Katsuichi's *A Journey to China*, p. 264.

[16] The monthly 『中国』, December 1971, quoted from Honda Katsuichi's 『南京への道』「百人斬り『超記録』」, *Asahi Shimbun*, Tokyo, 4th printed version, April 30th, 1987, p. 130.

the "100-man killing contest" was reported in the newspapers as heroic episode. These reports were the words of that era that the leaders of media kept adding this kind of records to the newspapers which bored people when they opened the newspaper.

It can be said that it would be better to consider A Journey to China in reverse and serialize it in greater length because today is not like that era in which it is not strange and reasonable for Second Lieutenant Noda to stand up and answer "Yes, I am the warrior of the time." Moreover, the people who gathered to listen to these words intentionally wanted to listen to the "great heroic episode".

However, he denied this "record". In other words, Second Lieutenant Noda said that the record of the so-called "100-man killing contest" was not a fact but a false report. His denial firstly appeared one year and four months after the report instead of in the war crimes tribunal.

Moreover, the other party was a student of a primary school student who knew the battlefield only through the false report in the newspaper, so he was able to correct the event in some extent. However, if the other party was an experienced hand-to-hand fighter, such correction could not be made, which was one aspect of that time. Things do have two sides. At that time, the "100-man killing contest" was seemingly valid as a fact, but in the "real" world, it was even more invalid as a fact than it is today.[17] (Here, the so-called "if the other party was an experienced hand-to-hand fighter, such correction could not be made" will be mentioned later in the work of Yamamoto, referring to the fact that some people will definitely ask "whether it was four or five persons".—noted by the citer)

Yamamoto's "calm" is really surprising when he drew such conclusions from Shishime Akira's words. I don't deny that Shishime's words are "very accurate testimony".[18] But isn't it more obvious that Noda Tsuyoshi—the epitome of the Imperial Army—was barbaric, cruel and inhuman? To kill an enemy in "hand-to-hand combat" may still be "understandable" from the perspective of war, but cheating and killing captives who laid down their arms and stopped resisting, as mentioned before, is absolutely unacceptable in the international law enacted in the era of great powers, not to mention violating the ethics and humanity of war. Moreover, in any case, Yamamoto's so-called "denial" cannot be held in any sense regarding the "100-man killing contest". There are two reasons: First, even if Mukai and Noda did not kill their enemies in the battlefield, the contest of killing captives could still continue, and the Tokyo Nichi Nichi Shimbun did not explicitly say that it was "hand-to-hand combat", and second, Noda told Shishime that there were mostly

---

[17] Yamamoto Shichihei, 『私の中の日本軍』下, Tokyo, 文藝春秋社, 3rd printed version, February 15th, 1976, pp. 69–71.

[18] The "accuracy" of Shishime Akira's retrospect should be reflected in the main plot instead of details. For example, the expression "it was all about me in the newspaper" is suspicious because the newspaper clearly published names and photos. It was a great honor at that time and "local people" must know it.

cheating and killing, which does not mean that he was also so honest with the Tokyo Nichi Nichi Shimbun. At that time, Noda and others formed bad habits in the Japanese army for a long time for their troops, for the "local people and families"[19] and after all, for their own "glory". Therefore, even if the media's exaggeration in the militaristic environment cannot be completely denied, it is not surprising that Noda and others were showing off their abilities.

4 IV

Yamamoto Shichihei's "detailed demonstration" is the "source" of many fictionalists' viewpoints later on. For example, both the above-mentioned The Alleged "Nanking Massacre" and The Truth of Nanjing Incident especially emphasized that the Japanese swords cannot be used to "chop" person on the basis of Yamamoto's "detailed demonstration". Therefore, we can draw inferences about other cases from reviewing Yamamoto's "demonstration". Yamamoto used more than 50 pages to explain the so-called "physical limitations" of Japanese swords[20] which were too complicated to be quoted. Here are some excerpted parts,

> …A Japanese sword is consumed very fast. In the real battle, a Japanese sword will almost become a waste matter after one use. Its greatest weakness is the hilt. There are still many Japanese swords in Japan. Since the Tokugawa era, they have not been used as weapons in the battlefield, but only used as a "ceremonial object" to show a samurai's identity. If it is used in a real combat, it can be said that it will be improved into a more practical product. But there is no such improvement at all. Japanese swords only develop towards "arts and crafts" in the same direction as harquebuses. Mr. R said so. (Yamamoto claims that "Mr. R" is a "Chinese" and in his letter he "expresses indignation at those who argue that '100-man killing contest' is a fact."—noted by the citer)

We will discuss later whether Japanese swords will become "waste" matter after being used once and whether they will only develop toward "arts and crafts" instead of being "practical" products. After this quotation, Mr. R talked a lot about the "Chinese broadswords (Green Dragon blades)" that were the "most practical" products for killing people. Then he said,

---

[19] According to the section eight "Cherishing Reputation" of the "Discipline in the War" issued by Japanese Secretary of State for War in wartime, soldiers were required to "often miss local people and families and try to meet their expectations with greater efforts", quoted from Tsuda Michio's *The Nanjing Massacre and Japanese Spiritual Structure*, Tokyo, Shakai Hyôronsha, 1st edition, June 15th, 1995, p. 53.

[20] 「日本刀神話の実態」、「白兵戦に適されない名刀」, Yamamoto Shichihei's 『私の中の日本軍』下, pp. 67–118.

Moreover, R's said: "The fatal defect of a Japanese sword has been pointed out in detail by Japanese Naruse Kanji (referring to an author who wrote a book about Japanese swords in wartime - noted by the citer). When it comes to swords, their advantages and disadvantages should be thoroughly compared with all other swords in the world. Moreover, the physical status should be studied on the basis of materials obtained from thorough practical investigations conducted by specialized experts on the spot. The unilateral assertion that the relevant records (the 100-man killing contest) are facts judging from the assertion that Japanese swords rank first in the world cannot but arouse strong dissatisfaction. It would be very fortunate to publish even Naruse's arguments…"

As always, the experts' arguments have been ignored, and the inexplicable and groundless unilateral lame arguments have been supported by all people … Why does this happen? It's confusing. Though Naruse claimed the defects of Japanese sword, in fact there was no improvement at all even at the end of the war.[21] Moreover, the existence of his work had also been forgotten by the Japanese and the "100-man killing contest" is still accepted as a fact today. (the emphasis marks are retained according to original texts)

The above is roughly the gist of R's words. I don't know about Chinese broadswords. However, I think that every defect of Japanese swords pointed out by R is correct. The Japanese do have an insurmountable "the myth of Japanese swords", and the idea of comparing Japanese and Chinese swords is totally absent in the past and present. Even today, the "100-man killing contest" is still spreading as a fact. It can be said that Japanese born after the war still believe this myth as a fact.

However, wielding a sword in the real battlefield has in fact been extremely rare since ancient times. In battles, the main weapon used in close combat has been a spear rather than a sword since ancient times regardless of in the oriental and western countries. Spears then developed into weapons like bayonets. In addition, it can be said that people use the gun itself rather than the special bayonet on it. As a result, this kind of weapons used in close combat can still be used in the Second World War. Not all the guns in the Japanese army are with bayonets. The artillery on the mainland is equipped with type 44 carbines that are bayonet-type, with long bayonets attached to the body of guns into spears.[22]

These remarks by Yamamoto Shichihei have nothing to do with the arguments of the "100-man killing contest". For example, no one has said that Japanese swords were the so-called "main weapons". Whether the Japanese swords were the "main weapons" did not hinder the killing competition. Besides, whether the Japanese swords had "fatal defects" did not hinder the

---

[21] In Japan, the expression "end of war" and "defeat in war" is strictly distinguished and both the left-wing groups and right-wing groups stick to the rule when use them. On the 50th anniversary of the Japan's defeat in August 1995, I wrote an afterword for *Monthly Journal of Chinese Affairs*, with the title of "Fifty Years after the End of War" (*Monthly Journal of Chinese Affairs*, Tokyo, Institute of Chinese Affairs, August 1995, pp. 70–72). After the publication, Yamane Yukio, a senior Japanese scholar, wrote a letter to me to point out that "instead of using 'End of War' like those uninformed Japanese, you should use 'Defeat in War' with a clear stand".

[22] Yamamoto Shichihei,『私の中の日本軍』下, pp. 78–79.

killing competition because, as Shishime Akira said in his "very accurate testimony," the vast majority of the killed were those captives who were disarmed. A brick, a whip or a wooden stick could be a lethal weapon, not to mention a Japanese sword.

However, the discussion of Yamamoto Shichihei's remarks does not lie in whether the remarks are relevant. If they are only irrelevant remarks, they are nothing but nonsense which need not be investigated. The special mention of Yamamoto Shichihei's remarks is because his description of the quality of Japanese swords was a "totally" false statement. The previous quotation that Yamamoto complained that "the experts' arguments have been ignored" is a good perspective. For such specialized problem, laymen can hardly discuss it. Let us see what a "specialist" said. Sato Kanichi (1907–1978), who served as deputy curator of the Japanese Sword Museum before his death, said in Introduction to Japanese Swords:

> The distinctive feature of Japanese swords is generally recognized as practicality because (1) they are not broken, (2) they are not bent, and (3) they are extremely sharp. So, how do these features come into being?
>
> First, it is the tempering of "Kawagane" on the surface of a sword. To be precise, "Japanese steel" is used as the material and is hammered repeatedly. While the steel reaches a proper hardness, the inclusions contained in the steel are also burnt out. Then hammers are used to make refined steel, especially to make the hardness of the steel uniform. This hard "Kawagane" is used to wrap the core bone made by repeatedly hammering soft iron, and then this combination is burned again and repeatedly hammered into a thin sword.
>
> The technique of (1) hammering repeatedly and (2) adding core bones cannot be found in other nations. It can be said that the above-mentioned features - not broken, not bent, and extremely sharp – come into being due to this technique.
>
> Second, all the surfaces of the basically formed swords are coated with mud called "burning blade soil" (the following is a discussion on the specific technique and therefore is omitted - noted by the citer)...
>
> Needless to say, Japanese swords were originally made as weapons. However, they are not used as weapons any more at present. The Japanese regard them as steel works of art that they are proud of around the world. They are not only practical but also beautiful.[23]

The features of Japanese swords "not broken, not bent, and extremely sharp" mentioned here are totally different from what Yamamoto said "a Japanese sword will almost become a waste matter after one use". Sato Kanichi was not only an "expert" in Japanese swords, but also an authority in the field of modern Japanese sword research. If we agree with Yamamoto Shichihei's words that we should listen to the "experts", then Mr. Kanichi

---

[23]Sato Kanichi,「日本刀概说」,『原色日本の美術』第25巻『甲冑と刀剣』, Tokyo, Shôgakukan, revised version, November 1st, 1980, pp. 216–217.

should win. Yamamoto used excuses such as "the experts' arguments have been ignored" to deny the facts—maybe his "experts" are not those recognized by the public but by only himself in accordance with his standards. If it is true, then I have nothing to say. I have also seen Japanese swords many times. The delicacy of Japanese swords is far better than that of "Green Dragon swords". The first impression is not delicacy, but sharpness. The special sharpness with chilly cold air cannot help but make people think that they are "murder weapons", a true weapon used to kill someone.

After the Meiji Restoration, there was a "decree of abolishing swords" and Japanese swords became "useless objects" for a time (Sato Kanichi). In Taishō and Shōwa era, the military sword craze began again. By the time the Sino-Japanese War broke out, the so-called "military sword climax" appeared.[24] In 1945, with Japan's defeat, the "decree of prohibition on the manufacture of weapons" explicitly prohibited the manufacture of Japanese swords. It was only after the 1950s that Japanese swords were allowed to be made again permitted by Japan's "Cultural Property Protection Committee" as "traditional culture". In other words, it was many years after the war that Japanese swords became what Yamamoto Shichihei called "arts and crafts". They were "weapons" for a long time before the war. However, as weapons they do not prevent some people from taking them as "fine arts", just as in the past noble ladies used pistols as decoration and even "toys" but these pistols still had function of weapons.

5   V

In conclusion, I think it is still too early to concede passively and admit that the "100-man killing contest" was a "heroic episode" produced by the media. The reason is that even if the so-called inside and outside "proofs" claimed by Japan's "fictionalists" are true—needless to say, the so-called "physical limitations" of the "Japanese swords" are contrary to the facts—they are not enough to have an impact on the records of the "100-man killing contest" in wartime. I am not saying that the records in wartime are true. But since I take the stand of affirming the "100-man killing contest", I have to more strictly examine records in wartime which is in accordance with basic objective requirement. I just want to say that there is no doubt about the "100-man killing contest" in regard of massive killings.

If we calmly analyze the reports of the wartime in the Tokyo Nichi Nichi Shimbun, it is not difficult for us to see the impact on the "facts" caused by the "reports". As far as "the reports" are concerned, in such hysterical environment at that time, it was almost inevitable to report the contest in the direction of "heroic episode". The report that the two carried out repeated (the Tokyo Nichi Nichi Shimbun said that the contest repeated three times)

---

[24] Sato Kanichi,「日本刀概説」,『原色日本の美術』第25巻『甲冑と刀剣』, p. 239.

killing contests without any physical injury is to show the "heroic" characteristic, which is close to a myth. Fortunately, there was "very accurate testimony" which Yamamoto Shichihei also admitted, accompanied by a large number of photos of killing disarmed captive in the world, so we can see Noda Tsuyoshi (same as Mukai Toshiaki) only killed the "fools" who laid down their arms (Noda's words) through the exaggerated report in the Tokyo Nichi Nichi Shimbun. If the truth is that they did not kill enemies, it would be too bland. However, it is more obvious that the Japanese army was against humanity.

Honda Katsuichi, member of the slaughter school whose opinions are most close to the original truth, has said recently: "At that time, 'trying swords' and killing captives by using Japanese swords were common for Japanese officers and soldiers. Because of the occasional apparentness, M and N (referring to Mukai Toshiaki and Noda Tsuyoshi) were sentenced to death. As far as the death sentences of the two men are concerned, there is indeed something worthy of sympathy".[25] From the standpoint of the victims, the so-called "sympathy" is absolutely unacceptable. Even from the academic perspective without personal feelings, the "100-man killing contest" is far from being overturned. Therefore, in any sense, this stand should not and need not be easily abandoned.

(Original published in *Jiangsu Social Sciences*, No. 6, 2002)

---

[25] Honda Katsuichi,「据えもの斬りや捕虜虐殺は日常茶飯だった」注1,『南京大虐殺否定論13のウソ』compiled by Nankin jiken chōsa kenkyūkai, Tokyo, Kashiwa Shobô, 4th printed version, March 30th, 2001, p. 115.

Re-examination of Ogawa Sekijiro's Testimony—Examination II of the Testimonies of the Defendants on Nanjing Atrocities in Tokyo Trial

The main reason for re-examining the testimonies of the defendants in the Tokyo Trial on Nanjing atrocities[1] is that due to the limitation of evidence, these testimonies were not effectively questioned by the prosecution and the court in the Tokyo Trial, thus not only affecting the judgment, but also to a certain extent affecting the Japanese people's understanding of the Tokyo Trial to this day. For a detailed explanation of this point, please refer to the introduction of my article "Re-evaluation of Iwane Matsui' s War Guilt - Verifications of one of the Testimonies on the Nanjing Massacre Given by the Defendants at the Tokyo War Crimes Trials".[2]

Ogawa Sekijiro was the justice minister of the 10th army that was one of the main forces of the Japanese army attacking Nanjing. He was the most senior full-time legal officer of the Japanese army at that time. Ogawa landed in Jinshan with the 10th army in November 1937. After that, the 10th army went west along Jiaxing, Pingwang and Huzhou to Nanjing.[3] At the end of December after the capture of Nanjing, the 10th army moved to Hangzhou and Ogawa never left the army. On January 7th of the following year, Ogawa went to Shanghai to form the council of military court of the Japanese Central China Area Army (the Area Army was the operational

---

[1] In the process of the Tokyo Trial and the Judgment, the original expression referring to the crimes committed by Japanese troops in Nanjing is "Nanjing Atrocities" while it is translated into Chinese as "Nanjing Massacre", such as the translation in *The Judgment of the International Military Tribunal for the Far East* (《远东国际军事法庭判决书》, Mass Press, February 1986) translated by Zhang Xiaolin and *The International Military Tribunal for the Far East* (《远东国际军事法庭判决书》, Law Press, July 2005) translated by Mei Rujing. This article uses the original expression "Nanjing Atrocities".

[2] *Modern Chinese History Studies*, No. 6, 2008, p. 423.

[3] The 6th and 114th divisions of the 10th army attacked Nanjing. The 18th division of the 10th army attacked Wuhu and was responsible for cutting off the retreat of the Chinese army on the upper reaches of the Yangtze River.

command organization coordinating the 10th army and the Shanghai Expeditionary Army, and there was no legal department). On February 14th, the system of the Japanese Central China Area Army and its 10th army and the Shanghai Expeditionary Army was abolished. A week later, Ogawa following the commander of the Japanese Central China Area Army Matsui Iwane, Chief of Staff Tsukada Osamu and others returned to Japan. Ogawa was a quite special witness among witnesses for the defense in the Tokyo Trial of the Nanjing atrocity case. The particularity of Ogawa is not that he was a witness and most of the witnesses at that time had experience of being in Nanjing at the scenes of incidents. The particularity of Ogawa is not that he had a higher title. At that time, the witnesses included not only low- and middle-title officers, but also high-title officers such as Iinuma Mamoru, Chief of Staff of the Shanghai Expeditionary Army. Ogawa's particularity lies in that he was the chief officer of the judicial departments of the 10th army and the Japanese Central China Area Army, and military discipline was his "specialty". His testimony is therefore more likely to be regarded as an "authoritative" testimony by a third party, at least be regarded as an "expert" testimony. Moreover, unlike many witnesses who denied that the Japanese army had committed atrocities, Ogawa admitted that the Japanese army had committed limited atrocities and, to a certain extent, his testimony is not totally fake. Although we cannot tell what role Ogawa's testimony played in determining the Japanese army's responsibility in the court on that day, it is of special significance that Ogawa's testimony was not questioned by the court and the prosecution. After examining the testimony of Matsui Iwane, the first person responsible for Nanjing atrocity crimes, I immediately chose Ogawa's testimony because of this "particularity". Moreover, I believe that Ogawa's testimony needs to be examined again apart from Matsui's testimony which "may" also an important reason. History focuses on seeking for truth. Humanistic evidence is different from scientific evidence in that the former cannot be "universally applicable". Therefore, humanistic conclusions are more easily limited by materials than conclusions of other disciplines. I mentioned in the previous quoted articles that the reason why the "Nanjing incident" has been in constant dispute in Japan lies in not only the "standpoint" that has nothing to do with academia, but also lies in the insufficient records at the time of the incident and the "loss" of firsthand documents. For example, the authenticity of the testimony given by the justice minister of the Shanghai Expeditionary Army Tsukamoto Hirotsugu at the Tokyo Trial can certainly be inferred from "indirect evidence" before the documents such as the log of the judicial department of the Shanghai Expeditionary Army and Tsukamoto's own diary are discovered. However, what one person saw cannot fundamentally replace what another person saw. Therefore, it is of insurmountable difficulty to judge the authenticity of Tsukamoto's testimony by inference. This is the same as the conclusion that a new judgment should be made according to the criminal records and new evidence. Ogawa's testimony is special because the most crucial public and private documents needed to examine Ogawa's testimony were rarely preserved by Ogawa himself. The reason for saying "rare" is that the log of the judicial department of the 10th army is the only log of all judicial departments of the whole Japanese army that can be seen today. Ogawa's diaries that were kept when he was in the 10th army and the Japanese Central China Area Army were preserved which surprised his daughter who lived with him in old age and she said that she "had no memory of it at all".[4] These two records of the first time of incidents, together with the log of the council of military court of the Japanese Central China Area Army which was also preserved by Ogawa, are the most powerful evidence for us that are used to compare Ogawa's testimony. Perhaps because the Tokyo Trial has made a judgment, no special examination of Ogawa's testimony has been made so far. I once wrote two articles using the diaries and logs left by Ogawa, which mentioned the falsehood of Ogawa's testimony, but only mentioned it incidentally.[5] This article intends to conduct a comprehensive examination of Ogawa's testimony.

First of all, here is the full translation of Ogawa's testimony.

1 OGAWA SEKIJIRO'S AFFIDAVIT

Ogawa Sekijiro's affidavit (Defense Document No. 2708, Court Evidence No. 3400):

1. I was appointed as the justice minister of the 10th army (the Commander was Lieutenant General Yanagawa) around the end of September 1937. I landed on the north bank of Hangzhou Bay and took part in the Nanjing battle. The 10th army was attached to the Japanese Central China Area Army on January 4th of the following year and I directly reported to Commander Matsui.
2. After the 10th army landed in Hangzhou Bay, it was under the command of the Japanese Central China Area Army. Commander Matsui ordered the army to strictly observe military discipline which certainly included the strict legal protection of the rights and interests of Chinese citizens and foreign countries.
3. During the period from in Hangzhou to in Nanjing, I had punished a total of 20 military discipline offenders. Among them, there was uncertainty between rape and adultery which was difficult to determine.

---

[4] Nagamori (Ogawa) Mitsuyo,「わが父、陸軍法務官　小川関治郎」, Ogawa Sekijiro, the appendix of *The Diary of a Military Solicitor*, Tokyo, Misuzu Shobô, 1st edition, August 10th, 2000, p. 210.

[5] "Ogawa Sekijiro and *The Diary of a Military Solicitor*", *Historical Review*, No. 1, 2004, pp. 92–105; and "Research on Military Discipline of Japanese Invaders—Focusing on the 10th army", *Modern Chinese History Studies*, No. 3, 2004, pp. 136–183.

The reason is that it was not uncommon for Chinese women to flirt with Japanese soldiers. Once the sexual intercourse was discovered by good citizens or others, the woman's attitude changed immediately and exaggeratedly claimed that it was rape. However, I would prosecute the case whether it was rape or not and dealt with each case according to the seriousness of the facts. If coercion was used, severe punishment would be imposed.

4. I entered Nanjing at noon on December 14th and only saw six or seven dead bodies of Chinese soldiers during my afternoon tour of parts of the 10th army garrison area (south of Nanjing). There were no other bodies. The 10th army withdrew from Nanjing on December 19th to attack Hangzhou. During my stay in Nanjing, I had neither heard of the illegal acts of the Japanese soldiers nor had I prosecuted illegal acts. The Japanese army was in war and its discipline was strict. Commanders Matsui's top-down order to allow illegal acts certainly did not exist, nor did an order to tolerate illegal acts.
5. The military police strictly abided by the command of Commanders Matsui. Lieutenant Colonel Kamisago (a military police) once protested against my decisions of not prosecuting minor crimes with too much tolerance. Illegal acts made by Japanese soldiers were severely banned.
6. On January 4th, 1938, I met with General Matsui in Shanghai headquarters where General Matsui requested in a particularly emphatic tone that "crimes should be severely punished". Under this order, I strictly carried out my tasks.

October 6th of the 22nd year of the Shōwa era (1947), Tokyo

Affidavit by Ogawa Sekijiro[6]

Ogawa's testimony was read out on the morning of November 7th, 1947. Unlike previous Iinuma Mamoru and subsequent Sakakibara Kazue who were repeatedly questioned by the prosecution, the prosecution and the court did not question Ogawa's testimony at all.

Ogawa Kanjiro's testimony is not very long among testimonies for the defense, and it is not true regarding Matsui ordering the army to strictly observe military discipline, a small amount of atrocities, "uncertainty" between the rape and "adultery", only six or seven dead bodies in Nanjing, no illegal acts being heard of, illegal acts being severely banned, and Matsui particularly emphasizing military discipline in person. Let us prove the conclusion by carefully comparing the logs of the judicial departments of the 10th army and the Japanese Central China Area Army and Ogawa's own records of the incidents.

---

[6] 『極東國際軍事裁判速記錄』 the 7th volume, compiled by Nitta Mitsuo, Tokyo, Yûshôdô Shoten, 1st edition, January 25th, 1968, p. 432.

2   Did "Commander Matsui" Order the Army to Strictly Observe Military Discipline?

At the Tokyo Trial, the defendants and Matsui Iwane had a tacit understanding. They all claimed that Matsui repeatedly emphasized the importance of military discipline when he led the army to China, which has been verified to be untrue after I examined Matsui's testimony. In order to examine Ogawa's testimony completely, I will not omit it here and will examine it with Ogawa's diary. Ogawa mentioned Matsui's talking about military discipline twice in his "affidavit": the first one is the "strictly observe" and "strict legal protection" and the second one is "particularly emphatic tone". Both of the talks were with cautious tone and were not daily routines or polite formulas. According to Ogawa's daily habit of keeping detailed records of people and matters, these instructions cannot be omitted. Therefore, when reading through Ogawa's whole diaries and finding no record of Matsui's similar words,[7] we can naturally conclude that the "testimony" is not true. The reason why I dare to assert that Ogawa's testimony is untrue is not only because there is no record in the diary, but also because the diary directly exposes Ogawa's "self-defeating" acts. Part 6 of the testimony says that "on January 4th, 1938, I met with General Matsui in Shanghai headquarters…" which is very specific in time, place and people. It is quite conceivable that the prosecution had no way to say anything at the trial. But it is precisely because of the specific accuracy that we can follow the trace and compare it with the diary. Ogawa's diary on January 4th recorded his second visit to Lieutenant General Yanagawa Heisuke, commander of the 10th army, to discuss the case of a certain Major (the names of all the people involved were intentionally hidden when the diaries were published) and his participation in farewell meetings of the armed forces, military doctors, veterinarians and judicial departments when he did not leave Hangzhou, the headquarters of the 10th army at all. Ogawa did not leave Hangzhou for Shanghai until the 7th to report to the Japanese Central China Area Army, and he did not see Matsui until the 15th. The diary on the 15th recorded the meeting with Matsui in detail. Matsui talked a lot about politics toward China, such as how to overthrow Chiang Kai-shek's regime, how to establish a pro-Japanese regime, how to realize the "a hundred-year plan for large numbers of Japanese immigrants to China" and so on, but there was not a word about military discipline. Not only they did not talk about military discipline, this diary also left a rather interesting record:

> Does the commander (original note: General Iwane Matsui) try to keep his dignity? Or is this his inherent arrogance? He is a little bit strange compared with other generals I have met so far. I believe that a chief executive should not stand on his dignity and make his own policies understood by his subordinates.

---

[7] In the log and diary, there are some records of Yanagawa Heisuke's talks, commander of the 10th army.

Such a gesture is entirely unnecessary. If someone is too arrogant, he cannot fully consider others' opinions and therefore subordinates' opinions cannot be understood by the superior. In particular, it is definitely not useless to listen to those who have opinions - between the superior and his subordinates, the subordinates fully understand the superior's opinions and the superior fully studies the subordinates' opinions… (the ellipsis is retained according to original texts - noted by the quoter) What is the reason for his arrogance?[8]

There were various descriptions of Matsui Iwane, but no one had ever said that he was "arrogant" or "stood upon the dignity". The reason why Matsui's impression on Ogawa is different is that, in my opinion, the military discipline put Matsui in an awkward position.

After the Japanese army entered Nanjing, western newspapers began to make a large number of reports on atrocities committed by the Japanese army since the first report issued on December 17th by F. Tillman Durdin, journalist of the New York Times who was expelled from Nanjing. On the third day after the Japanese army entered Nanjing, the westerners of the International Committee for the Nanking Safety Zones began to submit daily complaints and protests to the Japanese embassy in Nanjing. These reports and protests reached the Japanese senior political and military officials in the first place. Under the pressure, the Japanese central army had to issue orders and sent officials to urge the Japanese Central China Area Army to observe military discipline.[9] The pressure from the Japanese senior political and military officials made Matsui very embarrassed. The joy of capturing the capital of the "enemy country" was thus swept away. Under such a background, the council of military court of the Japanese Central China Area Army was formed in

---

[8] Ogawa Sekijiro, *The Diary of a Military Solicitor*, pp. 153–154.

[9] Some people in Japan have always thought that some historical facts did not exist and they even have used lame arguments regardless of contradictions. I would like to mention one case that has not been mentioned by others: Matsui Iwane once told Hanayama Shinshou, a "trymoaris" at the Sugamo Detention House, that the performance of division heads during the "Nanjing Incident" was worse than that of division heads during the Japan-Russia War. It is said that Matsui's dissatisfaction was mainly directed at the head of the 16th division, Nakashima Kesago. This matter is well-known. Therefore, in the first part (chapter) "the Bureau of Military Affairs of the Ministry of the Army" of the memo, the last director of the Bureau of Military Affairs of the Ministry of the Army before the end of the war, pointed that: "Commander Matsui tearfully told Director Anami (Anami Korechika, who was then the director of the Bureau of Military Affairs) the peace of Japan and human love with the intention to criticize the head of the 16th division Nakashima Kesago who was reckless. But he absolutely did not say that the division heads were worse in morality than the division heads in the Japan-Russia war". However, in the third part of the same book "The Images of Army Generals", Nukata Tan clearly recorded a passage like this: "On New Year's Day of the 13th year of the Shōwa era (1937), I was following the Director of Personnel Anami who was reporting to Commander of the Army Matsui. He said, 'the battle guidance of the 16th division led by Nakashima Kesago violated humanity' and therefore condemned it and lamented the decadence of Bushido". (Nukata Tan, 『陸軍省人事局長の回想』, Tokyo, Fuyo Shobo Publishing, 1st edition, May 1st, 1977, pp. 20 and 322) "The decadence of Bushido" is the very synonym of "bad" "morality", isn't it?

a short time. For Matsui, the formation of the council was not his original intention. Therefore, Matsui's unusual behavior of showing "arrogance" and "standing upon the dignity" toward Ogawa, who was of similar age and had similar seniority, is nothing more than a resistance to the pressure of improving military discipline, whether his behavior was genuine or not.

3 Was There Uncertainty Between Rape and "Adultery"?

The atrocities of rape of the Japanese army have been deeply rooted in Chinese national memory through various records, especially in literary and artistic works. However, the situation in Japan is different. In addition to the "slaughter school" which has few members and the "fabrication school" which is opposed to the slaughter school, the mainstream society has always avoided mentioning it. This can be reflected by the general account of the "Nanjing incident" that only recorded killings without the atrocities of rape. The denial of rapes of the "fabrication school" began to be strengthened after the 1990s. They not only called the records of incidents as "rumors" and resolutely denied them, but also further thought that "the truth of rapes" was the voluntary prostitution, or the behavior of "the Chinese soldiers who disguised as Japanese soldiers", or "disrupting the work of the Japanese by the Chinese soldiers".[10] Although the denial of rapes has become more and more prominent in the recent years, the source can be found in the Tokyo Trial as the denial of other atrocities. The so-called "uncertainty" of rape and "adultery" by Ogawa was the beginning of the current denial of rape.

The denial of rapes was closely related to victims' few accusations. I was said in article "The lack of Accusations by the Victims Cannot Deny the Japanese Sexual Atrocities"[11] that reason for "not taking actions" is, apart from the weak position of facing the occupying forces, related to Chinese

---

[10] 详见日本会議国際広報委員会編『再審「南京大虐殺」——世界に訴える日本の冤罪』第二章「強姦事件の真相」小节, 東京, 明成社2000年11月25日第2次印刷版, 第85–87页;藤岡信勝、東中野修道著『ザ・レイプ・オブ・南京の研究——中国における「情報戦」の手口と戦略』第三章「真実は安全地帯の住民が知っいた」小节, 東京, 祥傳社1999年9月10日第1版, 第168–170页; 東中野修道著『「南京虐殺」の徹底検証』第十二章「南京安全地帯の記録」, 東京, 展転社2000年7月8日第4次印刷版, 第257–282页. The above discussion is based on 361 cases of rape and attempted rape recorded by the International Committee for the Nanking Safety Zones. After the fall of Nanjing, Chinese officers and soldiers who laid down their arms swallowed humiliation and bore a heavy load when they faced the disaster. They kept a low profile in order to reduce unnecessary sacrifice. In the face of the search for residual Chinese soldiers by the Japanese army, the abolishment of the safety zone and the imposition of the "Self-governing Committee" and the "Reform Government", the so-called "lurking" soldiers (including citizens) all silently accepted. Therefore, the so-called "disguising as Japanese soldiers" and the so-called "disrupting the work" do not make sense and, moreover, have no foundation in fact.

[11] For details, please see my article the section fourteen of "Notes on the Nanjing Massacre", Shanghai, *Historical Review*, No. 1, 2003, pp. 117–119.

view on virtues and chastity. The Chinese people always put emphasis on the "righteousness" since ancient times. When it comes to moral integrity, they have no alternative but to sacrifice their lives for righteousness. A woman's duty of "righteousness" is her "supreme" "chastity" (When Guo Qi discussed the atrocities of rape of the Japanese army in Record of Blood and Tears in the Captured Capital, he said that "a woman's chastity was beyond everything".[12]) Therefore, if a Chinese woman was raped, especially by a "brutish soldier", her whole life was completely destroyed. Even if she did not commit suicide, she could only swallow the insult and humiliation silently rather than stand out to initiate an accusation. As a result, a report to the Japanese occupying forces was a doomed request, so few people intended to find justice with their real names after the war.[13] There was indeed the difficulty of finding evidence. However, with a rough reading of the diary and the log, there were not only a large number of rape cases in Shanghai, Hangzhou and Huzhou, but also the detailed records of pleadings and judgments made by the council of military court as well as the accusations and statements of the two parties. The latter was quite surprising. So the aforementioned reason of "not taking actions" is untenable and the "not taking actions" itself is untenable. Therefore, the so-called "uncertainty" of rape and "adultery" and the so-called "the rape was only hearsay" are self-destructive.

We could quote some related materials as evidence.

The 10th army began to land in Jinshan on November 5th, 1937. On November 8th, Ogawa landed with the headquarters. On the same day, the judicial department received the report "Plunder and Other Atrocities Violating Military Discipline near Jinshan" submitted by the leader of the military police, Kamisago Shoshichi. Later, there were constant reports of fires and plunders. The log of the judicial department of the 10th army on

---

[12] *Historical Materials of the Nanjing Massacre Made by Japanese Invaders*, compiled by the Editorial Board of Historical Materials of the Nanjing Massacre Made by Japanese Invaders and Nanjing Library, Jiangsu Ancient Books Publishing House, 1st edition, 5th printed version, February 1998, p. 8. Guo Qi, commander of the garrison when the Japanese army attacked Nanjing, was in captured Nanjing for three months. This article was written after he escaped Nanjing and was published in *Xijing Pingbao* the same year.

[13] After the war, a survey of the national government found that the vast majority of the rape victims identified by family members, neighbors and other witnesses had died or disappeared. A small number of women who stated that they were the victims often had their family members killed or their men in the families killed and had difficult lives. For example, Xuhong Shi, who lived in Dabaihua Lane, Nanjing, jumped into the well after being raped but survived. In addition to her daughter who also jumped into the well and her 70-year-old mother, the whole family was killed. She "lived with shame and had an extremely difficult life". Finally, she agreed to show up and ask for wiping out the "national humiliation and family hatred" (*Archives of the Nanjing Massacre Made by Japanese Invaders*, compiled by the Second Historical Archives of China and Nanjing Municipal Archives, Jiangsu Ancient Books Publishing House, 3rd printed version, December 1997, p. 354). The significance of the victims' complaints since the 1980s is obvious from a moral point of view but these complaints are of little significance from a legal and academic point of view.

November 15th firstly mentioned the "compulsory indecent" event reported by the military police. It clearly recorded that the rape happened next day:

> At 8:30 in the morning, Lieutenant Colonel Kamisago who was the leader of the military police came to discuss about the prosecution of the frequent occurrence of the plunders and rapes with Ogawa.[14]

The phrase "frequent occurrence" here is very noteworthy. In the past, when we talked about the "cause" of the Japanese army's atrocities, in addition to emphasizing the "barbarous character" of the so-called militarism of the Japanese army, we mostly regarded the "fierce fighting" and the "revenge" as objective causes. It could be seen from the log of the judicial department that the "rapes" were accompanied by the Japanese army from the beginning. The external cause was not of importance.

The first rape case was recorded in the diary on November 25th:

> At 3:30 in the morning, Senior Captain Matsuoka who was the leader of the military police of the Jinshan military station came to contact Minister Ogawa and accepted search command because of the case of five corporal soldiers of the army under the jurisdiction of the 6th Division committing rape and attempted murder.[15]

In the diary of the same day, Ogawa ordered Tajima Riuichi, a member of the judicial department, to search the crime scene at Ding Jia Lou in the morning. The case was tried on December 22nd. People involved in the case were the secret service soldier Shima□□□ of the small luggage[16] of the third battalion of the 13th Regiment of the 6th Division (in consideration of the "reputation" of the parties, only small part of the full name is kept in the publication and the rest is replaced by boxes), Private First Class Tana□□□ of the 12th Squadron of the same battalion, Leader Uchi□□□ and Tsuru□□□ of the 9th Squadron of the same battalion. There was the detailed record in the judgment left in the log of the council of military court of the Japanese Central China Area Army. Therefore, this case was very typical and here is the main case:

Firstly, at about 10 o'clock in the morning on November 24th of the same year, defendant Uchi□□□ was near the foregoing empty room. Defendants Shima□□□, Tana□□□, Tsuru□□□ and the aforementioned deceased Fuji□□□

---

[14] 『第十軍(柳川兵團)法務部陣中日誌』, 高橋正衛編集、解説 『続·現代史資料』6「軍事警察」, Tokyo, Misuzu Shobô, 1st edition, February 26th, 1982, p. 36.

[15] 『第十軍(柳川兵團)法務部陣中日誌』, 高橋正衛編集、解説 『続●現代史資料』6「軍事警察」, p. 38.

[16] The Japanese "small luggage" (and "large luggage") refers to the troops that transport goods for troops at or above battalion level. The small luggage is responsible for transporting ammunition and other goods directly related to the battle (the large luggage is responsible for transporting hay and other goods not directly related to the battle).

(He was a Private First Class of the 12th Squadron who met the other defendants on his way from Jinshan to Fengjing. According to Ogawa's diary, he committed suicide later—noted by the quoter) went to the nearby villages and sought for Chinese coolies in order to transport their luggage. Tsuru□□□ went back to Uchi□□□ on the way. Other defendants jointly planned to seek for and kidnap Chinese women for rape.

a. At about 11 o'clock in the morning of the same day, the defendant Shima□□□ was near the house of Pan △△ (18 years old) on the Din Jia Road in the same county (referring to the Ding Jia Lou recorded in the log of the judicial department of the 10th army—noted by the quoter). He found the woman who escaped because she saw the defendants. So he chased after her, aiming at her with the rifle carried and threatened her. Then he brought her by force when she gave up running away because of fear. At 4 o'clock in the afternoon of the same day, he entered the house of Li △△ (18 years old) in the same village. He also brought this resistant woman by force.

b. At noon of the same day, when the defendant Tana□□□ sought for Chinese women in the foregoing village, he saw Zhang △△ (20 years old). So he chased after her and threatened her with the bayonet carried. Then he brought her by force when she gave up running away because of fear.

c. At 4 o'clock in the afternoon of the same day, the deceased Fuji□□□ found that Zuo △△ (23 years old) and Zuo ◎◎ (22 years old) were working in a boat moored in a small river near the foregoing village. He approached them and threatened them with the gun carried. Then he brought them by force when they gave up running away because of fear. Then he entered the house of Lu △△ (16 years old) at the same time. He said to the woman: "Come! Come!" The woman disobeyed, so he kicked her several times and brought her by force when she was afraid of him.

The aforementioned six Chinese women were hijacked to the empty house that was the foregoing camp over one mile from the same village by boat, which made the defendants achieve their goal of plunder.

Secondly, at about 8 o'clock in the afternoon of the same day, the defendants Uchi□□□ and Tsuru□□□ went back to the foregoing dormitory and saw several Chinese women in the room. They knew that these women were plundered by the aforementioned defendants for lust. The deceased Fuji□□□ said that "everyone raped one woman". The defendant Uchi□□□ obtained Pan △△ for the purpose of rape and the defendant Tsuru□□□ obtained Zuo ◎◎ for the purpose of rape.

Thirdly, the defendants Shima□□□, Tana□□□, Uchi□□□, Tsuru□□□ and the deceased Fuji□□□ jointly planned to rape the foregoing Chinese women at about 9:30 in the afternoon of the same day in the foregoing empty house when these women were too afraid of the defendants' threaten to resist them. The defendant Shima□□□ raped Li △△. The defendant Tana□□□ raped Zhang △△. The defendant Uchi□□□ raped Pan △△. The defendant Tsuru□□□ raped Zuo ◎◎. The deceased Fuji□□□ raped Zuo △△.

Fourthly, the defendant Shima□□□

a. At about 11 o'clock in the morning of the same day, he was near the foregoing house of Pan △△. He saw Tan Youlin (53 years old), so he beckoned to her and asked her to come over. The woman did not agree and the defendant attempted to kill her. He shot the woman with the rifle carried and hit her heart in the left breast. The woman died immediately because of the perforating gunshot wounds.

b. At about 2 o'clock in the afternoon of the same day, he saw He-chen Shi (26 years old) in the vestibule of her house and said: "Come! Come!" The woman fled to the house because of fear, so the defendant attempted to kill her. He shot at the back of the woman with the rifle carried. The woman's right thigh was not wounded by the perforating gunshot wounds. Therefore, the defendant did not achieve his goal of killing.

c. At about 5 o'clock in the afternoon of the same day, when monitoring the Chinese women plundered in the foregoing boat, he saw that one unnamed Chinese showed up near the boat and led the way for soldiers who intended to arrest him. So he concluded that they came to retake the foregoing women and attempted to kill them. Then he shot them twice with the rifle carried, but he missed twice and did not achieve his goal of killing.

......

On November 24th, there was the report of the plunder and killing of Chinese women by the Japanese soldiers in the Shajiabang, Jinshan County, Jiangsu province. The result of the search was the arrest of the aforementioned defendants and Fuji□□□ who raped those Chinese women at about 11:40 in the afternoon of the same day in the house of Lu Longqing near Ding Jia Road.[17]

The characteristics of the case were not only the collective rape, but also no sign of resistance of Tan and He. As long as Shima□□□ was not satisfied, he would wantonly shoot other people by gun. The characteristic of "compulsion" was especially remarkable. The records in the diary of the 10th army and the Japanese Central China Area Army concerning this case proved that the "uncertainty" of "rape" and "adultery" Ogawa said in the Tokyo Trial; according to the diary of the 10th army, Ogawa was clear that the leader of

---

[17] 『中支那方面軍軍法会議陣中日誌』、髙橋正衛編集、解説『続・現代史資料』6「軍事警察」、pp. 175–177.

the military police accepted his instructions and he sent people to do the research.

Then, was it possible that the records in the diary were not accurate and Ogawa may not know the truth? This should not have been a problem because no matter whether the diary was personally recorded by Ogawa, its reservation by Ogawa should rule out the possibility that he did not know the truth. However, in accordance with the consistent performance of the so-called "indirect evidence" of the Japan's fabrication school, they must think that it could not be concluded whether Ogawa know the truth. Fortunately, we can still see the diary of Ogawa which is the most direct evidence today. Compared with the brief record of the judicial department of the 10th army on November 25th, Ogawa's diary recorded not only more detailed information of the same day, but also retained his psychological feelings at that time:

> Last night at 3:30, Senior Captain Matsuoka of the military police reported a major event late at night that five soldiers of the 6th Division (including one leader) hijacked several women ranging from teenage girls to 26-year-old women in a village about three miles away and wantonly raped them in an empty house. Meanwhile, a 55-year-old woman who escaped was shot and killed and another woman's right thigh was shot and injured. The extent of their violation of the bearing and discipline of the army was too appalling to depict.
>
> △ (the original symbol in the diary - noted by the quoter) The Japanese government declared that even if it was against the Chinese government, it would not be hostile to the nationals in the future. However, what the Japanese soldiers did to the people who had no guilt was extremely appalling. How did they think about the further anti-Japanese ideology of the Chinese people after such behavior? The consideration of the future of the Japanese Empire made people creepy.[18]

Not only did they "wantonly rape" Chinese women but also the extent was "too appalling to depict". The similar expression of "pain and sorrow" was not rare in the diary of Ogawa. Here were other two examples before the foregoing day and after the foregoing day for proof. Ogawa recorded in the aforementioned diary on November 23rd:

> It was unspeakable humiliation that the Japanese soldiers wantonly raped Chinese women wherever they went and did not regard predatory or arson as the wrongful acts. As Japanese, especially the young men who would be the support of Japan, what effect would be on the future ideology of the whole Japan if they made a triumphant return with such an unscrupulous

---

[18] The diary of that day also recorded that when the Military Police arrested the perpetrators, the villagers gave a pig and ten chickens "in token of gratitude" and Ogawa felt that "the ways of the world" were same everywhere. Ogawa Sekijiro, *The Diary of a Military Solicitor*, pp. 62–63.

psychological habit? The consideration made people creepy. I thought that the Japanese government should make a research and implement a comprehensive reform in ideological issues. This was a slightly extreme statement. However, as someone said, Japanese soldiers were more brutal than China soldiers, which made us sob. I heard that the Chinese people called Japanese the beasts and called Japanese soldiers the beast soldiers. From the perspective of Chinese people, it was indeed the truth. As Japanese, the regrettable examples of the actual behavior of the Japanese soldiers were countless.[19]

In his diary on November 26th:

From all aspects of observation, not only the frontline troops but also the cunning soldiers of the rear troops were deliberately left behind to enter the houses of civilians and do evil things. The aforementioned defendants of murder, robbery and rape were this kind of people. As a result, the honest and serious soldiers who fought bravely in the front line died because of a little negligence. It was not too much to call the cunning fellows who act wantonly and never participate in any battle traitors, opponents or black sheep, which gave people deeper feelings.

(the middle part is omitted) As soon as they saw the Japanese soldiers, they fled at once. Women and children seemed to be extremely afraid of the Japanese soldiers, which was resulted from the evil things did by the Japanese soldiers. If they never did any evil things, Chinese people would not escape. It was indeed a pity.

What was the dignity of the Imperial Army? Japanese themselves could not judge the beginning of the so-called war. However, in terms of the foregoing Chinese feelings of Japanese, the impact of the quality of Japanese soldiers on young men in the future would only be disappointing.[20]

Judging from Ogawa's "creepy" feeling, "regret" and "disappointment" over "wanton rape" and other atrocities, Ogawa's testimony of the "uncertainty" of rape and adultery in the Tokyo court was definitely perjury.

4 Did Ogawa See Only Six or Seven Dead Bodies of Chinese Soldiers in Nanjing?

The heated debate on the "Nanjing incident" in Japan was basically different from our attention to the Nanjing Massacre. For example, were the dead soldiers or civilians? Were the soldiers killed by the combatants in the battle or the captives who had laid down their weapons? Did the "executed" captives abide by the obligations of the captives stipulated in the international law? Was there a "legal trial"? Did the killed civilians resist? Could they be regarded as neutral "civilians"? And so on. These problems were not only under no consideration, but also were hardly accepted by our emotions.

---

[19] Ogawa Sekijiro, *The Diary of a Military Solicitor*, p. 59.
[20] Ogawa Sekijiro, *The Diary of a Military Solicitor*, pp. 65–66.

But no matter how to interpret these issues, the fabrication school always attempts to decrease the number of the dead as much as possible. This attempt also started from the defense of the Tokyo Trial. The so-called testimony of Ogawa that he "only saw six or seven dead bodies of the Chinese soldiers" in Nanjing was also a typical example.

At the end of the war, Japan handed down orders to destroy official document files, especially those of the army, so the relevant information hardly remained. However, only few Japanese documents could still prove that there were a large number of dead bodies[21] when the Japanese army conquered Nanjing. Therefore, it might contribute to our understanding of this event by quoting the diary of Navy Medical Officer Colonel Yasuyama Koudou, Chief Medical Officer of the Headquarters of the "China Fleet".

Yasuyama Koudou arrived in Nanjing on December 16th by seaplane. At two o'clock in the afternoon, he visited the battlefield with "Chief of Fleet Forces" and "Chief Accountant". He wrote in the diary of this day:

> From the Hsiakwan Dock, we were driving on the vast and straight road. The road was strewn with rifle bullets like brass-covered sand. The <u>dead Chinese soldiers, flesh and blood</u>, were lying in the grass beside the road.
>
> Soon, from the Hsiakwan area to Yijiang Gate leading to Nanjing, under the towering stone gate was an arched road, about one third of which was buried with soil. When entering the gate, there was a ramp in the Hsiakwan area. We drove slowly forward, feeling that we drove slowly forward on a rubber bag filled with air. The car was actually driving on bodies of <u>countless buried enemies</u>. Somehow we drove on a plot with thin soil layer, and meat pieces were suddenly secreted out of the soil when we drove. The miserable situation was too hard to be described.[22]
>
> Finally, through the doorway the army entered in Nanjing. There are <u>numerous enemies' bodies</u> that were charred. Iron pockets and bayonets were also blackened. Metal wires of barbed wires overlapped residual burnt-down doorposts. The piled was also burnt to black. The scene was too mess and smelt acrid to describe.
>
> On the hillock at the right head of the doorway, there were engraved words "China and Japan cannot coexist", showing Chiang Kai-shek's propaganda against Japan. When we were close to the downtown, plain blue-cloth cotton-padded jackets abandoned by enemies made the road look like ragged clothes while the <u>bodies of enemy officers</u>, dressed in khaki military uniforms with vigorous leather leggings, could be seen everywhere, lying on their backs with stiff and rigid hands and feet.

---

[21] For the records of the Japanese officers and soldiers, see the section five of "Is the Nanjing Massacre a Fabrication Made by Tokyo Trial?", *Modern Chinese History Studies*, No. 6, 2002, pp. 1–7), and for the records of the Japanese troops, see section five of "A Study of the Massacre Order for Japanese Troops", *Historical Research*, No. 6, 2002, pp. 68–79.

[22] Yasuyama Koudou, 「上海戦従軍日誌」, 南京戦史編集委員会編『南京戦史資料集』, pp. 527–528.

The above quotation is only a part seen by Yasuyama Koudou's on his first day in Nanjing. During his three days in Nanjing, he encountered a large number of bodies everywhere. For example, on the morning of the second day (the 17th), he saw "numerous bodies" in other two places in Hsiakwan area. And he personally saw a Chinese soldier "bleeding" and "begging for mercy" being shot dead by a "reserve soldier" who just stood behind him. In the morning, he saw "numerous bodies" along Zhongshan North Road. In the afternoon, he with Ōkawachi Denshichi, Commander of the Shanghai Special Marine Corps "inspected" the plain in lower reaches of Hsiakwan area, seeing "countless blackened enemy bodies" and "60 or 70 enemy bodies that 'tasted Japanese machetes'" in the dyke. On the 18th, in Lion Forest Garden, he first saw "bodies abandoned everywhere by enemies". Then outside the barracks that were stationed in the foothills, he saw "scattered bodies". When arriving at Zhongshan Park, He also saw "scattered enemy bodies".[23]

Yasuyama Koudou's testimony and other similar testimony could completely prove that Ogawa's testimony of "six or seven dead bodies of Chinese soldiers" was not true. There was no doubt about this. The question remained to be solved in this section was whether Ogawa intended to commit perjury for himself or whether Ogawa "only saw six or seven dead bodies of Chinese soldiers". We continued to examine the diary of Ogawa. His testimony stated that the date of entering Nanjing was December 14th. Let us check the diary of Ogawa of the same day. The diary of this day was fairly detailed. When he "entered Nanjing", the situation was as follows:

> The Chinese regular soldiers (the words "dead bodies" were mentioned in the foregoing same sentence and may be omitted in this sentence - noted by the quoter) on sides of the road were overlapped and burnt by fire. It seemed that the Japanese soldier were used to the dead bodies under their feet. We could see that soldiers who passed through the burning dead bodies due to heavy traffic became totally used to human dead bodies. We gradually arrived at the south gate. The walls completely constructed by the stones were about three feet high and the battle of yesterday had destroyed part of the walls. However, the wall was as thick as the car road, so the ordinary artillery was hard to collapse them. As soon as I entered the door, I saw numerous dead bodies of the Chinese soldiers on the both sides.[24]

---

[23] Yasuyama Koudou, 「上海戦従軍日誌」, 南京戦史編集委員会編『南京戦史資料集』, pp. 528, pp. 528–530 and p. 531. Nowadays, Higashinakano Shūdō regardless of the numerous records of Yasuyama Koudou's "numerous bodies", Japan unexpectedly said that "In detailed diaries from 17th to 19th of Navy Medical Officer Yasuyama Koudou who then stayed in Hsiakwan area, these bodies were not even mentioned. Even if there were drifting bodies, they must come from the upper reaches. It is too indiscreet to link it with the assumption that Japanese army threw bodies into the river" (「南京事件最新報告·問題は『捕虜処断』をどう見るか」, Tokyo, *Shokun*, Bungei Shunjû, February 2001, p. 129). The records are crystal clear. How dare Higashinakano Shūdō fool the readers by saying no "bodies thrown into the river"!

[24] Ogawa Sekijiro, *The Diary of a Military Solicitor*, pp. 111–112.

In fact, although Ogawa claimed that he "only saw six or seven dead bodies of the Chinese soldiers", what he truly saw was "numerous dead bodies". No matter what motivated him to testify, his testimony could only be considered as perjury compared with his diary.

Actually, since he landed in Jinshan, Ogawa had encountered dead bodies of the Chinese almost everywhere. For example, when Ogawa was on the way to Zhang Yan town on the morning on November 14th, "there are countless dead bodies in the rivers, pools and fields". When he arrived at Jin Shan in the afternoon, there were even some "naked" dead bodies. On November 17th, "there were still dead bodies of the Chinese". On November 28th, when he was on the way to Huzhou, he saw "numerous dead bodies" and quite a few of them wore civilian clothes. On December 10th, he recorded that there were "countless dead bodies of the Chinese here and there". Such a large number of dead bodies made him feel numb, as he said in his diary of December 11th,

> When I first set out from the house of Li to Jinshan and saw the dead bodies of the China people on the way, I always had a strange feeling. However, when I gradually saw a large number of dead bodies, I became accustomed to them. The feeling at this time was like seeing the remains of dogs in Japan.[25]

Ogawa's feeling for the body was from "feeling strange" to "being accustomed to them", but he would not ignore them or eliminate them from the memory. Particularly, he would not change the memory into a opposed memory.

As the justice minister, Ogawa was not in the frontline of the battle, so there was no fierce competition in his diary. However, in his diary there was no lack of the record that he personally saw the Japanese soldiers abused the Chinese people. The aforementioned diary on November 25th, he recorded,

> I saw the Japanese soldiers enslaving the Chinese people and pointing to them with rifles and they *exactly treated them like cats and dogs*...[26]

The diary on November 29th recorded,

> Some soldiers made the Chinese people carry their luggage... As long as the Chinese people showed a little disobedience or disobedience, they would be immediately punished, which made people speechless. I saw on the way that two soldiers pulled out the swords and stabbed a Chinese person lying on the back. Another Chinese person was filled with blood and pain. Confronted with this scene, I extremely felt pity for the nationals of the defeated country.

---

[25] Ogawa Sekijiro, *The Diary of a Military Solicitor*, pp. 27, 30, 44, 102, 107 and 192.

[26] Ogawa Sekijiro, *The Diary of a Military Solicitor*, p. 63.

It was very common that the Chinese people were forced into slave labor with the army at that time. He wrote on December 11th,

> These Chinese people tried their best to carry the luggage and a considerable number of them were <u>old people</u>. There was no one more fortunate than those who lost their country. On such an occasion, they would <u>be punished immediately</u> by our soldiers as long as they showed a little disobedience. If they had escaped, they would have <u>been executed immediately</u>. Therefore, the Chinese people were in a dilemma and had to obey every order.[27]

Although "if they had escaped" was "subjunctive mood", Ogawa's inference from his own personal experience was not baseless.[28] The 10th army was not strongly resisted after landing, so a considerable number of the corpses left behind by the 10th army were the victims of random "executions". Ogawa also recorded in the diary of the second day:

> According to the report of Lieutenant Colonel Kamisago who was the leader of the military police in the afternoon, the situation near Jinshan was that the plunder of the city was serious and the <u>useless killing was extremely miserable</u>. If this was the case, it would be a great and <u>disturbing</u> problem.[29]

The "useless killing" was "extremely miserable", which can be associated with Ogawa's every strong "regret" and "disappointment" of the Japanese army in his diary. Although he did not resolutely say that he had "not seen" any corpses in the Tokyo court, he had deliberately tried to commit perjury.

5 The So-called Severe Prohibition of the Wrongful Acts of the Japanese Soldiers

The basic position of the defense in the Tokyo Trial was the denial of a large scale of atrocities of the Japanese army in Nanjing and the "severe punishment" of the limited "wrongful acts" of the Japanese army. Wakisaka Jiro who was the captain of the 36th Regiment said that there was a most typical example that his subordinate was punished by the military discipline because he picked up a shoe.[30] Due to the limitation of the evidence, although the prosecutor put forward quite a number of opposite evidence, the words of the

---

[27] Ogawa Sekijiro, *The Diary of a Military Solicitor*, pp. 78, 105 and 106.

[28] There are many such records in Ogawa's diaries. On his way from Nanjing to Huzhou, Ogawa saw the difficult steps of the porter who was serving for the Japanese army, and he said: "If he refused, he would have been shot dead immediately. It would have been the same result if he escaped, so he can only follow the order". Ogawa Sekijiro, *The Diary of a Military Solicitor*, p. 121.

[29] Ogawa Sekijiro, *The Diary of a Military Solicitor*, p. 18.

[30] 『極東國際軍事裁判速記錄』第七卷, compiled by Nitta Mitsuo, p. 420.

prosecutor were almost "against" those of the defense. The prosecutor had not accordingly interrogated the other similar testimony of the defendant, so today in Japan there were still people who think that the treatment of the evidence of two parties in the Tokyo Trial was "extremely unfair".[31]

Ogawa entered Nanjing on December 14th and went to Huzhou on the morning of December 19th. In Nanjing, he participated in the "ceremony of entering the city", "spiritual consolation ceremony" and other activities. He also met with the officers from the bureau of justice of the Ministry of the Army and the justice minister of the Shanghai Expeditionary Army. Ogawa's diary when he was in Nanjing did not record the "wrongful acts" of the Japanese army except the fires. Therefore, that the "wrongful acts of the Japanese army were severely prohibited" and the "severe punishment" in his testimony referred to not Nanjing but other places. The Tokyo Trial did not investigate the atrocities of the two armies under the jurisdiction of the Japanese Central China Area Army outside Nanjing. Ogawa's testimony aimed at proving the internal evidence by the external evidence. He intended to prove that there were no atrocities in Nanjing because there was no "wrongful act" outside Nanjing. It was meaningless at all. The reason was very simple because no "wrongful act" outside Nanjing was not equivalent to no atrocity in Nanjing. However, Ogawa's testimony could not prove "the atrocities of Nanjing", but it provided an important basis for us to verify the authenticity of Ogawa's testimony.

The foregoing content mentioned that when Ogawa still stayed in Jinshan on November 25th, he sent a member of judicial department Tajima Riuichi to investigate the rape case of Ding Jia Lou. In his diary of the next day, Ogawa wrote that "the situation of the field investigation was much worse than my imagination".[32] There were a quantity of records in Ogawa's diary about the "wrongful acts" of the Japanese army and his "regret" and "disappointment" as mentioned before. So were all of these "wrongful acts" "punished severely"?

There were 118 people involved in the cases recorded in the log of the judicial department of the 10th army.[33] 60 people of them were not prosecuted, accounting for over half of the people. Besides, 16 people were not

---

[31] For example, Fuji Nobuo's *How the Nanking Massacre Was Manufactured—Deception of the Tokyo Trial* said that "Neither the evidence presented by the defense nor the defense's final argument had any effect on the trial", "the court's judgment was based on the evidence presented by the prosecution and the prosecution's final statement". "I'm not saying that the evidence presented by the prosecution was all wrong and the evidence presented by the defense was all right. I just want to say that as a Japanese with common sense, when I read the evidence of the prosecution and the defense, I felt deeply that the evidence presented by the prosecution contained much distortion, exaggeration and fabrication, and at the same time I felt that the evidence presented by the defense was more reasonable". Fuji Nobuo, *How the Nanking Massacre Was Manufactured— Deception of the Tokyo Trial*, Tokyo, 展転社, 1st edition, April 29th, 1995, pp. 291 and 348.

[32] Ogawa Sekijiro, *The Diary of a Military Solicitor*, p. 66.

[33] In addition, there were two other "violations of the military discipline" called by the Chinese.

dealt with promptly when the construction of the 10th army was revoked, so the actual processing rate was less than 36%. The people involved in the cases who were immune from prosecution included 24 murders, one person who abetted the murder, five people who assisted the murder, one person who injured and caused death of others, one person who raped and intentionally injured others, one person who plundered and raped others, three rapists, seven plunderers, one person who committed the atrocity, one person who intentionally injured others, two arsonists, one person who committed compulsory indecent crimes, three people who acted indecently toward others, two thieves, one person who threatened and plundered the chief due to the atrocities of the chief, one person who insulted and coerced the chief into preparing the murder and caused negligence injury, two people who violated the rules of convening the army, and three people who violated of the rules of the enforcement of military service. We could see that felonies such as murder, rape, plunder and arson accounted for most of the crimes, except a few conflicts between the Japanese officers and soldiers.

Let us look at three specific cases of the immunity from prosecution.

a. The Massacre by Second Lieutenant Youshi □□□ from the 4th Battalion of the 4th Group of the Reserve Infantry of the 10th Army and Other People

(1) When Second Lieutenant Oka □□ worked in the Jinshan branch of the field clothing and grain factory, he was driven by the uneasiness and complained to Second Lieutenant Youshi □□□ who was also the police chief because many Chinese who inhabited near his dormitory seemed to have the unsafe words and deeds or steal articles. (2) Therefore, Youshi □□□ ordered 26 subordinates to arrest the aforementioned 26 Chinese people on December 15th of the 12th year of Shōwa era. On the way back to the same Military Police station, the attempt to escape of the arrested Chinese people made him generating the intention to kill them. (the list of murderers and people who assisted the murder would be listed in detail later - noted by the quoter)[34]

All 26 people were killed in the case. Jinshan was the "stable rear" of the Japanese army at that time, so no one would dare to "beard the lion in his den" (my mother lived in Zhapu, which was not far away from Jinshan and she said that the general public was avoiding the Japanese army rather than irritating them).[35] Even if the doubt of Oka □□ was true, the Chinese

---

[34]「第十軍法務部陣中日誌」, 高橋正衛編集、解説『続•現代史資料』6「軍事警察」, pp. 67–68.

[35] Ogawa's diaries contained many records of people's "obedience" wherever they went. For example, Ogawa's record when he was in Jinshan said that "After arriving at Jinshan, the local Chinese residents look like bodhisattvas and are really obedient. They saluted us humbly, especially the children who gave the highest salute in an immobile manner. We cannot help but feel compassion for them". Ogawa Sekijiro, *The Diary of a Military Solicitor*, p. 59.

residents were just "stealing objects", which was "still doubtful". There was no reason to kill people due to the so-called doubt; since the "crime" was not enough to be punished, the so-called "attempt" to "escape" also could not be a crime; and when 26 soldiers escorted the same number of civilians (during the Nanking Massacre, the number of the people under escort was often a dozen times as many as the number of Japanese and they were all soldiers), any people with a little reason would not attempt to escape. If there was an attempt, it would not be implemented. Even if someone truly escaped, it was impossible for the rest to continue to run away regardless of their lives as long as the Japanese soldiers fired their guns or shot any person. Therefore, although it was obvious that the statement of the complaint tried to plead for the Japanese army, it was still impossible to cover up the facts of deliberate massacre.

b. The Killing by the Private First Class Tsuzi□□ from the 1st Battalion of the Reserve Artillery:

> At about 5 o'clock on the afternoon on November 29th of the 12th year of Shōwa era (1937), the defendant was completely drunk because of the Chinese wine in the camp of Jiaxing. Driven by the strong hatred, he produced evil thought and killed three passing Chinese people with the bayonet carried.[36]

It was difficult to imagine that a person who was "completely drunk" could kill three people by using a "bayonet" unless the victims had been caught. Moreover, if a person was "completely drunk", he would not recognize or care about any people. The statement of the defendant that he was "driven by the strong hatred" only aimed at the immunity from the crime. The record of the judgment was entirely based on the facts. Even if it is not partial to or tolerate the defendant, the defendant would not be able to get rid of the fact that he assisted the murder or was not conscientious enough.

c. The Compulsory Indecent Crimes by the First Private Class Taka□□□□ from the 1st Battalion of the 114th Regiment of the Engineers of the 114th Division:

> The defendant was in the camp of Huzhou at about 2:30 on the afternoon of December 31st of the 12th year of Shōwa era. When he was near the Tai Liang Bridge in the Huzhou city, he saw a passing Chinese girl (8 years old) and brought her to the nearby empty house to rape her by his blandishments (the name of this case was "Rape" - noted by the quoter). Then he was arrested by the military police.[37]

---

[36] 「第十軍法務部陣中日誌」, 高橋正衛編集、解説『続・現代史資料』6「軍事警察」, p. 46.
[37] 「第十軍法務部陣中日誌」, 高橋正衛編集、解説『続・現代史資料』6「軍事警察」, p. 75.

During the Japanese occupation of Nanjing, the age of the victims of the sexual violence ranging from grandmothers to granddaughters. For example, Miner Searle Bates demonstrated in his literature that "women aged from 11 to 53 years old were raped".[38] A lot of such records were recorded in Western literature at that time. For example, James McCallum wrote in the letter that "girls aged 11 or 12 and women aged 50 also did not escape (the sexual violence)".[39] It was appalling that girls aged 11 or 12 were raped. However, the case of Taka□□□ recorded in the diary showed that it was not the lowest limit of age. Even if the defendant used "blandishments" to induce and deceive an innocent girl without violence, it was still "rape".

Through the above three cases of serious crimes that were immune from prosecution, it was self-evident whether the "wrongful acts" of the Japanese army had been "severely punished". In fact, even without the most convincing cases immune from prosecution, we could also prove that the "severe punishment" was not true by only three cases that had "been punished".

a. The Rape and Killing by Private First Class Chi□□□ from the 10th Battalion of the 6th Regiment of the Engineers of the 6th Division. Chi□□□ committed the gang rape of a woman whose surname was Cai with his colleague on December 14th. Then they went back again,

> At about 3 o'clock on the afternoon of December 17th, Chi□□□ felt obsessed with the foregoing woman whose surname was Cai, so he left the dormitory to commit the rape again. He met the aforementioned Fuji□□□ (one of the former Gang Raptor - noted by the quoter) and asked him to go to the house of Cai △△ together. They called the woman out of the house. Her husband Cai ○○ happened to be at the door. He walked towards the defendants as he screamed out something. (The defendants) promptly judged that he was trying to stop them, so they attempted to kill her husband. The defendants continuously fired three shots to the man and two shots hit the back of his head and his left chest. As a result, the man died immediately because of the non-perforating gunshot wounds.[40]

They were too rampant to open the rape and "call the woman" on a public occasion. Besides, when they saw the husband of the victim, they not only had no sense of shame but also shot him at once. Such an abominable crime was only sentenced to four years in prison.

---

[38] *Archives of the Nanjing Massacre Made by Japanese Invaders*, compiled by the Second Historical Archives of China and Nanjing Municipal Archives, Jiangsu Ancient Books Publishing House, 1997, p. 694.

[39] 转引自「一九三七—一九三八年冬季の日本軍の南京虐殺に関する報告」, 南京事件調査研究会編訳:『南京事件資料集』1『アメリカ関係資料編』, Tokyo, Aoki Shoten, 1st edition, October 15th, 1992, p. 258.

[40] 『中支那方面軍軍法会議陣中日誌』, 高橋正衛編集、解説『続・現代史資料』6「軍事警察」, p. 164.

b. The "Rape and Intentional Injury" by the Private First Class Huru□□□ from the 13th Regiment of the 6th Division and the Rape by Kawa□□□:

> The two defendants were in the camp of Jinshan in Jinshan County. (1) On December 25th of the 12th year of Shōwa era, when the defendant Huru□□□ was in an unknown village which was three kilometers north of Jinshan in order to confiscate the vegetables, he intimidated an unknown woman (18 or 19 years old) in a Chinese farmhouse of the same village. Then he raped the woman when she could not resist him because of fear. (2) On December 27th of the same year, the defendant Huru□□□ also came to Cao Jia Bang in Jinshan County to confiscate the vegetables. He captured a Chinese boat because he worried that the assembled over 40 people might detained him. When he withdrew, he shot the assembled people with the gun carried in order to prevent them, which caused the waist of a Chinese man was shot but the bullet did not come out of his body. In the same night, when the defendant slept in a farmhouse in the Shi Jia Lou in Jinshan County, he invaded the neighborhood in the middle night and raped a Chinese woman (32 years old) who was sleeping with violence. The foregoing defendant Kawa□□□ had once slept in the house of a Chinese woman. After he knew that Huru□□□ raped a Chinese woman in the neighborhood, he came to the same house immediately. Then he threatened the same woman by the bayonet carried, frightening her and raped her.[41]

In this case, Huru□□□ was a recidivist because he raped the Chinese women twice. He even captured a boat and intentionally injured other people in the second time. However, he was only sentenced to two years in prison and Kawa□□□ was only sentenced to one year in prison.

c. The Killing Committed by Private First Class Asa□□□ from the 4th Squadron of the 124th Regiment of the 18th Division:

> The defendant was in the Huzhou quarter. On November 29th of the 12th year of the Shōwa era, he went to collect vegetables with his colleagues. They picked about 5kanmes (1 kanme is about 3,75 kilograms - noted by the quoter) of vegetables grown in a nearby field. The defendant went to the nearby farmhouse and demanded three Chinese women to wash the vegetables. One of the Chinese women (named Liu Asheng according to the log of the Area Army - noted by the quoter) said something quickly, as if she was reluctant. [The defendant] considered this as a scorn towards the Japanese soldiers, so he shot her dead with his rifle.[42]

Apparently, the defendant did not understand what the victim was saying, but he shot her dead in any case. This voluntary manslaughter was only sentenced to one and a half years in prison.

---

[41]「第十軍法務部陣中日誌」, 高橋正衛編集、解説『続・現代史資料』6「軍事警察」, p. 77.
[42]「第十軍法務部陣中日誌」, 高橋正衛編集、解説『続・現代史資料』6「軍事警察」, pp. 60–61.

According to the Japanese Criminal Law in wartime, murder and rape were felonies. "Robbery and rape", for instance, should be sentenced to "life imprisonment or punishment of over seven years" (Article 86 of the Army Criminal Law). Therefore, the case prosecuted by the judicial department of the 10th army received lenient judgments which were not in line with the crimes. The soldiers were not "severely punished" at all.

6 Confusion of the Chief of the Judicial Department

How to deal with crimes committed by Japanese troops was a difficult problem that deeply troubled Japanese justice minister Ogawa Sekijiro. Ogawa kept a large number of relevant records in his diary. I would like to make a brief summary on the basis of the proven untrue testimony of Ogawa, which can deepen the understanding of the legal department's inability to face the Japanese army's arrogant soldiers and the institutional conflict between the functions of the legal department and the Japanese army itself, and further see that Ogawa has no possibility of "forgetting" during the Tokyo Trial.

The Japanese court martial was composed of members of the judicial department (professional military law officers) and the so-called "judges with sword" (military personnel). Nominally speaking, there was no difference between the powers of military judges and those of "judges with swords".[43] However, as the editor of Modern History of Japan: the Military Police said, the "judicial officers could only serve as the weak commissioners where the military officers were equal to the 'judges with sword'". Besides, the Japanese council of military court provided that only the commanders or the chiefs of the divisions "could serve" as its chief, which "demonstrated the consistency between the jurisdiction and the command of the army".[44] This institutional provision restricted the professional legal officers from the rule of law.

In addition to the institutional provision, it was fairly serious that the headquarters did not attach the importance to the judicial department. There was a quantity of records in Ogawa's diary that the ministry of adjutants intentionally did not allow the judicial department to go along with the commander and the judicial department was discriminated in terms of the treatment, etc. The final jurisdiction of the Japanese council of military court was in the hands of the commanders at all levels who served as its chief. Therefore, as the ministry that was responsible for the daily affairs, it was necessary for the judicial department to maintain close contact with the commander at any time. It aimed at not only the high-efficient function but also the normal operation. Ministries of staff, adjutants, management, weapons, managers, military doctors, veterinarians and justice should have gone along

---

[43] 日高巳雄述著《陸軍軍法会議法講義》, 油印本, 无版权页, p. 41, 转引自高橋正衛編集、解説『続•現代史資料』6「前言」, p. 26.

[44] 高橋正衛編集、解説『続•現代史資料』6「前言」, page 27.

with the commander. So the judicial department should have been next to the commander unless it was deliberately arranged. However, based on the diary of Ogawa, the ministry of adjutants repeatedly tried to separate the judicial department from the army and Ogawa was very dissatisfied with this. For example, he wrote on November 24th:

> We should proceed to Jiaxing tomorrow, but it was postponed suddenly to the day after tomorrow because of the unknown reason. We protested against it for the following reasons.
> …
> Secondly, all affairs of the council of military court depended on the jurisdiction of the command, so our affairs could not be carried out without the commander. If the commander was separated from us, then we would not be informed of the decision of the commander and the most important procedures of the council of military court would be delayed. Now, we detained three suspects of arson. Although the investigation of the prosecutor had ended, it could not be prosecuted without the order of the commander, so the disposal of the incident could only be delayed.

In addition to this section, there was:

> Our position was not exclusive. However, it was a pity if people thought we were useless.[45]

The so-called "uselessness" was not the unwarranted suspicion of Ogawa, because it could be seen from many things that the judicial department was so ignored that it was unpopular. The following trivial matter was taken as an example of the treatment of the ministry of justice. The headquarters of the 10th army went from Huzhou to Lishui on December 10th. Many ministers and adjutants flew by the plane, but Ogawa was arranged to take a bus. So, he thought it was "discrimination" and wrote down his "indignation" in his diary that day. This situation was indeed related to the general low status of the civil service. The following account of Ogawa's diary on December 12th was a true portrayal of this:

> Our civil officers had no alternative but to accept this kind of discrimination. (In particular, the power of the army was increasingly fierce and extremely arbitrary. The original note: the original text in brackets was removed.) If we only depended on the bestowal, we might be the object of jealousy. However, we were actually regarded as encumbrance on any occasion.[46]

However, the "discrimination" against the judicial department was not only because the military officials often disdained the civil officials, but also

---

[45] Ogawa Sekijiro, *The Diary of a Military Solicitor*, pp. 61–62.
[46] Ogawa Sekijiro, *The Diary of a Military Solicitor*, p. 109.

because the function of the judicial department was in conflict with the bearing and discipline of the Japanese army. So the military officials might deliberately disdain the civil officials.

The diary of Ogawa recorded on December 8th that Minister Tsukamoto "negatively treated everything and did not implement anything". Tsukamoto referred to the aforementioned Tsukamoto Hirotsugu who was the justice minister of the Shanghai Expeditionary Army. According to Ogawa's diary, the reason for the "non-implementation" and "negative treatment" was the "lack of the internal harmony".[47] But at that time, it was hard to imagine that the non-implementation of everything was only because of the "interpersonal relationships". I believe that the reason for the "non-implementation" should be associated with that the operation of the judicial department was obstructed. Not a few Japanese soldiers mentioned the protests made by various troops to the judicial department in the Tokyo Trial, including Tsukamoto Hirotsugu. The reason was that the punishment of the judicial department was too severe. He said: "all the troops blamed the judicial department of the Shanghai Expeditionary Army for its severe punishment and its correction of misdemeanors".[48] Iinuma Mamoru who was the chief of the Shanghai Expeditionary Army also said that the "16th division protested against the judicial department because the military discipline was extremely upright (it should mean that the military discipline was overly strict in accordance with the context - noted by the quoter)".[49] The so-called "strictness" was completely nonsense based on a large number of cases of minor punishment or impunity recorded in the diary. However, even if the judicial department was very tolerable, its nature still determined that it could not be accepted by the Japanese military officials and soldiers.

The "blame" said by Minister Tsukamoto could be proved through the experience of Ogawa. When Ogawa visited the Area Army in January 1938, he felt that the difference between the Area Army and other armies was that there was no force directly under the jurisdiction, so it was not necessary to consider the "interpersonal relationships":

> (When I was in the army,) it was necessary to take into account that the army should bear the direct responsibility of the crimes committed by the subordinates and the chief had certain opinions on the subordinates in terms of the interpersonal relationships. Therefore, we had to think deeply and cautiously about the opinions of the chief.[50]

The so-called "certain opinions" referred to the "blame" of "various troops" said by Tsukamoto Hirotsugu. The professional legal officers were

---

[47] Ogawa Sekijiro, the Appendix of *The Diary of a Military Solicitor*, p. 97.
[48] 『極東國際軍事裁判速記錄』第五卷, compiled by Nitta Mitsuo, p. 228.
[49] 『極東國際軍事裁判速記錄』第七卷, compiled by Nitta Mitsuo, p. 426.
[50] Ogawa Sekijiro, *The Diary of a Military Solicitor*, p. 149.

in a weak position at that time. When the daughter of Ogawa was young, she had a symbolic experience. Mitsuyo (Ogawa) Nagamori said that when she was in primary school, the color of her father's official collar and the hat were special (white; red symbolized the army; black symbolized the navy; green symbolized the cavalry; blue symbolized the air force) and their number was rare, so people were always curious. Her classmates even asked: "Is your father a Chinese soldier?" For this reason, the teenager Nagamori was very upset. She thought: "I would be so proud if my father was an ordinary soldier, but I think I was very poor".[51]

Tsukamoto Hirotsugu "had no alternative but to negatively treat everything" and not to implement anything and the reason was explained above. The situation of the 10th army was better than that of the Shanghai Expeditionary Army, but the judicial department was still in a dilemma. So many cases could only be ignored by the judicial department, which caused the dissatisfaction of the military police of law enforcement. Ogawa wrote on December 25th:

> Lieutenant Colonel Kamisago came to consult some affairs. He said that most of the recent rape cases were not prosecuted and the laborious accusation of the military police was wasted in the end. I answered that it might be true. However, I thought that we could not ignore the situation of the war, the mentality of the prisoners, the view on chastity of the Chinese women, the number of crimes so far (the original note: the actual number was quite large), the comparison between the number of the people who were not accused and the number of the people who were occasionally accused, etc. In addition, theoretically, we could not assert that all the victims of the rape at that time were the so-called people who were unable to resist in conformity with Article 1, 7 and 8 of the criminal law. We should take into account that some people were easy to accept the requirements. Thus, it was hasty to define rape immediately when people were raped. The circumstances of the crimes should be further considered and then the disposal could be decided. Therefore, I did not immediately agree with the requirements of the Lieutenant Colonel.
>
> In addition, I was as worried as the Lieutenant Colonel about that the number of the [rape] cases would increase after the truce in the future, which would affect the conciliation. I might think so. On the other hand, the establishment of the comfort facilities might be able to prevent the increase. Moreover, it was unnecessary for people to give their lives away in war. The contact with women was like facing the last test of impulse. So it was unnecessary to worry about the increase of the rape cases after the truce.[52]

---

[51] Nagamori (Ogawa) Mitsuyo,「わが父、陸軍法務官　小川関治郎」, Ogawa Sekijiro, the appendix of *The Diary of a Military Solicitor*, pp. 205 and 206.

[52] Ogawa Sekijiro, *The Diary of a Military Solicitor*, pp. 127–128.

The leader of the military police, Kamisago Shoshichi, had said in Thirty-one Years of the Military Police[53] that some Japanese veterans were disinterested about the corruption of the bearing and discipline of the 10th army and thought it was a lie. For example, Major Yoshinaga Sunao who was the staff officer of the 10th army said: "The statement of Kamisago was a pity".[54] The foregoing record of Kamisago himself could prove that the denial of the memory of Kamisago was a slander.

At that time, it was often the case that the military police was dissatisfied with the non-prosecution. For example, on the next day (the 26th) that Kamisago came to the judicial department, Senior Captain Matsuoka expressed his dissatisfaction with the non-prosecution of a major:

> It was unfair that the cadres were not investigated. If the captain did not properly deal with it, I would not report any incidents of his soldiers in the future.[55]

There were a lot of repeated records in the diary of Ogawa that he was not reconciled to be ignored by the judicial department. We quoted the diary of Ogawa in the third section to prove that he knew the rape. However, when he was confronted with the dissatisfaction of the military police, he pretended to be a considerate man. At that time, this was the only way Ogawa could take whether he truly thought that some "rapes" might be adulteries. We could see that he was in a dilemma in his diary of December 3rd:

> If I did not have many works and was leisure, other people would consider that the judicial department was useless and despise it. However, if I had a lot of works and was busy, it would at least upset the relevant parties. I would rather say that it was inevitable to <u>be criticized</u> if we were too serious.[56]

Two days before Kamisago expressed his dissatisfaction with the non-prosecution of the rape cases, the diary also left an important "guideline" which was not found in the diary (the 23rd):

> As for rape cases, we adopted the policy that we only prosecuted the most vicious cases so far in order to deal <u>with the negative standpoint</u>. If the similar events continued to occur frequently, we had no alternative but to consider the related disposal.[57]

---

[53] Kamisago Shōshichi, 『憲兵三十一年』, Tokyo, ライフ社, 1st edition, April 10th, 1955.

[54] 『「南京事件」日本人48人の証言』, compiled by Ara Kenichi, Tokyo, Shôgakukan, 1st edition, January 1st, 2002, p. 164.

[55] Ogawa Sekijiro, *The Diary of a Military Solicitor*, p. 129.

[56] Ogawa Sekijiro, *The Diary of a Military Solicitor*, p. 85.

[57] Ogawa Sekijiro, *The Diary of a Military Solicitor*, p. 125.

It was not important that this policy was the decision of the chief or the self-determination of Ogawa or the judicial department. It was of importance that it told us that the military law system of the Japanese army indeed had a clear policy of indulging the atrocities.[58]

7 Conclusion

In conclusion, a general conclusion can be drawn that the falsehoods in Ogawa Sekijiro's testimony at the Tokyo Trial are not caused by occasional memory errors, but are intentional misrepresentations.

(Originally published in Jianghai Academic Diary, No. 4, 2010)

---

[58] Ogawa's emotion should not have too much conflict with the "negative" "punishment" "standpoint". Although he was very disappointed with the crimes committed by the Japanese army, he did have regret and sympathy for those officers and soldiers who committed crimes, which can be seen from Ogawa's comment on crimes committed by the Japanese officers and soldiers as "The lack of one basketful of earth spoils the entire effort to build a nine-ren mountain" (Ogawa Sekijiro, *The Diary of a Military Solicitor*, p. 179).

Ogawa Sekijiro and Diary of a Military Legal Affairs Officer

After the defeat of Japanese army and before the Tokyo Trial, a large number of documents were burnt, making the historical truth more elusive—Japanese scholars who are devoted to affirming Japanese armies' atrocities in wartime often say and so do those who deny the atrocities. For instance, Kenichi Matsumoto (a professor with Reitaku University) who holds a centrist view said "there remain such a few official documents on Japan's engagement in the Battle of Nanjing that Mr. Hora (Note: Hora Tomi, the late forerunner of the Great Slaughter School) denies China's claim of 30,000 people killed for not based on any specific statistics or documents, but instead argues for a death toll of 20,000 people and gains popularity".[1] I have shared a similar opinion in recent-year search for Japanese documents in response to Japanese fabrication school. When searching for books in Tokyo at the end of last year, I got surprised at the diary of Ogawa Sekijiro, the chief of Judicial Affairs Department of the 10th Army (which was one of the main forces attacking and capturing Nanjing and the Yangtze Delta) and regretted for my carelessness (as I had gone there for books many times in the past two years after the publication of the diary).

Okawas's diary has long been unknown and even Okawa's daughter who lived with him in his late years got "surprised" and "had no memory of it at all".[2] The diary starts with the issue of the mobilization order by the No. 7 Army (i.e., the 10th Army) on October 12th, 1937 and ends with his departure from Shanghai with General Iwane Matsui, commander of the Japanese

---

[1] 秦郁彦、東中野修道、松本健一「問題は捕虜処断をどう見るか」、『諸君!』、東京、文藝春秋社、2001 年第 2 期、第 132 頁。

[2] 長森光代著「わが父、陸軍法務官小川関治郎」、小川関治郎著『ある軍法務官の日記』「附録」、東京、みすず書房 2000 年 8 月 10 日第 1 版、第 210 頁。

© The Author(s) 2020
Z. Cheng, *The Nanjing Massacre and Sino-Japanese Relations*,
https://doi.org/10.1007/978-981-15-7887-8_9

Central China Area Army (CCAA), by ship on February 21st 1938. After his landing in Jin Shan Wei on November 7th, what mentioned in the diary were his experiences in China, which matters a lot to learning about the several-month operations of the 10th Army in China, especially the "military discipline" of the Japanese army. As Ogawa Sekijiro was most senior among Japanese legal officers at that time and his experiences have something with the theme of this article, this article will thus be divided into two parts, of which the former introduces Ogawa Sekijiro while the latter part, the focus of this article, argues for the importance of his book.

1 Part I Ogawa Sekijiro: Chief of Judicial Affairs Department of the 10th Army

Ogawa Sekijiro was born in 1875 (the 8th Year of the Meiji Era) in Kiori Village, Kaito County, Aichi Prefecture, Japan (which is now in 5, Miyanokoshi, Kiori, Miwa-cho, Ama-gun). In 1898, Ogawa was admitted to the Meiji Law School (now known as Meji University). He was appointed assistant prosecutor in 1904 and reserve judge in 1906 by the ministry of justice and became a member of the Judicial Affairs Department of the 16th Division on the appointment of the Army Ministry and then spent his career in various postings. When the 10th Army was founded in October 1937, he was appointed the chief of the judicial department. And in the next year, he was transferred to the command of CCAA in January and promoted to first-grade senior official (the top rank of military senior officials, equivalent of lieutenant general) in March but resigned in that month. After the Word War II, he worked as member of civil mediation council and so on. And he passed away in 1966 (the 41st Year of the Showa era). From the last years of the Taisho Era to the early years of the Showa era, Ogawa heard many serious cases and those of the Amakasu Incident (also called "Osugi Incident"), Aizawa Incident and 2-26 Incident matter most. In these cases, the defendants were all extreme right-wing soldiers[3] and became renowned "heroes"[4] as

---

[3] "Right-wing" is a catch-all term. On the one hand, the Imperial Way Faction in the Aizawa Incident and the February 26 Incident regarded the Mikado as the God of all generations and advocated that the whole country and even the world would be unified under the control of their Majesty, which in fact promoted the militarization of Japan. Therefore, they belonged to the right-wing forces. On the other hand, they hated the disparity between the rich and the poor and the corruption of the upper class and were devoted to changing the society through eliminating senior officials, warlords and plutocracy by force, which cannot be described as right-wing activities.

[4] Even today some people still hold this opinion. For example, the film "Turmoil" taken in the 1970s was based on the February 26 Incident and taking the position of the perpetrators, described the Imperial Way Faction as heroes who sacrificed themselves to save the country and people, with a love story starring popular actor and actress Katakura Ten and Yoshinaga Sayuri, which was so sad that moved Japanese audience into tears.

ultra-nationalism was prevailing at that time. Hence, it was a tough choice to put them on trial against the fad.

The Amakasu Incident occurred on September 16th 1923 (the 12th Year of the Taisho Era) in which anarchists Osugi Sakae and his wife Ito Noe, along with Ohsugi's young nephew, were killed by a squad of military police led by Captain Amakasu Masahiko who was in charge of the Shibuya-ku detachment and the Kojimachi detachment of Tokyo military police. Amakasu later confessed that the murder was for "personal reasons". In that case, however, two cars of the military police were dispatched, the three people were killed and hidden in the headquarter of the military police, and Amkasu then served as the detachment leader of military police—all these signs just indicate that there was organizational involvement behind the "personal reasons" but the military shirked from admitting and intended to cover it up. Ogawa investigated the case in a serious manner which not only was "against the fad" but also disturbed the military plan, and thus was replaced by the military after the first session on the ground that "the defendant challenged him for cause". The defendant claimed that Ogawa and the victims "came from a place and were distant relatives". This ridiculous reason fooled nobody and by an irony, Ogawa was said to be "the grandson of the foster home where the cousin of brother-in-law of sister-in-law of Osugi's brother-in-law was sent".[5] Subject to the will of the Military, Amakasu was sentenced for 10-year imprisonment but released after only three years and later became the chairman of Kabushikigaisha Manshueigakokai, the most important propaganda agency in Japanese overseas conquests.

On August 12th, 1935, an Imperial Way Faction officer, Lieutenant Colonel Saburo Aizawa, assassinated Major General Tetsuzan Nagata, leader of Toseiha Faction in Military Affairs Bureau of the Army Ministry, which came to be known as the Aizawa Incident. This incident involved in a tussle between different factions in the Army Ministry and became the contributing factor to the subsequent military coup on February 26th. The February 26 Incident is the most important coup in Japanese history and still a household name nowadays, in which many senior officials were killed and it shook the military and political circles. Both the cases were tried by Ogawa. Needless to say, the perpetrators were convicted, but the trail of General Masaki Jinzaburo, who was suspected behind the 2-26 Incident, was noteworthy. Masaki was the Inspector-General of Military Education—having a starting rank of general, as high as the army minister and the chief of staff—but transferred to a sinecure as member of the Supreme War Council (Gunji sangiin) on July 15th 1934, which became the direct cause of the Aizawa Incident (because the Imperial Way Faction believed the whole affair was a trap laid

---

[5] 山崎今朝弥 (律师) 著『地震、憲兵、火事、巡査』, 转引自小川関治郎著『ある軍法務官の日記』附录, 第 222 页。

by their rivals, the Toseiha Faction, but in fact it was for supporting Prince Kan'in Kotohito, Chief of the Imperial Japanese Army General Staff). Masaki had started to win support of junior ranks of the Imperial Japanese Army officer corps since he graduated from the military academy by the end of the Taisho Era and had been in frequent contact with the Imperial Way Faction until the 2-26 Incident. Therefore, he was also tried. But his role in the incident still remains uncertain. Masaki once tried to justify himself in a statement made one year before his death:

> I don't, as widely acknowledged, have anything to do with the February 26 Incident. To be more specific, I did not know the plan until the incident took place and the report came as a rude shock when I noticed the report on that morning. However, the prorogation that Masaki was brain behind the well-designed emergency have convinced the general public as well as the royal family.
>
> The military conference against him (Note: Masaki) took a year and three months and released him based on a thorough investigation.
>
> I would be anything but released if I had anything to with the incident. There's no need for a review of the entire investigation. But it must be noted that as Masaki enjoyed strong support from junior military officials, the authority at that time suspected he was more or less involved and then launched a half-a-year-long investigation and even postponed the execution of three people on the ground that they were taken as witness, which set a precedent in the world legal history, to buy time for gathering evidence against Masaki. However, time did not bring existence and all was in vain.[6]

Although Masaki's role remains uncertain, it is certainly not true that his so-called "anything but released" had he been involved, because recent year has seen the evidence that his release was subject to the political interests of Japanese military. According to General Matsuki Naosuke's diary, Isomura Toshi, Ogawa Sekijiro and he were judges in the Masaki case and held different opinions: Matsuki thought Masaki had the "intent" and was the "plotter"; Ogawa thought Masaki not only had the "intent" and was the "plotter" but also "tactfully encouraged those rebels" in the incident (which, if true, can be strong evidence to convict Masaki of collaboration); Isomura did not think Masaki had the "intention" and was the "plotter". They, especially Isomura and Ogawa, held firm opinions which conflicted with each other and broke up in acrimony. Eventually Isomura, pleading illness, resigned and the "special" military conference was dismissed (according to the diary on September 3rd, 1937). And (according to the diary on September 14th) many people like Oyama Ayao, director of the Judicial Bureau of the Army

---

[6] 真崎甚三郎記録「暗黒裁判二・二六事件」, 文藝春秋編『「文藝春秋」にみる昭和史』第一巻, 東京, 文藝春秋社 1988 年 1 月 10 日第 1 版, 第 309 頁. (此记录最初载于『文藝春秋』月刊, 1957 年 4 月号)

Ministry, stepped in to "persuade" Ogawa to "write a majority opinion without open trial" and the Army authority then revised Ogawa's Judgment, so Masaki was acquitted,[7] from which Ogama was still smarting in his late years.[8]

We do not need to judge the case and Ogawa's opinion was partly based on "morality" (as Ogawa once told his daughter that he despised Masaki for his abject cowardice, not daring to assume the responsibility). But generally, we can see from the case that Ogawa was a military legal affairs officer who strictly enforced the rules. As Ogawa was the chief of judicial department of the 10th Army, his case can help us get an idea of the Japanese military judicial officials and Ogawa's diary, no matter whether he was exceptional in the Japanese army.

2 PART II THE HISTORICAL VALUE OF DIARY OF A MILITARY LEGAL AFFAIRS OFFICER

This part is omitted.[9]

---

[7]桂川光政著「二・二六『真崎判決』はこう作られた」、「松木日誌(抄)」,『世界』, 東京, 岩波書店, 1994 年 3 月号, 第 289 299 页。

[8]Masuyama Takao, the doctor who made a diagnosis before Ogawa died, once said he was "greatly impressed" at the contact with Ogawa as Ogawa told him "Masaki really was a super asshole". (小川関治郎著『ある軍法務官の日記』附录, 第 226 页) We can see this mattered a lot to Ogawa so that he could not help telling someone he met for the first time.

[9]This part is omitted and please refer to my third note for the specific reason.

The Study on Some Issues Concerning the Nanjing Massacre

After the Mid-Autumn Festival 2009, Modern Chinese History Studies held a seminar with the theme of "The Thirty Years of Modern Chinese History Studies: Our Past Experience and The Potential Future". As the seminar was intended to review the past and look forward to the future, issues proposed were not supposed to be very specific. But I have not gone into modern Chinese history except the marginal issues of the Nanjing Massacre and the Tokyo Trial, so I had to consult Mr. Xu Xiuli, one of the sponsors, whether these two issues are appropriate. Mr Xu thought these two issues were of great importance but did not agree with me on the point that the Tokyo Trial matters more than the Nanjing Massacre outside China as he thought comparatively speaking, the Nanjing Massacre matters more to Chinese than the Tokyo Trial. I also phoned Mr. Xie who was one of the organizers and was told the seminar was intended to figure out the shortcomings through looking back. I agreed that it was more meaningful to find out the existing problems than to present the results in a conference that was intended to make a conclusion. Hence, I provided the seminar with a basic outline proposed from the perspective of looking back over the past and looking forward to the future instead of a complete article as demanded mainly because it was one thing to widely discuss about the existing problems of the Nanjing Massacre studies in a seminar but another thing as to whether it would be a well-time action to write into an article. A few days ago, I learned from the seminar's letter that the seminar proceedings would be published and the participants were again demanded to submit their own articles. I hereby explain this considering this topic is too wide to be fully covered today and thus this article is written under external pressure rather than at a right time.

In order to record my original idea, this article is based on the original outline without any structural changes.

1   A Brief Review on the History of Studies

In the outline proposed to the seminar, this section is divided into three parts. The second part deals with Chinese studies, titled "No Controversies involving Antagonistic Ideas in the Circle of Chinese Studies", which focuses on "no controversies" to compare itself with the fierce controversies among different schools in Japan. And it can be further divided into three points: One is the silence before the 1980s and the increasing growth of the writings and collections of documents since the mid-1980s. Another is the introduction of Documents on the Nanjing Massacre, one of the most important achievements, of which 55 volumes have been published and others are editing. The third is a brief account of recent-year reflections mainly by Nanjing middle-generation scholars. As for references, there have been many systematic reviews of Chinese Studies in the Nanjing Massacre, this point will not be discussed in detail. And Japanese studies have been mentioned in my recent-year monographs but without an overall introduction, so this article intends to make a summary with the focus on several important issues. Besides, Western studies in the Nanjing Massacre, which has a short history and has not caught our attention, will also be included. But subject to a limited knowledge, the introduction thereof might be incomplete and just for reference.

The Origin and The Status of the Controversies Among the Slaughter School, the Fabrication School and the Middle-of-the-Road School

The controversy over the Nanjing Massacre originated in the Tokyo Trial and most important controversial issues later can be dated back to the court debate. But Japan, in a weak position as vanquished and faced with all things in disrepair, could only debate with winners over the most important issues that concern the fundamental interests of the nation, such as maintaining tenonism, so the debate over the Nanjing Massacre was limited to the trial. And the Nanjing Massacre became the subject of the debate in Japan in the 1970s. When it comes to Japanese studies in the Nanjing Massacre, one scholar cannot be ignored and we will start with the introduction of him.

Hora Tomio: The First Researcher in the World

Hora Tomio has been a professor with the Waseda University since he graduated from Waseda University's literature department in 1931 and retired in 1977. He lived such a long academic life that he even published Bakumatsu Ishin no ibunka kōryū: Gaiatsu o yomitoku in 1995 when he was ninety years old. His studies focus on Japanese history but the most influential one is that in the Nanjing Massacre. His first article concerning the Nanjing Massacre was published in 1967 which was later included as the first chapter of Kindai senshi no nazo (Riddles of Modern War History) and that is also the first writing concerning the Nanjing Massacre based on empirical research in the world. And Hora's Nankin Jiken (The Nanjing Incident) published in 1972 is the first monograph on this subject.[1] Hora Tomio has contributed a lot to the Studies of the Nanjing Massacre and his "pioneering writings" matter most. Besides, Hora Tomio has discussed a wide range of issues concerning the Nanjing Massacre. In his magnum opus Nankin daigyakusatsu: ketteiban (Authorized Edition: The Nanking Massacre) and Nankin Daigyakusatsu no Shomei (Proof of the Great Nanking Massacre), Hora put forward some issues and refuted the arguments of the fabrication school, which has set the basic framework for the studies of the Nanjing Massacre and pointed out how to resolve the challenges from the fabrication school. And thirdly, as early as in 1973, Hora edited and published the first collection Nankin jiken (The Nanjing Incident) which consists of two volumes (The first volume covers excerpts concerning the Nanjing Incident from the shorthand record of the Tokyo Trial while the second volume deals with the early documents edited by H. J. Timperley, Shu-His Hsu, Lewis S. C. Smythe and F. Tillman Durdin) and has been frequently cited by Japanese scholars. Therefore, the basic framework set by Hora Tomio has remained generally unchanged, although part of his specific conclusions has been overruled or revised with the development of the Nanjing Massacre studies both in range and depth.

Travels in China: Sparkling Controversy in the 1970s
Hora Tomio was the forerunner of the Nanjing Massacre studies but it was a news report that arouse a wide discussion on the Nanjing Massacre in Japan. The report was written by Honda Katsuichi, a journalist with the Asahi Shinbunsha, who was permitted to visit China in 1971 and stayed for over 40 days from the June to July, during which he searched for traces of Japanese atrocities and surviving victims in many places such as Guangzhou, Changsha, Beijing, Shenyang, Fushun, Anshan, Tangshan, Jinan, Nanjing and Shanghai. And it was based on Honda Katsuichi's experiences in China and named as "Travels in China", serialized not only in Asahi Shinbunsha from August to September in 1971 but also in Asahi Special and Asahi Weekly and part of photos were published in Asahi Graph. In the next year, Asahi Shuppansha published an offprint of Travels in China, which includes some new chapters such as "Chinese Impression on Japan: Militarism", "The Workshops of Early Sumitomo", "The Center of Correction", "Bacteriological Experiments on Chinese and Vivisection", "Fushun", "The Massacre concerning Epidemic Prevention", "Anshan and the Early Kubota Chuzo", "The Neighbourhood of the Marco Polo Bridge",

---

[1] Although Niijima Atsuyoshi's The Nanking Massacre was published one year earlier, the book was limited to common pamphlets printed by his group.

"The Mandatory Escort to Japan", "Shanghai", "The Harbor", "The Real Situation of the Attacks and Bombings" and so on, in addition to the original "Pingding Mountain", "The Mass Grave (The Hushi Ditch)", "Nanking" and "Burn All, Kill All, Loot All". We can see from the titles that "Nanking" is merely one of the chapters of Travels in China. That is to say, Travels in China is a critique of Japanese troops' atrocities, including but not limited to the Nanjing Massacre. But only the Nanjing Massacre aroused a wide discussion, whose cause will not be detailed here. Honda Katsuichi made such a harsh criticism and Asahi Shinbunsha was so influential that "the Nanjing Massacre" became a "reality" that Japanese had to face. It cannot be easily determined whether the "reality" sparked a self-examination or aversion. But its great impact became unsettling news to those who oppose the so-called "Tokyo Trial view of history" and the driving force to the trends of denying the Nanjing Massacre.

The Illusion of the "Nanjing Massacre": The First Monograph to Deny the Nanjing Massacre

Suzuki Aki, who first worked for a private radio station and later became a freelance writer, was the first to "refute" the argument of Honda Katsuichi. In 1972, he published an article "Nankin daigyakusatsu" no ma boroshi (The Illusion of the "Nanjing Massacre") (hereafter referred to as "Illusion") in the April-Issue of Shokun and also named his memoir after this one in the next year. And the title of "Illusion" has a little story behind it. The Japanese translation of the word "illusion" is "まぼろし". As the "Illusion" denies the Nanking Massacre, the Japanese word "まぼろし", after the publication thereof, became a synonym for the Kanji "虛構", a label for the fabrication school. And for a long time, the Chinese translation of Sukuzi's book often used the word "fabrication", in addition to "illusion", "hypocrisy" or "fiction". But in Shin Nankin Daigyakusatsu No Maboroshi (New Edition: The Illusion of the "Nanking Massacre" published nearly thirty years later, Suzuki Aki specially pointed out that the original translation was "obviously incorrect". He said, "The Japanese word 'まぼろし' not only involves the meaning of Chinese character '虛' (fiction), '実' (reality) and '秀' (show) but also refers to something dreamy that goes beyond words. I think this title is such a typical Japanese-style, emotional expression that cannot be correctly translated into Chinese". He also cited the example of Sakaguchi Ango's Illusion of Asuka published in Bungei Shunjû (July 1951), in which the word "illusion" means unsolved historical mystery, and said "that is why I titled my book 'まぼろし'".[2] I once criticized Suzuki's explanation to be a far-fetched

---

[2]鈴木明著『新「南京大虐殺」のまぼろし』,東京,飛鳥新社1999年6月3日第1版,第31–32頁.

one "in response to undeniable fact"[3] but in fact it was not fair to accuse him of this because although Suzuki Aki was the forerunner of the fabrication school, he did not mention any specific figures and never claimed to be a member of the fabrication school, except raising questions in a gentle manner. "Nankin daigyakusatsu" no ma boroshi does raise questions concerning the 16th Division, like the corpse bridge, but mainly challenges the "murder race", which was the focus of controversy before the wide debate over the Nanjing Massacre in the 1970s. On one side, the leading ones were Hora Tomio and Honda Katsuichi and on the other side were Suzuki Aki and Yamamoto Shichihei.[4]

The Outstanding Achievements and Major Opponents of the Slaughter School in the 1980s

The debate over the Nanjing Massacre gone at full tilt in the 1980s. And the textbook incident raised wide concern and became the external driving force to stimulate the controversy. In 1984, the slaughter school established the Nankin Jiken Chosa Kenkyu Kai (Research Committee on the Nanjing Incident), including not only Hora Tomio and Honda Katsuichi but also their predecessor Fujiwara Akira as well as twenty middle-generation scholars such as Yoshida Yutaka, Kasahara Tokushi and so on, whose jobs vary from teacher to journalist and lawyer. The 1980s has seen the great achievements of the slaughter school and their prevailing in the debate with the fabrication school. In addition to Hora Tomio's Authorized Edition: The Nanking Massacre and The Proof of the Nanking Massacre that have been mentioned above, many important works came out in this period, including Nankin daigyakusatsu (The Great Nanking Massacre) written by Fujiwara Akira, Tenno no Guntai to Nanking Jiken (The Emperor's Military and the Nanjing Incident) written by Yoshida Yutaka, Nankin he no Michi (The Road to Nanking) and The Nanking Massacre on Trail written by Honda Katsuichi, Nankin jiken o kangaeru (Thinking about the Nanjing Incident) and Nankin daigyakusatsu no genba e (To the site of the great massacre of Nanjing) edited by Hora, Fujiwara and Honda and so on. The development of Japanese studies in the Nanjing Massacre was closely connected with the increasing challenges from the fabrication school and the fabrication school was also growing facing the provocation from the slaughter school. In the

---

[3] A Scrutiny of The Scrutiny of John Rabe's Diary. *Modern Chinese History Studies* 2002(2): p. 166.

[4] The controversy over the "murder race" still remains today and the most detailed discussion in the 1970s was that by Yamamoto Shichihei. See 『私の中の日本軍』下, 東京, 文藝春秋社 1975年12月15日第1版.

1980s, the major opponent of the slaughter school was Tanaka Masaaki, who worked for the Association for Greater East Asia and was henchman of Matsui Iwane in wartime. Tanaka Masaaki advocated militarism, which did not date from the 1980s but can be date back to 1963 when he published the Paru Hakase no Nihon Muzai-ron (Justice Pal's Theory of Japan's Innocence) which was later reprinted for over 20 times. Tanaka's argument against the Nanjing Massacre mainly can be seen in "Nankin gyakusatsu" no kyokō (The Fabrication of the "Nanking Massacre") and Nanking Jiken no Sokatsu (An Overview of the Nanjing Incident), which deny that Japanese troops perpetrated the massacre and other atrocities from every perspective: The sharp increase of Nanjing's population and after-war refugees; Japanese who entered Nanjing not see any corpse; The false and true points of the Safety Zone Committee reports; The peaceful refugee area and thank-you notes; The fabrication of slaughtering a large number of POWs; The untrue statement of corpses buried in Chongshan Tang; No mass killing according to Lewis S. C. Smythe's investigation; Not mentioned in Chinese military conference; No record from Chinese Community Party; Not a issue of League of Nations; No protest from the United States, Britain and France, etc.; Few US-Britain media reports; No Gagging Order; No Witness; Historical materials based on the so-called hearsay; The forged photos. Tanaka completely denied the Nanjing Massacre through introducing certain questionable points, which greatly distinguished himself from the previous fictionalists. He not only refuted the argument of the slaughter school, but also disagreed with the middle-of-the-road school (whose introduction can be seen in next section). Although the fabrication school always declared to be the prevailing one,[5] that was not the case in this round of debate, at least in terms of strength. More importantly than the foregoing writings, the slaughter school in this period widely searched for historical documents, which laid a foundation for affirming the atrocities of Japanese troops, especially the Nanjing Massacre. And this period also saw the publication of Hora Tomio's Nicchū sensō Nankin daizangyaku jiken shiryōshū (Documents on the Nanjing Massacre in the Second Sino-Japanese War), which had been published in 1973 under the name "The Nanking Incident", and the writing of Documents on American Relationships, the first volume and the most important volume of Documents on the Nanjing Incident which was later published in the early 1990s.

---

[5] For example, upon the publication of The Fabrication of the "Nanking Massacre", Japanese right-wing scholar Watanabe Shoichi who has long active in Japan, put in his comment that "those who use the word 'the Nanjing Massacre', if having read this book, will be labeled as anti-Japan left-wing forces." See 田中正明『「南京虐殺」の虚 構―――松井大将の日記をめぐって』腰封, 東京, 日本教文社1984年6月25日第1版.

The Contention Between the Middle-of-the-Road School and Other Schools and The Gradual Merge of the Middle-of-the-Road School and the Fabrication School

Japanese middle-of-the-road school is a very broad concept that covers those who claim that the death toll of the Nanjing Massacre was around ten thousand to tens of thousands. In recent years, those who argue around 10,000 people were killed have been further classified as the small slaughter school while those who argue 40,000 people were killed as the middle slaughter school.[6] The middle-of-the-road school includes those who argue for a death toll between 10,000 and 40,000 and they take a political stand far more complicate than that of the fabrication school and the slaughter school. For example, Sakurai Yoshiko belongs to the small slaughter school in terms of her advocacy of the death toll but has been carrying a anti-China banner, not far removed from the fabrication school; Ikuhiko Hata who belongs to the middle slaughter school, however, has a similar view[7] to the slaughter school. The middle-of-the-road school has long been contending with both the fabrication school and the slaughter school, but generally they more aimed at the fabrication school in the middle of the 1980s. For instance, after the publication of Matsui Iwane Taishō no jinchū nikki (The Battlefield Diary of General Matsui Iwane) edited by Tanaka Masaaki, Yoshiaki Itakura, a member of the small slaughter school, checked off and pointed out the quotations that had been tempered with, which amounted to over 900.[8] In Ikuhikko's memory, Shokun convened a meeting of representatives of three schools to discuss on the Nanjing Massacre in the spring of 1985 and Hora Tomio, Suzuki Aki, Tanaka Masaaki and he were present. "In the 8-hour-long discussion with only coffee for us, Hora, Ikuhikko and Suzuki shared a view that a large amount of people were killed, regardless of the scale and thus isolated Tanaka who denied the Nanjing Massacre".[9] It can be said, not accurate as it is, that the role of the middle-of-the-road school in the 1980s was epitomized by the discussion. The 1980s also seen their great achievement in documents. And the most important were the Documents on the Battle of Nanjing edited and published by Kikosha, a Japanese organization of retired military servicemen, and the Documents on the Battle of Nanjing:

---

[6] As for the name of "small slaughter school" and "middle slaughter school", please see 石川水穂著『徹底検証「南京論点整理学Ｉ」』,『諸君!』, 東京, 文藝春秋, 2001年2月号, 第147页.

[7] kuhiko Hata did not change the following statement in The Nanking Incident which has been reprinted many times: " I as a Japanese apologize to Chinese" "for Japanese aggression against China, including the huge pain and loss Chinese suffered from the Nanjing Incident". See 秦郁彦著『南京事件―――虐殺の構造』, 東京, 中央公論新社1986年2月25日第1版, 第244页.

[8] 『松井石根大!「陣中日誌」改篡の怪』,『歴史と人物』, 東京, 中央公論社, 1985年12月号.

[9] 秦郁彦著『南京事件―――虐殺の構造』増補版第九章「南京事件論争史」上, 東京, 中央公論新社2007年7月25日増補版, 第274页.

Volume II published in the 1990s. Strictly, documents on the battle do not directly deal with the "Nanjing Massacre" or the "Nanking Incident", but as an indirect source, it is still of value to showing in a broad sense what Japanese troops perpetrated, since most of the wartime documents have been burned. Documents on the Battle of Nanjing matters a lot to studies in the Nanjing Massacre and the most one lies in that the remaining Japanese military records prove that Japanese troops did killed the POWs in a large scale.[10] It includes diaries of military soldiers from all ranks, including but not limited to the generals, greatly different from those edited by the slaughter school, which only include those of soldiers and officials at low ranks. In the 1990s, the middle-of-the-road school still had a tendency to technically study the Massacre. For example, Hara Takeshi, a member of the National Institute for Defense Studies (NIDS), gave a death toll between 20,000 and 30,000 instead of the original 10,000 after reexamining the separate cases such as slaughtering POWs at Mufushan. But in general, the middle-of-the-road school has leaned toward the right-wing since the 1990s. Take Unemoto Masaki as example. He who belongs to the small slaughter school claimed the purpose of his writing is to "rebut" the "condemnations" of Japanese army.[11] And so is Yoshiaki Itakura. He once criticized Tanaka Masaaki tempered with the historical documents in the 1980s but his last (posthumous) work Hontö wa kö datta Nankin jiken (The Truth about the Nanjing Incident) includes a memorial article titled "Yoshiaki Itakura: The Enemy of the Slaughter School".[12] Even Ikuhiko Hata has mentioned many times that "only God knows the exact figure".[13] Nowadays, since the fabrication school has dominated, the middle-of-the-road role of the middle-of-the-road school has been greatly weakened.

The Catch-Up of the Fabrication School After the Mid-1990s

The increasing growth of the fabrication school since the 1990s, especially in recent years, has a lot to do with the comeback of the conservative forces. And in this period, several changes occurred to the fabrication school: The first was the dominance of right-wing "scholars". Representatives of the fabrication school after the mid-1990s, no matter Higashinakano Shudo and

---

[10] As for the argument that the so-called "bodies enemies left" in Japanese documents were captives killed by Japanese army, please refer to my article A Study of the Massacre Order for Japanese Troops in Historical Research. [Chen Zhaoqi. A Study of the Massacre Order for Japanese Troops in Historical Research. *Historical Research* 2002(6).]

[11] See my article A Scrutiny of The Scrutiny of John Rabe's Diary.

[12] 上杉千年著「南京大虐殺派の天敵　板倉由明先生を偲ぶ」, 板倉由明著『本当はこうだった南京事件』, 東京, 日本図書刊行会2000年1月20日第2次印刷版, 第506页. It is clearly put on the cover that "this book indicates 'the Nanjing Incident' cannot equate to 'the Nanjing Massacre".

[13] See「南京事件の真実」,『産経新聞』, 東京, 産経新聞社, 1994年7月1日.

Nobukatsu Fujioka who had obvious ideological bias or Kitamura Minoru who was a professional scholar, were professors who taught in the university for a long time while before the mid-1990s, in addition to Suzuki Aki who had been engaged in media and publishing and Ara Kenichi, the fabrication school mainly included the wartime generation, such as Tanaka Masaaki who once followed Matsui Iwane and Yamamoto Shichihei who had been a soldier. The second was the "systematization" of the fabrication school. Unlike the slaughter school who established the Nankin Jiken Chosa Kenkyu Kai as early as in the 1980s, fictionalists had been unorganized. Until recent years, they started to join together and established the Nihon "Nankin" gakkai (Japan Association for "Nanjing" Studies) in 2002. The third was the connection between the fabrication school and the political circle. Before the mid-1990s, politicians were not directly involved in the activities of the fabrication school, except for some occasionally "ill-considered remarks" on the historical issues. But in recent years, both the Nanking Issue Subcommittee of the Young Diet Member's League to Consider Japan's Future and History Education (Nippon no Zento to to Rekishi Kyoikuwo Kangaeru Giin no Kai) founded by the Liberal Democratic Party and the non-partisan Committee for the Examination of the Facts about the Nanking Incident (Nankin Jiken no Shinjitsu wo Kensho-suru Kai)[14] founded by Japan's House of Representatives and House of Councilors have frequently and closely interacted with the fabrication school.[15] The fourth was the contribution from mainstream TV stations. For a long time, denial of the Nanjing Massacre sometimes appeared on Japan mainstream TV stations, such as the talk show of TV Tokyo (Channel-12) hosted by Watanabe Shoichi (Emeritus Professor of Sophia University), but no special programs. Special programs on the Nanjing Massacre did not arrive until recent years. In those programs, the slaughter school never appeared[16] (from which we can what a stressful thing to appear on TV to confront Japan's national shame) while the fabrication school was well-prepared. Unequal opportunities brought about the situation where the fabrication school always prevailed based on "evidence" in the conflicts with the slaughter school. Therefore, such programs were more useful to fictionalists than one-sided propaganda. The fifth was the overall development of fictionalists' views. The fabrication school merely raised some basic questions in the period of Suzuki Aki and began to develop when

---

[14] In the first "Study Session" of the Committee for the Examination of the Facts about the Nanking Incident held on February 26th, 2007, a total of 48 members and representatives of the Liberal Democratic Party and the Democratic Party appeared and Nobukatsu Fujioka, the pioneer of the fabrication school, gave a lecture.

[15] Kasahara Tokushi said we then entered a period of "the politicization of 'contention'". See 笠原十九司著『南京事件論争史』, 東京, 平凡社2007年12月10日第1版, 第226 227頁.

[16] In a pay television called Japan Cultural Channel Sakura, which has been focusing on the topic of the Nanjing Incident, the host has repeatedly "invited" the slaughter school them to have a public debate in the program.

Tanaka Masaaki denied the Nanjing Massacre in its totality. In this period, the fabrication school widely searched for information and overall reinforce their original advocacy. Such examples were not rare: Tanaka Massaki mentioned the forged photos in the end of Nanking Jiken no Sokatsu and other fictionalists such as Higashinakano Shudo further claimed to have examined all the photos: "The 43 photos, the 'photo evidence', have been thoroughly examined and none can be taken as evidence".[17] Suzuki Aki "learned" that H. J. Timperley was an "adviser" with the International Propaganda Division of the Kuomintang's Central Propaganda Bureau (which was mistaken for the "Intelligence department") and then based on this, Kitamura Minoru wrote a monograph claiming to have proven the so-called "Nanjing Massacre" was "tightly interwoven" with "KMT's international publicity and foreign policy strategy in nature, which won undivided admiration among fictionalists.[18] The sixth was the publication of new writings one after one and next was Truth of Nanking (planed as a trilogy and the first one finished), the first film on this subject. And the last was output to the Western world, especially the United States.[19] Through such wide-ranging activities, arguments of the fabrication school then carried unparalleled weight.

The Struggle of the Slaughter School
The slaughter school made stout resistance against the all-out attack from the fabrication school. In the 1990s, except for the Nanking Daigyakusatsu Hiteiron 13 no Uso (Thirteen lies in the Nanjing Massacre Deniers' Claims) published by the Research Committee on the Nanjing Incident, they no longer joined up with each other as they did in the 1980s but almost separately argued from different perspectives. In this period, Kasahara Tokushi made the most outstanding achievement in terms of empirical research, Ishida Yuji, a member of the Research Committee on the Nanjing Incident, translated and edited the Nanking Daigyakusatsu o Kirokushita Kogun Heishitach (Documents: The Nanjing Incident as Seen by German Diplomats), the first collection on German official documents, and Ono Kenji edited the Nanking Daigyakusatsu o Kirokushita Kogun Heishitach (Imperial Army Soldiers Who Recorded the Nanjing Massacre) which, most importantly, proved

---

[17]東中野修道、小林進、福永慎次郎著『南京事件「証拠写真」を検証する』腰封、東京、草思社2005年2月8日第1版。

[18]北村稔著『「南京事件」の探究―――その実像をもとめて』第一部「国民党国際宣傳処と戰時対外戦略」、東京、文藝春秋社2001年11月20日第1版、第25 64頁。

[19] *The Alleged "Nanking Massacre"* published by Japan Conference in 2002 was written in both English and Japanese and subtitled "Japan's Rebuttal to China's Forged Claims". Since then, there has frequently come out English versions of Japanese writings. For example, books such as written by Tanaka Masaaki and Higashinakano Shudo have been translated into English and widely given away to American politicians, media professional, universities and community libraries.

most of 140,000 Chinese soldiers and people captured by the "Morozuno Detachment"[20] at Mufushan were shot dead as reported in wartime. In addition to the contribution from research committee members, Nankinsen—tozasareta kioku o tazunete (The Battle of Nanjing: Searching for Forbidden Memories) edited by Matsuoka Tamaki saved the memory of the most witnesses, including interviews on 102 veterans who mostly served in the 16th Division. And among a few writings other than Kasahara Tokushi's, I think worth mentioning is Tsuda Michio's Nankin daigyakusatsu to Nihonjin no seishin kozo, which is not rarely known as its Chinese version has been published in China (not only Chinese mainland but also Taiwan Province, Hongkong SAR and Macao SAR), for it has been ignored even by the slaughter school. The reason for the ignorance certainly lies in the fact that this book "obviously" depends on the "existence" of the Nanjing Massacre—the historical fact where the schools disagree, but I also think it has something to do with its harsh criticism on Japanese common people. The internal collaboration and external contention among Japanese schools is an old problem and it can be said both the dominance of the slaughter school in the 1980s and the prevailing of the fabrication school in the 1990s are the result of members of a school joining up to fight against other ones. The declining influence of the slaughter school in the 1990s thus cannot be said to have nothing to do with their separately fighting, although it has something to do with the background where society at large was leaning toward the right-wing forces.[21]

The history of Japanese studies in the Nanjing Massacre is a history of constant controversies. It can be said that the debates among schools are the major driving force for the development of studies. The fabrication school now has an overwhelming advantage but it has not and also cannot sweep away all others.[22] Since Japanese schools almost approach the limit of major historical materials on the Nanjing Massacre, it is no doubt that none of them can score an overwhelming victory and become the only voice, although the influence of different schools will wane and wax for the foreseeable future.

---

[20] The 65th Regiment of the 13th Division (whose head was Colonel Morozuno Sakuhajime).

[21] Kasahara Tokushi's *Nankin jiken ronsōshi: nihonjin wa shijitsu o dō ninshiki shite kitaka*, a book of over 300 text pages, does not mention any work of Tsuda Michio, Matsuoka Tamaki and others. They not only disregard but also do not recognize each other's works. For example, *Nankinsen - tozasareta kioku o tazunete* edited by Nankinsen - tozasareta kioku o tazunete was harshly criticized by members of Nankin Jiken Chosa Kenkyu Kai after the publication: Honda Katsuichi regarded it as "an unreliable book devoid of any truthful content" and "to the advantage of opponents"; Ono Kenji detailed the evidence, claiming that "it is rare to see so many mistakes and unbelievable statements in a book and that this book crossed the bottom line, although, as the say goes, to error is human" (see 「南京大虐殺をめぐる二つの空しい書物」、「『南京戦』何が問題か」,『金曜日週刊』, 東京, 株式会社金曜日, 2002年12月20日).

[22] You can get a brief idea of it from the fact that the Japanese reports on the China-Japan joint history research mostly adopt the viewpoints of Ikuhiko Hata.

A Brief Introduction of Western Studies in the Nanjing Massacre

The Involvement of Western Scholars in Recent Years

Western studies in the Nanjing Massacre began late but got a unique style. It was in the Nanjing Group Meeting organized by Yang Daqing (The George Washington University) of the Annual Conference of Association for Asian Studies (AAS) that Western scholars discussed on the Nanjing Massacre for the first time. The Proceedings of the Meeting, The Nanjing Massacre in History and Historiography[23] argues from the perspective of history and memory, politics and morality as well as methodology, whose focus and point of view are so different from existing Chinese and Japanese writings that it embarks on a new path among various works on the Nanjing Massacre. In recent years, noteworthy are works of three Japan-born scholars. One is Yamamoto Masahiro's (University of Wyoming) Nanking: Anatomy of an Atrocity published in 2001, another is Yoshida Takashi's (Western Michigan University) The Making of the "Rape of Nanking": History and Memory in Japan, China, and the United States published in 2006 and the third is Bob Tadashi Wakabayashi's (University of York) The Nanking Atrocity-Complicate the Picture published in 2007. These books intend to re-examine existing documents in a careful manner to affirm the facts about the Nanjing Massacre. Opinions vary on whether the purpose has been realized, but it is certain that they have highlighted the problems of previous Chinese studies.

Polarized Response to The Rape of Nanking

In the same year but shortly after the first discussion on the Nanjing Massacre, Iris Chang's The Rape of Nanjing was published in the United States which was the first one to fully reflect the "Nanjing atrocity" in the west and topped the best-selling list as soon as published. And it is still the best seller among Chinese and Japanese writings on this subject. But meanwhile, opinions are unprecedentedly divided on this book. It was a foregone conclusion that this book would be highly appreciated in China and severely challenged by Japanese fictionalists. But it was unexpected that Joshua A. Fogel who wrote "The Nanking Massacre in Historiography" (which has been included in a collection of the same name, i.e., The Nanjing Massacre in

---

[23] This book includes the following articles: "Foreword" by Charles Maler, who was then (the same below) a professor with the Harvard University), "Introduction: The Nanjing Massacre in History" by Joshua A. Fogel, a professor with University of California, Santa Barbara, "Aggression, Victimization, and Chinese Historiography of the Nanjing Massacre" by Mark S. Eykholt, a professor with the Massachusetts Institute of Technology, "A Battle over History: The Nanjing Massacre in Japan" by Yoshida Takashi, a doctoral student of the Columbia University and "The Challenges of the Nanjing Massacre: Reflection on Historical Inquiry" by Daqing Yang, a professor with Washington University. See ジョシュア・A・フォーゲル編『歴史学のなかの南京大虐殺』, 東京, 柏書房2000年5月25日第1版.

History and Historiography) made harsh criticism and especially unexpected was the severe frustration of Japanese slaughter school. According to the questionnaire of Shokun! afterwards, main members of the slaughter school like Fujiwara Akira, Kasahara Tokushi and Takasaki Ryuji, positive outlook as they presented on a limited part of the book, thought there were "too many mistakes" with the historical facts while like Rguchi Keiichi, Inoue Hisashi, Himeta Mitsuyoshi and Yoshida Yutaka made negative comments.[24] The leading members of the slaughter school and the author of the book were locked in disagreement over the supplement, leading to the delayed publication of Japanese version. Consequently, this book had no local publication in Japan but received mere criticism for a long time. The Japanese version did not come out until ten years after the original publication of the English version. And to accompany the publication of Japanese version, Shoĭ koĭ Fu, who translated the book, published Za reipu obu nankin o yomu at the same time. Iris Chang is a native speaker who was born in America. And it is a similar case with Shoi Koi Fu: He is a native speaker who has Chinese origin but was born in Japan. He is neither a translator or a researcher. The driving force for translating the book was his "instinctive", special feeling about "drawing near over" but "not assimilated into" the "motherland" and the "host country" (as put by Yamada Masayuki, a professor with Osaka Kyoiku University—the commentator for the Za reipu obu nankin o yomu). According to his mental experiences, he is strongly against the "memory of war" that Japan has been purposely pretending to be a victim to cover up wrong actions since 1970s and cannot tolerate "forgetting" such history of "cruel" and "inhuman" actions as the Nanjing atrocity. In his opinion, although there are some mistakes in The Rape of Nanking, those cannot outweigh the great importance of the book. He put as follows in the translation note: "Language contains messages, including not only the facts but also the speaker's passion, feeling, hope and sense of justice". The "basic requirements" for translating this book are "identification with the author's intention implied in the book" and "identification with the personality of the author, "without [which] it is impossible to finish the translation of this book".[25] He who places more value on "righteousness" than on "details" is much different from the slaughter school, featured by valuing empirical research.[26] The viewpoints of the translator for Japanese version (which has not carried much weight) are mentioned in this introduction to the work of Iris Chang with a special consideration: Many years ago I wrote the Dissent on and Reflection from "The Rape of

---

[24]「まぼろし派、中間派、大虐殺派三派合同大アンケート」，『諸君!』，東京，文藝春秋，2001年2月号，第164 203頁。中译见上引拙著附录之四第511–553.

[25] 巫召鴻著『「ザ・レイプ・オブ・南京」を読む』，同時代社2007年12月10日第1版，第14–15頁.

[26] Yamada Masayuki, who once "interpreted" Shoĭ koĭ Fu's book, also said that translating *the Rape of Nanking* into Japanese is "a resistance force against oblivion" based on "conscience and duty". See 山田正行解說《忘却への抵抗と良知の責務》，巫召鴻著『「ザ・レイプ・オブ・南京」を読む』，第151–189頁.

Nanking"[27] which introduces the criticism of Japanese and American scholars on The Rape of Nanking and certainly includes my viewpoints of how to deal with emotion and historical facts. The book sticks to the issue but unexpectedly it has often become a reference to justify the criticism on the author of The Rape of Nanking and on some Chinese scholars. Therefore, I would hereby proclaim that as my affirmation of the slaughter school's criticism on The Rape of Nanking does not mean I would refute Shoi Koi Fu and Yamada Masayuki's high appreciation for it, this article should not be interpreted without basis, especially since Iris Chang has passed away.

2 Issues Concerning Studies in the Nanjing Massacre

Confusion Arising from Not Stepping Back into "History"

"Contemporary History" is a so-called concept in Japan to distinguish from those pieces of history that have nothing to do with nowadays. It has been over 70 years since the Nanjing Massacre, but it still falls into the category of "contemporary history" which is emotionally connected to us. It is anything but uncommon in human history that conflicts over race, religion, "hierarchy", power and interests give rise to atrocities which greatly impress victims and the most impressing is harm from a difference race. For example, after "Emperor Hui Zong and Qin Zong (Note: the eighth and the ninth emperor of the Northern Song dynasty) were captured to northern China", Zhu Xi (Note: one of the most important philosophers of the Neo-Confucian School in the Song and Ming Dynasty) once said, "Hui Zong and Qin Zong were captured by the Jin (Jurchens) and taken to Manchuria in the Jingkang Incident. Courtiers were so irritated that they would take revenge no matter how time-consuming".[28] He also said that "He who leads to the death of my father or My Majesty is my sworn enemy".[29] Usually, courtiers in the period of Zhu Xi took a position that they would "take revenge no matter how time-consuming" and "never reconcile with their sworn enemy". And when it comes to the memory of "Yangzhou Ten-day Slaughter" and "Jiading Three-day Slaughter", such position was also not rare until the fall of Qing Dynasty. These examples of traditional dynasties are not mentioned because they matter as much as the Nanjing Massacre. Nowadays, "righteousness" and "law" taking a leading position, we can, for convenience but not breaking our principle, magnanimously take a position that "a handful of militarists"

---

[27] See *Historical review* 2002(3). And in Chen Zhaoqi. Study on the Nanjing Massacre. Shanghai Lexicographical Publishing House. 1st Edition published in December 2002, pp. 264–270.

[28] Chapter 75 "Preface to Right Statements of the Shuwu Year". In *The Collection of Zhuwen Gong*. In *Four Series* (Compact Edition), Vol. 7th. Shanghai Commercial Press, p. 1385.

[29] Zhu Xi also said he who leads to the death of my father or My Majesty is "my sworn enemy". See Chapter 13 "Documents of Chuigong Years". In *The Collection of Zhuwen Gong*, Vol. 1st, p. 188.

cannot speak for "the majority of Japanese common people" and a positive way to "memorize" the Nanjing Massacre has always been cherishing peace instead of "remembering" hatred. However, although the Nanjing Massacre as well as other atrocities can bring awareness such as of "cherishing peace", the trouble is that "irritation" can be the more direct or more likely result of this bad memory, which can be proved by the overwhelming amount of such words as hating "Japs" "forever" (which is not a prediction, but because such words as "often" cannot indicate the intensity of the emotion) in online topics.[30] Hence, if there's anything other than academic element that the Nanjing Massacre studies have been bound up by, such emotion (often mistaken for "national sentiment") which can affect the government and people's tolerance and has become a more insurmountable problem than political correctness must be one of the most important elements.

The Nanjing Massacre and the Tokyo Trial

In the proceedings of the Tokyo Trial, the defendants in fact were not charged with "crimes against humanity" but Japanese fictionalists still claim the Nanjing Massacre was "fabricated" to satisfy the elements of "crime against humanity". And the Nanjing Massacre was classified into the category of conventional war crimes (common war crimes) in trail, causing it difficult to distinguish Class-A war criminals from Class-B and Class-C ones. These issues have been dwelt on in another article[31] and thus will not be detailed here. Throughout the Tokyo Trial, the trial of the Nanjing Massacre has touched on the issue of legal principles but more "influential' is the issue of evidence. Japanese right-wing forces focus on the Nanjing Massacre among Japanese army's atrocities partly because the so-called evidence in the Tokyo Trial was "not true".[32] Certainly, it went without saying that the fabrication

---

[30] Although "public opinion online" may not speak for all people, online posts, which allow free speech to the most extent, will not go farther from the reality than opinion polls published. And whether those opinions have been shaped is quite another matter.

[31] See "Section 1: The Issue of Nulla Poena Sine Lege", "Section 2: The Issue of Conspiracy" and "Section 3: The Issue of Crimes against Humanity". In Chen Zhaoqi. *From the Film The Tokyo Trial to the Trial in Tokyo. Historical Review* 2007(5). Also see "Section 1: Problems Pointed out". In Chen Zhaoqi. *Re-evaluation of Iwane Matsui's War Guilt: Verifications of One of the Testimonies on the Nanjing Massacre Given by the Defendants at the Tokyo War Crimes Trials. Modern Chinese History Studies* 2008(6).

[32] Tanaka Masaaki said the evidence presented by the prosecution was nothing more than "rumor, speculation and exaggeration in the Tokyo Trial" (see 田中正明『東京裁判とは何か』, 東京, 日本工業新聞社1983年5月20日第1版, 第195页). And Fuji Nobuo who was a staff in the Tokyo Trial and claimed to have been at the public gallery during most of court sessions said, " As a Japanese with common sense, when examining the evidence presented by both parties, I felt that there were many problems, such as distortion, exaggeration and fabrication, with evidence presented by the prosecution while evidence presented by the defendants was much more reasonable (see 冨士信夫著『「南京大虐殺」はこうして作られた——東京裁判の欺瞞』, 東京, 展転社1995年4月29日第1版, 第348页).

school has been biased, but it does not mean evidence presented by the prosecution cannot be challenged. Dispassionately examined, the prosecution evidence does have a tendency toward "exaggeration". Let us take an obvious example. It is put as follows in No. 1702 Prosecution Document (Written Evidence):

> According to Lu Su's testimony provided to the prosecutor of Nanjing District Court:
> After entering the city, Japanese army raked our national army that was retreating as well as refugees regardless gender and age, totaling 5748 people, with machine gun fire and then stuck them with bayonet. At last, Japanese army poured kerosene on and burned them. The remaining corpses were pushed into the Yangtze River.

Lu Su claimed he was "hiding in a toilet at the Shangyuan Gate and witnessed the terrible scene just meters away and thus could bear a witness".[33] A slightly rational person, even if having deep sympathy to victims, definitely will doubt how he who was in a hideaway could calculate such an exact, big figure. And in terms of the tendency of "exaggeration", on the top of the list is the statistics of Chongshan Tang which society buried most people in the massacre.[34] Evidence could not be convincing—this, to a large extent, resulted in that in the Tokyo Trial all the charges were not approved and that the verdict on the number of atrocities was not similar to that of the Nanjing Trial. And the inconsistent[35] judgment of the Tokyo Trial more indicated that judge were confused at sketchy evidence. Hence, it is no coincidence that the viewpoints of the fabrication school can be dated back to the Tokyo Trial.

[33] 新田満夫編集『極東國際軍事裁判速記錄』第一巻，東京，雄松堂書店1968年1月25日第1版，第751頁。

[34] There is a great disparity between Chongshan Tang's records and The Red Swastika Society's records. Members of Chongshan Tang daily buried 150 bodies per capita while The Red Swastika Society's daily record of bodies buried is merely 11 bodies per capita, even if the highest on record. And the burial records of the Red Swastika Society was made during the time of the incident but those by Chongshan Tang were made during the Nanjing Trial, ten years after the incident. Therefore, I am doubtful about Chongshan Tang's records. For details of statistics, please refer to the 200th Note of "Section 1·Part II·The Value of Japan's Historical Material". In *Research on Japan's Existing Historical Material of the Nanjing Massacre*. Shanghai People's Publishing House. 1st Edition published in August 2008, p. 110.

[35] For example, in terms of death toll of the massacre, it is claimed to be "over 200,000" in the section of the Nanjing Atrocities, Chapter 8 "Conventional War Crimes" of the Judgement, and be "over 100,000" in the judgement for Matsui Iwane, Chapter 10 of the Judgement. And as put in the judgement for Hirota Koki, "Hundreds of people were killed every day" (see 新田満夫編集『極東國際軍事裁判速記錄』第十巻，第768、797、800頁). But the judgement for Hirota Koki in *Judgement of the International Military Tribunal for the Far East* translated by Zhang Xiaolin has changed the statement as "thousands of people killed" "every day" (People's Publishing House. 1st Edition published in February 1986, p. 578) for some reason. These three records contradict with each other on a same period (almost five or six weeks), not matter the last record is "hundreds of" or "thousands of".

On the other hand, we also feel pity for the "insufficiency" in addition to the tendency of "exaggeration". Let me give you an example. Matsui Iwane who commanded the capture of Nanjing is the first one who shall take responsible for the Nanjing Massacre. He was not only the most active war hawk among Japanese senior generals at the beginning of war but also the first to propose the capture of Chinese capital. It was inevitable that Matsui was found guilty of "aggression against China" (the 27th cause of action) but he was not and acquitted due to weak evidence presented by the prosecution.[36] (The court found Matsui Iwane guilty of "inaction", the 55th cause of action, which fell into the category of conventional war crimes, and sentenced him to death by hanging, the highest category of penalty. The penalty does not fit with the crime, somewhat justifying those who cry foul.) Due to the insufficiency of evidence, many war criminals were acquitted or sentenced to a penalty that did not fit with the crime. Hence, from the perspective of the "tendency of exaggeration" and "insufficiency", the Tokyo Trial of the Nanjing Massacre has left many serious problems, although it laid an international-law foundation for the existence of the Nanjing Massacre whose great significance cannot be ignored.

Not-Powerful-Enough Criticism of Japanese Slaughter School

When walking into a Japanese bookshop, you will find none of the writings on other historical events involving China can be bracketed with those on the Nanjing Incident in terms of quantity. In China, there are not only organizations double as research institution, such as the Memorial Hall of the Victims in Nanjing Massacre by Japanese Invaders, but also specialized research institutions like the Nanjing Massacre Research Institute (Nanjing University) and the Nanjing Massacre Research Center (Nanjing Normal University) and also there have long been researchers specially for the studies in the Institute of History of Jiangsu Provincial Academy of Social Sciences. The Nanjing Massacre has raised great concern both in China and Japan—not because it is one of the historical events—but because it is a special indicator, or "symbol"[37] as Japanese scholars named, of Japanese atrocities. Should the Nanjing Massacre be an ordinary event in history, neither China nor Japan would put so many efforts in it. Therefore, we don't need to take the judgment of the Tokyo Trial, especially that of the trial of the Nanking Atrocities, as a "standard", but should response to challenges, if necessary, from Japanese

---

[36]The judge says in the Judgement, "In order to justify the 27th cause of action, the prosecution has the obligation to present reasonable evidence from which we can infer that Matsui Iwanne had knew the nature of war as crime, but they failed" (see 新田満夫編集『極東國際軍事裁判速記錄』第十卷, 第800頁).

[37]For example, Ikuhiko Hata once said, "The Nanjing Massacre can be a symbol for incidents where Japan was perpetrator" (秦郁彦、佐藤昌盛、常石敬一「戦争犯罪ワースト20を選んだ――――いまなお続く『戦争と虐殺の世紀』を徹底検証」,『文藝春秋』, 東京, 文藝春秋社, 2002年8月号, 第160頁).

fabrication school. We have long focused on criticizing "notions" of the fabrication school, neglecting the rebuttal of materials. Fictionalists do have an obvious ideological bias but they have more than slogans. It was after he, via a circuitous route, found Timperley's obituary in Manchester Guardian that Suzuki Aki affirmed that Timperley was an "adviser" with China; The Top-secret Chinese Nationalist Documents Reveal the Truth about the Nanking Incident written by Higashinakano Shudo was based on The Summary of Operations of the International Propaganda Division of the Central Propaganda Bureau "discovered" in Kuomintang Party History Museum. Almost every important work of the fabrication school has included newly discovered materials. Although misinterpretation of historical texts and chicanery are not rare in these works, we cannot successfully "refute" if disregarding materials they based on. The fabrication school has been flaunting that they argue based on historical materials, so the most effective way to challenge them is to "refute them with their own argument". There are many examples of this, both positive and negative. Here is one that has been mentioned in my essay. After the publication of Nankin jiken "shoko shashin" wo kensho suru (Analyzing the "photographic evidence" of the Nanking Massacre) (hereafter referred to as "Analysis") edited by Higashinakano Shudo and other scholars, I heard about a rebuttal of the book based on convincing reasons, whose notion gained my appreciation, once in a conference. But meanwhile, to reason things out, I supposed, was a way that pulls his punches. And later I read a long article called The Sino-Japanese War as Seen in Camera[38] written by Watanabe Hisashi, a Japanese middle-school teacher, examining the Analysis in a simple way—It tracks the historical development of original texts and takes for reference both written and video materials to seek the truth. Let me take an example. As the Analysis claims a photo to be forged by China because there are no epaulets on Japanese military uniforms in that photo, Watanabe then searched for photos at the time of the incident and found there was also no epaulette in a photo titled "Captain Tanaka toasting for the occupation of radio station" in The China Incident Pictorial published by The Manichi (Osaka) on October 21st, 1937, with which the argument of the Analysis no longer held. But Wantanbe did not stop and further found in the literature an announcement issued by Umezu Yoshijiro, Secretary of the Army Ministry on August 29th of the same year, saying that all troops can take epaulets off "in case of spy". Based on Umezu's announcement, the conclusion can no longer be challenged. Watanabe neither launched a withering attack nor spoke with eloquence, but his article will give you the feeling of power after reading it. As the saying goes, "Facts speaker louder than words". To deal with the challenges from Japanese rightwing forces, the most powerful and effective way is to argue based on reliable evidence.

[38] 渡辺久志著「カメラが目撃した日中戦争」, 季刊『中帰連』, 2006年10月2007年7月, 第38–41期.

The Issue concerning Quantitative Research

Lacking quantitative research is a big problem with the Nanjing Massacre studies. Two major reasons can account for it. For one thing, some argue that studies in the Nanjing Massacre involve determining the nature rather than the "figure". But disregard for figure cannot mean the nonexistence of the problem. I have been asked many times why we stick to the figure since it is not a matter of quantity. This question puzzles more than Japanese fictionalists and even than Japanese people. I think there exists a unnecessary dispute over as well as a tendency of exaggeration of the figure when we emphasize the nature. It is unnecessary because the Nanjing Massacre is not our glory, shame of Japan as it is. For another, quantitative research does have trouble getting enough documents. Except for the limited survey by Lewis S. C. Smythe on which opinions vary widely, there was not and could not be a thorough investigation on atrocities committed by Japanese troops. The figure determined in the Tokyo Trial and the Trial of the Nanjing Massacre cannot be inferred from early records about Japanese atrocities, even the burial reports by the Red Swastika Society. And other first-handed evidence, like the remaining bodies that theoretically can be all discovered and then become hard evidence (in fact also involving identification), matters little to statistically justifying the token figure. The quantity issue focuses on not only the massacre but also the rape, robbery and other atrocities. In other words, the issue touches on whether atrocities committed by Japanese troops could be infinite. To cover Japanese atrocities, the fabrication school have provided "positive" "counter-evidence" like the thank-note for Japanese army and the "peace" of refugee area, etc. Over the years, I have criticized this for many times. For example, with regard to the thank letter from Chen Hansen, director of Baota Street Shelter, to Doi Shinji, captain of Japanese Hira Gunboat, for food assistance, I have put as follows in Review of Japanese Right-wing Writings on the Nanjing Massacre:

> Lieutenant Colonel Doi Shinji, captain of Japanese Hira Gunboat, "volunteered to clean up the area (Note: it refers to the Baotaqiao Street near Xiaguan)"[39] and renamed Baotaqiao Street as "Heiwa" Street, a Japanese name. And Director Chen took Showa as new year name, which indicates the misery facing people of a conquered nation, in addition to the loss of self-esteem. So are the words such as so-called "reward" and "great blessing". We can not ask refugees to reject food given in a disrespectful manner; We also need not criticize those like Chen Hansen who subjected themselves to the enemy; We even can set aside the purpose and operations of Doi Shinji– the epitome of Japanese

---

[39] 田中正明著『南京事件の総括―――虐殺否定十五の論拠』, 第179頁.

army– to establish a colony like the Manchukoko. However, we ought not ignore the fact that it was Japanese army that led to refugees in "Heiwa" Street Shelter and even all throughout the Nanjing City starving to death.[40]

I cite my previous article here—not to argue against wrong statements—but to draw attention to the fact that when it came to the Nanjing Massacre, concerned were savage people who killed every they saw, like Mukai Tashiakai and Noda Takeshi, long neglecting those conquered in a soft manner like the Doi Shinji. In a broad sense, we certainly can say that Japanese army brought themselves to our land without permission and all of their actions were invasion. But Doi's operations and similar actions are different from heinous crimes. Admitting this, we have to face a challenge, that is, is there a quantitative "line" for atrocities Japanese army committed in Nanjing? In other words, were Japanese atrocities infinite actions involving troops at all levels at all times and all places or limited to certain troop at certain time or place? Of course, we can argue that a quantitative line cannot refute the fact that Japanese atrocities violated the international law and went against humanity in nature. However, the notion of the Nanjing Massacre, to some extent, might inevitably change.

The Issue Concerning a Different "Common Sense"

The bones of contention over the Nanjing Incident in Japan are very different from our focus on the Nanjing Massacre, like whether the dead were soldiers or civilians, whether soldiers died in fighting or as disarmed captives, whether POWs executed performed the duty of captives provided in the international law and went through a "legal" trial and even whether civilians killed participated in resistance and then could be regarded as middle of the road, etc. These issues are not our concern and we can hardly accept such wording for emotional reasons. The reason for such difference lies in our different perception of international law. In our mind, since anti-aggression is a natural right, nationwide war of resistance against Japanese aggression is right and all killings committed by Japanese army are crimes. In addition to a few people who totally agree with us, such as Tsuda Michio, the majority of the slaughter school stress that Japanese troops committed "illegal" killing. For example, Yoshida Yutaka believes that Japanese army "violated the law" considering they killed soldiers in military uniform or plain clothes "without a trial" but it was necessarily up to the military court to determine the "punishment".[41] This statement is aimed at the fabrication school, but Tsuda Michio once expressed concern that the opposite side of "violation of law" is "legitimacy" but no killing in a war of aggression is "legitimate" (In private

---

[40]Cheng Zhaoqi. A Study on the Nanjing Massacre, p. 304.
[41]吉田裕『国際法の解釈で事件を正当化できるか』, 南京事件調査研究会編『南京大虐殺否定論13のウソ』, 東京, 柏書房1999年10月25日第1版, 第160–176页.

talks) the difference between Chinese and Japanese notions also touches on further like the perception of modern history. For example, Hata Ikuhiko, a middle-of-the-road school member, wrote the Rokōkyō Jiken no kenkyū (A Study on Marco Polo Bridge Incident),[42] a pretty thick scroll which studies "the first gun" in details. As our habitual thinking goes, such study is in vain no matter how detailed—unauthorized presence in the Marco Polo Bridge cannot be justified since the Marco Polo Bridge belongs to us. Japanese do not agree. They believe that it was beyond reproach that Japanese army stationed at the Marco Polo Bridge subject to the Final Protocol for the Settlement of the Disturbances of 1900 (Boxer Protocol), a legal, international treaty recognized by the KMT government, disregard that it is a notorious, unjust treaty unrecognized by the government of the People's Republic of China. In a different context, even the slaughter school will differ from us in the notion of issues, the basis of the argument as well as the manner of wording. And I think we will have to deal with such difference of "common sense" sooner or later. The Tokyo Trial took place early after World War II when there was an atmosphere of "widely supporting punishment", but had to leave room for the defendants to tangle over seemly absurd issues just because no one, even a "righteous" party, can "win" without producing evidence or demand blood for blood.

The Issue concerning Documents and Oral Material

In recent years, some scholars in Nanjing have started to review our previous studies. But meanwhile, some argue that "issues concerning the Nanjing Massacre cannot be solved merely based on historical materials". This statement does not imply the insufficiency of historical materials which is a common problem, but concerns the so-called "emotion and memory". My original proposal included a section about "emotion and memory" but finally excluded this topic for future discussion, considering it is not proper to incidentally and briefly mention a big complicated one that can be easily misunderstood. I admit the particularity of the Nanjing Massacre, but documents-centered historical materials (including writings, oral ones, video, objects and so on) are still indispensable to exploring the original appearance of it—in a way applicable to all historical events since it is one of them. Japanese schools are unanimous in their support to this point, stressing that they themselves have placed high value on historical materials and accusing opponents of misinterpreting, tempering with and even fabricate historical materials. Generally speaking, the contention among different schools shows a benefit in forcing a careful use of historical materials in addition to the increasing discovery. However, those schools, in widely different positions, inevitably have their own preference in terms of interpreting and

---

[42] 『盧溝橋事件の研究』, 東京, 東京大学出版会1996年12月10日第1版.

choosing materials. They prefer to put to good use those to their advantage and disregard those not, since normally one will inevitably focus on what he needs. In terms of "what we need", the obvious question is lacking a fundamental identification of historical materials. What do some documents exactly mean? What they can prove? To what extent? What is the significance of the entire document? Does the excerpt agree with the whole spirit? Is the material itself reliable? In particular, is the veracity of oral records likely to be challenged, such as the interview environment? Have the interviewer guided or dropped some hints to the interviewee? Is what the interviewee said realistic?—All these have not been carefully examined by historical standards. And thus, even having a good sense of righteousness and justice, some outsiders (such as Western scholars) inevitably think that both arguments can hold.

The Issue concerning Photos

The issue concerning photos is separately dealt with because the fabrication school has been most proud of the "examination" of "photos" among all the "achievements", boasting that "none of the photos can be taken as evidence" (see the forgoing section). As historical materials, photos are of special value to the recovery of historical truth as they can duplicate and get across information of physical objects other than "spirit" in an accurate manner that cannot be copied by writings. However, it is also due to this obvious nature that readers outside who have not knew the truth are easily convinced or misled. Nowadays when opinions widely vary (merely in Japan), confirming the veracity has a priority over right and wrong. The issues concerning photos raised by Japanese fictionalists generally involve "political" elements and the foregoing photo where there are no epaulets on military uniform is just an example of it. Meanwhile, there is a problem of arbitrariness with the interpretation of many photos. For example, in Memoir of Japanese Atrocities published in 1938, there is a photo titled "Rural Chinese women from the Jiangnan region who are being abducted by the Japanese army to the Japanese Command, later insulted, gang-raped and shot dead" (Note: Jiangnan region is the areas along the coastline to the south of the Yangtze River), which was long displayed in some museums. But in fact, this one first appeared in Asahi Graph published on November 10th, 1937, originally titled "a group of women and children who are returning to the village from farm work with the assistance of our troops". And it belongs to a series of photos and others are the photographs of picking cotton, with Japanese soldiers after returning to village and so on, which were taken by Japanese army obviously for propagation. We can be forgiven for borrowing this photo to encourage resistance at the most difficult time during the anti-Japanese war, but this does not mean we are justified in ignoring this mistake. Therefore, in order to recover the truth or simply in case of being caught out, it is necessary to thoroughly examine the source and content as well as the interpretation of every so-called "forged" photo. A few years ago, I once planned to explore the source of this photo, but has delayed it for some reason. Based on my general understanding, these photos fall into four categories: The first are those reflecting Japanese atrocities in Nanjing, whose origins are clear, taken by westerns in Nanjing, Japanese journalists and Japanese soldiers; the next are those reflecting Japanese atrocities outside Nanjing or not during the Nanjing Massacre; the third are those specially used for propagation by sections such as the International Propaganda Division of the Kuomintang's Central Propaganda Bureau; and the last are those that need further examination as the veracity is unclear. In addition to photos of atrocities, noticed are those taken as "counter-evidence" presented by Japanese scholars to prove the so-called "non-existence of atrocities". These photos mainly reflect the "close relationship" between Japanese army and Nanjing people, the "peaceful" atmosphere in Nanjing and so on. We can certainly say such photos were taken for propagation which went against the truth. And even if some photos show "real scenes", they merely focus on "certain place", whose situation cannot equate to that of many other places and of the whole country. Hence, these photos cannot be taken as "evidence" to deny the atrocities. Conversely, considering they were taken at the time of the incident, we also cannot disregard them and at least should figure out whether they show performances against the reality designed by a director or real scenes of certain place (even if it is a small corner), which will help us get a full idea of the whole thing. In a word, the fabrication school has "pioneered" the discussion over the issue of photos and it is our duty to give a strong argument against them.

3 Conclusion

As the saying goes, "One can predict the future by reviewing the past". Based on this, the theme of the seminar has included another key word "Potential Trend", which I have annotated as "which might be inevitable trend" in my proposal. Due to the limited space, three points mentioned in my proposal are copied here as a conclusion: First, it has been over seventy years since the incident and historical researchers can study the Nanjing Massacre as a historical event without having to devote themselves to "emotions"; second, we cannot refute the "evidence" presented by Japanese deniers merely based on "righteousness"; third, the recovery of the truth about the Nanjing Massacre cannot be confined to excerpts from materials to our advantage and negative evidence must be dealt with as well. If not so, the actual communication and contention between different opinions at least cannot be realized and then it was unlikely to realize the recovery of historical truth.

(Included in the Proceedings of the Conference on "Chinese Modern History Studies of the Past Thirty Years", Social Sciences Academic Press [CHINA]: 2010./published in *Historical Review*, 2010[4].)

An Introduction to Japan's Existing Historical Material on the Nanjing Massacre

In one year our center (Center for the Tokyo Trial Studies) held a symposium on "8-13 'Songhu Battle'", discussing about a series of photos of the incident acquired by Professor Xiong Yuezhi during his visit to Germany. On Mr. Xiong's invitation, I lectured and at the end, incidentally mentioned Fujioka Nobukatsu's claim of the so-called "forged" photos of Japanese atrocities. I said that importance should be attached to this issue but immediately got interrupted by a retired scholar who believed that "it has nothing to do with Japanese but is up to our Chinese" to determine the facts. As similar opinions were not in the minority and had been heard on many other occasions, I relied there and then, to the effect that we can write off Japanese right-wing scholars' self-justification but cannot ignore the issue itself and that it is necessary to thoroughly study the source, content and "interpretation" of each of the photos that Japanese scholars claimed to be "forged", not only because we are facing the "problem" of being challenged by right-wing scholars but also because photos inherited from previous generations, which will still be "adopted" (this word had no negative connotation when used) in the future, are due for a comprehensive study on the "source" in these days—ten years after the incident. Although I was then talking about the photos, I think we should do the same to other materials such as writings and objects and Japan's relevant studies, especially those involving disagreement. The biggest difference between the Nanjing Incident and other historical events is that it, in the words of previous scholars, involves "the issue of righteousness". But as a historical event, the Nanjing Massacre should permit challenges. Convinced of the truth of the incident, we should not worry about any academic scrutiny and it does not need exemption from scrutiny from the perspective of "practical advantage". By the end of last year when the Documents on the Nanjing Massacre, 28-volume set, was published, Nanjing

University, Nanjing Normal University and other institutions jointly held the "International Academic Seminar on the Historical Material of the Nanjing Massacre", where some "notions that had been widely acknowledged" were discussed for the first time, which means there is "a possibility to have a discussion" on this famous historical event which has been the concern of more than the academic circle. I have been convinced that should we adhere to academic standards and allow more "flexibility", many viewpoints of Japanese right-wing scholars would not hold at all, at least not as popular as now. That is mainly what I have learned from my years of following at the development of relevant Japanese studies and is one of the important reasons why I have been.

"Historical material of the Nanjing Massacre" mentioned here is a usual, broad concept. And there are several points that need explaining in advance. First, the "Nanjing Massacre" is not a popular name in Japan, although the majority of Japanese slaughter school used to take it as the official name for the historical incident which occurred after the fall of Nanjing in 1937, like the work of Hora Tomio. In the Tokyo Trial, this historical event was referred to as "南京暴虐事件" in Kanji (the same as Chinese characters, or as "Nanjing Atrocities" in English or as "南京アトロシティーズ"). Nowadays, in addition to some scholars, such as Tsuda Michio and Ono Kenji, insisting on the "Nanjing Massacre", the majority of Japanese slaughter school refer to it as the "Nanjing Incident". Japanese fabrication school definitely put the words "Nanjing Massacre", if used, in quotes to indicate "the so-called" massacre. And in recent years, some even put the word "incident" in quotes to imply that there was no such "incident" as merely "fabricated". But in general, the "Nanjing Incident" has been "widely acknowledged" in Japan and "material about the Nanjing Massacre" referred to in this article is what Japanese call "documents on the Nanjing Incident", which is not inconsistent with what we usually call. Second, Chinese academic circle has given a clear, strict definition of the Nanjing Massacre, especially of some key points such as the death toll, but has been "easy on" the material used. As for the exact meaning of some material, what can they prove? To what extent? What is the significance of the entire document? Does the excerpt agree with the whole spirit? Is the material itself reliable? And in particular, is the veracity of oral records likely to be challenged, such as whether the interview environment encourages the "freedom of speech"? Have the interviewer guided or dropped some hints to the interviewee? Is what the interviewee said realistic?—All these questions cannot be said to have been strictly examined and well solved from the perspective of history. And that is why different and even contradict conclusions can be reached based on a piece of material. Therefore, this article will not "judge a book from the cover" and all major writings about the "Nanjing Incident" will be discussed, regardless of school.

This article will be divided into two parts, of which the former briefly introduces Japan's relevant historical material while the latter, the key focus of this article, argues for the value of Japan's historical material.

Part I

Opinions on the Nanjing Incident in Japan are usually divided into three schools of thought (the slaughter school, the middle-of-the-road school and the fabrication school) and they all have their own collections as the basis for their argument. The collections can be classified as written documents and oral records in form and as Japanese official and private documents and Japanese versions of Western and Chinese documents according to the sources. And their collections will be, respectively, introduced in chronological order.

The Slaughter School:

1 NANKIN JIKEN

Nankin Jiken (*The Nanjing Incident*) was edited by Hora Tomio and published by Kawade Shobô Shinsha in 1973. This book consists of two volumes and has been included in the *Documents on the Second Sino-Japanese War* (as Volume VIII and IX).[1] Volume I includes the Japanese-language records of the International Military Tribunal for the Far East on the "Nanjing Incident", which can be divided into five parts, namely indictment, shorthand TR, Unpresented Court Evidence (documentary evidence submitted by the prosecution), Unsubmitted Documentary Evidence (by the Prosecution and Defense) and Sentence.

Hora Tomio has devoted a major section of Volume I to an introduction of shorthanded TR, from the answers of Robert O. Wilson (who was then, similarly hereinafter) a doctor at the original University of Nanking Hospital, in the cross-examination by the prosecution and defense on July 25th, 1946, to the 26 issues of the final debate between the prosecution and defense over Matsui Iwane, commander of the Japanese Central China Area Army (CCAA),[2] on April 9th, 1948. And this section can be summarized into five main parts: (1) Wilson, Xu Chuanyin, vice president of the Red Swastika Society, Chen Bao Fu, who was then a resident in Nanjing (the same below, unless otherwise specified), Professor Miner Searle Bates, Captain LIANG Tingfang at Chinese Army Medical Service Corps [sic], Matsui Iwane, Ambassador-at-large Ito Nobumi, Colonel Muto Akira, Deputy Chief of Staff of CCAA, John Gillespie Magee, a priest of Anglican Church, Major Nakayama Yasuto, a staff officer of CCAA, Hidaka Shinrokuro, Counselor of

---

[1] This edition was slightly revised and is still divided into two volumes. It was reprinted by Aoki Bookstore in November 1985 and October of the following year. The title was changed to "Collection of the Nanjing Massacre during Japan-China War".

[2] The reasons why 中支那方面军 cannot be translated into 华中方面军 can refer to my article Ogawa Sekijiro and Diary of A Military Legal Affairs Officer, Shanghai, Historical Review, 2204(1), p. 92, Note 3.

Japanese embassy in Nanjing, Tsukamoto Hirotsugu, a senior official as Chief of Judicial Affairs Department of Shanghai Expeditionary Army (SEF), Ishii Itaro, Director-general of the East Asian Affairs Bureau of Japanese Ministry of Foreign Affairs, Colonel Nakasawa Mitsuo, Chief of Staff of the 16th Division, Major General Iinuma Mamoru, Chief of Staff of SEF, and Okada Takashi, a special assistant of SEF, take the witness stand for the cross-examination by the prosecution, the defense or both sides. (2) The prosecution presents the written testimony of Shang Deyi, Wu Changde, Chen Fubao, Liang Tingfang, Professor Lewis S. C. Smythe at the University of Nanking, George A. Fitch, member of Young Men's Christian Association, Chen Ruifang James H. McCallum, a priest of American Christian Mission, Sun Yongcheng, Li Disheng, Luosong-shi, Wu Jingcai, Zhu Diwen & Zhang Dixiang (recorded in a document), Wangkang-shi, Hu Duxin, Wangchen-shi, Wu Zhuoqing, Yin Wangze,[3] Wangpan-shi, Wuzhang-shi and Chenjia-shi as well as Matsui Iwane's statement issued on December 19th, 1937; in second part also included are the report of Japanese atrocities[4] presented by Xiang Rongjun and other people on behalf of the prosecution, the *Documents of the Nanking Safety Zone* edited by Hsu Shu-hsi,[5] Jasu's testimony in the report of Nanjing District Court prosecution, the report of American embassy in Nanjing on the situation of Nanjing from December 1937 to the next year, Muto Akira's interrogation record and a summary of Proceedings of the 73rd Budget Committee Meeting of the House of Councillors of the National Diet of Japan (where Okura Kinmochi is the questioner while Kido Koichi is the answerer). (3) The court meet to discuss whether Matsui Iwane's statement on December 18th, 1937, and "Message to Urge the Surrender of Nanking" on December 9th of the same year as well as the speech delivered by the director of Intelligence Department of the Ministry of Foreign Affairs of Japan published in *The Japan Times* on December 1st, 1937, and the report on Matsui's "assistance" to the establishment of Nanking Safety Zone by Jaquinot and other people published in *Tokyo Nichi Nichi Shimbun* on November 16th of the same year can be taken as evidence for the defendants (which turns out to be dismissed). (4) Attorneys for the defense present the written testimony of Hidaka Shinrokuro, Tsukamoto Hirotsugu, Nakayama Yasuto, Ishii Itaro, Kido Koichi, minister of Education, Second Lieutenant Ohsugi Hiroshi, Leader of the Observation Squad of the 1st Battalion of the 3rd Field Artillery Regiment of the 3rd Division, Second

---

[3] Tomio Hora believed it as the misunderstanding of the Yin Wangze. 『日中戦争史資料』8「南京事件」I written by Tomio Hora, Tokyo, 河出書房, November 25th, 1973, the 1st version, P137.

[4] The "sadistic" behavior can generally be equated with atrocity. The two were used together in the Tokyo Trial, but the meanings are different. So the original text in this article will not be changed.

[5] The Chinese name is 南京安全区档案.

Lieutenant Ouchi Yoshihide, acting leader the 7th Squadron of the 9th Mountain Artillery Regiment of the 9th Division, Colonel Wakisaka Jiro, leader of the 36th Regiment of the 9th Division, Major Nishijima Tsuyoshi, leader of the 1st Battalion of the 19th Infantry Regiment, Nakasawa Mitsuo, Iinuma Mamoru, Ogawa Sekijiro, a senior official as Chief of Judicial Affairs Department of the 10th Army, Major Sakakibara Kazue, a staff officer of SEF, and Shimonaka Yasaburo, a member of Japanese Greater Asia Association Council, the letter of John D. Rabe, chairman of International Committee for the Nanking Safety Zone (Abstract), the written testimony of James H. McCallum (Abstract), the report by James Espy, a vice-consul of American embassy in Nanjing, the telegram from Joseph Clark Grew, the US ambassador to Japan, to the US Department of State on February 4th, 1938, Matsui Iwane's "Instructions" issued on December 18th, 1937, and the "Jinshan Temple Notice" issued by SEF, the photo of the ordination platform of Guanyin Hall built by Matsui Iwane, his statement on December 18th, 1937, and his "Message to the People of Republic of China". (5) The prosecution and defense present their cases and argue over them.

Unpresented court evidence includes (1) the slaughter of enemies reported by Nanjing charity and Jasu, (2) the Statistics of Suzendo Burial Team on Corpses Buried and (3) the Statistics of the Burial Squad of the Rescue Team of the Red Swastika Society on Corpses Buried.

Documentary evidence unsubmitted involves both the prosecution and the defense. The former includes: (1) the report of murder race in *Tokyo Nichi Nichi Shimbun*, (2) Okada Katsuo's sworn affidavit, (3) the deposition of Witness Huang Junxiang, (4) Frank Tillman Durdin's statement, (5) the *Truth about Japanese Troops' Slaughtering Nanjing Civilians and Disarming Soldiers and The Red Swastika Society's Burying Bodies*, (6) the *Photographs of the Burial Site of the Victims of the 1937 Nanjing Massacre* and (7) China's Confirmation of Crimes against Humanity Committed by Japanese Army (the original copy of the letter of Chinese government). And the latter includes (1) an abstract of a report in *Tokyo Nichi Nichi Shimbun* on December 10th, 1937 (titled "Wounded Soldiers Shut Out – Inhuman Chinese Army"), (2) an abstract of a report in *Tokyo Nichi Nichi Shimbun* on December 10th, 1937 (titled "The Crazy Destruction of the Chinese Army Surprising Foreign Military Experts") and (3) an abstract of a report in *Tokyo Nichi Nichi Shimbun* (North China Edition) on April 16th, 1938 (titled "Corpse Disposal Facing the Rampant Epidemic and the Active Actions of the Epidemic Prevention Commission").

And "Sentence" covers (1) the indictment in Section 8 of Chapter 2 Law (delivered on November 4th, 1948), (2) the part that deals with the Nanking Massacre in Chapter 8 Conventional War Crimes, (3) the sentence of Matsui Iwane in Chapter 10 Judgment and (4) the Part II "'Precise' War Crimes and the 54th and 55th Cause of Action concerning Ordinary People in Areas Occupied by Japan" of Section 6 "Precise War Crimes" of the Dissenting Opinions of Judge Radha Binod Pal.

Volume II involves four kinds of documents, in addition to interpretations. They are (1) *What War Means: the Japanese Terror in China* by H. J. Timperley,[6] (2) *Documents of the Nanking Safety Zone* edited by Hsu Shuhsi, *War Damage in the Nanking Area, December 1937 to March 1938: Urban and Rural Surveys* edited by Lewis S. C. Smyth and (4) the reports by F. T. Durdin, the Nanjing correspondent for the *New York Times*.

This book includes the materials on which the initial determination of the "Nanjing Incident" was based but opinions vary on the interpretation of those materials. Its case is similar to the Tokyo Trial. The Tokyo Trial has been questioned and resented[7] since the beginning, but one, regardless of his stand, has to confront the evidence and conclusions of the Tokyo Trial because it is an "internationally acknowledged" authority. In terms of the disputes over the Nanjing Massacre in Japan, almost all major arguments can be dated back to the Tokyo Trial. That is to say, this book is still of irreplaceable value, although the understanding of the Nanjing Massacre has developed with more leeway for discussion due to the increasing discovery of various documents, especially the change from court debate to that of the "academic circle".[8]

---

[6] The Chinese name is "外人目睹中之日军暴行".

[7] It is widely known that at the Tokyo Trial, Justice Radha Binod Pal argued that all defendants shall be acquitted (Pal is "widely respected" in Japan and many places have his monument, such as Yasukuni Shrine, Kyoto Lingshan Patriotic Shrine, Hiroshima Honsuji Temple and Toyama Patriotic Shrine). In fact, Pal was not alone. Major General Charles A. Willoughby, who was head of the 2nd Section (G II) under General Staff of American Occupation Forces and known as MacArthur's confidant, once said to Holland Justice B. V. A. Rling of the Tokyo Trial, "This Trial is an unprecedented show of the worst kind of hypocrisy"(小菅信行訳 & 粟原憲太郎解説『レーリンク判事の東京裁判』. Tokyo: Shinchôsha. 1st Edition published on August 31, 1996: p. 140). And Ruling himself, after seeing the "scorched earth" due to air bombardment in Japan, also think the Tokyo Trial, as Higashijo has claimed, is a party of winning states" since the winning states will not be judged by the law of war but the defeated will (ibid., p. 143). Besides, there is also another kind of "dissatisfaction" with the Tokyo Trial. For example, Chinese Justice Mei Ju-ao said, "The trial of the first case was prolonged and the US was increasingly eager to restore Japanese militarism. The Supreme Commander of the Allied Forces MacArthur instructed the International Inspection Service (an agency entirely controlled by the USA) to release, without authorization, the remaining 40 Class A war criminals in two batches on the excuse of "inadequate evidence and thus exemption from prosecution" (Mei Ju-ao. On Hisao Tani, Matsui Iwane and The Nanjing Incident. In Committee of Literature and Historical Material Research of CPPCC. (Ed.), Selected Cultural and Historical Materials: Volume 22. Beijing: China Literature and History Publishing House. 1st Edition published in December of 1986, p. 22). The Communist Party of Japan still criticizes the emperor's exemption. For example, some people said, "The Emperor Showa was the only person responsible for the whole process of the Japanese war from the invasion of Northeast China in 1931 (the so-called Manchurian Incident) to the defeat in 1945. But it was decided from the beginning that he would be exempted … This can be said to be the weakness of the Tokyo trial"(「東京裁判は『勝者の裁き』という意見をどう考える?」,『赤旗』2005年7月9日).

[8] Both Japanese left-wing and right-wing claimed to stick to the "academic" standard and accused the other side of politicization.

2   Documents on the Nanjing Incident

Documents on the Nanjing Incident was edited by Nankin Jiken Chosa Kenkyu Kai (Research Committee on the Nanjing Incident)[9] and published by Aoki Shoten in October 1992. It consists of two volumes, "American Documents" and "Chinese Documents".

Volume I includes an introductory remark, Part I "The Nanjing Incident as Recorded in Documents", Part II "The Nanjing Incident as Seen in News" and an appendix "Interview Materials by F. T. Durdin and Archibald T. Steele". And Part I examines (1) air raids on Nanjing, (2) USS Panay and Ladybird Incident, (3) situation in Nanjing, (4) Nanking International Safety Zone and (5) atrocities committed by Japanese army. Volume II covers an introductory remark, Part I "The Nanjing Incident as Recorded in News", Part II "The Nanjing Incident as seen in Writings", Part III "Burial Records", Part IV "Documents on the Nanjing Trial", Appendix I "Chinese Documents concerning the Nanjing Incident" and Appendix II "Content of Major Chinese Documents".

Volume II is mainly based on *Historical Material of The Nanjing Massacre Perpetrated by Japanese Invaders* edited by Nanjing Library, *Documents on the Nanjing Massacre Perpetrated by Japanese Invaders* co-edited by the Second Historical Archives of China and Nanjing (SHAC) and the Nanjing Municipal Archives, *The Battle of Nanjing: A Former KMT General's Personal Experience* edited by Committee of Cultural and Historical Data of CPPCC and Documents of Revolutions edited by KMT Party History Committee as well as some newspapers such as *Ta Kung Pao*.

It is the first time[10] that most of the Material, for which it is a tough thing to search, in Volume I has been mentioned. And edited by neither Chinese nor Japanese, this volume at least will not have a bias towards either side just because of "national sentiment". That is why it has a special significance.

3   Nankin Jiken Kyoto Shidan kankei shiryoshu

Nankin Jiken Kyoto Shidan kankei shiryoshu was edited by Iguchi kazuki, Kisaka Junjiro and Shimozato Masaki and published by Aoki Shoten in December 1989. This book includes the diaries of Masuda Rokusuke, Ueba Takeichiro, Kitayama Kazu, Makihara Nobuo and Azuma Shiro, who were soldiers of the 20th Infantry Regiment (Fukuchiyama) of the 16th Division (Kyoto) of the Imperial Japanese Army, notes of Masuda Rokusuke,

---

[9] Nankin Jiken Chosa Kenkyu Kai (Research Committee on the Nanjing Incident) is a research group of Japanese slaughter school. It was founded in March 1984 and consists of over 20 members, including teacher, journalist, lawyer and so on. Small as it is, it has had great achievements.

[10] For a long time, Japan has been ahead of us in material collection and related research. For example, Yale University's documents, such as the one of Miner Selle Betas, were often reported as major discoveries when introduced or compiled in China. But in fact, Japanese scholars have already used them, and "we" happen to "share a opinion".

Ueba Takeichiro's notes, the wartime log of the 4th Squadron of the 20th Regiment and the after-war report of the 12th Squadron of the 20th Regiment. Besides, there are also two explanatory articles, namely "The War Exhibit Movement in Kyoto and Documents Discovered" by Iguchi kazuki and "The Capture of Nanking and Junior Soldiers" by Shimozato Masaki.

This book is the first one to have original wartime records of Japanese soldiers to be aired in large quantities.[11] And since the 16th Division was one of major Japanese forces who attacked Nanjing, it is said to be the "voluntary confession" of those perpetrators. Therefore, we can actually learn about the "direct and indirect causes"[12] for the Nanjing Massacre from this book, as Shimozato Masaki, one of the editors, puts it.

4 NANKING DAIGYAKUSATSU O KIROKUSHITA KOGUN HEISHITACH

Nanking Daigyakusatsu o Kirokushita Kogun Heishitach (*Imperial Army Soldiers Who Recorded the Nanjing Massacre*) was edited by Ono Kenji, Fujiwara Akira and Honda Katsuichi and was published by Otsuki Shoten in March 1996. This book includes 19 diaries of junior officers and soldiers, of which sixteen (such as Saito Jiro) were from the 65th Infantry Regiment (Aizuwakamatsu) of the Yamada Detachment[13] and three (such as Kondo Eijiro)[14] were from the 19th Mountain Artillery Regiment (Echigo-takada) of the 13th Division (Sendai) of Imperial Japanese Army.

The chief editor of this book, Ono Kenji, is a researcher beyond academic circles (and claims to be a "worker"). And interviews and material gathering which took him many years were carried out in his leisure time, which is not an easy task[15] and thus is appreciated. This book most importantly proves most of 140,000 Chinese soldiers captured by the "Morozuno Detachment"[16] at Mufushan were shot dead as reported in wartime.[17]

---

[11] There were some books written based on the diaries of soldiers of the 20th Regiment before, but they did not include the original text (下里正樹著『隠された聯隊史＿＿20i下級兵士の見た南京事件の実相』、東京、青木書店,1987年11月30日第1版;同氏著『続·隠された聯隊史＿＿MG中隊員の見た南京事件の実相』、東京,青木書店,1988年7月15日第1版).

[12] 下里正樹著「南京攻略と下級兵士＿＿資料解題を兼ねて」、井口和起、木坂順一郎、下里正樹編『南京事件京都師団関係資料集』、東京,青木書店,1989年12月5日第1版、第485頁).

[13] It was a troop of the 103rd Brigade and the team leader was Major-General Yamada Senji. The 65th Infantry Regiment (Aizuwakamatsu) and the 19th Mountain Artillery Regiment (Echigo-takada) (the 3rd Battalion thereunder attended the battle of Nanjing) were under its command.

[14] The authors of the diaries included in this book are all replaced with pseudonym and thus will not be listed one by one.

[15] I once asked Mr. Ono whether he felt any pressure. And he matter-of-factly told me that he had been used to the "cold eyes" and the comment as "weird".

[16] The leader of the 65th Regiment was Morozuno Sakuhajime.

[17] According to Japanese middle-of-the-road school, "On December 14, the Yamada detachment captured a group of 14,000 surrenders near the Mufushan Fortress. And then 6,000 non-combatants were released and the remaining approximately 8,000 were taken prisoner. But

5   *Nankinsen-tozasareta kioku o tazunete: moto heishi 102-nin no shogen*

Nankinsen-tozasareta kioku o tazunete: moto heishi 102-nin no shogen (*The Battle of Nanjing: Searching for Forbidden Memories- Testimonies of 102 veterans*) was edited by Matsuoka Tamaki and was published by Shakai Hyôronsha in August 2002. This book consists of testimonies from 102 Japanese veterans, six from the 9th Division (Kanazawa), five from the 3rd Division (Nogoya), one from the 6th Division (Kumamoto), four from the 2nd Anchorage of the 38th Brigade and most (85) from the 16th Division, of which 59 served in the 33rd Regiment.

This book covers interviews of the largest number of people and thus the efforts Ms Matsuoka Tamaki and Lin Boyao, a Chinese businessman in Japan, made "against the main trend" are appreciated. However, there is also a different voice on this book among Japanese slaughter school.[18]

The Middle-of-the-road School:

6   Documents on the Battle of Nanjing

Documents on the Battle of Nanjing was edited by Battle of Nanking Editorial Committee and published by Kaikosha in November 1989. This book is divided into seven parts, namely diaries, battle orders, notes/instructions/combat briefings/wartime ten-day reports/detailed combat reports/wartime logs, Chinese intelligence, third-party intelligence, notes of war history researches and international rules and customs of warfare, of which the former three parts matter most.

Part I Diaries includes *Matsui Iwane Taishono jinchu nikki* (*The Battlefield Diary of General Matsui Iwane*), *General Matsui and Excerpts of The Marco Polo Bridge Incident Journal*, *General Hata Shunroku's Diary (Abstract)*,

---

on the evening of the 15th, a fire broke out in the asylum, and about half of them fled, leaving only about 4,000 people. In order to release these 4,000 people, they were brought to the vicinity of Guanyin Gate in the evening on the 17th. But a riot somewhat happened and caused the sacrifice of one official and six soldiers. At self-defense, the escort troop had the rioting prisoners raked with GM. About 1,000 people were killed and others fled" (南京戦史編輯委員会編纂『南京戦史』, 非売品, 東京, 偕行社1989年11月3日第1版, 第324325頁). This statement has been included in Japanese authoritative war history writing (for details, please refer to防衛庁防衛研修所戦史室編『戦史叢書支那事変陸軍作戦〈1〉昭和13年1月まで』, 東京, 朝雲新聞社1975年7月20日第1版, 第437頁).

[18]The right-wing group greatly criticized this book, which was only to be expected. However, upon the publication, it also received criticism from the left-wing group. See An Analysis on the Annual of the Japan Association for Nanjing Studies. Beijing: Modern History Studies, 2003 (6), p. 189, Note 1.

Sugiyama[19]*'s Letters, Iinuma Mamoru's Diary, Uemura Toshimichi's Diary, Sergeant Kanemaru Yoshio's Notes, Major General Sasaki Toichi's Diary, Yamazaki Masao's Diary, Kisaki Hisashi's Diary, Izu Kazuo's Diary, Oriono Suetaro's Dairy, Orita Mamoru's Diary, Second Lieutenant Maeda Yoshihiko's Dairy, Ike Yuichi's Diary, A First-year Soldier's Diary, Mizutani Sho's Diary, Makihara Shouta's Diary, Shoji (Yoshida) Masaaki's Diary, Masuda Rokusuke's Dairy* and *Navy Doctor Colonel Yasuyama Koudou's Diary Kept During the Shanghai Battle.* Part II Combat Orders include orders issued by the central agencies (such as General Staff Office and headquarter), the area armies, divisions directly thereunder and brigades. And the third part covers relevant documents from the central to grassroots levels (battalion and squadron).

This book was edited by a Japanese organization of retired military servicemen and its editorial board members were veterans except Itakura Yoshiaki (who wrote the *Honto wa ko datta Nankin jiken*). As we can learn from the title, this book, strictly speaking, is not a collection of documents on the "Nanjing Massacre" or on the "Nanjing Incident". But since only a few relevant documents remain after Japanese authority issued top-down orders to burn down wartime documents both at the end of the war and before the Tokyo Trial, such documents concerning "the battle", are still of value to showing in a broad sense what Japanese troops perpetrated. And a feature of the diaries in this book is that they were written by military soldiers from all ranks, including but not limited to the generals, greatly different from those edited by the slaughter school, which only include those of soldiers and officials at low ranks.

7 DOCUMENTS ON THE BATTLE OF NANJING: VOLUME II

Documents on the Battle of Nanjing: Volume II was edited by Battle of Nanking Editorial Committee and published by Kaikosha in December 1993. It's mainly diaries but also includes some other documents. And although it is titled "Volume II", it was not a scheduled one when *Documents on the Battle of Nanjing* was edited as *Documents on the Battle of Nanjing* was not titled "Volume I" and there is some repetition between two books. This book includes *Matsui Iwane Taishō no jinchū nikki* (in full), *General Matsui and Excerpts of The Marco Polo Bridge Incident Journal* (the same as in former book), *General Hata Shunroku's Diary (Abstract)* (same as above), *Sugiyama's Letters* (same as above), *Conversations between General Matsui and Yamamoto Sanehiko, Major General Kawabe Torashiro's Memoir, Central-government Policies and Strategies Against China, Uemura Toshimichi's Diary* (which starts from December 1st in former book while from August 15th in this one), *Yamada Senji's Diary, Morozuno Sakuhajime's Notes, Arasaka Sumurai's Diary, Otera Kawamura's Diary, Sugawara*

---

[19] It refers to General Sugiyama Hajime who was then the minister of the Army.

Shigetoshi's Diary, Wartime Log of the 12th Squadron of the 36th Infantry Regiment, Wartime Log of the 47th Infantry Regiment, Operations of the 1st Chariot Squadron, Ota Toshio's Confession, Takayuyi Takeo's Diary, Rules of Treatment as to POWs, Official List of Relations in China Incident, Imperial Japanese Headquarter of The Army Officer—Lieutenant Colonel Nishi Yoshiaki's Report, The Design, Construction and Function of the Fortifications in Nanjing, Shanghai and Hangzhou, The Construction of Nanjing Reserve Positions and the Battle of Guarding the City, "Joining the Army is a Walking Tour"—Sato Shinju's Dairy and *Nankin! Nankin!—A Piece of Anonymous, Monthly News Review.*

Japanese right-wing forces always say it's "unfortunate" that wartime documents have been burnt. They seem to think they can redress wrongs done to Japanese army if those documents have not.[20] But at that time, Japanese military and political authority as well as those involved regarded those documents as a potential danger that needed destroying, fearing any one of them missed. For instance, Matsui Iwane claimed his diary had been burned in Tokyo Trial but in fact had not. The "full text"[21] of Matsui Iwane's diary included in this book was "discovered" after the publication of the former book by Hara Takeshi (who belongs to small slaughter school), a researcher of The Office of War History of the National Institute for Defense Studies under Ministry of Defense. And other diaries of Japanese senior officials included both in this book and the former book matter a lot in developing a thorough understanding of the background of the "Nanjing Incident" and the decisions of the highest level of Japanese army, especially CCAA and SEF.

The Fabrication School:

8 NANJING INCIDENT-THEY TOLD US

Nanjing Incident-They Told Us was edited by Ara Kenichi and published by Tosho Shuppansha in August 1987. This book includes 35 interviews and an addendum. The interviews include *The Testimony of Captain Onishi Hajime, Staff Officer of Shanghai Expeditionary Army, The testimony of Mr. Okada Takashi, Attached to General Matsui, The Testimony Major Okada Yuji, Staff Officer of Special Duty Department of SEF, The Testimony of Mr. Kanazawa Yoshio, Photographer of Tokyo Nichi Nichi Shimbun, The Testimony of Mr. Jiro Futamura, Photographer of Hochi Shimbun Newspaper, The Testimony of Mr. Goto Kosaku, Reporter of Osaka Mainichi Shimbun,*

---

[20] For instance, Kenichi Matsumoto (a professor with Reitaku University) who holds a centrist view said, "there remain such a few official documents on Japan's engagement in the Battle of Nanjing that Mr. Hora denies China's claim of 30000 people killed which was not based on any specific statistics or documents, but instead argues for a death toll of 20,000 people and gains popularity"(秦郁彦、東中野修道、松本健一「問題は捕虜処断をどう見るか」, 『諸君!』, 東京, 文藝春秋社, 2001年第2期, 第132页).

[21] The "missing" part of Matsui's diary is from August 15 to October 31.

The Testimony of Major Yoshinaga Sunao, Staff Officer of the 10th Army, *The Testimony of Colonel Tanida Isamu, Staff Officer of the 10th Army*, *The Testimony of Captain Kaneko Rinsuke, Staff Officer, 10th Army*, *The Testimony of Mr. Suzuki Jiro, Reporter of Tokyo Nichi Nichi Shimbun*, *The Testimony of Mr. Sato Shinju, Photographer of Tokyo Nichi Nichi Shimbun*, *The Testimony of Mr. Arai Masayoshi, Reporter of Domei Tsushin*, *The Testimony of Mr. Asai Tatsuzo, Photographer of Domei Tsushin*, *The Testimony of Mr. Adachi Kazuo, Reporter of Tokyo Asahi Shimbun*, *The Testimony of Mr. Tomisaburo Hashimoto, Vice-chief of Shanghai Branch of Asahi Shimbun*, *The Testimony of Mr. Taguchi Risuke, Reporter of Hochi Shimbun Newspaper*, *The Testimony of Mr. Koike Shuyo, Reporter of Miyako Shimbun*, *The Testimony of Mr. Higuchi Tetsuo, Film Operator of Yomiuri Shimbun Newspaper*, *The Testimony of Mr. Hosonami Takashi, Radio Operator of Domei Tsushin*, *The Testimony of Lieutenant Commander Terasaki Takaharu, Captain of the Gunboat Seta*, *The Testimony of Mr. Mitoma Mikinosuke, Reporter of Fukuoka Nichinichi Shimbun*, *The Testimony of Mr. Sumitani Iwane, Painter and Naval Correspondent*, *The Testimony of Commander Doi Shinji, Captain of the Gunboat Hira*, *The Testimony of Mr. Watanabe Yoshio, Photographer of Information Department of Ministry of Foreign Affairs*, *The Testimony of Mr. Yamamoto Osamu, Staff of Shanghai Branch of Osaka Asahi Shimbun*, *The Testimony of Mr. Mori Hiroshi, Photographer of Yomiuri Shimbun Newspaper*, *The Testimony of Lieutenant Shigemura Minoru, Member of Press Bureau of Shanghai Military Office in the Navy*, *The Testimony of Mr. Matsumoto Shigeharu, Chief of Shanghai Branch of Domei Tsushin*, *The Testimony of Mr. Yauchi Shogoro, Reporter of Fukushima Minpo*, *The Testimony of Lieutenant Commander Genda Minoru, Staff Officer of the 2nd Combined Air Group*, *The Testimony of Mr. Okada Yoshimasa, Officer of Planning Board*, *The Testimony of Mr. Eiichi Iwai, Assistant Consulate*, *The Testimony of Mr. Koyanagi Jiichi, Member of the Press Corps of Japanese Army*, *The Testimony of Mr. Kasuya Yoshio, Assistant Consulate*, and *The Testimony of Colonel Mikuni Naofuku, Commander of the 22nd Field Artillery Regiment*. And the part of addendum introduces the circumstances of getting in contact with 32 persons who were in Nanjing and were still alive, such as Colonel Matsuda Chiaki, Staff Officer of SEF. Some persons themselves refused the interview or their families refused considering their old age, some passed away during the process of getting in contact and a few gave a brief answer. Among those who refused the interview, most believed it was of no use to talk about the nonexistent "Nanjing Massacre" while a few were not willing to talk about the topic as they doubt about Ara Kenichi's position. For example, Asami Kazuo, reporter of Tokyo Nichi Nichi Shimbun, who reported the "murder race" (whose perpetrators were sentenced to death in Nanjing Trial after the war) at the time of the incident, specially explained when refusing, "I hope you will not go for a chorus of militarism that denies this 'century' massacre".[22]

[22] 阿羅健一編『聞き書南京事件』, 東京, 図書出版社1987年8月15日第1版, 第294页。

9 THE NANJING INCIDENT: JAPANESE EYEWITNESS ACCOUNTS— TESTIMONY FROM 48 JAPANESE WHO WERE THERE

The Nanjing Incident: Japanese Eyewitness Accounts—Testimony from 48 Japanese Who Were There were edited by Ara kenichi and published by Shogakukan Bunko in January 2002. This book was a new revised edition based on *Nanjing Incident-They Told Us* (bunko edition),[23] where some parts of a few interviews and the full text of *The Testimony of Mr. Matsumoto Shigeharu, Chief of Shanghai Branch of Domei Tsushin* were deleted. Besides, some additional statements were included in this book, namely the testimonies[24] of Mr. Minami Masayoshi, Reporter of Shin-Aichi Shimbun, Colonel Isayama Haruki, Chief of General Affairs of General Staff Headquarters, and Major Otsuki Akira, Officer of Military Formation Team of Military Affairs Section of the Military Affairs Bureau of the Ministry of the Army as well as an introduction by Ms. Sakurai Yoshiko, an article "Facing the Popularity of the Bunko Edition" by the publisher and a new postscript by Ara Kenichi. Sakurai Yoshiko regards this book as "Class-A material" on the "Nanjing Incident". And Ara Kenichi specially emphasizes in the new postscript that Japanese army in Nanjing did "execute" soldiers but did not commit any crime against civilians, which makes the biggest difference between the new postscript and the original one.

There are also documents collection that are the mere translation of existing Chinese documents or Chinese field reports, like the *Shogen Nankin daigyakusatsu: senso to wa nani ka* translated by Kagami Mitsuyuki and Himeta Mitsuyoshi (1st Edition published by Aoki Shoten in 1984) and the *Nankin jiken genchi chōsa hōkokusho* (Field Report on the Nanjing Incident) (published by Nankin Jiken Chosa Kenkyukai and Yoshida Lab, Department of Sociology, Hitotsubashi University in 1985), which will not be further discussed.

In addition to collections, there are also separate articles, diaries, memoirs and interviews, etc. They are in large quantities and mostly cover a part of the topic. Those which create a more complete narrative have been widely spread in China (such as *Azuma Shiro's Diary*[25] whose Chinese version was

---

[23] Japanese bunko edition is roughly the size of a postcard. It is designed to be portable, ensuring you can read it in intervals during work or between public and private affairs. The Bunko edition has a high circulation in Japan, to some extent, indicating the view of fictionalists were more popular before.

[24] The main part includes 37 "testimonies" and the Addendum includes 11 short letters.

[25] The well-known "Trial of Azuma Shiro" in recent years is a debate over Azuma's account (『わが南京プラトーン』 was based on the diary and published in 1987. And the diary was published later, Chinese version in 1999 and Japanese version in 2001). After the publication, Azuma gave me one. I then compared it with various historical materials and felt that it was generally credible. However, since the diary was compiled and transcribed after the war and some of the later content was also occasionally included, the mainstream of the slaughter school mostly do not adopt it. (In the Trial of Azuma Shiro, neither Japanese communist party nor Social Democratic Party supported the diary.)

published earlier than its original version and *Diary of the Japanese-Chinese War—The Battlefield Experiences of A Transportation Regiment Soldier*[26] which has been selected and translated) and others are translation versions of foreign documents (such as Hirano Kyoko's *Nankin no shinjitsu*[27] which was partly translated from John Rabe's Diary). I thus introduce three kinds of materials that have not attracted enough attention in Japan, and others will be referred to in Part II.

Journal of Judicial Affairs Department of the 10th Army of Imperial Japanese Army

Journal of Judicial Affairs Department of the 10th Army of Imperial Japanese Army was included in Takahashi Masae's *Special Issue of Documents on the Modern History*, Chapter 6 "Military Police", the edition published by Misuzu Shobô in 1982. This book basically does not deal with Nanjing and thus Japanese schools of thought do not pay attention to it. But as mentioned above, considering a large quantities of Japanese documents were burned when Japan was defeated, this book, the "last remaining"[28] journal of Judicial Affairs Department of the 10th Army, under which troops were all involved in the "Nanjing Incident" (of which the 6th and 114th division were the major forces attacking Nanjing while the 18th division and Kunisaki detachment,[29] respectively, captured Wuhu and Pukou so as to cut off Nanjing from reinforcements) matters a lot: The performance of the 10th Army before capturing Nanjing not only plays a significant role in showing general condition of Japanese military discipline but also can be used as a yardstick by which to compare the operations of the 10th Army, even of SEF, after capturing Nanjing.[30]

---

[26]江口圭一、芝原拓自編『日中戦争従軍日記――一輜重兵の戦場体験』, 東京, 法律文化出版社1989年4月25日第1版。

[27]This book is an abridged translation but includes the complete report to Hitler that Rabe wrote after returning from China (ジョン・ラーベ著, エルヴィン・ヴィッケルト編, 平野卿子訳『南京の真実』, 東京, 講談社1997年10月9日第1版, 第289321頁). And the so-called "complete report" in the Chinese version of John Rabe's Diary is a letter before the report. See John Rabe's Diary. Jiangsu People's Publishing House & Jiangsu Education Publishing House. 1st Edition published in August 1997, p. 704. (And the Documents on the Nanjing Massacre Vol.13 John Rabe's Diary are also the letter rather than the complete report. See 1st Edition published by Jiangsu People's Publishing House in January 2006: p. 588.)

[28]It is a generalization that the editor of Japanese Modern History Documents claimed it to be "the last remaining" (高橋正衛編集、解説『続・現代史資料』6『軍事警察』, 東京, みすず書房1982年2月26日第1版, 前言第32頁) since the Proceeding of Court Martial of CCAA can be taken as, not as it is, the journal of the Judicial Affairs Department.

[29]It originally belonged to the 9th Infantry Brigade of the 5th Division of the Northern China Area Army and was incorporated into the 10th Army after its establishment. And the team leader was Major General Kunizaki Nobunaga, head of the Brigade.

[30]See my article "A Study of the Bearing and Discipline of the Japanese Army Invading China: Centered on The Tenth Army", Modern Chinese History Studies, 2004(3): pp. 136–183.

Proceedings of Court Martial of CCAA

Proceedings of Court Martial of CCAA was also included in Takahashi Masae's book. CCAA did not have a judicial affairs department and thus the court martial existed as an agency less than a month. The *Proceedings* mostly includes the cases of the 10th Army as well as a few "deserter" cases of SEF, which can be a complement to the former book.

Diary of a Military Legal Affairs Officer

Diary of A Military Legal Affairs Officer was not aired until recent days. The diary of Ogawa Sekijiro, who was Chief of Judicial Affairs Department of the 10th Army, just can be cross-referenced to the journal of Judicial Affairs Department of the 10th Army. And his diary is more than a record of the military discipline of the 10th Army. It can be a proof that Ogawa's testimony for the defense in Tokyo Trial was not truthful (which will be further discussed later) and that Japanese military records in the wartime had misrepresented the facts.[31]

Part II

It is undeniable that the long-standing controversy in Japan over the Nanjing Massacre has some thing to do with the "stance". But the shortage of first-hand documents can be said to have left much leeway for "different opinions". Then what can Japan's existing materials argue for? And to what extent? Which are still in doubt? Which need further proof?—These will be summarized with significance taken into account.

10 SECTION 1

Attacking Nanjing Was Predetermined or "Unexpected" by Shanghai Expeditionary Army?

It has been accepted by many domestic scholars that the August-13 Incident was a proactive action initiated by China.[32] But it was far from the fact that Japanese massive forces were sent to Shanghai to reactively "protect Japanese in China", although they failed to steal a march. The argument that Japanese

---

[31] See my article "Ogawa Sekijiro and Diary of A Military Legal Affairs Officer", Historical Review, pp. 92–105.

[32] First, the word "accept" does not mean this has long been the claim of Japanese mainstream (now the mainstream of Western academic circles also considers China to be the initiator, such as "Cambridge History of China, Vol. 12: Republic China") but implies China always claimed Japan to be the initiator from the beginning of the war to the early 1980s. For example, the Chinese commander at the beginning of the battle later recalled the plan and attack to "seize the initiative" (For details, please see the first and the fifth subsection of Section 5 "Another Anti-Japanese Operation: The August-13 Incident and The Battle of Shanghai" of Memoirs of Zhang Zhizhong, Chinese Literature and History Press. 1st Edition published in

military was reactive can be dated back to the defense for and the representation of Matsui Iwane in Tokyo Trial.[33] And this argument has made its mark in the controversy over the Nanjing Massacre as it implies that attacking Nanjing was not predetermined but was a "unexpected" decision subject to the war situation and thus "a few" atrocities in Nanjing, if any, were accidents in that background.

We do not have to deny that Japan did deliver a speech of "protecting the life, property and interests of Japanese in China" when sending troops and that General Staff Headquarter issued two notices of bounder limits.[34] However, this does not mean attacking Nanjing was an "unexpected" or "forced" choice. We had better place this issue in a broader context. We can learn that "gekokujo" had long been a common phenomenon in Japanese military since the Showa era. And it became a constant reality that front army "went uncontrolled". This cannot be simply summarized into the saying that "a field commander must decide even against king's order". And to say that by that time Japan had established the "autonomy system" of front army is anything but an exaggeration.[35] A series of events, from the Huanggutun and Liutiaogou explosions to the establishment of Manchukuo, are obvious examples where the grassroots level initiated the action and then the central government "had to" confirm it. And it was the same case after the Marco

---

February 1985, pp. 111–122). However, in the "Telegraph on the War of Resistance Against Japan", Zhang said, "In the afternoon of the 13th, the brutal Japanese army invaded Shanghai. Its fleet suddenly bombarded Zhabei with heavy artillery, and then the infantry crossed the border and attacked the defense positions of our General Security Regiment. Our regiment could not stand it and opened fire. Zhizhong was ordered to lead his soldiers to support to defend our land that our ancestors had striven hard for and to fight for the survival of 45 million descendants of Yan Di and Huang Di—Chinese people without living with Japanese." (See the issue of Shun Pao on August 15, 1938. Cited in The Historical Research Office of Shanghai Academy of Social Sciences (Ed.), Selected Historical Materials on the August-13 Battle Against Japanese Aggression. Shanghai People's Publishing House. 1st Edition published in May 1986, p. 34.) We of course can say that was the spirit of anti-aggression shall be above the means but this is another issue. Second, agreeing on the intention of "seizing the initiative", some people definitely say "the August-13 battle was launched by China" (Ma Zhendu. On the causes of the Songhu Battle on August 13. Modern Chinese History Studies. 1986(6): p. 223). While others think it was both Japan's "long-planned strategic attempt" and China's "good step to seize the initiative" (Yu Zidao & Zhang Yun. The Battle of Shanghai on August 13. Shanghai People's Publishing House. 1st Edition published in November 2011, pp. 10+75).

[33] See「松井石根最終弁論」中「第二節上海および南京戦における松井大!大辛苦経営」、「第三節中支那方面軍の編成並に南京攻撃を決した事情」、「松井石根口供書」中「(1)江南出兵の動機」、「(4) 中支那方面軍の編成と南京攻撃事情」、洞富雄編『日中戦争史資料』8「南京事件」I, 第34-348、273、275頁。

[34] It was ordered not to cross the Suzhou-Jiaxing Line and then the Wuxi-Huzhou Line.

[35] This was the comment of Soichiro Tahara, a famous Japanese political critic. And the situation at that time have been briefly dealt with in his book『日本の戦争＿＿＿なぜ、戦いに踏み切ったか?』「第5章昭和維新」、「第6章五族協和」(Tokyo: Shôgakukan. 1st Edition published in November 20, 2000, pp. 246–381.)

Polo Bridge Incident. A vivid example was that Colonel Shibayama Kaneshiro who was then Chief of Military Service Bureau of the Army Ministry and Major General Nakajima Tetsuo who was Head of General Affairs Section of General Staff put across the central policy of "not expanding the battle" to Lieutenant General Katsuki Kiyoshi, commander of the China Garrison Army (Shina Chutongun), but the policy was rejected and reprimanded, as Shibayama Kaneshiro recalled.[36] Considering this, whether it was a central decision cannot be an appropriate basis on which to judge the operations of Japanese army.

However, it is not inferred from common cases but based on strong evidence that Japan's attack against Nanjing was not "accidental". *Documents on the Battle of Nanjing*, a collection of documents on "war history" edited by a Japanese organization of retired military servicemen, was intended to "justify" Japanese army but as mentioned above, those diaries of senior military officials included therein are of value in helping us learn about the decisions of Japanese army. From *Iinuma Mamoru's Diary*, we can learn that before SEF set off, Commander Matsui Iwane had clearly stated "the policy of not expanding the battle beyond but ceasing fire swiftly and peacefully shall be abandoned". He instead advocated "a quick win based on the decisive use of necessary force and more forces sent against Nanjing rather than Northern China". He also said [we shall] "capture Nanjing in a quick manner"[37]—these totally go against what he said in the Tokyo Trial. His plans and thoughts were dwelt on in the newly "discovered" diaries before October that have been included in *Documents on the Battle of Nanjing: Volume II*. On August 14th, Matsui learned from General Sugiyama Hajime, the Army Minister, that he would be appointed commander of SEF and then "was deeply worried" that General Staff Headquarter did not take "central China" as the key battlefield. And the next day, he expressed his "great concern" in the diary, saying that "powerful measure shall be taken as soon as possible to force Chinese government face the reality". On August 16th, he intended to persuade Major General Ishiwara Kanji, director of the 1st Department of General Staff Headquarter, but failed and then turned to Major General Homma Masaharu, head of the 2nd Section of General Staff Headquarter, and General Sugiyama Hajime, the Army Minister. He said [we] "should act for the purpose of capturing Nanjing" and "need oppress Nanjing KMT government through not only forces but also economic and financial sanction, so as to more effectively destroy the Nanjing KMT government".[38] The

---

[36] Katsuki made it clear that he "had been given important tasks and will not accept instructions from the minister of the Army". See 柴山兼四郎著「日支事変勃発前後の経緯」之「盧溝橋事件の勃発」,『現代史資料月報』, 東京, みすず書房1965年12月, 第3頁.

[37] 「飯沼守日記」, 南京戦史編集委員会編『南京戦史資料集』, 非売品, 東京, 偕行社1989年11月3日 第1版, 第67-68頁.

[38] 「松井石根大!戦陣日記」, 南京戦史編集委員会編『南京戦史資料集』II, 非売品, 東京, 偕行社1993年12月8日第1版, 第46頁.

"purposed" mentioned here had been Matsui's pursuit throughout his career as commander of SEF and then-established 10th Army. Hence, "capturing Nanjing" was a constant policy binding the 10th Army, although the central order of "capturing Nanjing" was issued later.

Did Japanese Army Intend to Enter the Nanjing City in a Peaceful Way?

There long has been an unproven statement popular in Japan, that is, "On December 9, Japanese army, having surrounded the city of Nanjing, scattered 'Bills advising surrender of the Chinese Army' into the city by the aircraft and asked KMT for a reply by noon the next day. And Major General Tsukada Osamu, Chief of Staff of CCAA, as well as three staff officers, Lieutenant Colonel Kimihira Masatake, Major Nakayama Neito and Okada Takashi, waited outside the Zhongshan Gate until 1: 00 p.m. on the 10th but the KMT did not reply and then the troops opened fire".[39] And nowadays, this bill is even said to "guarantee opening the gates to the city in a peaceful manner" "in accordance with the international law".[40] This statement has been widely popular among the fabrication school and the middle-of-the-road school. It implies, as Watanabe Shoichi has put, that "if the KMT had accepted Japanese summons, nothing would happen". And Watanabe Shoichi also claims that that is why Chiang Kai-shek, leader of the national KMT government, did not actively publicize the Nanjing Massacre around the world.[41] Japanese fabrication school attaches such great importance to this bill that *The Truth about the Nanjing Incident* even regarded *John Rabe's Diary* as untruthful because it does not deal with this matter.[42] Apparently, this argument cannot hold merely based on no reference to a certain matter and thus debate over it is pointless. But we need to figure out whether Japanese army waited "in the peace" from December 9th to 10th—from which we can judge whether Japanese army would not attack if Chinese army retreated.

It is not difficult to figure out whether the Japanese army stopped attacking according to the records of foreign people in Nanjing at that time. At the beginning of *John Rabe's Diary* on December 9th, it is put that "air raids have started since the early morning". And air bombardment did not stop even later. According to the diary of the next day, "the heavy sound of artillery, rifle and GM fire could be heard from 8 p.m.

---

[39] The defendants mentioned this several times during the Tokyo trial and Okada Takashi gave the most details. See洞富雄編『日中戦争史資料』8「南京事件」I, 第262頁.

[40] 竹本忠雄、大原康男著, 日本会議国際広報委員会編集『再審「南京大虐殺」＿＿世界に訴える日本の冤罪』, 東京, 明成社2000年11月25日第1版, 第24頁.

[41] 小室直樹、渡部昇一著『封印の昭和史＿＿「戦後五〇年」自虐の終焉』, 東京, 徳間書店1995年10月15日第4次印刷版, 第69頁.

[42] 畝本正己著『真相·南京事件＿＿ラーベ日記を検証して』, 東京, 文京出版1999年2月1日第2次印刷版, 第39頁。I once specially wrote an article to refute this book. See Cheng Zhaoqi. Is The Diaries of John Rabe an "Unfounded Fabrication"?. Modern Chinese History Studies. 2002(2): pp. 150–183.

yesterday to 4 a.m. this morning" and "the city was under aerial bombings all the day".[43] The diary on this day also mentions that Japanese army very nearly captured the Guanghua Gate and advanced to the waterworks along the riverside on the night before (December 9th). In *The Diary of Minnie Vautrin*, it is put on December 9th that "a big bomb was dropped at the Xijiekou when we were attending the news conference tonight whose explosion forced us to stand up". According to her diary of the next day, "gunfire could be heard throughout the night".[44] And George A. Fitch also wrote a "diary" during his stay in Nanjing before the "Christmas eve of 1937". The diary starts from December 10th and it puts on the 10th as follows: "heavy artillery opened fire against southern Gates of Nanjing and bombings exploded inside the city".[45] This record does not mention the exact time and thus it is hard to judge whether the attack was launched before the noon as specified in the "Bill". But this record and foregoing ones can be cross-referenced to be a piece of evidence. Japanese army did not stop the attack after issuing the Bills on December 9th, which is also referred to in Chinese documents. In *Three Months of Nanking's Ordeal*, author Jiang Gong-gu wrote: "(On December 9th) Enemies are said to have attacked the area of Qilin Gate and approach the city wall. Gunfire has grown more continuous and closer than yesterday's. And Bafutang area has been under the gunfire. … After the mid-night, gunfire gets more heavier and bombs are dropped inside the city. A glimmer of white can be seen flit past the window from time to time".[46] The "hearsay" that Japanese army attacked the Qilin Gate proves to be true through Japanese records[47] and the attacks on the morning of the next day has been dwelt on in *Three Months of Nanking's Ordeal*.[48] From the experiences of both Chinese and foreign people who are disconnected, we can see that Japanese army are two-faced: After issuing the so-called Bills advising the surrender of Chinese army, Japanese army not only did not stop their attack

---

[43] The Good Man of Nanking: The Diaries of John Rabe, pp. 154 + 158 + 163.

[44] Minnie Vautrin. The Diary of Minnie Vautrin (The Nanjing Massacre Research Center of Nanjing Normal University Trans.). Jiangsu People's Publishing House. 1st Edition published in October 2000, pp. 184 + 185. Minnie Vautrin was then a professor with Ginling College of Arts and Sciences.

[45] My Eighty Years in China. In The State Archives Administration of P.R.C. (Ed.), The Nanjing Massacre. China Publishing House. 1sst Edition published in July 1995, pp. 1022 + 1025.

[46] Three Months of Nanking's Ordeal. In The State Archives Administration of P.R.C. (Ed.), The Nanjing Massacre, p. 191.

[47] The 1st Squadron of the 1st Chariot Battalion directly under the Shanghai Expeditionary Army "arrived at about 150 meters east of Qilin Gate at around 4:50 p.m." (「戦車第一大隊第一中隊行動記録」, 南京戦史編集委員会編『南京戦史資料集』II, 第405頁). And the 9th Division command also mentioned the 16th Division shall, as planned, "arrived near the Qinlin Gate" "at dusk (of the 19th)" (南京戦史編集委員会編『南京戦史資料集』, 第546頁).

[48] Three Months of Nanking's Ordeal. In The State Archives Administration of P.R.C. (Ed.), The Nanjing Massacre, pp. 192 + 193.

against Nanjing but also hit the city with direct artillery fire in addition to air bombardment.

Japanese army did not keep their words. But why do fictionalists always mention it? Perhaps "the Fabrication school" thinks senior military officials advocated a "peaceful" manner and bombings were due to the failure to get across the order to rank-and-file troops. Then, let us figure out whether there existed a "misunderstanding" based on Japanese military records. The 9th Division of Imperial Japanese Army issued the following order at 4 p.m. on the 9th, i.e., after scattering the "Bills advising the surrender of Chinese army":

......
2. The Division shall <u>take the advantage of the darkness of the night to occupy the city wall</u>.
3. Flanking Forces shall capture the city wall by night and the leader of left-flanking force shall leave two Light Armor platoons in the charge of the leader of right-flanking force.
4. The artillery regiments shall support the operations of flanking forces.
5. The engineer regiments mostly support the operations of right-flanking force.
6. And the other units continue to carry out their previous tasks.[49]

Behind their waiting for "opening the gates to Nanjing in a peaceful manner" was the intention to "capture the city wall by night"![50] Then was this operation an "accident" limited to the 9th Division? Let us continue to examine relevant Japanese military documents. According to "Wartime Ten-day Reports" of the 6th Division,

At the mid-night of December 9th, troops at the frontline set off. And intended to avail ourselves of the <u>night-time attack</u>, our commander arrived at the Dongshan Bridge at 6 a.m. and ordered the reserve force and the artillery force to advance towards the Teixin Bridge.[51]

The 6th Division also took participate in the "night-time attack". The "Battle Report" of the 114th Division put as follows:

"On the evening of December 9th, the Akiyama Brigade pierced enemy lines near the Jiangjun Mountain and chased the enemies. By the morning of the

---

[49] 「九師作命甲第百二十五号」, 南京戦史編集委員会編『南京戦史資料集』, 第546頁.

[50] The 36th Regiment of the left flank (the 18th Infantry Brigade) was in charge of capturing the Guanghua Gate. The attack began as soon as they arrived at dawn of the 9th but did not succeed due to outside trench, the barriers before the gate and the firepower on the city wall. At the night, engineers then used the cover of darkness to blow up the gate. See南京戦史編集委員会編纂『南京戦史』, 第175頁.

[51] 第六師団「戦時旬報」第十三、十四号, 南京戦史編集委員会編『南京戦史資料集』, 第689頁.

next day, they had captured the positions near Yu Hua Tai and approached the enemies. And then they immediately launched an attack."[52]

The Akiyama Brigade is the 127th Infantry Brigade under the 114th Division. And both the "Battle Report" and the "Wartime Ten-day Report" have detailed the continuous attacks from the evening of December 9th to the noon of the next day.[53] In addition to such division-level documents, documents of rank-and-file troops also mentioned it. For example, according to the "Battle Report" of the 33rd Infantry Regiment under the 16th Division,

"On the evening of December 9th, our regiment carried out the order of the Division, which provides that the 33rd Infantry Regiment (without the 1st Battalion, the 5th and 8th Squadron) shall attack the northern area of the main road (including the main road) in alignment with detachments on the right attacking Wuqi Jiang Ziwen Temple and the north-east corner of the city, 500 meters away from the Xuanwu Lake. And with the great mission of capturing highlands around the Zijin Mountain, soldiers had even more tremendous spirit."[54]

Base on the forgoing documents, it can be concluded that after issuing the Bills advising the surrender of Chinese army, Japanese army did not keep their words that they would wait for the reply but instead launched attacks by night. The so-called statement that "Japanese army did not launch all-round attacks" until the deadline by which KMT did not reply, which can be dated back to the Tokyo Trial, totally goes against the truth.[55]

Were There Many Bodies Slaughtered by Japanese Army Around Nanjing?

In the past 30 years, especially the recent ten years, it has becoming increasingly difficult to deny Japanese atrocities in its totality, with the publication of some important documents. Some Japanese thus have to make some changes to their strategy. They confirm some "less-serious-crime" charges but still

---

[52]「第百十四師団作戦経過ノ概要」、南京戦史編集委員会編『南京戦史資料集』、第653頁。

[53]第百十四師団「戦闘詳報」、「戦時旬報」、南京戦史編集委員会編『南京戦史資料集』、第654、664頁。

[54]歩兵第三十二聯隊「南京附近戦闘詳報」、南京戦史編集委員会編『南京戦史資料集』、第596頁。

[55] Not only was this the fact, but the Japanese army even did not think about the treatment if Chinese government gave up resisting. The Rules of Capture of the Walled City of Nanking, which was issued earlier than the Bill of advising the surrender of Chinese army, explicitly provides that as China would accept our offer, "each division shall select an infantry brigade as a backbone force to enter the city in advance and have mopping-up operations in the city". See 「南京城攻略要領」、南京戦史編集委員会編『南京戦史資料集』、第539頁。

completely deny the "massacre", the major and symbolic crime. Ooi Mitsuru, a member of the fabrication school, is a typical scholar who advocates giving up a rook to save the king. He puts in *Shikumareta "Nankin Daigyakusatsu"* (*The Fabricated Nanjing Massacre*), "Of course, I do not mean that Japanese army did not commit any crime. As is universally acknowledged, it was impossible that a troop of seven thousand soldiers did nothing. Staff Officer Mr. Onishi slapped the soldier who committed the rape and sent him to the Military Police. This case took place everywhere".[56] And in the questionnaire of *Shokun!*, he wrote "12"[57] which means as close to zero as it could when it comes to the first question of casualties count.

The slaughtered bodies in Nanjing were eventually buried, burned or thrown into the Yangtze River, etc. but had been exposed for a long time, which has been the major obstacle to deny the Nanjing Massacre and a main focus of the "rebuttal" of the fabrication school. The *First-six-Month Battles after the China Incident* wrote by Major Sumi Yoshiharu, Matsui Iwane's regular adjutant, in his late years was not published during his lifetime for mentioning the mass killing perpetrated by Japanese army (and later published in the January-issue of *Kaikou*, which was sponsored by a group of retired servicemen, in 1988) but aroused controversy as soon as published due to the special status of Sumi Yoshiharu. The biggest issue focused on the statement of "twelve or thirteen thousand bodies around Xiaguan".[58] Sumi Yoshiharu said it was the 6th Division committed the killing but the order was issued by Lieutenant Colonel Isamu Cho, director of the 2nd department of the Staff of SEF and also claimed to be present when Isamu Cho gave the order.[59] Both the fabrication school and the middle-of-the-road school have expressed incredulity at this point. *The Battle of Nanjing* says "there are many contradictions denting the credibility" of Sumi Yoshiharu's memory.[60] And the "Notes of War-history Researches" attached to the *Documents on the Battle of Nanjing* expresses the same opinion, saying that "there are numerous

---

[56]大井満著『仕組まれた「南京大虐殺」——攻略作戦の全貌とマスコミ報道の怖さ』，東京, 展転社1998年6月6日第3次印刷版, 第297页.

[57]「まぼろし派、中間派、大虐殺派三派合同大アンケート」, 『諸君!』, 東京, 文藝春秋社,2001年2月号, 第179页.

[58]See《支那事变当初六ヵ月間の戦闘》"三二、关于清除下关附近的尸体", 南京战史编集委员会编『南京戦史資料集』, 第760页. Hora Tomio said, "Regardless of the date or place, the testimonies of Sumi and Jusu are good explanation for the same event." (洞富雄著『南京大虐殺の証明』, 東京, 朝日新聞社1986年3月5日第1版, 第324页.) And Yoshida Yutaka agreed with him. (吉田裕著『天皇の軍隊と南京事件』, 東京, 青木書店1986年1月2日第1版, 第166页.)

[59]The statement that the order was issued by Isamu Cho can be dated back to the memoirs of Tanaka Ryukich, who was Head of Military Affairs Bureau of the Army Ministry (『裁かれざる歴史』1950年版, 转引自秦郁彦著『南京事件——虐殺の構造』, 東京, 中央公論新社1999年8月20日第20次印刷版, 第143144页). And no more direct evidence has been found yet.

[60]南京戦史編集委員会編纂『南京戦史』, 第163页.

misunderstandings, prejudices and errors in Sumi's memory".⁶¹ However, Sumi Yoshiharu was not alone.

There is a record in Matsui Iwane's diary that can be a positive proof. Matsui Iwane wrote on December 20th,

> "I set off at 10 a.m. to inspect the Xiaguan near the Yijiang Gate, <u>a disaster area of bodies thrown as they were</u>. Those bodies must be disposed later."⁶²

And Major Yamazaki Masao, a staff officer of the 10th Army, wrote in his diary on December 17th,

> "I arrived at the <u>Zhongshan Wharf</u>. … There were <u>numerous bodies</u> along the riverside and immersed in the River. The number that the so-called "<u>piles of bodies</u>" implies is uncertain but <u>that of bodies along the Yangtze River must top the list</u>. And those bodies, if piled at a place, really can form a so-called "<u>mountain of bodies</u>". But <u>having seen so many bodies</u>, I was not surprised at it at all.⁶³

The area of "Zhongshan Wharf" is just the place Sumi Yoshiharu refers to. Navy Doctor Colonel Yasuyama Koudou, chief medical officer of "China Area Fleet" Command, took a seaplane to Nanjing on December 16th and "visited" the battlefield along with the "commanding officer" and the "Comptroller" of the Fleet at 2 p.m. In his diary on that day, he wrote

> "Driving on the wide, straight road from the <u>Xiaguan Wharf</u>, I saw numerous rifle bullets scattering on the road as if paved with brass sands. And on the road-side grass were scattering <u>the bodies of Chinese soldiers, exposed</u>.
>
> It did not take a long time to drive <u>from Xiaguan to the Yijiang Gate of Nanjing</u>. Under the towering stone gate was an arched road, of which one third close to the earth was soil. On the other side of the Gate was a road that sloped down to Xiaguan, on which the car moved slowly as if on an inflated rubber bag. But in fact, it was a road under which buried <u>numerous enemy bodies</u>. And it was likely drove to a place where the soil was so thin that some body parts buried suddenly got exposed. The terrible scene was really beyond words.⁶⁴

The area from "Xiaguan Wharf" to "Yijiang Gate" is also the place Sumi Yoshiharu referred to. Since different, disconnected people kept similar records, the truthfulness of this matter shall not be questionable any more. And at least "piles of bodies" were definitely the result of slaughtering

---

⁶¹南京戦史編集委員会編『南京戦史資料集』, 第764页.
⁶²「松井石根大将戦陣日記」, 南京戦史編集委員会編『南京戦史資料集』, 第21-22页.
⁶³「山崎正男日記」, 南京戦史編集委員会編『南京戦史資料集』, 第408页.
⁶⁴泰山弘道著「上海戦従軍日誌」, 南京戦史編集委員会編『南京戦史資料集』, 第527528页.

captives since bodies were along the riverside rather than on the battlefield, regardless of whether there were civilians.

The "Notes of War-history Researches" attached to the *Documents on the Battle of Nanjing* specially "criticizes" one of Sumi Yoshiharu's statements. It said, "it is astonishing that 'the commander drove silently for two kilometers on the road where piles of bodies scattered and was so sad that his tears streamed down his face'. A general who loves or loved China will never drive on the bodies of the battlefield and a car with low-built chassis is unable to move two kilometers in that condition. I thus believe and every one will conclude this was totally made up".[65] However, such "conclusion" is ill-based not only because there is positive proof such as Yasuyama Koudou's statement[66] of "driving" on "numerous bodies", but also because it is an anomaly to make up something that can be easily exploded.

There are many records of Japanese soldiers that can reflect whether the slaughter was a widespread action. And let us examine Yasuyama Koudou's following parts of his diary on the 16th.

> On the other side of the Gate to Nanjing, we saw piles of charred enemy bodies as well as blackened iron helmets and bayonets. The gateposts that had been burned down were against the blackened wire fence. And the soil had also been blackened by fire. It was really a mess and was inexpressibly poignant.
>
> The hillock on the right of the gate was engraved "Japan is the natural enemy of China", a sign of KMT's anti-Japanese propaganda. And on the road approaching the city center were scattering blue wadded jacket left by enemies, making the road look like clothes tattered. Besides, stiff <u>bodies of enemy officers</u> in khaki suits and gaiters that had been confined to the supine position <u>could be seen here and there</u>.

The above passage just deals with part of what Yasuyama Koudou saw in Nanjing on the first day. During his three-day stay, Yasuyama Koudou saw a

---

[65] 「『角証言』の信憑性について」, 南京戦史編集委員会編『南京戦史資料集』, 第764頁.

[66] Durdin, Nanjing special correspondent of The New York Times, said in his report on December 18, "The Japanese army occupied Xiaguan and massacred the garrison. The bodies of Chinese soldiers were stacked between sandbags, forming a six-feet-high bomb. The Japanese army still had not cleared the dead bodies by the middle of the night of the 15th and the military vehicles traveled frequently during the two days, rolling on the bodies of people and dogs and horses."(洞富雄編『日中戦争史資料』9「南京事件」II, 東京, 河出書房新社1973年11月30日第1版, 第283頁.) Although Suzuki Aki's The Illusion of the "Nanjing Massacre" is the first monograph to deny the Nanjing Massacre, it mentions an important oral record that can prove this. Fuji Shinichi (the video recordist of the movie "Nanking") who followed the army to Nanjing said, "There were a large number of bodies near Yijiang Gate. And on bodies were wooden boards that cars could ran on". (鈴木明著『「南京大虐殺」のまぼろし』, 東京, 文藝春秋社1989年5月30日第15次印刷版, 第228頁.) This oral record can be unquestionable evidence because Suzuki Aki's interviews were carried out in the early 1970s when this matter had not raised a "controversy" and thus it was unlikely to be knowingly "coincidence". And it is just because this had not yet raised a "controversy" that this piece of evidence against the fictionalists can be preserved through Suzuki's writing.

large number of bodies wherever he went. For example, in the morning of the next day (December 17th), he saw "piles of bodies" in other two places of Xiaguan and saw a blood-drenched Chinese soldier who was begging for mercy shoot in the back at close range by a "reservist"[67]; he also saw "piles of bodies" along the North Zhongshan Road in that morning; and in the afternoon, he along with Okawachi Denshichi, commander of Shanghai Special Naval Landing Force, "inspected" the area downriver from Xiaguan where he saw "numerous charred enemy bodies" and there were "sixty or seventy enemy bodies lying along the river embankment, all bayoneted". On the 18th, Yasuyama Koudou saw that there were "enemy bodies everywhere" in Lion Forest Garden and "bodies scattering" outside the camps in the foothill; And at the Zhongshan Park, came into sight also "scattered enemy bodies".[68]

Such firsthand documents written at the time of the incident are most powerful proof that there were at least a large number of bodies of Chinese soldiers—in fact, not only Chinese soldiers, which will be further discussed later—around Nanjing. So, were those soldiers killed in the battle or in the slaughter? This issue has been much debated in Japan. And to solve it, we had better check whether senior officials of Japanese army issued the order of killing prisoners of war.

Did Senior Officials of Japanese Army Issue the Order of Killing Prisoners of War?

Was the slaughter of Chinese captives perpetrated by Japanese troops in Nanjing subject to an order from senior officials or independent action took by rank-and-file troops? This is a tricky one to answer because existing documents provide incomplete information. Japanese fabrication school, of course, denies the order of killing POWs since they do not confirm any charge of

---

[67] It was widely acknowledged in Japan that older soldiers who were enlisted again after their service as their service in regular army expired were less disciplined than regular soldiers. At that time, Tanaka Shinichi, head of the Military Division of the Military Affairs Bureau of the Army Ministry, was deeply concerned about these old recruits. He said, "The root cause of the decadence of military discipline lies in the recruit of older soldiers." (See 「田中新一/支那事変記録 其の四」, 转引自笠原十九司著『南京事件』, 東京, 岩波書店1997年11月20日第1版, 第62页.)

[68] 泰山弘道著「上海戦従軍日誌」, 南京戦史編集委員会編『南京戦史資料集』, 第528、528530、531页. Nowadays, Higashinakano Shudo who has the most achievements among the Japanese fictionalists ignores the recurrent words as "piles of bodies" in Yasuyama Koudou's records but said, "Nany Doctor Yasuyama Koudou's detailed diary from the 17th to the 19th does not mention the existence of these bodies at all. If any, those were from the upstream reach. It is reckless to conclude that those were pushed into the River by the Japanese soldiers" (「南京事件最新報告」「問題は『捕虜処断』をどう見るか」, 東京, 『諸君!』, 文藝春秋社,2001年2月号, 第129页). Regardless of the obvious records, how dare Higashinakano Shudo to conclude there were no "bodies pushed into the Rive"!

killing.[69] "The series of books on war history", the representative writings of Japanese war history circles, as well as *The Battle of Nanjing* also does not confirm or tends to deny the slaughter was subject to a top-down order.[70]

Among existing documents, there are three records that explicitly mention the order of killing prisoners of war. One is the diary of Nakajima Kesago, commanding officer of the 16th Division, on December 13th:

> "In principle, we would not take prisoners, so they were dealt with in the first place."[71]

Another is the diary of Yamada Senji, the commanding officer of the 103th Infantry Brigade of the 13th Division, on December 15th:

> A cavalry second lieutenant was sent to Nanjing to report on the issues concerning disposal of captives.
> The reply was killing all of them.
> It is confusing that troops at all levels have no reserve of food.[72]

And the last is the battle report of the 1st Battalion of the 66th Regiment of the 114th Division:

> Eighth, the following orders were received from the Head of superior battalion at 2 p.m..
> They can be summarized as follows:
> 1. Kill all the captives in accordance with the order from the Brigade;
> You can divide captives into groups of 10 and then shoot them group by group. How do you like it?
> 2. Collect the weapons and send troops for surveillance before receiving new instructions;
> …
> Ninth, in accordance with orders mentioned above, the first and the fourth Squadron were ordered to collect all the weapons and send soldiers for surveillance.

---

[69] For example, The Alleged "Nanking Massacre" claims that the "plain-clothes soldiers" were "anything but executed" even if their execution was "well-founded". See竹本忠雄、大原康男著、日本会議国際広報委員会編『再審「南京大虐殺」――世界に訴える日本の冤罪』，東京、明成社2000年11月25日第2次印刷版, 第73页.

[70] The Army Operations In the China Incident argues that "most of the bodies near Nanjing were killed in the battle and thus cannot conclude there were a planned, systematic 'slaughter'" (防衛庁防衛研修所戦史室著戦史叢書『支那事変陸軍作戦』〈1〉，東京、朝雲新聞社1975年7月25日第1版, 第437页). And The Battle of Nanjing thinks "many remain unknown". After listing five cases of prisoners, it says, "It can be inferred that the Japanese army acted subject to the task, or due to the riot or great concern for a riot. But such specific explanation was hardly mentioned in the battle report" (南京戦史編集委員会編纂『南京戦史』, 第336页).

[71] 「中島今朝吾日記」，南京戦史編集委員会編『南京戦史資料集』, 第326页.

[72] 南京戦史編集委員会編『南京戦史資料集』II, 第331页.

At 3.30 p.m., heads of the squadrons were gathered to discuss how to execute those captives. And it was decided that captives were distributed equally to the squadrons (the 1st, 3rd and 4th Squadron) and taken out of the cells in batches of 50 one by one to certain place and then killed them. The 1st Squadron took captives to the valley on the south of the camp, the 3rd Squadron took them to the hollow on the southwest of the camp and the 4th Squadron took them to the valley on the south-east of the camp.

But please mind that send soldiers to guard the cells and put them on alert and make sure captives do not know why they were taken out. Squadrons had prepared them by 5 p.m. and then started to kill them. The slaughter ended at 7.30 p.m.

Then report was submitted to the Regiment.

The 1st Squadron did not follow the schedule proposed and intended to incarnate the captives in a place and burned them but failed.

Some captives learned what would happen and became no longer afraid: Their heads were erect and their backs were straight before the sabers and bayonets, totally in a calm manner. Also there were some lamenting and begging for mercy. Especially when squadron heads came to make an inspection, laments could be heard here and there.[73]

Since these three records were kept in wartime, they, as firsthand material, play a special role in figuring out whether the slaughter of POWs was subject to an order. Hence, Japanese fabrication school and some members of the middle-of-the-road school wrote in a way that was extremely detailed, "arguing" that the records of Nakajima Kesago and Yamada Senji have nothing to with the order of killing prisoners of war and that the battle report of the 1st Battalion under the 66th Regiment is fabricated because it goes against the truth in terms the timing and content.

Through searching for a wide range of documents of that time, I have argued deductively from the texts as well as some memoirs of people who participated in the war that the foregoing records are powerful evidence to the existence of the order of killing POWs.[74] And the arguments can be summarized as follows: First, the order of "not allowed to take prisoners until there is a [new] division instruction"[75] issued by the 30th Brigade under the 16th Division is consistent with the spirit of Nakajima's diary. And then it can be concluded the order means killing all the captives based on the memory of Major Kodama Yoshio, an adjutant of the 38th Regiment under the 30th Brigade. Major Kodama Yoshio wrote,

> "It was when we were involved in a terrible fight against enemies once or two kilometers away from Nanjing that the division adjutant phoned and gave the

[73]步兵第六十六聯隊第一大隊「戦闘詳報」, 南京戦史編集委員会編『南京戦史資料集』, 第673-674页.

[74]See my article A Study of the Massacre Order for Japanese Troops. Beijing: Historical Research. 2002(6): pp. 68–79.

[75]「步兵第三十旅団命令」之六, 南京戦史編集委員会編『南京戦史資料集』, 第545页.

order that <u>Chinese soldiers who surrendered were not allowed to be taken prisoners but disposed</u>. It was surprising to receive such an order. Although Lieutenant General Kesago Nakajima, the director of the Division, was a great-hearted general with charm, we could be anything but pleased to accept this order. Surprised and confused as the whole army was, we still had to pass the order to the battalions. And then no battalion reported on this matter any more."[76]

Yoshio Kodama's account was written before Kesago Nakajima's diary and thus cannot be directed against any issue. His account of "not allowed" is just the most direct and clearest evidence that the order for "not allowed to take prisoners" was issued by the 30th Division. And taken into account the situation in that time and the documents that have remained, the order can only be understood as killing all the captives. Kesago Nakajima's diary, the order of the 30th Division and Yoshio Kodama's account are of a piece and completely involve all the levels up to down, i.e., the division, the brigade and the battalions. Hence, the record in Kesago Nakajima's diary is reliable without any doubt. Second, there is no contradictions in Yamada's diary in terms of the "context".[77] And the 65th Regiment of the 103rd Brigade did kill a large number of captives at the neighboring area of the Navy Wharf and in the place 4 kilometers on the east of Shangyuan Gate.[78] Third, the 10th Army issued the order of "wiping out the enemies in the Walled City of Nanjing" at 8.30 a.m. on the 13th[79]; receiving the order, the 114th Division thereunder issued the order of "wiping out enemies by all means"[80]; and then the 128th Brigade thereunder issued the order of "wiping out the enemies

---

[76] Battle of Nanking Editorial Committee (Ed.). The Battle of Nanking, pp. 341–344 (A Table occupies two pages).

[77] Having compared with all records, it is found that the fabrication school has tampered with key words. For example, Suzuki Aki replaced the words "all killed" with "from the beginning" when citing the diary of Yamada on December 15th. This change can be dated back to the 1st Edition published in 1973 and then have remained till today. (See 『「南京大虐殺」のまぼろし』, 第193页.) And because the word "dispose" in the same sentence was also modified with the word "from the beginning", it is not easy to explain the difference between two adverbials. This problem was not solved until the publication of Documents on the Battle of Nanjing (Volume II). Ono Kenji further suspected that "Yamada's diary included in Documents on the Battle of Nanjing (Volume II) is likely to have been partly deleted." See「虐殺か解放か——山田支隊捕虜約二万の行方」, 南京事件調査研究会編『南京大虐殺否定論13のウソ』, 東京, 柏書房2001年3月30日第4次印刷版, 第146-147页.

[78] The records and photos about this matter were immediately published in Japanese newspapers. For the record, please refer to「両角部隊大武勲——敵軍一萬五千餘を捕虜」,『東京朝日新聞号外』1937年12月16日;「両角部隊大殊勲——壹萬五千の敵軍餘を捕虜」,『福島民友新聞』1937年12月17日. And for photos, please refer to『アサヒグラフ』1938年1月5日、『アサヒグラフ臨時増刊・支那事変畫報』1938年1月27日.

[79]「丁集作命甲号外」之二, 南京戦史編集委員会編『南京戦史資料集』, 第554页。在前日下达的「丁集作命甲第六十六号」之三中有「国崎支队以主力占领浦口附近捕捉歼灭残敌」。

[80]「一一四師作命甲第六十二号」, 南京戦史編集委員会編『南京戦史資料集』, 第556页。

at all costs and if necessary" at 12[81] (Note: The 66th Regiment was in fact directly under the 127th Brigade of the 114th Division, whose documents, however, have been burned. Considering the 128th Brigade under the same division was also in Nanjing, the order issued from the brigade level shall be the same). Hence, it makes sense that the 66th Regiment, as put in the battle report, received the order at 2 p.m. and there is no so-called contradiction as Japanese fictionalists have claimed between the timing and the content. And the slaughter committed by the 66th Regiment was really subject to the order from a superior level, regardless of whether the order was explicit.

In a word, we can certain conclude that Japanese troops' slaughtering captives during the process of capturing Nanjing was based on a top-down order instead of being the so-called "accidental, sporadic event limited to individual soldiers".[82] Through this article, we can sure that Japanese military at the division level did issue a massacre order, although the massacre order issued by the army who captured Nanjing and by the Area Army cannot be affirmed.[83]

Were the Large Number of Chinese-Soldier Bodies Around Nanjing Killed in the Battle or in the Slaughter?

Japanese army did issue the order of killing prisoners of war, which can be concluded not only from the "contextual logic" of existing documents but, more importantly, based on the facts that there were a large number of Chinese-solider bodies around Nanjing, as mentioned above. Therefore, in addition to a minority, most of the slaughter school specially emphasize that those outside Nanjing were killed in the "battle" rather than "slaughter". However, after examining existing Japanese battle reports and wartime

---

[81]「步第一二八旅命第六十六号」,南京戦史編集委員会編『南京戦史資料集』,第557頁。

[82] This is Nakamura Akira's argument. See his book「過去の歴史を反省すべきは中国の方だ」,『正論』,東京,産經新聞社,2001年7月号,第67頁。

[83] That is not to say that there is no clue to be followed. After the publication of this article, I found two pieces of records that can be indirect evidence to suggest that Major General Iinuma Mamoru, Chief of Staff for Shanghai Expeditionary Army, had known and acquiesced in the slaughter of captives as early as when attacking Baoshan. (See Cheng Zhaoqi. The Record of Historical Documents Concerning the Defensive Battle of Baoshan. In On the History and Classics. Shanghai: Shanghai Classics Publishing House. 1st Edition published in August 2004, pp. 448–459.) Iinuma Mamoru had no time lost in learning that Yamada Detachment slaughtered the captives and on December 21 he wrote, "it was said that Yamada Column under the Rippei Army captured over ten thousand people and killed them one by one with bayonet. And on the following day many people were taken to the same place and a riot occurred. Yamada Column then had no choice but to sprayed them with machine gun. Several of Yamada Column soldiers were killed in the fusillade of bullets and many people fled." (See「飯沼守日記」,南京戦史編集委員会編『南京戦史資料集』,第222頁.) And the statement "Kill… one by one with bayonet" is almost the same as what was mentioned in the battle report by the 1st Battalion of the 66th Regiment, which proves the large-scale slaughter of captives was not limited to certain troop at that time.

journal of troops at different levels, we can see that the so-called operation of "wiping out enemies" that many Japanese troops had was in fact killing prisoners of war, subject to the order of SEF and the 10th Army on "mopping up" and "wiping out" "enemies".

The 7th Regiment, attached to the 9th Division of SEF, recorded "no captive" but 505 "corpses of enemies" in the List of Captives (December 7–13).[84] Considering soldiers who surrendered followed one after another, the reason why there were no captives alive must be that the 7th Regiment did "not take any prisoners". Section 2 of The List of Mopping-up Operations in the Nanjing city (December 13–24) read "6670 'defeated soldiers' stabbed to death,[85] and no prisoner". The No.111 Combat Order of the 7th Infantry Regiment expressly provided that "remaining defeated troops shall be thoroughly captured and wiped up"[86]—"Wiping-up" could mean "capture" but considering the foregoing order and the follow-up, the "wiping-up" measure taken by the 7th Regiment when attacking and after entering Nanjing, no doubt, meant physical annihilation. And the number of soldiers killed showed a surprisingly sharp increase when Chinese troops surrendered after the fall of Nanjing on December 13th. This increase cannot be justified unless on the slaughter of captives.

The 16th Division of Shanghai Expeditionary Army was the main force attacking Nanjing and his subordinate troop, the 33rd Regiment put as follows in Report on the Battle near Nanjing:

> At 2.30 p.m. on December 13th, the advance guard arrived at Xiaguan and searched for enemies. And it was found that many defeated soldiers were on rafts fashioned from bamboo and others down the Yangtze River. The Regiment then organized the advance guard to shoot them with high-velocity gun and annihilate almost 2000 soldiers in two hours.[87]

---

[84] The 7th Infantry Regiment. Appendix to the Battle Report. In Battle of Nanking Editorial Committee (Ed.). Documents on the Battle of Nanjing, p. 629.

[85] The 7th Infantry Regiment. The List of Mopping-up Operations in the Nanjing City. In Battle of Nanking Editorial Committee (Ed.). Documents on the Battle of Nanjing, p. 630.

[86] No.111 Class-A Combat Order of the 7th Infantry Regiment. In Battle of Nanking Editorial Committee (Ed.). Documents on the Battle of Nanjing, p. 622.

[87] The 33rd Infantry Regiment. The Report on the Battle near Nanjing. In Battle of Nanking Editorial Committee (Ed.). Documents on the Battle of Nanjing, p. 601. There are many records concerning the seaborne "mopping-up operations against enemies" in Japanese official and private documents. For example, the 1st Seaborne Mopping-up Platoon wrote in A Summary of Seaborne Operations near Nanjing, "We go down from Wulong Mountain to Xiaguan of Nanjing. And at 13: 23, the advance guard left the port to bombard the enemy position on the north-shore of the Yangtze River. We broke the blockade and launched a fierce assault on the major enemy force on the shore and those who tried to flee on ships and rafts, killing almost 10000 enemies." (The Education Department under the Ministry of the Navy. 『事変関係掃海研究会記録』. cited in Kasahara Tokushi, The Nanking Incident. Tokyo: Iwanami Shoten. 1st Edition on December 20, 1997: p. 159). This has proved by Major General Iinuma Mamoru's diary, which mentions Major General Eijiro Kondo, commander of the 11th Navy

In Annex 3 "Reference" to the above-mentioned battle report, it was recorded that from December 10th to 13th, defeated soldiers that were executed and corpses of enemies were up to 6830.[88] The 38th Infantry Regiment, also attached to the 16th Division, took charge of "thoroughly mopping up" the city and clearly stated in Annex 5 to *Report on the Battle in Nanjing (December 14th)* that "enemies were all wiped out", although it did not list the exact number of "copse remained" or "soldiers killed".[89]

The 114th Division attached to the 10th Army recorded a total of 6000 "corpses of enemies remained" in 3rd Annex to the battle report on December 15th and a total of 229 Japanese soldiers killed or injured in 1st Annex, with numbers of Table 1, 2 and 3 added up.

And it was the same case with the 1st Battalion of the 66th Infantry Regiment attached to the 114th Division. 9 of their soldiers were killed but they killed "700 enemies who fiercely resisted the day" before they entered Nanjing (December 12th)[90]; from December 10th to 13th, 17 of their soldiers were killed but they killed over 80 times as many "enemies", almost up to 1400.

The 11th Squadron of the 45th Regiment, attached to the 6th Division of the 10th Army, encountered enemies at the Jiangdong Gate and had 3300 "enemies killed" but their own soldiers killed and injured were just totally 80. The battle at the Jiangdong Gate was not the only case. According to the battle report by the 6th Division, during the battle from the Xiahe Town to Xiaguan, the 2nd and 3rd Battalion of the 45th Regiment, one troop of the 2nd Mountain Gun Regiment directly under the 10th Army, and one troop

---

Army claimed "about 10000 enemies were killed". (Battle of Nanking Editorial Committee (Ed.). Documents on the Battle of Nanjing, p. 217.) And Tatsuzo Ishikawa, a famous Japanese writer, once followed Japanese troops entering Nanjing and a month later wrote the Living Soldiers, which was forbidden to be published in wartime. "Japanese troops did not attack the Yijiang Gate, so defeated troops in the city fled to Xiaguan Wharf via this only gate. But then facing them was the vast river without any ferryboat and no alternative land route, and they had to swim across the vast river to the Pukou Wharf with floating objects such as table, log or door plank, of which the number was up to 50000 -- it seemed there was a dark cloud floating on the river. But when they approached the opposite shore, awaiting them was Japanese MG Column. Japanese soldiers opened fire and the rain of bullets broke the silence of the water. They also could not swim back as it is the case with the Xiaguan Wharf. Then Japanese destroyer delivered coup de grace to those defeated soldiers adrift in the river."(Tatsuzo Ishikawa. 著「生きている兵隊」, 昭和戦争文学全集3『果てしなき中国戦線』. Tokyo: Shûeisha. 1st Edition on June 30, 1965: p. 78.) Although it is a novel, Living Soldiers is based on personal experience and thus has special information value.

[88] The 33rd Infantry Regiment. The Report on the Battle near Nanjing. In Battle of Nanking Editorial Committee (Ed.). Documents on the Battle of Nanjing, p. 605.

[89] No.82 Battle Report of the 38th Infantry Regiment: The Report On the Battle in the Walled City Of Nanjing. The Condition Report of the 16th Division. In Battle of Nanking Editorial Committee (Ed.). Documents on the Battle of Nanjing, p. 591.

[90] The 1st Battalion of the 66th Infantry Regiment. The Battle Report. In Battle of Nanking Editorial Committee (Ed.). Documents on the Battle of Nanjing, pp. 668–689.

of the 6th Infantry Regiment of the 6th Division defeated Chinese troops with one-ten of their forces and killed 11,000 "enemies" but only 58 of their soldiers were killed, almost one hundred and ninety to one.[91]

In terms of the foregoing materials, noteworthy are two points: One is that there were no captives but "corpses of enemies"; another is that there was a big gap between the number of "corpses of enemies" and that of Japanese soldiers killed. This could not happen in a fight unless there existed a contrast between their weapons or on one side were captives disarmed. With the materials that remain, it will not be difficult to figure out the case. For instance, we can know the Battle of the Jiangdong Gate was a "close combat" and a "hand-to-hand combat", both sides with the same weapons.[92] SEF's Deputy Chief of Staff Colonel Uemura Toshimichi got surprised at the scale of underground bunkers after shown around the defensive facilities on southern highland of Yijiang Gate and the battery at Fugui Mountain on December 26th. But on January 6th of the next year (1937), he visited the 16th Division for the "proof firing of weapons captured" and recorded it in his diary on that day.

> This afternoon I accompanied the Prince to the 16th D and watched the "proof firing of weapons captured" (Note: The Prince refers to Lieutenant General Yasuhiko Asaka, commander of Shanghai Expeditionary Army and "D" means division). Sadly, equipment such as automatic rifle, rifle, pistol, LG, MG (Note: LG refers to light machine gun while MG refers to heavy machine gun), artillery, worked as well as ours.[93]

Major Ninomiya Yoshikiyo, a member of the 3rd Department attached to the General Staff, visited China and wrote an investigation report. He said, "Compared to Chinese troops, [Japanese troops] were at a disadvantage in the quality or in the quantity of weapons used in close combat".[94] When Shanghai Expeditionary Army fought at Baoshan in October, it occurred many times that 240 mm mortar shell and 300 mm carronade shell failed to explode after fired. After crossing the Suzhou River in November, it occurred many times that 240 mm mortar shells exploded in the barrel—Japanese troops were apparently not competitive in heavy weapons. And when it comes to small arms, things got worse. Colonel Sahishige Nagatsu, who served as Head of China-concerned Department under the General Staff before

---

[91] The 6th Division. No.13 and No.14 Battle Report. In Battle of Nanking Editorial Committee (Ed.). Documents on the Battle of Nanjing, p. 692.

[92] In this battle, Japanese troops and Chinese soldiers were both armed with Sanpachi-shiki hohei-ju.(Battle of Nanking Editorial Committee (Ed.). Documents on the Battle of Nanjing, p. 692.)

[93] Uemura Toshimichi's Dairy. In Battle of Nanking Editorial Committee (Ed.). Documents on the Battle of Nanjing, pp. 279+286.

[94] Battle of Nanking Editorial Committee (Ed.). The Battle of Nanjing, p. 6.

attacking Shanghai and then as commander of the 22th Regiment after the outbreak of war, once got fussed at Captain Onishi Hajime, the staff officer of Shanghai Expeditionary Army due to the poor quality of grenade which would not explode after thrown out. Coincidentally, Captain Haruo Kano, commander of 101st Regiment under the 101st Division who was killed in the battle near the Baoshan Section of Wenzao River on October 11th, mentioned the problem that grenade "could not be fully fired" in his letter to the division Chief of Staff. Such was the case not only with regular weapons but with "high-tech" ones. Flaks shipped from German to Nanjing before the battle and set up on eastern highland of the Jiming Temple had an electric aiming system and were the most advanced ones at that time. They were a great threat to Japanese naval aircrafts. Lieutenant Hanae Shou, who was the 3rd Squadron leader under the 1st Battalion of the 20th Infantry Regiment, once said German's military aid to Chinese troops, in his suppose, dealt a "German blow" to Japan.[95] These materials are not intended to prove Chinese military equipment of advantage over Japanese—in general, it was Japanese troops that got an advantage, especially in terms of heavy weapons such as aircraft, heavy artillery and tank, and they can take advantage of this mainly in uphill battles and remote sabotage—but to prove in close combat, hand-to-hand combat and night battle, a Japanese soldier could not magically defeat ten or hundred enemies.

Therefore, I can see no other explanation for the gap between the death toll of two sides in the battle near Nanjing except that Japanese troops slaughtered captives disarmed. And the so-called "battle", the so-called "close combat" and "hand-to-hand combat" were the excuse troops at different levels gave to claim more credit.

Military documents have proved once and for all the bodies both inside and outside Nanjing were those killed in the slaughter. And meanwhile, there are records of rank-and-file soldiers at the frontline that mostly deal with their personal experiences and what they saw. We might as well examine these relevant materials. Second Lieutenant Maeda Kitsuhiko, a team leader of the 7th squadron of the 45th regiment, wrote in his diary on December 15th:

> The cause was only a small matter. The road was narrow and thus Japanese soldiers with bayoneted guns on two sides were squeezed or slipped into the pond. [Japanese soldiers] were outraged and decided to beat or scold those prisoners. Prisoners were afraid and suddenly dodged aside. The guard soldiers there also jumped up. Weapons are long called dangerous tools. The guard soldiers swore "you bastard", shaking their bayoneted guns, beating and stabbing prisoners. Prisoners got panicked began to escape. "No," they said, firing and shouting, "Prisoners are not allowed to escape" and "Shoot who escape"– This must have been the case at that time. It is said that such a small misunderstanding led to a

---

[95] Hanae Shou. Preface Three to The Truth about the Nanjing Incident: Scrutiny of John Rabe's Diary, p. 7.

great tragedy. ... I have to say that this has tarnished the image of the Imperial Army. In order to conceal this tragic incident, those reserve soldiers stayed up all night and it was not until this morning that they buried almost all the bodies. This is an real example of immoral behaviors in "extraordinary" or extreme conditions that one cannot imagine in his common sense.[96]

Such "manslaughter" occurred frequently at that time. This article thus will not discuss whether they were "accidentally killed".

Private First-Class Makihara Shouta of the 3rd Machine Gun Squadron of the 20th Regiment wrote in his diary on December 14th:

At half past eight in the morning, the 1st detachment cooperated with the 12th squadron to have a mopping up operation in the area of Maqun. Hearing the residual enemies have staggered out because of lacking food, they immediately set off by bus. Upon their arrival, they quickly shot all about 300 enemies disarmed by the rifle squadron who had been waiting there and then came back. ... On the side of the railway bifurcation, there were more than one hundred Chinese soldiers attacked and all killed by our cavalry in the night. ... At 6 p.m. ... six defeated soldiers were caught and shot dead. ... Today, the most unusual thing is that 150 or 160 enemies were poured with gasoline and burned to death at a garage. But now we have been indifferent, no matter how many bodies.[97]

In just one day, Makihara Shouta and his detachment saw and committed so many slaughters. This was not for the special "luck" of Makihara Shouta and his companions, but it was a miniature of the whole Japanese army in Nanjing at that time. Yasuyama Koudou wrote in his diary on December 19th that "It is said that the number of Chinese soldiers who remained to defend Nanjing to the end was about 100,000 and about 80,000 were killed...".[98] Most of the "80,000 people" are those "disarmed" as mentioned above.

---

[96] 「前田吉彦少尉日記」, 南京戦史編集委員会編『南京戦史資料集』, p. 464.
[97] 「牧原信夫日記」, 南京戦史編集委員会編『南京戦史資料集』, pp. 511–512.
[98] Yasuyama Koudou, 「上海戦従軍日誌」, 南京戦史編集委員会編『南京戦史資料集』, p. 532. The number "80,000" seemed to be a "statement" at that time. For example, Nanjing's War Traces and Places of Interest compiled by the "Reporting Department of the China Dispatch" said wiping out "80,000" enemy troops (quoted form 『南京』第七篇第二章「南京攻略史」, compiled by Ichiki Yoshimichi, 南京日本商工会議所, September 1st, 1941, 1st edition, p. 626). For example, Nanjing, the collection of "verses" published in 1940, contains "Song" written by Senior Captain Horikawa Shizuo, the team leader of the military police, which also has the words "80,000 abandoned bodies" (quoted form 『南京事件を考える』, p. 206). "The Diary of Iinuma Mamoru" said on December 17th that "According to today's judgment, there are about 20 divisions and 100,000 people in the vicinity of Nanjing, with about 50,000 of them destroyed by our dispatching divisions, about 30,000 of them destroyed by the navy and the 10th Army, and about 20,000 scattering. The number of destroyed troops is expected to increase in the future." (「飯沼守日記」, 南京戦史編集委員会編『南京戦史資料集』, p. 217).

Private First-Class Matachi Ike of the 2nd squadron of the 7th regiment wrote in his diary on December 16th:

> We went out again in the afternoon and caught 335 young men... These 335 defeated soldiers were brought to the Yangtze River and <u>shot dead</u> by other soldiers.[99]

Shoji (Yoshida) Masaaki, the 4th Detachment Leader under the 1st Platoon of the 3rd Squadron of the 20th Regiment, mentioned killings many times in his diary. In his diary on the 24th, it was mentioned 7000 "prisoners" were taken to an area near the Yangtze River and shot dead—in his words, "foregoing 7,000 prisoners also became <u>fish food</u>".[100] There are two points worth noting in Shoji Masaaki's records. First, as mentioned above, Yasuyama Koudou, Yamazaki Masao and others stated a large number of bodies were found along the river on the 16th and 17th and that prisoners were still killed near the river on the 24th—This indicates the riverside area had become a abattoir at that time. Second, Japanese right-wing groups take the denial of pushing bodies into the river as a key to deny the slaughters near the river (if bodies were not pushed into the river, there must be remains there). And the so-called "fish food" mentioned here proves once again that Japanese army would push bodies into the river after the slaughter.

The foregoing details of the slaughter in Yoshihiko Tanaka's records are just "hearsay". But Matachi Ike has dealt with his personal experience in his diary on December 22nd:

> When it was getting dark at 5 p.m., we gathered at the headquarter of the Battalion to kill the residual defeated soldiers. We saw 161 Chinese in the courtyard of the headquarter, waiting for the gods and looking at us without knowing death was coming to them. We took them out and shouted at them at the Foreigner Street of Nanjing, where we can see our destination, the important place near Gulin Temple where machine guns had been hidden. As the sun sank low, only moving figures could be seen and houses also became black dots. Prisoners were took to a house in the middle of a pond (Note: maybe lake? The exact meaning is not clear). Five people were took out of the house and stabbed dead. The five people walked, screaming, muttering or crying. Apparently, they had already known what was awaiting them and thus were sacred out of their scared out of their skulls. <u>Defeated soldiers are doomed to be killed by Japanese soldiers</u>! They would be beaten by sticks while walking, wrists and necks tied with iron wires. There were also some brave soldiers singing and walking. Some soldiers pretended to be dead after being stabbed. Some jumped into the water and gasped for breath. Some hid on the roof in order to escape. But since they firmly refused to come down, we poured petrol and set fire on them. With the fire burning, two or three people jumped down and were stabbed to death.

[99] 「井家又一日記」，南京戦史編集委員会編『南京戦史資料集』，p. 476.
[100] 「林正明日記」，南京戦史編集委員会編『南京戦史資料集』，p. 519.

> In the darkness, we tried hard to stab and shoot guys who tried to escape. This place was a hell at that moment. All seemed killed, we poured petrol on the bodies lying on the ground and set a fire. Those who were still alive started to move in the fire and then we killed them. The fire grew stronger. And tiles on the roof all fell down, sending sparks flying. When we looked back on our way back, the fire was still burning.[101]

If Kisaki Hisashi and other people who, as mentioned above, demonstrated "righteous indignation" can be said to still have a sense of humanity, Matachi Ike's position is totally against humanity.

Most of the foregoing records are from *Documents on the Battle of Nanjing* which was published by a group of retired military servicemen called "Kaikōsha". Although Kaikosha denies Japanese army committed the atrocities in Nanjing, it is possible to ensure documents in the collection "steer clear" of any word that confirm the atrocities, since the atrocities Japanese army committed in Nanjing were not "sporadic" individual action. And there are similar pieces of material in relevant records of different publications.

Ohara Koutarou, who served the 19th Squad of the 4th Detachment of the 2nd Platoon of the 4th squadron of the 16th regiment of the transportation crop, was a primary school teacher in Chiba County before he was enlisted. He kept a diary from September 1st, 1937, the day he joined the army, to August 7th, 1939, the day he left the army. He wrote in his diary on December 15th, 1937,

> That area seems to be Nanjing. At the other side of the mountain, there was a village on slightly flat terrain, where I saw astonishing scenes. It was astonishing that as many as 2,000 prisoners were in a square surrounded by bamboo fences, carefully guarded by our army. I later knew that they were prisoners captured during the attack against Nanjing. It was said there were about 7,000 prisoners. They came with white flags and were disarmed. Of course, some of them were captured in the battle or in other circumstances. Some even wore military uniforms under plain clothes. They were all checked and then the army decided to shoot, enslave or release them. It is said that in the mountain behind, <u>bodies of prisoners who were shot dead have been piled up as a hill</u>. But most in Nanjing seem to have been cleaned up.

His diary on December 17th has detailed the bloody process of killing "defeated soldiers" found when they went to "collect" hay. And he also wrote,

> The prisoners, those saw in the village yesterday, were taken here. And about a squad with bayonets was walking in the procession. The procession was too long to count. I ran over and asked about the amount. I was told there were 4,000 prisoners and all were captured by the 33rd, 38th and 20th Regiment in

[101]「井家又一日記」, 南京戦史編集委員会編『南京戦史資料集』, p. 479.

the battles of this area. The guards were also from these regiments. What for? Were they brought to Nanjing? Some said all would be shot dead while Others said they were taken to Nanjing to serve. Anyway, no one certainly knew the answer. There were 20,000 prisons but now only these remain to be disposed.

On his way to Nanjing on the 18th, Ohara Koutarou also encountered a large number of corpses. In his diary on that day, he wrote that "The bodies are piled up like mountains. I could imagine [our army] climbing over the bodies and chasing the enemy all the way to Nanjing".[102] The "mountainous" bodies were, of course, the prisoners the narrator had seen.

Private First-Class Kitayama Atae who served in the 3rd MG Squadron of the 20th Regiment had been arrested in the early 1930s for joining a left-wing organization before he was recruited on August 31st, 1937. His diary was checked by his squadron. In his diary on December 13th, Kitayama Atae mentioned a Chinese student soldier who "begged" Japanese soldiers to shoot him in the throat because he could not bear the atrocities. Kitayama Atae said,

> Killing such one who did not resist, pointing at his own throat and begging to "shoot here", was a disgrace to Japanese soldiers.

In the diary on December 14th, Kitayama Atae also mentioned the killing of prisoners:

> After twelve o'clock in the evening, the mopping-up operation was over and all came back. It seemed that 800 soldiers had been disarmed and all were killed. Enemy soldiers might not think they would be killed. Most of them seemed to be students and I heard many were college students.[103]

In addition to records of that time, recent years have occasionally seen some people involved who no longer broke their silence and testified. For example, a soldier from the 3rd Battalion of the 19th Regiment of the 13th Division (in his word, "his name cannot be made public in case of intimidation") testified that:

> [On the way to Nanjing] The army was stationed in a village. All men of the village were taken out of houses and shot with pistols or rifles. Women and children were all locked up in the room and would be raped at night. I didn't do such things, but I think many others had committed rape. And on the next morning, all the raped women and children were killed and even the houses were burned down. This is a march accompany with killings leaving no residences for ourselves if return. I could not believe why we were so stupid. The

---

[102]江口圭一、芝原拓自編『日中戦争従軍日記——一輜重兵の戦場体験』, pp. 134 + 136 + 137.
[103]Iguchi Kazuki et al., 『南京事件京都師団関係資料集』. Tokyo: Aoki Shoten. 1st Edition published in December 5, 1989: p. 71.

answer I got was that the anti-Japanese thought was quite popular in this area, so we were ordered to kill them all. In short, this is a sinful war of arson, robbery, rape and murder.

I think this is a war we really should apologize for. By the time when we arrived at Mufu Mountain near Nanjing, the number of prisoners had been incalculable. The 65th Morozuno Regiment (Note: "Morozuno" refers to Colonel Morozuno Sakuhajime, head of the regiment; at that time, the main force of the 13th Division was in the north of the Yangtze River, and only the 65th Regiment was sent to attack Nanjing along with one part of the 19th regiment) captured about 20,000 people. These "prisoners" included all men, ranging from 12-year-old children to wrinkled old men.

… [5,000 prisoners were tied up and confined under the forts of Mufu Mountain] This time, they were marching in a two-column row for somewhere in the direction of the Yangtze River. Two or three meters away from the two sides of the row were Japanese soldiers armed with ammunition and pulling ropes. Suddenly, one prisoner fell down and other ones fell down one after another. Before they could get up, they were all stabbed dead with bayonets.

Prisoners behind had to make a detour and walked four kilometers, which ought to be one kilometer walk, to the Yangzi River. When we arrived, it was already evening, so I was not sure whether it was a soldier shed or other building standing on the south of the Yangtze River. Five thousand prisoners were sitting there in the square and there were infantries with guns pointed at them from windows of second and first floors. In the north was a several meter-high stone wall which was so high that I could feel it even though it was late at night. No prisoners thus could escape from the side of wall. They all sat there. Some Japanese soldiers wanted to pull prisoners out for beheading in order to try their military swords while others wanted to stab them with bayonets, and all did as they wanted.

In fact, I have not decapitated anyone since my war service began. I borrowed a sergeant major's machete to cut a sleeping prisoner, but was stuck in half. It was really not easy to cut off one's head. I could not manage it even with all my strength. Then, there was a screaming and [prisoners] all stood up. We should not have shot them without the command of the machine gun team leader. However, at that time, five thousand prisoners stood up but we can hardly control the situation. Machine guns thus were fired without the "shooting" command. I also wanted to have a try and I did, but I did not continue because I thought it was dangerous. Sprayed with machine gun fire, 5000 captured soldiers all fell.

Then, we used bayonets to stab them because there might be someone alive. I was not holding a Japanese gun, but a Chinese gun, which could not be equipped with Japanese bayonet. So I had to borrow my comrade's Japanese gun, with my Chinese gun on the back. I walked on the bodies and stabbed over 30 people. The next morning, I fell to lift my sore arms up.[104]

The specific statement made by the former Japanese soldier, whose name cannot be made public in case of "intimidation", is another strong evidence

---

[104] 南京大虐殺の真相を明らかにする全国聯絡会編『南京大虐殺＿＿日本人への告発』, Tokyo, Tôhô Shuppan, 1st edition published on September 21st, 1992, pp. 34–37.

that Japanese army not only violated international law but were totally against war ethics.

Among all the atrocities committed by the Japanese army, the killings of prisoners are the most well-documented in existing Japanese historical material. These materials having been examined and explained, I think Japanese fictionalists should have no more words if they did conclude, as they have advertised, based on historical facts.

How Was the Military Discipline of Japanese Army When Attacking Nanjing?

Japanese fabrication school, middle-of-the-road school and great slaughter school have different opinions on the operations of Japanese army after capturing Nanjing. The diaries and memoirs of Japanese veterans and related Western documents that have been compiled by the slaughter school involve many records of murders, arsons, robberies and rapes committed by Japanese army; the fabrication school denies Japanese army committed any atrocity; the middle-of-the-road school does not deny the atrocities in its totality but since they only confirm charges of a small amount of "occasional" crimes, they, in terms of overall judgment, are no different from the fabrication school—the fabrication school has been emphasizing that the armies of the United States, the Soviet Union and other countries are not well-disciplined, and thus the atrocities of Japanese army cannot become a special problem if only "a small amount" of atrocities. Such argument that Japanese army was not guilty[105] had been repeated as early as by the Tokyo Trial and has long lasting impact on not only the opinions of the Japanese mainstream but also third parties other than China and Japan (such as above-mentioned the Indian Justice R. B. Pal and Holland Justice B. V. A. Rolling of the Tokyo Trial and C. A. Willoughby, head of the 2nd Section of Staff of US Army). And since there are always some Japanese who believe that Chinese and Western documents are not objective as propaganda of "enemy" and his allies, it is hard to avoid the debate over the truthfulness, unless arguments made based on Japanese documents.

As mentioned above, the journal of the Judicial Affairs Department of SEF does not remain today and that of the 10th Army, which "accidentally" remain today, does not mention the operations of Japanese army after capturing Nanjing. But although records of operations taken after capturing Nanjing do not remain, the operations of Japanese army outside Nanjing

---

[105] It is said that "Japanese army has the lowest crime rate in the world" (小室直樹、渡部昇一著『封印の昭和史＿＿＿「戦後五〇年」自虐の終焉』、『国際法から見た「南京大屠殺」の疑問』, 東京, 徳間書店1995年10月15日第4次印刷版, 第107页). Also, someone claims that "most of the Japanese soldiers who were charged are kind" (畝本正己著『真相·南京事件＿＿＿ラーべ日記を検証して』第230页, And in the preface of this book, Hanae Shou claims Japanese army was "immaculately clean". See p. 11).

were well-documented. Under a force at the same time, the military discipline of Japanese army outside Nanjing can reflect that of those inside Nanjing.

Based on the journals of Judicial Affairs Department at two levels, respectively, under the 10th Army and SEF, as well as documents such as Ogawa's diary, we can reach the following conclusions: First, during the several months that the 10th Army stayed in China, Japanese troop "comparatively steadily"[106] controlled the southern China because both Kuomintang (Nationalist Party) and Communist Party didn't organize large-scale resistance. If the Japanese soldiers' atrocities are related to the so-called "revenge",[107] the number of atrocities should be the smallest during the war. However, the 10th Army still committed severe atrocities. Second, the Japanese troop's atrocities include reckless murder, arson, looting and rape. Among these crimes, rape was frequently and ubiquitously committed. Third, since the military law office responsible for regulating military discipline was small and limited to certain functions, and in particular the number of military police was small, a lot of atrocities were not and were unlikely to be seen by the police. As a result, the cases submitted to the military law office and the atrocities recorded in the journals and diaries account for only a tip of the iceberg of the crimes committed by the Japanese soldiers. Fourth, the Japanese army set a military law office to maintain military discipline. On the one side, wrongful acts were really circumstanced. On the other hand, it has some side effects as the soldiers resist it and the leaders at different levels purposely shied their soldiers, which imposed another constraint on the operation of the military law office, in addition to mechanical limits. Fifth, it was the military law office that had responsibility to maintain military order and discipline. But, as a part of the Japanese army, it primarily could not "do harm to" the army. Many criminals were acquitted or sentenced to a light punishment mainly because the military law office volunteered to make some concessions, although it did suffer from external "pressure". The office heard limited or even a handful of cases on the atrocities committed by Japanese army and did not launch a thorough investigation and then apportion blame. Objectively speaking, it was the connivance of the office that encouraged Japanese soldiers to commit crimes on a broader scale. Sixth, compare to the connivance in Japanese soldiers' atrocities, Japanese military law office imposed extremely cruel penalty on Chinese who "violated the law".

---

[106] Although the 10th Army was established when China and Japan were stuck in fierce battles, the Chinese army guarding Shanghai had begun to retreat when it landed from Jinshanwei on November 5. During the months in China, the 10th Army did not encounter fierce resistance or have casualties as heavy as that of SEF. Except for capturing Nanjing by an absolute advantage of forces, there was almost no battle later. For example, when occupying Hangzhou, they "entered the city with no casualty" and without opening fire.

[107] It has been widely acknowledged that the main reason for the Japanese atrocities lies in the vengeance inspired by the tough fighting and heavy casualties. And the performance of the 10th Army outside Nanjing is especially typical of its normal status.

(The most powerful evidence is that according to the limited records in the remaining journal and diaries, Chinese who were suspected to have tried to escape all ended up being executed.) And in daily regulation, Chinese who showed a hint of rebellion were severely punished by the Japanese police in a much more violent manner. Therefore, for Chinese, the Japanese military law office is a machine to brutally suppress them. And last, we thus can draw a general conclusion that the so-called "strict military discipline of the Japanese troop" and "the lowest crime rate" still cannot make sense even if they are arguments based on the firsthand documents left by Japanese troops.[108]

Were Operations of Japanese Army After the Capture of Nanjing Unknown to Japanese Military Authority?

Japanese right-wing forces always think the Tokyo Trial was "a party for winning states". In their opinion, the "Nanjing Massacre" was not known to the world until the Tokyo Trial and so was the atrocities committed by Japanese, such as large-scale looting, rapes and arson—the reason why they were "unknown" is "non-existence" and thus the "Nanjing Massacre" was the fabrication of the Tokyo Trial. This argument has existed for a long time and began to be emphasized in the 1980s.[109] We need not bother to refute this argument due to the following simple reasons: First, "being unknown" does not mean "non-existence"; second, as put in history studies, "to prove is easier than to deny". One can witness a mere part and thus cannot draw an overall conclusion, no matter whether what he said is what he saw. And this does not mean the argument that they were "unknown" can hold.

Japanese army entered Nanjing on December 13th. At that time, some citizens and foreigners in Nanjing were expecting that Japanese would save them from the bombings since mid-August, especially the looting and arson committed by defeated soldiers before the fall of Nanjing, and would restore the order of Nanjing. However, operations of Japanese army after entering Nanjing were beyond their expectations. F. Tillman Durdin, a reporter of *New York Times*, was ordered to leave Nanjing by Japanese army on December 15th. He issued his first report on the 17th on an American

---

[108] See my article A Study of the Bearing and Discipline of the Japanese Army Invading China: Centered on The Tenth Army.

[109] For example, there is a section called "Knowing the 'Nanjing Massare' for the first Time" in Chapter 7 "The Tokyo Trial" of "Nankin gyakusatsu" no kyokō. (See田中正明著『「南京虐殺」の虚構＿＿松井大将の日記をめぐって』, 東京, 日本教文社1984年6月25日第1版, pp. 287–289.) The History As Not Seen in Textbook claims that the Nanjing Massacre was "suddenly put forward" at the Tokyo Trial. (藤岡信勝、自由主義史観研究会編『教科書が教えない歴史』2, 東京, 産経新聞社1996年12月30日第1版, p. 72). Takemoto Tadao and Oohara Yasuo said that "there was no Japanese senior official knowing about this". (See『再審「南京大虐殺」＿＿世界に訴える日本の冤罪』, p. 65.) And Matsumura Toshio said that from the Tokyo Trial to the Nanjing Trial, "we clearly see how a rumor became increasing powerful". (See『「南京虐殺」への大疑問』, 東京, 展転社1998年12月13日第1版, p. 396.)

warship moored in Shanghai, which was also the first report by a Western reporter on Japanese atrocities. This report dealt with the disenchantment of Chinese people with the possibility of leaving in peace.

> However, the wait-and-see attitude towards the situation has to change with only three-day occupation by Japanese army. Crimes happen anywhere in Nanjing, such as large-scale looting, violence against women, slaughter of ordinary citizens, their expulsion from houses, collective execution of prisoners and forcible capture of adult men. Nanjing has been gripped by a horror of such crimes.[110]

The operations of Japanese army spread like wildfire and soon spread to the outside world. Judging from the available documents, Japan's top officials also learned the truth almost at the same time. Japan's local military and political authorities learned about the situation of Japanese army mainly through two channels. One was the extensive coverage in foreign media and the other was the information obtained by Japanese embassy and consulates, mainly the embassy in Nanjing and other institutions. And the sources of information can be roughly classified as the grievances reports, protests and other documents received by Japanese embassy and consulates and the various types of information collected by Japanese embassy and consulates, Japanese news agencies and other institutions.

As can be learned from *The Good Man of Nanking: The Diaries of John Rabe* as well as other records, the next day after Japanese army entered Nanjing, John H. D. Rabe drafted letters in the name of the chairman of the International Committee for the Nanking Safety Zone and planned to submit them to the Japanese army. On the 15th, Rabe met with officials of Japanese army and Japanese embassy and, respectively, gave them a letter, hoping that they would maintain order in Nanjing and gave Chinese soldiers who laid down their arms "lenient treatment". Since the 16th, the International Committee began to report every day to the Japanese embassy officials on the atrocities committed by Japanese troops.[111] At that time, the embassy officials contacting with Rabe and other people were mainly alternate official

---

[110] Hora Tomio (Ed.). 『日中戦争史資料』9「南京事件」II, p. 280. This record included in Hora Tomio's book is slightly different from that included in Hata Ikuhiko's Nankin Jiken. For example, there is an additional sentence "even some citizens greeted the Japanese spearhead with cheers at the end of the first paragraph and the "only three days" is replaced with "only two days" in the second paragraph". (See Hata Ikuhiko. 『南京事件____虐殺の構造』, Tokyo: Chûô Kôronsha. 20th Edition published on August 20th, 1999: p. 3.)

[111] For example, Bates said, "We visited the Japanese embassy every day and submitted the reports of our protests, our requests, and accurate records of violence and crimes." (The National Archives Administration of China, the Second Historical Archives of China & Jilin Provincial Academy of Social Sciences. (Eds.), The Anthology of Documents on Japanese Invasion of China: The Nanjing Massacre. Beijing: The Book Company. 1st Edition published in July 1995: p. 1023.)

Fukuda Tokuyasu,[112] Consul General of Shanghai Okazaki Katsuo,[113] Second Secretary Fukui Kiyoshi[114] and others.

Fukuda Tokuyasu once said in an interview:

> I became the recipient of their dissatisfaction (Note: referring to the International Committee for the Nanking Safety Zone). They protested everything and the protests were half truths. It is my role to convey protests to the military like "Something happens and please deal with it no matter in what way."[115]

Such a large number of protests were conveyed to the local army as well as to the top military and political authorities in Japan. On December 22nd, Major General Anami Korechika, Head of Personnel Bureau, after attending the directors' meeting of the Army Ministry, wrote down the following words in his notes, "the Nakashima Division has treated women (Note: this is the original expression and means rapes or violence against women), committed killing and violated military discipline in a way that is despicable beyond words, leading to the decadence of the national morality and the tragic situation of the war".[116] The South China battle targeting Guangdong, which was scheduled on December 25th, had to be canceled, which seemed to have something to do with pressure from public opinion on the Nanjing atrocities.[117]

---

[112] The Chinese version of The Good Man of Nanking: The Diaries of John Rabe mistakenly translated it into "Fukuda Tokuko", such as line 2 on page 180. After Fukuda Tokuyasu became the secretary of the Prime Minister Yoshida Shigeru, he had served as the chief of the Defense Department, the chief of the Administrative Department, the Postmaster General and other positions as well as a member of parliament.

[113] The Chinese version of The Good Man of Nanking: The Diaries of John Rabe mistakenly translated it into "Okazaki Katsutake", such as the line 7 by counting backwards on page 190 and the line 6 by counting backwards on page 191. Okazaki Katsuo served as the Minister for Foreign Affairs in the 1950s.

[114] The Chinese version of The Good Man of Nanking: The Diaries of John Rabe mistakenly translated it into "Fukui K", such as line 13 and line 16 on page 191, line 10 on page 201. At present, in many historical data collections, the name is mistakenly translated as "Fuguyi" (the pronunciation of the surname "Fukui"), such as Selected Archives of Japanese Aggression against China: Nanjing Massacre, line 4 on page 1034; Archives of Nanjing Massacre Made by Japanese Invaders jointly compiled by the Second Historical Archives of China and Nanjing Municipal Archives, line 18 on page 657, edition produced in December 1997. Fukui Kiyoshi was serving as Consul General of Japan in Nanjing.

[115] Tanaka Masaaki, 『「南京虐殺」の虚構──松井人!の日記をめぐって』, p. 36.

[116] Cited in Hata Ikuhiko, 『南京事件──虐殺の構造』, p. 172.

[117] In general, much emphasis has been placed on harming the interests of the west, like said, "The reason is that the U.S. ship Panay was sunk and a British ship was shelled during Japanese attack on Nanjing. Diplomatic negotiations on this incident are under way. Now the relationships with Britain and the United States are very dangerous. Therefore, the implementation of this operation will be considered seriously." (Imoto Kumao, 『作戦日誌で綴る支那事変』, Tokyo: Fuyo Shobo Publishing, 1st edition published on June 30th, 1978, p. 184.) However, judging

According to *From Ichigayadai-machi to Ichigayadai-machi*, the memoir of Colonel Kawabe Torashiro, who was then Chief of the War Instruction Section of the first division (Operations Department) of the General Staff Headquarter, he then drafted a "serious warning" to Matsui Iwane in the name of Chief of Staff Prince Kan'in Kotohito.[118] The so-called "serious warning" is the "Ultimatum on Military Discipline" issued on January 4th, 1938. The ultimatum raised the Japanese atrocities to the level of "harming the great cause of the entire army".[119] In *The Battle of Nanjing*, this event is titled "Special and Significant expectation of the Chief of Staff",[120] which can reveal its great significance. Meanwhile, as early as on December 28th, 1937, there was an ultimatum "Reinforce and Maintain the Military Discipline" jointly signed by the Chief of Staff and the Secretary of State for War. And at the same day, the Deputy of the Ministry of the Army also phoned the Chief of Staff and the Director of Secret Service Department of CCAA for the issue of Japanese atrocities. At the end of December, Japanese military sent Anami Korechika to China. Nukata Tan who then was Anami Korechika's retinue later recalled,

"On the New Year's Day of the 13th year of the Shōwa Era (1937), I followed Mr. Anami, Head of Personnel Bureau, to Nanjing and reported to the Army Commander Mr. Matsui. 'The battle instructions issued by Nakashima Kesago, the commanding officer of the 16th Division, were against humanity.' Mr Anami said. And thus he condemned it and lamented the decadence of Bushido."[121]

At the end of January of the following year, Major General Honma Masaharu,[122] Head of 2nd Section (Intelligence Department) of General

---

from the original documents, this matter should also be connected with the Japanese atrocities, as in the Iinuma Mamoru's diary on December 30th: "Staff Officer Nakayama of the Area Army has come to convey the regret to see Japanese army' illegal acts against foreign embassies and other violations of military discipline to the Chief of staff, which is frightening. He showed a telegram jointly issued by Secretary of State for War and Chief of Staff with the main idea that the Area Army is requested to be careful when the movements of various countries are extremely delicate. There is a tone that the Guangdong battle has been consequently suspended." (「飯沼守日記」, 南京戦史編集委員会編『南京戦史資料集』, 非売品, Tokyo, Kaikōsha, 1st edition published on November 3rd, 1989, pp. 229–230.) At that time, Japanese atrocities were an important aspect to cause severe international public opinion.

[118] Kawabe Torashiro.『"ケ谷台から"ケ谷台へ』, Tokyo: Jiji Tsûshinsha, 1st edition published on Novemmber5, 1962, p. 153.

[119]「軍紀風紀に関する件通牒」, 南京戦史編集委員会編『南京戦史資料集』, p. 565.

[120] 南京戦史編集委員会編纂『南京戦史』, 非売品, Tokyo: Kaikōsha, 1st edition published on November 3rd, 1989, p. 398.

[121] 額田坦著『陸軍省人事局長の回想』, 東京, 芙蓉書房1977年5月1日第1版, pp. 321–322.

[122] Honma Masaharu later defeated MacArthur in the Philippines and was then quickly executed after Japanese defeat. Tanaka Masaaki was very dissatisfied with the execution and said, MacArthur "was extremely keen on revenge for Lieutenant General Honma Masaharu who

Staff, visited China and one of his missions was also investigating the discipline of Japanese army.

Aiyi Tanjiri who was then the first Secretary of the Japanese embassy in China said,

> I was personally told about Japanese atrocities by Okazaki Katsuo who (later became the Minister of Foreign Affairs but) then followed General Iwane Matsui and took preventative measures in cooperation with foreign missionaries and professors in Nanjing. And the atrocities committed by Japanese Army after they entered the city of Nanjing, such as looting and abuse, were too cruel to hear.[123]

Ishii Itaro, who was then Chief of East Asian Affairs Bureau of the Ministry of Foreign Affairs, testified in the Tokyo Trial and detailed the situation after the news of Nanjing atrocities came to Tokyo:

> On December 13th, our army entered Nanjing city, and then our Acting Consul General of Nanjing (Fukui Kiyoshi) returned to Nanjing from Shanghai. The Acting Consul General's original local report to the Ministry was about our army's atrocities. And the report by telegram was then immediately submitted by the East Asia Affairs Bureau to the Chief of the Military Affairs Bureau of the Army Ministry. At that time, the Foreign Minister was astonished and worried about the report. He told me measures must be taken to deal with it as soon as possible. I then replied since the report had been sent to the Ministry of the Army, it should be me to warn the military authority in the liaison meeting of Ministries of Army, Navy and Foreign Affairs. (It was a practice that the meeting would be held in the office of Head of the East Asia Bureau at any time when necessary. Heads of the Military Affairs Bureau of the Army Ministry and the Navy Ministry as well as Head of the East Asia Affairs Bureau should have attended the meeting. But in fact, it was the first Section Chiefs of the Military Affairs Bureau of the Army Ministry and the Navy Ministry that attended the meeting which was hosted by Head of the East Asia Affairs Bureau.) At the meeting, I told the foregoing issue of atrocities to the first Section Chief of the Military Affairs Bureau of the Army Ministry, saying that since it was called holy war and Imperial Army, severe measures should be rapidly and firmly taken in reaction to such a serious situation. The Section Chief totally agreed with me and accepted my proposal. Shortly thereafter, a written report was submitted to the ministry from the Acting Consul General of Nanjing. The detailed report on the atrocities of our army was printed in English by the International Committee for the Nanking Safety Zone which was organized by third-country

---

caused MacArthur's failure and loss of face in the Philippines. The Lieutenant General Honma was executed only two months after the trial began. Moreover, both the judges and the prosecutors of this trial were his subordinates, so the trail was tantamount to lynching." (田中正明著『南京事件の総括____虐殺否定十五の論拠』, p. 24).

[123]Tajiri Akiyoshi, 『田尻愛義回想録』, Tokyo: Hara Shobô, 1st edition on October 11th, 1977, p. 62.

citizens who resided in Nanjing. It was sent to my Ministry by our Consulate General of Nanjing upon receiving it. After carefully reading through the report, I reported the gist to the Minister. As the minister intended, at the next liaison meeting, I mentioned this report to the Head of the 1st Section under the Military Affairs Bureau of the Army Ministry and proposed to take severe measures. And the military authority said that it had already instructed the front army to pay strict attention to military discipline. Later, the atrocities committed by the local army have greatly decreased. I remember that around the end of January of the next year, the central authority of the Army specially dispatched personnel to the front army. I know it was Major General Honma. Since then, the atrocities in Nanjing ended.[124]

Ishii Itaro later wrote in his memoir,

Nanjing fell on the December 13th. I was later amazed at the telegraphed report of Consul Fukui who followed our army back to Nanjing and the written report of Shanghai Consul which were submitted one and another. Words came that Japanese troops which entered Nanjing committed looting, rape, arson and murder against Chinese. And military police were too few to regulate the military discipline. It was reported that even Consul Fukui was in danger due to his attempt to stop it. In the diary on January 6th, 1938, he wrote,
  A letter from Shanghai reported in detail the atrocities committed by our army in Nanjing, including looting and rape, which were horrible. Alas, is this still the Imperial Army?[125]

One of the records of the Tokyo Trial said that Lieutenant Colonel Hirota Minoru was sent to China and specially served as the staff SEF due to the issue of military discipline. According to the memory of Utsunomiya Naokata (Minister of Foreign Military Affairs, who was succeeded by Hirota Minoru), Hirota Minoru once told him, "Japanese consuls in Nanjing and I knew merely from the clearest information that there were many married women and young women suffering from violence and killed in the University of Nanking. Such a regrettable fact is really shameful".[126] Lieutenant General Okamura Yasuji, who came to China as commander of the 11th Army in June 1938, said that "In Tokyo, I once heard large scale atrocities were said to be committed during the Battle of Nanjing". After arriving in Shanghai in July, he confirmed the following facts:

During the Battle of Nanjing, Japanese army committed atrocities, such as looting and rape, against ten thousands of citizens.

---

[124] Hora Tomio (Ed.).『日中戦争史資料』8「南京事件」I, Tokyo: Kawade Shobô Shinsha. 1st edition on November 25th, 1973, p. 220.

[125] Ishii Itaro.『外交官の一生』、東京、中央公論社1986年10月25日第1版、第332页。Tokyo: Chûô Kôronsha. 1st Edition on October 25, 1986, p. 267.

[126] Utsunomiya Naokatak.『黄河、揚子江、珠江＿＿＿中国勤務の思い出』. Edition published in1(Not For Sale). Cited in南京戦史編集委員会編纂『南京戦史』, pp. 402–403.

The troops at the front were guilty of killing prisoners or captives due to the shortage of supplies.[127]

Shigemitsu Mamoru, the later ambassador to Nanjing, also put in his memoir which was written in Sugamo prison after the war, "[Japanese atrocities] were known to the world and became an international issue. Japan was thus discredited".[128]

From the foregoing documents, we can learn that the atrocities committed by Japanese army after entering Nanjing were reported to the top military authority in Tokyo as soon. Hence, the argument that atrocities were not known to the Japanese authority until the Tokyo Trial totally goes against the truth. (Japanese right-wing forces claim atrocities were "unknown" to not only senior military officials but also all in Nanjing including those reporters. I have refuted this argument in detail in my another article, which thus will not be further discussed.[129])

Were the Testimonies to the Innocence of Japanese Soldiers Who Participated in the Capture of Nanjing and Took the Stand in Tokyo Trial Reliable?

When the Tokyo Trial heard the Nanjing atrocities, the witnesses for the defense and the defendants who participated in the attack against Nanjing did not argue along the same line. Some denied the atrocities in its totality, leaving no room for correcting themselves. Most typically, Wakisaka Jiro, leader of the 36th Regiment, said one of his subordinates was jailed for picking up a shoe.[130] And others admitted there were problems with "individual" military disciplines[131] but unanimously argued that the Nanjing atrocities presented by the prosecution had not been heard or seen, even if they do not completely deny that Japanese army had some problems with military discipline. As mentioned above, whether they had heard about the atrocities isn't equal

---

[127] Inaba Masao (Ed.).『岡村寧次大将資料』(上). Hara Shobô. The Edition in 1970. Cited in『南京大虐殺否定論13のウソ』, p. 32.

[128] 重光葵著『昭和の動乱』上巻，東京，中央公論社1952年3月20日，第175頁。The performance of the Japanese army in Nanjing, even completely from the standpoint of Japan, was "regrettable" to some extent. As Horiba Kazuo said in a summary of "national governance" in the late 1940s, "The invasion of Nanjing brought up ten years of hatred and hurt the prestige of the Japanese army." (堀場一雄著『支那事変戦争指導史』, Tokyo: Jiji Tsûshinsha. 1st edition on September 10th, 1962, p. 111).

[129] See my article "Is the Nanjing Massacre a Fabrication Made by Tokyo Trial?". Modern Chinese History Studies. 2002(6): pp. 1–57.

[130] 洞富雄編『日中戦争史資料』8「南京事件」I，東京，河出書房1973年11月25日第1版, p. 239.

[131] For example, Ogawa Senjiro's "Affidavit" (No. 2708 Document of the Defense) says, "By the time [he] arrived in Nanjing, [he] had punished the wrongdoers in the case of military or moral discipline offense, a total of 20 cases." See 洞富雄編『日中戦争史資料』8「南京事件」I, p. 256.

to whether it is true. But if we say a certain amount of different people's similar accounts are all not truthful, it is necessary to prove it. Hence, it is necessary to directly respond to this issue not just because the fabrication school has always argued based on foregoing statements. Maybe it is because the Tokyo Trial has reached a conclusion or some people think these "testimonies" will be overturned as long as the facts can be clarified; there is so far no specific examination of these "testimonies". I have analyzed the doubts about the important testimonies of the defendants that were not questioned in the Tokyo Trial, but did not have a thorough examination of the testimonies. Recently, I have compared the testimonies of the defendants and witnesses in Tokyo Trial with their diaries later published and have found there exist inconsistencies which are not accidental "errors" but differences by nature. Two key figures will be taken as example, namely Iinuma Mamoru, Chief of Staff of SEF and Ogawa Sekijiro, Chief of the Judicial Affairs Department of the 10th Army, to have a brief idea of what are the differences between their testimonies and the documents at the time of the incident.

Iinuma Mamoru

Iinuma Mamoru's "Affidavit" (i.e. No. 2626 Document for the Defense and No. 3399 Court Evidence) mainly deals with as follows: First, according to General Matsui's Instructions after the Establishment of Shanghai Expeditionary Army, "battles in Shanghai shall be targeted against Chinese troops that have specially challenged me. You shall protect Chinese soldiers and civilians and not involve foreign residents and troops in". Second, "Those who fall down with infectious diseases shall be treated without distinction and provided with medicine". Third, "Bombing shall not be dropped in downtown areas (of both Shanghai and Nanjing)". Fourth, "General Matsui issued a detailed instruction on attacking against Nanjing, which provides that … enemies who do not resist and common people shall be treated with mercy". Fifth, "there were no dorms for Japanese soldiers as houses outside the city had almost been burned, so more troops than planned entered Nanjing. And on December 19th, General Matsui ordered all troops except the 16th Division to retreat to the eastern area of Nanjing and to strictly observe military rules and discipline so as to maintain the order of Nanjing". Sixth, "he had a inspection tour on December 16th, on the 20th and at the end of the year. During his tours, no bodies were seen in the city but only around ten bodies who killed in the battle at Xiaguan. The slaughter of ten thousand of people even could not happen in his wildest dream". Seventh, "there were small fires but no systematic arson as had not been seen or reported. Only a handful of houses inside the city were burned down and most remained as what they were". Eighth, "after entering Nanjing, General Matsui received the reports of a small amount of looting and atrocities and felt pity as he had forbidden such acts for many times. And then he ordered all soldiers to prevent any wrongful acts and advocated imposing severe punishment for wrongful acts. Since then, the military rules were so rigorous that the 16th Division protested against Judicial Affairs Department's disposal of such matter". Ninth, troops "offered damages" to those who were levied and "put up the certificate of paying damages" if the owner were absent. Tenth, one could not enter the safety zone without permission as it is under protection and thus there were "no collective, systematic and long-lasting looting". And last, "I did not know the Nanjing Security Zone Committee had protested a lot, and no one reported it to General Matsui".[132]

Since the establishment of Shanghai Expeditionary Army, Matsui Iwane has always emphasized on the "strict observance" of military discipline, to which the testimonies of witnesses for the defense can be consistent evidence. And among the testimonies, that of Iinuma Mamoru is particularly powerful evidence—not only because he was Chief of Staff—but because he claimed some "instructions" were passed on by him (such as that on December 4th). However, *Iinuma Mamoru's Diary* from August 15th to December 17th (1937) does not mention that Matsui Iwane demanded for a good military discipline. Generally speaking, whether there is a record cannot be equated to whether it is a fact. If the diary is rough, something irrelevant is likely to be omitted. But since *Iinuma Mamoru's Diary* distinguishes itself out for a wide coverage of details and more importantly, Iinuma as well as other witnesses claimed Matsui Iwane attached great importance to the "instructions", relevant records were unlikely to completely omit them. There is no possibility of being omitted, but there exists no relevant records—the only answer is Iinuma lied and perjured himself in the Tokyo Trial. As for why he mentioned the issue of military discipline in his diary on December 18th, I suppose Japanese top military and political authorities suffered from the pressure due to the protests of Western media and foreigners in China, especially those in Nanjing, on the atrocities of Japanese army after entering Nanjing.

The diary also does not mention the so-called "treatment without distinction" of infectious diseases as claimed in the testimony. Moreover, in the diary is recorded the treatment in opposite. For example, there are many records of the so-called "disposal" (which means "slaughter") of prisoners in the diary: Respectively on September 6th and 7th, about 600 prisoners were slaughtered inside and outside the Baoshan Fortress; on September 9th, "some of the bodies... were killed with hands tied up"; on October 19th, "when the 3rd D (Note: D means division) occupied the house of Huangs, they disposed eleven captives who were wounded".[133] Such records can still go on. Logically, since they refused to release anyone, were they likely to give "treatment without distinction"? Lieutenant General Nakashima Kesago, the commanding officer of the 16th Division, mentioned the "disposal" of prisoners and wrote his "concern" that prisoners would "riot" in the diary on

---

[132] 洞富雄編『日中戦争史資料』8「南京事件」I, pp. 251–252.
[133] 「飯沼守日記」, 南京戦史編集委員会編『南京戦史資料集』, pp. 99–100 + 105 + 155.

December 13th.[134] In the diary of Yamada Senji, the commanding officer of the 103th Infantry Brigade, on December 15th, it is mentioned prisoners would "all be killed", which had something to do with the confusing thing that there was "no reserve of food". Therefore, the fabrication school often takes the foregoing records as their "arguments". For instance, *The Illusion of the "Nanjing Massacre"*, the first monograph to deny the Nanjing Massacre, has "tampered with" the original words when citing Yamada's diary, turning "no reserve of food" to be the direct reason for "disposing prisoners". Although Japanese army shall not be allowed to "dispose" prisoners due to any "concern" or "confusion" in accordance with the rules of civilized society, it is certainly not surprising that an army lack of awareness of international law[135] regarded prisoners as their burden. As for the so-called "treatment without distinction", it totally goes against the "personality" of Japanese army and cannot be truthful, so it is not surprising that no record can be found.

From the records of both Chinese and foreigners in Nanjing that have been mentioned in the 2nd Section, we can see that Nanjing was under bombing attacks. Hence, Iinuma Mamoru's so-called testimony that Japanese army tried to avoid dropping bombing into the city does not make sense because it goes against the truth. And to the least, were the bombing attacks unknown to Iinuma Mamoru? Apparently, the answer is negative based on *Iinuma Mamoru's Diary*: On September 11th, he wrote "the Navy (Note: by that time the Japanese air force had not yet become an independent force) bombed Nanshi"; on September 15th, it was written at the beginning that "the Navy will attack Hankou, Nanchang and other important cities, in addition to heavier bombing attacks against Nanjing", which implies that Iinuma Mamoru knew not only the bombings but also Japanese army's bombing plan against "cites". In addition to the records of bombings, in his diary are also mentioned the specific targets and consequences of the bombing attacks. For example, he wrote on September 20th that "the Navy attacked Nanjing and at about noon, 16 war planes bombed the enemy General Staff Headquarter, the national KMT government and so on". And on October 30th, the foreign confessions were bombed, raising the protests from Western missions:

> At 10 a.m., Major General Harada reported as follows: At 4 o'clock on the 29th, our army dropped eight bombs into the Jessfield Park and were asked to stop. But today at 4:00, another ten bombs were also dropped there, having three English soldiers killed and several wounded. And thus we have received

---

[134] 「中島今朝吾日記」, 南京戦史編集委員会編『南京戦史資料集』, p. 326.

[135] The Japanese army nominally had a consultant for international law, and the consultant for the Chinese Army was Dr. Saito Yoshie. However, Japanese left-wing scholars have severely criticized the Japanese army as a "barbaric", "premodern" army, such as Tsuda Michio's The Nanjing Massacre and The Japanese Mental Structure (Cheng Zhaoqi &Liu Yan Trans. Hong Kong: The Commercial Press. 1st Edition published in June 2000, p. 89).

serious protests (perhaps from the Britain) and been asked for a solution. Italy claimed his border with the British police was bombed at 4:00 and friendly asked us to stop. And we were also asked to stop the bombing attacks by France and the USA, respectively for a bomb dropped between the Avenue Jofire Confession and the railway lines at 7:00 and one dropped at the Columbia Road at the same time.

Since the frequent bombing attacks had raised protests from Western countries, Japanese military felt much pressure. On November 2nd, Matsui Iwane stated that "[we] should pay careful attention to the potential damage". But at that time, Matsui referred to the "rights of countries" excluding China. And a record in this dairy is noteworthy. It is written that "The Army minister made it clear that the British plane that flew over our area yesterday afternoon should be shot down".[136] It thus can be inferred that the Japanese army's attitude towards the West was not as they claimed in the Tokyo Trial.

The foregoing examples have proven Iinuma Mamoru's testimony, cross-referenced with his own diary, cannot make sense at all. And let's move on to the most important issue, that is, what did Iinuma Mamoru think of the operations of Japanese at that time and whether the operations were "extremely lawful" as he claimed in the Tokyo Trial. As mentioned above, "Yamada Detachment captured over ten thousand people and killed them one by one with bayonet". This in fact can be the most powerful evidence that Japanese army broke all the international laws. But considering Iinuma Mamoru as well as other soldiers regarded such acts as "combat operations", we will set aside this issue and focus on the operations after the battle. On December 19th, "the military police reported, the buildings in Sun Yat-sen Mausoleum were set on fire the day before and the fire was still burning. Also, some officials along with his soldiers entered the safety zone and committed rapes". It was not mentioned who set the fire, but considering the function of military police was to report on the acts of ill-disciplined army and Chinese soldiers who escaped had to hide themselves in face of the city-wide manhunt, it could be nobody but Japanese soldiers that set the fire. Iinuma Mamoru affirmed in the Tokyo Trial that he had not received any report—it cannot make sense that "he forgot it" because one would not reply with finality had he forgotten about something. Let us go back to the records. In his diary on February 24th (1937), he wrote "Vicious looting was mainly committed by soldiers. Measures must be taken to restore the military discipline and the spirit of the Imperial Army". On January 14th (1938), he was filled with "extreme indignation" at those military officials who had wrongful acts and thus were arrested by the military police; on January 21st, he was "really sorry" about the robberies and rapes; on January

---

[136] 「飯沼守日記」. In 南京戦史編集委員会 (Ed.), 『南京戦史資料集』, pp. 106 + 111 + 118 + 168 + 174 + 175.

26th, "squadron leader Amano" of the 8th Squadron of the 45th Regiment along with his soldiers committed rapes; on January 29th, Chief of the Judicial Affairs Department submitted a report on rape, injury and especially on seizure; on February 12th, he "was really embarrassed at" the wrongful acts reported by the military police. And at that time, Iinuma Mamoru also frequently mentioned military discipline in his later diaries. For example, on December 30th, adjutants stationed in Nanjing and nearby areas were required to pay "serious attention" to military discipline (Nanjing garrison commander Major General Sasaki Toichi [head of the 30th infantry brigade] also gave "words of advice and expectation" on the same occasion), and Major Nakayama Yasuto, Staff officer of CCAA, said the Area Army "deeply regretted" the "wrongful" and "ill-disciplined" acts; on January 6th, "great attention" was paid to the "military discipline".[137] And certainly, it was not pointless for Iinuma Mamoru to frequently mention such words as "regret" and "indignation" and to emphasize the "military discipline".

Iinuma Mamoru was filled with "regret" and "indignation"—not because he was sensitive—but because the operations of Japanese army could not be justified even if as an "Imperial army" in accordance with the lowest standards.[138] And the perception of his colleagues can be positive proof and I will take one as example. Colonel Uemura Toshimichi, Deputy Chief of Staff of SEF, also recorded the operations of Japanese army in his diary. As early as on December 12th, the day before the Japanese army entered Nanjing, he wrote in the diary, "I have heard and deeply regret that the Imperial Army have not been subject to the military discipline". In the diary on December 16th, he wrote that "it is a pity that nothing but criticism has been given when it comes to the military discipline of the army inside the city". In the diary on December 27th, it was written that "the precious cultural relics with academic value in Nanjing city were gradually destroyed by the soldiers who were seeking goods and materials to satisfy the demand of the 2nd section (subject to the order of Colonel Kazahaya, who was then a lieutenant colonel)".[139] The so-called "demand of the 2nd section" indicates that looting,

---

[137]「飯沼守日記」. In 南京戦史編集委員会 (Ed.),『南京戦史資料集』, pp. 220 + 224 + 237 + 237 + 248 + 229–230 + 234.

[138] Toshio Matsumura was sued by Li Xiuying, a victim of Nanjing atrocities for his inappropriate words in his book. At the beginning of the book, he said "the Central Army" "maintained discipline" and "had nothing to do with the atrocities", as contrast to the "inappropriate actions" of "the Chinese army then" (村俊夫著『「南京虐殺」への大疑問』, 東京, 展転社1998年12月13日第1版, 第1936頁[正文起自19頁]). Toshio Matsumura "question" was intended to justify Japanese Army. He gave examples of the "damages" caused by Chinese army, such as strengthening the defenses and destroying everything in the fields, because he wants to pass the buck. But considering the Japanese statement that the United States and Soviet troops also had atrocities, behind the "challenges" from the Japanese right-wing group is their "concession", implying that don't be too strict with Japanese army.

[139]「上村利道日記」, 南京戦史編集委員会編『南京戦史資料集』, pp. 270 + 272 + 280.

for the Japanese army, is more than "individual" act.[140] And he wrote in the diary on January 8th, "According to the report of the military police, there were quite a number of ill-disciplined soldiers. And thus second lieutenants and warrant officers were called in. I very much regret the shameless behaviors".[141]

From such words as "deeply regret" and "very much regret", we can see the writer of diary had thought highly of but then was openly disappointed at the Japanese army. His stand in favor of the Japanese army makes the records more reliable. But his strong sentiment has been a strike contrast to his understatement of the so-called "a handful of" atrocities made in the Tokyo Trial. I believe which is truthful has been self-evident.

Ogawa Sekijiro

Ogawa Sekijiro's affidavit (No. 2708 Defense Document and No. 3400 Court Evidence) testified for the following facts: First, "Commander Matsui certainly ordered the army to strictly observe the military discipline, including the protection of the rights and interests of Chinese citizens and foreign countries and the strict application of laws and rules"; second, "By the time [he] arrived in Nanjing, [he] had punished the wrongdoers in the case of military or moral discipline offense, a total of 20 cases. And it was difficult to deal with the moral discipline offense due to the ambiguity between rape and adultery"; third, "[he] entered Nanjing at noon on December 14th … and there were no other bodies but only six or seven bodies of Chinese soldiers that could be seen. … During [his] stay in Nanjing, neither [he] heard about the wrongful acts of the Japanese soldiers nor cases of wrongful acts were brought to the court. And the Japanese army was in a state of warfare and the military discipline was strict" (which is the original text and means they were well-disciplined); fourth, "the Military police were strictly abide by the orders of Commander Matsui and wrongful acts were strictly forbidden"; fifth, "On January 4th, 1938, [he] met with General Matsui in Shanghai and General Matsui particularly emphasized that 'crimes should be severely punished'".[142]

Ogawa Sekijiro, as a senior legal officer, was appointed Chief of Judicial Affairs Department of the 10th Army and was "professional" in military discipline. Some outsiders thus tend to take his testimony as "authoritative" evidence. In that case, his testimony ought to be carefully examined. However, his testimony was neither examined by the prosecution in the Tokyo Trial nor questioned before the publication of the foregoing article. As for why the

---

[140] As to plundering daily necessities, it was a "work" of the Japanese army. For example, in the "Results Table" of the 7th infantry regiment recorded from December 13th to 24th, there are tens of thousands of "seized things", in all 77 kinds ranging from various types of vehicles (32) to compressed biscuits (1600 cases) (步兵第七聯隊〈南京城内掃蕩成果表〉, 南京戰史編集委員会編『南京戰史資料集』, p. 630).

[141]「上村利道日記」, 南京戰史編集委員会編『南京戰史資料集』, p. 287.

[142] 洞富雄編『日中戦争史資料』8「南京事件」I, pp. 256–257.

Tokyo Trial is said to be subject to the winning states in Japan and even in the west, I always suppose an important reason has been that the testimonies such as Ogawa's have not been examined. And a key reason why they have not been examined is lack of powerful "inner evidence". As individual horizon varies, what he saw cannot represent or be a basis to deny what others saw. And thus merely based on external documents, arguments are bound to be not powerful enough. At this point, the publication of Ogawa's diary[143] provides the most reliable reference to his testimony.

The following sections will examine whether the testimony of Ogawa Sekijiro at the Tokyo Trial was consistent with what he heard at the time of the incident. In Ogawa's Affidavit, it is mentioned that Matsui Iwane talked about the discipline twice, respectively, using such words as "strictly abide" "strict observance" and "specially emphasize", which implies that Matsui was not perfunctory but serious. Considering Ogawa would record everything he met with, such instructions were unlikely to be omitted. But throughout his diary, there is no record of such address delivered by Matsui Iwane, so we can conclude the "testimony" was not truthful. And moreover, the diary turns out to be direct, negative proof against Ogawa. Take as example the foregoing fifth record, which reads that "On January 4th, 1938, [he] met with General Matsui in Shanghai". As you can imagine, the prosecution failed to challenge Ogawa's testimony because he was specific about the time, place and character. But with such specific, clear information, we can easily check his testimony compared with his diary. In his diary on January 4th, Ogawa recorded his second visit to Major General Yanagawa Heisuke, commander of the 10th Army, for the discussion on the case of a certain Major and for the farewell meetings of the armed forces, military doctors, veterinarians and judicial departments. And thus Ogawa did not leave Hangzhou (where the headquarter of the 10th army located) at all. It was on January 7th that he left for Shanghai to report to CCAA[144] and not until January 15th did he met with Matsui Iwane. His diary on the 15th detailed his meeting with Matsui Iwane: Matsui Iwane talked about the policies and strategies against China, how to overthrow the Chiang Kai-shek government, how to establish a pro-Japanese regime and how to implement the "Hundred-Year Plan on the Immigration of A large number of Japanese to China" and so on, with no word about the military discipline. Moreover, there is an interesting record of his feeling in the diary on this day:

> Was the commander (Original Note: General Iwane Matsui) trying to be intimidating? Or was he a man of natural arrogance? He is a little bit strange,

---

[143] Okawa's diary has long been unknown and even Okawa's daughter who lived with him in his late years got "surprised" and "had no memory of it at all". 長森光代著「わが父、陸軍法務官小川関治郎」，小川関治郎著『ある軍法務官の日記』附録，東京，みすず書房2000年8月10日第1版，第210頁.

[144] The Central China Area Army did not have a legal department and Ogawa was responsible for the daily affairs of the court martial.

compared with other generals I have met so far. I believe a good chief executive will not stand on his dignity and must be able to get across his own policies to his subordinates. Such a gesture is entirely unnecessary. An arrogant man will not fully consider others' opinions and also will fail to get across his worries to his superior. It is definitely not useless to listen to those who have different opinions – This is particular the case for the superior and his subordinates. The subordinates shall fully understand the superior's opinions while the superior fully studies the subordinates' opinions ... (Note: The ellipsis is retained according to original texts) why was he so arrogant?[145]

There were various descriptions of Matsui Iwane, such as the untruthful witnesses testimonies of the Tokyo Trial, but no one had ever said that he was "arrogant" or "stood on the dignity". The reason why Matsui left a different impression on Ogawa, I suppose, lies in the military discipline which put Matsui in an awkward position at that time. Under the pressure from Western countries, Japanese military and political authorities had to urge the Japanese Central China Area Army to observe military discipline. And the joy of capturing the capital of the "enemy country" was thus swept away. In this context, the council of military court of CCAA was founded in a short time. For Matsui, the foundation of the council was against his intention (According to the diaries of Hata Shunroku (Matsui's successor) and others, Matsui's dismissal had something to do with the military discipline of the Army[146]). Therefore, simply intended to show his resentment to the pressure on improving military discipline, Matsui "stood on the dignity" and was unusually "arrogant" to Ogawa, who is of similar seniority but he held no grudge against, regardless of whether he was born or pretended to be so.

Ogawa also mentioned another specific date in his testimony, saying that he "entered Nanjing at noon on December 14th" and "only saw six or seven bodies of Chinese soldiers at that time". But his diary on that day detailed what he saw. When "entering Nanjing", he saw as follows:

> On the roadside were Chinese regular soldiers (Note: it refers to "corpse" and this word is omitted here as it has been repeated in former, same sentence), piled up and on fire. At the sight of the bodies, Japanese still seemed to feel nothing. Soldiers had to walk over the burning bodies due to the congestion and soon became indifferent to the bodies. We gradually approached the South Gate. The city wall is about three meters high and made up of stone. Some parts were hit by our shells in the battle of yesterday. The thickness of the wall is equated to the width of a road that a car can run through, so ordinary shells cannot destroy it. <u>On entering the gate</u>, I saw <u>piles of Chinese-soldier bodies</u> lying on both sides.[147]

---

[145] Ogawa Sekijiro.『ある軍法務官の日記』, pp. 153–154.

[146]「陸軍大将畑俊六日誌」, 南京戦史編集委員会編『南京戦史資料集』, 第52頁. The diary was marked "January 29" of 1938. But since it involves the matters on February 5th and 6th, and the next diary is marked February 7th, so it should be diary for January 29th to February 6th.

[147] Ogawa Sekijiro『ある軍法務官の日記』, pp. 111–112.

Ogawa claimed there were "six or seven" bodies but wrote "piles of bodies" in the record of what he saw! As the saying goes, facts speaker louder than words. His diary can only be said to belie his testimony, regardless of his motive.

Unlike Japanese commanding officers in the battle (such as the foregoing Wakisaka Jiro, leader of the 36th Regiment) who denied it in its totality, Ogawa confirmed a handful of cases of "military discipline offense" and "moral discipline offense"—"whether it was rape or adultery uncertain". His testimony thus seemed to be objective to some extent. As a result, it is necessary to examine his diary to finally determine whether the "military discipline was strict", although the foregoing two examples can belie Ogawa's testimony.

In his diary on November 24th, he wrote that:

> It was an <u>unspeakable humiliation</u> that the Japanese soldiers <u>wantonly raped</u> Chinese women wherever they went and did not regard <u>looting</u> or <u>arson</u> as wrongful acts. As Japanese, especially the young men who would be the mainstay of Japan, they were unscrupulous. And then what would they bring to the future ideology of the whole Japan if they made a triumphant return in this mind-set? I <u>quailed</u> at the thought. I think our Japanese government shall make a research and implement a comprehensive, ideological reform. This statement may be a little bit extreme. However, as someone has said, we Japanese will <u>have mixed feelings</u>, hearing Japanese soldiers were more brutal than Chinese soldiers. It is said Chinese people has called Japanese the <u>beasts</u> and called Japanese soldiers the fearsome <u>beast soldiers</u>. For Chinese people, it is indeed the truth. But as Japanese, we <u>have seen and very much regret numerous acts of Japanese soldiers</u>.

Ogawa does not think such words as "beasts" and "beast soldiers" are vilification just because "[he has] seen and regret numerous acts of Japanese soldiers". As a professional legal officer, he certainly will "have mixed feelings".

In his diary on November 25th, he wrote that:

> Last night at 3:30, late as it is, Senior Captain Matsuoka of the military police reported a major event that five soldiers of the 6th Division (including one leader) abducted several women ranging from teenage girls to 26-year-old women in a village about three li (Note: 1 li is around 4 km) away and wantonly raped them in an empty house. Meanwhile, a 55-year-old woman who escaped was shot to death and another woman was shot in right thigh. Their acts are serious breach of military discipline and were despicable beyond words.
>
> △ (Note: the original symbol in the diary) The Japanese government declared that even if it was against the Chinese government, it would not be hostile to the nationals in the future. However, what the Japanese soldiers did to the innocent people was despicable beyond words. In this context, what do we think about the further anti-Japanese thought of the Chinese people? I quailed at the thought of the future of the Japanese Empire.

(The middle part has been omitted) I saw the Japanese soldiers enslaving Chinese people and pointing their guns at them as if they were treating cats or dogs. As Chinese, they did not resist. What would happen if Chinese and Japanese trade positions?

In a cruel war, abusing soldiers sometimes cannot be completely avoided. But abusing "innocent civilians" can never be justified. Hence, Ogawa put himself in other guy's shoes at least because he had not lose his conscience. But more importantly, it was because the acts of Japanese army were so "despicable beyond words" that he was inevitably shocked.

In his diary on November 26th, he wrote that:

Taking an all-round observation, I found not only the frontline troops but also some cunning soldiers of the rear troops who deliberately left behind had entered the houses of civilians and done evil things. So were the aforementioned defendants who had been charged with murder, robbery and rape. In this context, the righteous and earnest soldiers fought bravely in the front line and died because of a little negligence while those cunning, unscrupulous ones did not participate in any battle, and thus it is not an exaggeration to call the latter traitor, betrayer or black sheep. At the thought of this, I always have mixed feelings.

(The middle part is omitted) As soon as they saw the Japanese soldiers, they would ran away. Women and children seemed to be extremely afraid of the Japanese soldiers. The reason lies in their wrongful acts. If they never did any evil things, Chinese people would not escape. I very much regret at them.

What is the dignity of the Imperial Army? What is the so-called war for? This is not clear. However, in terms of the foregoing Chinese feelings against Japanese and the impact of the quality of Japanese soldiers on young men in the further, the answer is absolutely disappointing.[148]

(The diary on this day recorded at the end that Tajima Riuichi, a member of judicial department, investigated the rape case which was mentioned in the diary on the 25th, saying that "the situation of the field investigation was much worse than imaged". It is noteworthy that Ogawa wrote there were three people killed and three people wounded in this case while the official document and judgment included in *Proceedings of Court Martial of CCAA* recorded only one people was killed and one people was wounded. Apparently, Japanese official documents in wartime had been tampered with in terms of facts.[149]) Chinese people were "extremely afraid" of Japanese

---

[148] Ogawa Sekijiro. 『ある軍法務官の日記』, pp. 59+62–63+65–66.

[149] I have carefully compared the diary of Ogawa with the journal of the Legal Department of the 10th Army and the proceedings of the court martial of CCAA. Based on the solid evidence of the Japanese army after Jinshanwei's landing, I argue that the journal had concealed the performance of the Japanese army; and the cases of the Chinese people, such as Zhou Jitang's, were not recorded and thus I inferred the journal today has been partly deleted. For details, please refer to Part II of Ogawa Sekijiro and Diary of A Military Legal Affairs Officer. To be specific, "From the records of the executions such as of Zhou Jitang, it can be seen that the Japanese

soldiers just "because of the wrongful acts committed by Japanese soldiers" and "I very much regret at them"—merely based on this statement, we can infer Ogawa's testimony at the Tokyo Trial was not truthful at all.

In his diary on November 29th, he wrote that:

> Some soldiers have the Chinese people carry their luggage ... As long as the Chinese people showed a little disobedience or had an act of disobedience, they would be <u>immediately punished</u>, which made people speechless. I saw on the way that two soldiers pulled out their swords and <u>stabbed a Chinese person lying on the back</u>. This is another case of blood-drenched Chinese suffering a lot. At sight of this, I extremely felt pity for the nationals of the defeated country.

It was very common that the Chinese people were forced into slave labor with the army at that time. He wrote on December 11th:

> These Chinese people tried their best to carry the luggage and a considerable number of them were <u>old people</u>. There was no one more unfortunate than those who lost their country. On this occasion, they would be <u>punished immediately</u> by our soldiers as long as they showed a little disobedience. If they tried to escape, they would be <u>executed immediately</u>[150]

At this point, I recalled that Japanese in the United States filed a claim against the US government for wartime containment several years ago.[151] And during the claim process, Japanese television broadcast the refugee camp video several times as evidence of so-called "inhuman" treatment. Compared to Ogawa's account and similar records, Chinese people endured pain and suffering that was as much as over a hundred times the "prosecution" of overseas Japanese!

---

army's sentencing to Chinese and Japanese was extremely unfair and thus the journal has been abridged" in Section 1; "The difference between the diary and the journal implies the not only the abridgment of the journal in terms of facts but also the important value of the diary" in Section 2.

[150] Ogawa Sekijiro. 『ある軍法務官の日記』, pp. 78 + 105 + 106.

[151] After the Pearl Harbor incident, the United States once centralized Japanese expatriates. This act was determined by the specific background at the time. As a hostile country, especially a hostile country that has suffered huge losses from its sneak attacks, Japan has no credit for the United States. Suspecting those Japanese in United States, it is natural and well-founded to for the United States take precautionary measures. However, things have changed. In an age without gunpowder smoke, people have forgotten the environment in which you have to live through killing others and the conflict between detention and modern nation-building concepts has become increasingly prominent. As a result, Japanese in the United States accused the US government of "inhuman treatment" during the war, demanding the US government to apologize and compensate them. Not only did they receive the unanimous support of the Japanese government, but the United States had to make concessions and give compensation.

Since the 10th Army did not encounter fierce resistance after landing, a large portion of the corpses left by the 10th Army must be the victims of such arbitrary "executions". After he landed at Jinshan, Ogawa saw the bodies of Chinese people almost everywhere he went. For example, in the morning of November 14th, he was on the way to Zhangyan Town and saw "numerous bodies" "lying everywhere in the rivers, pools and fields"; in the afternoon, he arrived at Jinshan and even saw some "totally naked" corpses. On November 17th, "there were still bodies of Chinese people" in the area of Jinshan. On November 28th, on his way to Huzhou, he saw "piles of bodies" of which many were wearing civilian clothes. And he wrote in his diary on December 10th, "I have seen innumerable bodies of Chinese people on the way". After seeing such a large number of dead bodies, he slumped into a state of torpor. As put in his diary of December 11th,

> On my way from the house of Li to Jinshan, at the sight of the dead bodies of Chinese people, I always had a strange feeling at first. But when I gradually saw a large number of dead bodies, I became accustomed to them. The feeling at this time was like seeing dog remains in Japan.

The most serious crime the 10th Army committed in China was murder or say depriving Chinese people of their life. Besides, there still remains a serious problem with "military discipline" by the time CCAA, SEF and the 10th Army were disbanded and about to retreat back to Japan.

> Legal Officer Tsukamoto arrived in Nanjing to hear the report of incidents in Nanjing, especially a detailed report on the case of the rape committed by Lieutenant Amano. … Rape has occurred frequently in various aspects, and how to prevent them is a matter that should be specially studied.[152]

The foregoing experiences are the most powerful evidence against the argument that the wrongful acts of Japanese army were unknown to Ogawa as he claimed at the Tokyo Trial. Although we cannot extend the example of Ogawa to others and thus conclude similar evidence at that time were all forged for purpose. However, those contradictory records in Ogawa's testimony and his diary at least can belie those testimonies similar to Ogawa's. And it is the same case with Iinuma's.

Was the Murder Race, a Symbol of the Nanjing Massacre, the Fabrication of Media?

The Nanjing Massacre has gained widespread attention in Japan since the 1970s. And the direct cause was *Travels in China*, a series of reports serialized

---

[152] 小川関治郎著『ある軍法務官の日記』, pp. 27+30+44+102+107+192.

in *Asahi Shimbun* from late August to December 1971.[153] The reports were written by Honda Katsuichi, a journalist with the *Asahi Shinbunsha*, who was permitted to visit China in 1971 and stayed for over 40 days from the June to July, during which he visited Guangzhou, Changsha, Beijing, Shenyang, Fushun, Anshan, Tangshan, Jinan, Nanjing, Shanghai and many other places. Everywhere he went, he searched for traces of Japanese atrocities and surviving victims. His experiences were all recorded in *Travels in China*. In his reports, Honda Katsuichi made such a harsh criticism and *Asahi Shinbunsha* was so influential that "the Nanjing Massacre" became a "reality" that Japanese had to face. Its great impact became unsettling news to those who oppose the so-called "Tokyo Trial view of history" and then became the driving force to the trends of denying the Nanjing Massacre. Suzuki Aki was the first to "refute" the argument of Honda Katsuichi. In 1972, he published an article "*Nankin daigyakusatsu" no ma boroshi (The Illusion of the "Nanjing Massacre")* in the April-Issue of *Shokun*, a famous Japanese right-wing journal, and also named his memoir after this one in the next year.[154] Since then, the word "illusion"[155] has had the same meaning as Chinese character "虚构" (fiction) and become the generic name of the "fabrication school" which denies the "Nanjing Massacre" in its totality. The first challenge posed by the *Illusion* to the *Travels in China* focused on the "murder race". The "murder race" refers to the killing contest between Second Lieutenant Noda Tsuyoshi, adjutant of the 3rd Battalion of the 9th Infantry Regiment of the 16th Division of SEF, and Second Lieutenant Mukai Toshiaki, leader of Infantry Gun Platoon under the same battalion, on their way to attacking Nanjing. The contest was famous at that time,[156] and the two were sentenced to death by Nanjing War Crimes Tribunal after the war. The *Illusion* argued that the "murder race" was the fabrication of the media and was not the truth. As a result, Japan's left-wing groups and right-wing groups have launched fierce debates. In response to a relevant questionnaire before his death, Fujiwara Akira, who was Hora Tomio's successor and became the leader of the "great slaughter school", once said that this contest "was concocted for the purpose

[153] Honda Katsuichi later said that "I have written all kinds of communications so far, but I have never had such a strong and profound reaction as that caused by the serial of A Journey to China." 本多勝一編『裁かれた南京大屠殺』, 東京, 晩聲社1989年6月1日第3次印刷版, 第85頁.

[154] Suzuki Aki.『「南京大虐杀」のまぼろし』. Tokyo: Bungei Shunjū. 1st edition published on March 10th, 1973.

[155] Regarding Suzuki's denial of the old translation of "まぼろし" and approval of the new translation "myth", please see the footnote of Section 3 of "Is The Good Man of Nanking: The Diaries of John Rabe an 'Unfounded Fabrication'? - An Examination of The Truth of Nanjing Incident: An Examination of John Rabe's Diaries". Modern Chinese History Studies, Beijing: 2002(2): pp. 166.

[156] The report was divided into four parts published in Tokyo Riichi Shimbun (the precursor of Mainichi Shimbun), respectively, on November 30, December 4, December 6 and December 13 of 1937. And the report on December 13 also had a large photo of the two soldiers pressing their Japanese swords down on the earth.

of writing heroic episode of the battle, but it can be said that some captives who did not resist were killed".[157] If we take the answer as a conclusion of the debate, as far as the "justice" of this matter is concerned, opinions still vary (on the so-called "killing" of captives); and as far as the matter itself is concerned, it has to be said that the "fabrication school" has won the game (due to the word as so-called "concocted"). Among the Japanese "great massacre school", Honda Katsuichi is the one who has hardly changed his opinion. He also said, "It was common in China at that time for Japanese soldiers to 'test their swords' through killing captives or just to perform a slaughter. Only a small part had sometimes been reported. Mr. M and Mr. N (referring to Mukai Toshiaki and Noda Tsuyoshi) was executed just because they were in the news and thus could receive some sympathy".[158] Although he does not deny the act of "testing the sword", he is inclined to think that the "contest" itself was the fabrication of the media.

The murder race is the so-called "symbolic incident"[159] of the Nanjing Massacre and moreover, the relevant discussions still can be furthered. Therefore, I think it is still too early to be negative and concede that the "murder race" was a "heroic episode" made up by the media. If calmly analyzing the wartime reports of the *Tokyo Nichi Nichi Shimbun*, we can easily see the "reports" were embellished with some "facts". Against the backdrop of hysterically undisciplined soldiers at that time, the "reports" almost were inevitably embellished in the direction of "heroic episode": The two Japanese officers competed many times (three times, according to *Tokyo Nichi Nichi Shimbun*) to see who could kill 100 Chinese soldiers but they themselves did not get wounded—such description implies more than the "heroic" characteristic, but nearly can be seen as a myth. But when Honda's Travels in China was serialized, an important memoir written by Shishime Akira was published in the September-Issue of *China*, a monthly magazine. Shishime Akira recalled what Noda Tsuyoshi said to him when Noda returned to his primary school in hometown:

> It was all about me in the newspaper, such as the warrior from a village and the warrior of the murder race ... In fact, there were only four or five people killed in the assault.
>
> Facing the enemy trenches that had been occupied by us, I shouted "You come, you come" (Note: He said "Ni Lai" in Chinese). The Chinese soldiers were fools and gradually came out. I asked them to stand in line and then kill one after another...
>
> The so-called "murder race" was actually like this...

[157]「まぼろし派、中間派、大虐殺派三派合同大アンケート」. Shokun!, p. 193.

[158] 本多勝一著「据えもの斬りや捕虜虐殺は日常茶飯だった」注1,『南京大虐殺否定論13のウソ』, p. 115.

[159] This word is from the recent questionnaire of Japanese journal Shokun!. See「まぼろし派、中間派、大虐殺派三派合同大アンケート」. Shokun!, p. 166.

Among those who denies the murder race, Yamamoto Shichihei's arguments have been the most "detailed".[160] However, he also admits this memory is a "very accurate and reliable testimony".[161] Considering this as well as the large number of photos of killing disarmed captive that have remained in the world, we can see further, no more limited to the exaggerated reports of *Tokyo Nichi Nichi Shimbun*, that Noda Tsuyoshi, as he claimed, only killed the "fools" who laid down their arms (and it can be inferred so was Mukai Toshiaki). If so, this truth may be too bland but better reveal how inhuman the Japanese army was.

I have thoroughly examined the arguments of Japanese right-wing group in my article *Re-discussion on the "Murder Race"*[162] and please refer to the article for further details. And my conclusion is even if the so-called inner and external "proofs" presented by Japanese "fictionalists" are true—needless to say, the so-called "physical limitations" of the "Japanese swords" are contrary to the facts—they are not enough to deny the wartime records of the "murder race". I am not saying that the records in wartime are completely true. But since I take the stand of affirming the "murder race", I have to examine those wartime records in a more strict manner. I just mean there is no doubt about the "murder race" in terms of the existence of massive killings. And from the standpoint of the victims, the so-called "sympathy" is absolutely unacceptable. Even from the academic perspective without personal feelings involved, the "murder race" is far from being overturned. Therefore, in any sense, this stand should not and need not be easily abandoned.

11 SECTION 2

Several Issues Concerning the Nanjing Massacre

The debate over the death toll of the massacre focuses on two aspects: the difference between those killed in the battle and those in the slaughter as well as the absolute number of deaths. And these two aspects might interlock. The fabrication school denies the massacre but does not deny the deaths in the battle. For instance, Ooi Mitsuru's statement as the so-called "as close to zero as it could" refers to the death toll of "unlawful slaughter", excluding those killed in the battles. And the slaughter school attaches importance to the massacre but will include those killed in the battles if counting the death toll. Japan's three schools of thought have different opinions on the death toll, not only due to the above-mentioned difference of their stands, but due to the unorganized, insufficient firsthand material. Japanese records of the massacre and corpses are in a large quantity, but there is no statistical data.

---

[160] 山本七平著『私の中の日本軍』下「日本刀神話の実態」「白兵戦に適されない名刀」, 東京, 文藝春秋社1975年12月15日第1版, pp. 67–118.

[161] Ibid., p. 70.

[162] Jiangsu Social Sciences. Nanjing. 2002(6): pp. 135–140.

There are many Western records on the atrocities, of which, however, a limited number have dealt with the death toll. In this sense, the identification of the death toll depends on Chinese material. Although, as we can see from the title, the focus of this article is Japanese material, it is still necessary to deal with the death toll of the Nanjing Incident as it is the most controversial one among all the issues.

As I once put in the last section of *A Study of the Order for Japanese Troops during Nanjing Slaughter in 1937*, the number of people killed in the massacre is of subordinate importance, considering the figures cannot deny the nature, that the bodies buried have been destroyed in decades of weathering, that large quantities of bodies were pushed into the Yangtze River at that time and that the documents reserved are incomplete. (This section was deleted before contribution for I suppose it is not prudent to discuss this issue, which is of great importance during the studies on the Nanjing Massacre, incidentally in an article of different theme.[163]) In addition to considering the objective limits, I made this conclusion more based on a point, i.e., too much emphasis on this issue is not conducive to further studies. The fabrication school has long fussed about verifying the number, but there is no doubt that the token number cannot deny the nature, be they increased or decreased. But this is not to say that the number of people killed counts for little.[164]

There are very different opinions on the death toll in Japan and all have claimed to be based on a faithful "examination". Generally speaking, the leading members of the fabrication school before the 1980s were those who were personally involved in the incident or engaged in media. Masaaki Tanaka[165] and Yamamoto Shichihei[166] fall within the former group while Suzuki Aki[167]

---

[163] This part was later taken as the postscript of A Study of the Order for Japanese Troops during Nanjing Slaughter in 1937 which was included in Studies on the Nanjing Massacre by Cheng Zhaoqi, the Edition published by Shanghai Lexicographical Publishing House in December 2002: pp. 101–104.

[164] At the end of last year, I had a talk with a Japanese scholar who not only was dismissive of the fictionalists' research on figures but did not agree with the relevant works of the school of slaughter. This is the most extreme view I have ever met. However, he cannot deny that disregard of figures to a full scale will make the issue of the Nanjing Massacre "vague".

[165] Masaaki Tanaka was the secretary of Iwane Matsui when at the Greater Asia Association. He along with Iwane Matsui visited the southwest area and Nanjing, etc. in the year before the Nanjing Massacre. He wrote 『「南京虐殺」の虚構̲̲̲̲松井大将の日記をめぐって』 (Tokyo: Nippon Kyobunsha. The 1st Edition published on June 25th, 1984) and 『南京事件の総括̲̲̲̲虐殺否定十五の論拠』 (Tokyo: 謙光社. The 1st Edition published on March 3rd 1987).

[166] Although Yamamoto Shichihei has nothing to do with the Nanjing Massacre, he was a member of the Japanese army in wartime (he used to be a second lieutenant of artillery of the 103 Division). He wrote the 『私の中の日本軍』 Volume I and Volume II (Tokyo: Bungei Shunju. The 1st Edition, respectively, published on January 30th, 1975, and on December 15th, 1975).

[167] Suzuki Aki first worked for a private radio station and later a freelancer after the Illusion of the Nanking Massacre became a hit. And please refer to the previous note for his writings.

and Ara Kenichi[168] belong to the latter. But since the 1990s till today, in addition to people of all kinds like Kobayashi Yoshinori,[169] the active members of the fabrication school have more been those institution scholars such as Higashinakano Shudo,[170] Nobukatsu Fujioka,[171] Watanabe Shoichi[172] and Kitamura Minoru,[173] a budding one.

Compared to the arguments of the fabrication school, the middle-of-the-road school has a more broad concept, in terms of the death toll and especially of the judgment on the incident. For example, those who argue around ten thousand to tens of thousands of people were unlawfully killed belong to the small slaughter school, but its members such as Unemoto Masaki[174] and Itakura Yoshiaki[175] have arguments quite similar to those of the fabrication school and Sakurai Yoshiko[176] in fact has been the top

---

[168] Ara Kenichi was employed in planning work of a publishing house. And he wrote the 『聞き書 南京事件＿＿日本人の見た南京虐殺事件』, (Tokyo: 図書出版社. The 1st Edition published on August 15 1987.)

[169] Kobayashi Yoshinori is a cartoonist who has been denying the Nanjing Massacre through comics and comments, like 『「個と公」論』(Tokyo: Gentosha. The 1st Edition published on May 5th 2000).

[170] Higashinakano Shudo is a professor at the Asia University and is the author of 『「南京虐殺」の徹底検証』(Tokyo: 展転社. The 1st Edition published on August 15th 1998).

[171] Fujioka Nobukatsu is a professor at the University of Tokyo and has wrote many writings denying the invasion. In terms of the Nanjing Massacre, he coauthored the 『ザ・レイプ・オブ・南京の研究＿＿中国における「情報戦」の手口と戦略』with Higashinakano Shudo.

[172] Watanabe Shoichi is a professor at the Sophia University and has wrote a number of writings denying the invasion. Although none of the books is on the Nanjing Massacre, he often lectures on different occasions due to his great reputation and thus is the most influential one of the fictionalists.

[173] Kitamura Minoru is a professor at the Ritsumeikan University and has wrote the 『「南京事件」の探究＿＿その実像をもとめて』(Tokyo: Bungei Shunju. The 1st Edition published on November 20th 2001). Kitamura belongs to the School of Fabrication due to the conclusion of his recent works. But he himself does not claim to be of either school as he has put in the postscript that he insists on " 'seeking truth from fact', the code of ethics that China has followed since Deng Xiaoping took part power" (p. 193). Besides, neither school has claimed to admit him up till now. And recently, some Japanese scholars have criticized him for his political persuasion. (See 山田要一.「歴史改ざんの新意匠＿＿北村稔『「南京事件」の探究』の実像」. In 『人権と教育』341号. Tokyo: 社会評論社. Published on May 20th 2002, pp. 139–149.)

[174] Unemoto Masaki was a leader of the Light Armored Convoy when Japanese troops captured Nanjing. Although he taught the war history at the National Defense Academy of Japan, he, as a general of the Japan Ground Self-Defense Force, distinguishes himself from other school scholars. He wrote the 「証言による南京戦史」1–11 (Tokyo: 『偕行』. Apr. 1984 - Feb. 1985).

[175] Itakura Youming is an operator of the manufacturing plant. Before his death, he specialized in amateur studies and was mainly dedicated to the research on the "Nanjing Incident". In the 1980s, he once pointed out Tanaka Masaaki had tampered with Matsui Iwane's diary. 著有『本当はこうだった南京事件』, 東京, 日本図書刊行会1999年12月8日第1版.

[176] Sakurai Yoshiko was a Japanese TV anchor and has a high popularity. Although she has not studied on the Nanjing Massacre, her denial has been the most influential one.

spokesman for the fabrication school. Ikuhiko Hata[177] argues for a death toll of around 40,000 and belongs to the middle slaughter school but has a similar view to the slaughter school. It is necessary to explain the case of Ikuhiko Hata as it is special to some extent. Ikuhiko Hata has extensively studied the "history of the Showa era", especially the period of the Second Sino-Japanese War. Although he gradually has had opinions different from that of the slaughter school in recent years,[178] he has long been contending with the fabrication school. His basic arguments in *Nankin Jiken: gyakusatsu no kōzō*, his representative work, has never changed so far. For example, facing the doubts of the fabrication school on the figure, he said,

> "Some people even falsify the first-hand data and insist that there never exists Nanjing Massacre. Some people merely care about the token figure of 30,000 or 40,000 people that the Chinese government insists on. Should the anti-Japanese group in the United States say that the number recorded in textbooks of people killed in the atomic bomb explosion is 'too large' or 'fabricated' (the real number is still unclear) and begin to protest, what would the victims think of it? The exact figure may be controversial, but the massacre and various illegal acts committed by the Japanese army in Nanjing are undeniable facts. As a Japanese, I, the author genuinely apologizes to the Chinese people."[179]

His "attitude" can be said to be almost the same as the slaughter school but far from that of the fabrication school.

Members of the slaughter school also have different opinions on the death toll of the massacre, ranging from the maximum "over 200 thousand" as estimated by Hora Tomio to "over 100 thousand". And unlike the middle-of-the-road school, they just have different opinions on the death toll as well as the probative force of material but agree with each other on the nature of the massacre.

A few years ago, Japanese representative right-wing journal "Shokun!" conducted a questionnaire survey,[180] of which the first question was about the death toll. The question and answers are as follows:

---

[177] Ikuhiko Hata was a professor with Nihon University and wrote the 『南京事件＿＿虐殺の構造』.

[178] See my article An Analysis on the Annual of the Japan Association for Nanjing Studies.

[179] Hata Ikuhiko. 『南京事件＿＿虐殺の構造』. Tokyo: Chuokoron-Shinsha. The 20th Edition published on August 20th 1999: p. 24. (The first edition was published on February 25th 1986 and later editions remain basically the same.)

[180] 「まぼろし派、中間派、大虐殺派三派合同大アンケート」, 『諸君!』, 第164203页. For the Chinese translation, see Appendix IV of Study on Nanjing Massacre by Cheng Zhaoqi, pp. 511–553. This survey did not include all the important figures in Japan, such as Hata Ikuhiko, the middle-of-the-road school, and Higashinakano Shūdō, the fabrication school, but all the schools of thought. The right-wing ideological background of Shokun! makes the questions with a clear tendency, but the basic positions of different Japanese schools on the "Nanjing Incident" are still reflected.

What is the appropriate number of Chinese people slaughtered (illegally killed) by Japanese army during the Nanjing Incident?

(1) Over 300 thousand; (2) around 300 thousand; (3) 200 thousand to 300 thousand; (4) 200 thousand; (5) over 100 thousand; (6) around 100 thousand; (7) 70 thousand to 90 thousand; (8) around 50 thousand; (9) 20 thousand to 30 thousand; (10) around 10 thousand; (11) thousands of; (12) as close to zero; (13) Other (around __).

Watanabe Shoichi	(13)	40 or 50 common people
Suzuki Aki	(13)	It cannot be imagined due to the shortage of historical documents
Ara Kenichi	(12)	
Kobayashi Yoshinori	(13)	The so-called firsthand information on massacres does not exist, so this question cannot be answered
Fuji Nobuo	(3)	I don't think there were people slaughtered
Takaike Katsuhiko	(12)	I don't think that the Japanese soldiers commit no wrong acts in Nanjing. But it is another matter that has nothing to do with the so-called Nanjing incident. The Nanjing Incident here refers to the Nanjing Massacre
Tanaka Masaaki	(12)	There is no evidence of the Nanjing massacre. For example, none of the fifteen members of the United States, Britain, Germany and Denmark who were resident in the safety zone and could inspect freely inside and outside Nanjing have seen the massacre, nor have they recorded the massacre. Moreover, they even have never mentioned it. The Jiang regime and the Communist Party of the opponent country did not mention the killings at the time of the incident
Ooi Mitsuru	(12)	
Matsumura Toshio	(13)	With "slaughter" as illegal killing, the Japanese army as well as the American occupation forces in Japan and the army of other countries cannot be said to have no offenders at all. As mentioned later, there are also some people mistakenly executed as plainclothes soldiers. The total number is unknown, but those who are mistaken should be less than "a hundred". The so-called 300,000 people were originally proposed by Timperley in the name of Priest Gach. Those who were killed in the battle or arrested after fleeing and executed in the safety zone as a combat act cannot be included in the death toll of the massacre
Fujioka Nobukatsu	(12)	
Hara Takeshi	(9)	Around 20 thousand prisoner and plainclothes soldiers and several thousand common people were illegally killed
Nakamura Akira	(10)	Several thousand to ten thousand, but in principle, excluding common people
Unemoto Masaki	(13)	Not systematic, planned killing of captives who surrendered and good citizens but individual, accident killings, including Mufushan captives killed on the way and ordinary citizens who were mistakenly executed during the mopping-up operations in the refugee area

Okazaki Hisahiko	(10)	The exact number of plainclothes soldiers killed was unknown, so select the number of ten thousand, in-between 300 and 30,000
Sakurai Yoshiko	(10)	
Tanabe Toshio	(10)	
Fujiwara Akira	(4)	The late Hora Tomio, who was the pioneer of the research on the incident, always claim "Chinese soldiers and civilians killed inside and outside Nanjing were not less than 200 thousand" (Nankin daigyakusatsu: ketteiban). And I also support him. The figure includes the war deaths, but most are killed illegally. It is extremely difficult to accurately calculate the number of dead people. In this sentence, the effort is still necessary
Rguchi Keiichi	(5)–(6)	
Inoue Hisashi	(13)	<u>At least</u> tens of thousands. (Note: Bullet points were originally added.)
Himeta Mitsuyoshi	(5)	
Kasahara Tokushi		From the existing research and data, it can be inferred that it is about 100,000 to 200,000. With the discovery and publication of documents as well as the development of the studies, the death toll might increase
Takasaki Ryuji	(4)	
Yoshida Yutaka	(13)	It now can be inferred to be at least 100,000 because the actual killings in the rural area, especially in the suburbs of Nanjing, are almost unknown

The difference between the fabrication school and other two schools is that the former basically deny the evidence presented by the prosecution at the Tokyo Trial and the Nanjing Trial, especially the objectivity of Chinese investigation and testimonies. And the difference between the middle-of-the-road school basically lies into what extent they admit the burial report of the Red Swastika Society and in whether they admit the burial activities of Suzendo as well as the testimonies such as Jusu's.

Among all the Chinese documents on the Massacre as evidence, the burial report of the Red Swastika Society is the only one that has not been completely denied.[181] Two reasons can account for it: One is that the report was written at the time of the incident. And the other is that Japanese special service department financed the burial activities of the Red Swastika Society, which has been recorded in some documents (such as the testimony of Maruyama Susumu). But as for how to interpret the burial activities of the Red Swastika Society, different schools have different opinions. The fabrication school does not admit that the bodies buried were killed

---

[181] For example, Higashinakano Shūdō said, "Only the Red Swastika Society was engaged in burying bodies". See 『「南京虐殺」の徹底検証』, p. 308.。

in the slaughter while the middle-of-the-road school and the fabrication school believe the report exaggerated the figure because Japanese special service department paid the Red Swastika Society on a piecework basis. And the middle-of-the-road school and the fabrication school do not admit any other burial activities, especially those of Suzendo which buried the most bodies (over 110 thousand) but the slaughter was on the contrary. In the above-mentioned article, I have argued from all perspectives that the denial of the fabrication school is ill-based. But this does not mean the death toll issue has been completely solved based on existing documents. Take Suzendo as example. There are two problems with its records: First, the number of the bodies was tallied after the war and the existing application form for auto parts submitted by Zhou Yiyu, who was in charge of Suzendo, do not mention the circumstance of burying bodies. Second, the statistics of the bodies buried cannot be said to be unquestionable and so are the testimonies.[182] For instance, as Jusu said, he took refuge in a big haystack at Shangyuan Gate and then "saw Japanese soldiers" slaughter or "freeze and starve people to death", having a total of 57,418 people killed. But it was physically impossible for him to work out such a huge, accurate number. And these have been the major reasons why the death toll confirmed at the Tokyo Trial is smaller

---

[182] The burial task of Suzendo was in the charge of four teams. In addition to a director, each team had a member who could get 8 cases of rice every day and ten members who every day could get 6 cases of rice. These figures are from the Appendix of the List of Suzeendo on the Burial Team Work which was compiled after the war. At that time, people were eager to reveal Japanese atrocities, so there was no possibility of underreporting. Among them, the first team buried 26,612 corpses from April 9 to 18 and each person, namely in all 12 people including the director, buried an average of nearly 222 every day; the second team buried 18,788 corpses from April 9 to 23, with an average of burying about 104 bodies per person per day; the third team buried 3828 corpses from April 9 to May 1, and the average burial was nearly 123 per person per day; the fourth team was buried a total of 25,490 corpses from April 7 to 20, with an average of burying 152 bodies per person per day. In all, the four teams buried 150 per capita per day during this period. But the biggest number of daily burials of the Red Swastika Society was 6468 on December 28, and 600 members had an average of less than 11 per capita (The number of the staff of the Red Swastika Society is not clear, but according to a post-war report, "another 600 members were sent". Although the additional members may not be sent on December 28, the burial work had started since the second day after the Japanese army entered the city [See the Section 2 of "Three questions concerning the Burial". In Cheng Zhaoqi, Study on the Nanjing Massacre, pp. 214–217) without any interruption. Therefore, the staff number and the number of people who buried bodies shall be basically proportional. And since additional members shall in fact be more than "600 additional members", there will not be a big difference if counting as 600 members.) Compared to the number of bodies daily buried, that of Suzendo was almost 40 times bigger than that of the Red Swastika Society. The gap is so big and there was also no mechanical equipment but entirely manpower at that time (The only remaining document, the application for auto parts submitted by Zhou Yiyu can also prove this.), so the figures are questionable. For the relevant materials, see The Archives on the Nanking Massacre committed by Japanese Invaders, pp. 446–462.

than that at the Nanjing Trial[183] and why the deaths confirmed by Japanese slaughter school is smaller than our token figure.

Is There a Limit to the Amount of Japanese Atrocities?

Over the years, Japanese fictionalists have been producing "counter-evidence" against the Japanese atrocities. And let me give you an example. Tanaka Masaaki once argued that the "refugee area" was " in peace" based on a "thank-you note". The note is as follows:

> In all,
> Ten cases of canned animal meat, ten packets of sugar, ten cases of salted fish, ten cases of soybean oil and ten packets of salt
> Twenty cases of biscuits
> Thanks to the captain for bringing a variety of food to the refugees. That has been a great blessing and you are such a merciful person. We are deeply grateful to the Captain of the Gunboat Hira for rewarding Baotaqiao Street Shelter, Xiaguan Branch of the World Red Swastika Society
>
> Chen Hansen
> Director of Heiwa Street Refugee Shelter
> of the World Red Swastika Society
> January 2, the 13th Year of Showa Era

As I have put in *Review of Japanese Right-wing Writings on the Nanjing Massacre*, "Lieutenant Colonel Doi Shinji, captain of Japanese Hira Gunboat, 'volunteered to clean up the area (Note: it refers to the Baotaqiao Street near Xiaguan)'[184] and renamed Baotaqiao Street as 'Heiwa' Street, a Japanese name. And Director Chen took Showa as new year name, which indicates the misery facing people of a conquered nation, in addition to the loss of self-esteem. So are the words such as so-called 'reward' and 'great blessing'.

---

[183] The 45th cause of action under the second type of "murder" in the indictment of the Tokyo Trial says that "subject to the unlawful killing order", the Japanese army "killed and slaughtered the following people as well as tens of thousands of Chinese civilians and disarmed soldiers whose number has not known yet when attacking Nanjing". The second section of the Appendix A of the Indictment states that "the Japanese army attacking Nanjing killed tens of thousands of civilians". The part that deals with the Nanking Massacre in Chapter 8 "Conventional War Crimes" of the Judgment says, "According to the estimate two days later, the total number of civilians and prisoners killed in Nanjing and surrounding areas during the first six weeks after Japanese army captured Nanjing was over 200,000". And the Section Matsui Iwane of Chapter 10 "Sentence" puts, "From the beginning of the capture of the city on December 13, 1937 to the end of February, 1938, thousands of women were raped and more than 100,000 were killed during this six or seven weeks". The Tokyo Trial did not confirm the conclusions of more than 300,000 people at the Nanjing trial.

[184] 田中正明著『南京事件の総括____虐殺否定十五の論拠』, p. 179.

We can not ask refugees to reject food given in a disrespectful manner; We also need not criticize those like Chen Hansen who subjected themselves to the enemy; We even can set aside the purpose and operations of Doi Shinji– the epitome of Japanese army– to establish a colony like the Manchukoku. However, we ought not ignore the fact that it was Japanese army that led to the refugees in 'Heiwa' Street Shelter and even all throughout the Nanjing City starving to death".

It has been my "daily routine" to refute such "evidence" of the fabrication school from the perspective of facts and reason. But I again mention this example—not to argue against wrong statements—but to draw attention to the fact that when it came to the Nanjing Massacre, concerned were savage people who killed every they saw, like Mukai Tashiakai and Noda Takeshi, long neglecting those conquered in a soft manner like the Doi Shinji. In a broad sense, we certainly can say that Japanese army brought themselves to our land without permission and all of their actions were invasion. But Doi's operations and similar actions are different from heinous crimes. Admitting this, we have to face a challenge, that is, is there a quantitative "line" for atrocities Japanese army committed in Nanjing? In other words, were Japanese atrocities infinite actions involving troops at all levels at all times and all places or limited to certain troop at certain time or place? Of course, we can argue that a quantitative line cannot refute the fact that Japanese atrocities violated the international law and went against humanity in nature. However, the notion of the Nanjing Massacre, to some extent, might inevitably change.

Was Matsui Iwane, Who Was Primarily Responsible for the Nanjing Massacre and Sentenced to Be Hanged at the Tokyo Trial, Reliable for Certain "Action"

At the Tokyo Trial, Iwane Matsui who was primarily responsible for the Nanjing Massacre was sentenced to be hanged, the severest punishment, which, however, was not for his "command, authorization and permission in an illegal manner" as the prosecution requested, but for his negative "inaction".[185] This judgment gave some leeway for Iwane Matsui to appeal his conviction and won the "sympathy" from outsiders since "failure to control" was a much lesser charge. Why did the court sentenced Matsui to the capital punishment without confirming the corresponding heavier charges? The major reason shall lie in the lack of direct evidence for his "action", which will be further discussed later. And I also think the seemly insignificant testimony that Matsui was a "pacifist" worked to some extent because all such testimonies were neither questioned by the court or the prosecution. But in fact, the

---

[185] "This court therefore finds the defendant Iwane Matsui guilty on the 55th cause of action, not guilty on the 27th, 29th and 31st, 32nd, 35th, 36th, and 5th cause of cation." See 洞富雄編『日中戦争史資料』8「南京事件」I, p. 399.

strategy behind such shared "testimony" was "deception".[186] Among all the relevant testimonies, the testimony of Okada Takashi, a special assistant of SEF, was the most "sincere" one, which spared no efforts to justify Matsui. Then, let us check what Okada said and whether the testimony was truthful.

Okada Takashi said that Iwane Matsui really loved China. For example, he said when he visited Iwane Matsui the next morning of "celebrating-the-victory party" (which was held in the evening December 17th), Iwane Matsui was not happy at all because his "consistent wish over the past 30 years has been to realize the peace between China and Japan" and he was "deeply sorry" for the "miseries" resulting from our battles. And he "felt much sympathy on General's mind when hearing these grave words". According to Okada, Matsui was accompanied by him to Qingliang Mountain and Nanjing Observatory on December 19th. He said Matsui "very much regretted the tragic setback that Generalissimo Chiang Kai-shek's reunification efforts suffered and thought if Generalissimo Chiang Kai-shek could wait for another two or three years without provoking wars, Japan would also realize the disadvantages of solving the Chinese problems by force, thus avoiding these unfortunate consequences". Okada also took as example the poem that Matsui wrote to him on the New Year's Day of 1938. The poem is as follows: "Dozens of autumns with northern horses and south boats, I am ashamed of being incapable to realize the peace and development of Asian countries. I will continue to pursue my dream and never give up even I die". Okada claimed this poem had "revealed the General's thought", that is, "pursuing the peace and development of Asian countries". Okada's testimony also mentioned when Matsui "inspected the refugee area", he "kindly comforted those refugees", issued an order of "never harming the kind civilians" and promised them "the era of peaceful and happy life would surely come in the near future".[187]

Indeed, if it were not for his comeback after retirement, there might have been a completely different historical evaluation of Iwane Matsui. Iwane Matsui individually had a bond with China in an early time when he served as a military officer in Beijing and Shanghai. He used to support Sun Yat-sen's revolutionary activities and he "loved" Chinese traditional culture, having knowledge of Chinese poetry and calligraphy. Although he was passionate about "Pan-Asianism and getting acquainted with Chinese dignitaries in his late years, he was very frugal and behaved well. In terms of his close relationship with China throughout his life, as Okada has said, it was "really rare".[188] But apparently, just as the personal morality doesn't matter much in the evaluation political

---

[186] The word "deception" is a common word used by Japanese fictionalists to deny the Nanjing Massacre and to accuse the Tokyo trial. For example, Fuji Nobuo's monograph to deny the Nanjing Massacre is subtitled "The Deception of the Tokyo Trial" (冨士信夫著『「南京大虐殺」はこうして作られた＿＿＿東京裁判の欺瞞』, 東京, 展転社1995年4月29第1版).

[187] 洞富雄編『日中戦争史資料』8「南京事件」I, pp. 263–264.

[188] 洞富雄編『日中戦争史資料』8「南京事件」I, p. 264.

figures, Iwane Matsui's "love" have nothing to do with his being responsible for Japanese atrocities. And I would like to specially point out that although the performance of Iwane Matsui described by Okada Takashi has never been questioned, it is still more suspicious than credible and we should not be easily convinced. And take a detail as example. It is strange that Iwane Matsui used the words "China and Japan" (which appear many times) in the foregoing records, because it is against Japanese expression habit, just like Chinese would not say "Japan and China". Even ordinary Japanese would not say in this manner in private and especially would not in formal occasions, let alone Matsui Iwane. Matsui Iwane was unlikely to use that word, but Okada Takashi said he did. Obviously, there is something worth examining. When I first read the defense testimonies of the Tokyo Trial on the Nanjing atrocities, I felt Okada Takashi was obviously different from others but did not much. Later, it occurred to me that Okada's testimony was well designed. Other witnesses, such as Wakisaka Jiro, head of the 36th Regiment of the 9th Division of SEF, and Nakasawa Mitsuo, Chief of Staff of the 16th Division, took a resolute and left no leeway, such as claiming the atrocities of the Chinese Army and using "Japan Chine" as long as they refer to China and Japan together. Okada Takashi was different because he tried to "touch the judge with emotion". In the "affidavit" (No. 2670 Document for the Defense and No. 3409 Court Evidence) and when testifying in the court, he understated everything and merely stressed Iwane Matsui committed to the peaceful relationship between Japan and China and was sad for the tragedy between Japan and China. In that case, "China and Japan" was thus used though it seemed to stress the status of China. Okada Takashi acted in this way because he was very eager to save Iwane Matsui. Subject to this, he sought to "turn the enemy into friend" when asked to talk or write and thus was very different from those witnesses who only cared their "integrity" but never cared about the situation of the defendants. The reason why Okada Takashi tried so hard is that Iwane Matsui is both like a farther and benefactor to him, that is, their relationship is much more closer than that between superior and subordinate. Therefore, what those insolent witnesses said is not credible and neither is what Okada Takashi said, even if his words are more mild. And the so-called "China and Japan" obviously has betrayed him.

Among the statements of Okada Takashi, there is another one that was not questioned by the prosecution at the Tokyo Trial and later became the main source of opinions of Masaaki Tanaka and others,[189] namely the so-called

---

[189] As Masaaki Tanaka said, Iwane Matsui spent his whole life pursuing for "Good relationship between Japan and China", "the unity of Asia": For example, he visited the southwest in 1936, "convinced the warlord era with Hu Hanmin as the core" in order to "follow the great mission of peaceful relationship between Japan and China, repair the two countries' relationship that has been in crisis". And he spread the opinions widely, "Promoting the unity and self-reliance of Asia, promoting the cultural renaissance of Asia and advocating that Asia should be the Asians' Asia is to realize the unfinished dream of Sun Yat-sen." (田中正明著『「南京虐殺」の虚構――松井大将の日記をめぐって』, 東京, 日本教文社. The 1st edition published on June 25, 1984, pp. 99+91).

"peace cause" led by Matsui Iwane. Matsui advised "people of all circles", especially "people of the financial circle" that

> Seeking another way to negotiate and sticking to a peaceful road under the guidance of a correct theory, you shall propose your own government to create an atmosphere of peace and end the state of warfare without dishonoring both governments. I think this is the most appropriate way.[190]

Okada Takahashi take as example the meeting with Soong Tse-ven. He and Li Tseh-i, as persuader, arrived in Hong Kong on January 10th, 1938, and had a talk with Soong Tse-ven. It was said "Mr. Song totally agreed on the suggestion and also thought the unfortunate incident between China and Japan was not only the misfortune of the two countries, but also a tragedy of the whole mankind". The proposal finally did not work because Fumimaro Konoe issued a statement of "not taking National KMT government as enemy" and Iwane Matsui was dismissed. When Okada mentioned this matter, the related parties were all present, so he was unlikely make a forgery. But it is not sure whether the talk between Iwane Matsui and Li Tseh-i, the talk between Li Tseh-i and Soong Tse-ven and what Soong Tse-ven agreed on were the same as Okada claimed. When saying the proposal failed because of Iwane Matsui's dismission, Okada used the expression "everything would be over".[191] It seemed that had not for this, China and Japan would be probably to turn hostility into friendship. But it depends. In terms of the whole China, Iwane Matsui's ambition was not realized. In terms of the Japan-occupied area, Liang Hongzhi, Wen Zongyao, Chen Qun, Chen Jintao, Ren Yuandao, Hu Yatai, Wang Zihui, Jiang Hongjie, Gu Cheng, Lian Yu and others, and then a larger group of "people from all walks of life" such as Wang Jingwei, Chen Gongbo, Zhou Fohai successively cooperated with the Japanese army "in the most appropriate way" to "eliminate the state of warfare" and "create an atmosphere of peace", and in this sense, Iwane Matsui's ambition can be said to have been realized. I think the original ambition of Iwane Matsui was to conquer the Chinese nation, and my thought is not subject to any personal emotion, but based on what Iwane Matsui said and wrote. As mentioned above, Matsui had advocated "occupying Nanjing in a short period" as early as he accepted the task and this had been a consistent demand before the senior officials of Japanese army decided to attack Nanjing. On November 15th, when Colonel Sadaaki Kagesa, Chief of Chief of 8th Section (Propaganda Strategy) of General Staff, and Colonel Shibayama Kenshirō, Chief of Military Service Bureau of the Army Ministry, visited Shanghai Expeditionary Army, Iwane Matsui emphasized the "necessity of occupying Nanjing". On November 22nd, CCAA stated again in the "Opinions on the Future Operations" that

---

[190]洞富雄編『日中戦争史資料』8「南京事件」I, p. 265.
[191]洞富雄編『日中戦争史資料』8「南京事件」I, pp. 265–266.

"[we] shall occupy Nanjing when the enemy is weak."(Iwane Matsui clearly noted in his diary of that day that the opinion of CCAA was "approval") On November 25th, Vice Chief of Staff Hayao Tada phoned and said the operations of CCAA can expand to Wuxi and Hizhou but should not extend further in the west. And Iwane Matsui denounced the order in his diary as "following old ruts and really unbelievable".[192]

During the Tokyo Trial, the defense took as evidence "Iwane Matsui's statement" on October 8th, 1937, which was later frequently cited by the fictionalists, due to the words "do not regard the civilians as the enemy" in the statement. But in fact, the statement begins as follows:

> Because of my position, I received Emperor's order and bore the heavy responsibility to lead the army to capture the victory of the war. Since we landed in the south of the Yangtze River, our army has been enriched and the brave troops have been sent, totally showing our power. Subject to the purpose of Japanese government's statement, our army shall protect the rights and interests of our country as well as our expatriates, punish the Nanjing government and the violent China and sweep away the red forces as well as anti-Japanese policies so as to establish a clear foundation for the peace of East Asia.[193]

"The Nanjing government", "red forces" and "violent China" refer to people except Liang Hongzhi and his partners and they shall all be "punished" and "swept up". It is obvious that Matsui Iwane intended "China" to surrender to Japan. Therefore, the above-mentioned Iwane Matsui's "regrets" for the war between China and Japan cannot make sense in terms of fact. Here I would like to cite a more important piece of evidence to veil the real intention of Iwane Matsui. The decision of the General Staff Office arrived at CCAA on November 28th and Iwane Matsui wrote his feelings down in his diary. "It is a great relief to me that my sincere proposal was approved".[194] This sentence is more valuable for us to understand Iwane Matsui than any other ones. It not only belies Okada's argument that Matsui was reluctant, but also reveals Matsui's great "passion" for attacking Nanjing. Someone may think Iwane Matsui's state of mind and even his understanding changed after the army occupied Nanjing, but whatever, it is impossible for Iwane Matsui to have a feeling of "loneliness" after entering the city which has indisputable evidence. And among the evidence, there is also Iwane

---

[192] 「松井石根大将戦陣日記」, 南京戦史編集委員会編『南京戦史資料集』, pp. 7+8+9.

[193] 洞富雄編『日中戦争史資料』8「南京事件」I, p. 269.

[194] 「松井石根大!戦陣日記」, 南京戦史編集委員会編『南京戦史資料集』, p. 10. After receiving the order "Be brave to fight, be determined to act, try to win with less armies, show the power of our nation to China and foreign countries, I would be grateful to your loyalty" from the emperor, Iwane Matsui expressed that he would "overcome all difficulties to show the power of the imperial army" in his response article. (同上引『南京戦史資料集』, pp. 196+197). Iwane Matsui has always been active.

Matsui's self-testimony. On December 18th, the day as Okada claimed Matsui had very much regret, Matsui wrote in "Feelings in Nanjing" that "Million Warriors marched with flying banners, and the great authority of Imperial Army reach everywhere".[195] And on December 21st, Iwane Matsui went back to Shanghai and wrote in his diary of that day as follows: "It has been two weeks since I left Shanghai and I have completed the feat of entering the Nanjing city, so I return with great happiness".[196] Matsui's diary provides a very different message from Okada's testimony.

In terms of the overall operations, Matsui Iwane cannot be said to a mere soldier. He was more actively advocate expanding the war and capturing Nanjing than the central authority of Japanese army and his soldiers always crossed the "border line" provided by the central authority. And unlike technical soldiers, Matsui had mature political views. "Great-Asianism" can be set aside. In terms of the views on the situation, he was far more radical than the Japanese government at that time. The statement of "not taking National KMT government issued by Fumimaro Konoe" signaled the denial of the Japanese government on National KMT government. This statement was issued on January 16th, 1938. Before that, the Chinese and Japanese parties secretly contacted for peaceful negotiation with German ambassadors in both countries as a go-between. However, as has been mentioned above, Matsui had a general plan to overthrow the national KMT government very early. On December 2nd, 1937, he had said, "The strategical aim in the future is primarily to overthrow the national KMT government and establish an independent regime in Jiangsu and Zhejiang, as well as Anhui if possible. And as a last resort, the remaining important officials of the national KMT government who stayed near Nanjing can be called to remould the government and establish a new one, independent from the Hankou government".[197]

Through revealing the original intention of Matsui Iwane, I would like to argue that the "negative" impression Matsui has left so far is the fabrication created by the prosecution of the Tokyo Trial. From the perspective of political responsibility, Matsui is responsible for the "Nanjing Incident" not only because of his "inaction". In this sense, the prosecution and the judges at the Tokyo Trial failed to see this and the "inaction" judgment is not appropriate. But on the other hand, we have to admit the evidence for his direct "action" against the atrocities, namely the evidence of the so-called "order,

---

[195] 「松井石根大!戦陣日記」，南京戦史編集委員会編『南京戦史資料集』，第21页。 Okada Takashi tried to prove Matsui "pursued" "peace" through Matsui's poems on the New Year's Eve of 1938. But in fact, the "the authority of Imperial Army Power" mentioned was his always pursuit. In his poem on the day he left for Shanghai, he said, "This autumn is publicize the royal way, and our hundred million soldiers would occupy the 400 states" (「松井石根大!戦陣日記」，南京戦史編集委員会編『南京戦史資料集』II, 第12页). Not only the spirit was the same as above-mentioned poem, but also the words.

[196] 「松井石根大!戦陣日記」，南京戦史編集委員会編『南京戦史資料集』, p. 23.

[197] 「松井石根大将戦陣日記」，南京戦史編集委員会編『南京戦史資料集』, p. 13.

authorization or permission", has never been found. From this case, we can learn that as long as we further examine and analyze the "material", including writings, oral records, videos and objects, it can be easily found that Japan's long-standing defense against the "Nanjing Incident" is contrary to the facts. Besides, we must be aware that many issues concerning the Nanjing Massacre remain to be solved.

12   Conclusion

As a separate one, this article has been too long, and thus it is impossible to follow the writing practice and summarize the outline of the full text. At the end of this article, there are also some words that should not be omitted: As a historical event, the complete restoration of the Nanjing Massacre still needs the unremitting efforts of scholars from various countries, especially Chinese historians. This effort cannot be offset by either the so-called "emotional memory" or the so-called "principle correctness".

(Published in Journal of Social Sciences: 2006(9), sponsored by Shanghai Academy of Social Sciences)

Essays

The "Legitimacy" That Cannot Be Self-justified

The Japanese attack on Nanjing was an extension of the attack on Shanghai, while the attack on Shanghai was a "natural" development of the whole trend after the Lugouqiao Incident. The trend is not something that can be easily changed by a few historical junctures. However, the Japanese "fictionalists" still defend for themselves by every means, resisting at every important juncture. As "Nanjing Massacre" has been recognized as a fact for a long time, if the Japanese "fictionalists" do not insist at every point that "Nanjing Massacre" is a "considered fact" created by people's words, it is impossible for them to win. Therefore, they stress that the first shot from Lugouqiao was just "provoked" by the Chinese side. According to *The Alleged Nanking Massacre*[1]:

---

[1] 『*The Alleged Nanking Massacre———confiding Japan's grievances to the world*』, written by Takemoto Tadao and Ohara Yasuo, compiled by 日本会議国際広報委員会 (Tokyo: 明成社. The 1st edition published on November 25, 2000). Among the works negating the "Nanjing Massacre" placed in prominent places in major Japanese bookstores nowadays, this book is a more special one. This kind of "special" is mainly manifested in: First, the complete negation of the Nanjing Massacre, which can be seen from its subtitle-*confiding Japan's grievances to the world*; second, different from other works which focus on "textual research", this book is basically a collection of views, quite a kind of "editorials". Third, different from other works which mainly take the "the School of Slaughter" in Japan as the discussion target, this book is published in both Japanese and English languages, shifting the target of "confiding" to the world, as is shown by the big word "the first rebuttal to the anti-Japanese propaganda on the American stage" at the first line in the endpaper. Fourth, although the "American stage" and so on has appeared in the endpaper, it is said in the preface: "the 'whistleblower' who is the object of our criticism…… is to rouse the attention on the Chinese government's theory of the Nanjing Massacre. The reason is……prove that the source of the international anti-Japan encirclement network that condemn Japan's brutal behaviors lies in the Chinese government. Fifth, the book often said that China has "anti-Japanese" sentiment, but the whole book is filled with its own anti-China sentiment, and even foul language, such as saying that China's point of view is "Chinese-style castration voice" ((「中国式金切り声」, claiming to be a "low, clear and fair statement"). Sixth, although Takemoto Tadao and Ohara Yasuo are signed on the cover of this

---

© The Author(s) 2020
Z. Cheng, *The Nanjing Massacre and Sino-Japanese Relations*,
https://doi.org/10.1007/978-981-15-7887-8_12

> On July 7th, 1937, when the Japanese garrisons were conducting a night manoeuvre near the Lugouqiao in the western vicinity of Beijing, several bullets were sent suddenly from the direction where the Chinese army was. Thus, the Japanese and Chinese armies clashed for this incident. This is the destined Lugouqiao Incident.[2]

According to *The Sealed Syou Wa History*:

> The Lugouqiao Incident was once considered "to be provoked by the Japanese army as the Japanese fired first", but now, "the CPC is the real criminal" is a common sense. It was Liu Shaoqi's entourage who fired on the Japanese army and Chiang Kai-shek's army at the same time, aiming to provoke a conflict between the two.[3]

According to *The History Not Taught in Textbooks*:

> You can immediately understand as long as you see who wins the war between the Japanese army and Chinese army. It is appropriate to think that the CPC army first fired in the Lugouqiao Incident.[4]

Who fired the first shot? I'm afraid that there will never be a unanimous conclusion. This is not to say that the facts can no longer be proved, but to say the influence of the "stance" on the question is too great, and it is difficult for the "truth" to gain a foothold-as the two sides have insisted on their own opinions from the very beginning, the materials left are too different: We think that there is no doubt about the matter, and the "fictionalists" also say that

---

book, the copyright page is signed by "日本会議国際広報委員会" and "on behalf of Takemoto Tadao". The "Japan Conference" is an important right-wing organization in Japan, so this book can also be regarded as an "official" book of the right wing of Japan.

[2] 『*The Alleged Nanking Massacre———confiding Japan's grievances to the world*』, written by Takemoto Tadao and Ohara Yasuo, compiled by 日本会議国際広報委員会(Tokyo: 明成社. The 1st edition published on November 25, 2000, p. 18).

[3] 『封印の昭和史———「戦後五〇年」自虐の終焉』, written by Komuro Naoki and Watanabe Shoichi (Tokyo: Tokuma Shoten. The 4th edition published on October 15, 1995, p. 92). This book is a collection of the dialogues between the two, the citation above is said by Watanabe Shoichi. Watanabe Shoichi is a senior rightist in Japan, according to 小室: "since the heyday of the left-wing and progressive culture, the Tokyo Trial has been thoroughly criticized" (same as the first sentence of the preface to 小室 on page 2). In the 1990s, 渡部 hosted a talk show at 10:00 every Sunday on Tokyo Television (Channel 12). I have been used to seeing such opinions as above quotes for a long time. But on one occasion, he unexpectedly said, "Liu Shaoqi's command to fire the first shot is recorded in Chinese primary and secondary school textbooks". It is really shocking that he can say such fake words. May be that is a distant reason why many people cross the line and make such irresponsible remarks today.

[4] 『教科書が教えない歴史』, compiled by Nobukatsu Fujioka and 自由主義史観研究会 (Tokyo: 产経新聞社. The 1st edition published on August 10, 1996, p. 188).

they have "Indisputable evidence".⁵ This incident does make people feel the limitations of "textual research". However, for the Chinese, this is not an issue of sufficient importance in that there is a more fundamental question beyond that, that is, the Lugouqiao is part of Chinese territory. The Japanese army not only came uninvited, but also used weapons such as swords and guns, which would never be accepted by the Chinese army, no matter in emotion or in reason. And that is the prior issue. In this regard, *The Alleged Nanking Massacre* has another argument, it believes that the stationing of Japanese garrisons has a "legal" basis so the matter has nothing to do with "Chinese territory":

> In 1899, taking the Boxer Rebellion as the opportunity, Britain, the United States, France, Italy and Japan, concluded the *Final Protocol on the Northern Qing Incident* with the Qing government in 1901. Because of this protocol, countries such as Japan and the United States stationed troops on the outskirts of Beijing in order to protect their expatriates.⁶

The *Final Protocol on the Northern Qing Incident* mentioned above is just the Boxer Protocol we call.

In the eyes of the Chinese, the Boxer Protocol is only a witness to the notorious history in that it can only evoke the worst memories of oppression, humiliation and so on. However, because it is a so-called "international treaty" and is related to the interests established by the West since modern times, its "legitimacy" has not been denied by the United States and other victorious countries even after the war. For example, instead of doubting the legitimacy of the stationing of the Japanese on the Chinese territory, the judgment of the Tokyo Trial only said: Qin Dechun, acting commander of the 29th Army, said that "the manoeuvre that night" was "illegal" because the Chinese side was not informed.⁷ However, although the "legitimacy"⁸

---

⁵Words from *The Fiction of Nanjing Massacre*. 『「南京虐殺」の 虚構――松井大!の 日記をめぐって』 (Tokyo: 日本教文社. The 1st edition published on June 25, 1984, p. 122).

⁶『*The Alleged Nanking Massacre――confiding Japan's grievances to the world*』, written by Takemoto Tadao and Ohara Yasuo, compiled by 日本会議国際広報委員会(Tokyo: 明成社. The 1st edition published on November 25, 2000, p. 18).

⁷*International Military Tribunal for the Far East Judgment*, translated by Zhang Xiaolin, Section 4, Part 2, *From the Lugouqiao Incident to Guardian Statement* (Mass Publishing House. The 1st edition published in February 1986, p. 333). The Tokyo Trial avoided the important points while focusing on the small things so that leave a way to overturn the case in the future. The Japanese "fictionalists" stress that the Japanese army used blank bombs in the manoeuvre that night so it didn't belong to the areas that should be "informed".

⁸This is a general stance of the Japanese "fictionalists", for example, according to *A thorough examination of the Nanjing Massacre*: "In 1937, to protect their expatriates, five countries including Japan, the United States, Britain, France and Italy stationed in the northern outskirts of Beijing. The army's right to station was decided in 1901 on the basis of the *Final Protocol on the Northern Qing Incident* signed by the several powers and Li Hongzhang after Boxer Protocol in 1900" (『「南京虐殺」の徹底検証』, written by HIGASHINAKANO Shudo, Tokyo:展転社. The 4th edition published on July 8, 2000, p. 14).

insisted by the Japanese "fictionalists" seems to be powerful, it is actually very reluctant because it does have a problem of self-justification.

The basis for the "fictionalists" to raise objections to the Tokyo Trial and the whole Western system originally lies in the negation of Western power. Nobukatsu Fujioka, a professor at the University of Tokyo who has been active in recent years, expressed a very different opinion, saying that the Meiji Restoration is a "great national revolution" aiming "to rid Japan of the colonial crisis of Western and European powers".[9] Watanabe Shoichi, a professor of Sophia University, said that Japan is a "model to get rid of the Western powers".[10] Kanji Nishio, a professor at The University of Electro-Communications, said: "In the pluralistic order of the 'international community' of Western countries, East Asia does not exist at all. In the eyes of East Asians, this is a demon wearing a mask of justice".[11] Such stances are preconditions to affirm the modern routes of Japan as well as negate the so-called "historical view of the Tokyo Trial". That is to say, in order to affirm Japan's behavior of "opposing the West", we must negate the rank order imposed by the West on the East. The two cannot run side by side. If we negate the order imposed by the West, we can only negate the imitating behavior of Japan. The latter negation is the natural development of the previous negation. In *The Truth of History*, Mae Tetsu, chairman of the Asian Economic Man Symposium, firmly denied that the "Greater East Asian War" was a war of aggression and that the "Greater East Asian War" was a "war against the ravages of the white race" and a "war against racial discrimination" but at the same time, he argued that Japan "must admit and reflect" on its aggression against China, and that reflection alone is not enough. He also used the words of his predecessors to say that Japan must be grateful to China:

> The predecessors who went to China felt that China's leniency could not be expressed in words. Mr. Kōzō Masuda of the chess circle and Mr. Yamaoka Sōhachi, a novelist, have all gone to China, and they often say to me, "to China, this kindness must not be forgotten. We must pass it on to our children and grandchildren."[12]

The "kindness" here has two meanings, first, China did not mistreat Japanese prisoners as well as Japanese nationals after the war, second, both

---

[9] 『污辱の近現代史―――いま 克服のとき』, written by Nobukatsu Fujioka (Tokyo: Tokuma Shoten. The 1st edition published on October 31, 1996, p. 148).

[10] 『封印の昭和史―――「戦後五〇年」自虐の終焉』, written by Komuro Naoki and Watanabe Shoichi,(Tokyo: Tokuma Shoten. The 4th edition published on October 15, 1995, p. 348).

[11] 『国民の 歴史』, written by NISHIO Kanji, compiled by 新しい歴史教科書をつくる (Tokyo: 扶桑社. The 1st edition published on October 30, 1999, p. 435).

[12] 『戦後・歴史の真実』the second chapter 「大東亜戦争は侵略戦争ではなかった」, written by Mae Tetsu (Tokyo: 経済界. The 3rd edition published on May 25, 2000, pp. 94, 106–107).

the two post-war Chinese governments gave up their claims for compensation. Although it is not sure whether Mae Tetsu's definition of the "Greater East Asian War" confirms to the fact or not, his stance has its own thread and is of consistency. However, some works such as *The Alleged Nanking Massacre strongly stress the "legitimacy"*, which can be said lacking evidence at least.

Impudently Take a Mistranslation as "Rebuttal Evidence"

When it comes to negating the outrages the Japanese army has committed, the Japanese "fictionalists" would be so impudent that there is no means that they cannot use. The opinion I have expressed is not out of "national" emotion or "ideological" stance, but out of the real reflection of the "fictionalists". I gave an example not long ago, pointing out that the current active figure of the "fictionalists" Higashinakano Shudo deliberately obscures the facts: Ignoring the detailed records of the large number of corpses near Xiaguan and Yijiangmen written in the dairies of Colonel Yasuyama Koudou, the Military Medical Officer of Chini Fleet, Higashinakano dared to say that "there are totally no records of these corpses" in Yasuyama Koudou's diaries![1] The practice of Higashinakano has gone beyond the bottom line that we can discuss, only leaving us aghast. The example cited in this article is only a wrong translation, which is of a different nature and does not need to be studied in detail, but the "fictionalists" exaggerate the wrong translation repeatedly, as if they have grasped the "evidence" of the Chinese side "framing" the Japanese army. And a big conclusion has been developed from the small mistranslation. Thus, it is about the great justice and we cannot just leave the problem behind.

Thirty years ago, Suzuki Aki named the "fictionalists" with the book 「南京大虐殺」のまぼろし,[2] then after twenty seven years, he added

---

[1] Refer to No. 134 annotation of my article *Is the Nanjing Massacre fabricated by the Tokyo Trial?* for more detail (Beijing: *Modern Chinese History Studies*, No. 6, 2002, p. 48).

[2] The book's original name is 『「南京大虐殺」のまぼろし』(Tokyo: 文藝春秋社. The 1st edition published on March 10th, 1973). Since then, "まぼろし" has been regarded as the translation of the Chinese words "虚幻" and "虚构", becoming the general usage of the fictionalists, who totally deny the existence of the Nanjing Massacre. But, the Chinese word "虚构" is also used in Japan such as the book 『「南京虐殺」の虚構 (Tokyo: 日本教文社. The 1st edition published on June 65, 1984) written by 田中正明. In this way, it is not easy to distinguish.

the word "new" to the old name and wrote *The New Mystery of Nanjing Massacre,* raising various new questions about the "Nanjing Massacre", one of which is:

> The report of "the tragedy of Nanjing", which was read during the "Tokyo Trial", has been left on the "Tokyo trial reports". Among them, the representative document is Chen Guangyu's long "affidavit" signed in the name of "Chief Prosecutor of Nanjing District Court". It is divided into "Previous text" and "This text". "This context" includes many items and numbers that are related to "massacre", but the real puzzling contents exist in the "Previous Text". First of all, the Japanese shorthand of the "Previous Text" starts from "the investigation course". On November 7, 1945 (about three months after the defeat of Japan), Nanjing District Court printed documents to inform the citizens that the atrocities committed by the Japanese army will be investigated. Fourteen departments including the Nanjing Central Bureau of Investigation was mobilized to hold the first meeting to start the investigation. Here is the quote from the shorthand:
>
> At present, due to the <u>deceit</u> and fierce <u>interference</u> of the enemy (the key points are added by the quoter, the following key points added by the quoter will not be annotated), most people feel depressed and few people are active to report the outrages. Even some people are investigated by the officers, they tend to keep silent out of fear or deny the facts. What's more, some people keep the outrages to themselves as their reputation is involved, some people leave their home and can't be founded, also, there are some others whose life and death are unknown and there is no way to explore.
>
> From the very beginning, the text says the investigation is very difficult. Since Japan has surrendered unconditionally, it is more normal that the citizens should be ecstatic and assist in "investigation". However, the Nanjing citizens not only refused to assist in the investigation, but also were afraid of the "deceit and fierce interference of the enemy". It has been three months since the victory of the Chinese side, what does "the fierce interference of the enemy" mean? Why do the citizens remain silent even if they are inquired by the officers?[3]

Considering the various evidence Suzuki has confronted in recent years, he has to say that the translating "まぼろし" into "虚幻" or others is an "obvious mistranslation": the Japanese word 'まぼろし' can be directly translated as '虚' '实' '秀' and other various Character words (the words have the equal meanings--the introducer). What' more, 'まぼろし' also has a meaning of trance that cannot be easily captured, so I think it is not possible to correctly translate the extremely Japanese and 'emotional' word in Chinese". Suzuki used to interpret the word "幻" in 坂口安吾's article 「飛鳥の 幻」, which was published on 『文藝春秋』in July 1952. He defined it as "the inexplicable mysteries of history". Now, Suzuki's interpretation of "まぼろし" seems to turn to a "puzzling" interpretation (of course, Suzuki would not acknowledge it himself). Refer to 『新「南京大虐殺」のまぼろし』 (Tokyo: 飛鳥新社. The 1st edition published on June 3rd, 1999, pp. 31, 32). Therefore, I used Suzuki's interpretation here instead of using the old translation.

[3] 『新「南京大虐殺」のまぼろし』, written by Suzuki Aki (Tokyo: 飛鳥新社. The 1st edition published on June 3rd, 1999, pp. 302–303).

It is easy to figure out the true meaning of Suzuki Aki, but he still doesn't make his words clear, as his normal behavior.[4] That is because as long as there is an opportunity, someone of the "fictionalists" will always find a way to "create an explanation", they are never afraid of "losing their talents". Sure enough, last year, Minoru Kitamura[5] made use of the word "the fierce interference of the enemy" to elaborate his own idea in his article Study on the Nanjing Incident:

It has been nearly ten years since the Japanese army occupied Nanjing and many citizens have left their house, never to be found. However, the description of "the deceit and fierce interference of the enemy, the citizens are depressed" is very confusing. The investigation was conducted from the winter of 1945 to February of 1946, three or four months after the "enemy" Japan surrendered, the national government of Chiang Kai-shek returned to Nanjing from Chongqing, the Japanese rule was swept away and members of Wang Jingwei regime, the Japan's puppet regime, have either been arrested or trialed. It is unimaginable that the shadow of the Japan would still have such a great impact on the citizens. The situation of the so-called "deceit and fierce interference of the enemy" doesn't exist at all.

But Chinese language pays little attention to the concept of time. Therefore, it is difficult to judge the tense of "fierce work". If it refers to the present, then it would be impossible that the Japanese side has done such works after the defeat. If it refers to the past, it seems unnatural that this kind of affect would last until after the defeat of Japan. Therefore, the article starting from "The deceit and interference of the enemy……" is nothing more than the investigators' arbitrary judgment of the situation at that time. In terms of the facts, the residents in Nanjing have no vivid memories of the atrocities or killing of the Japanese soldiers. What's more, it is understandable that "people keep the outrages to themselves as their reputation is involved", but the description of "people keep silent out of fear or deny the facts" is quite confusing. "Keep silent out of fear" means daring not to say something out of fear, but what make them fearful? More importantly, why do they deny the "facts" what the investigators think real? The description of "people keep silent out of fear" tells us that most of the residents aren't willing to report

---

[4] Although Suzuki Aki was the pioneer of the "fictionalists" in the 1970s, his tine was not as intense as that of the latter.

[5] Kitamura Minoru was born in 1948 and now a literature professor of Ritsumeikan University, he majors in modern and contemporary Chinese history. He is a "freshman" in the research of "Nanjing Massacre". The basis for classifying him into the "fictionalists" lies in his recent works. Maybe he wouldn't recognize himself belonging to any school and no one in Japan has classified him into any school yet. Recently, some Japanese scholars have criticized his "political" tendency of his works (Refer to 「歴史改ざんの新意匠―――Minoru Kitamura『「南京事件」の探究』の実像」, No. 341 of 『人権と 教育』 written by 山田要一. Tokyo: 社会評論社. Published on May 20th, 2002, pp. 139–149).

the fasts to the investigators and even faced with investigators' inducement, most of the residents deny the facts.[6]

Compared to Suzuki Aki's words, Kitamura Minoru adds "work" to the cited parts, making the "investigation course" described by Chen Guangyu's "affidavit" more complex to understand. Since Japan has surrendered, why can they continue to "deceive and interfere", and even "fierce work"? Is it true that Japan surrendered but not retreated? But how can it be true? There is no such thing! Even Chen Guangyu tells a lie, it is not convincing—if there is only "The Japanese Shorthand" of the Tokyo Trial, probably everyone would think in the same way.

Fortunately, the original Chinese Text of the "investigation course" still exist in the world, avoiding Chen Guangyu as well as the then Chinese government taking the blame for something inexplicable. It turns out that the original text of the so-called "the deceit and fierce interference of the enemy" and "the work of the deceit and interference of the enemy is fierce" is just:

Only in this place, people are depressed because they have suffered most from the torments committed by the enemy......[7]

The meaning of this sentence is very clear, it has nothing to do with the "concept of time" and some other points put forward by Minoru Kitamura. Also, the question "what does 'the interference of the enemy' mean" put forward by Suzuki Aki lost its value. The "fictionalists" think that they have grasped rebuttal evidence, but in fact the so-called evidence is just a translation that is misunderstood.

However, if it is only an unintentional misunderstanding, we shall not criticize it because it is normal for people to make mistakes. But the "fictionalists" are not that easy. It does not just mean that the "misunderstanding" of the "fictionalists" is always a one-way misunderstanding, for example, when it comes to the number of people the Japanese have killed, the "fictionalists" will only misunderstand it in the direction of less, and when it comes to whether the Japanese army has committed the crime, the "fictionalists" will only misunderstand in the direction of no crime. Moreover, the "fictionalists" are trying to "find ways" to misunderstand, or we can say they are afraid of there being no ways to misunderstand. Just take Minoru Kitamura's *Study on Nanjing Incident* as an example, the whole article is trying to grasp "the School of Slaughter's misunderstanding" that can be used as rebuttal evidence. For example, Tomio Hora translated the "observe" in H. J. Timperley's book *What war means: The Japanese Atrocities in China*(Its

---

[6] 『南京事件の探究―――その実像をもとめて』, written by Minoru Kitamura (Tokyo: 文藝春秋社. The 1st edition published on November 20th, 2001, pp. 143–144).

[7] *Reports of the enemy's crimes investigated by the Procuratorate of the Nanjing Capital District Court, (I)"Investigation Course", Selected Archives of Japanese imperialist invasion of China--Nanjing Massacre*, jointly compiled by The State Archives Administration of the People's Republic of China, Secondary Historical Archives of China, Jilin Academy of Social Sciences, Zhonghua Book Company, the 1st edition published in July 1995, p. 404.

Chinese name has been changed into 《外人目睹中之日军暴行》) as "watch", Kitamura Minoru remarks:

The words equal to "watch" should be "witness" and "eyewitness", the correct translation of "observe" should be "perceive" or "monitor". If "observe" is translated as "watch", the incidents caused by the Japanese army and reported by the European and Americans will all be misinterpreted as "being witnessed".[8]

However, the reason Tomio Hora why used the word "watch" is because the Chinese version, which was published with the English version at the same time in 1938, used the word "watch", and during the wartime, the Japanese version [9] translated from the Chinese version (there is a little difference between English version and Chinese version) by unknown also used the word "watch". Therefore, Tomio Hora just followed the convention, completely different from Suzuki Aki's creation.

Minoru Kitamura's new book reflects "carefulness" in several places. The Chinese version of *Selected Archives of Japanese imperialist invasion of China–Nanjing Massacre* was not a rare book and it was also a book Kitamura Minoru must read if he decided to write such a book. The Chinese and Japanese versions of Chen Guangyu's "Investigation Course" were different, he could easily find that when he looked through these materials as long as he was a little "careful". However, he not only failed to find the difference, but used it as "rebuttal evidence" to elaborate on his own idea, how can people not suspect that he made the mistake intentionally?

---

[8] 『南京事件の探究―――その実像をもとめて』, written by Minoru Kitamura (Tokyo: 文藝春秋社. The 1st edition published on November 20th, 2001, p. 117).

[9] There is no record of the publishing matter of this version, according to Tomio Hora's deduction: "It was probably a top secret publication translated, printed and distributed by the Military Department to a very small number of high-level people in Japan at that time." 『日中戦争史資料』9「南京事件」2「解題」』, compiled by Tomio Hora (Tokyo: 河出書房新社. The 1st edition published on November 30th, 1973, p. 7). I used to think Tomio Hora's deduction is correct. But I started to doubt its rightness in last summer. At that time, when the "textbook incident" was reviving, the Shanghai Dictionary Publishing House Library (the foundation of the dictionary library came from the old Zhonghua Book Company, except for universities and libraries at or above the provincial level, it has the most books) happened to find a batch of prewar Japanese textbooks in the warehouse, and curator Wang Youpeng wanted me to say a few words to the media, so I roughly checked these books. In addition to textbooks and teaching aids, there is also a joint publication in English and Japanese, with excellent sheets of paper and excellent printing, without the editor, bookstore or publication date, it contains a collection of aggressive remarks in all kinds of Japanese textbooks. Since the Chinese version of Timperley's book was operated by the Propaganda Department of the Kuomintang at that time, I suspect that the Japanese version of Tian's book, this book and the Chinese version of Tian's book may have the same origin.

How Can There Be "Not Expansion"

After the July 7th Incident, the Japanese officers had differences on the next strategy of the war, Major General Kanji Ishiwara, Chief of G-1, General Staff Office (Operations Section), determinedly proposed the strategy of "no expansion",[1] but most of Japanese officers thought it was a great opportunity to attack China, and these officers took the overwhelmingly account. Although the anti-Japanese momentum had been very strong in the Chinese side at that time, the Japanese army sending out a large number of troops was still the priority reason that the war expanded day by day and formed a national scale. However, *The Alleged "Nanking Massacre"* said:

> At that time, the Japanese Army didn't prepare to have a war with China, Hirohito also expected that there was no expansion after the incident so he ordered that the Japanese garrisons on the spot "not expand, but to resolve locally", after four days later, an armistice agreement was concluded, but the Chinese side didn't abide by the armistice agreement. Faced with this danger, on July 27th, the Japanese Army sent three divisions in the mainland to North China. Two days later, on July 29th, the "Tongzhou Incident" happened, in which the Chinese military units attacked Tongzhou's Japanese residential zone and more than 210 Japanese residents were slaughtered.

---

[1] Kanji Ishiwara's "thinking mode" can refer to my article The Way to Pearl Harbor, Historical Monthly (Taipei, 歷史智庫出版公司. Published in December, 2001). According to the recollection of Tanaka Shinichi, who supported war: after the happening of the "Langfang Incident" at one o'clock on July 26th, he had received one call from Kanji, Kanji said: "We can only mobilize the division in mainland. Expansion will destroy everything". In this regard, 《大本営陸軍部》 said "Even Major General Kanji, who totally oppose expansion, think it is impossible" (『大本営陸軍部』, compiled by 防衛庁防衛研修所戦史室 (Tokyo: 朝雲新聞社. The 1st edition published on September 25th, 1967, page 455). But Kanji never changed the basic idea even after the defeat in the end of September.

© The Author(s) 2020
Z. Cheng, *The Nanjing Massacre and Sino-Japanese Relations*,
https://doi.org/10.1007/978-981-15-7887-8_14

It's inevitable that the above quotation will lead to conflicts, such as the different opinions on the "Tongzhou Incident", but the more important thing is how to determine the facts of this incident. Hirohito committed himself to the war and was highly engaged. He was "very satisfied" with the fact that the Japanese army had occupied Nanjing and the fact that the Japanese soldiers were willing to sacrifice themselves to express their gratitude to "emperor benevolence". As these things about Hirohito have been discussed on another article,[2] I will not tell more here. (It is close to Japanese scholar Tsuda Michio's new book *Aggressive war and sexual violence*, which makes a detailed analysis of the promotion of war at the "moral" level made by the "Emperor".)[3] In fact, there is not much room for discussion on whether the Japanese military and political leaders and the troops stationed are "unwilling" to start the war and whether they have made "substantial concessions".

In the book *Japan's War*, written by Soichiro Tahara, Japan's most influential critic in recent years, there is a paragraph that summarizes the reaction of the Japanese army after the news of the Lugouqiao Incident was sent to them. I will use the description in order to avoid soliciting the complex raw materials:

> When the report was received, the Ministry of the Army was holding regular meeting, almost all of the attenders showed their positive attitudes towards the situation, and most of them thought that they should resolutely attack China. Among them, Colonel Tanaka Shinichi, head of the Military Division of the Military Bureau, strongly advocated the tough policy. Colonel Akira Mutō (Head of the Third Military Division, and later he became the Director of Military Affairs of Ministry of the Army and was executed after the war) was Tanaka's contemporary in the Hellenic Military Academy, he told Colonel Tarashiro Kawabe (Head of the Second Military Division): "A pleasant thing happened". That is to say, most people in Army Central Committee advocated of "completely attacking China".[4]

---

[2] *Was the Nanjing Massacre Fabricated by the Tokyo Trial?*, Beijing, *The Study of Modern History*, Issue 6, 2002, page 1–57.

[3] 『侵略戦争と 性暴力―――軍隊は民衆をまもらない』, written by Tsuda Michio, section "天皇による 道徳的價値の独占" of IV 「天皇社会と 中国・中国人蔑視」 (Tokyo, 社会評論社. The 1st edition published on June 15th, 2002, page 177–180). With regard to the moral responsibility of the emperor, among the Japanese right-wing scholars who completely deny that the emperor bears the "legal" and "political" responsibility, there are also Japanese right-wing scholars who think in the opposite direction: "The emperor does not bear the responsibility for war, but bear the responsibility for failure morally", it is commensurate with the position of the emperor", and "it can be considered that there has been a way to assume responsibility in the form of abdication" (『国民の 道徳』, written by Susumu Nishibe, compiled by 新しい 歴史教科書をつくる, Tokyo: 扶桑社. The 1st edition published on October 30th, 2000, page 134).

[4] 『日本の戦争―――なぜ、戦いに踏み切ったか?』, written by 田原総一郎 (Tokyo: 小学館. The 1st edition published on November 20th, 2000, page 375).

The word "pleasant" comes from the memory of Tarashiro Kawabe and has been cited by many Japanese works; it can be regarded as the symbol of the mainstream mentality of the Japanese army even the Japan as a whole. Under this kind of mentality, it is not strange that the opinion of "completely attacking China" takes "large account". Therefore, the so-called "no expansion" can only be empty no matter it is decided by which level of military officers. Just after the Japanese cabinet passed the resolution of "not expansion" on July 9th, it sent more troops to North China the next day. Of course, "sending more troops" could only be a "precaution", which did not necessarily run counter to "not expansion", but at that time, there were only a few people who truly advocated "not expansion", including Kanji Ishiwara, Tarashiro Kawabe (Head of War Guidance Division), Major General NAKAJIMA Tetsuzo, Minister of General Affairs of General Staff Office, Colonel SHIBAYAMA Kenshiro, Head of Military Affairs of Ministry of the Army and someone else. Therefore, "not expansion" was just a "word", what the actual behavior the Japanese army did was the opposite "expansion". Major Takeo Imai, who was the Japanese military attache in Peiping, had once participated in the mediation after the war; he said in his recollection:

> At two o'clock in the afternoon (July 11th), I felt the atmosphere of the room suddenly changed when I stepped into the secret service. At that time, an emergency call came from the Tianjin General Staff Office, I immediately got the call and found it was from an officer in the General Staff Office, the content of the call was: "Today the Tokyo Cabinet decided that except the power force of the Kwantung Army and the Korean Army, another three divisions would be mobilized from the mainland, therefore, <u>it is even more unnecessary to negotiate and reach an agreement. If an agreement has been made, it must be given up!</u>"[5]

Takeo Imai is the one who personally participated in this incident, his memories have special values as firsthand information, as the "power force" would come, it is "unnecessary to negotiate and reach an agreement", even "the agreement has been made", it "must be given up", we can see that the "peaceful" negotiation was just a stalling tactic made by the Japanese army without sincerity.

After Japan entered the period of Showa, it became the common practice that "the lower class rebelled against the upper class" in the army, so some Japanese would say that what the "officer in the General Staff Office" said reflects just "an individual will". But the key point is, even if the decision-making level made the "not expansion" decision, their real action didn't supplement to it. On the contrary, they only took the "expansion" measure. Therefore, it doesn't matter what they have said. Later,

---

[5]「盧溝橋事件の現地交渉」, written by 今井武夫, compiled by 日本國際政治学会・太平洋戦争原因研究部編『太平洋戦争への道』第4巻付録 (Tokyo: 朝日新聞社. The 1st edition published on January 15th, 1963, page 3).

SHIBAYAMA Kenshiro recounted the situation when he and NAKAJIMA Tetsuzo conveyed the "not expansion" policy to Lieutenant General Kiyoshi Katsuki, Commander of the Japanese China Garrison Army. That is a material worthy of reference:

> In mid-July, I visited Lieutenant General Kiyoshi Katsuki on the upper floor of Kaikosha in Tianjin, which then served as the military headquarters and the dormitory. I conveyed the policy to Lieutenant General Kiyoshi Katsuki and his Chief of Staff who were with him at that time. But on that day, for some reason, the military commander was in a very bad mood, after I conveyed the "not expansion" policy, he started to loudly insult NAKAJIMA Tetsuzo and SHIBAYAMA Kenshiro. I can't remember the exact reason right now, the general reasons are: on the one hand, they claim a not expansion policy, however, on the other hand, isn't the Central Cabinet sending more troops to northern parts? With such a contradiction, what's the meaning of not expansion? Such being the case, I can't accept if we not expand the war. You say it is the policy of the Central Cabinet, what is the so-called Central Cabinet? I accept instructions from the commander system rather than the Ministry of the Army of the Military Government. As the military commander who assume the important responsibility to decide the foreign policy. The above are the main reasons of Nakajjima and SHIBAYAMA Kenshiro being insulted.[6]

The reasons that Kiyoshi Katsuki can insult the envoy of the central government is not only because he bears the responsibility of deciding "foreign policy" or he has a higher military rank, but also because the mission given to him by General Staff Office is originally a "combat mission".[7] In fact, on July 11th, the "power force" (refers to the independent blend of the departments such as the First and the Eleventh Brigades as well as the Twentieth Division) of the Kwantung Army and the Korean Army introduced by "some general staff officer" to Takeo Imai has been placed under the command of Kiyoshi Katsuki, what' more, on the same day, an agreement has been concluded between Imperial Japanese Navy General Staff (Navy) and General Staff Office: "The Kwantung Army and the mainland send troops to Peiping and Tianjin to strengthen the Japanese China Garrison Army, the battle on

---

[6] 「日支事変勃発前後の経緯」之「盧溝橋事件の勃発」, written by 柴山兼四郎, 『現代史資料月報』(Tokyo, みすず書房. December 1965, page 3).

[7] Kiyoshi Katsuki didn't record the insults in his memoirs, but he recorded the then situation in detail, saying that he accepted "the definite task about the use of military forces from Chief of Staff". The memoirs also recorded the "aspiration of a junior officer", who made the final statement that day: "If the not expansion policy is used, the army (refers to the Japanese China Garrison Army—the quoter) is not properly handled, or the center government can't bear the worries, then it is necessary to first replace the commander of the general with a more capable one" (The memoirs of Kiyoshi Katsuk, 「支那事変回想録摘記」,小林龍夫等解説『現代史資料』12『日中戦争』4 (Tokyo: みすず書房. The 1st edition published on December 15th, 1965, page 567, 568). The dissatisfaction with the War Department's "not expansion" is overstated.

the right (refers to the Peiping and Tianjin area–the quoter) is mainly conducted by the Army, the Navy is responsible for transporting and defending the Army and cooperating with the Army to fight in Tianjin".[8] The battle plan formulated on July 15th stipulated that at the first stage, the 29th Chinese Army should be "promptly punished by military force" and "sweep the enemy in the outskirts of Peiping west of the Yongding River", at the second stage, "The current troops remain on the front line of Baoding and Renqiu to have more troops to fight a decisive war with the Central Army on the front line of Shimen and Dexian".[9] On July 26th, Chief of Staff General Kan'in Kotohito abolished July 8's "prevent expansion" instruction of "temporary order No.400" with "temporary order No.418".[10]

Of course, it is undeniable that the present Japanese army does have a high "enterprising spirit". When the Japanese army formed the Shanghai Expeditionary Army after "8.13 Incident", it was declared that the war would "not expand" outside Shanghai, but Army Commander Senior General said: "We should abandon the strategy of local solution and not expansion", "We should resolutely use the necessary forces with the traditional spirit to make a quick fight. The main forces should be used in Nanjing rather than in the North Branch", "We should occupy Nanjing in a very short time".[11] The active behavior of the present Japanese army has indeed played a great role in promoting the war. However, the real key to the fact that the present Japanese army is able to fight a bigger and bigger war is that the Japanese central government continues to "send more troops to the North Branch" and other places, while the reason of the continuous increase of troops lies in "the overwhelming majority of opinions on giving China a decisive strike". Under the guidance of such an "overwhelming majority", Japan's policy can only be "expansion", rather than the opposite. (Although Watanabe Shoichi's partner Naoki Komuro, who has been mentioned before, stressed that "At that time, China resolutely wanted to fight, it never thought about not expansion, it only had the attempt to expand thoroughly", he had to admit that "It is possible that the [Japan] government, military headquarters really adopted the 'not expansion policy' at that time".[12] [The key point is from the original text].)

[8] 昭和12年7月1日軍令部、参謀本部「北支作戦に関する 海陸軍協定」,臼井勝美等解説『現代史資料』9「日中戦争」2 (Tokyo: みすず書房. The 1st edition published on September 30th, 1964, page 5).

[9] 「支那駐屯軍ノ 作戦計画策定」,臼井勝美等解説『現代史資料』9「日中戦争」2 (Tokyo: みすず書房. The 1st edition published on September 30th, 1964, page 15).

[10] 「臨命第四一八号指示」,臼井勝美等解説『現代史資料』9「日中戦争」2 (Tokyo: みすず書房. The 1st edition published on September 30th, 1964). "指示" is one of the forms of the orders of the Japanese army.

[11] 「飯沼守日記」,南京戦史編集委員会編『南京戦史資料集』,非売品 (Tokyo: 偕行社. The 1st edition published on November 3rd, 1989, page 67, 68).

[12] 小室直樹著『大東亜戦争ここに 甦る———戦争と 軍隊、そして 国運の 大研究』(Tokyo: クレスト社. The 1st edition published on September 30th, 1995, page 118).

Therefore, even if there really exists a "not expansion, local solution" thought as *The Alleged "Nanking Massacre"* said—but it can never come from Hirohito—it is just a flower in a mirror.

The Truth of "Substantial Concessions"

Besides the above quotation, *The Alleged Nanking Massacre* continues to say:

> Even so, the Japanese Government still thoroughly sought a peaceful solution as well as a peace proposal. The Japanese side made substantial concessions to this peace proposal, completely abandoning Japan's rights and interests in China since the Manchurian incident.[1]

The so-called "substantial concessions" here refer to the strategies before the "8.13 Incident". From the point of view of *The Alleged Nanking Massacre*, Japan's efforts to "seek peace" were ruined by the Lieutenant OYAMA Isao and Private First Class 斎藤屿藏's "being killed" on August 9th. Indeed, after the outbreak of the Lugouqiao Incident, China had no choice but to rise up. On July 17th, Chiang Kai-shek published *The Last Moment,* and the next day he recorded his "determination" in his diary, expressing that the last resort to Japan is also the "only" resort.[2] From the diary we can see that *The Last Moment* is not a performance of a politician. However, although Chiang Kai-shek himself has decided to resist against Japan, he is compelled to make the decision because "righteousness shall no longer be humiliated". Moreover, at that time, the diplomatic channel between China and Japan didn't break off that time, on the third day of the publishing of *The Last Moment*, Xu Shiying, the Chinese Ambassador to Japan, visited Japanese Minister for Foreign Affairs Kōki Hirota. Even if the Japanese side didn't make "substantial concessions", as long as they would not bully the Chinese too much, the Chinese government at that time—even if it was under the pressure of opposition

---

[1] 竹本忠雄、大原康男著,日本会議国際広報委員会編集『再審「南京大虐殺」———世界に訴える 日本の冤罪』,第18頁。

[2] サンケイ 新聞社著『蔣介石秘録』（下),東京,サンケイ 出版1985年10月31日改訂特裝版,第205頁。

forces to resist against Japan, it was still unwilling to make a complete break with Japan.

As mentioned above, the Japanese army rapidly expanded its war in North China, Peiping, Tianjin and other places fell one after another at the end of July, and even before OYAMA Isao and others were "killed", Japan had been ready to open up a battlefield in Shanghai and other places. In the battle plan formulated by the highest level of the Japanese army on July 29th, "Shanghai Nearby" had been listed as one of the areas where war would begin "according to the situation".[3] On August 4th, Lieutenant General Kiyoshi Hasegawa, commander of the Third Fleet, suggested to the Imperial Japanese Navy General Staff: "In view of the pressing circumstances, the Special Marine Corps should be secretly sent to Shanghai gradually". On August 8th, the Third Fleet "made a new deployment of troops based on the instructions of the central authorities in order to complete all preparations to adapt to the expansion of the situation".[4] In other words, OYAMA Isao was no more than a fuse, even if there were no OYAMA Isao, there would be others or some other things.

At the same time, the Japanese government was indeed "seeking peace", shortly before OYAMA Isao and some other people were "being killed", the Japanese government indeed drew up a "peace proposal", but this proposal was only one of the two-pronged approaches synchronized with the Japanese army, which had nothing to do with the so-called "substantial concessions" in *The Alleged Nanking Massacre*:

(In the evening of August 6)
One. Political Aspects

I. China promised euphemistically that it would not regard "Manchukuo" as an issue in the future.[5]
II. Japan and China signed an Anti-Communist Party Pact (the defense of the Communist Party in unarmed zones must of course be realized and it should be particularly strictly banned in the same zone).
III. Apart from dispelling troops from Jidong and Jicha under the conditions of armistice, Japan would negotiate with Nanjing on the issues of Inner Mongolia and Suiyuan. Nanjing must accept our legitimate request and exclude Nanjing's forces in the same respect.

---

[3]「中央統帥部ノ 対支作戦計画」,臼井勝美等解説『現代史資料』9「日中戦争」2 (Tokyo: みすず書房. The 1st edition published on September 30, 1964, page 25). "统帅部" refers to General Staff Office.

[4] 軍令部編『大東亜戦争海軍戦史』,转引自防衛庁防衛研修所戦史室編『支那事変陸軍作戦』1 (Tokyo: 朝雲新聞社. The 1st edition published on July 25, 1975, page 257, 258).

[5] Some works add "recognize Manchukuo or......" after "China" when they make the quotation, such as秦郁彦著『日中戦争史』(Tokyo: 河出書房新社. The 3rd edition published on September 30th, 1977, page 227).

IV. China must strictly ban the resistance against Japan and exclusion of Japan throughout the country, thoroughly implementing the decree on the rapprochement of diplomatic relations.[6]

In this case, there are also "military aspects" and "economic aspects", which share the same attitudes with "political aspects", so I will not give a quotation here. The Kuomintang government abandoned the Northeast and blindly suppressed the Communist Party, in a very long time, it had been opposed by officers' suggestions an indicator of the mood of the Chinese people.[7] Moreover, just because Chiang Kai-shek made a guarantee to all the Chinese people that he would resist against Japan and tolerate the Communist Party, he was released the year before when he had just provoked a mutiny. In particular, the evolution of events after "The 7.7 Incident" made it even more impossible for Chiang Kai-shek to give up his political commitment. Japan required recognition of "Manchukuo"—whether explicit or "euphemistic", requested to defend against the Communist Party, demanded a strict ban on resistance against Japan, and demanded the "exclusion of Nanjing's forces" from Inner Mongolia and Suiyuan, that is to say, Japan requested to turn the whole of China into "Manchukuo", large or small. Not to mention all of these requirements, even it was a small requirement among them, it had completely exceeded the acceptable bottom line of the Chinese government as well as Chiang Kai-shek himself.[8] If this can be regarded as "substantial concession", how can there be no concession in the world?

[6]「日支國交全般的調整案要綱」,外務省編纂『日本外交年表竝主要文書1840—1945』(下) (Tokyo: 原書房. The 6th edition published on February 10th, 1978, page 367).

[7]Refer to my article「中國大陸的日本觀」,『歷史月刊』 (Taipei, 歷史智庫出版公司. No. 6, 2001).

[8]On the eve of the Japanese attack on Nanjing in December of that year, German Ambassador to China Trautmann once mediated between the two countries, he described the conditions of the Japanese side to Chiang Kai-shek including "recognition of Manchukuo" and so on, which were roughly the same as those proposed by Japan in August. Song Xilian heard from Jiang's secretary Xiao Zicheng: "Trautman came to Beijing to see Generalissimo this time in order to mediate the war between China and Japan by German, he conveyed six conditions of truce proposed by Japan: (1) Admit the independence of Manchukuo and Inner Mongolia; (2) Expand 'Hemei Agreement', regulate North China as a non-garrison area; (3) Expand the unarmed area provided by 'Songhu Agreement'; (4) Economic cooperation between China and Japan; (5) China and Japan resist against the Communist Party together; (6) Totally ban anti-Japanese activities. Generalissimo asked opinions from Chongxi, Tang Shengzhi, Gu Zhutong, Xu Yongchang and other people, they expressed their acceptance. E-commerce merchant Yan Xishan also accepted these conditions. Generalissimo told Trautmann that these conditions can be used as the basis for the negotiations but he can not believe the Japanese, the Japanese can regret, but since German is a good friend, German should always involve in the mediation". He also said: " Japan doesn't want to have a long time war against China, it adopts a strategy of successive annexation, so it is very likely that a peace negotiation will be conducted. And if a negotiation is to be conducted, it needs some time, Japan may not attack Nanjing during this period. So, we can use this opportunity to strengthen our troops". Song Xilian said: "Although I heard these words from Xiao Zicheng, they are in fact Chiang Kai-shek's opinions" (《南京守城战役亲历记》, written by Song Xilian, compiled by Research Committee on Cultural and Historical Materials of the

About the year before last, Japanese female writer Kamisaka Toko published a new book with a big title 《我は苦難の道を行く》. Take a look at it, there is a line of small words besides the main topic on the cover: "汪兆銘の真実". At that time, the words "as it is" came up in my mind. Usually, I would not buy this kind of book, but as the book only sold for half price with a good quality and it was almost brand new, so I still bought it. Prior to the main content, there are the photos of Wang and his books, in addition, there are many photos of Wang's descendants in the United States, Hong Kong and Indonesia. Only after reading it did I know that the title of the book has its origin. It is a free translation of the last four words of the eight words "You do easy things, I accept hard ones" Wang left to Chiang Kai-shek when he left Chongqing. The book is full of mournful sympathy for Wang and generally regards Wang's life as "revolutionist" and "patriot". (As I thought this book is not so useful, I didn't bring it back when I left for Shanghai, so please forgive me that I can't indicate the page number according to the specification.) It is not strange that Ms. Kamisaka Toko and some like-minded Japanese have this kind of opinions, but unfortunately, in China, the step taken by Wang in China violates an absolute taboo—From this point, it is not excessive to describe it as "hardship". Chinese People, whether they are modern people who have been educated about patriotism, or the people of the Song Dynasty, the Tang Dynasty and the Republic of China, there is absolutely no possibility of "forgiveness" by "putting themselves in one's shoes". Therefore, as long as they choose the road of "hardships", even if they have the capital of "revolutionists", they will inevitably end up utterly discredited. This is true of Wang Jingwei, Qin Hui as well as Wu Sangui. I suddenly digress to say this only to express: "substantial concessions" recognized by *The Alleged Nanking Massacre* are acceptable to Wang Jingwei but never to Chinese people who cherish true love for their native land.

National Committee of the Chinese People's Political Consultative Conference. *Selected Works of Literature and History*, No. 12. Beijing: China Literature and History Press. The 1st edition published in December 1986, page 22, 23). Bai, Tang, Gu, Xu and Yan all said that the Japanese conditions were "acceptable". At that time, the Shanghai garrison collapsed, the situation was completely different from that in the Summer and Autumn, and Chiang Kai-shek wanted to "take advantage of the opportunity" to "strengthen" the troops. It can be said that it is also a delaying tactic. The situations are different so they can't be judged in the same way.

The Insincere "Peacefully Opening the City"

According to *The Alleged Nanking Massacre*:

> On December 1, the Japanese Army decided to attack Nanjing, then, on December 9, the Army distributed the "Recommendation on Peacefully Opening the City" to the city by plane. The Recommendation was made on the basis of "Occupation strategy", which was completed through consultation with international law scholars. It noticed the Chinese side: In accordance with international law, if the city is declared to be open as an "unfortified city", which means "a city without any defense", the city will not be attacked.
>
> But there was no answer at all by one 'clock in the afternoon of the next day, then the Japanese Army started the general offensive.[1]

This argument originated from the Tokyo Trial. For example, Iwane Matsui's "Private", Shanghai Expeditionary Army OKADA Takashi (Iwane is both a father and benefactor to OKADA Takashi) said in the "affidavit under oath": "On December 9, the Surrender Recommendation was made and distributed to the Nanjing city by plane, what's more, an order was issued around December 9 to ask all the Japanese Army to stop the general offensive and get consolidated around the Nanjing city, waiting for the order of general offensive".[2] Also, Colonel MUTO Akira, Deputy Chief of Staff (Vice Chief of Staff) of Shanghai Expeditionary Army Colonel testified in court: On December 8, "General Iwane issued the following orders: First: the first line should be stopped at the first line three or four kilometers outside the Nanjing city; Second: Distribute the leaflets by plane in order to advise the

---

[1] 竹本忠雄、大原康男著，日本会議国際広報委員会編集『再審「南京大虐殺」―――世界に訴える 日本の冤罪』，第24页.

[2] Tomio Hora, *Battle History of Japan and China 8 Nanjing Incident I*, Tokyo, 河出書房新社, the 1st edition published on November 25th, 1973, p. 262.

© The Author(s) 2020
Z. Cheng, *The Nanjing Massacre and Sino-Japanese Relations*,
https://doi.org/10.1007/978-981-15-7887-8_16

Nanjing garrisons to surrender;......Fourth: Attack Nanjing on December 10 if the Chinese Army don't surrender at that time".[3] This argument has since been very popular among the Japanese "fictionalists", its subtexts, in the words of Watanabe Shoichi, are "If China surrendered at that time, nothing would have happened. Also, Watanabe Shoichi claimed: "This is the reason why Chiang Kai-shek, who led the National Government at that time, never confides in the world about the Nanjing Massacre".[4] The massacre took place only because China did not accept the "Recommendation of peacefully opening the city"! The thinking mode of the Japanese "fictionalists" is always so surprising that it confuses the normal people.

The "fictionalists" pay much importance to this "Surrender Recommendation" (the original words of the "fictionalists"[5]). Taking the fact that *The Diaries of John Rabe* doesn't record the "Surrender Recommendation" as an evidence, *The Truth· Nanjing Incident* regards *The Diaries of John Rabe* as a false diary.[6] I have once written an article specifically to criticize *The Truth· Nanjing Incident* for greatly framing *The Diaries of John Rabe*.[7] But since it was already unreasonable for *The Truth· Nanjing Incident* to take the fact that the diary didn't record something as an evidence, I thought there was no need to argue about it, so I didn't place this incident into my article. Now think about it, although there is no need to argue about the unreasonable behavior, whether the Japanese army has "peacefully" waited for a day during the limited period between December 9th to December 10th—which can see whether the Japanese army has the sincerity of "not attacking" if the Chinese Army really withdrew—is still necessary to be figured out.

From the standpoint of the invaded, refusing to accept the recommendation of surrender is not only a natural right, but also an unshirkable obligation. I think it is not an extra act to state a "political" attitude before clarifying the matter.

The Diaries of John Rabe didn't record the "Recommendation on Peacefully Opening the City", just like many people in the Nanjing city at that time such as Vautrin, a professor of Jinling Woman College of Arts

---

[3] Quoted from 『「南京大虐殺」はこうして作られた———東京裁判の欺瞞』, written by 富士信夫 (Tokyo, 展転社. The 4th edition published on November 23rd, 1998, pp. 224–225).

[4] 小室直樹、渡部昇一著『封印の昭和史———「戦後五〇年」自虐の終焉』(Tokyo, 德間書店. The 4th edition published on November 15th, 1995, p. 69).

[5] 大井満著『仕組まれた「南京大虐殺」———攻略作戦の 全貌とマスコミ 報道の 怖さ』(Tokyo, 展転社. The 3rd edition published on June 6th, 1998, p. 32).

[6] 畝本正己著『真相・南京事件———ラーベ日記を検証して』(Tokyo, 文京出版. The 2nd edition published on February 1st, 1999, p. 39. 畝本正己 has been subdivided as a "centrist" according to Japan, and here he is classified as the fictionalist because he regarded the Nanjing Massacre as a "fiction".

[7] My article 《〈拉贝日记〉是"无根的编造"么?》, Beijing, *Studies of Modern History*, Issue 2, 2002, pp. 150, 183.

and Science, didn't write the thing in their diaries. Maybe they didn't know the thing, maybe they knew the thing but they didn't write it down. John Rabe said about the protest against the Japanese bombing in his diary on September 27th: "No one will believe that the Japanese Army will pay attention to the protest"![8] Now that the promise of the Japanese army is no longer believed, it is entirely possible for the Chinese Army to ignore the "recommendation" of the Japanese army in such an urgent moment when the disaster is approaching.

So, does the Japanese really have the sincerity of "not attacking"? We might as well take a look at what they did after the "recommendation" was issued.

The Diaries of John Rabe begins with this:

> Airstrikes keep happening from early in the morning. Chinese planes no longer come here, but anti-aircraft warfare is still firing. A large number of bombs have fallen in the south of the city and a huge column of smoke can be seen there, a large fire is spreading in the south.[9]

The Japanese bombing didn't stop later. Rabe continued the diary next day:

> It was very restless last night. The rumble of gunfire, rifles and machine guns went off from 8:00 p.m. yesterday to 4:00 a.m. Today. ......The city was bombed all day today, and the windows were rattled by the bombing.[10]

The diary that day also recorded how the Japanese army nearly occupied Guanghua Gate and advanced to the waterworks along the Yangtze River the night before (the night of the December 9th). The Japanese "fictionalists" think that Rabe lacks justice, so that the diary is "intertwined with truth and falsehood".[11] I have refuted it in the above-mentioned article (footnote 49). However, *The Diaries of John Rabe* is indeed reorganized after Rabe returns home, so we can not draw a conclusion as to whether it is completely in line with the facts right now.

---

[8] *The Diaries of John Rabe*, written by John Rabe, translated by 同书翻译组. Jiangsu People's Publishing, Jiangsu Education Publishing. The 1st edition published in August 1997, p. 23.

[9] *The Diaries of John Rabe*, written by John Rabe, translated by 同书翻译组, p. 194.

[10] *The Diaries of John Rabe*, written by John Rabe, translated by 同书翻译组, pp. 158, 163.

[11] 畝本正己著『真相・南京事件―――ラーベ日記を検証して』前言 (Tokyo, 文京出版. The 2nd edition published on February 1st, 1999, p. 1 総括, p. 220). Most of other fictionalists also hold the same opinion, for example, 東中野修道 believes: "From the point of conclusion, Rabe's *The Truth of Nanjing* has four following features: (1) Description on the basis of facts; (2) Description of the over-polished facts; (3) Removal of the description of key facts; (4) Description of Chinese's rumors that are regarded as facts" (『「南京虐殺」の徹底検証』付章"改めて'ラーベ日記「を読む」. Tokyo, 展転社. The 4th edition published on July 8th, 2000, p. 385).

The Diaries of Vautrin recorded on December 9th:

When we were attending press conference this evening, a huge artillery shell fell in the Xin Jie Kou, the sound of the explosion made us all stand up from our seats, and some people turned pale because of fear. This is the first time we have been bombarded by artillery shells.

The Diaries of Vautrin recorded on December 10th:

When I was eating breakfast, other people said that the gunfire kept bombing until 4:00 in the morning, obviously I was too tired to hear the sound.[12]

George A. Fitch's "Destruction of Nanjing" "begins on December 10", it recorded on December 10th: "Heavy artillery bombarded the southern gate of the Nanjing city and the bombs blossomed in the city".[13] Although this record didn't indicate the specific time and it is hard to judge whether it was recorded before the time one o'clock of the "recommendation", it can still be used as an evidence with the reference of the above quotation.

After Japan's "recommendation" was issued on December 9th, Japan did not stop its attack, which can also be seen in the records of Chinese countrymen. Jiang Gonggu recorded in *Records of the Three Months after the Fell of Nanjing*:

(December 9th) I heard that the enemy has attacked the area of Qilinmen and approached the city wall. Compared to yesterday, the sound of gunfire has been denser and clearer. Bafutang in the southern side of the city had been bombarded by the enemy......After twelve o'clock at night, the gunfire intensified and shot into the city; white light flashed through the windows from time to time.

(December 10th) At about nine o'clock, Qi Mingjing (Dean of the First, Second and Third hospitals) came, when I was going downstairs to the Zhongyang Road with him, he suddenly received a call from Gulou Hospital, saying: "The enemy are bombarding the northern area of Xin Jie kou, there are many dead and wounded citizens and soldiers alongside the road, measures should be taken immediately". When they were talking, we heard a bomb exploded very close to us, Qi and I looked out the window quickly, finding that the bomb was just behind our house and there was still a cloud of smoke. Later, the enemy still kept bombing Fu Chang, three or four bombs fell into the front door, and the water tank on the roof was also bombed. We all thought that we had to leave this dangerous place so we went downstairs together. When we ran out of the door, we caught a glimpse of our car, which had been burning, then

---

[12] *The Diaries of Vautrin*, written by Minnie Vautrin, translated by Nanjing Massacre Research Center of Nanjing Normal University, Jiangsu People's Publishing House, the 1st edition published on November 2000, pp. 184, 185.

[13] *My Eighty Years in China*, written by George A. Fitch, *Nanjing Massacre*, compiled by State Archives Administration, pp. 1022,1025.

we turned to the north side quickly and we entered into Huaqiao Road, then I suddenly got separated from him. I stood at the door and waited for about four or five minutes before he arrived. At that moment, the enemy are still shooting at our direction. The people along the way were all running northward like a flood. Since we didn't have a targeted direction, we ran following them.[14]

The "hearing" of the enemy coming to Qilinmen can be proved by the record of the Japanese army.[15] And on the whole, the sincere tone of this record is completely trustworthy. From these records of unrelated Chinese and foreign personages, we can see that what the Japanese army said and did was totally opposite. After the so-called "recommendation" was issued, the Nanjing city was not only faced with bombing, but because of the arrival of the Japanese army, it was also bombed directly by cannons besides the air-dropped bombs.

The Japanese army was so untrustworthy, those who know the shame would only hide the fact, but why did the "fictionalists" have the courage to quote the record? Maybe the "fictionalists" think that the senior officers of the Japanese army intended to keep "peace" and the bombing order was not given to the lower officers. Then, let's check the Japanese army's own records to see if there are some "misunderstandings". The Ninth Division of the Japanese army issued the following orders at 4:00 p.m. on December 9th after the "Recommendation of peacefully opening the city" was issued:

> ……
> Second. The division <u>takes the advantage of the darkness of the night to occupy the city wall.</u>
> Third. The two-wing troops should take advantage of the darkness of the night to occupy the city wall. The left-wing captain should put two teams of light armored vehicles under the command of the right-wing captain.
> Fourth. The artillery units should assist the two-wing troops in combat as needed.
> Fifth. The engineer troops should mainly assist the right-wing troops in combat.
> Sixth. Other units should continue to finish prior tasks.[16]

---

[14] *Records of the Three Months after the Fell of Nanjing*, written by Jiang Gonggu, *Nanjing Massacre*, compiled by State Archives Administration, pp. 191, 192, 193.

[15] "The Sixteenth Division Arrived Near Qilinmen in the Evening of December 9", refer to *Documents on the Battle of Nanjing*, compiled by Battle of Nanking Editorial Committee, p. 546.

[16] 《九師作命甲第百二十五号》, *Documents on the Battle of Nanjing*, compiled by Battle of Nanking Editorial Committee, p. 546.

Behind the waiting for the response of the "Recommendation of peacefully opening the city",[17] the real intention was "taking the advantage of the darkness of the night to occupy the city wall"! In this way, how could there be any sincerity? But was this kind of action only limited to the Ninth Division, or was it just an "accident"? Let's continue to examine the relevant materials of the Japanese army. According to the "wartime records" of the Sixth Division:

> In the middle night of December 9, the front-line troops determined to take action. In order to immediately take the advantages of night attack outcome, the head of the division came to Dongshan Bridge at six o'clock in the morning and ordered the reserved and artillery troops to advance towards the Tiexin Bridge.[18]

The Sixth Division also had a "night attack". According to the "combat process" recorded by the 114th Division:

> In the evening of December 9th, Akiyama Brigade broke through the enemy's positions near the Jiangjun Mountain and chased the enemy quickly. In the morning of December 10th, the brigade occupied the positions near Yuhuatai and reached the enemy. They soon started the attack.[19]

Akiyama Brigade is just the Infantry 127th Brigade belonging to the 114th Division. There are detailed records of the uninterrupted attacks from the evening of the December 9th to noon on the December 10th in the "detailed report of the war" and the "wartime records" of the division.[20] In addition to the documents at the division level, there also the relevant records at the grassroots level. For example, the 33rd infantry regiment belonging to the 16th Division recorded in the "detailed report of the war":

> At the night of December 9th, in accordance with the order "the 33rd infantry regiment (lacking the 1st Battalion and the 5th, 8th Company) should advance and attack as right-wing troops from the north side of the main road

---

[17] The 36th regiment of the left-wing troops (The 18th Brigade of Infantry) was responsible for attacking the Guanghuamen, they started to attack when they arrived in the morning of December 9th, but they made no great progress because of the obstacles in the outer trenches and doorways as well as the firepower of the city wall. At that night, the engineer troops take the advantage of the darkness to start bombing with large number of explosives. You can refer to *Battle of Nanjing*, compiled by Battle of Nanking Editorial Committee, not for sale (Tokyo, 偕行社. The 1st edition published on November 3rd, 1989, p. 175).

[18] Issue 13,14 of *Wartime Records* of the Sixth Division, *Documents on the Battle of Nanjing*, compiled by Battle of Nanking Editorial Committee, p. 689.

[19] 「第百十四師団作戦経過ノ概要」, *Documents on the Battle of Nanjing*, compiled by Battle of Nanking Editorial Committee, p. 653.

[20] 第百十四師団「戦闘詳報」, 「戦時旬報」, *Documents on the Battle of Nanjing*, compiled by Battle of Nanking Editorial Committee, pp. 654, 664.

(including the main road). Then they should connect to the battle area of the right detachment, which includes Wuqi Jiangwang Temple, the 500 meters east of the Xuanwu Lake, the northeast corner of the Nanjing city and form a line (including the right line). The soldiers honorably accept the major task of "attacking the highlands around the Purple Mountain, becoming more and more high-spirited.[21]

It can be seen from above that after the Japanese army issued the "recommendation of peacefully opening the city", they never stopped taking the advantage of the darkness of the night to launch attacks. The so-called "The Japanese Army started the attack" only after the Chinese side failed to response during the limited time, which originated from the Tokyo Trial, was totally a falsehood.[22]

---

[21] The 33rd infantry regiment, 「南京附近戦闘詳報」, *Documents on the Battle of Nanjing*, compiled by Battle of Nanking Editorial Committee, p. 596.

[22] In addition to the fact, the Japanese army did not even think about what they would give the Chinese side if they retreated, in the "Strategy of occupying the Nanjing city" issued before the "recommendation", it is clearly said: When the Chinese Army accept the recommendation, "Each division selects a infantry battalion as a basic unit, first enter the city and then sweep within the city". 「南京城攻略要領」, *Documents on the Battle of Nanjing*, compiled by Battle of Nanking Editorial Committee, p. 539.

Three Questions on the Burial

1 Whether "Only the Red Swastika Society Was Engaged in Burial"?

After the Japanese army occupied Nanjing, many charity organizations took part in burying the corpses, but only the Red Swastika Society was admitted by the Japanese "fictionalists". *A Thorough Examination of the "Nanjing Massacre"* holds: "Only the Red Swastika Society was engaged in the burial".[1] But there is something wrong with the basis on which it is based. It doesn't mean that the basis itself is unreliable, it means the conclusion cannot be drawn from the basis. For example, Maruyama Susumu, one member of the Japanese Secret Service Organization, once said:

> Chongshantang and other small organizations submitted their applications to the Autonomous Committee, as the Autonomous Committee had already entrusted the burial matters to the Red Swastika Society, it didn't accept these organizations' applications. Even these organizations engaged in the burial as subcontractors, the amount of the corpses they buried was included in the work of the Red Swastika Society.[2]

Even if Maruyama Susumu's words were real, it only meant that the "work volume" couldn't be counted outside the works of the Red Swastika Society, so the conclusion "only the Red Swastika Society was engaged in the burial" couldn't be drawn from his words.

This conclusion has another main basis, that is the following paragraph said by M. S. Bates in "The Rescue Situation in Nanjing":

---

[1] *Thorough Examination of the Nanjing Massacre*, written by Shūdō Higashinakano (Tokyo, 展転. The 4th edition published on July 8th, 2000, p. 308).

[2] *Thorough Examination of the Nanjing Massacre*, written by Shūdō Higashinakano, p. 307.

© The Author(s) 2020
Z. Cheng, *The Nanjing Massacre and Sino-Japanese Relations*,
https://doi.org/10.1007/978-981-15-7887-8_17

All of our relief efforts were conducted under the control of the International Committee, which was organized in the security zone……From the beginning, we had very excellent cooperation with local organizations of <u>the Red Swastika Society of China</u> on the operation of large-scale <u>free canteens</u>. What's more, we cooperated with <u>the Red Swastika Society</u> on two large-scale <u>free canteens</u> and the operation of <u>the burial of corpses</u>. (the key points are from the original text)

Therefore, *A Thorough Examination of the "Nanjing Massacre"* said: "Bates listed all the relief efforts conducted by the International Committee. From this point, only the Red Swastika Society was engaged in the burial of corpses".[3] This conclusion may make people wonder: What Bates said was just "we" and just "our" "cooperation", there were no exclusive records besides "we", and he didn't say "we" had "cooperated" on "all rescue undertakings"; of course, we can judge "all our relief undertakings", but how can we judge "all rescue undertakings" after giving up "we"?

2 When Did the Burial Work of the Red Swastika Society Begin?

The Red Swastika Society is the only organization admitted by the Japanese "fictionalists" to engage in the burial work, but when the burial work began is directly related to the number of dead people, so there is a debate on when the burial work began. After *The Truth of Nanjing* (The Japanese name of *The Diaries of John Rabe*) was published, the "fictionalists" found a "new basis" from this book:

Everyday of December(especially around the Christmas), we literally walk over the corpses. That is because the burial is prohibited until February 1st. Not far from the door of our house, there are the Chinese soldiers' who have been killed with their hands and feet tied up. They are tied into a bamboo stretcher and placed on the road. From December 13th to the end of January, we have applied to bury the corpses or move the corpses to somewhere for many times, but all of our applications have been refused. Our applications weren't admitted until February 1st.[4]

(This was what Rabe said in his report to Hitler after returning home. Some statements in this report are quite different from current domestic views, I wonder if it is the reason of the Chinese version of *The Diaries of John Rabe* not involving the statement?[5]) *A Thorough Examination of*

---

[3] *Thorough Examination of the Nanjing Massacre*, written by Shūdō Higashinakano, p. 310.

[4] ジョン．ラーベ著，エルヴィン．ヴィッケルト 編，平野卿子訳『南京の 真実』(Tokyo, 講談社. The 3rd edition published on November 21st, 1997, p. 317).

[5] The "full text of the report" attached to the Chinese version of *The Diaries of John Rabe* is actually only one of the letters before the report, not the "full text of the report" *The Diaries of John Rabe*, written by John Rabe, translated by 同书翻译组, p. 704.

the "Nanjing Massacre" thinks that with the combination of the above quotation and Maruyama Susumu's word "starting from the early February", it can be proved that "The burial work of the Red Swastika Society started on February 1st".[6] In response, Inoue Hisashi, one member of the school of slaughter, used the following two statements to refute, these statements are from the February and March reports in 1938 of Nanjing Secret Service Organization:

> The burial team of the Red Swastika Society has been burying the corpses within and outside the city under the guidance of the secret service organization since early January. At present, in the end of February, around five thousand corpses have been buried. It can be regarded as a great outcome. (February report)

> It has been three months since the burial work (of the Red Swastika Society) began. (March report)

Yinoue believes that "this report is a top secret internal report and there is no need to lie intentionally".[7]

"The early January" refers to the time when the Japanese Secret Service Organization started to provide funding, the actual "burial work" should begin earlier. In its request for funding from the Red Swastika Society to the Nanjing Autonomous Committee on April 4th, the Red Swastika said that the burial work had begun "since the autumn last year".[8] The Japanese army started to bomb Nanjing since August 15th, causing the continuous death of people, and the Red Swastika collected and buried the corpses whenever they saw them until Nanjing fell. There is no doubt about that. But there is still room to discuss when the Red Swastika Society's burial work began after the Japanese army entered into the city. Since the Red Swastika put forward that the burial work started on December 22nd, 1937, in the Tokyo Trial, this date is generally regarded as the beginning date. Yinoue's article also holds the same opinion.

In fact, December 22nd is not the beginning date. I noticed this when I was reading the letter from the Japanese Embassy signed by Rabe: "From <u>Tuesday</u> morning, the Red Swastika Society under our leadership will send

---

[6] *Thorough Examination of the Nanjing Massacre*, written by Shūdō Higashinakano, pp. 302, 304.

[7] 井上久士著「遺体埋葬記録は偽造史料ではない」, Nankin jiken chōsa kenkyūkai compiled 『南京大虐殺否定論13のウソ』 (Tokyo, 柏書房. The 4th edition published on March 30th, 2001, p. 129).

[8] *Archives of the Nanjing Massacre Made by Japanese Invaders*, compiled by the Second Historical Archives of China and Nanjing Municipal Archives, Jiangsu Ancient Books Publishing House. The 3rd edition published in December 1997, p. 460.

cars to collect and bury corpses in the safe zone".[9] This letter from the International Committee is concluded in various data sets. I didn't notice that because none domestic data sets have translated the meaning of "Tuesday", they just mentioned "the Red Swastika Society under our leadership" and so on.[10] Therefore, although I thought the beginning date should be before December 22nd, I didn't make more investigation because the date was uncertain. A few days ago, I read the same letter included in the Japanese data sets, finding that the word "Tuesday morning" is also included. But the meaning of the whole sentence is a little different from that of the Chinese version of *The Diaries of John Rabe*. It said: "On Tuesday morning, the Red Swastika Society (the organization under the leadership of this committee) sent cars to collect and bury corpses".[11] Although this sentence mentioned "Tuesday", it doesn't have the meaning of "starting from Tuesday morning" that *The Diaries of John Rabe* indicates. As the Japanese version is from Timperley's *What Is War (What War Means: The Japanese Terror in China)*, the book is in fact translated twice, so we should still refer to The Diaries of John Rabe. However, the translator may easily make this minor difference without attention; therefore, if you have the Germany version on your hand, you'd better check it again. But in any case, it can be proved that the Red Swastika Society began to "collect and bury" the corpses at least on Tuesday. December 14th is "Tuesday", we can know that the burial work of the Red Swastika at least began on the second day after the Japanese army entered into the city.[12]

3   Were Chongshantang Not Involved in the Burial Work?

According to the materials provided by Chongshantang in the trial after the war, it buried more than 110 thousand corpses. The number is more than the total number of the corpses that the Red Swastika and Red Cross and other

---

[9] *The Diaries of John Rabe*, written by John Rabe, translated by 同书翻译组译, p. 193. The Japanese version of *The Diaries of John Rabe The Truth of Nanjing* doesn't include this letter.

[10] For example, *Nanjing Massacre Archives of Japanese Troops Invading China*, co-compiled by the Second Historical Archives of China, the Nanjing Archives, page 598; Selection and Compilation of Japanese Imperialist Invasion of China· Nanjing Massacre, co-compiled by the State Archives, the Second Historical Archives of China, and Jilin Academy of Social Sciences, p. 81.

[11] Tomio Hora, *Battle History of Japan and China 9 Nanjing Incident II*, p. 126.

[12] After the book was published, I read *A Thorough Examination of the "Nanjing Massacre"*, finding that there is a simple argument about this thing. It said: According to No. 9 Document, the burial work seemed to start on December 14th, but it is impossible. The most important reason is that people couldn't go outside the city to bury the bodies because the city gate was closed then" (*Thorough Examination of the Nanjing Massacre*, written by Shūdō Higashinakano, p. 296). But the No. 9 Document, as Rabe said, only said "collect and bury bodies in the safety zone", did it have anything with "can't go outside the city"? Maybe Higashinakano means that the corpses needed to be transferred to the outside the city to be buried (the article doesn't have the meaning), even it is the fact, evidence should be listed to make the words clear.

organizations that had buried. But as many related materials are collected after the war[13] (such as the burial form), these materials can't be regarded as "first-hand" materials, so Chongshantang's burial operations are always negated by the Japanese "fictionalists". However, Chongshantang also has some authentic materials from the spot, such as the request article for funding written by the dean ZHOU Yiyu. Although this article didn't reflect the burial scale, the negation put forward by the "fictionalists" can't be established.

However, the fictionalists still have something to say. The Alleged "Nanking Massacre" said:

> The original work of Chongshantang included "providing substances(giving clothes), saving those who need help(saving the widows), nurturing(feeding the babies", "burial work" was not included. Moreover, according to *Nanjing*(it was published by Japanese Society of Commerce and Industry in Nanjing in 1941), which is compiled by Shilai Yidao, chongsantang stopped its activities from December 1937 to next year's August. There is no evidence that Chongshantang was engaged in the burial work at that time.[14]

("saving those who need help", according to its literal meaning, it includes widowers, widows and orphans, the "saving those who need help" of Chongshantang mainly includes widowers and orphans, not just only "widows", the citation notes are not appropriate so I will not discuss it). If the "stopping activities" stressed by *Nanjing* is true, it would be a big problem.[15] Because the request article of dean Zhou was signed on December 6th, 1938, it was not within the scope of the above. But we cannot get a conclusion of whether the records in *Nanjing* are true or whether we should trust them just from the only one person, because there are still some questions on the book compiled by Shilai. For example, in its form of charity organizations "after the

---

[13] Refer to the "Proceedings of the Latest Research Achievements Exchange Meeting" of the Nanjing Massacre, the first page article says: "It has been more than 60 years since the Nanjing Massacre, the names of countless victims are still sealed in the old paper of the archives, the victims are still silent, the Japanese right-wing forces are still denying and obliterating historical facts. These are the things we cannot tolerate, and we must fight back to recover the rightness of history and uphold the justice of mankind" (Proceedings of the Latest Research Achievements Exchange Meeting of Nanjing Massacre, compiled by Zhu Chengshan, Nanjing University Publishing House, the 1st edition published in April 2001, p. 2). I cannot tolerate "denying and obliterating historical facts. But it is our own responsibility that these names "are sealed in the old paper of archives" and it has nothing to do with the Japanese right-wing forces.

[14] 竹本忠雄、大原康男著, 日本会議国際広報委員会編『再審「南京大虐殺」―――世界に訴える 日本の冤罪』, 第46页.

[15] The question was first "found" by Ara Kenichi(「崇善堂の埋葬活動はなかった」,『サンケイ 新聞』1985年8月10日社会版), later, the fictionalists often refer to it, for example, 田中正明 wrote 『南京事件の総括』第六章「虐殺否定十五の論拠」之七「崇善堂の十一万埋葬のウソ」(Tokyo, 謙光社. The 1st edition published on March 7th, 1987, pp. 190, 199. And retired police 吉本栄 wrote 『南京大虐殺の虚構を 砕け』第五章「虐殺数の 問題」二「崇善堂の 嘘」(Tokyo, 新風書房. The 1st edition published on June 1st, 1998, pp. 92 and 94).

incident", there is Chongshantang, there is Red Cross, but it "misses" the Red Swastika Society.[16] Tao Xishan, the head of the Red Swastika Society, was also "Chairman" of the "Nanjing Autonomous Committee"—the first "government" after the fall of Nanjing. He was regarded as the main leader at that time, and he did a lot of hard work in the burial work of the Red Swastika Society, so there is no reason that he is not recorded in the book. Therefore, I think that what is mentioned in *Nanjing* may not be reliable, and second, there is a question of how to understand it.

A few days ago, I compared the *General form of Charity Organizations in Nanjing*[17] recorded in *Current Situation of Reformed Government* with form of charity organizations in *Nanjing*, finding that there are some differences between the two. There are 26 organizations recorded in *Nanjing*, and *Current Situation* recorded 27. The ones recorded in *Nanjing* but not recorded in *Current Situation* are "Nanjing Branch of the Red Swastika Society", "Board of Directors of Charity Society", "Chinese Science and Education Association" and "Private Charitable Warehouse". What's more, the "Nanjing Buddhist Charity School" and "Nanjing Peishantang" in *Nanjing* are called simply as "Buddhist Charity School" and "Peishantang", and "Guangli Charity Hall" is called "Guangli Charity Society" in *Current Situation*. The *General Form* in *Current Situation* indicates it is "at present, the end of the January of the Republic of China"; the time is basically the same as that recorded in *Nanjing*. However, as *Current Situation* was edited by "Propaganda Office of the Executive Yuan" and the publishing time is more close to the time mentioned above ("Shangzi", March 28th, 1939); therefore, *Current Situation* should be more accurate than *Nanjing*, which is written by a individual long time ago. But my main purpose of citing this example is not to judge whether Nanjing is right or wrong, but to illustrate the danger of the Japanese "fictionalists" "reviewing the history with personal theories" as well as the deviation from facts brought the practical attitude of the Japanese "fictionalists".[18]

---

[16] *Nanjing*, compiled by 市来義道編, Japanese Society of Commerce and Industry in Nanjing, the 1st edition published on September 1st, 1941, p. 236.

[17] 行政院宣傳局編纂『維新政府之現況―――成立一周年紀念』, 行政院宣傳局, the 1st edition published on August 1st, 1939, p. 584.

[18] In fact, not only are the Japanese fictionalists seeking excerpts from the materials to match with their own ideas, many veterans are still strict in their statements so as to not lose face for the "Nihon-gun". 山田正行, a professor of Akita University in Japan, has repeatedly interviewed an elderly Qindian veteran (who was a lieutenant at that time), the veteran totally denied the existence of "comfort women", saying that he had never heard such a thing, but when they talked about other topics, the old lieutenant inadvertently said: "Usually the army provided condoms, but when the weapons, ammunition and food could not be replenished, condoms naturally could not be distributed. Soldiers had to wash those used condoms and dried them so as to use them again". 山田 said mockingly after this sentence: "He didn't know the meaning of 'comfort women in the army' but he knew the meaning of 'distributing the condoms to soldiers'" (山田正行著『アイデンティティと戦争―――戦中期中国雲南省滇西地区の心理歴史研究』, 鹿沼"[栃木], グリーンビース出版会. The 1st edition published on May 20th, 2002, pp. 103, 104).

Now let's go back to have a brief discussion on the request article of Zhou Yiyu and how we should view the so-called "stopping the activities" in *Nanjing*.

> In order to ask for subsidies to relieve the difficulties so as to continue to do charitable work, according to the instructions of Deputy Junhui on charity work: taking our hall to handle charity work, such as giving relief, baby care, medical treatment, medicine, materials on credit, giving rice and subsidizing poor children to study, and so on. There has been no interruption for more than a hundred years since the pre-Qing Dynasty. Even in this incident, our hall has also set up clinics in refugee areas, organized burial teams and handled other relief matters. The refugee area is scattered, the disaster caused by shortage of food and clothing can be seen everywhere, philanthropy in the urban area is be much needed than before, and the difficulties we feel in our hall are now twice as in the past...[19]

The request article clearly indicates that Chongshantang has not involved in the burial work since pre-Qing Dynasty, it started to "organize burial teams" after "this incident". So why did it make an exception for "this incident"? Because "compatriots are poorly dead everywhere".[20] The request article was submitted to "Jiangsu Zhenwu Committee" and it was an urgent incident, so it was impossible to make a false report.

In fact, even if there was no request article from Zhou Yiyu, it was useless for the fictionalists to negate the later "burial work" by "original" "activities", because the organizations such as "Shengxin Jishantang" "Xiaguan Leshantang" recorded by Nanjing "after the incident" were engaged in the "burial work"! If Chongshantang's work can be negated by "original", Jishan, Leshan and others can be affirmed by the "original"? I'm afraid the "fictionalists" may not admit it. (Admitting that means they are doing useless job.)

Shantang does charity work, which has a deep foundation in Chinese society, just as today's Japanese volunteers, they do the work out of dedication, but they are often praised by officials because their behaviors are in line with the mainstream values of Chinese society. But the official subsidies are limited by financial conditions so there is a question of whether the government has the capability. After the "Nanjing Autonomous Committee" was established, the financial condition was quite difficult. Matsui Iwane, the supreme commander of the Japanese army who occupied Nanjing, once expressed his feelings:

---

[19] *Nanjing Massacre Archives of Japanese Troops Invading China*, co-compiled by the Second Historical Archives of China, the Nanjing Archives, p. 449. In *The Collection of Nanjing Incident China Relations*, compiled by Nanjing Incident Investigation Society of Japan (青木 Bookstore), a letter written on February 6th, 1938, by Zhou Yiyu is included. It is indicated that the letter is from the Nanjing Archives. I can't help but worry because the Chinese data set don't collect it.

[20] *Nanjing Massacre Archives of Japanese Troops Invading China*, co-compiled by the Second Historical Archives of China, the Nanjing Archives, p. 448.

......The members of the Autonomous Committee look poorer and weaker, one of the reasons is that they have no financial resources and equitable facilities.[21]

Matsui Iwane says the above sentence in his diary on February 7, when the "autonomous committee" has established for more than one month. Later, the "autonomous committee" had been too busy to take care of itself and never got rid of its financial difficulties until it was replaced by Reformed Government, let alone free up its hands to subsidize non-governmental charitable activities. After the "Reformed Government" was established on March 28th, the situation seemed to be better, however, due to the great damage done to Nanjing, as Chen Jintao, the "Finance Minister" of "Reformed Government" said, "all organizations were damaged no matter they are governmental or non-governmental"[22] (He definitely dared not to directly blame the Japanese army, he just blurred the word by saying "after the quick military act"), the situation was not getting better and it was impossible for the situation to get better immediately. *Nanjing* contains a comparison of Nanjing's income and expenditure between 1935 and 1938, the annual income of 1935 was 8,360,563 yuan and the annual income of 1938 was 1,167,613 yuan, the latter was less than 1/7 of the former.[23] But even Reformed Government had some "deficiency", it was a little better than the autonomous committee's nothing. From May that year, the "Executive yuan" started to allocate funds to the "Zhenwu Committee of the Nanjing Municipal People's Office", from Zhongzhi Fushantang, some charity organizations were funded successively. *Nanjing* holds the opinion that some charity organizations "receive the funds from Zhenwu Committee, gradually like the past",[24] receiving the funds is the fact while "gradually like the past" is like asking for compliment. *Nanjing* equates the acceptance of subsidies with practical activities, this statement cannot be said to be in line with the actual situation.

---

[21] 「松井石根大!戦陣日記」, *Documents on the Battle of Nanjing*, compiled by Battle of Nanking Editorial Committee, p. 40.

[22] 『財政部概要・周年回顧』, 行政院宣傳局編纂『維新政府之現況———成立一周年紀念』, 行政院宣傳局. The 1st edition published on August 1st, 1939, p. 298.

[23] Nanjing, compiled by Shilaiyidao, p. 138.

[24] Nanjing, compiled by Shilaiyidao, p. 236.

Does Iwane Matsui Have Any Grievance to Tell?—An Analysis of OKADA Takashi's Arguments

OKADA Takashi, the dispatched member of Shanghai Expeditionary Army, joined the army because of his father's intimate relationship with Iwane Matsui. During the Tokyo Trial, OKADA Takashi appeared in court to defend for Iwane Matsui and tried his best to excuse him by saying "sincere" words, which had an impact on the court's final decision.[1] According to OKADA Takashi, Iwane Matsui really loved China, for example, when he visited Iwane Matsui the next morning of December 17th, when they "celebrated the victory" that night, Iwane Matsui was not happy at all, saying:

> For more than 30 years, my consistent wish is to achieve peace between China and Japan. However, this time, we brought Nanjing the most miserable results that I never wanted even in my dreams. As long as I think that many of my Chinese fiends who live in Nanjing will leave Nanjing with very bad mood, I feel infinite sadness. What's more, I worry about the future relationship between Japan and China, I am too lonely to indulge in the happiness of victory.

---

[1] Although the Tokyo Trial finally sentenced Iwane Matsui to the highest punishment-hanging, the punishment was only for a negative "responsibility for inaction" and denied the defendant's "illegal order, authorization and permission" put forward by the public prosecutor. That is to say, "this court finds that the defendant Matsui is guilty in item 55 of the cause of action, and the first, twenty-seventh, twenty-ninth, thirty-first, thirty-second, thirty-fifth, thirty-sixth and fifty-fourth of the cause of action are not guilty" (Tomio Hora, *Battle History of Japan and China 8 Nanjing Incident I*, p. 399). In the indictment filed by the public prosecutor in the Tokyo Trial, the forty-fifth item was the Nanjing Massacre. The court called it "ambiguous" and "not necessary" in terms of "adequacy", and classified its "occasions of violating the Law of War" in the 54th and 55th cause of action. The 54th item refers to" illegal authorization, order, permission", and the 55th item refers to "responsibility for inaction".

© The Author(s) 2020
Z. Cheng, *The Nanjing Massacre and Sino-Japanese Relations*,
https://doi.org/10.1007/978-981-15-7887-8_18

OKADA Takashi said:

I felt very sympathy for general's inner feelings when I was listening to these grave words......I often think, general Matsui is an unusual figure who has been promoted to general only because of his relationship with China since his youth. It is rare for a soldier like general to have so many Chinese friends.

When greeting the victorious New Year's Day in 1938, general wrote the following poem, which revealed his mood.

Dozens of autumn with northern horses and south boats, I am ashamed of being incapable to realize the peace and development of Asian countries. I will continue to pursue my dream and never give up even I die.

This poem was presented by general when I went to his official residence on New Year's Day. Its meaning is as follows:

"Over the past decades of my journey in China with my army, all I prayed for was the peace and development of Asian countries. I was deeply ashamed of my powerlessness when I look back on the past. Today, I unexpectedly ushered in the age of 61 in the military, and it is already difficult to realize my dream which I had since a very young age. However, I will never forget that dream even I die".

On December 19th, commander Matsui and his staff boarded Qingliangshan and the Observatory in Nanjing. While listening to the instructions of his staff, he looked inside and outside the city. At that time, commander looked at the Dr. Sun Yat-sen's Mausoleum first and expressed his wishes for its peace. What's more, he expressed his regret that Generalissimo Chiang Kai-shek's reunification efforts had suffered a tragic setback, thinking that if Generalissimo Chiang Kai-shek could endure for another two or three years without provoking wars, Japan would also realize the disadvantages of using military forces to solve the Chinese problems, and today's unfortunate results of brotherly rivalry would not occur, it is such a pity. I was listening by his side when commander Matsui said these words to his serious staff.

On the way home, the army commander suddenly said that he wanted to inspect the situation of the refugees nearby, and then he inspected the refugee area, which made his staff amazed. During that time, general inquired the refugees about many things such as the dangers of the war and he kindly comforted those refugees, what's more, he also told them that the Japanese Army had issued a strict order that it would never harm the kind and great civilians. Although it had caused much trouble because of language difficulties and other reasons, the era of living and working in peace and contentment would surely come in the near future. I directly translated general's words sentence by sentence.[2]

OKADA Takashi's testimony is quoted in detail because the Japanese fictionalists claim it is a grievance that Iwane Matsui was sentenced to hanging by the Tokyo Trial and many unrelated people feel sympathy for Iwane Matsui, and OKADA Takashi's testimony is an important basis of these

---

[2] Tomio Hora, *Battle History of Japan and China 8 Nanjing Incident I*, p. 263, 264.

reactions, therefore, it is necessary to discuss his testimony. Indeed, if it were not for his comeback after retirement, history might have made a completely different assessment of Iwane Matsui. From the point of individual, Iwane Matsui had a bond with China in an early time when he was a military officer in Beijing and Shanghai, he used to support Sun Yat-sen's revolutionary activities and he "liked" Chinese traditional culture, he had knowledge of Chinese poetry and calligraphy, although he was passionate about "Pan-Asianism: in his late years and was quite acquainted with Chinese dignitaries, he was very frugal himself and behaved well". In terms of his close relationship with China in his life, just as OKADA Takashi said, it is "truly rare". However, just as the personal morality doesn't play an important in evaluating political figures, Iwane Matsui's "like" should have nothing to do with being responsible for Japanese atrocities and that is easy to understand. I would like to point out in particular that although the performance of Iwane Matsui described by OKADA Takashi has never been questioned, it is still more suspicious than credible and we can't trust it easily. I cite an obvious example here as proof. In the above two quotations of Iwane Matsui, "China and Japan" appears twice, which is very strange. Because although it is a little change to turn "Japan and China" into "China and Japan", it is not in line with the Japanese habit, just like Chinese would not say "Japan and China". Iwane Matsui would not say that, nor the normal Japanese. They would not say that in private, especially not in formal occasions. They would not say that, but OKADA Takashi said that, so there is much to discuss. When I first read the testimony for the defendants in the Tokyo Trial about the atrocities in Nanjing, I felt OKADA Takashi was obviously different from others. Other witnesses, including WAKISAKA Jiro, the head of the 36th Regiment of the 9th Division of Shanghai Expeditionary Army and NAKASAWA Mitsuo, chief of staff of the 16th Division, took a resolute and left no leeway, such as alleging the atrocities of the Chinese Army, calling "Japan Chili" as long as they need to say China and Japan together. OKADA Takashi was different because he tried to "touch the judge with emotion", and he understated himself both in "affidavit statement" (No. 2670 Defender's instrument, No. 3409 Court testimony) and testimony, he only stressed that Iwane Matsui committed to the peaceful relationship between Japan and China and was saddened by the tragedy between Japan and China, therefore, the "China and Japan" was naturally used though it seemed to stress the status of China. OKADA Takashi acted in this way because he was very eager to save Iwane Matsui. Because he wanted to save him, he just sought to "turn the enemy into friend" as long as he needed to talk or write, which surely was very different from those witnesses who only cared their "integrity" but never cared about the situation of the defendants. The reason why OKADA Takashi tried so hard is that Iwane Matsui is both like a father and benefactor to him, their relationship is much closer that between superior and subordinate. What those insolent witnesses say is not credible, neither is what OKADA Takashi says, even his words are more mild, the so-called "China and Japan" here is an obvious flaw.

The above words put forward by OKADA Takashi, which he claimed to be said by Iwane Matsui, were not doubted by the procuratorate in the Tokyo Trial and they later became the main source of opinions of Masaaki Tanaka and others,[3] the following example is an important one. OKADA Takashi said that Iwane Matsui left Nanjing on December 21st by destroyer,[4] stayed at Wulong Mountain and Zhenjiang on the way and went back to Shanghai on December 23rd; during this journey, Matsui told him the following words:

> The unfortunate scourge of war between China and Japan should not be expanded. Since the Manchurian Incident, China has implemented anti-Japanese education, and that strengthen the anti-Japanese mentality of the military and young students, and the interests of Japan and the property and lives of its expatriates have been threatened. Therefore, the army was sent for safety. Under that situation, the war between China and Japan was obviously fierce, our army had to march on Nanjing, the capital of China. However, the resort to force is not the fundamental solution to the problems of our two countries, it is just a temporary way. I'm convinced that in any case, if the misunderstanding between our countries can't be solved fundamentally by peaceful means (diplomatic means), it will lead to great misfortune for both countries in the future. As a military commander, I was sent to China not for fighting like today, but for the peaceful work in the future, I will make devote myself wholeheartedly to the realization of this mission in the future. If the war is our focus, there is no need to let me comeback since I am retired, because there are many excellent generals at present. In this regard, it is difficult for the military of the two countries to negotiate because of the war, so I think people in financial or cultural circle may come forward to negotiate, and if it is possible, people from the financial circle are the best to participate in the negotiation. And the negotiation conducted be these people is a totally different path. In this way, a peaceful path will be started on the basis of the correct theory. They can speak to their own government so as to naturally create a peaceful atmosphere, I think it is the best way to eliminate the war without harming the face of the two governments.[5]

OKADA Takashi said, they chose Song Ziwen at that time, he and Li Zeyi, who was then a lobbyist, arrived in Hong Kong on January 10th, 1938 and had a talk with Song Ziwen, it was said that "Mr. Song totally agreed on the

---

[3] As Masaaki Tanaka said, Iwane Matsui spent his whole life pursuing for "Good relationship between Japan and China", "the unity of Asia": for example, he visited the southwest in 1936, "convinced the warlord era with Hu Hanmin as the core" in order to "follow the great mission of peaceful relationship between Japan and China, repair the two countries' relationship that has been in crisis". And he spread the opinions widely, "Promoting the unity and self-reliance of Asia, promoting the cultural renaissance of Asia and advocating that Asia should be the Asians' Asia is to realize the unfinished dream of Sun Yat-sen" (Masaaki Tanaka 『「南京虐殺」の虚構―――松井大将の日記をめぐって』, 東京, 日本教文社. The 1st edition published on June 25th, 1984, pp. 99, 91).

[4] According to the diaries of Iwane Matsui, it should be Torpedo boat ("Hong").

[5] Tomio Hora, *Battle History of Japan and China 8 Nanjing Incident I*, p. 265.

suggestion and he also thought that the ominous war between China and Japan was not only the misfortune of the two countries, but also a tragedy of the whole mankind".[6] The proposal finally failed because Fumimaro Konoe issued a statement that "do not take Chiang Kai-shek as an opponent" and Iwane Matsui was dismissed. When OKADA Takashi raised the matter, the related parties were all there so it is not likely that he would make a forgery. But there are still some doubts about whether the talk between Iwane Matsui and Li Zeyi, the talk between Li Zeyi and Song Ziwen and the content what Song Ziwen agreed on were the same as the above quotation. When OKADA Takashi said the proposal failed because Iwane Matsui was dismissed, he used the expression "everything would be over".[7] It seemed that if it were not for this, there would be great possibility that China and Japan would turn hostility into friendship. That depends on how we look at it. If we look from the perspective of the whole China, Iwane Matsui's ambition was not realized, but from the perspective of the Japanese-occupied area, there were Liang Hongzhi, Wen Zongyao, Chen Qun, Chen Jintao, Ren Yuandao, Hu Yatai, Wang Zihui, Jiang Hongjie, Gu Cheng, Lian Yu and others, later, a larger group of "people from all walks of life" such as Wang Jingwei, Chen Gongbo, Zhou Fohai successively cooperated with the Japanese army "in the most appropriate way" to "eliminate the state of war" and "create an atmosphere of peace", thus, Iwane Matsui's ambition can be said to have been realized. I have said that the original ambition of Iwane Matsui was to conquer the Chinese nation, and I said that not out of any personal emotion, the basis of my opinion lies in what Iwane Matsui said and wrote. In *How can there be "not expansion"*, I have cited 饭沼守's diaries, according to the diaries, when Iwane Matsui accepted the task, he opposed the Japanese army limiting the war in Shanghai and suggested that "occupy Nanjing in a short period".[8] That was also Iwane Matsui's consistent demand before the Japanese army decided to attack Nanjing. On November 15th, when Colonel Sadaaki Kagesa, Chief of strategy of General Staff Office and Colonel Kenshirō Shibayama, Director of military affairs of Ministry of the Army went to visit Shanghai Expeditionary Army, Iwane Matsui resolutely explained the "necessity of occupying Nanjing". On November 22nd, Japanese China Area Army expressed again in "Letter of opinion on future operations": "We should occupy Nanjing when the enemy is weak". (Iwane Matsui clearly noted in his diary that the opinion of Japanese China Area Army was "approve".) On November 25th, Vice Chief of staff Hayao Tada called, saying that the operation of Japanese China Area Army can expand to Wuxi and Hizhou but

---

[6] Tomio Hora, *Battle History of Japan and China 8 Nanjing Incident I*, p. 266.
[7] Tomio Hora, *Battle History of Japan and China 8 Nanjing Incident I*, p. 266.
[8] Refer to *One of the Notes of Nanjing Massacre* III.

should not extend further in the west direction. Iwane Matsui denounced the order in his diary "pursue for palliative, really unbelievable".[9]

During the Tokyo Trial, the defense party cited "Iwane Matsui" on October 8th, 1937, aiming to use the words "do not regard the civilians as the enemy" in the statement, but the statement begins with the following argument:

> Because of my position, I received Emperor's order and bore the heavy responsibility to lead the army to capture the victory of the war. Since we landed in the south of the Yangtze River, our army has been enriched and the brave troops have been sent, totally showing our power. The mission of our army is to protect the rights and interests of our country and to protect our expatriates on the basis of the Japanese government's statement as well as punish the Nanjing government and the violent China, sweep away the red forces and the anti-Japanese policies that coexist with them so as to establish a clear foundation for the peace of East Asia.[10]

"The Nanjing government" "red forces" and "violent China"—refers to the people besides Liang Hongzhi and his partners and they are the objects of their "punishment" "sweeping", it is obvious that Iwane Matsui's only purpose is to make "China" surrender to Japan. Therefore, the above citation of Iwane Matsui's "regrets" for the war between China and Japan cannot stand the test of facts at all. Here, I would like to cite a more important piece of evidence to veil the real intention of Iwane Matsui. The decision of the General Staff Office arrived at the Japanese China Area Army on November 28th, Iwane Matsui wrote his feelings down in his diary: "It is a great relief to me that the suggestion I strongly offered was approved".[11] This sentence is more valuable for us to understand Iwane Matsui than any other ones. Somebody may think that Iwane Matsui's state of mind and even his understanding have changed after the army occupied Nanjing, but whatever, it is impossible for Iwane Matsui to have a feeling of "loneliness" after entering the city and that can be proved by indisputable evidence. And the evidence is also proved by Iwane Matsui's self-testimony. On December 21st, Iwane Matsui went back to Shanghai, he wrote the following sentence in his diary of that day: "It has been two weeks since I left Shanghai and I have completed

---

[9] 「松井石根大!戦陣日記」, *Documents on the Battle of Nanjing*, compiled by Battle of Nanking Editorial Committee, pp. 7,8,9.

[10] Tomio Hora *Battle History of Japan and China 8 Nanjing Incident I*, p. 269.

[11] 「松井石根大!戦陣日記」, *Documents on the Battle of Nanjing*, compiled by Battle of Nanking Editorial Committee, p. 10. After receiving the order "Be brave to fight, be determined to act, try to win with less armies, show the power of our nation to China and foreign countries, I would be grateful to your loyalty" from the emperor, Iwane Matsui expressed that he will "overcome all difficulties to show the power of the imperial army" in his response article. (同上引『南京戦史資料集』, pp. 196, 197), Iwane Matsui's active performance is consistent.

the feat of entering the Nanjing city, so I am particularly happy to come back here".[12] Thus, the regret feeling of Iwane Matsui described by OKADA Takashi has been totally destroyed, Iwane Matsui's "enthusiastic" desire to quickly attack Nanjing has been exposed clearly by the sentence.[13]

What OKADA Takashi said only referred to Iwane Matsui and he did not deny the atrocities in Nanjing, may be because he had deep worries so he didn't easily change the words, it was difficult to clear the responsibility of Iwane Matsui, but it was more difficult to deny the atrocities in Nanjing, so it is understandable that he said the less serious one. However, Iwane Matsui had a lot to do with the atrocities in Nanjing. He was convicted for the atrocities in Nanjing, the two were closely related to each other, so was there any grievance?

---

[12] 「松井石根大!戦陣日記」, *Documents on the Battle of Nanjing*, compiled by Battle of Nanking Editorial Committee, p. 23.

[13] Reviewing the whole performance of Iwane Matsui, we can see that he is not a simple soldier, so not only he is more active than the Japanese central government on whether to enlarge the war and whether attack Nanjing, and the army under his command constantly broke through the "commanding line" set by the central government, furthermore, compared to skilled soldiers, Iwane Matsui has his own "mature" ideas in politics. Let's not discuss "Pan-Asianism" here; he was much more radical than the then Japanese government on the propositions for the current situation. The symbol of the Japanese government's denial of the nationalist government is Fumimaro Konoe's statement "Do not regard Chiang Kai-shek as the enemy", which was published on January 16th, 1938. Previously, China and Japan had been in secret contact on peace negotiations by the German Ambassador to China, but Iwane Matsui had considered to exclude the nationalist government for a long time. He expressed on December 2nd, 1937: "The first strategic goal in the future is to expel the nationalist government and establish an independent regime in Jiangsu, Zhejiang and if possible, Anhui. If there is no other way, we transform the nationalist government with the remaining dignitaries near Nanjing, so as to establish a nationalist government separated from Hankou government" (「松井石根大!戦陣日記」, *Documents on the Battle of Nanjing*, compiled by Battle of Nanking Editorial Committee, p. 13).

Was What Fitch Said "Wrong"?

The Thorough Examination of "Nanjing Massacre" questioned Fitch (George Fitch)'s letter to Timperley:

What is War (i.e., *What War Means: the Japanese Terror in China*—by the citer) compiled by Timperley in Shanghai was urgently published without any verification on the basis of letters from Fitch and Bates. In the first chapter, Fitch, the writer, wrote:

> At 11 o'clock on December 13, I heard for the first time that <u>Japanese troops had been found in the safety zone. Two members of the international committee</u> and I went to visit them by a car. We encountered a small detachment <u>at the southern entrance to the security zone</u>. At that time, the Japanese troops did not show any hostility, but they <u>soon shot twenty refugees who had fled in panic because of the appearance of the Japanese Army</u>. (The key points are from the original text—citer)

The shooting of refugees by Japanese troops took place around noon on December 13, just in front of Fitch at the southern end of the safety zone. But apart from what Fitch said, <u>there are no such records in Japan, the United States, Germany and other countries</u>. (The key points are added by the citer, the following ones will no longer be noted.)

That is in line with the fact. The Japanese Army hasn't arrived at the spot (the safety zone) <u>around noon on December 13. The Japanese Army entered the safety zone on December 14, the next day, to sweep.</u>

......It is clear that what Fitch recorded is totally wrong.[1]

When *The Thorough Examination of "Nanjing Massacre"* cited Tian's work, some expressions were exaggerated, for example, "I heard for the first

---

[1] *Thorough Examination of the Nanjing Massacre,* written by Shūdō Higashinakano, pp. 201, 202.

time that the Japanese troops had been found in the safety zone", the original expression in the Japanese collection was "I heard for the first time that the Japanese Army entered the safety zone",[2] there was no unnatural "had been found", and in the Chinese version and of Fitch's memories, which were published simultaneously with the English version, the translation of this sentence was also the same as the Japanese collection. *The Thorough Examination of "Nanjing Massacre"* intended to give a different translation at this unimportant point and created some knot, nothing more than to leave some questions on the materials that are not conducive to the Japanese army. These tricks are commonly used by the fictionalists, for example, when Masaaki Tanaka compiled Iwane Matsui's wartime records; he personally changed more than nine hundred places.[3] I will not discuss these places one by one as there are no key differences.

The above quotation "the Japanese Army hasn't arrived at the spot around noon on December 13rd" is a wrong description, but this mistake may not be made by Fitch, because it takes time for everyone to know the matter. Fitch said that he "heard for the first time", so it is very likely that he heard the matter earlier than any other westerners; it is also not strange that the Japanese side didn't record this matter, because if the Japanese army consisted of a small group of troops, they may not record everything in detail—if it was not allowed, they certainly would not record. This is from a reasonable point of view. As far as the fact is concerned, the so-called "there are no such records in Japan, the United States and Germany" is an arbitrary conclusion, because besides the American Fitch, whether there are records in Japan and Germany is not as what Shūdō Higashinakano said. For example, the records of *The Diaries of John Rabe* on December 13th have a lot to do with this matter, so although the contents are long, I copied here:

> Early in the morning, when I was awakened by the air raid again, I felt very disappointed. The bombs felt down again like hails. The Japanese only captured a few city gates last night and haven't entered into the city.
> After arriving at the headquarters of the committee, we established an international Red Cross Society in ten minutes and I became the member of the council of that organization. John Magee assumed chairman of Red Cross, and he has been planning to set up a Red Cross Society for weeks. Three members of the council drove to several military hospitals established in the Ministry of

---

[2] Tomio Hora『日中戦争史資料』9「南京事件」II, p. 29.

[3]「『南京虐殺』史料に改ざん ／900所原文とズレ」、「『南京虐殺』ひたすら 隠す／ 田中氏の 松井大!の日誌改ざん」, Tokyo, Asahi Shimbun, November 24, 25 of 1985. As for the facts of the changes made by Tanaka Masaaki, refer to 《南京大虐殺の証明》 written by Tomio Hora, Tokyo, 朝日新聞社, the 1st edition published on March 5, 1986, pp. 210, 222, and as for Tanaka Masaak's refutes, can refer to his『南京事件の総括』, Tokyo, 謙光社, the 2nd edition published on July 10, 1987, pp. 340, 341, Tomio Hora's another response can refer to his「松井大!陣中日誌竄あとさき」, Tomio Hora、藤原彰、本多勝一編『南京事件を考える』, Tokyo, 大月書店, the 1st edition published on August 20, 1987, pp. 55, 68.

Foreign Affairs, Ministry of Military Affairs and Ministry of Railways. Through their inspection, we were convinced of the miserable condition of these hospitals, and the medical staff of the hospital. Through their inspection, we were convinced of the miserable condition of these hospitals and the medical personnel of the hospital fled during the fierce fire, leaving the patients unattended. Therefore, we quickly got a Red Cross flag and hang it over the Ministry of Foreign Affairs, we also recalled a considerable number of personnel, who dared to return home only after seeing the Red Cross flag flying over the Ministry of Foreign Affairs. On the road to and outside the Ministry of Foreign Affairs, there were casualties lying everywhere. In the courtyard, discarded weapons and equipment were littered like Zhongshan Road. There was a pile of shapeless thing on a wheelbarrow parked at the gate, the thing was like a corpse and the exposed feet showed that he was not dead. We drove cautiously down the street and were in danger of being blown up by grenades scattered on the ground all the time. We turned into Shanghai Road, where dead civilians lying all over the street, then we drove forward and met the advancing Japanese Army. The unit told us through a doctor who can speak German that the commander of the Japanese Army would not arrive until two days later. As the Japanese Army were advancing northward through Xinjiekou, we bypassed the Japanese troops quickly and drove away quickly. [4]

The above paragraph of the diary did not note the specific time, but it should be in the morning that Rabe arrived at the "headquarters of the committee" and he later went out after the election of the Red Cross, "three members of the committee" inspected the military in the Ministry of Foreign Affairs and other places, whose address should be from the north to south along "Shanghai Road", not far from "Xinjiekou"—roughly near Hanzhong Road—and met the Japanese army. Judging from the whole situation, this was properly the time when they met Fitch. I would like to make a guess here, which is not a really "bold" hypothesis: Rabe and Fitch were together. The first reason is that Fitch and his companions were the three members of the International Committee (Fitch was not on the initial list of the International Committee, but he was indeed an important member), and Rabe and his companions were also the three members of the International Committee; the second reason is that Fitch and his companions met the Japanese army at the "southern entrance to the safety zone", Rabe and his companions also met them at the southern end of the safety zone; the third reason is that the situation after Fitch returned to the headquarter of the International Committee was the same as the situation after Rabe returned to the headquarter of the International Committee. Fitch recorded the situation after he returned to the headquarter in his memoirs:

---

[4] *The Diaries of John Rabe*, written by John Rabe, translated by 本书翻译组, Nanjing, Jiangsu People's Publishing House, Jiangsu Education Publishing House, the 1st edition published on August 1, 1997, p. 171.

We were busy in the office disarming Chinese soldiers who could no longer escape and came to the "safety zone" to sought refuge. We guaranteed that if they could put down their weapons, their lives would be pardoned by the Japanese Army.[5]

The Diaries of John Rabe recorded the situation after returning to the headquarter as follows:

When I returned to the headquarter, I found that the gate was very crowded with a large number of Chinese soldiers who could not cross the river. They all accepted our request and had dropped down their weapons, later, they were placed in various parts of the safety zone.[6]

The thing recorded by these two people was roughly the same, we can conjecture that what Fitch had told Timperley was the record of the facts. Even what Rabe described was not the same thing as what Fitch said, they both met the Japanese army at about the same time and the same place, so the so-called "Apart from Fitch……there are no such records" has lost its foundation. Mr. Higashinakano is a scholar with experience in teaching in Western schools such as the University of Washington, he should understand the characteristics of the history industry: "It is easy to say some materials exist but it is difficult to say some materials don't exist". Maybe Mr. Higashinakano has read all of the Japanese collections and inadvertently "included" Germany just because Japan "doesn't have such records". If it is the fact, although he was not careful enough, he can be forgiven in that occasional mistakes are inevitable. Unfortunately, this is far from the fact: the so-called Japan "doesn't have" is totally untrue.

After the Japanese army captured the gates of Nanjing around dawn of December 13th, they swarmed into the city in the morning. According to the route of the Japanese army, the troops that Fitch and Rabe met were the 23rd, 47th and 13th Regiment of the infantry. According to the "wartime records" of the 6th Division of the Japanese army:

At 8:30 a.m. of December 13, the 3rd battalion of the 23rd regime of the infantry occupied Shuiximen, the 1st unit entered the city and started to sweep.
One battalion of the 47th regime of the infantry entered the city and started to sweep around 10:00 a.m.[7]

---

[5] George Fitch, *My Eighty Years in China*, Archives of the Nanjing Massacre Made by Japanese Invaders, compiled by the Second Historical Archives of China and Nanjing Municipal Archives, Jiangsu Ancient Books Publishing House, Nanjing, Jiangsu Ancient Books Publishing House, the 3rd edition published in December 1997, p. 651.

[6] The Diaries of John Rabe, written by John Rabe, translated by 本书翻译组, p. 173.

[7] *"Wartime Records" of the 6th Division, No. 13, 14, Documents on the Battle of Nanjing*, compiled by Battle of Nanking Editorial Committee, p. 691.

Orita Mamoru, second lieutenant of the infantry and the team leader of the mortar team of the 2nd battalion of the 23rd regime of the infantry, recorded the situation of that day in his diary:

> At about 10:30 a.m., all of the team have entered the city. Because the horses couldn't pass the gate (the Chinese defenders block the gate in order to guard against the Japanese attack—the citer), we left four horses and three soldiers and put the remains of Private first class here. The battalion advanced at 11:00 a.m. to sweep the city and attack Qingliangshan. We thought it would be an urban warfare like in Shanghai, but it turned out to be extremely stable and we only heard a small number of gunshots that seemed to be fired when someone is chasing others.
>
> After entering the bustling urban area, we took a short break and later we continued to advance. During the process, we only saw two or three weak soldiers. However, we encountered 13i (i refers to infantry; 13i refers to the 13th regiment of the infantry—the citer), 47i and other troops and they were also advancing to the same direction. We heard that we were all advancing from Qingliangshan to Lion Rock. While dissatisfied with the disunity of the instructions of D (D refers to division—the citer), we continued to advance.
>
> We successively arrived at Qingliangshan at around 15:00 p.m. R commander (R refers to regiment, R commander refers to the commander of the regiment—the citer) came to our place and decided to stop attack and camp on the spot.[8]

The troops Fitch and others heard from might be the 3rd Battalion that entered the city before Orita Mamoru's team and also might be the Orita Mamoru's team that entered the city at 10:30 a.m. No matter which team it was, the so-called "Japan doesn't have such records" in *The Thorough Examination of "Nanjing Massacre"* can no longer be established. And the so-called "the Japanese Army hadn't arrived at the spot (the safety zone)" can be basically denied. I added the limitation "basically" because, on the one hand, if the 6th Division entered the city, they had to go through Zhonghuamen and Shuiximen, and the safety zone was a shortcut to Qingliangshan and Lion Rock, and there was no prohibition on passing through the safety zone from orders at all levels, the Japanese enforcement forces had no reason to avoid the safety zone and chose a longer way; on the other hand, if the area of the safety zone was regarded as the boundary, the above citation materials alone cannot prove that the Japanese army had entered the safety zone, because whether the "southern end" "xinjiekou" was beside or outside the boundary—it's already boring to be so "penny-pinching"—cannot be completely asserted.[9]

---

[8] 「折田護日記」; *Documents on the Battle of Nanjing*, compiled by Battle of Nanking Editorial Committee, p. 447.

[9] 森英生, who have been active in recent years, was the leader of the 3rd company of the 20th Regiment, he claimed that he saw a large number of discarded military uniforms. He said that day was "14", and he stressed that "they didn't enter the zone". (森英生著『ラーベの日記「

If we can go to verify whether the Japanese army had entered the safety zone at the "noon of December 13th" and we can put the truth aside, the "the next day December 14th" claimed by *The Thorough Examination of "Nanjing Massacre"* a totally falsehood. "The Japanese Army didn't enter the safety zone" is the unanimous conclusion of the Japanese army. When I "examined" *The Truth-Nanjing Incident*, I have listed some specific records of Jiang Gonggu and Wei Telin to refute,[10] I can cite another two unquestionable evidence left by the Japanese army to prove my argument. Private First Class Matachi Ike, who belonged to the 2nd company of the 7th Regiment, listed "6:00 p.m." particularly in his diary on December 13th, which records:

> Starting from 6:00 p.m. and approaching 8:00 p.m. (The original text is this– the citer), we finally went to the international refuge area to sweep the left enemy. On the way, we passed some splendid roads such as Zhongshan Road and Shanghai Road, along which are magnificent buildings such as Great Hall of the People. We came back at 2:00 a.m. I'm extremely tired.[11]

After the Japanese army occupied Nanjing, the task of sweeping the city was mainly carried out by the 9th Division and the 16th Division which the Shanghai Expeditionary Army belonged to, and the areas under the control of the 9th Division and the 16th Division, which were, respectively, southwest and northeast areas of the city, were bounded by Zhongshan Road, and the 7th Division that Matachi belonged to was just the unit that was responsible for sweeping the security zone. We can confirm that the area the Japanese army entered recorded by Matachi in his diary was the safety zone, that is not only because the "the international refuge zone" was just the safety zone, but also because "Shanghai Road" was just within the safety zone. But the fictionalists may also raise questions on whether Matachi wrote a wrong time, because he returned home at 2 o'clock in the evening, and he was "extremely

---

南京の真実」を読んで」, 畝本正己著『真相・南京事件―――ラーベ日記を検証して』序章之三, 東京, 文京出版1999年2月1日第2版, 第8頁.) 森英生 said that because he planned to send 東史郎 to court not long ago and he had a strong sense of "realistic politics", whether he said was beneficial to the current situation needs to be decided. In fact, what he saw was that happened on December 13, because the 20th regiment had entered the city to sweep on December 13, "the company entered the city through Zhongshanmen at 1:40 p.m. and started to sweep to the west" (步兵第二十聯隊第四中隊《陣中日誌》第五号, 南京戦史編集委員会編『南京戦史資料集』, p. 610). Although the above diary was the 4th company's diary, the action should be under the same order of the 3rd company, which can be proved by 吉田正明's diary, who was in the same company with 森英生. In this diary, 吉田証明 recorded the fact that they entered the city to sweep on December 13.

[10] Refer to my article *The Examination of The Truth-Nanjing Incident--Examine The Diaries of John Rabe*.

[11] 「井家又一日記」, 南京戦史編集委員会編『南京戦史資料集』, p. 475.

tired", this record is very likely made up later, and it is not completely impossible that the time was wrongly wrote down. The reason why I dare to conclude that this record is "absolutely not suspicious" is because there is another solid evidence to prove this record.

The Japanese's records were incomplete due to the incineration during the defeat. Fortunately, the records of the 7th Regiment still exist. Apart from the records of the 7th Division, the related records of the 6th Brigade of the senior infantry of the regiment, the records of the senior 9th Division of the brigade also exist. Today, we can still see the consistent records from division to regiment. The 9th Division issued a sweeping order at noon on December 13th (Ninth Division Jia No. 131), the 6th Division issued a sweeping order at 16:30 p.m. on December 13th (Sixth Division Jia No. 138), the 7th Division received an order at 5 o'clock and they immediately deploy the implementation. The "wartime records" of the 7th Division recorded the thing as follows:

> December 13th, sunny
> At around 5:00 p.m. we received the Sixth Division No. 138 order to sweep in the city (with another paper). Jia No. 105 order was immediately ordered. Regiment (The 3rd Division returned,[12] one company of the infantry[miss one unit], one company of chariot[miss one unit] immediately assembled their troops in the western area of the airport and began sweeping. At around 3:00 p.m. on December 14th, the troops successively finished and returned.[13]

This record of the 7th Regiment is indeed beyond doubt, and it is in the coincidence with the "6:00 p.m." recorded by the Matachi Ike, the reliability of this matter has been unbreakable. The so-called "the Japanese Army didn't enter the safety zone on December 13th" claimed by the Japanese fictionalists has been completely overthrown.

---

[12] The third Battalion served as a reserve for the brigade when it attacked Nanjing and did not act with the Seventh Regime.
[13] 「步兵第七聯隊戦闘詳報」, *Documents on the Battle of Nanjing*, compiled by Battle of Nanking Editorial Committee, p. 619.

Questions on the Query Against Rabe

The Thorough Examination of "Nanjing Massacre" has some special sections to criticize the above citation from what Rade recorded in his diary on December 13th, claiming:

> Rabe turned into Shanghai Road about 200 meters from the Ministry of Foreign Affairs. And the Japanese Army came from ahead of Shanghai Road.
>
> As we all know, Shanghai Road is within the safety zone. As mentioned in the previous chapter, this area is the sweeping area of the 7th Regiment of the infantry.
>
> The 7th Regiment of the infantry entered the safety zone on December 14th, the next day. On December 13th, which remains some doubts, the 7th Regiment only reached the west side of the airport in the city about two kilometers after entering the Zhongshan Gate.
>
> Moreover, the combat medic was not in field hospital but in the forefront of the battle, was there such an army? The combat medic is always set up in the field hospital in the rear when or after the fiercest battle. At that time, the field hospital should be in the foothills of Zijin Mountain so the combat medic should be there. There is no reason for the combat medic to be in the Shanghai Road.
>
> If it was the Japanese combat medic, they may had studied German. If the combat medic could speak German language, Rabe might be able to speak with them—the "combat medic who can speak German language" may be created for the readers.
>
> However, even we assume that there is combat medic in the Shanghai Road, the assumption itself is strange because there is no reason for the combat medic to know the commander's entry into the city. The "Diaries of IINUMA Mamoru" on December 14th recorded, "The Chief of Staff of the Front Army called, hoping to sweep the city on December 17". According to this record,

the date on which the commander would enter the city had not been decided on December 13th. This description must be recorded on the basis of his own imagination after he knew about the entry of the city.[1]

This section is quite debatable: I. The date recorded in *The Thorough Examination of "Nanjing Massacre"* cannot stand the test of the fact, which has been discussed before, it is obvious that we cannot draw a conclusion in line with the facts if we judge the authenticity on the basis of this false premise; II. although hospital sets a position for combat medic, it is not strange that combat medic goes to the battlefield with the army, especially when the "battle is at its fiercest"; III. all the units of the Japanese army in the front line had their own combat medic originally, for example, the 7th Regiment mentioned before had its exclusive combat medic lieutenant Yikuo Hashi, as long as one has a little common sense of the military history of the Japanese army, he should not say such layman's words. If one doesn't know the history but blame others at his own will, he would make a clear a mistake, and readers would criticize the mistake, if one knows the history but still says that, it will become a moral issue; IV. Unemoto Masaki and others have all questioned the fact that the Japanese army could speak German language,[2] that is also unreasonable. After Meiji Restoration in Japan, compulsory education became common, the Japanese soldiers were all educated in school and German language was also the most important language besides English, and when the Japanese army entered the city, considering the "rights and interests of foreign countries", they particularly selected those soldiers who could speak foreign languages to take part in the "sweeping", and in the sweeping order of the 7th Regiment, there was also a requirement of "choosing the soldiers who can learn languages quickly",[3] so it is not strange that the soldiers could speak German language. And modern Japanese medicine learned mainly from German so it is more common that the combat medic could use German language. V. The Japanese commander mentioned in *The Diaries of John Rabe* (the so-called "commander" in *The Thorough Examination of "Nanjing Massacre"*) might not be the supreme commander, but could be commander at all levels. On December 13th, the divisions and brigades might not enter the city, for example, the first unit that arrived at the safety zone—at least the edge-the 6th Division, the commander department of its 36th Brigade stationed outside the Shuiximen gate, the commander department of the division stationed at the farther Andemen, and the main commander of the regiment didn't enter the city

---

[1] *Thorough Examination of the Nanjing Massacre*, written by Shūdō Higashinakano, pp. 204–205.

[2] Unemoto Masaki asserted that "there are no German-speaking military doctors" and used it as a basis for the falsehood of Rabe's diary. (畝本正己著『真相·南京事件———ラーベ日記を検証して』第2部,第67页。)

[3] 步兵第七聯隊「捕虜、外国権益に対する 注意」, *the Battle of Nanjing*, compiled by Battle of Nanking Editorial Committee, not for sale, Tokyo, 偕行社, the edition published on November 3, 1989, p. 193.

with the first batch of the basic military units. Therefore, the basic military units of the Japanese army said the commander could only arrive "two days later", the commander could be of the regiment, and also could be the officer of brigade and division, so the commander didn't have to be Iwane Matsui.[4] And even the person referred to the supreme commander, the Japanese soldiers didn't have the obligation to tell others whether they knew the truth or not, during the wartime, it is very normal that people casually tell lies. The Thorough Examination of "Nanjing Massacre" think all Rabe had written was wrong, in fact, it doesn't list any convincing evidence and reason.[5]

---

[4] In a letter to the Japanese embassy signed by Rabe on December 16th, it was stated that "the supreme commander of the Japanese army arrived in Nanjing yesterday" (written by John Rabe and translated by the translation team of this book, The Diaries of John Rabe, p. 186). There is no possibility of intentional falsification in the letter to the Japanese Embassy, and this conclusive material proves that Rabe did not know at that time (Ishigen Matsui arrived in Ningxia on the 17th).

[5] 检证》 pointed one the so-called "change" on the translation of the Japanese version, that "the copious bodies of the citizens (the Chinese version is "dead civilians lied everywhere, refer to the earlier citation) should be translated as v e r s c h i e d e n e t o t e Z i v i l i s t e n" (*Thorough Examination of the Nanjing Massacre*, written by Shūdō Higashinakano, p. 204), but this has nothing to do with Rabe.

How Magee's Explanation Became Contradictory

The atrocities of the Japanese army in the safety zone were mainly recorded on the documents sent to the Japanese side by the International Committee, and thus these things were known to people around the world. Among these documents, *What War Means: the Japanese Terror in China* compiled by Timperley and *Documents of the Nanking Safety Zone* compiled by Xu Shuxi were the two important ones. Therefore, the Japanese fictionalists regard these two documents as the particular targets that they can attack.

The most important reason for *The Thorough Examination of "Nanjing Massacre"* to negate the two books is "Ninety percent of the contents is hearsay".[1] To prove this, *The Thorough Examination of "Nanjing Massacre"* cited the "case 219" in the documents of the International Committee and "Magee's another explanation of case 219", using the differences between the two to prove that Magee (John Magee)'s statement was untrue. Apart from the unjustifiable reasons such as the so-called "incredible" things in common sense, the key to the untrue statement was that 11 out 13 people were killed in "case 219", while Magee's "another explanation" was that 12 out of 14 people were killed. *The Thorough Examination of "Nanjing Massacre"* wanted to use this example to overthrow two books at one time, which is of course impossible. If one document can be totally negated just by these small discrepancies, no document can be useful since each collection might have these minor errors. Under such a dangerous situation at that time, it is very normal that there are some small doubts in the large number of the atrocities recorded by the International Committee. But this does not mean that "case 219" has really been proved wrong by *The Thorough*

---

[1] *Thorough Examination of the Nanjing Massacre*, written by Shūdō Higashinakano, p. 239.

Examination of "Nanjing Massacre", because the exact number of the people who were killed cannot be affirmed just by the assertion of The Thorough Examination of "Nanjing Massacre", and it is necessary to check the original text to get a conclusion.

Magee's "explanation" involved two families and was made in hasty, although the relationship between the two was clear; it is still possible that the number might be wrongly counted. So it is not convincing to determine the "explanation" is wrong just because of the lack of one person. According to the case 219 of Japanese atrocities recorded by the International Committee, 11 out of 13 were killed. On this matter, Georg Rosen, secretary of the German embassy, said in his report (No. 2722/1011/38) to the Ministry of Foreign Affairs on February 1st: "The 13 people of one family were almost all killed, the two surviving children were adopted by neighbors".[2] It is very unlikely that the number of people would both be counted wrong if they had not copy the statement of one person. Therefore, to solve this doubt, we still need to see how *The Thorough Examination of "Nanjing Massacre"* counted more people in "Magee's another explanation":

> On December 13, about 30 soldiers came to a Chinese household at the new intersection Five(It should be No.5—the citer) of southeast of Nanjing and asked to enter.
>
> The owner of the Islamist family whose surname was Ma(1) opened the door in the porch and was shot dead by a pistol on the spot. A man named Xia(2) knelt beside Ma's body and begged them not to kill again, but he was also shot dead. Ma's wife(3) asked the soldiers why they killed her husband, later she was also killed.
>
> Xia's wife(4) hid the one-year-old baby(5) under the table in the living room and later she was dragged out after being found. She was stripped, raped by many men and then stabbed into the chest with a bayonet and killed. The soldiers also inserted a bottle into her vulva, and the baby was also stabbed to death.
>
> Later, several soldiers went to the next room. Xia's wife's parents, who were respectively 76 years old(6) and 74 years old, were in that room as well as her 16-year-old(8) and 14-year-old(9) daughters. When the soldiers were going to rape the girls, their grandfather tried to protect her granddaughter and was shot. Grandfather grabbed his wife's body and was also killed.
>
> Next, two girls were stripped naked, the older girl was raped by two or three soldiers and the younger girl was raped by three soldiers. After the older girl was stabbed, her vulva was inserted by s stem, and the younger girl was not treated as miserably as her mother and sister was treated.

---

[2] Selected Archives of Japanese Imperialist Invasion of China Nanjing Massacre (co-compiled by The State Archives Administration of the People's Republic of China, Secondary Historical Archives of China and Jilin Academy of Social Sciences, Beijing, Zhonghua Book Company, the 1st edition published in July 1995, p. 151.

The soldiers stabbed their sister who was seven or eight years old(10) in this room.

The last people of this family to be killed were Ma's two children(gender unknown) who were respectively four years old(11) and two years old(12). The older one was stabbed to death and the younger one was split in half by a bayonet.

After being injured, the eight-year-old(13) girl climbed into the room where her dead mother was in and stayed there for 14 days with her four-year-old sister(14) who had escaped unharmed. The two children made a living by eating steamed rice.[3]

According to the figured marked by *The Thorough Examination of "Nanjing Massacre"*, the 14 people were all listed and there seemed to be no doubt. But if we carefully discern the meaning of the text, we would find that there should be a preposition of "After being injured, the eight-year-old girl(13)". Thus, could it be one of the people mentioned earlier. If it was someone mentioned earlier, which one was it? If being arranged by age, (10) "the seven-year-old or the eight-year-old" was undoubtedly the closet. However, the first, (13) was "eight" certainly, (10) was the uncertain "seven-year-old or eight-year-old"; the second, the above twelve people were all killed, while (13) was just "injured". Therefore, with this contradiction, although the matter was still doubtful, it was not appropriate to get a conclusion quickly. Recently, I read again the Magee's "explanation" cited by *The Diaries of John Rabe*, and I suddenly noticed that the citation of *The Thorough Examination of "Nanjing Massacre"* was probably inaccurate.

Later, the soldiers stabbed Ms. Xia's another seven-year-old or eight-year-old daughter by a bayonet who was also in the room......The seven-year-old or eight-year-old girl climbed into the next room after being injured, where her dead mother lied.[4]

So it is! If this version is correct,[5] the "stabbed" and "seven-year-old or eight-year-old" are clearly written, the doubt of the age and the question whether the people were killed should not exist, they are totally created by *The Thorough Examination of "Nanjing Massacre"*!

---

[3] *Thorough Examination of the Nanjing Massacre*, written by Shūdō Higashinakano, pp. 241, 242.

[4] *The Diaries of John Rabe*, written by John·Rabe, translated by 本书翻译组, p. 629.

[5] I used "probably inaccurate" "if" to express that the truth of the matter should refer to the original text; however, according to common sense, there is no "problem consciousness" in the Chinese version, and the "eight-year-girl" cited by 东中野 has its corresponding source, so my opinion should be right.

Had the Population of the Safety Zone "Increased"?

The issue of population is one entangled by the fictionalists, because the more they can prove the population at that time was less, the more they can negate the massacre, so they "get straight to the point" regardless of the existing materials, claiming that there was no one outside the safety zone. And since there was no one outside the safety zone, as long as it is proved that the number of people in the safety zone was limited, their goal of denying the massacre can be achieved. As the saying goes "A liter bottle of wine, no matter how much it is filled, a liter bottle of wine is still a liter. If there were only 200, 000 people, it can't be that 300, 000 people were killed".[1] Therefore, *The Thorough Examination of "Nanjing Massacre"* finds various reasons to prove that the safety zone could only accommodate a small number of people, for example, it says that the safety zone is only four times that of the Kokyo Gaien National Garden in Japan, since the area was very limited, the number of people it could accommodate was also very limited.

It is true that the safety zone is not large, but there is no question of whether it can accommodate hundreds of thousands of people. Whether there is enough space or not depends on the situation. During the special period when people's lives are endangered, congestion cannot be the reason to prevent the refugees from swarming into the safety zone. To be extreme, a square that is much smaller than the safety zone can hold a large assembly of millions of people, so it is totally possible for the much larger safety zone to accommodate much fewer people. Even if we judge it according to the population distribution in the normal period, the proportion of population in different districts is originally very different because of the degree of development, whether it is suitable for human habitation and so on. For example, according to the investigation conducted by the Nanjing government in June

---

[1] 田中正明著『南京事件の総括―――虐殺否定十五の論拠』, p. 159.

1935, although the Fourth District's area was the smallest in all of the districts, its population was the largest, with the population density about 196 times that of the rural areas (Swallow Rock, Shangxinhe and Xiaolingwei),[2] which was much beyond the so-called "common sense" claimed by the Japanese fictionalists. So it makes no sense that the fictionalists intentionally interpret the population density.

Similarly, although the population in the safety zone was related to the massacre, it was just related to it, not equal to it. The fictionalists, without exception, deliberately confuse this distinction. Because number of the massacres mentioned by the school of slaughter refers to the people who were killed in Nanjing administrative areas, including the area within the city, Xiaguan and Pukou, Xiaoweiling, Swallow Rock, Shangxinhe, Lingyuan in suburbs as well as the six surrounding counties such as Jiangning, Jurong, Liyang, Jiangpu, Liuhe and Gaochun, it is not the number of people killed in the safety, neither the number of people killed in the Nanjing city, the Japanese scholars have already conducted an appropriate discussion.[3] Therefore, grasping the population of Nanjing, which is actually the population of the safety zone, is of no significance to the understanding of the massacres.

The Thorough Examination of "Nanjing Massacre" has another section "the increase of the population in the safety zone", which says:

> The population of the safety zone is gradually expanding. Moreover, according to *The Nanjing Relief International Committee Report*, *The Diaries of John Rabe* and other records, the civilians who remained in Nanjing were "the poorest of the civilians". Therefore, the food problem became the urgent problem. The international committee was very sensitive to the issue of population and had mentioned it for many times.
>
> The initial document that mentioned the population issue was the No. 9 document of the international committee (December 17th), which complained that a considerable majority of the 200,000 citizens were at risk of "starving to death" because of insufficient food.

---

[2] The Fourth District had an area of 2.1726 square kilometers and a population of 153,422, the population density was 70,617 people per square kilometer; the rural districts had an area of 411.9020 square kilometers and a population of 148,557, the population density was 361 people per square kilometer. Refer to 市米義道編『南京』, 上海, 南京日本商工會議#1941年9月1日第1版, 第23頁.

[3] For example, Tomio Hora said: "In 1965, I visited Nanjing with delegation of Association of Returnees from China, Wangliangshi of the Foreign Culture Association of Nanjing said that there were more than 100,000 refugees swarming into the city, and these people had nowhere to hide because all families closed their doors. The streets were filled with crowds and they all became victims of raids by the Japanese Army. I think most of what Wangliangshi said is an exaggeration". Tomio Hora《南京大虐殺の証明》, 東京, 朝日新聞社, the 1st edition published on March 5th, 1986, p. 173. Tomio Hora is the founder of the "School of Slaughter", he criticizes the view of the fictionalists most strongly but he can maintain a clear consciousness, thus he is very fair.

Where did the figure of 200,000 come from? This was unknown for a long time and was finally figured out through The Diaries of John Rabe. And the police director Wang Gupan's speech "200,000 civilians still live in Nanjing" became the basis of the International Committee.

The director's speech was on November 28th in the 12th year of shōwa. The population on December 17 was still the same as that of 20 days ago, when the Nanjing fell on December 13. The International Committee also realized that the population of civilians didn't change after the fall of the Nanjing city.

On December 18, the No. 10 document said: "We, 22 Europeans, are unable to provide food to 20 Chinese civilians." Therefore, they asked assistance from the Japanese Army.

On December 21st, because of the inability to provide food and fuel to 200,000 people, the No. 20 document made the lamentation that "Under the current situation, the food shortage became more and more serious".

We can see from the three documents that the population of Nanjing remained unchanged from the late November to December 21st. Because there was no slaughter, so the population didn't decrease.[4]

How many people were there in the safety zone, and were those people staying in Nanjing "the poorest people among the residents"? The fact will not change according to the argument of *The Thorough Examination of "Nanjing Massacre"*. For example, Minnie Vautrin went to Shuiximen to check the houses of Presbyterian church on December 14th, they saw "Many poor and rich people hung the Japanese flags at the door of their homes, people made the Japanese flags in advance and hung them up in order to get better treatment".[5] The "rich" families here cannot rule out the possibility that the Japanese soldiers occupied the houses, however, there must be evidence to prove that the people there were not the original residents. I think that although it is right that the people who left Nanjing at that time were mainly the rich ones, the rich ones should be mainly the political and military figures and their families who had close ties with the officials. There should be plenty of rich people in Nanjing. Because no one expected the performance of the Japanese army after they entered the city. Smith, a reporter of Reuters, said in related reports:

> With the emergence of the Japanese, the Chinese people also felt a sigh of relief. "If the Japanese are civilized, the Chinese would like to come out to welcome them".[6]

[4] *The Thorough Examination of "Nanjing Massacre"*, written by Shūdō Higashinakano, pp. 232-233.

[5] Diaries of Vautrin, written by Minnie· Vautrin, translated by Nanjing Massacre Research Center of Nanjing Normal University. Nanjing, Jiangsu People Publishing House, the 1st edition published in October 2000, p. 193.

[6] Attached to the report of German Ambassador to China Todd Mann to the German Ministry of Foreign Affairs, *Archives of the Nanjing Massacre Made by Japanese Invaders*, compiled by the Second Historical Archives of China and Nanjing Municipal Archives, Jiangsu Ancient Books Publishing House, p. 619.

The words "Welcome" and others are quite different from the traditional "integrity" and the so-called "national rightness" in modern times, but Smith's inference is not a barrier to the feelings of the Chinese people, because for the most civilians, although the instinct to survive may not be superior to the negative conduct, for example, they may betray their friends to seek glory, but must precede the noble rightness such as dying for the country. Today, it is actually not necessary to accuse the people of failing to keep their integrity for the country. The Chinese civilians are often the victims of the "country", especially in the time of emergency. Regardless of other people's rejection, Chiang Kai-shek and Tang Shengzhi proposed that they should try every possible means to defend Nanjing, of course, their action was beyond reproach, but the problem is, their reasons were just something like "the capital was where the mausoleum of the founding father located",[7] they had never considered the lives and property of hundreds of thousands of civilians. Since the Chinese people couldn't got the effective protection from their government, and the performance of the Japanese army was not as they had expected, "the emergence of the Japanese" made them "breathe a sigh of relief" was a very natural thing. Therefore, the large number of civilians who were not related to the politics would not leave quickly to ruin their basic life and the people who stayed in Nanjing then should be not only the "poorest people among the residents". If this judgment is

---

[7] Li Zongren said he, Bai Chongxi and Germany advisers advocate abandoning defense, He Yingqin and Xu Yongchang "conducting everything based on the will of the Chairman", "Mr. Jiang said, in his opinion, Nanjing is the capital city and where the mausoleum of the founding father is located, so there is no reason to retreat without battle. He advocates defending...... Finally, the Chairman asked Tang Shengzhi, Tang stood up and shouted: "Now the enemy is approaching the capital. The capital is where the mausoleum of the founding father is located. At this period, when the enemy is approaching, if we do not sacrifice one or two great generals in Nanjing, we are not only sorry to the Prime Minister's spirit in heaven, but also sorry to our chief commander. I advocate sticking to Nanjing and fighting with the enemy to the end!" When Tang said this, his voice was fierce and he was very inspiring with a great willing to bleed". (*Memoirs of Li Zongren*, Volume 2, Nanning, Literature and History Committee of Guangxi Zhuang Autonomous Region Committee of the Chinese People's Political Consultative Conference, 1st edition, June 1980, pp. 699, 700.) Zhou Zhenqiang, deputy chief commander of the elite unit guarding Nanjing, said differently, he said that Tang Shengzhi was not so inspiring, and it was because Chiang Kai-shek who personally "persuaded" Tang that Tang agreed to serve as a guard general. (*Chiang Kai-shek's Iron Guard-Teaching Corps*, Selected Collection of Literary and Historical Materials compiled by the Literature and History Research Committee of the National Committee of the Chinese People's Political Consultative Conference, Beijing, the 1st edition published in December 1986, Chinese Literature and History Publishing House, p. 49.) But I heard this from others when I was attended a meeting this weekend, so there was no evidence to support. Liu Fei, head of the base camp combat group who attended the meeting at that time, had the same memories as Li Zongren, and records of Song Xilian, Wang Yaowu, who didn't attend the meeting but took part in the defense of Nanjing, were also the same as those of Li, therefore, Li's statements should be accurate. On December 4th, Chiang Kai-shek convened a meeting of cadres at and above the division level and talked about the six principles of defending Nanjing, but none of these was related to the civilians in Nanjing.

right, then the 200,000 hungry people to be rescued, which the International Committee often mentions, should not be the full number of people in the safety zone, and even should not be the "original people" in the safety zone. After the Battle of Shanghai, Nanjing also entered an extraordinary period because of the air raid, and by the time the Japanese army approached the city, every household had already stored many grains; therefore, the original residents seemed not to be the 200,000 people who had to "be provided with food and fuel" as mentioned by the International Committee, and even should not be the people who were faced with "starvation to death" on December 17th.

It is a big problem that *The Thorough Examination of "Nanjing Massacre"* uses three times the number of population to prove that "the population of Nanjing has not changed", because under such a chaotic situation at that time, it was impossible to conduct any effective investigation. In Rabe's diaries, whether the "200,000 people" said by Wang Gupan (Diary on November 28th, 1937), the "250,000 people" (refers to the number when the Japanese army "entered the city") reported by Japanese secret service organization Nanjing Class in February 1938, the "400,000 people" mentioned in *The People in the Dark Hell* of *The Atrocities of the Enemy* in March 1938, the "around 500,000 people" in the letter from the Nanjing Municipal Government to the Military Commission of the National Government on November 23rd, 1937, the "530,000 people" in the letter from the Consulate General of Japan in Shanghai to Minister for Foreign Affairs on October 27th, 1937 and so on, all the statements that exist today are just references. It is in fact far-fetched[8] to choose one of these statements in order to conform to one's own views. *The Thorough Examination of "Nanjing Massacre"* adheres to the "200,000 people" but turns a blind eye to other theories and made no explanation, how can it reach a realistic conclusion?

Since there are some doubts on the "200,000 people", the conclusion would of course be not reliable if it is made on the basis of the premise "200,000 people". *The Thorough Examination of "Nanjing Massacre"* said:

> According to the report of November 14th next year (No. 41 Document), the total population was 250,000 (refers to the safety zone—the citer). Around 50,000 people were added. That also indicates that there was no slaughter.[9]

---

[8] The Japanese fictionalists acted in this way, so were the other theorists. For example, the "530,000 people" was originally well-founded (it was clearly stated in the letter that it was "according to the investigation of the Police Bureau"), and some works tried to strengthen the reliability of this argument but ended up self-defeating. As noted in the Chinese version of *The Diaries of John Rabe:* "The official letter is the result of an investigation conducted by spies sent by the Japanese Consul General in Shanghai to Nanjing". (The Diaries of John Rabe, written by John Rabe, translated by本书翻译组, p. 115.) Spies might be successful, but how could they make such "investigations" that could not be done or kept secret without great labor? especially under such circumstances at that time.

[9] *Thorough Examination of the Nanjing Massacre*, written by Shūdō Higashinakano, p. 235.

"Around 50,000 people were added", where did they come from? After the fall of Nanjing, the Japanese army strictly guarded the city gate, and many accounts said that the gate was like a ghost gate.[10] One article in the Ta Kung Pao of February 21st said: "On the surface, the authorities of the enemy displayed the post to comfort the civilians and announced that Beijing and Shanghai would be open to traffic, but in fact, Chinese and foreign passengers who went to take the train were all refused, the so-called opening to traffic was only the enemy's tool to conduct aggression".[11] Li Kehen, an office employee at the time when Nanjing fell, was not able to escape until June 3rd and was still subject to strict inspection, he said:

> The news of the opening to traffic between Beijing and Shanghai inspired everyone's heart, but the enemy did not allow our compatriots to take the train, later, after the negotiation of the international committee, it was finally agreed that 60 tickets could be sold every train.
>
> People who wanted to leave Nanjing must first use his "residence card" to obtain a "relocation permit", many compatriots were willing to get out of this hell on earth but all their money had been robbed, so how could they afford to take the train? I made a lot of efforts and all my money was not robbed, which was really lucky for me, and I left Nanjing on June 3.
>
> When you got on the train at Xiaguan station, you had to go through close inspection, even the outsiders had no exception......[12]

It was difficult to leave Nanjing and it was also difficult to enter Nanjing. There were many people who "were willing to get out of this hell", but there were very few people who were willing to throw themselves into the net. This was a common situation at that time. Therefore, it was absolutely impossible that the Nanjing city "increased" 50,000 people.[13] Then, why did the

---

[10] As recorded in Guo Qi's Record of Blood and Tears in the Captured Capital, although there are dramatic elements (such as the genitals were cut off when a monk passed through the Zhonghua Gate), the difficulty of passing the gate can still be seen from it.

[11] *The Tragedy of Nanjing after the Fall, Selected Archives of Japanese Imperialist Invasion of China Nanjing Massacre* (co-compiled by The State Archives Administration of the People's Republic of China, Secondary Historical Archives of China and Jilin Academy of Social Sciences, p. 173.

[12] 《沦京五月记》 written by Li Kehen, compiled by Editorial Committee of the Historical Materials of the Nanjing Massacre of the Japanese Invaders and Nanjing Library; *Historical Materials of the Nanjing Massacre Made by Japanese Invaders*, Jiangsu Ancient Books Publishing House, the 1st edition and 5th printed edition published in February 1998, p. 115. This record is a strong negation of the so-called "free entry and exit allowed after February 25" in the second report of the "Nanjing Class" of the Japanese secret service organization.

[13] Shūdō Higashinakano himself said: "Nanjing is surrounded by huge city walls so it is actually impossible to walk into or outside the city".(The Thorough Examination of "Nanjing Massacre", written by 東中野修道, p. 291.) 东中野 said this to prove the dilemma that "the China Area Army lurking in the safety zone could not escape outside the city when Nanjing conducted population registration and issuing civilian cards, at this time, it was necessary to protect the Japanese Army so he forgot another argument—"increase" theory, this is another example of 东中野's taking opinions first and then the facts.

International Committee record more people than before? I think there were only four possibilities: I. The previous estimate was incorrect but latter it had been revised. II. The International Committee mentioned this in the letter mainly to seek food supply,[14] the residents in the safety zone who did not rely on assistance became the hungry residents after one month; III. The situation of the area within the Nanjing city and outside the safety zone was too bad, those people who did not leave their home because of fluke previously had to come to the safety zone to seek shelter. IV. The supply of the safety zone depended on the Japanese army while the performance of the Japanese army could not be trusted; therefore, the International Committee intended to report more people. Among these possibilities, the first three were more possible.

The "250,000 people" said by The Thorough Examination of "Nanjing Massacre" was not the original number of No. 41 Document. The original number of No. 41 Document was "250,000 people to 300,000 people". In theory, "300,000 people" "increased" more and could better show that "there was so slaughter", The Thorough Examination of "Nanjing Massacre" did not take the upper number but chose the low number of "250,000", which indeed had some intentions. Because the purpose of The Thorough Examination of "Nanjing Massacre" was to prove that the people in the Nanjing city only increased and the key lied in the more people, therefore, although the more the better, if there were too many, people would doubt the possibility. Thus, it would be better to be prudent and the lower number was taken. And the reason why it didn't take the original number was that the 50,000 people between "250,000 people and 300,000 people" was too large and it was easy to leave behind the impression that the figure was just a rough estimate, which was not conducive to the conclusion that "there was no slaughter".

To sum up, *The Thorough Examination of "Nanjing Massacre"* attempted to negate the slaughter on the basis that the population in Nanjing didn't decrease and even increased, and that was totally untenable.

---

[14] H.J.ティンパーリ―編「戦争とはなにか. 第十九号文書」(即徐淑希編《南京安全区檔案·第四十一号文書》), 洞富雄編『日中戦争史資料』9「南京事件」II, 第142 144页.

There "Should Have Been No" Civilians Outside the Safety Zone

The Thorough Examination of "Nanjing Massacre" mentioned that "outside the safety zone, everyone was banned from going out on December 8th. In the dangerous period after the fall of Nanjing, there should be no civilians outside the safety zone to the safe area that may become a battlefield". The author takes the testimony of Yasumura Junnitu as an example to analyze detailedly and refutes the statement "outside the safety zone, there is no citizen".

The Thorough Examination of "Nanjing Massacre" quotes the testimony of the military painter 住谷盤根 and the diaries of Colonel Yasuyama Koudou, the Surgeon General of the third fleet to prove that there was nobody outside the safety zone(the so-called "silence"), and it was as silent as a "dead street". But as Tōichi Sasaki(the Brigade Major of the 30th brigade of the 16th Division, major general) said in his diary on December 14th about the left "lurking" soldiers, when he recorded the sweeping in the city: "Those who didn't obey and resisted would be killed immediately without mercy, <u>gun shots were heard all day long everywhere</u>".[1] The 30th brigade commanded by Tōichi Sasaki was one of the main forces sweeping in the city and his records were fully reliable. Because there are various similar records including Tōichi Sasaki's diaries, it is not necessary to cite other evidences here. 住谷's testimony is a recollection after decades of years, which doesn't have the effect to negate the reliable records of that time. Overall, Yasuyama Koudou's diary is highly reliable, but he arrived in Nanjing in the afternoon of December 16th and left Nanjing in the morning of December 19th, and this period was when the Japanese army held "the ceremony of entering the city" (December 17th) and "Sacrifices of God" (December 18),

---

[1] 「佐佐木到一少!私記」, *Documents on the Battle of Nanjing*, compiled by Battle of Nanking Editorial Committee, p. 379.

and a large number of Japanese dignitaries headed by Iwane Matsui were in Nanjing, so it was not strange that the Nanjing city was relatively "quiet". Moreover, when Yasuyama Koudou arrived in Nanjing, in addition to participating in the Japanese ceremony, he also visited many places of interest outside the city, such as Dr. Sun Yat-sen's Mausoleum and Ming Xiaoling Mausoleum, and he only drove to some limited places in the urban area; moreover, his words "totally a dead city" on December 19th quoted by *The Thorough Examination of "Nanjing Massacre"* were his feelings of looking out on the river.[2] Moreover, what is more important, the Japanese army conducted successive dragnet sweeping after they entered the city on December 13th for the ceremony of entering the city on December 17 and especially for the "safety" of Lieutenant General Prince Yasuhiko Asaka—"gunshots were heard all day long everywhere" came from this and so it was not strange that Nanjing had become a "dead city" when Yasuyama Koudou arrived in Nanjing.

The Thorough Examination of "Nanjing Massacre" also quoted the letter sent to the Japanese Consulate General of Japan by the International Committee on December 17th: "When your troops entered Nanjing on December 13th, all civilians were almost all crowded in the refugee area", and it also said Euphemistically:

> Moreover, "outside" the safety zone, everyone was banned going out on December 8th. Of course, in the dangerous period after the fall of Nanjing, there should be no civilians "outside" the safety zone to the safe area that may become a battlefield. The testimony of the Japanese soldiers that they didn't see the civilians when the Nanjing fell was totally reliable.
>
> Therefore, if someone was "outside" the safety zone, he should not be a civilian but a soldier. Moreover, if there was a corpse "outside" the safety zone, it was not a corpse of a civilian but a corpse of a soldier.[3]

Whether there were any civilians outside the safety zone can be proved by the statements of the victims collected by the following kinds of data sets that are easy to see nowadays and a large number of cases of the victims outside the safety zone recounted by others. Here, I would like to cite the testimony of one witness recently as the evidence. The 38th Regiment of the 16th Division of the infantry was responsible for the sweeping of the northeast area of Nanjing (the triangle area of the northeast of the safety zone and the area west of Xuanwu Lake), Yasumura Junichi, the 3rd company of machine gun of the 38th Regiment, said:

---

[2] "The anchor was lifted at 9 o'clock in the morning and went into the river. Nanjing has completely become a dead city viewed from the river." Yasuyama Koudou「上海戦従軍日誌」, *Documents on the Battle of Nanjing*, compiled by Battle of Nanking Editorial Committee, p. 532.

[3] *The Thorough Examination of "Nanjing Massacre"*, written by Shūdō Higashinakano, pp. 191, 192.

On the next day of the fall of Nanjing, the raids were also conducted within the city. The operation was carried out by small units, all of the soldiers of the 3rd company of machine gun took part. There were still enemies the next day and they still held weapons. Their weapons were mainly rifles. Those people with guns would hide somewhere, and they would arrest and handed over to the captive troops if they went out. There were captive troops everyone and all the captives were gathered together. Someone were tied up with ropes and taken there. They were all sent to the rear troops but in fact I don't know the places where they would be sent because we didn't deal with the prisoners.

<u>Raids were carried out everyday.</u> (soldier or civilian) is not clear. As long as they were seen, they would be taken away, no matter they were men or women. Women would also resist and they were very resistant.

The troops dealing with (captives) were different ones and I haven't seen them. The captives would be taken outside the city. After that, they would be dealt with by the captive troops,[4] we can't imagine how they would be dealt with. Dead or alive, probably they would not get some good results. As their troops have nothing to do with me, so dead or alive……

I am only responsible for killing the enemy in the battle and I never heard of captives being executed in large numbers even after the war. The Nanjing Massacre is totally nonsense. That's my opinion. There is no reason that 300000 people have died.

I didn't kill people like that, shooting about ten or twenty people with machine guns. That's not an ordinary way to kill. It is probably gathering Chinese people together and opened fire at once. I've never done anything like this. When the raids are carried out, ten or twenty people are gathering together and they are killed by machine guns, this has happened. The number of dead people published by the General Staff Office was 84000, which was probably a mistake. There was a repetition number which was published by the regiment. I do not believe as much as I want others to believe in the number of dead people in the report. (Because it was published by the army) of course I would not negate.[5]

---

[4] For the facts about the slaughter of Chinese prisoners committed by the Japanese army, please refer to the article Is the Nanjing Massacre a fabrication of the Tokyo Trial?—Fifth, Beijing, The Study of Modern History, No. 6, 2002; for the top-down order of the massacre, please refer to The Study of the Japanese Massacre Order, Beijing, Historical Studies, No. 6, 2002; for symbolic cases of the massacre, please refer to my article Again on "The 100-man Killing Contest", Nanjing, Jiangsu Social Sciences, No. 6, 2002.

[5] 安村純一口述「兵士と　思ったら、男も　女も　若いのはみんな引っ張った」, 松岡環編著『南京戦―――閉ざされた記憶を尋ねて』, 東京, 社会評論社, the 1st edition published on August 15, 2002, pp. 186, 187. The Chinese translation of this book will be published by Shanghai Lexicographical Publishing House. Japanese scholar Tsuda Michio recently wrote an article to affirm the "precious value" of this book and at the same time pointed out that because the book "does not see essential self-reflection", "let Chinese readers read such a book, as a Japanese, I cannot help feeling shudder." (津田道夫著「歴史の真実―――松岡環編著『南京戦―――閉ざされた記憶を尋ねて』読む」, 東京, 『図書新聞』, the 2nd edition published on October 12, 2002.)

From Yasumura's dictation, we can see that Yasumura and his companions arrested everyone they saw, although they defended for themselves that they "didn't know" whether these people were soldiers or civilians—in fact, they of course knew, because these women[6] couldn't be soldiers—but anyway, they dared not to say that there were no civilians outside the safety zone. Yasumura, the party concerned, only dared to say "didn't know", why did Higashi-Nakano say repeatedly that "there shouldn't be"? The reliability of Yasumura's statement lies in his negative attitude toward the Nanjing Massacre, since he emphasized that the Nanjing Massacre was a "nonsense", he would certainly not add suspicion to the Japanese army. The 1st and 3rd Battalion of the 38th Regiment took part in the sweeping of this area, each battalion included four companies and one company of machine gun, one small mortar team, each company included three small teams and one small team included six squads, the "small team" said by Yasumura should be the team smaller than company and even smaller, that is to say, at that time, in the small triangle area northeast of the safety zone and west of Xuanwu Lake, there were dozens of hundreds "small teams" engaged in operations. If the situation Yasumura met was quite common at that time, every small team sent a large number of captives to the "captive troops", and the small batch of "ten or twenty people" were either handed over or executed on the spot, how many civilians were killed for no reason in this area alone?

As for the statement that the corpses can't be divided outside or inside the safety zone, it is of course right and there is no need to argue because even if there were no civilians outside the safety zone, the fact that the victims were constantly brought out of the safety zone can be proved by many public or private Chinese or foreign records such as that of the International Committee.

---

[6] 山田忠义, who also belonged to the 3rd company of machine gun of the 38th regiment, said: "There are corpses everywhere in the city, many of which are women". 「捕虜に食わす物がないので処分せざるをえず」, 松岡環編著『南京戦―――閉ざされた記憶を尋ねて』, p. 190.

The Japanese Army's Sex Atrocities Cannot Be Denied Even If Victims Have Never Accused

After the Japanese army occupied Nanjing, a large-scale rape happened. Guo Qi, who later moved to Taiwan with the army and served as a military instructor at National Taiwan University, was then a battalion major of the army guarding Nanjing when the Japanese army attacked Nanjing, he had been trapped in the city for three months and after fleeing, he wrote the famous *Records of the Blood and Tears of the Fallen Capital*, which was published in the Xijing Daily. It says:

> Since ancient times, there has been a difference between men and women in China and we attach great importance to ethics. Woman's chastity is more important than anything. Our country pays more importance to the courtesy than any other country. However, wherever the beast soldiers went, everything was destroyed, I don't know whether their country is the world of man or the world of beasts!
>
> ……This kind of rape is more hated by the common people than any burning and looting. The Japanese have given a course to awaken the public in China this time, and we can say that the Chinese would not be thoroughly awakened without this course![1]

Because rape does special harm to woman's body and mind, and because Chinese people are particularly sensitive to "chastity" and "ethics", the "rape" is mostly hated by the Chinese people.

On the basis of relevant evidence, the Tokyo Trial found that the Japanese army committed as many as 20,000 sexual crimes in Nanjing. Some people in Japan expressed their dissatisfaction with the finding during the Tokyo Trial

---

[1] Recited from *Historical Materials of the Nanjing Massacre Made by Japanese Invaders*, which was compiled by 同书编委会, Nanjing Library, Jiangsu Ancient Books Publishing House, the 5th edition published in February 1998, pp. 8, 14.

and they thought that the finding was fabricated against the Japanese army. For example, Colonel WAKISAKA Jiro, the regime major of the 36th regime of the 9th Division which took part in attacking Nanjing, claimed that the Japanese army had committed no crime against Nanjing when he was testifying in court at the Tokyo Trial; NAKASAWA Mitsuo, Chief of Staff of the 16th Division, said when testifying in court:

> The planned rape carried out by the Japanese Army in Nanjing is totally untrue. We had some soldiers committed crimes, but all these actions have been punished by the law.[2]

In recent years, the "fictionalists"'s negation of the Japanese army's rape has inherited this caliber but has also developed. Documents of the Nanking Safety zone compiled by Xu Shuxi said in No. 192 case that the Japanese army came to Jinling University to ask for women, on January 16th, "there was no one willing to go", the Japanese army returned the next day and took away seven women, Bates was at the scene and he watched the process, "understand that it was an action based entirely on free will, one of the women went there out of her own will".[3] The Japanese army deduced from this that the Japanese army did not rape, for example, *The Alleged Nanking Massacre* said:

> Was it really a rape?
> Instead, this scene should be regarded as that the Chinese known to the Japanese, recruit women who were willing to prostitute themselves at the shelter set up in the Jinling Woman's College of Arts and Science in the safety zone, and these women went to prostitute themselves "happily". Bates mistook this consensual prostitution for organized rape.[4]

It was noted that the quotation of *The Alleged Nanking Massacre* was from the *Data Set* compiled by Tomio Hora, while the *Data Set* recorded "a young

---

[2] *Records of the History of War between Japan and China 8 Nanjing Incident*, compiled by Hora Tomio, p. 245.

[3] Data Set on the Nanjing Disputed between Japan and China, Volume II, "English Material Set", compiled by Hora Tomio, Tokyo, 青木書店, the 2nd edition published on November 15th, 1986, p. 182. Selected Archives of Japanese Imperialist Invasion of China· Nanjing Massacre (co-compiled by The State Archives Administration of the People's Republic of China, Secondary Historical Archives of China and Jilin Academy of Social Sciences, p. 122), the same sentence is not recorded in Historical Materials of the Nanjing Massacre Made by Japanese Invaders (compiled by Editorial Committee of Historical Materials of Nanjing Massacre Made by Japanese's Invaders, Nanjing Library, Jiangsu Ancient Books Publishing House, the 5th edition published in February 1998, p. 373).

[4] 『再審「南京大虐殺」————世界に訴える 日本の冤罪』, compiled by International Committee of the Japan Conference, 東京, 明成社, the 2nd edition published on November 25th, 2000, p. 86.

woman went there out of her own will", *The Alleged Nanking Massacre* strengthened it as "a young woman went there happily". "Out of her own will" and "happily" have the same aspects because they both showed a positive attitude, but "out of her own will" could be self-sacrifice and "happily" was just a willingness to do it, the two were totally different. From the whole tendency of *The Alleged Nanking Massacre*, it was not an accidental mistake that this book changed the original meaning.

The Study of Nanjing Atrocities believes that rape is a part of the "anti-Japanese disruption" conducted by Chinese senior military officials lurking in the safety zone, and it says:

> Put these materials together, the truth of the matter can be clearly seen in general. The actual situation of "rape" accused by the Chinese, which is unknown to the witnesses and recorders, is in fact a scam of "the Japanese soldiers" played by the Chinese, and the possibility can be said to be infinite.[5] (It is from the original text—the citer)

This kind of "voluntary" theory, "scam theory" has been previously put forward by *The Thorough Examination of "Nanjing Massacre"*,[6] and has become a "consensus" among the "fictionalists". And in recent years, the fictionalists have even emphasized that if there is a large-scale rape, there should be a large number of mixed-blood children. However, there are no such mixed-blooded children in Nanjing, so there is no evidence to prove the existence of Nanjing, for example, Big Questions about the Nanjing Massacre said:

> The most incredible thing is that 20,000 cases of rape are believed to happen, and after one year, and even now, there are no reports of mixed-blood children. There are no rumors or private letters and other documents related to mixed-blood children.
> ......
> According to the School of Slaughter, at that time the men in Nanjing were either killed or enslaved by the Japanese Army, and those born in Nanjing around October 1938 were supposed to be mixed-blood children with the Japanese soldiers. But the mixed-blood children left by the Japanese Army in the south(refers to the South East Asia—the citer) has become a problem, and in Nanjing as well as other parts of the mainland that are long time occupied by the Japanese Army, no such children were born.
> Today, people who advocate the Japanese sexual violence against women, including the Japanese themselves, do not pay attention to this strange

---

[5] 藤岡信勝、Shūdō Higashinakano 著『ザ・レイプ・オブ・南京の研究―――中国における「情報戦」の手口と戦略』, 東京, 祥傳社, the 1st edition published on September 10th, 1999, p. 169.

[6] Shūdō Higashinakano 著『「南京虐殺」の徹底検証』第十二章「南京安全地帯の記録」, 東京, 展転社, the 4th edition published on July 8th, 2000, pp. 257, 282.

phenomenon. Moreover, even if the pregnant women had abortions, the underground doctors should be a lot, but we never heard something about this.[7]

Such an argument, in the words of the major force of the School of Slaughter, "is a double and triple harm to the slain Chinese women and a serious harm to the reputation of the Chinese people".[8] This harm is like blasphemy, which can best arouse anger and accumulate hatred. The reason why the Japanese fictionalists dare to challenge in this most sensitive place and never care about the feelings of the victims is based on their standing, but their own reason is the so-called all events are "accumulation of rumors".[9] Therefore, although the basis for peaceful discussion with the fictionalists no longer exists, I do not think it is absolutely unnecessary to give an answer to the general readers in Japan.

Sexual violence is the most difficult to recover among the Japanese atrocities. Chinese people attach great importance to "rightness" all the time and they would sacrifice their lives for rightness at big joints, even if some Chinese people "pretend to betray China" and endure humiliation, they will inevitably be branded as traitors and national thieves. This is completely different from Japan, even if in wartime, there is no such expression as "Japanese traitor". Although there is indeed a word "traitor", it is not a common word and its tone is not as strong as that of Chinese. When "rightness" turns into the obligation of women, it means the heavier "chastity" that is "higher above all" said by Guo Qi. This is also completely different from Japan, where a considerable number of women are willing to go with the army to "comfort" them in the wartime and the pressure of engaging in sex profession is not as great as that of China in peacetime. Therefore, in China, if a woman is raped, especially by a "beast soldier", her whole life is almost ruined, even if she doesn't choose to kill herself, she can only cry and swallow the bitterness by herself, and it is very difficult for her to complain in public. Just for this reason, informing the Japanese army of rape is like discussing with a tiger to peel off its skin, even after the war, there are few people coming out to redress their

---

[7]松村俊夫著『「南京虐殺」への大疑問』, 東京, 展転社, the 1st edition published on December 13th, 1998, pp. 185 and 186. According to *Nanjing Municipal Survey* of Nanjing Secret Service Organization, in 1939, 723 corpses were buried, including 152 male corpses, 45 female corpses and 526 children's corpses (recited from *Research on the Number of Bodies of Compatriots Buried by the Puppet Regime in Nanjing* written by Cao Bihong, *The Symposium on the Latest Research Achievements in the History of the Nanjing Massacre made by Japanese Invaders in China*, compiled by Zhu Chengshan, the 1st edition published in April 2001, p. 84). It is worth noting that the proportion of dead children is so high. I think it is related to the mass rape made by the Japanese army. China's concept of chastity would not allow the consequences of enemy's rape to survive; therefore, these dead children should be abandoned babies.

[8]笠原十九司著『妄想が産み出した「反日攪乱工作隊」説』, compiled by Nankin jiken chōsa kenkyūkai, p. 217.

[9]田中正明著『「南京虐殺」の虚構———松井大!の日記をめぐって』「伝聞の 集積」, 東京, 日本教文社, the 1st edition published on June 25th, 1984, pp. 28, 30.

grievances under their real names.[10] This is also "one of the reasons" why the westerners in Nanjing did not use their real names when they submitted the rape cases to the Consulate General of Japan.

On the other hand, because "rape" is a special matter of "shameless", it is also nominally rejected by the military rules of the Japanese army. For example, major general Iinuma Mamoru, Chief of Staff of the Shanghai Expeditionary Army, repeatedly expressed his "great indignation" about the rape and other matters in his diary,[11] Colonel Toshimichi Uemura, Deputy Chief of Staff of the Shanghai Expeditionary Army, felt "very regretful" for the fact that lieutenant Nakano of the 33rd Regiment lead others to rape,[12] Senior General Shunroku Hata, the successor of Senior General Iwane Matsui the Commander of "Japanese Central China Area Army", said in his diary that the rape happened in Nanjing is "very abominable act".[13] Even at the grassroots level, the situation is the same. For example, Private First Class soldier of the 1st company of the 7th Regiment of the infantry recorded the commandment of the "village leader" in his diary on December 19th: "We should be especially prudent to the shameless behaviors such as arson and rape".[14] Among all the crimes, rape is the most difficult to talk about. Killing can often be "complacency words" (Japanese words and are close to Chinese); Robbery, since the acquiescence of "conscription",[15] have not only

---

[10] According to the investigation conducted by Nationalist Government after the war, most of those identified by their families, neighbors and other witnesses were dead or missing, and a very small number of victims who reported themselves had all their families or male families killed or missing, and all their situation was very difficult. For example, Xu Hong, who lived in Dabaihua Lane in Nanjing, tried to jump in a well to kill herself after being raped but failed, and later, all her families were killed except for her 70-year-old mother and her daughter who also jumped in a well. They then lived in "a very shameful and difficult life" and so they dared to come out to clear the "national shame and family feud". *Archives of Japanese Imperialist Invasion of China*, compiled by Secondary Historical Archives of China, Nanjing Archives, p. 354.

[11] As stated on January 14 after the military police arrested the officer who broke the law, *Iinuma Mamoru's Diary, Documents on the Battle of Nanjing*, compiled by Battle of Nanking Editorial Committee, p. 237.

[12] 「上村利道日記」, *Documents on the Battle of Nanjing*, compiled by Battle of Nanking Editorial Committee, p. 292.

[13] 「陸軍大!畑俊六日誌」, *Documents on the Battle of Nanjing*, compiled by Battle of Nanking Editorial Committee, p. 52.

[14] 水谷莊著「戦塵」, *Documents on the Battle of Nanjing*, compiled by Battle of Nanking Editorial Committee, p. 503.

[15] After the war in Shanghai, the Japanese Army marched to Nanjing but because of the "rapid progress", supplies could not keep up with the army. Iwane Matsui would record this in his diary, for example, he recorded On November 8th, the supplies could be provided to the 10th Army were only enough for "a few days" and was caught in a "difficult situation". Therefore, the Japanese army basically relied on the "requisition" on the spot, and he recorded on November 18th, they "don't need to worry about the food" because they occupied Taicang and other places. 「松井石根大!戦陣日記」, *Documents on the Battle of Nanjing*, compiled by Battle of Nanking Editorial Committee, pp. 5, 8.

been namely rejected by the military rules, but also become a very common phenomenon; therefore, in the records of the Japanese armies and officials, rape leaves the least trace.

Because of these two reasons, it is impossible to fully recreate the Japanese sexual atrocities through existing materials and it is also extremely difficult to roughly describe the sexual atrocities.

Only Truth Has Power

A few days ago, I received a call from Zhang Lianhong, director of the Nanjing Massacre Research Center of Nanjing Normal University, he praised the film *Nanjing* a lot and thought the film had achieved quite outstanding results among the films with similar themes. Just a few days ago, one of my friend who was concerned about the Nanjing Massacre talked about the film *Nanjing Nightmare,* which was also made by Americans, he said that there were various mistakes in this film and referred to some hot debates between the two sides online. The affirmative side thinks that the film's "stance" is correct and the rest doesn't have to be discussed since its main idea is correct; and the negative side believes that if the historical records are not correct, it will only give an excuse to others—such as the Japanese right-wing groups. As I haven't watched these two films, I can't judge them now. But from this point, I think although the topic regarding which one is more important between "correct" and "truth" when dealing with the special historical events that cannot be separated from our emotions, values and "beliefs" is a cliché, it can still be discussed.

Ni Zhengyu, who participated in the Tokyo Trial, wrote the *Standing in the Hague Calmly* in his late years, in which he cited such an example when he wrote about the fact that it was difficult for Chinese Procuratorate to comply because of the strict requirements for evidence: "When Qin Dechun, the then Vice Minister of the Ministry of National Defense of Nationalist Government, testified in court, he said that the Japanese Army 'set fire everywhere and did everything bad', his words were regarded as groundless and he was almost bombarded". Qin Dechun's enthusiasm in condemning the Japanese army was conceivable, but as Ni Zhengyu said, the "empty words have no basis", even if we do not call these words harmful and useless, they have no benefits to the trial. If we say that it was in chaotic times when Qin appeared in court and it was understandable that collecting evidence was

© The Author(s) 2020
Z. Cheng, *The Nanjing Massacre and Sino-Japanese Relations,*
https://doi.org/10.1007/978-981-15-7887-8_25

difficult. Today, I am afraid that we cannot be successful if we only rely on "righteous indignation".

Over the years, when I carefully read the relevant works of the Japanese right-wing groups (I mean all those who negate Japanese atrocities, and the Japanese do not use the name in this way), I have a prominent feeling that in addition to the limited dissemination, one of the reasons why a large number of our criticisms failed to clarify the facts and failed to "awaken" the majority of Japanese civilians was that most of our criticisms were based on "opinions" and didn't pay enough attention to the evidence—It doesn't mean that we do not use evidence, it is about the evidence itself, for example, what is the exact meaning of one document, and what can it prove? To what extent can it prove? What is the meaning of one whole article? Does a passage extracted coincide with the spirit of the whole article? Is the material itself reliable? Especially the authenticity of some oral records, for example, is it possible that the interview environment is fake? Does the interviewer have any guidance or hint to the interviewee? Is what the interviewee said in line with the reality? If measured by the yardstick of history, these materials cannot be said to have been strictly inspected. So even if your sense of criticism is high-spirited, outsiders (such as some Western scholars) can't help but think that people can have different attitudes toward these materials.

The Japanese right-wing groups have made a fuss about the image materials about the Nanjing Massacre, and a reprinted special book *Examine the Photos of Evidence of the Nanjing Incident* published the year before last claims that none of the 143 relevant photos is true. After the publication of this book, I heard a refutation to this book at a meeting, which gave people the impression that the refutation was justified and commendable. But from another point of view, when the case is investigated with "reasoning", it is difficult to "refute". Recently, I received a long article *The War between Japan and China Witnessed by Cameras* written by a high school teacher Watanabe Kushi (serialized in the quarterly journal). In this article, it "checked" every example listed by *The Examination*. And the method of verification is very simple, that is, to seek historical source of the original version and refer to the relevant text and image in order to restore its original appearance. I cite an example here. *The Examination* claims a photo fake on the grounds that the Japanese military uniform in the photo doesn't have epaulets, so it asserts that it was a "forgery" created by China. When Watanabe searched for photos of the incident, he found that in the *China Incident Pictorial* published by Osaka Daily News Agency on October 21, 1937, there was a photo named "A toast to the commander of the Tanaka who occupied the radio station", the Japanese military uniform also had no epaulets. Having this contrast, what is said in *The Examination* can be destroyed without attack. But Watanabe didn't stop here. He also found in the documents that deputy officer of Ministry of the Army Yoshijirō Umezu issued a notice on August 29 the same year, stating clear that all troops could remove their epaulets in order to "defend against espionage". With the Yoshijirō Umezu's statement, there is no doubt about the case. There is neither high-pitched momentum nor fancy words in Watanabe's writings, but after reading it in one breath, I can't help but feel the power of being steady. As the saying goes, "facts speak louder than words", I think the most powerful response to the Japanese right-wing group's challenge is to speak with reliable evidence.

(Originally published on Xinmin Evening News, September 2, 2007)

Afterword

At the Shanghai Book Fair this summer, a young reader took a hardcover of *The Nanjing Massacre Research—Criticism of Japanese Fiction School* and asked for my signature. The book was hastily compiled on the 65th anniversary of the Nanjing Massacre in 2002. At that time, two versions were printed and few hardcovers were available. Both versions were out of stock for a long time. Over the years, there have been several requests for reprints. Yu Lan, one of the editors of the first edition, also told me the wish of buying the copyright by a Japanese publishing house. Since the original compilation is only part of my plan and I always want to finish the whole plan someday unhurriedly, there has been no plan to reprint it. Editor Cui Xia, who was also at the Book Fair that day, said that "this year is the 80th anniversary of the Nanjing Massacre and how about publishing a new edition?" I believed it was a good idea. After a small discussion, the publication schedule for the 80th anniversary edition was confirmed on the spot. The purpose of explaining the motive of this edition is to show that the book is also a "temporary" compilation and not a mature achievement.

The dispute of the Nanjing Massacre in Japan is discussed in detail in my article "*Issues concerning the Nanjing Massacre Studies*", which is inappropriate to elaborate in the afterword and thus omitted here. However, I still want to make a brief explanation of one point. Not long ago, at a seminar, when talking about Japan's "fabrication school", a Japanese scholar said that "Japan's mainstream academia has not denied the Nanjing Massacre" and "Japan's mainstream historical journals have not issued articles denying the Nanjing Massacre", which implied that our criticism was aimless and fruitless. This is not the first time I have heard such words in public seminars, so I did not hesitate to say what I did not have to say on the spot which embarrassed both the speaker and the listeners. The main points are as follows: First, we criticized Japan's fabrication school instead of the "Japan's mainstream academia"; second, since the 1990s, the most active fictionalists are university professors including "professors of Tokyo University" instead of folk writers outside the "mainstream academia"; third, apart from a few people, such as the late senior scholars Hora Tomio (former professor of the Waseda University), Akira Fujiwara (former professor of the Hitotsubashi University) and the junior scholars Kasahara Tokushi (former professor of the Tsuru University), the Japanese "mainstream scholars" who claimed not to deny the Nanjing Massacre have not made any criticism of the claims of the fictionalists, nor have they made even little analysis of the so-called evidence put forward by the fictionalists; and fourth, it is true that Japan's "mainstream historical journals" have not published articles denying the Nanjing Massacre, but they have also not published articles refuting the fabrication school, let alone articles affirming that the Nanjing Massacre is true. It is true that a scholar, whether he is in the "mainstream academia" or not, can do whatever he wants, which is entirely personal freedom. Moreover, we don't have to pay any attention to the connection between the indifference of "Japan's mainstream academia" and the rampant spread of fictionalists' claims in Japan. However, once the fabrication school was criticized, there were words "Japan's mainstream academia did not deny it" and it was the "Japan's mainstream academia" that kept resisting it and was reluctant to face the explicit revelation of Japanese atrocities in Nanjing. In light of this, this book, which was published again today under its former name 15 years ago, still has an uncovered value, albeit limited. (Domestic research on the Nanjing Massacre has made remarkable progress in recent years in both breadth and depth, but there is no purposeful criticism of the fiction school.)

Compared with the old edition, the new one has great additions and deletions. The new edition deletes some articles in the original edition, such as the most voluminous article "Comments on the Works of the Japan's Fabrication School" (more than 130 pages), "Objections and Reflections on Nanjing Atrocities" in "Essays and Miscellaneous Notes" and "Chronicles of Events" and "Compiled Tables for Japanese Attacks on Nanjing" as the background in the appendixes. The new edition adds "*An Analysis of the Annual Report of the Japanese Nanjing Society*", "A Study of the Bearing and Discipline of the Japanese Army Invading China: Centered on The Tenth Army", "Re-evaluation of Iwane Matsui' s War Guilt", "Re-examination of Ogawa Sekijiro's Testimony", "Ogawa Kanjiro and the Diary of A Military Justice Officer", "*Issues concerning the Nanjing Massacre Studies*", "*An Introduction to Japan's Existing Historical Material on the Nanjing Massacre*", "*Postscript of Japan's Existing Historical Material on the Nanjing Massacre*" and the short essay "Truth has Power". Since nearly seventy percent of the content is new, it can be said as a new book.

Asking someone to write a preface is tantamount to asking for complement, which is the most embarrassing thing. Cui Xia asked me if I could ask two representative colleagues to write prefaces. I have no option but to bother Mr. Sun Zhaiwei, who has studied the Nanjing Massacre for the longest time among Chinese scholars, and Curator Zhang Jianjun, who is busy with taking charge of the Memorial Hall of the Victims in Nanjing Massacre by Japanese Invaders and the Research Institute. I sincerely give gratitude and thanks to them! Thanks go to managing editors Cui Xia and Feng Yuan who forced themselves to read through this dull manuscript and to Chen Lina who also worked hard to compile the index. During the new compilation, the former edition was found out and I noticed that there was no mention of the editors' hard work but only the process of finishing the book in the Afterword. Apart from their hard work, there will not be this new compilation without the sincere help of the managing editors Mr. Xu Zhongyi and Mr. Yu Lan. It also occurred to me that most articles in this edition were mostly published in *Modern Chinese History Studies*. The main reviewer, Mr. Du Chengjun (Jidong) and the editor-in-chief Mr. Xu Xiuli, also put forward valuable suggestions then, which still makes me feel moved and grateful.

Cheng Zhaoqi
October 10th, 2017

Besides, on the eve of the publication, Cui Xia once again stated that the issues discussed in this book came from overseas, and she advised me to invite two Japanese and Western scholars to make a brief review on the back cover. The editor spares no effort to promote my work and I cannot fail to live up to the good intentions even if I feel a little bit embarrassed… Among Western scholars, Mr. Yang Daqing, who organized the first discussion of Nanjing Massacre in the United States and has been paying close attention to relevant research in China, Japan and the United States for many years, has a last say. Among the living Japanese scholars, Mr. Hata Ikuhiko, an expert and senior scholar of the Sino-Japanese War history who wrote *The Nanjing Incident* that has the most copies and Mr. Kasahara Tokushi, a scholar who "specializes in" the Nanjing Massacre, would have been the most qualified people to make comments. However, although I have known them for a long time, and I have also received their masterpieces many times, I seldom contact with them. Therefore, I can only cite the comments in *After Reading Cheng Zhaoqi's Articles* of the late scholar Mr. Tsuda Michio, the author of *The Nanjing Massacre and Japanese Spiritual Structure*.[1] Thanks also go to him here.

---

[1] Mr. Tsuda once severely criticized "Japan's mainstream academia" for its following the footsteps of the fabrication school and replacing the "Nanjing Massacre" with the "Nanjing Incident". Mr. Kasahara Tokushi always fights in the front line—at present he is almost alone. Not inviting Mr. Kasahara may be due to certain reason and other people were not invited because they did not stick to the standpoint and were reluctant to face the diffuse claims of the fabrication school.

Appendix

Dissecting the Spiritual World of Japanese Without Fear— Comments After Reading *Nanjing Massacre and the Spiritual Structure of the Japanese*[1]

Even measured by the strictest standard of "freedom of speech", Japan is still regarded as a country with "complete freedom of speech". However, because there has never been a national reflection on war crime in Japan and because the Mikado-Worship, which was deeply rooted in the Japanese people after Meiji, was saved from liquidation with the preservation of the system of Japanese emperor, talking about the emperor's war crime in Japan is still an "obstruction" (タブー). Tsuda Michio's *Nanjing Massacre and the Spiritual Structure of the Japanese* raises a very strict with the emperor; he says in the postscript:

> It is true that the emperor didn't directly lead the massacre and give the order to kill captives, but he was the only head of the Empire of Japan and also the "Generalissimo" of the army and navy of the Empire. After the Mukden Incident, the general name of the Japanese army changed from "national army" to "imperial army" and the war of aggression against China was carried out as a "Jihad" in the name of the emperor. This policy of "Jihad" complements the sense of contempt for China, dispels the sense of guilt and rationalizes all acts of cruelty. Therefore, there is no doubt that the emperor must at least bear the highest moral responsibility for the Nanjing Atrocities. (アトロシティーズ)

---

[1] *Nanjing Massacre and the Spiritual Structure of the Japanese*, translated by Cheng Zhaoqi and Liu Yan, The Commercial Press (Hong Kong) Limited, the 1st edition published in June 2000.

In a country where popular thinking is becoming increasingly fascist (author's words) and faced with rolling turbid current, if an author can make resistance efforts and keep a tough attitude, I think he or she should be paid special respect. This is also one of the main reasons why I translated and introduced this book to my countrymen and wrote this article.

This book shows no leniency to the emperor and repeatedly emphasizes his unshakable responsibility for war, but the purpose of this book is not to criticize the emperor or the wartime rulers, as the title shows, it is not satisfied with simple criticism—if the Japanese are regarded as one part, it can be self-criticism—it is also not satisfied with the general "historical" analysis; instead, "from outside to the inside", it explores human roots of atrocities from the "spiritual structure" of the Japanese public. As the author said: "My question is, why the Japanese commoners, such as 'kind laborers', 'fathers of ordinary families', 'well-mannered people' in their daily life, would become so brutal in the battlefield in China. I think it is not enough to explain the phenomenon with the reasons such as "abnormal psychology", to revenge through the incident, to revenge for the comrade-in-arms who died in the war. I think it is related to the 'special spiritual structure of the Japanese public'".

The book has a detailed discussion and analysis of the "spiritual structure" of the Japanese public; I can only give a general summary here.

The Calculation and Nihilism of the Commoners

The "Nanjing Massacre" is usually called "Nanjing Atrocities" by the Japanese. Hora Tomio, Akira Fujiwara and others call it "Nanjing Atrocities Incident" or directly use the transliteration アトロシティーズ, which is the match version of Nanking Atrocities. *The Spiritual Structure* also uses "Nanjing Atrocities" or アトロシティーズ a lot. Because what happened in Nanjing was not only a slaughter, but also included rape, plunder and other acts of cruelty; therefore, "atrocities" are indeed more summarized than "massacre". To explain the consciousness of the maker of the "atrocities", so far, the Japanese academic circles have mostly taken the perspective of "battlefield psychology" or the so-called "abnormal psychology" of the battlefield. In this regard, the author doesn't deny it, but thinks the various aspects of the "Nanking Atrocities" cannot be explained just by "battlefield psychology" and "abnormal psychology". The author thinks that the Japanese public already have the sadistic embryos in the thought of an sich, so they had such sadistic behaviors in the desperate experience of the front line of the war of aggression and could still happily talk with complacency attitudes ("tegarabanashi") about the atrocities after they returned to the rear and became "kind labors", "fathers of ordinary families" "well-mannered people" again. Wataru Kaji, who worked in Political Design Committee of the Nationalist Government when he fled to China in wartime, recorded one of his colleagues in Tokyo Police Station as early as in 1938 in the preface he wrote for the Japanese version of the *War? The Records of the Japanese Atrocities* compiled by Timperley. The person was "surprisingly numb to the morality" but was also a "warrior" with "outstanding war achievements". Wataru Kaji said emotionally: "I can't help thinking about what the so-called 'warrior' is. I don't see any moral difference between the shameless nature of the man's normal words and behaviors and the boldness of his atrocities on the battlefield". In his eyes, both the good citizens of Tokyo and the residents in the mainland are the objects of brutality. It's because that the latter are the Chinese and are different from the ordinary people, so he can enjoy the pleasure of free disposal without legal restrictions on the battlefield.

Wataru Kaji was released on bail in October 1935. The author thinks that before the outbreak of Japan's full-scale war of aggression against China, Wataru Kaji had found a "bold basis for the loss of humanity in massacres on the battlefield" from the mental state showed in a "rascal"'s "shameless normal words and behaviors". The author further points out: In the Nanjing Atrocities Incident, not only such "rascals", but also the "good citizens of Tokyo" and even the male mass of the whole Japan appeared on the stage as the main body of cruelty.

Kōzaburō Tachibana, one of the pre-war right-wing leaders, heard the dialogue of "a group of simple countrymen": "'Anyway, it is better that the war between Japan and the United States start as soon as possible.' 'In that case, the situation will probably be better. But can we win? The United States is strong!' 'I don't know, but the Japanese Army is the strongest in the world.' 'Of course, it ranks number one in the world. But although our soldiers are the strongest in the world, our military funds can not catch up.' 'Hmm……' 'You can't fight with a hungry stomach.' 'Of course. But let's not care about the defeat or victory, we fight first. If we win, the victory belongs to us we can grab as much money as we want. If we lose, it's not a big deal to lose to such an opponent like the United States. It may be better to become a dependent country to the United States'".

Kōzaburō Tachibana "was at a loss when he heard about the dialogues among the simple countrymen". This matter is recorded on *The Original Meaning of Japanese Patriotic Innovation,* an illegal "underground" publication. It was published in the 7th Shōwa year, which was shortly after the Mukden Incident and the first Shanghai Incident. At that time, "Shōwa panic" was prevailing", the cities were full of the unemployed and the hardship of the countryside could be symbolized by "娘身売り" (selling daughters and hungry children). Under that situation, self-abandonment pervaded people who couldn't find the way out. And the above citation just appeared against that background. Therefore, although it was only an isolated case, it was a portrayal of the general state of mind of the people at that time.

Although what the "words of simple countrymen" showed was not self-conscious thought, the actual state of the public thought was usually not self-conscious. The dialogue of these countrymen fully demonstrated the sinking, helplessness, pragmatic thinking, snobbery and cunning of the

Japanese public in confusion at that time. The author summarizes this state of mind as "the calculation and nihilism of the commoners (ニヒリズム).[2] He believes that "under the Shōwa panic, nihilism has become an outlet for emotional venting and its pinnacle is the emergence of the parasitic ronin consciousness of using "army" and "war"".

The author quotes a lot wartime diaries ("diaries in the battlefield"), among which there are many contents of "seizing" trophies. If the idea of "robbing as much money as we want" from the United States was more or less the "simple old countrymen"'s joke word for spiritual venting, the "seizing" in the "diaries in the battlefield" was a real plunder and a plunder plan. The author believes that "the so-called 'jihad' policy of "punishing the Chinese" is hereby combined with the calculations of the commoners—the "seizure" and also the "plunder plan". "I don't think the 'jihad' policy can be separated from the real commoners' self (エゴ), that is to say, the slogan of "punishing the Chinese atrocities" is just the political formalization of the commoners' egoism (エゴイズム)". Moreover, behind the commoners' calculation is the shadow of mass nihilism.

Mass Nihilism and the Intellectual's Nihilism

The Japanese army showed extreme "cruelty" in Nanjing and even in China as a whole, and what is more special was that this kind of "cruelty" was often very "pointless". A large number of "diaries in the battlefield" have various records of it. The Chinese version of *The Diary of Azuma Shiro* published last year (1999),[3] for example, records a lot of arson and senseless killing just for relieving boredom. On December 4th, 1937, it recorded as follows: "Arson is really nothing to us these days and it is more interesting than children's playing with fire. 'Hey. It is cold today.' 'Then, let's burn a house to keep warm'". On March 23rd, 1938, it recorded: "There is an old man among the coolies". His appearance is cold and annoying. Private First-Class Aramaya said, "your face is disgusting. If you die, you will not be able to dangle around in front of me". After saying that, he quickly stabbed him with a knife. He may have stabbed the old man's lung, blood vomited from his mouth, and he struggled for a while, later he died. This kind of senseless killing Chinese non-combatants is called "irresponsible mass nihilism" by the author.

---

[2] Nihilism (ニヒリズム) is one of the key words used by the author to explain the state of mind of the Japanese public in his book. Its meaning is slightly different from that of the Chinese word and it mainly refers to the mental state of self-abandonment in an uncontrollable environment.

[3] This is the first publication of Shiro Azuma's "diaries in the battlefield". After 《わが南京プラトーン》, which was written on the basis of the diaries, was published by Aoyama Book Center in 1987, it was besieged by the right-wing groups of Japan. In recent years, the famous "Shiro Azuma trial" is a twist around this book. In this regard, it is still difficult to publish the diaries in Japan.

Different from the irrational nihilism of the commoners, the intellectual's nihilism shows complete self-consciousness. The author gives the example of Heisuke Sugiyama. Heisuke Sugiyama is a literary critic with the reputation of "social conscience". He traveled to North and Central China from October 1937 to January of the following year. In these years of the fall of Nanjing, he had a long conversation with a reporter from the Nanjing branch of the Asahi Shimbun. The situation at that time was recorded by Sugiyama in *China and the Chinese and the Japanese*. There are words like this: "I think that once the war begins, it will be all right to take any means to win and to ensure the outcome of the war. Under such circumstances, morality is not only powerless, but also incompetent. In the future war, it is impossible to distinguish between combatants and non-combatants in a strict sense. Rapid annihilation is also a kind of mercy. It's just that there are still technical problems here. Cruelty as a force must be used".

The author believes that "Sugiyama shows astonishingly active nihilism". As a man of knowledge, Sugiyama has full self-consciousness, and his "nihilism" has reached a terrifying degree.

In the same article, Sugiyama described the experience of an old "Chinese" woman who wept bitterly with her son's corpse in her arms. Sugiyama remarked with emotion: "Are people's troubles so empty? Even if everything in this world is empty, only exclamations and troubles seem to have something substantial, and we can easily think about it. Will heaven be indifferent to the troubles and sighs of the common people? However, the heaven is indeed indifferent! The earth is also indifferent! People's sighs are nothing. The worries5 and groans of hundreds of millions of people are hollower than the wind in the twinkling of an eye to nature. We humans may be too arrogant! It's a little boring to talk too much about one's own troubles. So I only sneered at the distress of this tearful Chinese. The lives of slaves are not worth mentioning, and neither are our lives. At present, for us, we have no choice but to work hard and risk our lives to defend Japan".

Heisuke Sugiyama doesn't have the slightest sense of morality. On the contrary, he has only the sense of killing people due to the war. This b*ecomes the reason for "great atrocities"*. The author has cited what Hikosaka Akira said in *How People Become Soldiers* "The greater sin of mass killing(ジェノサイド) lies in the obliteration of everyone's value(人の重み)"; he doubted the expression "the tragic degree of the 'disaster' is determined by the number, the 'Holocaust' is determined on the basis of the number of the dead and injured, and if the document doesn't have a clear record of the amount, it can only be regarded as not existing". When the author quoted the above word of Sugiyama, he said: "the real criminal character of mass killing is the complete obliteration of human values, personal 'annoyance and exclamation' and personal misery. What Sugiyama said above is nothing more than a mysterious reason for mass killing". "This is just the last words of the nihilism of the intellectuals who have self-consciousness".

China and the Chinese and Japanese was first published in the comprehensive magazine *Transformation*. And the Transformation has always had the reputation of "progress", and Sugiyama is the so-called "conscience of the society". In this regard, we can see the extent to which the spirit of the whole Japanese people has fallen during the war.

The Egoism of the Commoners

The author thinks that the calculation and nihilism of the common people shown in the "Nanjing Atrocities Incident" are "nothing more than the expression of the common people's egoism (エゴイズム) of the Japanese masses" and the another aspect of the "common people's egoism". However, it is understandable that the common people's egoism is presented by "calculation", while it is slightly tortuous to present egoism by nihilism (Wataru Kaji calls it "cunning robbery", "sense of gaining without giving", "looting in troubled situation" and "the destructive behavior of ruffians"). Because not only the public, who are forced by life and give up themselves, cannot find a way to vent their emotions, the reason for the naturally occurring nihilism is rampant lies in the fact that the emotion coincides with the policy of "punishing the violent Chinese".[4]

The author says that the "common people's egoism" he refers to is different from "the 'private' egoism of civil society in modern times, which is as the driving force of political liberation".

The egoism among the masses with the peasants as the main body was released only after Japan entered into "modern times" with Meiji Restoration. The author believes that this egoism "does not sublimate to the height of human rights, but only shows the narrow calculation of the common people = material desire. The theory of civil rights, which once attracted people's attention in the early Meiji period, was soon absorbed by the theory of state power. Moreover, this mass materialism has been "invariably" transformed into the "motive force" of aggression. The modern nationalism in Western Europe sublimates the citizens' 'private' egoism to the level of national consciousness through the media of human rights thought, but Japan's nationalism — imperial nationalism was formed under the negation and suppression of human rights thought. Therefore, the various forms of common people's egoism of the Japanese public are different from the modern classical egoism that purifies itself to the thought of human rights. In this way, the opportunity for self-selection at the level of public consciousness must be lacking".

At the same time, the author thinks that the common people's egoism "does not exist only with the explicit self-proposition of materialism. In fact, the existence form, I think, is the tribal consciousness regulated by the order

---

[4] "暴支应惩", Japan's wartime slogan, "支" refers to China.

of the family tribal community = the rural party consciousness". The "tribe" or "village" mentioned here ("ムラ", the author distinguishes it from the Chinese character "village") is quite different from the administrative village after Meiji. The "village" mentioned by the author refers to "the 'village'= 'natural village' which is composed of the 'local people' who bear the tribute rent under the bakuhan taisei". This kind of "village" is regulated by the community, and the common use of its water and the common land of the "village" are the important economic foundation of the life of different families. However, "with the development of capitalism and the penetration of the commodity economy, the entity of the natural village gradually disintegrated, and the disparity between the rich and the poor among small families began to appear (the formation of parasitic landlord system), the consciousness of the "village" as a fantasy system·community consciousness, the acceptance of a large number of variants and tenacious regeneration, and all of these things make the ideological mechanism of the warm community order work out. I think that the rebirth of the consciousness of the "village" as a fantasy system·community consciousness, on the one hand, is related to the economic foundation that is gradually disintegrating but still surviving, on the other hand, it can be seen as the common intuition of self-defense of open common people's egoism (on the basis of the entity, that is, peasant egoism).

The author continues to analyze: "Even if there is a sense of community within the 'village', once outward, it will still turn into an extreme sense of xenophobia and hostility. Moreover, the outward hostile consciousness will eventually turn to the inside, turning small families into enemies, which, as a negative factor, will inevitably have an effect on the community order based on the fantasy system. For this negative factor, the ideological mechanism for maintaining the order of the 'village' is familism. This kind of familism, according to the view of Fukushima Jiro, because it comes from the principle of the kinship combination, was formed with the 'one-family's parental leading power as the center; therefore, in modern times, it refers to extending from the small families in the virtual tribe to the whole order of the 'village' and virtualizes the opposition between the tenants and farmers within the 'village' as the relationship between the original family and the branch family. Therefore, the *Battle Training* appeals to 'always think about the family and community, and work harder to meet the expectation' on the basis of the existence of this kind of common people's egoism".

Such "familism" has also been brought into the army. The frequent group-scale snatching of meritorious service at the front, the scramble for trophies and the fiercer confrontation in a state of despair, not to mention the group tyranny against the "enemy" including innocent non-military personnel, are all related to this "familial" ethics. Thus, when the military discipline was abolished after fierce fighting, the grassroots level of the army turned into a "ruffian (ごろつき) family".

As a member of this "family", it is very difficult to get rid of the shackles of familial ethics and refuse to participate in rape and plunder, because that is tantamount to leaving the "family", and the consequence of leaving the "family" means being isolated and becoming a stranger for other members of the "family". Moreover, individual guilt can be easily absorbed by the silent norms cultivated by such group actions. The mental state of such "group action-dependent syndrome" like this still exists among some Japanese people today, 50 years after the war. As the author said: "Some words such as 'ヤルパック' (like ya lu ba cu)—I didn't hear about them until recently from a student who had a clumsy speech at a private university—can be said that they are the performance of such a way of action, such as buying spring travel, and so on, and the dependence of group action when traveling overseas, they can be said to be its performance. The only difference is that weapons have been exchanged to money, and the arrogant sense of great power that supports the two has something in common. The famous saying I hate very much 'If you run a red light together, you will not be afraid' is indeed a symbol of the above-mentioned state of mind".

Emperor Worships and the Thought of Contempt for China

The above opinions touch on the basis of the mass consciousness that represents the "great atrocities". But the author believes that this alone is not enough to explain the whole basis of the chilling violence committed by the Japanese army in China. "There is a spiritual driving force caused by special history. Only on this point, the emperor worships and the thought of 'jihad' based on it were combined with the thought of contempt for China and even the Chinese people, and coupled with the egoism of the common people, the 'great atrocities' was routinized in the spirit of the soldiers".

The author believes that the particularity of the formation of the Meiji absolute monarchy is quite different from the "classical absolutism" of Western Europe. The classical absolutism of Western Europe was baptized by the fierce struggle among Roman bishops, churches and feudal princes, and established political authority through its own hands. In contrast, Japan's absolute monarchy was formed in the power struggle of restoration reform, when the political forces of one side pushed the relatively "free" traditional authoritative emperor into the leader of the unified power of the whole country. Specifically, that is, "the instructors of the Meiji hambatsu government who are 'still sober-conscious' about the emperor (Shikano Masano, *Meiji Thought*), take the witchcraft (シャーマニズム) worship for emperor and emperor families cultivated among the Japanese public since ancient and medieval times and the close relationship as an opportunity to create the authority of the emperor, thus creating an ideological imperial system".

Even so, "The ideology of the system of self-justification for orthodoxy (divine right of kings) is not fully developed. As a result, there are myths and legends of the Emperor, which began with the "divine order" of "boundless heaven". Moreover, the Japanese imperial system takes this myth as the central axis, creating a special ideology of the self-justifying concept of "family country". It directly extends the principle of "family" of paternalism to the "country", taking the royal family as the "head of family" of the subjects and the emperor as the "great imperial relative". In addition, it makes up the "subjects" as the so-called "innocent son" and compares the country to a big family. "There is no doubt that such an ideology is promoted from the consciousness of the "village" ·community consciousness on the basis of the principle of 'family' and the myth of 'infinite heaven' and the thought of Confucianism is the medium".

Tribal consciousness was elevated to national consciousness, which promoted the aggression against neighboring small and weak nations. As mentioned earlier, under the domination of the emperor system, the consciousness of "village" is a breakwater to prevent "common people's egoism" from turning into anti-system tide. At the same time, the author thinks that it is also "maintained and formed as the real form of common people's egoism". However, the disintegration tendency of the entity of the natural village will inevitably induce the internal tension of the old order maintained by the "village" consciousness based on the "fantasy system" and the internal tension is transformed to the external tension, which, together with the gentle tendency to the old order, becomes the social basis for recreating the rule of the state. Therefore, the author said: "It can be said that with the opportunity of foreign aggression, the 'village' consciousness is constantly raised to the level of national consciousness. As a result, in Japan, patriotism is often transformed into the so-called 'loyalty and patriotism' of xenophobia".

The other pole of the "jihad" consciousness of "loyalty and patriotism" is the contempt for China and even the Chinese people. The so-called "ちゃん", "ちゃんちゃん", "ちゃんころ" and other contempt words for the Chinese people were popular in Japan after their victory in the First Sino-Japanese War. But as early as before the First Sino-Japanese War, the old admiration for China has been gone away. After the Opium War, China was repeatedly humiliated by the Western people, and the Japanese had started the contempt for China in addition to the shocking feeling.[5]

After the First Sino-Japanese War, the sense of contempt for China has become "universal", and even Natsume Sōseki's works have frequently shown the expression of "ちゃんちゃん". For example, in his book 坊ちゃん, there is such a narration of the character ちゃん when he quarreled, "In the case of the Sino-Japanese War, you would be ちゃんちゃん". From this, we can see the general feelings of the Japanese people. The author quotes a large number of his father's diaries, in which there are not only records and feelings

---

[5]According to Japanese common saying, the Japanese who went to the United States in the middle of the nineteenth century were surprised at first and then despised when they saw the Chinese workers building roads in the west-"piglets"-enduring hardship and humiliation.

of the wartime scenes, but also a lot of newspaper clippings and letters, and the disdain can be seen everywhere. For example, the author's cousin on the North China front sent a letter from near Taiyuan (it was sent on December 17th, 1937, the date of arriving not recorded) with this passage: "'Anti-Japanese National Salvation, the people of Shanxi should get up and join the army' is written on the dilapidated wall, two meters trenches creep on both sides of the road, and the donkey walk slowly. The ちゃんころ who have been shouting anti-Japanese even on yesterday came sparsely with the banner of welcoming Greater Japan". The author said, "I don't think I'm the only one who feels the weak and cunning disdain for the 'ちゃんころ' here. My father also accepts this feeling and is proud of his nephew who is fighting at the front".

The author concludes: "Such insulting thoughts and feelings to China, except for a few foresights, have spread to the scale of the country. And the policy of 'jihad'—'punishing the violent Chinese'—combined with this sense of contempt, the 'great atrocities incident' vented by the egoism of the common people was accepted by almost all the officers and soldiers without a sense of resistance. We are burdened with the reality of such an ideological history and are positioned in this history". The author summarizes "some elements of Japanese popular thoughts" which caused the "Nanjing Atrocities Incident" into the following picture:

The jihad in the name of emperor

Calculation—the egoism of the common people—nihilism

The contempt for China

There are no less works on the Nanjing Massacre in Japan than in China, and there have been no less than 60 special books since the 1980s, but it is still a unique description from the perspective of "spiritual structure". The author's explanation may be incomplete, but there is no doubt that it is generally effective. The conspicuous facts such as the Nanjing Massacre are still blatantly negated (the fictionalists) or obliterated (the "objective" school); the Japanese "national character" analyzed by the author can be used as a present example to prove the past.

The Japanese version of this book is divided into two parts. First part, in addition to the above, gives a detailed description of how the "war policy of Japanese imperialism" and "the political strategy of the Japanese Military Department" absorb "common people's egoism" and as a result become particularly "savage, predatory and speculative". There is also a detailed analysis of the spiritual harmony between the Japanese public and the Japanese atrocities during the war (such as "rationalizing" the "publishing" because of the killing of Japanese expatriates in Tongzhou). The second part of this book is a criticism of the national character of Japan today; the author believes that because Japan has never conducted a national introspection on the progress of the war of aggression after the war, so that in the 50 years after the war (when the Japanese version is published), there is still no regret for the war today—there not only no regrets, all kinds of strange theories for the grievances of the war become very popular. Several articles have been added to the Chinese version of the book, mainly to supplement the thinking of the Japanese public since 1995. From the title of one of the articles "Criticism of the Reactionary State of Thought in Modern Japan-the 145th Fascist Movement in the Congress Grass-roots level", we can see the totally different attitude that the author has from the current opinions.

Born in 1929, the author is a generation with firsthand experience of war. Shortly after the war, he devoted himself to the democratic movement in Japan. For a long time, the author has consistently criticized arbitrariness, oppression, injustice, discrimination, beautification of aggression and slander of the Asian people, and never slackened his self-examination of his own nation. The writer is now the editor-in-chief of the monthly magazine *Education and Human Rights*. The author's main works include: *Modern Trotskyism* (Aoki Shoten Publishing Co., 1960), *Modern Marxism* (Aoki Shoten Publishing Co., 1963), *Hegel and Marx* (Seasonal Society, 1970), *(Supplement) Japanese Nationalism* (Fukumura Publishing, 1978), *(Supplement) Restoration of the State Theory* (Fukumura Publishing, 1978), *The Theory of the State and Revolution* (Lunchuang Press, 1979), *Cognition and Education* (Sanyi study, 1979), *Education Movement for the Disabled* (Sanyi study, 1981), *Shigeo Kamiyama in the History of Showa Thought* (Social Review Agency, 1983), *The Road towards Practice* (Lunchuang Press, 1984), *Ichitaro Kokubun* (Sanyi study, 1986), *Impression and Willingness* (Social Review Agency, 1989), *The Collapse of Revolutionary Russia* (Social Review Agency, 1992), *Nanjing Massacre and the Spiritual Structure of the Japanese* (Social Review Agency, 1995), *Dialectical Restoration of Dialectic* (Social Review Agency, 2000), *War of Aggression and Sexual Atrocities* (Social Review Agency 2002).

(Originally published on *Study of the Anti-Japanese War*, No. 4, 2000; Japanese translation was published on No. 335, *Human Rights and Education*, Japanese Social Review Agency)

Recollection of Tsuda Michio

I received the new issue of *Human Rights and Education* before the New Year, and when I found that Mr. Tsuda MichioI's name was not on the cover, I had a sense of foreboding. Then, I immediately turned to the editor's postscript page; sure enough, the first sentence was: "In the process of compiling this issue, Tsuda Michio, editor-in-chief and publisher YAMADA EIZO died of illness......". *Human Rights and Education* is a minority left-wing publication in Japan. Although the main purpose of the publication is to safeguard the right to education of the disabled, there are also critical reviews of Japan's domestic and foreign affairs and various social issues from time to time. The publication was founded in the early 1970s; in addition to a simple monthly newsletter of the same name, the official issue is published every half a year. It has existed for decades as a publication run by members of editing department, from which we can see the perseverance of Mr. Tsuda and his colleagues.

I met Mr. Tsuda late. In the mid-1990s, Mr. Wu Guangyi from the Chinese Academy of Social Sciences invited me to visit Mr. Tsuda in Kuki City, Saitama County. On that day, Mr. Tsuda sang *National Anthem of the People's Republic of China* and *L'Internationale* when he drank high. We were in a quiet town and it was midnight. I thought it might disturb the neighbors, so I said, should we be quieter? Mr. Tsuda said "Don't care about that" and started to shout the slogan "Down with the Japanese Imperialism". Since then, I have more and more contacts with Mr. Tsuda, and I have learned more about his maverick and the big difference between him and the reserved introverted ordinary Japanese. One time, I had a walk with Mr. Tsuda and we were walking through a graveyard not far from home. Mr. Tsuda kicked away a bunch of flowers in front of a tombstone, I was really surprised and he told me that it was his "father" sleeping there and he stressed that his father was "a militarist". Mr. Tsuda has consistently criticized the "militarism" and stood on the opposite side of his father in political standpoint. In his late eighties, he compiled a very special book named The Diary of a Military Teacher, which mainly criticizes his father's diaries. I asked Mr. Tsuda who sent the flowers? He said they were sent by his "stupid" brother. His brother graduated from Tokyo University and was a professor at Chiba University Nishi-Chiba Campus. Mr. Tsuda was once expelled from the Japanese Communist Party and he had no contact with his brother, who was also a member of the Japanese Communist Party. Therefore, although Mr. Tsuda belongs to "left-wing", he does not fit in with the mainstream left-wing groups.

Mr. Tsuda was also the backbone of the "Association for the Realization of the Right to Education for the Disabled" from participating in the student movement when he was young to his later years, and he never left the "movement" all his life. At the same time, he is also a scholar who has never left his study all his life. Over the years, I have received more than 20 kinds of tome pamphlets sent by Mr. Tsuda, such as *State and Will-Reading Capitalism and Philosophy of Law from the Perspective of Will* published at his age of 77, *Ichitaro Kokubun—Movement Connected to the Life of Resistance*, *Recollection of Shigeharu Nakano* which was revised after his age of 80 and *The Collection of Voluntarism—The Deficiency of Marxist in the 20th Century* he edited for Miura, an influential Marxist scholar in the Showa period. Because most of these books are outside my focus, they have become the "collection of books" on the shelf after being received.

The Nanjing Massacre is a joint research object between me and Mr. Tsuda. At the end of the 1990s, Ms. Liu Yanzi, who accompanied Mr. Azuma Shiro to China many times to repent, called me and invited me to translate Mr. Tsuda's *Nanjing Massacre and the Spiritual Structure of the Japanese* with her. At that time, I had paid attention to the debate on Japan's so-called "Nanjing Incident", but I was only a "bystander" and had no intention of delving into it. Looking back, translating Mr. Tsuda's book was a cause that I unwittingly stepped into the review ranks.

Nanjing Massacre and the Spiritual Structure of the Japanese is a very special kind of book related to Japan. There are disputes among the school of slaughter, the fictionalists and the centrist over the Nanjing Massacre; whether they are arguing about the "number" or the "existing or not", they all have something to do with the facts. Mr. Tsuda believes that the fact that Nanjing Massacre exists is self-evident, so he thinks this kind of argument is "meaningless". Mr. Tsuda's book discusses the responsibility of the "Japanese public". Mr. Tsuda disagrees with the popular saying that the responsibility for Nanjing atrocities—expanding to an entire war—should only be borne by "a small handful of militarists" and that the "Japanese public" are also "victims". In this book, he explains in detail the "egoism" and "nihilism" the Japanese calculate about and the special "spiritual structure" mixed with "emperor worship" and "disdain feelings for China"; he stressed that the Japanese public during the war were much more like promoters than the "victims" so they had unshirkable responsibilities.

Mr. Tsuda is very strict not only to the Japanese public, but also to the emperor. He believes that Japan's invasion of China was carried out in the name of "jihad", so "there is no doubt that the emperor should at least be morally responsible". It is conceivable that Mr. Tsuda's stern attitude is difficult to be accepted by the "Japanese public", what is more difficult to understand is why the mainstream left-wing groups in Japan, which seems to be consistent in the right direction, have turned a blind eye to Mr. Tsuda's book. Mr. Tokushi Kasahara is the school of slaughter who contributes the most to the study of Nanjing Massacre in the world after Mr. Tomio Hora who first started the study of Nanjing Massacre. His *Controversial History of the Nanjing Incident* is nearly 300 pages, but there is no mention of Mr. Tsuda's book. If we do not look at it from the perspective of "origin", there are certainly reasons for the difference between "textual research" and "reasoning", or the reason why there is not only "what to say" but also "how to say". However, Mr. Tsuda believes that between him and the academic school of the school of slaughter, there is not only a difference in perspective and method, but also a difference in principle. Mr. Tsuda said to me more than once that "It is not possible for Kasahara and others to replace the 'Nanjing Massacre' with the 'Nanjing Incident'. This is a major matter of right and wrong, not a simple problem of the usage of noun. They are more backward than Mr. Hora on this point".

What Mr. Tsuda said about "not a problem of the usage of noun", I also had the experience of being "well-educated" once. On August 23rd, 2007, the Asahi Shimbun made a special report on the "70th Anniversary" on the relevant situation of China and Japan under the title of *The Rekindling of the Debate over Nanjing Incident*. The Chinese side mainly introduces the difficulties to prove the conclusion of the Nanjing Trial that I mentioned in an article. At noon that day, Mr. Tsuda Michio called me in a strict tone, and his first sentence was, "I call you not to criticize you". Mr. Tsuda said on the phone: "Things like the Nanjing Massacre cannot be solved academically. I also do not believe that the conclusion of the Nanjing Trial is in line with reality, but we should see that the Japanese army has done too many bad things in China. Apart from the direct victims, what is more important is that the foundation of life of countless Chinese families has been destroyed. And these countless tragedies cannot be quantified. Just like if the United States questions the number of deaths in Hiroshima and Nagasaki, which arouses the anger of the Japanese people. So in this matter, what Chinese people said is always right!" As a matter of fact, this is the consistent attitude that Mr. Tsuda expressed to me a long time ago. The main idea of my answer at that time was that I was working in historiography, which was not at the same level as what Mr. Tsuda said. That night, Mr. Tsuda called again in a gentle tone, saying that he did not deny the value of empirical research, but empirical research could not replace emotional memory. Later, he talked about it in the article *The 300000 People as Emotional Memory—Nanjing Massacre* (*Human Rights and Education,* No. 407, November 10th, 2007); in particular, he said: "The 300000 people as emotional memory and the work as empirical research are unified within his mind". I think that rather regarding this as a good intention of Mr. Tsuda, it is better to regard this as his "hope" for me not to go too far.

Although I have always thought that at present, more than 70 years later, historians should have the right to study the atrocities such as the Nanjing Massacre as "historical events", Mr. Tsuda's thorough reflection on the war is still admirable. I think in terms of "reflection" alone, Japan's mainstream society, which cannot satisfy the people of China and South Korea, is not too bad after all, and it is more or less inseparable from Mr. Tsuda's and some other people's efforts. On the occasion of Mr. Tsuda's death, I think we should pay special tribute to such a friend who has been struggling with the right-wing groups of Japan all his life.

Originally published on *Wen Wei Po*, April 16, 2015, the 7th issue.

A Postscript to *The Study of the Existing Historical Materials of the Nanjing Massacre in Japan*

"Involvement" in the study of the Nanjing Massacre was something that I had not expected before I entered the Institute of History, and it can be said to be an "accident". When I reported to the Institute of History in the spring of 2000, it coincided with the declaration of the National Social Science Fund that year, and the institute party hoped that everyone would participate, saying that funding was on the one hand, and the "national project" itself was a kind of evaluation. I had no intention of applying for the project at all. Because although I have various interests and have written some relevant articles over the years, I still have a lot of courses to make up if I want to specialize in a single subject. Moreover, I thought "evaluation" should be measured by the results. Moreover, at that time, I had a prejudice against the form of the "project", thinking that if we want to complete an academic project with quality, it cannot be as time-limited as the production of material products. However, the tone of the institute side was very sincere and made people think that it is their duty to strive for it. At the beginning, I planned to declare a project on the incident between Song and Jin; this was not because I had any special experience in this field, but I don't remember why I chose the topic of Nanjing Massacre. It seems that one of my colleagues said that filling out the form was a troublesome task; in order to avoid working fruitlessly, we should choose a topic with high probability. In retrospect today, it was a bit daring to declare such a topic when the "preliminary results" were blank.

At that time, I didn't even have the most superficial understanding of the Nanjing Massacre, but for many years when I was browsing through some discussions about Nanjing Massacre in Japanese right-wing publications such as *Gentlemen* and *Theories,* apart from the feeling that they are "unconvincing", they indeed leave me the impression that "it has yet to be answered". If we say that the choice of this subject in the future is not entirely accidental, this double impression is an important reason. If I only felt that they were "nonsense" or "absolutely correct", it was unlikely that I would have the motivation to review this subject.

After the project was approved, my first step was to take care of more than 20 kinds of related works, including Suzuki Aki's *The Mystery of the Nanjing Massacre*, Masaaki Tanaka's *The Fiction of the Nanjing Massacre* and the works of the fictionalists such as Higashinakano Shudo's *The Great doubt about the Nanjing Massacre,* and the centrist works whose views are close to the fictionalists such as Itakura Yoshiaki's *The Truth is such a Nanjing Incident* and Unemoto Masaki's *The Truth-Nanjing Incident.* Then, I organized the materials on which these works are based to see whether they were reliable and whether they could prove their conclusions, and to what extent they could prove them. The project I declared was originally entitled *Research on*

Collections of Nanjing Massacre in Japan, and the review of the fictionalists was the focus but not all. After embarking on it, I found that the problems to be discussed were much more than originally expected, so I had to shrink the battle line and limit the scope to the review of the works of the fictionalists. When this work was later compiled into a book, it was entitled *Nanjing Massacre Studies-Criticism for the Japanese Fictionalists*. However, since the publication of the book coincided with the 65th anniversary of the Nanjing Massacre, and the publishing house hoped that the book could be listed in time for the anniversary, although the book has more than 500 pages, the review of the fictionalists has not yet been completed. For this reason, after concluding the project, I continued to apply to the National Social Science Fund for a new project entitled *Research on the Existing Historical Data of the Nanjing Massacre in Japan*. This thin pamphlet is the final report of this project. Originally, the study of historical materials should take a lot of space, and the reason of the "hasty end" that has not been laid out in detail is mainly due to the fact that different to the past, I have other opinions on the direction of the study of Nanjing Massacre Research Institute. Let's talk about this later.

With regard to Japan's war crimes, only the Nanjing Massacre in Japan has been debated for a long time. Walking into Japanese bookstores, we can see that no other historical events related to China have been written as much as the Nanjing Incident, which shows that this debate is no longer limited to a narrow professional scope and has become a topic of considerable social concern. Why are there so much debates only on Nanjing Massacre in Japan? What we can easily think of is that the Nanjing Massacre is the largest of all the atrocities committed by the Japanese army, and the second is that the Nanjing Massacre is regarded as a "symbol" of the "historical entanglement" between the two countries. The third is that the Nanjing Massacre was decided by the postwar trial (at that time, the trial and use of chemical and biological weapons had not yet been exposed and had not become a charge). Fourth, there have always been people in Japan who claim that the Nanjing Massacre is a "fabrication" that corresponds to "crimes against humanity". These reasons are all related to the "position" that has nothing to do with academia. Indeed, without the factor of position, the Nanjing Massacre could not have caused so much controversy. At the same time, if it's just a difference in position, it would not form a lasting debate. I think the reason why the Nanjing Massacre has become a continuing "hot spot" is indeed related to the inadequate records at the time of the incident and the "loss" of firsthand literature. The insufficient record at the time of the incident means that there was no and could not be a comprehensive investigation and record of Japanese atrocities at that time; the "loss" of firsthand documents refers to the non-transmission of Japanese documents such as the logs of the Ministry of Justice of the Shanghai Expeditionary Army. These documents are said to be "lost" rather than destroyed because the documents may still exist in the world, just as the logs of the Legal Department of the 10th Army are actually not destroyed but have not been known for a long time. Since some people insist that the problem of Nanjing Massacre has been solved on the Nanjing Trial and there should be no doubt anymore, so it is necessary to make a special explanation on this point: First, the materials about the Nanjing Massacre—including words, physical objects, images and oral transmission—are not in the minority today. For example, the *Collection of Historical Materials on the Nanjing Massacre* published the year before last and renewed recently has reached 55 volumes. The insufficient I said is limited to the records of "the first time" and "firsthand" documents in the sense of history. Second, "insufficient" does not mean that the evidence of Japanese atrocities in Nanjing is not sufficient, but that the basis for the conclusion of the Tokyo Trial, especially the Nanjing Trial, needs to be further enriched. And that should be an important reason why the Nanjing Massacre still has the value of research as a historical event. On the contrary, it can also be said that if the problem of the Nanjing Massacre has been solved by the Nanjing Trial, not only today's efforts to dig up new historical materials will become meaningless, but also the study of the Nanjing Massacre will become unnecessary. In this sense, whether there is a right-wing challenge in Japan or not is not the same thing as whether it needs to be studied today.

In 2003, Nanjing Massacre Research Center of Nanjing Normal University organized relevant scholars from Nanjing area, such as Nanjing University, Nanjing Normal University, Jiangsu Academy of Social Sciences, Jiangsu Provincial Party School and so on, to hold a Nanjing Massacre Research Salon. Mr. Zhang Lianhong, director of the center, invited me to give the first lecture. I mainly talked about the origin and current situation of the debate in Japan, and incidentally mentioned the problems we face. The so-called "our" problem was actually the difference between me and some domestic scholars, among which there was no lack of my prejudices. However, Nanjing scholars were tolerant and magnanimous and gave the kindest understanding. That day, Mr. Sun Zhaiwei specially came from the suburbs. Mr. Sun is a representative scholar in the study of the Nanjing Massacre in China, but he expressed his special thanks after I finished my speech. That night, Mr. Jing Shenghong of Nanjing Normal University came to my hotel and talked about his relevant research, saying that according to what I called "the context of the material" his previous paper did have the problem of giving priority to conclusions. Until during the second Nanjing Massacre Historical Data Discussion Session this year, Mr. Zhang Sheng of Nanjing University told me that the photo issue I talked about at that time had changed his view on this issue. I was deeply impressed by the frankness of Nanjing scholars. Later, with the increase of contacts with scholars in Nanjing, I further feel that the actual ideas of Nanjing scholars have made a great breakthrough compared with the published writings. For example, the views of Mr. Wang Weixing of the Jiangsu Academy of Social Sciences and

Mr. Yang Xiaoming of the Jiangsu Institute of Administration have basically got rid of the shackles outside the academic. At the beginning of this year, Mr. Zhang Lianhong and I visited Tokyo, Kyoto and other places in Japan at the invitation of the Tokyo consortium, and we had the opportunity to have a leisurely conversation, although some of our views were still different. However, there was no difference at all on the point that the Nanjing Massacre, as a historical event, should also be tested by historical data.

The knowledgeable attitude of Nanjing scholars has led to a subtle change in the study of the Nanjing Massacre in China in recent years, which can be seen in the *Collection of Historical Materials of the Nanjing Massacre* and the Second Symposium on the Historical Materials of the Nanjing Massacre chaired by Mr. Zhang Xianwen. The value of the *Collection of Historical Materials of the Nanjing Massacre* has been discussed in many articles, and I will only mention one point that goes unnoticed here. Volume 12 of the *Collection of Historical Materials of the Nanjing Massacre* contains the writings of the autonomous committee. If it was in the past, it was impossible for these documents to be included, the first reason was that the autonomous committee would be marked with "pseudo" marks, while most of the contents of the documents were related to activities about the people's livelihood, which were no different from the functions of the general public regime. Second, the content about Japanese atrocities was very diluted and there were even contrary contents such as a petition asking the protection from Japanese gendarmerie (even if the request for protection can be interpreted as preventing Japanese atrocities, it is still very different when it comes to the fact that the gendarmerie has been used as an accomplice to the atrocities). In a narrow sense, these documents did not add points to the exposure of Japanese atrocities, but they did contribute to a comprehensive understanding of the reality of Nanjing at that time. I have mentioned a little about the first discussion of historical materials in introduction note 2 of this book. Here, I would like to take two speeches at the beginning and end of the second seminar as examples to take a look at the new trends in the study of the Nanjing Massacre in China. The speaker of the first session of the meeting was Mr. Sun Zhaiwei. The title of his report was *On the Two-Way Effect of the New Historical Materials of the Nanjing Massacre-Centering on Burying Corpses*. As I said earlier, Mr. Sun is a representative scholar in the study of the Nanjing Massacre in China, and he is also the main object of questioning by the Japanese centrists and fictionalists, but Mr.Sun is not stubborn and he admitted that "we" had the problem of double numbering on burying bodies in the past and he specifically stated that "any valuable academic achievements do not need to be artificially 'safeguarded' and 'defended'". At the end of the meeting, Mr. Zhang Xianwen delivered a closing speech. Different from the usual closing speech that is composed of conclusions and thanks, the main purpose of Mr. Zhang's speech is to emphasize that the study of the Nanjing Massacre should remain independent from non-academic factors. Somehow, the atmosphere of that day made people feel very moved. If you have never been involved in the study of the Nanjing Massacre, you may think that these words are not very meaningful, but if you are in the position, you will certainly realize the responsibility for such self-reflection on this event that is most entangled with national feelings.

I mentioned earlier that I had different opinions on the direction of the study Nanjing Massacre Research Institute should focus, and the trigger was largely due to the above changes. Judging from the existing "research" results of the Nanjing Massacre in China, if we ignore the critical articles on past "Japanese militarism" and the Japanese right wing today, the research so far has mainly focused on two aspects, one is to explore the material and spiritual damage caused by Japanese atrocities to the Chinese people, and the other is to explore the "causes" and "nature". The former is almost an incremental work in one direction, while the latter, strictly speaking, is not a kind of historical work because the determination of the facts is based on the existing conclusions. Therefore, although the number of relevant works is considerable, the comprehensive reconstruction of the historical facts of the Nanjing Massacre in the historical sense has not yet begun. I think the most basic work to rebuild the historical facts of the Nanjing Massacre is to establish the evidence by studying the historical data centered on the literature—rather than "looking" for the root evidence that I need, and on this basis to test the conclusions of the Tokyo Trial, especially the Nanjing Trial. Only in this way can the historical facts of the Nanjing Massacre be irrefutable. This work couldn't be done in the past, and there were some reasons, including the reasons within the disciplines such as the failure of accumulation of historical data and the degree of research, as well as reasons outside the disciplines such as the bearing capacity of the government, but the most important reason was the "consciousness" of the researchers themselves. Nowadays, due to the above-mentioned changes in recent years, I think it's time to use academic means to solve the problem of Nanjing Massacre. Therefore, although it was necessary to review the Japanese materials and the views of the fictionalists, today it seems too circuitous and too slow to help.

At this point, I think of some words said by a senior scholar this summer. On August 23rd, 2007, the Asahi Shimbun made a special report on the "70th Anniversary" on the relevant situation of China and Japan under the title of *The Rekindling of the Debate over Nanjing Incident*. The Chinese side mainly introduces the difficulties to prove the conclusion of the Nanjing Trial that I mentioned in an article. At noon that day, Mr. Tsuda Michio, who wrote *Nanjing Massacre and the Spiritual Structure of the Japanese* and other books, called me in a strict tone, and his first sentence was, "I call you not to criticize you". Mr. Tsuda said on the phone: "Things like the Nanjing Massacre cannot be solved "academically". I also do not believe that the conclusion of the Nanjing Trial is in line with reality, but we should see that the Japanese army has done too many bad things in China. Apart from the direct victims, what is more important is that the foundation of life of countless Chinese families has been destroyed. And these countless tragedies cannot be quantified. Just like if the United States questions the number of deaths in Hiroshima and Nagasaki will arouse the anger of the Japanese people. So in this matter, what Chinese people said is always right!" As a matter of fact, this is the consistent attitude that Mr. Tsuda expressed to me a long time ago. The main idea of my answer at that time was that I was working in historiography, which was not at the same level as what Mr. Tsuda said. That night, Mr. Tsuda called again in a gentle tone, saying that he did not deny the value of empirical research, but empirical research could not replace emotional memory. Later, he talked about it in the article The 300000 People as Emotional Memory—Nanjing Massacre (*Human Rights and Education*, No. 407, page 113, November 10th, 2007); in particular, he said: "The 300000 people as emotional memory and the work as empirical research are unified within his mind". I think that rather regarding this as a good intention of Mr. Tsuda, it is better to regard this as his "hope" for me not to go too far. Mr. Tsuda is one of the very few members who had the most thorough introspection of the war in Japan, and he has always been respected by me. However, I think that today, 70 years later, historians should have the right to regard the Nanjing Massacre as a "historical event".

This postscript is relatively long. In addition to explaining the cause of my research on the Nanjing Massacre, I also want to make up for the haste "attitude" at the body content. There is one more thing that needs to be mentioned before concluding this postscript. Mr. David Askew, an Australian scholar from Ritsumeikan University, once mentioned "the maximization of corpse numbers" in an article when he referred to my work, but I had never mentioned body numbers in my works; what's more, this article was published in the Japanese right-wing publication *Gentlemen!* (Issue December 2005), and the title was also *The dead of the Nanjing Massacre*, so I used the word "ridiculous" when talking about it (see Note 220 in this book). During my speech at the Tokyo consortium at the beginning of this year, Mr. Askew came all the way from Oita to attend the lecture and then attended two seminars in Tokyo and Kyoto. On the break of the Tokyo seminar, I said to him, "you fictionalists……", before I had finished my words, he interrupted: "I am not a fictionalist. Except for the Japanese, there will be no fictionalists in other countries!" When I mentioned this at the Kyoto seminar the next day, Mr. Askew mocked himself: "I am mainly dissatisfied with the conclusions of the school of slaughter. Since I have caused such a misunderstanding, I will start to write articles to criticize the fictionalists". (The host of that day was Mr. Minoru Kitamura, the only expert in modern Chinese history among the fictionalists; the host of the Tokyo seminar was Qin Yuyan, a main person of the centrist.) Later, when Mr. Askew wrote about the criticism of relevant Japanese research in my speech, he specifically said that "he had no objection" (Gentlemen! Issue April 2007, p. 174). The original manuscript of Mr. Askew's article was entitled Changes in the Interpretation of Nanjing Atrocities in Chinese Academic Circles. The original title of my speech was Cheng Zhaoqi's Speech. Although the content was not changed when it was published, the title of the article and excerpt had been intentionally changed out of context, so we can see the "the ideological stand of *Chukun*!" From this, I thought that the words "the dead", which made me classify Mr. Askew as the fictionalist, should also be the change made by *Chukun*!. But why Mr. Askew, who doesn't want to have anything to do with the fictionalists, would publish his article on the fictionalists' headquarter Gentlemen!? The question is still puzzling......

Finally, I would like to thank all the gentlemen mentioned in this book, especially Mr. Xiong Yuezhi, Mr. Zhang Lianhong, Mr. Du Chengjun and Mr. Xu Zhongyi!

In the evening of December 13th, 2007
(*The Study of the Existing Historical Materials of the Nanjing Massacre in Japan*, written by Cheng Zhaoqi, published by Shanghai People's Press in 2008)

QUESTIONNAIRES OF JAPANESE FICTIONALIST, CENTRIST AND SLAUGHTER SCHOOL

Preface: This survey was published in Japan's *Chokun!* in February 2001, pp. 164–203. Although it does not include all the important figures, such as Hata Ikuhiko of centrist school and Higashinakano Shudo of fictionalist school in Japan, the various factions are still quite specific. Although the questions are obviously inclined due to the ideological background of the right wing contained in *Chokun!*, the basic stance of Japanese parties on the so-called "Nanking Incident" is still reflected, so it is specially translated as an appendix for the reference of domestic readers. For inconsistencies in style, such as "Nanking Incident", when quoted, and when not, such as reference books, or note the author, or omitted; the differences in cultural atmosphere, such as the long sentences of Matsumura Toshio, are all in accordance with the original appearance and will not be changed.

Watanabe Shoichi (Professor of Sophia University), Suzuki Aki (Non-fiction writer), Ara Kenichi (Media Worker), Kobayashi Yoshinori (Cartoonist), Fuji Nobuo (Tokyo Trial Researcher), Takaike Katsuhiko (Lawyer), Tanaka Masaaki (Chairman of "the Association of Guarding Xingya Kuan-yin[Built by General Matsui]"), Ooi Mitsuru (War History Researcher), Matsumura Toshio (Nanking Incident Researcher), Nobukatsu Fujioka (Professor of University of Tokyo), Hara Takeshi(Chief Research Officer, War History Department, Former Defense Research Institute), Nakamura Akira (Professor of Dokkyo University), Unemoto Masaki (War History Researcher), Okazaki Hisahiko (Director of the Hakuhodo Okazaki Research Institute), Sakurai Yoshiko (Media Worker), Tanabe Toshio (Showa

History Researcher), Fujiwara Akira (Honorary Professor, Hitotsubashi University), Rguchi Keiichi (Professor of Ochi University), Inoue Hisashi (Professor of Chuntaihe University), Himeta Mitsuyoshi (Professor of Chuo University), Kasahara Tokushi (Professor, Tokyo Metropolitan University of Arts), Takasaki Ryuji (Critic), Yoshida Yutaka (Professor of Hitotsubashi University).

Researchers who are deeply concerned about the Nanking issue conducted a questionnaire survey with the following items.

1. How many people do you think are appropriate for the number of Chinese killed (illegally killed) by the Japanese troops in the Nanjing Incident?
   (1) Over 300, 000
   (2) About 300, 000
   (3) 200, 000-300, 000
   (4) 200, 000
   (5) Tens of thousands
   (6) About 100, 000
   (7) 70, 000-90, 000
   (8) About 50, 000
   (9) 20, 000-30, 000
   (10) About 10, 000
   (11) Thousands
   (12) Infinitely close to zero
   (13) Other (About)

2. Regarding the scope of its victims.
   (1) Because the old Japanese army invaded China, the Chinese in the Nanking Incident were all slaughtered.
   (2) It could have been a war of aggression, but the number of people killed in China should not include those killed as a result of ordinary acts of war.
   (3) Many of those killed in the "Nanjing Incident" took off their uniforms and fled to the safety zone, where they were found and executed by the Japanese army. These people should not be counted as being slaughtered.
   (4) Other.

3. From when to when the so-called "Nanking Incident" happened?
   (1) From the mid-November of the Showa 12th year, in which the Japanese troops took control of Shanghai and began pursuing the Chinese army that had retreated to Nanjing, to the end of January of the Showa 13th year, in which the remnants of Nanjing were basically ended. (More than two months)
   (2) From the fall of Nanking around December 13th, Showa 12th year, to the end of January of the Showa 13th year when the remnants of Nanjing were swept. (About six weeks)

(3) From December 13th, Showa 12th year, before and after the fall of Nanking, to the 17th of the same month when General Iwane Matsui and others entered the city. (A few days)
(4) Other.
4. Where should the Nanking Incident refer to geographically?
(1) Including Shanghai controlled by the Japanese troops, Suzhou and Wuxi near Nanking to which the Chinese Army retreated because of the pursuit of the Japanese troops.
(2) Including Zijin Mountain and other suburbs of Nanking where fierce fighting took place before the Japanese troops captured Nanking.
(3) Only in Nanking.
(4) Only in the Nanking Security Zone where refugees are pouring in.
(5) Other.
5. What does the "slaughter" refer to in the "Nanking Incident"? Please explain.
6. The Chinese soldiers who escaped into the safety zone changed their uniforms into plain clothes. Do you think such Chinese soldiers are plainclothes soldiers? Or regulars? Or citizens?
(1) Plainclothes soldiers
(2) Regulars
(3) Citizens
(4) Other.
7. Continue with the previous question and ask the people whose answer is the plainclothes soldier.
In accordance with wartime international law (p. 113, Junpei Nobuo's *Shanghai Campaign and International Law* was published in the 7th year of Showa, by Maruzen Publishing), plainclothes soldiers are "people who, dressed in clothes similar to those of ordinary citizens, sneak into places where many locals live, hide in residents, suddenly shoot and snipe at the enemy". Do you think the Chinese soldiers in Nanking after the fall were like this?
8. If there are any definite historical records regarding the punishment of the Japanese army as a violation of international law, please advise.
Only the first-level historical data (records made by relevant personnel at the scene of the incident at the time of the incident) and the second-level historical data (records made at the scene of the incident although it is relatively late from the time of the incident). For the third-level and below historical data made from the first-level and second-level historical data, please advise if there is sufficient evidence.
9. What do you think of the responsibility of Japanese General Iwane Matsui in the "Nanking Incident"?
10. What do you think of the role of China's Tang Shengzhi in the same incident?

11. When do you think the so-called "Nanking Massacre" began in Japan?
    (1) After Nanking campaign in the 12th year of Showa.
    (2) After the Tokyo Trial.
    (3) Starting from the second half of the Showa era 40s, the Asahi Shimbun serialized "Nanking Massacre" under the title "Journey to China".
    (4) After the 57th year of Showa, it was turbulent because the textbook description was changed to "aggression → in and out".
    (5) Other.
12. As a symbol of the Nanking Incident, is it true that two second lieutenants, Mukai Toshiaki and Noda Tsuyoshi, were known to the world for their killing contest?
13. How to evaluate Iris Chang's *The Rape of Nanking*? (*The Rape of Nanking: The Forgotten Holocaust of War II*)
14. How do you evaluate *Nanking Reality* in the diary of John Rabe, the Chairman of the Safe Area of the "Nanking Incident"? (Japanese Version Title-Translator)
15. How should the textbook on the historical interfluve of Japan in the "Nanking Incident" be recorded?
16. Is the "Nanking Incident" a crime similar to the holocaust? Or is it the usual act of war? Is it rather excessive as an act of war? Or is it a bit excessive? How do you think about it?
17. Finally, after answering the above questions, is there any change in your evaluation on the "Nanking Incident" changed now?

If any, please indicate at what point (e.g., the number of deaths) and the reasons for the change (books or discovery of new facts, etc.). In addition, please list the important works (limited to five volumes) that are of referential value to the "Nanking Incident".

The answers are published below.

Watanabe Shoichi
1. (13) Forty to fifty ordinary citizens.
2. (4) Only ordinary citizens.
3. (1)
4. (3)
5. The killing of citizens who were mistaken for guerrillas (plainclothes teams) and other ordinary citizens involved can be considered a massacre.
6. (1)
7. I don't know. There are people like this, and there are also people who want to be saved, but do not want to resist, so they pretend to be citizens.
8. Is there such a thing? I don't know.
9. Considering pre-war standards, it is certain that Matsui was ashamed of the behavior of Japanese soldiers. Because out of the ethics that Japanese

soldiers received before the war, it was a shame for soldiers to rape women. However, such acts are not subject to international sanctions and there is no need to be punished by the death penalty.

10. Tang Shengzhi bore the greatest responsibility. First, Japan did not want to wage street fightings, and it advised China to surrender. Therefore, he should open Nanking, in which case there would be no fierce fighting in the city and no such chaos. When Chinese soldiers failed to guard the city, the General should raise the white flag to surrender as soon as possible. If it is the prisoners who surrender in this way that are slaughtered, then the circumstances are very serious, but Nanking is not the case. There should be a leader among the captured prisoners, but Zhina soldiers (Chinese soldiers) do not have such a leader, which is worthy of sympathy. In fact, there were no reports of ordinary citizens being massacred in Beijing and Hankou, which had surrendered before.
11. (2)
12. It is not true absolutely. The views of Yamamoto Shichihei and Honda Katsuichi have completely refuted this statement. The Katana cannot kill people that way.
13. Iris Chang's book, obviously, is a deception in order to cheat Chinese and extort money from Japan. Publishing such a book is the response of Chinese Americans to this "Nanking Incident". In addition, as Americans, their psychological burden of Hiroshima and Nagasaki's atomic bombing is no less than that of Hitler's massacre of Jews. In terms of the potential consciousness of discovering the reasons for the Japanese massacre, *The Rape of Nanking* thus became popular and became a best seller. For such a book, the Japanese government's failure to seriously respond is dereliction of duty.
14. Rabe is an agent of Siemens, so he has a reason to hate the Japanese in business. However, his vision is limited. Since he is the chairman of the safety zone, he does not understand the meaning of the safety zone. Chinese soldiers entered the safe zone with weapons, so the Japanese army conducted a weapon search, which is a legitimate act, so it is strange to criticize it. In this diary, the only certainty in his behavior is the gratitude expressed by the Japanese troops when they entered the city.
15. The textbook should include the Japanese military's claims. The Chinese side rejected Japan's proposed surrender, especially the fleeing of General Tang, leading to street fighting, which eventually resulted in the innocent citizens being killed to some extent.
16. It is completely ridiculous to compare with holocaust. The "Nanking Incident" was a common fighting act. Compared with the tragic street fighting like the Warsaw riots, the number of ordinary citizens killed in the Nanking Incident, as a street-based battle, is small.
17. In terms of evaluation, there is no change.

Recommended books are:
  (1) Tanaka Masaaki: *Summary of the Nanking Incident——Fifteen Arguments for Denying the Slaughter* (Qianguang-Sha)
  (2) Higashinakano Shudo: *Thorough Inspection of "Nanjing Massacre"* (Zhanzhuang-Sha)
  (3) Edited by Nanjing War History Compilation Committee: *History of Nanjing War* (Kaikōsha)
  (4) Maggie's testimony in *Records of International Military Trial for the Far East* published by Yushodo
  (5) Ara Kenichi: *Records · Nanjing Incident* (Book Publishing House).

Suzuki Aki
1. Choose (13). Because of the lack of historical data, it is completely unimaginable.
2. It should be between (2) and (3). Japan may start the war of aggression, but compared to the history of the last hundred years, it is not a "unilateral war of aggression". Both sides have a reason to quarrel when they quarrel.
3. Choose (4). From mid-November in the 12th year of Showa to New Year's Day in the 13th year of Showa. Because the self-government committee composed of Chinese, which was the predecessor of the Nanjing Reform Government, was set up in New Year's Day, so it was thought to have happened before that.
4. The Chinese side advocates (3), but I choose (1). The battle in Nanjing was derived from the result of the battle in Shanghai.
5. Death in battle cannot be called slaughter, but shootings and assassinations carried out when the battle is almost over are massacres.
6. Choose (4). Many of the Chinese soldiers in Nanjing are recruited from the peasants in the suburbs, and they are not adequately trained. So there are both regular soldiers and simple citizens. (From the perspective of context, the "citizen" here should include the aforementioned "peasants" translator.)
7. In such a place like "Nanjing", it is impossible to define plainclothes soldiers.
8. It is impossible to answer this question when the whole picture of the incident is not clear.
9. Iwane Matsui is in a sense a conservative idealist. He thinks that they should carry out a clean war, so it must be a pity for him to find brutalities such as rape. However, as the supreme responsible person, he is responsible for the ominous things of his subordinates. For example, according to the current standards, it is also natural for the chairman of the company to take the blame and resign for the ominous things that have happened. In the case of Iwane Matsui, we should first study what kind of contact he has had with the General Staff Office of his country.
10. Tang's action can be said to be correct on the surface and in military law. He also gave instructions to his subordinates to flee, so he is not to blame. The person who has the highest responsibility is Chiang Kai-shek.

11. As a general understanding, choose (3). However, it has spread in Europe and the United States that "Massacre has happened in Nanjing" from the end of the 12th year to the 13th and 14th year of Showa. Timperley's What War Means: The Japanese Terror in China was published by Gao Lanci Limited Bookstore in England in July 1938. The Chinese version of the book was also published in Hankou at the same time.
12. When writing *The Illusion of the Nanjing Massacre*, it has been shown that it is gray infinitely close to white, and there is no problem with the innocence.
13. I have never read Zhang's book, and I have no interest in reading it in the future.
14. The Diaries of John Rabe, as far as the part published in Japan, can be used for reference. However, what was published as an affidavit in the Tokyo Trial should be paid more attention as a contemporary testimony. The details will not be mentioned here.
15. It's not a problem that teenagers can understand. It should be taught in the course of Japanese history for college students. The secondary and senior high school students only need to say "The Japanese occupied Nanjing in December of the 12th year of Showa during the Japanese-Chinese War"; I do not think it is necessary for them to know more.
16. They are completely heterogeneous. Holocaust implies unlimited slaughter of specific ethnic groups, and it is clear that Japan has no such consideration for China. It is just that as an act of war, it is true that there are some excessive behaviors.
17. I have written two books on this topic, *The Illusion of the Nanjing Massacre* and *The Illusion of the Nanjing Massacre* (New), because after nearly 30 years, the first (1972) and the second (1999) have a large difference. Since the first edition was published before the resumption of diplomatic relations, it was impossible to interview the Chinese people, so almost all of the interviews were done with the Japanese who were still alive, and the second edition was mainly based on Chinese publications. A particularly important point is that the Dictionary of Names published by the Chinese Academy of Social Sciences clearly states that Timperley "was sent to Britain and the United States by the Nationalist Government after the Lugou Bridge Incident to do propaganda work, and subsequently served as an adviser to the Propaganda Department of the Nationalist Government". There are almost the same records of deaths in British newspapers. Of course, there are still some differences in some aspects of these records; what is the basis of these historical sources has not been made public (e.g., the date of death is not recorded in China, but it is clearly recorded in the British newspapers). In China, books that are really important and of reference value will appear only when there the information can be open and free. I think Edgar Snow's

War in Asia and Timperley's What War Means: The Japanese Terror in China are important materials, but I hope to read their contents critically. In the materials on Nanjing relations published by the Chinese side, there are no books worthy of reference in the real sense.

Kenichi Ara
1. Choose (12)
2. Choose (3)
3. Choose (2)
4. Choose (3)
5. The Tokyo Trial began to say that the Tokyo Trial regarded it as massacre. The killing of citizens and defeated soldiers.
6. Choose (1)
7. After the fall of Nanjing, Chinese soldiers in Nanjing were the same as plainclothes soldiers.
8. There were no firsthand historical materials.
9. The Nanjing Incident was fabricated, so General Iwane Matsui was not responsible. I think it is a pity that there are problems around the rights and interests of third countries.
10. Referring to Chinese history, it is a common performance for a commander, and I don't think he should bear any special responsibility.
11. Choose (2)
12. It's a story made up by the newspaper.
13. I was surprised when I read the Emperor's Conspiracy of バーガミニ, and I felt the same way when I read Iris Chang. Even if it is said that there is freedom of description and publication, the media bear great responsibility for the evaluation of such books.
14. It is valuable to know the actual state of the safety zone. In addition, it is clear that Rabe is responsible for the chaos in the security zone.
15. The description of textbooks is wrong as historical facts.
16. The "Nanjing Incident" is a common act of war.
17. No changes.

The recommended books are:
(1) Suzuki Aki, *The Illusion of the Nanjing Massacre* (Wenchun Wenku)
(2) Suzuki Akis, *The Illusion of the Nanjing Massacre* (New), Asukashinsha Publishing Co., Ltd.
(3) *The History of the War in Nanjing* (Kaikosha).

Yoshinori Kobayashi
1. Choose (13). The so-called firsthand information about the massacre does not exist, so this question cannot be answered.
2. Choose (4). This is also impossible to answer without firsthand information.
3. (3) If it has to be answered.

4. Choose (5). The origin of the so-called Nanjing Incident is not even clear, the topic of the period from when to when is really incredible so there is no need to answer.
5. There is also no need to answer.
6. If you change into civilian clothes, of course, you can only be plainclothes soldiers, so it can only be (1) plainclothes soldiers.
7. If you become a plainclothes soldier, of course, it can only bring the possibility of danger, arson and sabotage, not just to ordinary people.
8. If so, I hope it can be taken out immediately in order to identify the truth immediately.
9. This is an addition to "the existence of the Nanjing Incident" and a botched question. I will not answer.
10. The Nanjing Incident and so on, from the point of view of causing chaos in Nanjing, this guy (Tang Shengzhi) shall take the biggest responsibility. The control of his subordinates was completely out of control, and I really wanted to say to him, "what on earth do you want?"
11. The Tokyo Trial began to say this, and the Asahi Shimbun's "Trip to China" began to popularize.
12. Such a thing is complete nonsense.
13. Chang's book was a nonsense from the beginning.
14. All of Rabe's diaries are analyzed, and the so-called killing of Chinese people is all rumors. He himself had never witnessed a crime that was committed by the Japanese army. Rumors may be of some value, but they are only information about how Rabe was demonized because of rumors. The greatest material value of Rabe's book is the letter received by Hora Tomio's data collection to the Japanese Consulate General in Nanjing asking for food support. Here, it was recorded that the population of Nanjing trapped in safety zone after the fall was 200,000, which increased to 250,000 a month later. This is firsthand information.
15. The Tokyo Trial cited the matter and said a lot of records that were taken as facts, but the basis for the matter has not been determined. The 300,000 of the figures put forward by the Chinese side is totally unfounded, and there is no need for textbooks to record the matters in dispute.
16. People who think they are similar are people who do not yet understand what war is. Generally speaking, today's teaching books, in the project of World War II, first introduce Anna Frank's diaries, Jewish tragedies, holocaust; these are words that have nothing to do with the war. This way of writing makes people misunderstand the Holocaust as war. As a national purification, the Holocaust is different from war, and Japan has never done such a thing to China. You can't even regard it as an excessive behavior of war.

17. Generally speaking, most Japanese are just having imaginary feelings about this problem. I used to be like this. In terms of image, you will more or less believe that not recognizing the Nanjing Massacre is the right wing. It was so until recently. Mr. Nobukatsu Fujioka repeatedly said in his speeches that the Nanjing Massacre was a lie, and I was worried that he would be mistaken for the right wing. However, upon careful reading of the materials, the theory of slaughter collapsed. The massacre and so on can no longer make people feel that it is untrue. Perhaps the view will change with the new firsthand information. The same is true of the questions about comfort women. There is not a single piece of information imposed by the state and the government. The same is true of the problem of Nanjing and the issue of comfort women.

The recommended books are:
(1) Masaaki Tanaka, *Summary of the Nanjing Incident-15 Arguments for Denying the Massacre* (Qianguang-Sha)
(2) Shūdō Higashinakano, *The Thorough Examination of the "Nanjing Massacre"* (Zhanzhuang-Sha).

Nobuo Fuji
1. Choose (13). I don't think there are people who have been slaughtered (illegally killed).
2. Choose (4). I don't think the Japanese invaded China. I think the reason for the war between the Japanese and Chinese armies is that the Japanese troops who were exercising at Lugou Bridge were shot out of nowhere. Therefore, the people who died in the war were the victims of war, not the slaughtered ones caused by the Japanese army. The Chinese soldiers took off their uniforms, changed into plain clothes (became plainclothes) and had been executed after being found. That could not be regarded as being slaughtered.
3. Choose (2)
4. Choose (3)
5. Because I don't think the Japanese army carried out a massacre in Nanjing, so I can't define "slaughter".
6. Choose (1)
7. After the fall of Nanjing, some Chinese soldiers seized the clothes of ordinary Chinese people and entered the security zone pretending to be ordinary people. After inspection by the Japanese army, they were found that they were not ordinary people and were executed. The Chinese soldiers who were dealt with in this way should be regarded as plainclothes soldiers.
8. I didn't know there were such historical materials.
9. General Matsui was not directly responsible for the Nanjing Incident, but some of his soldiers had ominous incidents (reported from the gendarmerie, etc.). As the supreme commander of the attack on Nanjing, he had to be held indirectly responsible.

10. General Tang Shengzhi fled Nanjing before the fall of Nanjing (did not accept the surrender advice of the Japanese army); his responsibility can be considered extremely heavy.
11. Choose (2). I learned about this through reports before the start of the Tokyo Trial.
12. I think it's a completely made-up story.
13. I think it is a work that is not worthy of evaluation at all. Iris Chang wrote the book based on the information instilled by anti-Japanese elements in the United States (mainly overseas Chinese in the United States). It is surprising that such books can become bestsellers in the United States.
14. The Diaries of John Rabe, I think, is hardly worthy of evaluation.
15. The textbook author wrote the "Nanjing Incident" in the current Japanese textbook on the basis of the judgments put forward by the prosecutor during the Tokyo Trial and the judgments were made according to fabricated evidence and conclusion, so they can only teach students wrong history. In order to correct this, the authors of the "Nanjing Incident" should study more of the relevant works of the Nanjing Incident, and it is very important to strive to understand the truth of the Nanjing Incident.
16. The "Nanjing Incident" was fabricated by prosecutors at the beginning of the Tokyo Trial (I think), so it cannot be compared with fascist holocaust. The war between Japan and China resulted in a large number of Chinese soldiers killed in Nanjing, and the "Nanjing Incident" was fabricated by prosecutors, so it is impossible to answer the question of whether it is too much as an act of war.
17. The "Nanjing Incident" was fabricated by prosecutors during the Tokyo Trial, and my view has been consistent from the beginning to the present.

The reference books for examining the "Nanjing Incident" are:
(1) Suzuki Aki, *The Illusion of the Nanjing Massacre* (New), Asukashinsha Publishing Co., Ltd.
(2) Shūdō Higashinakano, *The Thorough Examination of the "Nanjing Massacre"* (Zhanzhuang-Sha).
(3) Ooi Mitsuru, Fabricated *"Nanjing Massacre"-The Whole Picture of the Attack and the Horror of the Media Reports* (Zhanzhuang-Sha).
(4) Masaaki Tanaka, *Summary of the Nanjing Incident-15 Arguments for Denying the Massacre* (Qianguang-Sha).
(5) Nobuo Fuji, *How the Nanking Massacre Was Manufactured—Deception of the Tokyo Trial* (Zhanzhuang-Sha).

Takaike Katsuhiko
 1. Choose (12). I don't think there isn't any illegal behavior of the Japanese soldiers in Nanjing. But this is another incident that has nothing to do with the so-called Nanjing Incident. What is called the Nanjing Incident here is the Nanjing Massacre.

2. Choose (2) (3). But it is not a war of aggression.
3. Choose (2). Because I advocate that there is no Nanjing Incident, so it is impossible to answer the question of when to start and when to end, but doesn't what is called the Nanjing Incident refer to (2)? (It is not my opinion, but the propositions of those who advocate the Nanjing Incident.)
4. Choose (5). Including the city of Nanjing and a number of surrounding areas. Here, too, because I think there is no Nanjing Incident, the question of where to go cannot be answered, but the original proposition of the affirmative theorists was including the city of Nanjing and some surrounding areas. "Nanjing City" is several times the vast area of the city.
5. The original proposition of the affirmative theorists refers to the fact that the Japanese collectively tied Chinese people's hands and feet with wire, pushed them into the river alive and killed them in large quantities by sadistic methods. At present, there has been some discussion on the consideration of how the prisoners should be punished. This is a question of pure academic research that should be conducted in accordance with international law at that time. I do not think it has anything to do with the massacre. It is possible that the result of the study may break the law.
6. As a general view, plainclothes soldiers.
7. The answer to the previous question "as a general view" is related to this question. In fact, a large number of weapons were collected from the refugee areas and the illegal act of framing the Japanese soldiers under the command of officers was carried out. In this sense, it is generally appropriate to regard the Chinese soldiers hidden in the refugee areas as plainclothes soldiers, but it is necessary to examine individual soldiers one by one. For this reason, the Japanese army has conducted screening.
8. I have no idea. I haven't seen it.
9. Because I do not recognize the Nanjing Incident, I do not think that he has any responsibility for the Nanjing Incident. From another angle, General Matsui's tearful instructions can be held responsible for a number of ominous things, but as seen in the general's instructions, he can be considered having bored the responsibility. Therefore, he has no responsibility.
10. This is the same as the previous point, because there is no Nanjing Incident, so there is no responsibility for the Nanjing Incident. But the responsibility for the death of Chinese soldiers is heavy. Because as a commander, he has the responsibility to give correct orders to fight and retreat. General Tang did not take responsibility for this at all.
11. Choose (4). Of course, (1) (2) (3) are also correct, but it is also written in the textbook that (4) is widely used as a propaganda tool by the Chinese side.
12. "The 100-men killing contest" is not a fact at all.

13. Iris Chang's book, as a history book, has no value at all. However, it should be sold so much in the United States and lied in the bookstores anywhere in the United States and airport bookstores; their organizing strength is amazing. One cannot help feeling the power behind it.
14. I think Rabe's diary is biased, but compared with other materials, the correct part can be evaluated.
15. There is absolutely no need for textbooks to write about it.
16. I think it's a normal act of war. This, as economists say, should be taken into account that the Japanese economy achieved full employment in the 10th year to 12th year of Showa, and Japan reached its highest economic state before the war. In other words, ordinary soldiers know that there are good jobs waiting for them when they return to Japan. It is inconceivable that such a soldier would give himself up.
17. No particular changes.

The recommended books are as follows:
(1) *The Battle of Nanjing*, compiled by Battle of Nanking Editorial Committee (Kaikōsha)
(2) Masaaki Tanaka, *Summary of the Nanjing Incident-15 Arguments for Denying the Massacre* (Qianguang-Sha)
(3) Shūdō Higashinakano, *The Thorough Examination of the "Nanjing Massacre"* (Zhanzhuang-Sha)
(4) Itakura Yoshiaki, *The Truth of Nanjing Incident* (Japanese Book Publishing Association)
(5) Kenichi Ara, *Reconstruction of Nanjing Incident* (Book Publishing House).

Tanaka Masaaki
1. Choose infinitely close to zero. There is no evidence of the Nanjing Massacre. For example, none of the fifteen commission members of the United States, Britain, Germany and Denmark who were in residence at the safety zone and were free to inspect inside and outside Nanjing did not see or record the massacre. Moreover, none of them mentioned the killings. Neither the opponent Chiang Kai-shek regime nor the Communist Party mentioned it at the time of the incident.
2. Choose (3). Soldiers who have taken off their military uniforms and fled to the safety zone were called plainclothes team or plainclothes soldiers. They violated the international rules and customs of warfare and thus their execution cannot be considered a massacre.
3. The explanation of (2) is correct. Among the majority of the slaughter school, such as Honda Katsuichi who was a journalist of *Asahi Shimbun*, some claim that the death toll of 300,000 in the Nanjing Massacre involves the period from the Shanghai Battle to the end of the Nanjing Battle, and the regions including counties around Nanjing. And it is wrong to extend the scope of time and area.

4. Choose (2). But the suburbs where had fierce fights are also included, such as the Zijin Mountain, Yuhuatai, Xinhe Town, Xiaguan and other regions around Nanjing.
5. The so-called "slaughter" refers to killing non-combatants based on order. And it was after the Tokyo Trial that the "Nanjing Massacre" or "Nanjing Incident" became a heated topic in Japan. The Tokyo Trial must confirm the Nanjing Massacre so as to convict Japan of "a crime against humanity". So Marshal MacArthur sent secret envoys to Nanjing and entrusted them to collect evidence. The Nanjing government gathered cadres from 14 groups including the Medical Association, the Law Society and the Chamber of Commerce and Trade to uncover the massacre perpetrated by the Japanese army. At first, they remained silent. But after all kinds of repeated coaxing, a man finally broke his silence, "I saw the bodies of 279,586 people". The death toll of 340,000 people was based on such nonsense and the calculation was also wrong. As a result, the Tokyo Trial shrunk this ridiculous figure and issued a dual sentence that the Japanese army slaughtered more than 200,000 people (but more than 100,000 in the sentence for General Matsui).
6. Choose (1) plainclothes soldiers.
7. On December 9th, the bills of General Matsui on advising Tang Shengzhi to "peacefully open the gate of Nanjing" were scattered but Tang did not reply. The general attack then began at noon the next day, the deadline. And Nanjing fell on the 13th. Command Tang fled Nanjing the night before. Without a commander, the Chinese soldiers took off their uniforms and hats, seized the clothes of residents and entered the safety zone. With weapons hidden, such as pistols, rifles and grenades, they waited for the opportunity to attack the Japanese soldiers. They violated the international rules and customs of warfare, and thus, their executions were well-founded. Shinobu Junpei agrees with me on this point.
8. The execution of plainclothes soldiers did not violate the international rules and customs of warfare at all. Nanjing University Professor M. S. Bates (who was member of the Commission for the Safety Zone) originally thought it "a breach of the international law and openly stated that the Japanese army slaughtered 40,000 people in the safety zone". Later, he realized it was not the case and canceled the figure. He is another example.
9. General Matsui Ishigen graduated with the first place from the Imperial Japanese Army Academy and volunteered to be as a military attache in China for 16 years. He supported Sun Yat-sen's second revolution and devoted his life to realize the "Asianism". He could be said to be the top China hand among the army. On August 13th, 1937, the Second Shanghai Incident broke out. And then the General Staff Headquarters ordered General Matsui to change from reserve to active duty and to establish the Shanghai Expeditionary Army with General Matsui as

commander. The 35,000 Japanese soldiers, against the Chinese combat power almost reaching 400,000, were gradually on the back foot. But things changed after the Yanagawa Company landed from the Hangzhou Bay. On December 1st, Deputy of Staff Tada flew from Japan to China and ordered to capture Nanjing. He appointed General Matsui commander of the CCAA, leading the SEF and the 10th Army (Yanagawa Company) to proceed toward Nanjing. General Matsui issued the bills advising Tang Shengzhi to "peacefully open the gate of Nanjing" but was refused. When the general attack began on December 10th, he issued an instruction, saying "it is an unprecedented event in history that the Imperial entered the foreign capital which will attract worldwide attention. All should be well-disciplined and upright, providing a model for the future". Soldiers were also given the sketch of Nanjing, with Sun Yat-sen's Mausoleum, Ming Xiaoling Mausoleum, foreign embassies and consulates marked, and forbidden to enter these guarded places. The general also ordered to "severely punish the plunderers and those who have caused fires even if unintentionally". As he claimed at the Tokyo Trial, "My mission was to command the SEF and the 10th Army and the divisions that have military police and legal departments were directly responsible for the supervision, disclosure, and punishment concerning military discipline". But as mentioned above, the massacre did not exist. Disregarding the hatred, General Matsui built the Kyin Kannon, which associated Japanese spirit with and Chinese god, at Atami in the 15th year of the Showa era. He thought, "The honorable sacrifice of the Japanese and Japanese armies is for the future revival of Asia".

10. Li Zongren, Bai Chongxi and other warlords believed that guarding Nanjing would require too much sacrifice and thus advocated abandoning the city. But Tang Shengzhi advocated defending Nanjing through a battle. His proposal was adopted by Chiang Kai-shek and he was then appointed as commander. General Matsui urged the peaceful opening of the city, but he still refused. On the eve of the fall of Nanjing (December 12th), he fled to Pukou at night, without taking his staff officer and soldiers. For a commander, this is the biggest shame and the biggest disgrace.

11. The same as the forgoing (2), it was after the Tokyo Trial. About 120 reporters and photographers (including five foreign reporters), who entered Nanjing at the time of the fall of Nanjing, did not see any slaughter, nor did they see the mountainous corpses or the blood river when they had interviews in Nanjing. The size of the city is about two-thirds of Tokyo's Setagaya Ward and equivalent to Kamakura City in the level of city. There were 120 journalists having interviews here. And later, fifteen people including writers and commentators, such as Soichi Otsuki, Saijo Hachijo and Hayashi Fumiko, also entered the city. None of them saw the massacre. Critic Ara Kenichi directly interviewed 36 officers, soldiers,

498   APPENDIX

journalists, critics, etc., who entered Nanjing and wrote the *Nanjing Incident-They Told Us*. But no one mentioned the killings or the mountainous bodies. Neither foreign media have not reported them, let alone the Nanjing Massacre.

12. It was a fabrication by the reporter of *Tokyo Nichi Nichi Shimbun (Mainichi Shimbun* today*)* Asami that the Lieutenant Mukai and Noda killed 100 men in order to raise Japanese national enthusiasm in war. Mukai was the commander of the field artillery and Noda was the adjutant of the brigade. Both of them couldn't kill 100 men in terms of their positions. Besides, it was physically impossible for a Japanese sword to cut a hundred people's heads.

13. For this, As the book *Study on the Nanjing Atrocities* written by Nobukatsu Fujioka and Higashinakano Shūdō said, Chang's book, published in the 9th year of Heisei and soon published more than 500.000 copies, got a great reputation in the USA. However, its content was full of mistakes. 34 photos in this book were fabricated and revised, none of which could prove the Nanjing Massacre. The subtitle of this book is Holocaust forgotten by World War II. The so-called Nanjing Incident said by Chang was a massacre of China by Japan, similar to the German fascists' war of exterminating Jews. This is a book dedicated to anti-Japanese propaganda by the Chinese, which can be seen as a reproduction of the "international intelligence war" of wartime propaganda after 60 years. The California Council, triggered by this book, passed a resolution demanding Japan to apologize and compensate. This book is dangerous for Japan to fall into the "dark legend".

14. The Japanese translation of "*Nanjing's Truth*", John Rabe's Diary, has been published. This is not his diary written in the era of "Chairman of the Security Council", but his writing after returning to Germany. As Indian judge Radha Binod Pal said during the Tokyo Trial, "diary" is not the same as "writing" after many years.   I also read "*The Truth of Nanjing*". There is no record of General Matsui's truce from December 9th to 10th and that Rabe's "expressed gratitude to the Japanese army for not shelling the security zone" and established the "Nanjing Autonomous Committee" on January 3rd to inherit the business of the security zone committee. The words of arson and rape are wild, which discredited anti-Japanese book.

15. The Sankei Shimbun reported "China's Pressure on Textbook Verification" in a prominent position on the front page of the first edition on October 6th, in the 12th year of Heisei. The subtitle was "The Nanjing Incident and Comfort Women" with "No Less Account" and it reported severe demands on the Ministry of Education, Culture and Sports and members of the ruling party. As far as I can remember, with the implementation of the new learning guidelines since the 14th year of Heisei, the self-abuse bias in history education among people has become

a problem. The "New History Textbook Compilation Association" has also been established, so China has once again intervened. These words "Japan is the worst country in the world" and "please don't treat me as a Japanese soldier like a wild animal" are written by Japanese public high school students after learning Japanese history. The Nanjing Incident, which did not exist, was written as a cruel massacre of more than 300,000 people. This was reported by Japanese textbooks. Which country educates its young people on the illegal and tyrannical practices that do not exist in the country? I want to say that China's interference can stop!

16. The fascist Jewish holocaust and the Nanjing War are totally different with no similarities. Anyone who looks at it will know that the Nanjing offensive is a common act of war. Moreover, this war is not excessive for the Japanese army. However, the differences from the common war are that from the very beginning, as the Japanese army worried, (1) the 3.8-square-kilometer (four times the square in front of palace) size of the security zone has neither natural obstacles such as rivers nor barbed wire that allows a large number of plainclothes soldiers to enter; (2) China's unique plainclothes soldiers changed their uniforms into plain clothes, hid their weapons and swarmed into the safety zone; (3) these plainclothes soldiers were exposed and punished (this does not violate wartime international law), which are not seen in common wars. The "Gacino Shenfu Security Zone" of the Shanghai War, which also set up a security zone, had no such disputes (this does not violate wartime international law), which are not seen in normal wars. The "Gacino Shenfu Security Zone" of the Shanghai War, which also set up a security zone, had no such disputes.

17. Views on the Nanjing Incident have been consistent and unchanged. I graduated from the "Revitalizing Asia School" in the 8th year of the Shōwa era. I was introduced by my mentor Mr. Shimonaka Yasaburo to General Iwane Matsui and then got a position in "Greater Asia Association" where the General served as president. I used to accompany the General to the army hospitals in Osaka, Nagoya, Kanazawa, Sendai and other places to visit the wounded former subordinates. Moreover, the General said to me that "I am worried about the security situation in Nanjing in the future. Can you go there and inspect it?" At that time, I was the editor of the association's publication the Great Asianism and got permission "military correspondent" from the Ministry of the Army. At the end of June of the 13th year of the Showa era, I went to Nanjing (about half a year after the fall of Nanjing). In Nanjing, I was introduced by General Matsui to visit, apart from the Nanking Safety Zones, former battlefields and refuges for prisoners and other places in such as Yuhuatai, Hsiakwan, Xinhe town, Straw Shoe Gorge, Zijin Mountain and other places. With a population of nearly 400,000, it was no longer dangerous

for a woman to go out alone and there was no need to worry about law and order. In the 10th year of the Shōwa era, Nagata, Chief of the Bureau of Military Affairs of the Ministry of the Army, was assassinated by Lieutenant Aizawa. General Matsui felt responsible as the senior in the army and retired voluntarily and joined in the reserve service. He was the first one of the five generals of the same term (referring to the same term in military academy—noted by the translator) to retire during the same period. In the next year, the "February 26th incident" occurred and the rest four generals were also arranged in the reserve service. At that time, Chiang Kai-shek's anti-Japanese campaign was vigorously launched, which would lead to a worrying situation for the Sino-Japanese War. In order to persuade the southwest warlords and Chiang Kai-shek, the General went to China and I accompanied him as a secretary in January of the 11th year of the Shōwa era. Warlords Hu Hanmin, Li Zongren and Bai Chongxi in the southwest were all disciples of Sun Yat-sen, Father of the Nation. The General told the three respectively the peaceful path between Japan and China. Sun Yat-sen, Father of the Nation once said that "Without China, there would be no Japan and Without Japan, there would be no China. Sino-Japanese relations are as close as lips and teeth". However, with the aid of the United States and the Soviet Union, Chiang adopted the policy of resisting Japan and insulting Japan. One joined in the Chiang's central government and wanted to change the policy. The General even went to Nanjing to persuade Chiang Kai-shek. In Nanjing, General He Yingqin and Foreign Minister Zhang Qun warmly welcomed the General. Chiang and Zhang were also taken care of by the General during their stay in Japan. The General talked about what he said during his visit to the southwest and also about the hope of ending the policy of resisting Japan and insulting Japan as well as other things such as the danger of associating with the Soviet Union. Two welcome receptions were held and Chiang accepted the General's advice. The General reported to Prime Minister Hirota on the course of his talks with Chiang Kai-shek and suggested that he hoped to implement a peace policy toward China. When General Matsui's Sino-Japanese peace work achieved success, Chiang Kai-shek, who went to Xi'an to supervise the war, became Zhang Xueliang's prisoner in December that year. Stalin sent a telegram asking to keep Chiang "alive" and Chiang was able to return to Nanjing after signing six vows including "Kuomintang-Communist cooperation" and "stop the civil war and cooperate to fight foreign enemies" proposed by Chou En-lai. In July of the following year, the Lugou Bridge Incident broke out and more than 200 Japanese were killed in Tongzhou. The war spread to Shanghai and the Sino-Japanese War expanded. As mentioned earlier, ironically, General Matsui returned to active service and was appointed commander of the Shanghai Expeditionary Army, and later became the general commander of the

Central China Area Army. He then completed the capture of Nanjing. At the Tokyo Trial after the war, General Matsui was sentenced to death for the non-existent Nanjing Massacre. In order to wash away this injustice, I studied on the Nanjing Incident. The outcomes of the study were published one after the other. They were three books: Fiction of the Nanjing Massacre (Nihon Kyôbunsha, in the 59th year of the Shōwa era); General Matsui's Diaries in the Wartime (Fuyo Shobo Publishing, in the 60th year of the Shōwa era); and Summaries of the Nanjing Incident—Fifteen Arguments Against the Massacre (Kenkōsha, in the 62nd year of the Shōwa era). The book Nanjing Atrocities written by Iris Chang in the United States has more than ninety mistakes, and the 34 photos inserted are also fake photos. The book claims that the Japanese army brutally killed more than 300,000 Chinese, which can be seen as the fascist holocaust. All of a sudden, the popularity of the book rose. Not only did the number of publications exceed 500,000, but the California Parliament even passed a resolution requiring Japan to apologize and compensate. Unfortunately, neither the government nor ordinary people have responded to this appropriately in English. The above-mentioned "Summary of the Nanjing Incident" is the essence of my study of Nanjing (the original text—noted by the translator). I plan to translate this essence into English and distribute it to about 3,000 influential politicians, scholars and journalists in the United States. Fortunately, with the assistance of translators, it is scheduled to be completed by the end of the 12th year of the Heisei era. Supporters of the plan are now being sought. First of all, the most important thing is to let Americans know that there was absolutely no holocaust in Nanjing, no massacre of more than 300,000 people and no rape of more than 80,000 people as Chang said. Second, the publication of the book is also very necessary for Japan's future. I would be very grateful if I could get agreement and support.

Ooi Mitsuru
1. Choose (12)
2. Choose (3)
3. Choose (3)
4. Choose (3)
5. Killing the common citizens.
6. Choose (1)
7. Paper
8. No.
9. Rape and acts that no army anywhere can avoid are the responsibility of the commander.
10. I have no responsibility.
11. Choose (3).

12. It is a story from the common sense. *The Illusion of the Nanjing Massacre* written by Suzuki Aki proves a fabrication. Don't ask such questions.
13. Chang's book is not worth discussing.
14. Rade's diary is the result of emotions and cannot be accepted.
15. No, Is it necessary for the fake to write down?
16. Maybe the execution was a little excessive. But the battlefields are different from the peacetime. War indeed is killing each other.
17. There is no change.

Matsumura Toshio
1. Choose (13). Regarding "massacres" as illegal killings, the Japanese army, like the US occupying forces in Japan and the troops of other countries, cannot be said to have no offenders at all. As mentioned later, there are also those who have been wrongfully executed as plainclothes soldiers. The total number is unknown, but those who are mistaken should be within hundred units. The so-called figure of 300,000 was originally put forward by Timperley in the name of Gacino Shenfu. A war dead or a soldier in a safe area who has been arrested and executed as a combat act after fleeing cannot be massacred.
2. Choose (4). Since the dead includes the dead in the battle and the condemned, the term "slain" cannot be used to refer to both.
3. Choose (3). From around December 13th, to mid-February in "*Nanjing Safe Zone Records* (i.e., *Nanjing Safe Zone Archives*—translator) and Timperley's *What is the War? Outsiders Witness the Atrocities of the Japanese Army*". Why? The "Nanjing Incident", which uses the "Nanjing International Commission" and some Americans as its source, is summarized through these two books. In addition, there was no "Nanjing Incident" at that time (this is the original text, which seems to refer to no one mentioned—translator). Deding's records are also based on the rumors of the International Commission Bates, and the records of Chinese newspapers come from the same source. Deding and Stall were not witnessed by themselves. (Except for the "sentence" at Nanjing Pier on December 15th.)
4. Choose (4). Almost all the information of foreigners is what happened in the safety zone. According to Smyth's investigation of the dead in rural areas, the perpetrators could not be specifically identified as the Japanese army. The expansion of the scope is the evidence produced by the national government for the Nanjing military trial. As for the Shanghai battle and so on, it is unreasonable to slaughter tens of thousands of people in a narrow range. This is what Japanese "Slaughter School" holds.
5. As mentioned in the previous No.2, it is wrong to regard "Nanjing Incident" as a "massacre". If this is a massacre, then those who died in the war in ancient and modern Japan and abroad can be called "massacred".

6. Refer to the following No.7.
7. At that time, the soldiers were divided into three types: (a) plainclothes soldiers who had been trained and planned to sneak into the safety zone from the beginning; (b) those who, as regular troops, changed into civilian clothes after the fall of Nanjing to try to make a comeback; and (c) those wrested civilian clothes from the refugees to escape into the safety zone, simply because they were desperate for their lives. These people cannot be said to have surrendered, nor can they be said to be citizens.
8. Refer to the previous No.7.
9. General Matsui, as already mentioned in No.1, issued a severe order to the soldiers that no crimes were allowed. He certainly did not have the responsibility for the "Nanjing Incident" just because of foreigners' propaganda.
10. From a tactical point of view, Tang Shengzhi arrogantly claimed to defend Nanjing, although it was Jiang Jieshi's order, but as Datin reported, there were no ships ready to cross the river and the elite troops would retreat soon. Thus, soldiers left in Nanjing were exhausted troops from Shanghai battle and urgent troops which were made up of able-bodied men and juvenile soldiers who were forced from the southern rural areas to fight against the Japanese army. Therefore, most of them would be out of control once they collapsed, especially the chaos that caused the Jiang River and Shimonoseki, and caused a large number of deaths; there was no organized surrender to the Japanese army, and they just wanted to escape.
11. Choose (5). The "Nanjing Massacre" was known by Ministry of Foreign Affairs of Japan through information from foreigners (a telegram to Foreign Minister Hirota), which is only a rumor (the sender is the Shanghai Consulate conveying the action of the national government worker Timperley). The Tokyo Trial used the evidence of the Nanjing Massacre produced by the Nanjing Trial. It was first heard in Japan and the world, so it disappeared after the judgment. In the 40s of the Showa era, propaganda led by the Asahi Shimbun recruited survivors from Nanjing citizens in China. The memorial was completed with the assistance of some Japanese.
12. As is known to all, this incident originated from the fictional memoir of Asahi reporter of the Tokyo Daily News on November 30th, December 4th, December 6th and 13th of the Showa era. It was reproduced by Japan advertiser, Chinaweekly, etc., and attracted Timperley's attention and then was included in the former citation *What is the war? Outsiders witnessed the atrocities of the Japanese and Chinese forces*, bringing bad luck to the two second lieutenants. The Nanjing Military Court took advantage of the "Nanjing Incident" as evidence of atrocities to punish the two second lieutenants. The prosecutors in Tokyo prepared to use this as one of the evidences, but did not submit it to the court. Honta

Masaru, who re-introduced the Japanese in the *Journey to China*, now describes the "hundreds of beheaded" of the two second lieutenants as "slaughtering captives and refugees who lost their resistance", making a completely irresponsible direction change. This is a correspondence that was made in order to support the argument that the two second lieutenants had the possibility of hand-to-hand combat and did not reach Nanjing city. The Japanese sword could not kill dozens of people in the battle.

13. Iris Chang's ignorance of history is needless to say, what is called information is all used for two military trials, including the records of foreigners' rumors in Nanjing and the prosecution evidence of Chinese testimonies, plus new testimony of the Chinese since the 1980s. Moreover, it is clear that it is several times longer than the original data, so it is easy to point out his change of direction. It can be said that this is a fake book.

14. Rabe's "The Truth of Nanjing" is valuable as a source of information about how rumors spread in Nanjing at that time. I don't think he is lying. However, he lacks insight into whether what they hear or see reflects the truth. On the one hand, he is a nice person used by American missionaries. On the other hand, he mistook all the prisoners who fled because they were afraid of revealing their true identity for simple Japanese soldiers who were scared of the "Hitler, Nazi Party Flag and German" light. But intensive reading of Rabe's diary, you will feel that it is a denial of the so-called "Nanjing Massacre".

15. Historical cognition is something that everyone understands historical facts, as long as it describes the "fall of Nanjing" as a fact. The so-called Nanjing Incident is the fabrication of foreigners based on the rumors against the Japanese army, including those plainclothes soldiers mentioned above as deserters, spread by national government officials who were in charge of disturbing the peace of the home front.

16. As mentioned before, the "Nanjing Incident" came to the world by foreigners mainly in missionaries in Nanjing, and Timperley, a staff member of Chiang Kai-shek, who had the same interest for two military trials after the war. Therefore, this question, which was premised on the existence of the "Nanjing Incident", cannot be answered. In the final debate on April 9th, 23 in Showa era, the defender of Tokyo Trial, Martes said quite completely. "China has always been good at propaganda and its methods are extremely clever. Anti-Japanese propaganda was initially directed by the staff of American and British schools, churches and hospitals in China. The unfortunate incident in Nanjing was quickly spread through exaggerated malicious propaganda without distinguishing of the Japanese army".

17. The reference of "before" is unclear. From the Nanjing Incident to 1995, which was almost unknown to me, I cannot judge. However, from the publishing of *The Great Question about the "Nanjing Massacre"*

in December 1998 to the present, the thoughts obtained mainly from a careful review of the foreigners at that time and the Chinese after the war were more profound with the previous answer.

Reference Books Helping to Understand the Reality of Nanjing Incident:
(1) Suzuki Aki, *The Illusion of the Nanjing Massacre* (Asukashinsha Publishing Co., Ltd.)
(2) Nobukatsu Fujioka and Higashinakano Shūdō, *Study on the Nanjing Atrocities* (Xiangchuan-Sha)
(3) Itakura Yoshiaki, *The Truth of Nanjing Incident* (Japanese Book Publishing Association)
(4) *Minnie Vautrin's Diary* (Ōtsuki Shoten)
(5) Matsumura Toshio, *Questions on the Nanjing Massacre* (Zhanzhuan-Sha).

Note: Vautrin's diary is not evidence of the Holocaust, but if one can grasp the essence, he can see the truth of the rampant spread in Nanjing at that time. On December 13th and 14th, there was no a massacre at all, and it was completely quiet in Nanjing. Even outside the security zone, Vautrin did not see the cruel behavior of the Japanese army and the bodies spread, which alone was useful evidence. However, if the reader still cannot understand this. In this case, it is recommended to read Tanaka Masaaki's Nanjing Incident (Qianguang-Sha).

Nobukatsu Fujioka
1. Choose (12).
2. Choose (3).
3. Choose (2).
4. Choose (4).
5. The so-called "massacre" (1) refers to the groundless killing of common citizens who are not combatants and (2) unlawful killing of prisoners in violation of wartime international law.
6. Choose (2).
7. Blank.
8. Blank.
9. As for the ulterior intelligence that a large-scale ominous event has taken place in the Japanese army in Nanjing, General Matsui is suspected of being trapped in a mistake. From this point of view, he is responsible for the future generations.
10. As Chinese textbooks once recorded, the "Nanjing Incident" was caused by Tang Shengzhi's escape, so he had the greatest responsibility.
11. Choose (3).
12. It can't be true.
13. Iris Chang's book is only a pseudograph of anti-Japanese propaganda.
14. Rabe's diary, contrary to his intention, has become the material for understanding the whole picture of the "Nanjing Incident".

15. If it is recorded in the textbook, as part of the Propaganda, it is only appropriate that the Tokyo Trial and other relevant measures be taken.
16. There are few excesses.
17. After receiving the description of the whole picture of the incident in the "Complete Examination of the Nanjing Massacre" by Higashinakano Shudo, the evaluation has changed greatly. The incident is the material for propaganda, and I hope to refer to the "Study of Nanjing Atrocities" jointly written by Nakano and Fujioka.

Hara Takeshi
1. Choose (9). About 20,000 prisoners and plainclothes soldiers were killed illegally and thousands of ordinary citizens were killed.
2. Choose (4). The first-line troops arbitrarily executed captives, plainclothes soldiers. And the soldiers (a small group) killed common citizens outside the fighting.
3. Choose (2).
4. Choose (2).
5. Illegal killing in violation of the laws and regulations of war. The first-line troops arbitrarily killed prisoners and plainclothes soldiers without going through the procedures of the military law meeting, which was unlawful killings. If plainclothes soldiers are not taken as prisoners, they should be interrogated and punished by the military law meeting.
6. Choose (2).
7. Blank.
8. "Wartime felons shall be interrogated by military courts or other courts arbitrarily designated by belligerents. However, it must be recognized that punishment without trial is prohibited by current international customary laws and regulations" (Tachi Sakutaro's "Wartime International Law", Japan Review Agency, Showa 13 Years, p. 49). I think that for the execution of the captured foreigners, we think that it was a legal execution after trial (don't know it is illegal executions), and thus, it was not clearly recorded as a violation of international law. I think, because a large number of executions were carried out at night on the banks of the Yangtze River, there were few witnesses.
9. The lack of concern for the issue of prisoners and the lack of a clear policy for dealing with prisoners are of great responsibility. Even in the event of an incident, it is natural to have capitulators in battle. However, it does not indicate the policy for dealing with capitulators. Both the chief of the army and the commander are blunders and irresponsible.
10. It is totally irresponsible to run away from Nanjing with the disposal of protecting the citizens. If the leaders who stayed in Nanjing surrendered, nothing would have happened.
11. Choose (2).
12. It did kill a lot of people, but the killing of a hundred people is an act of ostentation. The two second lieutenants' wish to be famous and the

shallow sea reporters' wish to be brave are consistent with the army's wish to improve their fighting will, which has led to such exaggerated propaganda far from the truth.
13. Iris Chang's book is a campaign product of the Nanjing Massacre. Moreover, there is no demonstration.
14. Rabe's diary made a relatively objective record of the situation at that time. It is a valuable document for researchers.
15. I think there have been massacres, but textbooks should clearly record that there are not such massacres as 200,000 or 300,000.
16. Compared with the common war, the Nanjing Incident is excessive. Japanese and Chinese leaders and military commanders have shown a weak view of international law.
17. With the research, we will understand the indifference of the Japanese military leaders to the prisoners and the Japanese people's profound contempt for China. The Holocaust theory in China and the fiction theory of some Japanese people are all empty and scanty arguments that lack empirical evidence.
18. Reference books:
    (1) Hora Tomio, *Data on the History of Japan-China War: Japan-China War I and II* (Kawade Shobo Shinsha)
    (2) Nanjing War History Editorial Committee compiles *Nanjing War History, Document Collection I and II* (Kaikōsha)
    (3) Nanjing Incident Investigation and Research Association compiles *Nanjing Incident Data Collection 1 and 2* (Aoki Bookstore)
    (4) John Rabe (Hirano Ko's Translation) *The Truth of Nanjing* (Kodansha).

Nakamura Akira

1. Choose (10). Thousands of people to around 10,000. However, as a principle, the common citizens are excluded.
2. Choose (2) and (4). But it is not considered a so-called "war of aggression". Most of those killed were soldiers who became prisoners.
3. Choose (2). However, it can be considered to be particularly focused on (3).
4. Choose (2). However, it should correctly include Zijin Mountain, which was the scene of fierce fighting on the eve of the Japanese army's fall in Nanjing, and the outskirts of Nanjing, which are adjacent to the city.
5. (Definition 1) Killed in a Cruel Way, regardless of whether it is legal or not. The so-called cruel method refers to a method accompanied by unnecessary suffering. ※. (Definition 2) Mass unlawful killings, regardless of whether the method of killing is cruel or not. ※.The so-called lawlessness has no justification for justifiable defense or emergency refuge.
6. Choose (1) and (2). It is plainclothes soldiers who can truly subordinate themselves to the organization (plainclothes team). It is regular soldiers who change into plain clothes just to escape. There are both cases.

7. It is certainly not that "infiltrate the place where most of the natives live", so this point cannot be compared with the plainclothes soldiers in Shanghai during the war. There are real plainclothes soldiers who belong to the plainclothes team, and there are not real plainclothes soldiers who just put on plain clothes for the purpose of escape. This must be distinguished from the "plain clothes" of slayers in civilian clothes in wartime international law. In addition, it must not be forgotten that plainclothes soldiers who can be executed immediately are limited to "current offenders".
8. Blank.
9. Commander Matsui paid great attention when entering the city and probably never dreamed of the execution of a large number of prisoners by the Imperial Army. If Commander Matsui had to go back, perhaps it was because he stubbornly insisted on holding the entry ceremony on December 17th. Because we can see that the troops are rushing to deal with the prisoners in order to hold the entry ceremony in time. Moreover, this causal relationship is undoubtedly not what General Matsui expected.
10. Both Tang Shengzhi and Chiang Kai-shek were the first responsible for the incident. On the one hand, he advocated to "defend" Nanjing, but on the other hand, he abandoned his troops and residents and ran away. Since they ignored the Japanese army's advice to surrender, or fought the war completely, or declared Nanjing an open city (unguarded city) and retreated with the troops.
11. Choose (2). However, the period of (3) was specifically mentioned.
12. It is hard to imagine that "cutting a hundred people" is a fact.
13. Chang's book is a ridiculous book written for anti-Japanese political purposes. It does not even have the value of serious criticism. The author's ignorance of history is surprising. It is only a book of anti-Japanese incitement and is not worth reading.
14. There are both true accounts and absurd rumors. However, since Rabe has kept a diary, he is sure to try his best to be fair.
15. The Imperial Army's mass execution of prisoners should be documented, and the Chinese side's claim that there were J-plans and organized killings of more than 300,000 citizens should be categorically rejected.
16. We have to admit that it is rather excessive as an act of war.
17. I have always held the position of "having had is having" since before, and this has not changed. I just used to call "Nanjing Incident" and tried to avoid "massacre" and "massacre incident", which contained the term "massacre", but now it is believed that there has been "massacre" of prisoners. This is the conclusion reached by modestly reviewing our army's combat, operational records and various testimonies based on the aforementioned "definition 1" and "definition 2" of the massacre.

18. Books that should be consulted: (1) Nanjing War History Editorial Committee compiles *Nanjing War History* (Xiexing Society), (2) Nanjing Incident Investigation and Research Association compiles *Nanjing Incident Information Collection* (Aoki Bookstore). (3) It is a book edited by the Massacre School, but things concerning the enemy should also be read carefully, the facts are accepted frankly, and nonsense can be dismissed as nonsense.

Unemoto Masaki
1. Choose (13). It is not an organized and planned killing of surrendered prisoners and good citizens, but an individual and sporadic killing, including those shogunate mountain captures who were killed during the liberation and ordinary citizens who were mistakenly dragged away and executed during the raid in the refugee area.
2. Choose (2) and (3).
3. Choose (4). From the fall of Nanjing (December 13th) to December 20th. The main body of the incident was (3) the incident (action) attached to Nanjing's strategic war (military operations) during the period from the occupation of Nanjing (into the city to wipe out the remnants of the enemy and the refugee areas) to the entry into the city. By December 20th of (4), the system of guarding and maintaining public order will be implemented, and the number of incidents (broadly speaking) that occurred after entering the city will be small.
4. Choose (5). From outside Nanjing to the safe area.
5. (1) Surrenders taken in by the Japanese army were killed illegally as formal prisoners. (2) Killing good citizens for no reason. (3) Good citizens wrongly involved in the raids in refugee areas.
6. Choose (1).
7. Not limited to shooting and blocking, concealing and carrying weapons and ammunition, they have always been in a state of being dangerous. There was no control at the time of the occupation.
8. Confirmed data (historical data) are unknown.
9. General Matsui is the commander of the army and has no responsibility to direct the normal military operations. If there is one, it is only a moral responsibility.
10. General Tang Shengzhi has a great responsibility. (1) The guidance of Nanjing guarding city operations. (2) The bungling of withdrawal operations. (3) Give up guarding the ground and leave the battlefield. (4) Rejecting General Matsui's peace proposal and Rabe's proposal, which brought great sacrifices to the army and the people.
11. (2) is the beginning. The uproar began after (4) (due to China's interference).
12. It is not true that "one hundred people are beheaded". Perhaps, Wells and Noda were impulsive, boasting "one hundred people are beheaded", but saber is unable to cut one hundred people.

13. Iris Chang's book is full of lies and prejudices, with zero credibility, but it is necessary to study countermeasures for Americans to read it. It should be criticized, denied and publicized correctly.
14. As for the relief of refugees, Rabe's diary is probably correct, but the accounts of the Japanese army, especially the brutal acts, are almost all based on hearsay and cannot be believed. Therefore, it is not "the reality of Nanjing". It is necessary to compare it with other historical materials. However, even in Rabe's Diary, there are no cases of organized killings.
15. During the attack on the capital Nanjing, the garrison commander Tang Shengzhi involved the citizens in "defending" and brought great damage to the army and the people. However, it should be admitted that some Japanese troops have committed excessive acts in this attack war.
16. The "Nanjing Incident" is completely different from the fascist holocaust. The attack on Nanjing, the capital, was a war of retreat backed by the great river and a war of annihilation led by the Japanese army (encircling 200,000 citizens). Therefore, in the process of attacking and occupying the capital, China did not formally surrender but carried out a thorough attack, causing a lot of damage to the army and the people. A war like this has to be considered too much. Rabe's comparison of the actions of the Japanese army to Genghis Khan's European expedition is absolutely absurd. The Japanese army was fighting in an open and honest manner, which can be understood by looking at the photos of entering the city at that time.
17. The evaluation of the Nanjing Incident has not changed much in the past or now. The Japanese army is not a disorderly army without military discipline. Not before and after the attack on Nanjing, 200,000–300,000 troops were massacred and 20,000 troops were raped. Making the "Nanjing Massacre" was the strategy of the "Tokyo Trial" and China's propaganda and disinformation after the war. At the time of the war, no matter Chiang Kai-shek, the national government, Mao Zedong or the communist party of China had any record, nor did they appeal to the League of Nations. Nor is there anything in He Yingqin's military report. It's only seen as being killed in battle. I am looking forward to Rabe's "Nanjing's Truth", but after intensive reading, I know it is nonsense and there is no credibility as historical data. Even the Japanese army's "detailed report of the battle" and "journal of the army" (with the highest credibility) at that time were exaggerated and boasted. It is necessary to give a considerable discount. I think it is a good way to criticize all kinds of historical materials according to common sense. Some people say that war makes people mad, but most people are ordinary people. How can a madman complete an organized military operation by a large army? The Nanjing War did great damage to the enemy. Taking it as an illegal massacre is just a transfer. The real illegal slaughter and illegal acts are extremely limited … This is my real feeling.

Okazaki Hisahiko

1. The exact number of plainclothes teams targeted for punishment is not known, so 10,000 out of 300 to 30,000(10) were chosen.
2. (2) is common sense.
3. Either way. Only my mind is (3).
4. The answer is the same as 3. But my mind is mainly (3).
5. The killings and atrocities of ordinary citizens, the killings of prisoners and the unjustified killings of plainclothes teams. Every point has difficulty in determining the numbers today.
6. (1) and (3), the specific problem, specific treatment (case by case).
7. The equivalent definition should exist.
8. Because it is a war that has not declared war, it is not considered to be applicable to the original wartime international law. It is up to one's opinion whether to consider it as a matter outside the application of international law or as a complete violation of international law.
9. There is no legal responsibility. But as leaders, they have political and ethical responsibilities.
10. There is political and ethical responsibility for the atrocities committed by the Chinese soldiers themselves before the occupation.
11. Well-informed people are in the period of (1) and ordinary Japanese are in the period of (2).
12. I don't know.
13. Chang's book is a curious and third-rate historical story.
14. Rabe's diary is unknown. Seems to be valuable information.
15. It is an epiphyte of war. According to the general principles of textbooks for primary and secondary schools in the world, it is not necessary to describe it. However, the problem is that publicity has reached such a level that it is necessary to give a low-key and negative explanation to a certain extent.
16. It is totally different from the fascist holocaust. If classified, the problem of ordinary citizens being killed in battle should fall into the same category as the barbaric acts of the Soviet troops in Tokyo, Dresden, Hiroshima, Nagasaki and Manchuria. It is indeed excessive. General Matsui said, "What did you do?" Stone shot Itaro said, "Alas, such a royal army!" Yoshio Horiuchi said, "It has attracted ten years of hatred and hurt the prestige of the Japanese army". Pal said, "Even after considering propaganda and exaggeration, the evidence of sadistic behavior ... is overwhelming". What these show is really "quite excessive".
17. The following three points have never been changed. (1) What happened. (2) Numbers cannot be specified. (3) 200,000 is against common sense.

    Documents:
    (1) Tokyo Trial records, especially "Pal's Judgment" (Academic Library of Kodansha)

512   APPENDIX

   (2)   *No Defence Documents Submitted in Tokyo Trial* (National Book Association), Volume III, IV (1) Nanjing Incident
   (3)   Fujioka Nobukatsu, Higashinakano Shudo *Study on Nanjing Atrocities* (Xiangchuan-Sha)

Sakurai Yoshiko
 1. Choose (10).
 2. Choose (2) and (3).
 3. Choose (3).
 4. Choose (4).
 5. The killing of ordinary non-military personnel during the search of plain-clothes soldiers who had infiltrated among refugees.
 6. Choose (2).
 7. Blank.
 8. Blank.
 9. General Matsui was sentenced to death at his trial in Tokyo, which was a wrong sentence. In the book *Dr. Pal's Defence of Japanese Innocence*, it was written that General Matsui instructed his army not to involve the general public when attacking Nanjing. After entering the city, he learned that there were violations of military regulations, he adjusted the military forces to guard against any violation of military regulations and punished those violators, etc. It was the same logic that blaming General Matsui as it was to blame the staff on his superior. General Matsui himself was strictly vigilant in the Nanjing Incident.
10. Blank.
11. Choose (3).
12. I didn't think "the slaughter of one hundred people" was a truth.
13. Chang's book had many mistakes in the identification of facts and could not be regarded as something written in a fair way, but it exerted a great influence on the international community led by the United States.
14. The origin of the number 50,000 or 60,000 in Rabe's diary was not known, so it was necessary to compare it with the content of the diary reported by T. Darting of the New York Times at that time.
15. It was not appropriate for history textbooks to record the opinions of one side as definitive facts. The description of the situation that 300,000 people in China were involved lacked evidence of facts, testimonies or records at that time. There was a big difference between the claims of Japan and China. Therefore, it was an event that had not yet been proved true. Japanese army attacked Nanjing was a fact, so was the killing of Chinese nationals. The matter itself could not be denied, but the very politicized treatment of the incident as a source of criticism of Japan should be recorded fairly. This was an issue that should be followed from the beginning with a dispassionate revisionism.

16. It was completely different from fascist Holocaust in nature, and it was not reasonable to talk about them together. It was a normal fighting behavior, but it could be considered excessive.
17. References:
    (1) Akira Suzuki. *Illusion of the "Nanjing Massacre"* (Wenchun Wenku).
    (2) Akira Suzuki. New Edition of *Illusory of the "Nanjing Massacre"* (Asukashinsha Publishing Co., Ltd.).
    (3) Masaaki Tanaka. Dr. Pal's *Defence of Japanese Innocence* (Hui Bunsha).
    (4) The Pal's Judgment (Tokyo Tribunal).

Tanabe Toshio
1. Choose (10).
2. Choose (2) (not confirmed about whether it was an aggressive war).
3. Choose (2).
4. Choose (2).
5. To kill "non-combatant without guards" (captives and civilians, etc.) on the basis of "combatant qualifications" under the "Hague Rules of Land Warfare". If it did not agree with the definition, it could only be judged by common sense. Judging by the standards of modern army in Europe and the United States, the Chinese army was pre-modern, and the Japanese army could be thought as the same. Therefore, it was considered as "the war of Asia".
6. Choose (1).
7. I thought it was obviously different. Although it could not be clearly stated, it could be considered as close to the "fugitive soldier". He only cared if he could survive, and he would not resist if there was no accident, but if he felt that his life was in danger, he would take up a weapon and fight. He could be said to be a "soldier who didn't want to involve in the war".
8. Blank.
9. Originally, there was the view that the Central Chinese Army was a decoration. Regardless of the organization chart, it was not clear how much command power it actually had. The arbitrary chasing of the 10th Army was not so much the acquiescence of Commander Matsui as the insubordination of Commander Yanagawa. One might think that no one could stop it. In this way, the responsibility was ambiguous, and in the end, the superior could not be irresponsible. Three conclusions could be drawn from the above:
    (1) Misjudging that the capture of Nanjing would put an end to the war, and proposing an aggressive offensive proposal to the central government that upheld the principle of non-expansion.

(2) There are no clear instructions on the treatment of captives (Having experience in the Shanghai War?).

(3) Ignoring the objections of instability in public order and rushing to hold the city-entering ceremony. This was one reason for harsh and cool mopping.

10. There was no awareness of protecting the residents, etc. As Rabe's diary also pointed out, this was the case with the Chinese army at the time. You could not force yourself to get something you didn't have, but here were two things you could wish for:

(1) Since guarding Nanjing city was not successful, it was necessary to anticipate what would happen after the guarding, so Japan's surrender advice should be accepted (December 9th).

(2) There was probably no will to fight to the end, so the decision during the retreat was too late (12th).

11. Choose (2).

12. I never thought it was true. The fact that Lieutenant Noda was the deputy of the brigade and that Lieutenant Muroi was the captain of the infantry artillery team was quite sufficient. The "rebuttal" and Lieutenant Muroi's "Diary in Prison" were submitted by the two Lieutenants to the Nanjing Court. I didn't think there was any room for disputes.

13. Iris Chang's book was a highly successful propaganda and fake book. And it was worthless as a history book. Only taking references from the source in Japan and China, from what people in Japan and China said, and from the source in Germany and other third countries, many people thought it was a fact-based history book, so did they accept. Knowing that this book has been well reported and commented on in the United States, it was a pity to think that this book would become basis for persecution of Japanese people in the future, but I thought it was a matter of course. It was the Japanese media, which for a long time had reported the atrocities of the Japanese army with impunity and pretended not to know if they had been proved wrong. On the other hand, it was because of the silence of those involved who did not refute them. Chang did nothing but utilized these reports from Japan. The perpetrators of the perjury proved and then appeared one after another, and it was amazing to see that "Tadokoro Kozo" (Takuno Kogyo) was charged with rapes. The witnesses appeared at "Asahi Literature and Art" were soldiers of the 102th wing, and the author even knew such people.

14. From the point that Rabe was considered a person with conscience who had a nationality other than the states concerned, it was first-class information. The so-called Nanjing Massacre of three hundred thousand people was a political issue, and I didn't think the gulf between the researchers and the countries involved could be bridged. In addition, judging by the progress of the Chinese propaganda that has turned to the United States, Japan was at a disadvantage. I wondered whether it might

be feasible to ignore the information found in Japan and China, and adopted only the information and testimonies left in the third countries to clarify the Nanjing issue. Probably, it was easier for foreigners, such as Americans, to understand the approximate number of "massacres". The so-called number of "50,000 - 60,000" and the name of Tsung Sin Tong did not appear. "Even if the first atrocity appeared, we did only listen to the Chinese side" (a letter from the German Embassy official). Without the reference from Rabe's diary, which provided such a valuable clue, I didn't think there would have been a chance.
15. Titles like "Nanjing Massacre" were no longer in textbooks; it should be "Nanjing Incident". There have been massacres. Would it be more appropriate to refer to numbers in terms of "opinions varied", or to write down everything from "three hundred thousand" to "zero"?
16. It was completely different from fascism. The fascist persecution of the Jews was a matter of planned national purification that was not directly related to the war. The Nanjing issue was not planned, but was something unexpected happened during the attack. Nonetheless, one could not but admit that it was quite excessive. Because it could be seen that the policy of "burn all, kill all, loot all" was analogous to the idea of Holocaust, so a few more words were added here. China called these campaigns initiated by the Japanese army as the "burn all, kill all, loot all" to censure its cruelty, but such operations were not originally initiated by the Japanese army. The "testimony" of the Japanese, who were detained in China as war criminals, played a decisive role in supporting China's claims, and the policy of "burn all, kill all, loot all" became an abnormal event in most history textbooks. I hope to refer to the *Request of Deleting the "Burn all, Kill all, Loot all" from the Textbooks* (*Theory*, December 1996) which was based on these evidences. Now, as the investigation progressed, we had sufficient facts to doubt China's claims and these "testimonies".
17. I have read more than ten major books; recently, I also read news Blank clippings and magazines. Regarding the facts, nothing has changed since. But here were what I thought. It was meaningful to pursue facts in the sense of learning. But as to the propaganda in wars, one could not help but question the value of the ever-arguing. The domestic dispute in Japanese, unless there was a particular new fact, was nothing more than a ripple in the cup. The stage should be the English-speaking world. It was urgent to establish a system that could send messages to the world in English. As for important books, after reading the introductory book, you should read *Nanjing War History* compiled by the Nanjing War History Compilation Committee (including materials, Kaikōsha) and other books containing many firsthand and second-hand information. Akira Suzuki's *New Edition of Illusory of the "Nanjing Massacre"* (Asukashinsha Publishing Co., Ltd.) was also worth reading.

Fujiwara Akira
1. Choose (4). I also supported the view of Tomio Hora, a pioneer in the study of events, that "no fewer than two hundred thousand Chinese civilians and soldiers have died inside and outside Nanjing" (the Nanjing Massacre). This also included the war dead, but there were more victims of illegal killing than the war dead. It was extremely difficult to accurately calculate the number of the dead, and future efforts in this regard would remain necessary.
2. Choose (4). Except for those who died in wars, soldiers and civilians were victims. That was to say, most of the captives, surrendered soldiers, captured soldiers and so on were killed illegally. And of course, the citizens were the victims of the massacre.
3. Choose (2). Almost during the same period, the starting point should start from the beginning of December when the attack on Nanjing began. Related to the next question.
4. Choose (5). Including the city of Nanjing and the outskirts of the six counties in the Administrative Region of Nanjing.
5. The same answer as that of 2.
6. Choose (4). Original disarmed soldiers.
7. Blank.
8. The problem was that Japan at the time, especially the military, lacked awareness of violations of international laws. Subordinate cadres and soldiers had no knowledge of international laws. Senior cadres had knowledge but they had no willingness to comply. So the responsibility for violating international law rest with senior cadres. In this regard, it might be helpful to refer to the educational content and its changes of Imperial Japanese Army Academy as well as the army's attitude toward The Hague and Geneva Conventions. Moreover, the following recent research results could be used as a reference. *Preface to the Study of the Illegality of War and Japan* by Toshiya Ika (Japan-China Historical Research Center, 1999 Annual Report).
9. Of course, there was responsibility. Matsui had concerns about the violation of British and American rights, but he hardly cared about killing captives and citizens.
10. As a commander, Tang gave up commanding and escaped, which was extremely irresponsible.
11. Choose (1). The upper ranks of the army and the Ministry of Foreign Affairs, as well as the upper ranks of the political circle, and journalists were informed at the time. There was a lot of evidence.
12. Stories made as tales of bravery in battles. But it could be considered to have killed defenseless captives.
13. Iris Chang's book had many errors in understanding historical facts, ignorance of Japanese research and many photographic problems. It has thus become an excellent target for the negation of the massacre. But

even with such shortcomings, this book was relevant for making the vivid facts of the Nanjing Massacre widely known in English world. Another aim of the book was to denounce right-wing attacks in Japan that sought to conceal and obliterate the truth, at which point a positive introduction and criticism were necessary.
14. Rabe's diary was narrow in scope, but it could be evaluated as a firsthand material. The report left by Secretary Rosen at the German Embassy in Nanjing at the time was then in the National Archives of the Old East Germany. It was scheduled to be published in the near future and it would be even more interesting than John Rabe's diary.
15. The retrogression of the description in history textbooks for middle school students in 2002 was a shame. It was a throwback to the past. This was because the publishers fear the liberal views from history research group. The historical accounts of two hundred thousand or three hundred thousand victims have been deleted, which was not appropriate.
16. Different from Holocaust. The so-called Holocaust was a national policy of obliterating specific ethnic groups from the very beginning. The Japanese army killed civilians and raped women indiscriminately due to the negligence of commanders and the willfulness of soldiers.
17. Almost nothing changed. He participated in the establishment of the Nanjing Incident Research Association in 1984 and then published the *Nanjing Massacre* (Sorin Iwanami) in 1985. Basically, his opinions have not changed since then. This was the most symbolic and largest war crime in aggressive war against China.

References:
(1) An interpretation by Tokushi Kasahara, *The Days and Nights of Nanjing Incident-Minnie Weitling's Diary* which was translated by Okada Ryunosuke and Ihara Yoko (Otsuki Book Store)
(2) Tokushi Kasahara, *Nanjing Incident* (Iwanami Shoten)
(3) Tokushi Kasahara, *The Nanjing Incident and the battle of "Burn all, Kill all, Loot all"*.

Rguchi Keiichi
1. Choose (5)–(6).
2. Choose (2).
3. Choose (1).
4. Still (1).
5. Except for the war dead in normal fighting behavior, the execution and killing of the surrendered soldiers who have surrendered without being given the opportunity of trial (unarmed, disarmed), surrendered, captured or soldiers (unarmed). And the killing of civilians.
6. Choose (4). Soldiers who were unarmed and lost their willingness to fight.

518   APPENDIX

7. Blank.
8. Blank.
9. The unjustifiable attack on Nanjing by Commander Matsui, who broke away from the central authorities, could be regarded as the greatest cause and bore the greatest responsibility.
10. The "Battle of the Qing-ye" and the wrong command, as well as the extremely clumsy operations, inevitably bore some responsibility for the incident.
11. Choose (1). But it was just rumors. It was officially (2).
12. This report was made up, but sufficient facts were telling that almost 100 people were killed.
13. Chang's book was full of simple mistakes and misunderstandings, and it could not be said to be an academic book.
14. Rabe's diary was highly valued because it was a vivid record at the time.
15. Textbooks should be written. But it should not be copied from what told in China. Incidentally, my high school textbook *History of Japan B* (Shijiao Publishing) stated: "The Japanese invaded and occupied the capital of Republic of China: Nanjing in December. At that time, the Japanese army killed many of the survivors and captives. The Japanese have plundered, set fire and committed atrocities (this sentence did not conform to the Chinese-speaking habits, and it was still based on the original translation). The Nanjing Massacre was criticized internationally. The number of the dead, including combatants before and after the occupation, was estimated to reach at least 100,000 people within several weeks".
16. Events like Holocaust were carried out in accordance with a prior plan, but these were incidents that occurred during the occupation of Nanjing. But as wars, they were clearly detached.
17. The number 300,000 people in China was said to be exaggerated, but there were many testimonies and detailed information. The truth of the tragedy has been understood to a considerable degree.

References:
(1) *The Days and Nights of Nanjing Incident-Minnie Weitling's Diary* (Otsuki Bookstore, 1999)
(2) Diary of John Rabe, *The Truth About Nanjing* (Kodansha,1997)
(3) Kenji Ono, I. Honda, *Emperor Soldiers Recording the Nanjing Massacre: A Diary in the Yamada Detachment of the Thirteenth Division* (Otsuki Bookstore, 1996).

Inoue Hisashi
1. Choose (1). At least 100,000 (The mark was in the original book—translator).
2. Choose (2). But not "it might be an aggressive war". Instead, we should recognize that "this was an aggressive war".

APPENDIX 519

3. Choose (4). From early December to March of the following year.
4. Choose (5). At that time, the jurisdiction of the Nanjing Municipal Government included (Pukou, Xiaoweiling, Yanziji, Shangxinhe and Lingyuan in Nanjing, and six counties (Jiangning, Jurong, Lishui, Jiangpu, Liuhe, Gaochun) in the suburbs.
5. The killing of captives included the killing of ordinary female citizens and farmers.
6. Select (4). The distinction between plainclothes and regular soldiers made no sense. Since it was a case of losing the willingness to fight and fleeing with weapons thrown away, in either case they should be treated as captives and never be killed without a military trial.
7. As to the reality of Nanjing after the occupation, the armed resistance of the plainclothes soldiers was almost non-existent.
8. In a report to the German Foreign Ministry on January 20th, 1938, Rawson, a German diplomat in Nanjing, made the following statement in connection with the killing of Chinese soldiers whom the Japanese had found out of the safe zone: "there was no trace of a military trial or similar procedure. Such a procedure would have been the custom of all wartime international laws and human decorum. And it was also not appropriate that Japanese army mocked". The killing of captives without a military trial was considered a problem, which was even agreed by diplomats of Japan's ally Germany.
9. Blank.
10. It was too late to issue a withdrawal order. On the 11th or the 12th of December when it was virtually impossible for Nanjing city to stand still, it was necessary to negotiate withdrawing and allow the Japanese army to enter the city without bloodshed at the final stage.
11. It was usually (2). The Ministry of Foreign Affairs of Tokyo knew about it at the time.
12. Blank.
13. As a Chinese American, I could understand the feelings of the author Chang who wrote about the impact of the Nanjing Massacre, but the facts were wrong and the photographs chosen were wrong. If as a historical work, I could not give a positive evaluation.
14. Evaluated as important historical materials. John Rabe could not grasp the whole situation of Nanjing at that time, so the comparison with other historical materials was indispensable.
15. The textbook should describe it in more detail. It was absolutely not allowed to reduce or cancel the description of the "Nanjing Incident".
16. And it could not be equally talked as Holocaust. It was true that there have been massacres, but it should be understood that the Japanese army did not occupy Nanjing for the sake of the massacres. The massacres occurred as a result.

17. Compared with knowing the scale of the massacre, etc., taking part in the investigation of "Nanjing Incident" made people feel more sympathy for the victims.

References:
(1) Nanjing Incident Investigation and Research Association, *13 Lies of Denying Nanking Massacre* (Bai Study)
(2) Sun Zhaiwei, *Nanjing Massacre* (Beijing Publishing House)
(3) Lee Enhan, *Study of Japanese Military Atrocities in War* (Taiwan Commercial Press)
(4) Kuji Inoue, *Materials on the work of Propaganda in central China* (Fifteen Years' Distinctive War Data Collection//n 13, Published by Fuji)
(5) Kuji Inoue, *Photographic Data in History-Occasions of the Nanjing Incident* (*Historical Review*, October 2000).

Himeda Mitsuyoshi
1. Choose (5).
2. Choose (1).
3. Choose (2).
4. Choose (2).
5. (1) Non-combatants (women, the elderly) and farmers working in the field. (2) Disarmed captives. (3) Soldiers who have lost the will to fight and the sense of resistance (including officials).
6. Choose (4). The "plainclothes soldiers" who actually resisted were a minority, almost all of them were soldiers changed into "plain-clothes" in order to escape.
7. Blank.
8. Based on the writings of Tomio Hora, Fujiwara and Yoshida. There was no specific study.
9. In modern times, there was a responsibility for supervision. But if you said that, even higher authorities (including the emperor) could hardly be exempted from responsibility.
10. Abandoning organized resistance and retreat bore great responsibility. But in this case, the highest responsibility rest in Chiang Kai-shek, and he should be held accountable for ambiguous orders (between defending and retreating).
11. Choose (2). Timperley's book (Guo Moruo's wrote preface) was the first to report on individual abuses both internationally and domestically, but not as "Nanjing Massacre" events.
12. It was a matter of symbols, not numbers. The public executions were for precepts.
13. I have not read Iris Chang's original book. I knew only from the writings of Tokushi Kasahara. And it was not conducive to scientific and objective arguments. It was only brewed from overseas "fanaticism" (the

extreme nationalism of Chinese); it ultimately rose the trend of Japanese negativism.
14. Rabe's diary was reliable in terms of the most and most direct words heard from the "refugees" of the time.
15. As an event in an aggressive war (an event of symbolic significance), it should be recorded.
16. As an act of war, it was excessive. What could be compared to the Holocaust was the later "burn all, kill all, loot all" event.
17. Little has changed, but we were tired of talking about "numbers". Theses were just inconclusive discussions. According to the Tokyo Trial, I thought it was about 100,000. Perhaps even more profound problem was raised by China that "35 million victims" were killed in the Japanese-Chinese War period. I knew that someone thought the figures cited by China were fake. But China was still investigating killings at the county level and that should be kept in mind. When perpetrators were obliterating, concealing records and memories, the testimony of the victims in China could not be ignored. In any case, we were peace-loving Japanese who had a deep aversion to violence. We should acknowledge the past as soon as possible and apologize for it in order to establish a new Japan-China relationship.

Kasahara Tokushi

1. From the existing research and data, it can be inferred that there are about 100,000 to 200,000 people. With the progress of data exploration, disclosure and research in the future, the number of slaughtered people may increase.
2. Choose (2). However, the war of aggression was officially recognized by the Japanese government, so the question should be "the war of aggression".
3. Choose (4). The Central China Army entered the Nanjing Theater around December 4th, 1937, until March 28th, 1938, when the Republic of China Reformed Government was established in Nanjing.
4. Select (5). It covers the whole area of Nanjing Special City, which is the administrative area of Nanjing city and six counties in the suburbs. This is the theater of the Nanjing attack and the area occupied by the Japanese army after Nanjing was lost.
5. Collective or individual killing of wounded, captured, surrendered (thrown weapons, unwarranted), Chinese soldiers who are prohibited from killing in accordance with the "Treaty on Conventions and Laws and Practices of Land War" prohibited by wartime international law. The civilians killed in the Japanese army's annihilation battle and the raids, and the adult men who were killed as original soldiers during the capture of the remnants, especially the civilians shot and assassinated by the Japanese soldiers on a sudden impulse. In the Nanjing Incident, rapes caused by Japanese soldiers occurred in large numbers, because the crime

of rape was personally charged, and the evidence was annihilated because the Japanese gendarmerie was not told. Especially in rural areas, many women were raped and gang raped, and then were killed. Such rape and gang killings are, of course, massacres.

6. Choose (4). Plainclothes soldiers are soldiers who are belligerent and openly armed. Chinese soldiers who have fled into the security zone have given up fighting because they are afraid of being killed as soldiers (Japanese soldiers also kill prisoners and surrendering soldiers). People throwing away weapons, taking off military uniforms and putting on civilian clothes are the defeated soldiers who want to live, which is obviously different from plainclothes soldiers. The International Commission of the security zone also disarmed the former Chinese soldiers and took them into the security zone as refugees.

7. Blank.

8. Is there the firsthand information of the "related person" of the Nanjing Incident and the China Army's related person then clearly recorded in the "Japanese army's punishment of Chinese prisoners' violation of international law"? This is the purpose of this question, in order to setting questions with ulterior motives. The verbal order issued by the Central China Army and the Shanghai dispatched military command that the "all prisoners are killed" and "all prisoners executed" will be considered as a "crime of disobedience" in the army criminal law if they are judged "contrary to international law". If it is not indicated, it will be considered as "insulting", so it is impossible to say from common sense. The original question should be to point out the firsthand historical data of the Japanese army violating "the Treaty on the laws and practices of land war" (signed by Japan in February 1912), which forbids the killing of captives and the "means of harming the enemy". In this case, the firsthand information will be numerous. It is pointed out the historical data of the foreigners who were detained in Nanjing at that time to witness the events, although they are not "related persons". It is a historical material that clearly records the punishment of "plainclothes soldiers" by the Japanese army who violated the provisions of international law that they must have the procedures of military trial.

    (1) Report to the German Ministry of Foreign Affairs by the Secretary General of the Nanjing Branch of the German Embassy (January 20th, 1938, German Federal Archives, provided by Ishida Yuji). There is no trace of military trials or similar procedures (for those who were forcibly took away, killed after throwing away weapons, take off their uniforms and escape into the security zone). Such formalities were the practice of all wartime international law and human etiquette, which was not commensurate with the practice of the Japanese army, which ridiculed it.

    (2) A. T. Steele, *Talking about the Bravery of Americans in Nanjing* (*Chicago Sun*, December 18th, 1937, compiled by Research

Committee on the Nanjing Incident, Aoki Shoten, *Nanjing Incident Data Collection 1, American Relations Data Series*): "The Japanese army arrested many people as plainclothes suspects. Only a few of them were able to come back. It is said that their companions who were arrested were slaughtered without a simple trial". *The Nanjing Incident I saw* (PHP Research Institute) by Okumiya Masatake clearly records the Japanese army's punishment of the Chinese people violating international law witnessed by him.

9. As recorded in the *Nanjing Incident* (Iwanami Shinsho), the Staff Headquarters dismissed the commander of the General Matsui Iwane in the Central Army and called it back because he knew that Matsui's inaction led to the Nanjing Incident and was handled internally. The German Embassy in Tokyo in its political report to the German Foreign Ministry (as of March 3rd, 1938) stated that "It is unclear whether Matsui's call was considered a scapegoat for the Nanjing massacre". It is illustrated that the insight that the General Matsui Iwane is a scapegoat in Nanjing Incident exists at that time (German Federal Archives, courtesy of Ishida Yuji). General Matsui's inaction responsibility as commander of the Central China Army cannot be waived, but there is indeed only one side of General Matsui who was used as a scapegoat. Originally, most commanders related to the Nanjing Incident, including Lieutenant General Chao Xianggong, commander of the Shanghai Expeditionary Army, were investigated to search for the full picture of the incident and determine that trials of all those responsible people were necessary.

10. As stated in manuscript *Nanjing Defense Forces and Chinese Forces* (*Research on Nanjing Massacre* compiled by Hora Tomio and others (Evening News Agency), as the commander in chief of Nanjing Defense War, he lacked experience and strength, failed to command the Chinese Army's retreat and lacked countermeasures to protect the lives of huge capitulators, captives, disabled soldiers, citizens and refugees. Therefore, he has more responsibility for the victims. However, the main responsible person of Nanjing Incident is the Japanese army that attacked Nanjing and killed illegally, which is the main premise of understanding.

11. Choose (5). Japan began to use the term "Nanjing Massacre" after the Tokyo Trial, but it cannot be said that "Nanjing Massacre" is a fabrication of the Tokyo Trial. As Yoshida Takashi said, "who really didn't know about the Nanjing Massacre?" *(Thirteen lies in the Nanjing Massacre Deniers' Claims* compiled by Research Committee on the Nanjing Incident, Kashiwa Shobo), Nanjing witnessed a considerable scale of massacre, which was known from the central guidance department of the army and diplomats who knew about foreign reports at the time of the Japanese-Chinese War. In July 1938, Lieutenant General Okamura Ningji confirmed that "when attacking Nanjing, there were great atrocities such as plundering and raping tens of thousands of citizens". "Tokyo air raid" is also a postwar name; no one said it was fabricated because it appeared

in the postwar time. The history of the event is true in the first place, the title is added later, and it is possible to change.

12. As detailed in Honda Katsuichi's "killing objects (using humans as living targets) and killing captives is commonplace" (previously cited by *Thirteen lies in the Nanjing Massacre Deniers' Claims*), Japanese military officers in order to boast to their subordinates with his own wrist strength, letting the non-resistance Chinese and the arrested Chinese soldiers sit and behead with Japanese swords is commonplace in many troops. It can be considered that the "Hundred People Cut" of the two lieutenants was based on such facts. As Suzuki Akira's *The Unreal of the Nanjing Massacre* (Literature Spring and Autumn) said, women who read the news note of "Hundred People Cut" look forward to "Nanjing Warriors" and send condolences bags to marry for the opportunity. We saw the feminine consciousness that regarded "hundred people as a hero" at that time.

13. The "Nanjing Massacre Controversy" that began in the first half of the 1970s and ended in the second half of the 1980s, as collated by the draft *Nanjing Massacre and Historical Research* (collected by the book The Japanese Army in Asia [Otsuki Shoten]). At the academic level, the flaws and failures of negation have been decided. However, in 1997, Iris Chang, *The Rape of Nanking: The Forgotten Holocaust of War II*, was published in the United States. Although the Japanese translation has not yet been published and ordinary citizens have no chance to read it, the negators still rushed to this book, criticizing the book for its flaws. The intention is to make the "Nanjing Holocaust" in Japan with the "Book of Holocaust" the same impression, so as to achieve the attempt to resurrect the influence of the negatives that have retreated and fallen in Japan. On the one hand, when the Japanese negated party to criticize and attack her, but in the United States, Iris Chang's impression of "fighting the right-wing of Japan" was enhanced, and the effects of evaluation and influence were enhanced.

14. It is the record of the chairman of the Nanjing Security Area International Committee at that time, which is limited to the regional considerations centered on the Nanjing Refugee Area. It is precious firsthand information about the Nanjing Incident. At the time of the Nanjing Incident, other members of the Nanjing Security Area International Committee who had directly and indirectly witnessed the incident left Nanjing city with many diaries, letters and documents, which were included in *Documents on the Nanjing Massacre in the Second Sino-Japanese War • Second Volume of English Resources* compiled by Hora Tomio (Aoki Shoten), formerly cited *Nanjing Incident Dataset 1 US Relations Data Compilation, Day and Night of Nanjing Incident-Minnie Weitling's Diary* (Otsuki Shoten), the German diplomat stationed in Nanjing in the second half of the event and the official document

Data • German Diplomatic Documents of the Nanjing Incident (tentative name, scheduled to be published by Aoki Shoten in the near future). The comparison with the records of these foreigners in Nanjing can prove the reliability of the contents of Rabe's diary. It's just that *Nanjing Reality* (Kodansha) is a translation of Erwin Victor's edited version. With strict records, it is hoped that the original diary, including the original documents and photos inserted into Rabe's diary, will be totally translated and published.

15. The textbook of the Japanese historical division is limited by the total number of pages, so the general history from ancient to modern times is just like a slightly detailed chronology. The descriptions of historical textbooks, such as those of many foreign textbooks, must be specifically described in order to give students as much impression as possible of historical events. Even with regard to the Nanjing Incident, it is not as few lines as the current history textbooks, but it should be a detailed description of the cause, process, content and impact of the Nanjing Incident on China and the world. Moreover, it is not just this article. As the study topics and discussion questions at the end of the chapter, the memory and knowledge of the Nanjing Incident should be compared and discussed on the differences between the Chinese nationals of the injured party and the Japanese nationals of the aggressor. Dialogue of Chinese young people is necessary.

16. As noted in the book *Nanjing Incident and Operation of Three Lights* (Otsuki Shoten), the "Three Lights Operation" of the Japanese army comparable to holocaust is appropriate. The Nanjing Incident, as clearly stated in the masterpiece, was the forcible attack on Nanjing because there was no combat preparation, and the war flocked in Shanghai caused the fatigue of the soldiers and the abolition of the military regulations, occurred overlappingly with the arbitrary command of the local military headquarters and the erroneous operation of the command and the other occasional factors. In this regard, the "Three Lights Operation" is based on the Japanese army's formal operations in an attempt to wipe out the soldiers and civilians in the liberated areas and guerrilla areas in order to carry out raid operations. As an exaggeration of warfare, it was precisely because the staff headquarters at that time also recognized that there was a change in the commander of the Central China Army, General Matsui Iwane, and it was confirmed by Lt. Gen. Okamura, who was appointed commander of the Second Army in June 1938: "When attacking Nanjing, there were atrocities such as looting and rape of tens of thousands of citizens". When occupying Wuhan in October of the same year, the chief of staff of the Central China Army sent a thorough instruction: "Looking forward to all kinds of illegal acts, especially plundering, arson and rape will never happen". Strive to prevent the "Wuhan Massacre" (Yoshida Takashi's *The Emperor's Military and the Nanjing Incident*, Aoki Shoten).

17. Reflecting internationalization, the United States and China discuss the Nanjing Incident through international conferences. Historians and social scientists in Europe and the United States have more opportunities to discuss the Nanjing Incident, which has increased than before, which indicates that the evaluation of "as the Nanjing Incident in world history" has been strengthened. To welcome the twenty-first century, as a view of the world history of human history that grasps the world as a whole, in the generalization, the academia and journalism in the United States, Germany, the United Kingdom and other European and American countries will regard the Nanjing Incident as a twentieth-century world history and compare the massacres in the world, such as the Armenian massacres in Turkey, the Jewish massifs in Fascist Germany, the massacres in Cambodia and the recent massacres in Rwanda and the Old Yugoslavia. Thus, a tendency to study the history of cruelty occurs. Among them, comparative studies of so-called "The eraser of memory" such as Auschwitz's negation, Nanjing Incident negation and Armenian massacre negation also appeared. The theories and movements of Japan's Nanjing Incident negation, the role and responsibility of the media which support them, and the psychological and war-knowledge of the people who accept the negation have all become the research objects of foreign researchers.

Reference works that have important reference value for the Nanjing Incident:
(1) Fujiwara Akira, *The Japanese Army in Nanjing—The Nanjing Massacre and Its background* (Otsuki Shoten)
(2) Honda Katsuichi, *Honda Katsuichi Episode 23 Nanjing Massacre* (Asahi Shinbunsha)
(3) Yoshida Yutaka, *The Emperor's Military and the Nanjing Incident* (Aoki Shoten)
(4) Kasahara Tokushi, *A Hundred Days in Nanjing Refugee Area-Foreigners Seeing the Massacre* (Iwana Shoten)
(5) *Thirteen lies in the Nanjing Massacre Deniers' Claims*, edited by Research Committee on the Nanjing Incident (Kashiwa Shobo).

Takasaki Ryuji
1. Choose (4).
2. Choose (4). Question 2 is "It may be a war of aggression", but my point is "It is a war of aggression". But I don't think that war dead caused by "common fighting behavior" should be included in the number of people massacred.
3. Choose (1).
4. Choose (1).
5. The killing of general citizens who are not resistant and the killing of captives who have surrendered.

6. Choose (2).
7. Blank.
8. Blank.
9. It is the responsibility as the person with the highest responsibility, but I think that whether it is General Matsui or not, no one can ignore the nature of the Japanese army.
10. As the commander, Tang should at least issue an asylum order to ordinary citizens in Nanjing (in the administrative region).
11. Choose (2).
12. The dissemination is not totally considered to be fact, but it can be presumed that similar behavior has been fact.
13. There are exaggerated parts in Chang's book. But from the standpoint of literary truth (emphasis is the original-translator), it can be affirmed.
14. There is quite a lot of content written according to rumors, but it is basically certain. Rabe said that the number of massacres in Nanjing was about 50,000. If it was limited to the city, it could be considered as close to the actual number.
15. On the grounds that the number of killers is uncertain, it is wrong to not even outline them, and at the same time, there is a negative argument about the killings, indicating that they have not been resolved. I think it is appropriate.
16. It is not considered to be comparable to holocaust of fascism, but as an event that can be taken as a reference, it is a crime that must not be allowed.
17. There is a little change. At the time, it was judged that the number of massacres was 150,000, but referring to the research results of other researchers, it was thought that nearly 200,000 was appropriate. In terms of reference materials, *The Field Post Flag* (by Sasaki Motochi, Press Conference of the Modern History Data Center) was the most important record at that time. In addition, the booklet entitled *The Experience of Soldiers in the Army* issued to the soldiers by the Ministry of the Army in August, Showa 13th year, is also important as relating to the incident.

Yoshida Takashi

1. Choose (13). The current stage can be inferred to be at least 100,000. The cause, especially the killings in the rural areas in the outskirts of Nanjing, is almost unknown.
2. Choose (4). It is a clear war of aggression, but since it is a war, war dead caused by normal fighting behavior should not be included in the massacres.
3. Choose (4). From December 1st, 1937, when the base camp ordered the attack on Nanjing, to the general restoration of law and order, March 1938.

4. Choose (5). The area controlled by the Central China Army within 3 answers. Therefore (1) cannot include, but cannot be limited to, Nanjing, and should include the entire area of Nanjing Special City (Nanjing area and the suburban countryside).
5. The killing of captives and surrenders. (2) Punishment of Chinese soldiers who have abandoned military uniforms and weapons and sneaked into the safe zone (captives should be the object of absorption. Even if there are hostilities, it is necessary for the punishment to go through military court procedures). (3) Killing of the disabled soldiers who have lost their war will (at least they should be managed as prisoners). (4) Killing of ordinary citizens.
6. Choose (4). The defeated soldiers of the regular army who had lost their war will. As a result of the execution without the formalities of a military court, ordinary citizens who were mistaken for soldiers were also executed.
7. Blank.
8. The interpretation of international law at that time is detailed in *Modern History and War Responsibility* (Aoki Shoten 1997) and *Thirteen lies in the Nanjing Massacre Deniers' Claims* (Kashiwa Shobo 1999). In addition, the Ministry of Military Affairs and Legal Affairs of Central China also executed military courts at least after January 1938 against Chinese who engaged in hostilities (Kogawa Seijiro, *Diary of a Military Legal Officer* みすず Shoten 2000). It can be said that it is necessary to go through the procedure of military court. To say a digression, this question was originally biased. If it is a neutral stance, you should also ask if there are historical records that the execution of the Japanese army is legal in international law. Please indicate.
9. (1) Responsibility for forcibly attacking Nanjing and normalizing the plunder without the support of the military station. (2) No responsibility for taking measures to protect captives, surrender soldiers or defeat soldiers. (3) Failure to take measures to prevent uncontrolled troops from entering the city. (4) Failure to take full responsibility for working with the International Commission for Safe Areas to protect refugees. (5) The premature implementation of the Japanese-Russian war-type war view into the city caused too much blame for the raid campaign. (6) Responsibility for deepening the puppet regime establishment and other political work, and not paying special attention to the original duties of military commanders.
10. (1) Responsibility for adopting an absolute obedience policy toward Nanjing with a large number of refugees and involving a large number of civilians. (2) Fleeing on the way to waive the responsibility of commander. As a result, there is much confusion.
11. Choose (5). The word "Nanjing Massacre" was only available after the war, but the incident was known at that time.

12. The numbers have an expanding side, but there are some such as cutting prisoners and losing soldiers.
13. Chang's book is completely ignorant of its research status in Japan, explaining the incident from the nationality of the Japanese, and ignoring the facts of the introspection trends in Japan and textbook description. It is a book with a lot of problems.
14. Rabe's diary, I think it is precious historical data. It is only necessary to analyze, for example, German diplomatic instruments to make the facts clearer.
15. In the sense of clarifying the responsibility of the Japanese government and the Japanese for harm, detailed records are necessary.
16. It is not a military operation with the purpose of annihilating in a specific area like the "Three Lights Operation", but a war crime that accompanies the attack on the capital, so it is frankly holocaust. I hope I can learn more about this.
17. Understanding the facts of the opium trade that violated international law by the Nanjing Puppet Government (participation of military secret services) and the war crimes committed by the Japanese navy made the understanding of the incident deeper. In this regard, it is a big doubt that this questionnaire focused only on the "massacre". At least it should include questions about rape and plunder.

There are five important references:
(1) Hata Ikuhiko, *The Nanjing Incident*
(2) *Documents on the Battle of Nanjing* edited by the Nanjing War History Editorial Committee (Kaikosha)
(3) Fujiwara Akira, *The Japanese Army in Nanjing* (Otsuki Shoten)
(4) Kasahara Tokushi, *The Nanjing Incident* (Iwanami Shinsho)
(5) *Thirteen lies in the Nanjing Massacre Deniers' Claims* compiled by Research Committee on the Nanjing Incident (Kashiwa Shobo).

References

Foreword: 1. Except for the special books on the Nanjing Massacre, the relevant works only include special historical materials, but the general historical materials are not included, such as "The War History of the 6th Division" instead of "Documents on Japanese Foreign Relations". 2. The list of reference books is limited to Japanese documents only. 3. The publication time of the books in the list of reference books collected refers to the first edition, which is different from the actual version of the paper part of this book. For example, Hata Ikuhiko's book "Nanjing Incident" has its first edition in 1986, while the paper part of this book is the 20th edition in 1999. 4. Japanese characters have also changed from numerous to simple. For example, 读卖 was used as 讀賣 during the war, which is the same as the traditional Chinese character. Now it is used as 読売. This list of reference book is based on the original book. 5. Except the order of the third part is according to the army sequence, the rest is according to the publication time.

I. Collection of Historical Documents

1. 『現代史資料』9「日中戦争」2,臼井勝美等解説,みすず書房,1964年
2. 『現代史資料』12「日中戦争」4,小林龍夫等解説,みすず書房,1965年
3. 洞富雄編『日中戦争史資料』8南京事件I,洞富雄編,河出書房新社,1973年
4. 洞富雄編『日中戦争史資料』9南京事件II,洞富雄編,河出書房新社,1973年
5. 『支那事変に関する造言飛語に就いて支那事変下に於おける不穏言動と其の対策に就いて』,社会問題資料研究会編,東洋文化社,1978年
6. 『資料日本現代史』1「軍隊内の反戦運動」,藤原彰編集、解説,大月書店,1980年

© Shanghai Jiao Tong University Press 2020
Z. Cheng, *The Nanjing Massacre and Sino-Japanese Relations*,
https://doi.org/10.1007/978-981-15-7887-8

7. 高橋正衛編集、解説『続・現代史資料』6「軍事警察」,高橋正衛編集,解説,みすず書房,1982年
8. 『資料日本現代史』10、11「日中戦争期の国民動員」,吉見義明等編,大月書店,1984年
9. 『日中戦争南京大殘虐事件資料集』1「極東国際軍事裁判南京事件関係記録」,洞富雄編,青木書店,1985年
10. 『日中戦争南京大殘虐事件資料集』2「英文資料編」,洞富雄編,青木書店,1985年
11. 『南京戦史資料集』,南京戦史編集委員会編,偕行社,非売品,1989年
12. 『華中宣撫工作十五年戦争極秘資料集第13集』,石井久士編,不二出版,1989年
13. 『南京事件京都師団関係資料集』,井口和起、木坂順一郎、下里正樹編,青木書店,1989年
14. 『南京事件資料集』「アメリカ関係資料編」,南京事件調査研究会編譯,青木書店,1992年
15. 『南京事件資料集』「中国関係資料編」,南京事件調査研究会編譯,青木書店,1992年
16. 『南京戦史資料集』II,南京戦史編集委員会編,偕行社,1993年
17. 『国際検察局尋問調書』,粟屋憲太朗、吉田裕編,日本図書センター,1993年
18. 『東京裁判却下未提出弁護側資料』,東京裁判資料刊行会編,図書刊行会,1995年
19. 『南京大虐殺を記録した皇軍兵士たち――第十三師団山田支隊兵士の陣中日記』,小野賢二、藤原彰、本多勝一編,大月書店,1996年
20. 『南京戦記映画復刻シリーズ21』,国書刊行会,1997年

II. Literature, Dairy and Recollection

21. 『十三年版最新支那要覧』,磯部榮一編,東亜研究会,1938年
22. 『新支那現勢要覧』,東亜同文会編,東亜同文会,1938年
23. 『支那事変戰蹟ノ栞』,陸軍畫報社編,陸軍恤兵部,1938年
24. 『南京城總攻撃』,高木義賢編,大日本雄辯会講談社,1938年
25. 『支那事変皇國之精華』,全國各縣代表新聞五十社協力執筆,上海毎日新聞社,1939年
26. 『維新政府之現況――成立一周年紀念』,行政院宣傳局編纂,行政院宣傳局,1939年
27. 『民國廿八年、昭和十四年中國年鑑』,上海日報社、野田經濟研究所編,上海日報社調査編纂部,1939年
28. 『華中現勢 昭和十四年』,上海毎日新聞社編,上海毎日新聞社,1939年
29. 『南京日本居留民誌』,莊司得二編,南京居留民団,1940年
30. 『南京』,市米義道編,南京日本商工会議所,1941年
31. 『支那事変實記』,讀賣新聞社編集局編,讀賣新聞社,1941年
32. 『朝日東亜年報昭和十三――十六年版』,朝日新聞社中央調査会編,朝日新聞社,1941年

33. 『南京市政概況』,南京特務機関調製,1942年
34. 『日本に與へる書』,蔣介石著,中國文化社(京都),1946年
35. 『失はれし政治』,近衛文麿,朝日新聞社,1946年
36. 『裁かれる歴史』,田中隆吉著,新風社,1948年
37. 『平和の発見』,花山信勝著,朝日新聞社,1949年
38. 『外交官の一生』,石射猪太郎著,読売新聞社,1950年
39. 『生きてゐる兵隊』,石川達三著,河出書房,1951年
40. 『昭和の動乱』上巻,重光葵著,中央公論社,1952年
41. 『新軍備と戦いの思い出』,渡辺卯七著,私家版,1952年
42. 『憲兵三十一年』,上砂勝七著,ライフ社,1955年
43. 『時間』,堀田善衛著,新潮社,1955年
44. 『みんなが知っている』,藤原審爾編,春陽堂,1957年
45. 『市ケ谷台から市ケ谷台へ』,河辺虎四郎著,時事通信社,1962年
46. 『第九師団経理部将校の回想』,渡辺卯七著,私家版,1963年
47. 『生きている兵隊』,石川達三著,集英社,1965年
48. 『南京作戦の真相』,下野一霍著,東京情報社,1966年
49. 『破滅への道——私の昭和史』,上村伸一著,鹿島研究所出版会,1966年
50. 『支那事変従軍記——われら華中戦線を征く』,佐佐木稔著,私家版,1966年
51. 『ある軍人の自傳』,佐佐木到一著,勁草書房,1967年
52. 『江南の春遠く』(歩四十五聯隊),赤星昂編,三田書房,1968年
53. 『榊谷仙次郎日記』,私家版,1969年
54. 『聖戦の思い出』,手塚清著,私家版,1969年
55. 『岡村寧次大将資料』(上),稲葉正夫編,原書房,1970年
56. 『どろんこの兵』,浜崎富蔵編,私家版,1970年
57. 『外国人の見た日本軍の暴行』,ティンパーリー編,龍渓書舎,1972年
58. 『想い出の進軍——南京、徐州、武漢三鎮』(山砲九聯隊),山本勇編,山九戦友会事務所,1973年
59. 『最後の殿様』,徳川義親著,講談社,1973年
60. 『野戦郵便旗』,佐佐木元勝著,現代史出版会,1973年
61. 『落日燃ゆ』,城山三郎著,新潮社,1973年
62. 『日中戦争裏方記』,岡田酉次著,東洋経済新聞社,1974年
63. 『日中十五年戦争と私』,遠藤三郎著,日中書林,1974年
64. 『男六十五年を歩く』,菊本輝雄著,私家版,1975年
65. 『花と詩——思い出の泉』,土井申二著,私家版,1976年
66. 『上海時代』,松本重治著,中央公論社,1977年
67. 『陸軍省人事局長の回想』,額田坦著,芙蓉書房,1977年
68. 『田尻愛義回想録』,田尻愛義著,原書房,1977年
69. 『ある作戦参謀の回想手記』,池谷半二郎編,私家版,1978年
70. 『大陸を戦う——観測小隊長の日記』(野重十四聯隊),尾村止著,私家版,1979年
71. 『河辺虎四郎回想録』,毎日新聞社,1979年

72. 『揚子江が哭いている——熊本第六師団大陸出兵の記録』,創價学会青年部反戦出版委員会編,第三文明社,1979年
73. 『戦地憲兵』,井上源吉著,図書出版社,1980年
74. 『黄河、揚子江、珠江——中国勤務の思い出』,宇都宮直賢著,私家版,1980年
75. 『軍務局長武藤章回想録』,上法快男編,芙蓉書房,1981年
76. 『命脈陣中日誌』,平本渥著,私家版,1981年
77. 『私の朝日新聞社史』,森恭三著,田畑書店,1981年
78. 『出版警察報』,内務省警保局編,不二出版,1982年
79. 『日本兵士の反戦運動』,鹿地亘著,同成社,1982年
80. 『侵掠』,小俣行男著,徳間書店,1982年
81. 『永遠への道』,花山信勝著,日本工業新聞社,1982年
82. 『戦争の流れの中に』,前田雄二著,善本社,1982年
83. 『支那事変大東亜戦争写真集』,鵜飼敏定編,歩兵第四十五聯隊史編纂委員会,1983年
84. 『記録と記憶私の眼で見た支那事変』,金丸吉生著,私家版,1983年
85. 『風雲南京城』,宮部一三著,蘞文社,1983年
86. 『史上最大の人事』,額田坦著,芙蓉書房,1983年
87. 『戦争を知らない世代へ(II8)鮮血染まる中国大陸』,創価学会青年部反戦出版委員会編,第三文明社,1983年
88. 『日中戦争日記』第一巻,村田和志郎著,鵬和出版,1984年
89. 『私記南京虐殺——戦史にのらない戦争の話』,曽根一夫著,彩流社1984年
90. 『続私記南京虐殺——戦史にのらない戦争の話』,曽根一夫著,彩流社1984年
91. 『侵略の告発——暴虐の上海戦線日記』,玉井清美著,教育出版センター,1984年
92. 『ある技術屋のロマン』,加賀山学,私家版,1984年
93. 『松井石根大将戦陣日誌』,田中正明編,芙蓉書房,1985年
94. 『一兵士の従軍記録』,山本武著,安田書店,1985年
95. 『南京事件現地調査報告書』,南京事件調査研究会,一橋大学社会学部吉田研究室,1985年
96. 『聞き書南京事件』,阿羅健一編,図書出版社,1987年
97. 『わが南京プラトーン』,東史郎著,青木書店,1987年
98. 『茶毘の烟殉国の士を悼みて』,赤尾純藏著,私家版,1987年
99. 『南京虐殺と戦争』,曽根一夫著,泰流社,1988年
100. 『続・重光葵手記』,伊藤隆、渡辺行太郎編,中央公論社,1988年
101. 『彷徨二千五百里兵上の機微』,斎藤忠三郎著,私家版,1988年
102. 『日中戦争従軍日記——一輜重兵の戦場体験』,愛知大学国学叢書1,江口圭一、芝原拓自編,法律文化出版社,1989年
103. 『昭和天皇独白録』,寺崎英成、マリコ・テラサキ・ミラ編,文藝春秋,1991年
104. 『南京大虐殺——日本人への告発』,南京大虐殺の真相を明らかにする全国連絡会編,東方出版,1992年

105. 『石射猪太郎日記』,伊藤隆、劉傑編,中央公論社,1993年
106. 『長江の水天をうち上海東亜同文書院大学第34期生通訊従軍記』,通訊従軍記編集委員会編,滬友会第34期生会,1993年
107. 『支那事変従軍写真帖』,寺本重樹編,私家版,1994年
108. 『南京大虐殺記録した皇軍兵士たち』,小野賢二、藤原彰、本多勝一編,大月書店,1996年
109. 『レーニン判事の東京裁判』,小菅信子訳、粟原憲太郎解説,新潮社,1996年
110. 『南京の真実』,ジョン・ラーベ著,平野卿子訳,講談社,1997年
111. 『侍従長の遺言』,徳川義寛著,朝日出版社,1997年
112. 『南京の真実』,ジョン・ラーベ著,平野卿子訳,講談社,1997年
113. 『南京事件の日々——ミニー・ヴォートリンの日記』,岡田良之助、伊原陽子訳,笠原十九司解説,大月書店,1999年
114. 『ある軍法務官の日記』,小川関治郎,みすず書房,2000年
115. 『東史郎日記』,熊本出版文化会館,2001年
116. 『資料ドイツ外交官の見た南京事件』,石田勇治著,大月書店,2001年
117. 『「南京事件」日本人48人の証言』,阿羅健一編,小学館,2002年
118. 『南京戦・閉ざされた記憶を尋ねて』,松岡環編,社会評論社,2002年
119. 『南京戦・切りされた受難者の魂被害者120人の証言』,松岡環編,社会評論社,2003年

III. History of the Japanese War and Japanese Army
120. 『南京戦史』,南京戦史編集委員会著,偕行社,1989年
121. 『戦史叢書大本営陸軍部<1>昭和15年5月まで』,防衛庁防衛研修所戦史室編,朝雲新聞社,1967年
122. 『戦史叢書中国方面海軍作戦<1>昭和13年3月まで』,防衛庁防衛研修所戦史室編,朝雲新聞社,1974年
123. 『戦史叢書支那事変陸軍部<1>昭和13年1月まで』,防衛庁防衛研修所戦史室編,朝雲新聞社,1975年
124. 『大本営陸軍部』1,防衛庁防衛研修所戦史室編,朝雲新聞社,1967年
125. 『支那事変陸軍作戦』1,防衛庁防衛研修所戦史室編,朝雲新聞社,1975年
126. 『第三師団戦史』,陸上自衛隊第十師団
127. 『広島師団史』(第五師団),陸上自衛隊第十三師団,1969年
128. 『熊本兵団戦史』支那事変編(第六師団),熊本日日新聞社,1965年
129. 『南京作戦の真相——熊本第六師団戦記』,五島広作編,東京情報社,1966年
130. 『第九師団戦史』,陸上自衛隊第十師団,1965年
131. 『騎兵第三聯隊史』,騎兵第三聯隊史編纂委員会編,騎兵第三聯隊史編纂委員会,1978年
132. 『歩兵第七聯隊史』,伊佐一男他編,歩七戦友会,1967年
133. 『金城聯隊史』(歩兵第七聯隊),歩七戦友会,1969年

134. 『山砲第九聯隊史』,荒谷金子編,第九師団砲兵会,1974年
135. 『追憶金沢輜重兵聯隊』(輜重兵第九聯隊),追憶金沢輜重兵聯隊編集委員会編,金沢輜重兵会,1976年
136. 『我が戦塵の懐古録』(山砲第九聯隊),九砲の集い,私家版,1979年
137. 『大陸踏破三万里——野戦重砲兵第十四聯隊史』,野戦重砲兵第十四聯隊史編纂委員会編,野戦重砲兵第十四聯隊史編纂委員会,1981年
138. 『われらの野重八』(独立野戦重砲兵第十五聯隊),野重八会編,野重八会,1976年
139. 『歩兵第十八聯隊史』,歩兵第十八聯隊史刊行会,1964年
140. 『敦賀聯隊史』(歩兵第十九聯隊),安川定義編,敦賀聯隊史蹟保存会,1964年
141. 『福知山聯隊史』(歩兵第二十聯隊),伊藤良一編,福知山聯隊史刊行会,1975年
142. 『福知山歩兵第二十聯隊第三中隊史』,大小田正雄著,福知山聯隊史刊行会,1982年
143. 『隠された聯隊史』(第二十聯隊),下里正樹,青木書店,1987年
144. 『続•隠された聯隊史』(第二十聯隊),下里正樹,青木書店,1988年
145. 『都城歩兵第二十三聯隊戦記』,歩兵第二十三聯隊戦記編纂委員会編,歩兵第二十三聯隊戦記編纂委員会,1978年
146. 『歩兵第三十三聯隊史』,島田勝己著,歩兵第三十三聯隊史刊行会,1972年
147. 『魁——郷土人物戦記』(歩兵第三十三聯隊),小林正雄編,伊勢新聞社,1984年
148. 『歩兵第三十四聯隊史』,歩兵第三十四聯隊史編纂委員会,1979年
149. 『富山聯隊史』(補第三十五聯隊),富山聯隊史刊行会編,富山聯隊史刊行会,1986年
150. 『鯖江歩兵第三十六聯隊史』,鯖江歩兵第三十六聯隊史編纂委員会編,鯖江歩兵第三十六聯隊史蹟保存会,1976年
151. 『歩兵第三十六聯隊中支方面ニ於ケル行動概要』,坂武徳,私家版,1983年
152. 『奈良聯隊戦記』(歩兵第三十八聯隊),野口俊夫著,大和タイムス社,1963年
153. 『歩兵第四十五聯隊史』,鵜飼敏定著,歩兵第四十五聯隊史編纂委員会,1981年
154. 『郷土部隊奮戦記』1—3(歩兵第四十七聯隊など),平松鷹史著,大分合同新聞社,1983年
155. 『郷土部隊戦記1——歩兵第六十五聯隊』,福島民友新聞社編,福島民友新聞社,1964年
156. 『ふくしま戦争と人間』1白虎編,福島民友新聞社編,福島民友新聞社,1982年
157. 『戦友の絆』(歩兵第六十五聯隊),白虎六光奉友会編,白虎六光奉友会,1980年
158. 『若松聯隊回想録』(歩兵第六十五聯隊)

159. 『步兵第六十八聯隊第一大隊戰史』,步兵第六十八聯隊第一大隊戰史編纂委員会編,步兵第六十八聯隊第一大隊戰史編纂委員会,1976年
160. 『步兵第五十聯隊史併記第百五十聯隊史』,堀越好雄著,私家版,1974年

IV. Works

161. 堀場一雄著『支那事変戦争指導史』,时事通信社,1962年
162. 洞富雄著『近代戦史の謎』,人物往来社,1967年
163. 田中正明著『パール博士の日本無罪論』,慧文社,1963年
164. 新島淳良著『南京大虐殺』,日中友好協会「正統」永福支部,1971年
165. 洞富雄著『南京事件』,新人物往来社,1972年
166. 本多勝一著『中国の旅』,朝日新聞社,1972年
167. 本多勝一著『中国の日本軍』,創樹社,1972年
168. 本多勝一著『殺す側の論理』,すずさわ書店,1972年
169. 鈴木明著『「南京大虐殺」のまぼろし』,文藝春秋社,1973年
170. 山本七平著『私の中の日本軍』上,下,文藝春秋社,1975年
171. 洞富雄著『南京大虐殺——「まぼろし化」工作批判』,現代史出版会,1975年
172. 森山康平著『証言記録三光作戦南京虐殺から満州崩壊』,新人物往来社,1975年
173. 松浦総三著『「文藝春秋」の研究』,晩聲社,1977年
174. 本多勝一編『ペンの陰謀』,潮出版社,1977年
175. 加登川幸太郎著『中国と日本陸軍』,圭文社,1978年
176. 井本熊男著『作戦日誌で綴る支那事変』,芙蓉書房,1978年
177. 江藤淳著『忘れたことと忘れさせられたこと』,文藝春秋社,1979年
178. 洞富雄著『決定版·南京大虐殺』,徳間書店,1982年
179. 浅見定雄著『にせユダヤ人と日本人』,朝日新聞社,1983年
180. 田中正明著『「南京虐殺」の虚構——松井大将の日記をめぐって』,日本教文社,1984年
181. 谷口巖著『南京大虐殺の研究』,Office PANO,1984年
182. 藤原彰著『南京大虐殺』,岩波ブックレット,1985年
183. 吉田裕著『天皇の軍隊と南京事件』,青木書店,1985年
184. 秦郁彦著『南京事件——虐殺の構造』,中央公論新社,1986年
185. 洞富雄著『南京大虐殺の証明』,朝日新聞社,1986年
186. 本多勝一著『南京への道』,朝日新聞社,1987年
187. 田中正明著『南京事件の総括——虐殺否定の十五の論拠』,謙光社,1987年
188. 阿羅健一著『聞き書南京事件』,図書出版社,1987年
189. 洞富雄、藤原彰、本多勝一編『南京事件を考える』,大月書店,1987年
190. 木村久邇典著『個性派将軍中島今朝吾』,光人社,1987年

191. 洞富雄、藤原彰、本多勝一編『南京大虐殺の現場へ』,朝日新聞社,1988年
192. 文藝春秋著『「文藝春秋」にみる昭和史』第一巻,文藝春秋社,1988年
193. 本多勝一著『裁かれた南京大虐殺』,晩聲社,1989年
194. 時野谷滋著『家永教科書裁判と南京事件』,日本教文社,1989年
195. 阿部輝郎著『南京の氷雨——虐殺の構造を追って』,教育書籍,1989年
196. 冨士信夫著『私の見た東京裁判』,講談社学術文庫,1989年
197. 板倉由明著『徹底検証南京事件の真実』,日本政策研究センタ事業部,1991年
198. 教科書検定訴訟を支援する全国連絡会編『家永·教科書裁判第三次訴訟地裁編第4巻南京大虐殺·七三一部隊』,ロング出版,1991年
199. 洞富雄、藤原彰、本多勝一編『南京大虐殺の研究』晩聲社,1992年
200. 畝本正己著『史実の歪曲』,閣文社,1992年
201. 南京大虐殺の真相を明らかにする全国聯絡会編『南京大虐殺——日本人への告発』,東方出版,1992年
202. 上羽修、中原道子著『昭和の消せない真実』,岩波書店,1992年
203. 滝谷二郎著『目撃者の南京事件、発見されたマギー牧師の日記』,三交社,1992年
204. 前川三郎著『真説·南京攻防戦』,日本図書刊行会,1993年
205. 笠原十九司著『南京难民区的百日』,岩波書店,1995年
206. 冨士信夫著『「南京大虐殺」はこうして作られた——東京裁判の欺瞞』,展転社,1995年
207. 津田道夫著『南京大虐殺と日本人の精神構造』,社会評論社,1995年
208. 小室直樹、渡部昇一著『封印の昭和史——「戦後五〇年」自虐の終焉』,徳間書店,1995年
209. 戦争犠牲者を心に刻む会編『南京大虐殺と原爆』,東方出版,1995年
210. 大井満著『仕組まれた「南京大虐殺」——攻略作戦の全貌とマスコミ報道の怖さ』,展転社,1995年
211. 小野賢二、藤原彰、本多勝一編『南京大虐殺記録した皇軍兵士たち』,大月書店,1996年
212. 藤岡信勝、自由主義史観研究会編『教科書が教えない歴史』2,産経新聞社,1996年
213. 教科書検定訴訟を支援する全国連絡会編『家永·教科書裁判第三次訴訟地裁編第2巻南京大虐殺·朝鮮人民の抵抗·七三一部隊』,民衆社,1997年
214. 渡辺寛著『南京虐殺と日本軍——幕府山の中国人捕虜殺害事件の真相』,明石書店,1997年
215. 奥宮正武著『私の見た南京事件』,PHP研究所,1997年
216. 藤原彰著『南京の日本軍南京大虐殺とその背景』,大月書店,1997年
217. 笠原十九司著『南京事件』,岩波書店,1997年

218. 本多勝一著『本多勝一集』第23巻『南京大虐殺』,朝日新聞社,1997年
219. 渡辺寛著『南京虐殺と日本軍』,明石書店,1997年
220. 笠原十九司、松村高夫ほか著『歴史の事実をどう認定しどう教えるか——検証731部隊・南京虐殺事件・「従軍慰安婦」』,教育資料出版会,1997年
221. 藤原彰編『南京事件をどうみるか——日、中、米研究者による検証』,青木書店,1998年
222. 東中野修道著『「南京虐殺」の徹底検証』,展転社,1998年
223. 松村俊夫著『「南京大虐殺」への大疑問——大虐殺外國資料を徹底分析する』,展転社,1998年
224. 畝本正己著『真相・南京事件——ラ—ベ日記を検証して』,文京出版,1998年
225. 吉本榮著『南京大虐殺の虚構を砕け』新風書房,1998年
226. クリストファ・バーナード著、加地永都子訳『南京虐殺は「おこった」のか―高校歴史教科書への言語学的批判』,筑摩書房,1998年
227. 鈴木明著『新「南京大虐殺」のまぼろし』,飛鳥新社,1999年
228. 秦郁彦著『現代史の光と影―南京事件から嫌煙権論争まで』,グラフ社,1999年
229. 笠原十九司著『南京事件と三光作戦——未来に生かす戦争の記憶』,大月書店,1999年
230. 西尾幹二著『国民の歴史』,産経新聞社,1999年
231. 東中野修道、藤岡信勝著『〈ザ・レイプ・オブ・南京〉の研究——中国における「情報戦」の手口と戦略』,祥傳社,1999年
232. 南京事件調査研究会編『南京大虐殺否定論13のウソ』,柏書房,1999年
233. 板倉由明著『本当はこうだった南京事件』,日本図書刊行会,1999年
234. 西岡香織著『報道戦線から見た日中戦争——陸軍報道部長馬淵逸雄の足跡』,芙蓉書房,1999年
235. 早瀬利之著『将軍之真実——松井石根人物傳』,光人社,1999年
236. 前田雄二著『南京大虐殺はなかった—「戦争の流れの中に」からの抜粋』,善本社,1999年
237. 小林よしのり著『「個と公」論』,幻冬舎,2000年
238. 早乙女勝元著『ふたたび南京へ』,草の根出版会,2000年
239. ジョシュア・A・フォーゲル編、岡田良之助訳『歴史学のなかの南京大虐殺』,柏書房,2000年
240. 五十嵐善之丞著『決定版南京事件の真実』,文芸社,2000年
241. 竹本忠雄、大原康男著,日本会議国際広報委員会編集『再審"南京大虐殺"——世界に訴える日本の冤罪』,明成社,2000年
242. 吉本栄著『南京大虐殺の大嘘—何故いつまで罷り通るか』,東京図書出版会,2001年
243. 田中正明著『南京事件の総括—虐殺否定の論拠』(復刊本), 展転社,2001年

244. 田中正明著『パール判事の日本無罪論』(復刊本),小学館,2001年
245. 北村稔著『南京事件の探究——その実像をもとめて』,文藝春秋社,2001年
246. 津田道夫著『侵略戦争と性暴力——軍隊は民衆をまもらない』,社会評論社,2002年
247. 松岡環編『南京戦——元兵士102人の証言』,社会評論社,2002年
248. 笠原十九司著『南京事件と日本人—戦争の記憶をめぐるナショナリズムとグローバリズム』,柏書房,2002年
249. 五十嵐善之丞著『南京事件の反省と平和の構築について』,文芸社,2002年
250. 津田道夫著『侵略戦争と性暴力——軍隊は民衆をまもらない』,社会評論社,2002年
251. 東中野修道編『南京「虐殺」研究の最前線<平成14年版>——日本「南京」学会年報』,展転社,2002年
252. 東中野修道編『南京「虐殺」研究の最前線<平成15年版>——日本「南京」学会年報』,展転社,2003年
253. 室谷守一著『南京翡翠の数珠』,文芸社,2003年
254. 田中正明著『朝日が明かす中国の嘘』,高木書房,2003年
255. 本多勝一著『南京大虐殺歴史改竄派の敗北——李秀英名誉損裁判から未来へ』,教育史料出版会,2003年
256. 富沢繁信著『南京事件の核心——データベースによる事件の解明』,展転社,2003年
257. 東中野修道編『1937南京攻略戦の真実—新資料発掘』,小学館,2003年
258. 村尾一郎著『プロハカノダ戦「南京事件」——秘録写真で見る「南京大虐殺」の真実』,光人社,2004年
259. 川田忠明著『それぞれの「戦争論」——そこにいた人たち——1937・南京—2004・イラク』,唯学書房,2004年
260. 富沢繁信著『南京安全地帯の記録完訳と研究』,展転社,2004年
261. 畠奈津子著『「百人斬り」報道を斬る—敵はシナ中共政府と我が国の偏向マスコミだ』,日新報道,2004年
262. 東中野修道編『南京「虐殺」研究の最前線<平成16年版>——日本「南京」学会年報』,展転社,2005年
263. 東中野修道、小林進、福永慎次郎著『南京事件「証拠写真」を検証する』,草思社,2005年
264. 三好誠著『戦争プロパガンダの嘘を暴く——「南京事件」からバターン「死の進行」まで』,展転社,2005年
265. 東中野修道編『南京「事件」研究の最前線<平成17・18年合併版>——日本「南京」学会年報』,展転社,2005年
266. 笠原十九司著『体験者27人が語る南京事件』,高文研,2006年
267. 笠原十九司、吉田裕編『現代歴史学と南京事件』,柏書房,2006年
268. 東中野修道著『南京事件——国民党極秘文書から読み解く』,草思社,2006年

269. 稲垣大紀著『25歳が読む「南京事件」——事件の究明と論争史』,東京財団,2006年
270. 鈴木明著『「南京大虐殺」のまぼろし』(改訂版),ワック,2006年
271. 富沢繁信著『「南京事件」発展史』,展転社,2007年
272. 東中野修道著『南京「百人斬り競争」の真実』,ワック,2007年
273. 東中野修道編『南京「事件」研究の最前線<平成19年版>——日本「南京」学会年報』,展転社,2007年
274. 津田道夫著『ある軍団教師の日記——民衆が戦争を支えた』,高文研,2007年
275. 稲田朋美著『百人斬り裁判から南京へ』,文藝春秋,2007年
276. 西村幸祐編『情報戦「慰安婦・南京」の真実<完全保存版>中国、朝鮮半島、反日メディアの連携を絶て!』,オークラ出版,2007年
277. 秦郁彦著『南京事件——「虐殺」の構造』(増補版),中央公論新社,2007年
278. 東中野修道著『再現——南京戦』,草思社,2007年
279. 阿羅健一著『再検証南京で本当は何が起こったのか』,徳間書店,2007年
280. 笠原十九司著『南京事件論争史——日本人は史実をどう認識してきたか』,平凡社,2007年

V. Videos
281. 『私の従軍中国戦線:一兵士が写した戦場の記録村瀬守保写真集』村瀬守保編,日本機関誌出版センター,1987年
282. 『支那事変従軍写真帖』寺本重樹編,私家版,1994年
283. 『写真集・南京大虐殺』,「写真集・南京大虐殺」を刊行するキリスト者の会編,1995年
284. 『南京戦記映画復刻シリーズ21』,日本映画新社,1997年
285. 『不許可写真集1』,毎日新聞社,1998年
286. 『不許可写真集2』,毎日新聞社,1999年
287. 『南京戦線後方記録映画』,東宝映画文化映画部製作、1938年(2004年発売)

Index

A
Abend, Hallet, 11, 16, 17
Agawa Sadayoshi (安川定义), 200
Aiyi Tanjiri (田尻爱义), 149, 341
Akira Mutō (武藤章), 388
Allison, John Moore, 16
Amakasu Masahiko (甘粕正彦), 268, 269
Anami Korechika (阿南惟几), 147–149, 159, 244, 339, 340
Ara Kenichi (阿罗健一/富中秀夫), 5, 24, 28, 144, 214, 265, 281, 307–309, 360, 362, 409, 483, 488, 490, 495, 497
Asabu (麻生), 168
Asaka Yasuhiko (朝香宫鸠彦), 128, 134, 328, 446
Asami Kazuo (浅海一男), 231, 308, 498
Azuma Shiro (东史郎), 178, 195, 223, 303, 309, 466, 475

B
Bates, Miner Searle (M.S. Bates), 259, 299

C
Cassese, Antonio, 86
Chaplin, 228
Chen Chung-fu (陈中孚), 97
Cheng Zhaoqi (程兆奇), 461, 483
Chen Pengren (陈鹏仁), 160
Chen Yi (陈毅), 97
Chiang Kai-shek (蒋介石), 96, 97, 110, 112, 140, 144, 178, 183, 243, 252, 314, 350, 367, 376, 383, 393, 395, 396, 398, 414, 417, 440, 488, 495, 497, 500, 504, 508, 510, 520
Coville, Cabot, 60, 216

D
Donowaki (堂之胁), 181

E
Eguchi Keiichi (加纳治雄), 189
Eiichi Kakuta (角田荣一), 129
Espy, 11, 16

F
Fansibo (范思伯), 33, 34
Fitch, George, 16, 163, 178, 208, 209, 214, 300, 315, 400, 421–425
Foster, 198
Fujii Shinichi (藤井慎一), 183
Fujimori Yukio (藤森幸男), 218
Fujimoto (藤本), 177
Fuji Nobuo (富士信夫), 4, 59, 70, 82, 92, 142, 216, 362, 483, 492, 493
Fujita Isamu (藤田勇), 183

Fujiwara Akira (藤原彰), 5, 154, 156, 169, 173, 226, 277, 285, 304, 356, 363, 464, 484, 516, 526, 529
Fukasawa Kanosamu (深泽千藏), 26, 129, 172
Fukuda Tokuyasu (福田笃泰), 147, 338, 339
Fukui Kiyoshi (福井喜代志), 147, 149, 339, 341
Fukuoka Yoshio (福冈义雄), 75
Fukushima Yasumasa (福岛安正), 110
Fumiko Hayashi (林芙美子), 142, 497
Funatsu Tasuichiro (船津辰一郎), 98

G

Gauss, Clarence E., 16
Genda Minoru (源田实), 40
Genghis khan (成吉思汗), 40, 116, 221, 510
George Atchison Jr., 11, 15, 16

H

Hanae Shou (森英生), 135, 195, 196, 199, 203–205, 214, 216, 329
Harada (原田), 99, 100, 104, 346
Harada Katsumasa (原田膝正), 174
Harako Shojo (原子昭三), 144
Hara Shiro (原四郎), 140, 161, 162
Hara Takeshi (原刚), 7, 35, 280, 307, 362, 483, 506
Haruo Kano (加诵英明), 135, 329
Hashimoto Kingoro (桥本欣五郎), 105
Hashimoto Tomisaburo (桥本登美三郎), 26, 308
Hayao Tada (多田骏), 370
Heisuke Sugiyama (杉山平助), 142, 467
Heisuke Yanagawa (柳川平助), 96, 126, 243, 350
Hideichi Noyori (野依秀市), 142
Hideki Tojo (东条英机), 110
Higashinakano Shudo (东中野修道), 4, 5, 7–9, 14, 21–32, 35, 41, 61, 115, 119–122, 130, 144, 145, 184, 193, 197, 218, 229, 253, 280, 282, 290, 321, 360, 361, 363, 377, 381, 405–408, 421, 422, 424, 430, 431, 433, 435, 439, 441, 442, 446, 451, 477, 483, 488, 492, 493, 495, 498, 505, 506, 512
Hijiya Masaharu (土屋正治), 200, 217
Hirai Akio (平井秋雄), 208
Hirohito (裕仁), 159, 160, 387, 388, 392
Hirota Koki (广田弘毅, 84, 105, 112, 160, 288
Hirota Koki(广田弘毅, 393
Hirota Minoru (广田丰), 150, 342
Hisashi Yamanaka (山中恒), 162
Hitler, 40, 116, 219, 406, 487, 504
Honda Katsuichi (本多胜一), 156, 172, 188, 225–227, 229, 231, 237, 275–277, 283, 304, 356, 357, 487, 495, 524, 526
Honma Hikotaro (本间彦太郎), 47, 87
Honma Masaharu (本间雅晴), 149, 150, 340–342
Horiba Kazuo (堀场一雄), 151, 343
Horikawa Shizuo (堀川静夫), 186, 330
Huang Jinrong (黄金荣), 210
Huang Wenxiong (黄文雄), 22
Huang Ziliang (黄子良), 201

I

Iba Masuo (伊庭益夫), 199, 217
Iguchi Kazuki (井口和起), 304
Iinuma Mamoru (饭沼守), 46, 93, 95, 96, 129, 133, 138, 148, 151, 152, 157, 159, 166, 167, 209–211, 216, 240, 242, 263, 300, 301, 306, 313, 325, 326, 340, 344–348, 355, 453
Ikuhiko Hata (秦郁彦), 6, 7, 35, 36, 171, 172, 279, 280, 293, 361, 461, 483, 529, 531
Imai Masayoshi (今井正刚), 26
Inaba Masao (稲葉正夫), 150, 162, 343
Inose Naoki (猪瀬直樹), 126, 171
Isa Kazuo (伊佐一男), 207
Isamu Cho (长勇), 128, 131, 181, 183, 318
Ishii Itaro (石射猪太郎), 49, 149, 151, 300, 341, 342
Ishikawa Tatsujo (石川达三), 24, 142, 174, 175
Isoda (矶田), 125
Isomura (矶村年), 270

Ito Noe (伊藤野枝), 269
Iwane Matsui (松井石根/松井岩根), 83–85, 88–98, 100–102, 104, 107, 108, 112, 137, 145, 155, 281, 299, 301, 307, 319, 345, 367, 419, 453, 488, 499

J

Jiang Genfu (姜根福), 227
Jiang Zhengyun (姜正云), 11, 12
John Magee, 197, 422, 433
Jusu (鲁甦), 363, 364

K

Kagesa Sadaaki (影佐祯昭), 369, 417
Kamisago Shoshichi (上砂胜七), 47, 242, 246, 247, 255, 264, 265
Kaneko Renji (金子廉二), 170, 173
Kanji Ishiwara (石原莞尔), 313, 387, 389
Kanji Nishio (西尾幹二), 145, 378
Kan'in Kotohito (闲院宫载仁), 148, 270, 340, 391
Katogawa Kotarou (加登川幸太郎), 172
Kawabe Torashiro (河边虎四郎), 148, 154, 306, 340, 388, 389
Kawagoe Shigeru (川越茂), 98, 113
Kayano (萱野), 97
Kazahaya (风早), 348
Kazuo Minamata (小俣行男), 171
Keenan (基南), 144
Kikuchi Masanori (菊地昌典), 163
Kimura Ki (木村毅), 142
Kisaki Hisashi (木佐木久), 176, 187, 199, 206, 332
Kitamura Minoru (北村稔), 4, 6, 32, 33, 36, 41, 88, 89, 169, 179, 202, 281, 282, 360, 383–385, 482
Kitayama Atae (北山), 178, 179, 189, 190, 333
Knatchbull-Hugesscn, S.M., 100
Kobayashi Katsuji (小林胜治), 47
Kondo Eijiro (近藤英次郎), 304
Kroeger, 168
Kusano Shinpei (草野心平), 142

L

Laden, Bin, 162
Little, 105, 106, 521
Liu Asheng (刘阿盛), 58, 74, 260
Liu Yan (刘燕), 463
Li Zeyi (李泽一), 97, 416, 417
Lu Liren (陆礼仁), 62
Lu Liru (陆礼如), 62
Lu Liwen (陆礼文), 62
Lu Longqing (陆龙庆), 57, 249
Luo Fuxiang (罗福祥), 223
Lu Xiaoyun (陆肖云), 62

M

Mabuchi Itsuo (马渊逸雄), 176
Maeda Yoshihiko (前田吉彦), 306
Maeda Yuji (前田雄二), 26, 129, 172
Makihara Nobuo (牧原信夫), 303
Mao Zedong (毛泽东), 144, 510
Marshal MacArthur, 496
Masaki Jinzaburo (真崎甚三郎), 269
Masayoshi Arai (新井正义), 26, 129, 172, 308
Masuyama Takao (增山隆雄), 271
Matachi Ike (井家又一), 186, 187, 205, 209, 215, 221, 331, 332, 426, 427
Matsumoto Shigeharu (松本重治), 171, 308, 309
Matsumura Toshio (松村俊夫), 4, 483, 502, 505
Matsuoka (松冈), 247, 250, 265, 352
Matsuoka Tamaki (松冈環), 283, 305
Ma Zhendu (马振犊), 90, 312
McCallum, James, 15, 16, 53, 259
Mei Ruao (梅汝璈), 86
Mikado (天皇), 463
Mills, 203
Mitsumasa Yonai (米内光政), 92
Mitsuyo (Okawa) Nagamori (畏森光代/小川光代), 47, 264
Mizutani Sho (水谷荘), 177, 306
Mori Kyojo (森恭三), 164
Morozuno Sakuhajime (两角业作), 190, 283, 304, 306, 334
Muguruma Masajiro (六车政次郎), 199, 205, 206, 221

Mukai Toshiaki (向井敏明), 173, 226–231, 237, 292, 356–358, 486

N
Nakai (中井), 98
Nakajima Tetsuo (中岛铁藏), 313, 389, 390
Nakamura Akira (中村粲), 117, 362, 483, 507
Nakasawa Mitsuo (中泽三夫), 300, 301, 368, 415, 450
Nakashima Kesago (中岛今朝吾), 153, 180, 340, 345
Nakayama Neito (中山宁人), 152, 156, 216, 314
Naokata Utsunomiya (宇都宫直贤), 150, 342
Naoki Komuro (小室直树), 40, 144, 376, 378, 391
Naosuke Matsuki (松木直亮), 270
Naruse Kanji (成濑关次), 234
Nishibe Susumu (西部迈), 115, 144, 388
Nishino Rumiko (西野瑠美子), 141
Nishioka Kaori (西冈香織), 161
Nishio Kanji (早尾盾雄), 378
Nisuk Ando (安藤仁介), 87
Nitta Mitsuo (新田满夫), 242, 255, 263
Noboru Kojima (儿岛襄), 128
Nobukatsu Fujioka (藤冈信胜), 4, 5, 144, 280, 297, 360, 362, 378, 483, 492, 498, 505, 512
Noda Tsuyoshi (野田毅), 173, 226–232, 237, 356–358, 486
Nomura Toshiaki (野村敏明), 215
Nukata Tan (额田坦), 340

O
Odagiri Hideo (小田切秀雄), 175
Ohara (小原), 185
Ohara Koutarou (小原孝太郎), 188, 189, 332, 333
Okada Takashi (冈田尚), 300, 307, 314, 367–369, 397, 413–417, 419
Okada Yuuji (冈田酉次), 153
Okamoto (冈本), 178
Okamura Yasuji (冈村宁次), 150, 342
Okazaki Katsuo (冈崎胜男), 147, 149, 339, 341

Ōkawachi Denshichi (大川内传七), 184, 253
Onishi Hajime (大西一), 307, 318, 329
Ono Kenji (小野贤二), 282, 298, 304, 518
Onuma Yasuaki (大沼保昭), 113
Oohara Yasuo (大原康男), 143, 230, 337
Ooi Mitsuru (大井满), 3, 23, 128, 129, 144, 180, 197, 207, 229, 318, 358, 362, 483, 493, 501
Orikono Suetaro (折小野末太郎), 200, 206, 215
Orita Mamoru (折田护), 177, 200, 206, 209, 306, 425
Osugi Sakae (大杉荣), 269
Oyama Ayao (大山文雄), 270

P
Pal, Radha Binod, 86, 113, 301, 302, 498
Pot, Pol, 116

Q
Qi Mingjing (祁明镜), 201, 400

R
Rabe, John H.D., 11, 15–18, 28, 34, 116, 146, 147, 167, 178, 194–196, 198, 208, 338, 399, 429, 486, 490, 493, 529
Rguchi Keiichi (江口圭一), 285, 363, 484
Roling, B.V.A., 86

S
Saburo Aizawa (相泽三郎), 269
Sadaharu Hirabayashi (平林贞治), 128
Sahishige Nagatsu (永津佐比重), 135, 328
Sakakibara Kazue (榊原主计), 242, 301
Sakurai (樱井), 24
Sasaki (笹木), 19, 20, 22, 121
Sato Kanichi (佐藤寒山), 235, 236
Sato Shinju (佐藤振寿), 230, 307, 308
Sayuri Yoshinaga (吉永小百合), 268
Scharffenber, 220

Sekiguchi Minami (关口鐮造), 207, 208
Shibayama Kaneshiro (柴山兼四郎), 94, 154, 313, 369, 389, 390, 417
Shigemitsu Mamoru (重光葵), 88, 151
Shimozato Masaki (下里正樹), 303, 304
Shinrokuro Hidaka (日高信六郎), 47, 108, 300
Shiratori Toshio (白鸟敏夫), 84
Shishime Akira (志志目彰), 231, 232, 235, 357
Shu-His Hsu (徐淑希), 275
Shunji Aida (相田俊二), 128
Shunroku Hata (畑俊六), 155, 157, 160, 305, 306, 351, 453
Smith, 197, 204, 439, 440
Smythe, Lewis S.C., 18, 147, 209, 275, 278, 291, 300, 302
Soejima (副島), 185
Soichiro Tahara (田原总一郎), 388
Soki Yoshinobu (曾木义信), 141
Sone Ichio (曾根一夫), 169, 179
Song Ziwen (宋子文), 416, 417
Sono Ayako (曾野绫子), 162
Stalin, 116, 500
Steele, Archibald T., 11, 15–17
Sugihara Chiune (杉原千亩), 35
Sugiyama Hajime (杉山元), 92, 313
Sumi Yoshiharu (角良晴), 131, 181–183, 318–320
Sunao Yoshinaga (吉永朴), 265, 308
Sun Yat-Sen (孙文), 109, 151, 347, 367, 414, 415, 446, 496, 497, 500
Sun Zhaiwei (孙宅巍), 461, 479, 480, 520
Susumu Maruyama (丸山进), 7, 363, 405, 407
Suzuki Aki (铃木明), 4, 5, 31, 32, 41, 93, 127, 128, 130, 143, 173, 183, 202, 226, 228, 230, 276, 277, 279, 281, 290, 320, 324, 356, 359, 362, 381–385, 477, 483, 488, 490, 493, 502, 505, 513, 515, 524
Suzuki Jiro, 231, 308

T

Tadao Yanaihara (矢内原忠雄), 175, 176
Tajima Riuichi (田岛隆犬), 247, 256, 353
Takahashi Eizo (高桥荣藏), 76

Takanashi Masaki (高梨正樹), 171
Takemoto Tadao (竹本忠雄), 40, 143, 229
Takigawa Masajiro (泷川政次郎), 28
Takuji Shibahara (芝原拓自), 189
Tame (溜), 185
Tanaka Masaaki (田中正明), 5, 22, 40, 91, 139, 155, 278–281, 359, 362, 365, 368, 416, 422, 477, 483, 488, 492, 493, 495, 513
Tanaka Ryukich (田中隆吉), 154
Tanaka Shinichi (田中新一), 388
Tang Shaoyi (唐绍仪), 97
Tang Shengzhi (唐生智), 220, 440, 485, 487, 491, 493, 496, 497, 503, 505, 508–510
Tan Youlin (谭友林), 56, 249
Tasawa (田泽博), 152
Tenya (天野), 152
Tillman Durdin, F., 11, 15–17, 29–31, 145, 169, 172, 183, 220, 244, 275, 301–303, 320, 337
Timperley, Harold John (H.J. Timperley), 201
Tokugawa Yoshichika (德川义亲), 183
Tokushi Kasahara (笠原十九司), 277, 282, 283, 285, 363, 460, 461, 475, 484, 517, 520, 521, 526, 529
Tomio Hora (洞富雄), xiii, 5, 14, 60, 91, 95–97, 146, 150, 152, 155, 156, 166, 168, 170, 183, 188, 216, 228, 229, 274, 275, 277–279, 298–300, 318, 338, 342, 356, 361, 363, 384, 385, 397, 408, 413, 414, 416–418, 422, 438, 450, 460, 464, 475, 491, 507, 516, 520, 523, 524
Tomizawa Shigenobu (富泽繁信), 7, 9–20, 22, 35
Toshimichi, Uemura (上村利道), 134, 152, 167, 306, 328, 348, 453
Touichi Sasaki (佐佐木到一), 19, 152, 208, 215, 306, 348, 445
Tsuda Michio (津田道夫), 283, 292, 298, 388, 461, 463, 473, 481
Tsuguichi Koyanagi (小柳次一), 214
Tsukada Osamu (冢田攻), 240, 314
Tsukamoto Hirotsugu (冢本浩次), 46, 47, 240, 263, 264, 300, 355
Tsuneishi Keiichi (常石敬一), 289

U

Unemoto Masaki (亩本正己), 5, 40, 116, 187, 194, 196–199, 202, 211, 280, 360, 362, 430, 477, 483, 509
Usui Katsumi (臼井膝美), 162

V

Vautrin, Minnie, 11, 16, 202, 205, 209, 210, 212, 214, 439
Victor, 194

W

Wachi (和知), 97, 98
Wakeman, 36
Wakisaka Jiro (胁坂次郎), 41, 42, 83, 255, 301, 343, 352, 368, 415, 450
Wang Jingwei (汪精卫/汪兆铭), 61, 369, 383, 396, 417
Watanabe Shoichi (渡部升一), 6, 8, 144, 194, 278, 281, 314, 360, 362, 376, 378, 391, 398, 483, 486
Wen Zongyao (温宗尧), 369, 417
Wilson, Robert O., 15, 16, 299
Wu Guangyi (吴广义), 474

X

Xu Chuanyin (许传音), 60, 299
Xuhong Shi (徐洪氏), 246
Xu Shiying (许世英), 112, 393
Xu Xianqing (徐先青), 201

Y

Yamada Eizo (山田英造), 473
Yamada Masayuki (山田正行), 285
Yamada Senji (山田栴二), 118, 127, 128, 130
Yamamoto Isoroku (山本五十六), 161
Yamamoto Shichihei (山本七平), 5, 105, 230, 231, 233–237, 277, 281, 306, 358, 359, 487
Yamamoto Yoshimasa (山本义正), 161
Yamane Yukio (山根幸夫), 234
Yamashita (山下), 87
Yamazaki Masao (山崎正男), 177, 181, 186, 209, 215, 221, 319, 331
Yang Xiaoming (杨夏鸣), 480
Yaso, Saijo, 142
Yasumura Junnitu (安村纯一), 20–22, 448
Yasuyama Koudou (泰山弘道), 182–184, 186, 252, 253, 306, 319–321, 330, 331, 381, 445, 446
Yinoue Kentaro (井上源吉), 48, 407
Yoshiaki Itakura (板仓由明), 119, 125, 126, 143, 168, 181, 188, 205, 230, 279, 280, 306, 307, 360, 477, 495, 505
Yoshikiyo Ninomiya (二宫义清), 134, 328
Yoshimoto (吉本荣), 3
Yoshinori Kobayashi (小林よしのり), 5, 8, 360, 362, 483, 490
Yoshio Kodama (儿玉义雄), 123, 323, 324
Yutaka Yoshida (吉田裕), 277, 285, 292, 363, 484, 526
Yu Zidao (余子道), 90, 312

Z

Zeng Xubai (曾虚白), 32–34
Zhang Xianwen (张宪文), 480
Zhang Xiaolin (张效林), 154, 239, 288, 377
Zhang Yun (张云), 90, 312
Zhang Zhizhong (张治中), 90
Zhou Jitang (周继棠), 353
Zivkovie, R., 86